Contents

PART II   Foundations of Inferential Statistics

Chapter 5 • z-Scores: Location of Scores and Standardized Distributions   123

Chapter 6 • Probability   149

Chapter 7 • Probability and Samples: The Distribution of Sample Means   175

PART III   Using *t* Statistics for Interferences About Population Means and Mean Differences

Preface

Many students in the behavioral sciences view the required statistics course as an intimidating obstacle that has been placed in the middle of an otherwise interesting curriculum. They want to learn about human behavior—not about math and science. As a result, the statistics course is seen as irrelevant to their education and career goals. However, as long as the behavioral sciences are founded in science, a knowledge of statistics will be necessary. Statistical procedures provide researchers with objective and systematic methods for describing and interpreting their research results. Scientific research is the system that we use to gather information, and statistics are the tools that we use to distill the information into sensible and justified conclusions. The goal of this book is not only to teach the methods of statistics but also to convey the basic principles of objectivity and logic that are essential for science and valuable for decision making in everyday life.

Those of you who are familiar with previous editions of *Essentials of Statistics for the Behavioral Sciences* will notice that some changes have been made. These changes are summarized in the section titled "To the Instructor." In revising this text, our students have been foremost in our minds. Over the years, they have provided honest and useful feedback. Their hard work and perseverance has made our writing and teaching most rewarding. We sincerely thank them. Students who are using this edition should please read the section of the preface titled "To the Student."

The book chapters are organized in the sequence that we use for our own statistics courses. We begin with descriptive statistics, and then examine a variety of statistical procedures focused on sample means and variance before moving on to correlational methods and nonparametric statistics. Information about modifying this sequence is presented in the "To the Instructor" section for individuals who prefer a different organization. Each chapter contains numerous examples—many based on actual research studies—along with learning checks, a summary and list of key terms, and a set of 20 to 30 problems.

TO THE INSTRUCTOR

Those of you familiar with the previous edition of *Essentials of Statistics for the Behavioral Sciences* will notice a number of changes in the eighth edition. Throughout the book, research examples have been updated, real-world examples have been added, and the end-of-chapter problems have been extensively revised. The book has been separated into five sections to emphasize the similarities among groups of statistical methods. Each section contains two to four chapters and begins with an introduction and concludes with a review, including review exercises. Major revisions for this edition include:

- The former Chapter 12 on estimation has been eliminated. In its place, sections on confidence intervals have been added to the three chapters presenting *t* statistics.

- A new appendix titled *Statistics Organizer: Finding the Right Statistics for Your Data,* discusses the process of selecting the correct statistics to be used with different categories of data and replaces the Statistics Organizer that appeared as an appendix in earlier editions.

Other specific and noteworthy revisions include:

Chapter 1   A separate section explains how statistical methods can be classified using the same categories that are used to group data structures and research methods.

Chapter 2   The discussion of histograms has been modified to differentiate discrete and continuous variables.

Chapter 3   A modified definition of the median acknowledges that this value is not algebraically defined and that determining the median, especially for discrete variables, can be somewhat subjective.

Chapter 4   Relatively minor editing for clarity. The section on variance and inferential statistics has been simplified.

Chapter 5   Relatively minor editing for clarity.

Chapter 6   The concepts of random sample and independent random sample have been clarified with separate definitions. A new figure helps demonstrate the process of using the unit normal table to find proportions for negative z-scores.

Chapter 7   Relatively minor editing for clarity.

Chapter 8   The chapter has been shortened by substantial editing that eliminated several pages of unnecessary text, particularly in the sections on errors (Type I and II) and power.

Chapter 9   The section describing how sample size and sample variance influence the outcome of a hypothesis test has been moved so that it appears immediately after the hypothesis test example. A new section introduces confidence intervals in the context of describing effect size, describes how confidence intervals are reported in the literature, and discusses factors affecting the width of a confidence interval.

Chapter 10   An expanded section discusses how sample variance and sample size influence the outcome of an independent-measures hypothesis test and measures of effect size. A new section introduces confidence intervals as an alternative for describing effect size. The relationship between a confidence interval and a hypothesis test is also discussed.

Chapter 11   The description of repeated-measures and matched-subjects designs has been clarified and we increased emphasis on the concept that all calculations for the related-samples test are done with the difference scores. A new section introduces confidence intervals as an alternative for describing effect size and discusses the relationship between a confidence interval and a hypothesis test.

The former Chapter 12 has been deleted. The content from this chapter discussing confidence intervals has been added to Chapters 9, 10, and 11.

Chapter 12   (former Chapter 13, introducing ANOVA) The discussion of testwise alpha levels versus experimentwise alpha levels has been moved from a box into the text, and definitions of the two terms have been added. To emphasize the concepts of ANOVA rather than the formulas, $SS_{\text{between treatments}}$ is routinely found by subtraction instead of being computed directly. Two alternative equations for $SS_{\text{between treatments}}$ have been moved from the text into a box.

Chapter 13   (former Chapter 14, introducing repeated-measures and two-factor ANOVA) A new section demonstrates the relationship between ANOVA and the t test when a repeated-measures study is comparing only two treatments. Extensive editing has shortened the chapter and simplified the presentation.

Chapter 14   (formerly Chapter 15, introducing correlation and regression) New sections present the t statistic for testing hypotheses about the Pearson correlation and demonstrate how the t test for significance of a correlation is equivalent to the F-ratio used for analysis of regression.

Chapter 15   (formerly Chapter 16, introducing chi-square tests) Relatively minor editing has shortened and clarified the chapter.

Matching the Text to Your Syllabus   We have tried to make separate chapters, and even sections of chapters, completely self-contained so that they can be deleted or reorganized to fit the syllabus for nearly any instructor. Some common examples are as follows:

- It is common for instructors to choose between emphasizing analysis of variance (Chapters 12 and 13) or emphasizing correlation/regression (Chapter 14). It is rare for a one-semester course to provide complete coverage of both topics.

- Although we choose to complete all the hypothesis tests for means and mean differences before introducing correlation (Chapter 14), many instructors prefer to place correlation much earlier in the sequence of course topics. To accommodate this, sections 14.1, 14.2, and 14.3 present the calculation and interpretation of the Pearson correlation and can be introduced immediately following Chapter 4 (variability). Other sections of Chapter 14 refer to hypothesis testing and should be delayed until the process of hypothesis testing (Chapter 8) has been introduced.

- It is also possible for instructors to present the chi-square tests (Chapter 15) much earlier in the sequence of course topics. Chapter 15, which presents hypothesis tests for proportions, can be presented immediately after Chapter 8, which introduces the process of hypothesis testing. If this is done, we also recommend that the Pearson correlation (Sections 14.1, 14.2, and 14.3) be presented early to provide a foundation for the chi-square test for independence.

TO THE STUDENT   A primary goal of this book is to make the task of learning statistics as easy and painless as possible. Among other things, you will notice that the book provides you with a number of opportunities to practice the techniques you will be learning in the form of learning checks, examples, demonstrations, and end-of-chapter problems. We encourage you to take advantage of these opportunities. Read the text rather than just memorize the formulas. We have taken care to present each statistical procedure in a conceptual context that explains why the procedure was developed and when it should be used. If you read this material and gain an understanding of the basic concepts underlying a statistical formula, you will find that learning the formula and how to use it will be much easier. In the following section, "Study Hints," we provide advice that we give our own students. Ask your instructor for advice as well; we are sure that other instructors will have ideas of their own.

Over the years, the students in our classes and other students using our book have given us valuable feedback. If you have any suggestions or comments about this book, you can write to either Professor Emeritus Frederick Gravetter or Professor Emeritus

Larry Wallnau at the Department of Psychology, SUNY College at Brockport, 350 New Campus Drive, Brockport, New York 14420. You can also contact Professor Emeritus Gravetter directly at fgravett@brockport.edu.

Study Hints   You may find some of these tips helpful, as our own students have reported.

- The key to success in a statistics course is to keep up with the material. Each new topic builds on previous topics. If you have learned the previous material, then the new topic is just one small step forward. Without the proper background, however, the new topic can be a complete mystery. If you find that you are falling behind, get help immediately.

- You will learn (and remember) much more if you study for short periods several times per week rather than try to condense all of your studying into one long session. For example, it is far more effective to study half an hour every night than to have a single $3\frac{1}{2}$-hour study session once a week. We cannot even work on *writing* this book without frequent rest breaks.

- Do some work before class. Keep a little ahead of the instructor by reading the appropriate sections before they are presented in class. Although you may not fully understand what you read, you will have a general idea of the topic, which will make the lecture easier to follow. Also, you can identify material that is particularly confusing and then be sure the topic is clarified in class.

- Pay attention and think during class. Although this advice seems obvious, often it is not practiced. Many students spend so much time trying to write down every example presented or every word spoken by the instructor that they do not actually understand and process what is being said. Check with your instructor—there may not be a need to copy every example presented in class, especially if there are many examples like it in the text. Sometimes, we tell our students to put their pens and pencils down for a moment and just listen.

- Test yourself regularly. Do not wait until the end of the chapter or the end of the week to check your knowledge. After each lecture, work some of the end-of-chapter problems and do the Learning Checks. Review the Demonstration Problems, and be sure you can define the Key Terms. If you are having trouble, get your questions answered *immediately* (reread the section, go to your instructor, or ask questions in class). By doing so, you will be able to move ahead to new material.

- Do not kid yourself! Avoid denial. Many students watch their instructor solve problems in class and think to themselves, "This looks easy—I understand it." Do you really understand it? Can you really do the problem on your own without having to leaf through the pages of a chapter? Although there is nothing wrong with using examples in the text as models for solving problems, you should try working a problem with your book closed to test your level of mastery.

- We realize that many students are embarrassed to ask for help. It is our biggest challenge as instructors. You must find a way to overcome this aversion. Perhaps contacting the instructor directly would be a good starting point, if asking questions in class is too anxiety-provoking. You could be pleasantly surprised to find that your instructor does not yell, scold, or bite! Also, your instructor might know of another student who can offer assistance. Peer tutoring can be very helpful.

ANCILLARIES   Ancillaries for this edition include the following:

- *Aplia Statistics for Psychology and the Behavioral Sciences:* An online interactive learning solution that ensures students stay involved with their coursework and master the basic tools and concepts of statistical analysis. Created by a research psychologist to help students excel, Aplia's content engages students with questions based on real-world scenarios that help students understand how statistics applies to everyday life. At the same time, all chapter assignments are automatically graded and provide students with detailed explanations, making sure they learn from and improve with every question.

- *Instructor's Manual with Test Bank:* Contains chapter outlines, annotated learning objectives, lecture suggestions, test items, and solutions to all end-of-chapter problems in the text. Test items are also available as a Word download or for ExamView computerized test bank software.

- *PowerLecture with ExamView®:* This CD includes the instructor's manual, test bank, lecture slides with book figures, and more. Featuring automatic grading, ExamView, also available within PowerLecture, allows you to create, deliver, and customize tests and study guides (both print and online) in minutes. Assessments appear onscreen exactly as they will print or display online; you can build tests of up to 250 questions using up to 12 question types, and you can enter an unlimited number of new questions or edit existing questions.

- *WebTutor on Blackboard and WebCT:* Jump-start your course with customizable, text-specific content within your Course Management System.

- *Psychology CourseMate:* Cengage Learning's Psychology CourseMate brings course concepts to life with interactive learning, study, and exam preparation tools that support the printed textbook. Go to www.cengagebrain.com. Psychology CourseMate includes:
- An interactive eBook;
- Interactive teaching and learning tools, including
    - quizzes,
    - flashcards,
    - videos,
    - and more; plus
- The Engagement Tracker, a first-of-its-kind tool that monitors student engagement in the course.

ACKNOWLEDGMENTS   It takes a lot of good, hardworking people to produce a book. Our friends at Wadsworth/Cengage Learning have made enormous contributions to this textbook. We thank: Jon-David Hague, Publisher; Tim Matray, Acquisitions Editor; Paige Leeds, Assistant Editor; Nicole Richards, Editorial Assistant; Charlene M. Carpentier, Content Project Manager; Jasmin Tokatlian, Media Editor; and Pam Galbreath, Art Director. Special thanks go to Liana Sarkisian and Arwen Petty, our Developmental Editors, and to Mike Ederer, who led us through production at Graphic World.

Reviewers play a very important role in the development of a manuscript. Accordingly, we offer our appreciation to the following colleagues for their assistance with the eighth edition: Patricia Tomich, Kent State University; Robert E. Wickham, University of Houston; Jessica Urschel, Western Michigan University; Wilson Chu, California State University, Long Beach; Melissa Platt, University of Oregon; Brian Detweiler-Bedell, Lewis and Clark College.

About the Authors

Frederick J Gravetter is Professor Emeritus of Psychology at the State University of New York College at Brockport. While teaching at Brockport, Dr. Gravetter specialized in statistics, experimental design, and cognitive psychology. He received his bachelor's degree in mathematics from M.I.T. and his Ph.D. in psychology from Duke University. In addition to publishing this textbook and several research articles, Dr. Gravetter co-authored *Research Methods for the Behavioral Sciences* and *Statistics for the Behavioral Sciences.*

Larry B. Wallnau is Professor Emeritus of Psychology at the State University of New York College at Brockport. At Brockport he taught courses relating to the biological basis of behavior and published numerous research articles, primarily in the field of biopsychology. With Dr. Gravetter, he co-authored *Statistics for the Behavioral Sciences.* He also has provided editorial consulting for a number of publishers and journals. He is an FCC-licensed amateur radio operator, and in his spare time he is seeking worldwide contacts with other radio enthusiasts.

PART

1

Introduction and Descriptive Statistics

We have divided this book into five sections, each covering a general topic area of statistics. The first section, consisting of Chapters 1 to 4, provides a broad overview of statistical methods and a more focused presentation of those methods that are classified as *descriptive statistics*.

By the time you finish the four chapters in this part, you should have a good understanding of the general goals of statistics and you should be familiar with the basic terminology and notation used in statistics. In addition, you should be familiar with the techniques of descriptive statistics that help researchers organize and summarize the results they obtain from their research. Specifically, you should be able to take a set of scores and present them in a table or in a graph that provides an overall picture of the complete set. Also, you should be able to summarize a set of scores by calculating one or two values (such as the average) that describe the entire set.

At the end of this section, there is a brief summary and a set of review problems that should help to integrate the elements from the separate chapters.

CHAPTER

1

Introduction to Statistics

aplia

Aplia for *Essentials of Statistics for the Behavioral Sciences*
After reading, go to "Resources" at the end of this chapter for an introduction on how to use Aplia's homework and learning resources.

1.1 STATISTICS, SCIENCE, AND OBSERVATIONS

OVERVIEW

Before we begin our discussion of statistics, we ask you to read the following paragraph taken from the philosophy of Wrong Shui (Candappa, 2000).

The Journey to Enlightenment

> In Wrong Shui, life is seen as a cosmic journey, a struggle to overcome unseen and unexpected obstacles at the end of which the traveler will find illumination and enlightenment. Replicate this quest in your home by moving light switches away from doors and over to the far side of each room.*

Why did we begin a statistics book with a bit of twisted philosophy? Actually, the paragraph is an excellent (and humorous) counterexample for the purpose of this book. Specifically, our goal is to help you avoid stumbling around in the dark by providing lots of easily available light switches and plenty of illumination as you journey through the world of statistics. To accomplish this, we try to present sufficient background and a clear statement of purpose as we introduce each new statistical procedure. Remember that all statistical procedures were developed to serve a purpose. If you understand why a new procedure is needed, you will find it much easier to learn.

As you read through the following chapters, keep in mind that the general topic of statistics follows a well-organized, logically developed progression that leads from basic concepts and definitions to increasingly sophisticated techniques. Thus, the material presented in the early chapters of this book serves as a foundation for the material that follows. The content of the first nine chapters, for example, provides an essential background and context for the statistical methods presented in Chapter 10. If you turn directly to Chapter 10 without reading the first nine chapters, you will find the material confusing and incomprehensible. However, we should reassure you that the progression from basic concepts to complex statistical techniques is a slow, step-by-step process. As you learn the basic background material, you will develop a good frame of reference for understanding and incorporating new, more sophisticated concepts as they are presented.

The objectives for this first chapter are to provide an introduction to the topic of statistics and to give you some background for the rest of the book. We discuss the role of statistics within the general field of scientific inquiry, and we introduce some of the vocabulary and notation that are necessary for the statistical methods that follow.

DEFINITIONS OF STATISTICS

Statistics are often defined as facts and figures, such as average income, crime rate, birth rate, baseball batting averages, and so on. These statistics are usually informative and time saving because they condense large quantities of information into a few simple figures. Later in this chapter we return to the notion of calculating statistics (facts and figures) but, for now, we concentrate on a much broader definition of statistics. Specifically, we use the term *statistics* to refer to a set of mathematical procedures. In this case, we are using the term *statistics* as a shortened version of *statistical procedures*. For example, you are probably using this book for a statistics course in which you will learn about the statistical techniques that are used for research in the behavioral sciences.

*Candappa, R. (2000). *The little book of wrong shui*. Kansas City: Andrews McMeel Publishing. Reprinted by permission.

Research in the behavioral sciences (and other fields) involves gathering information. To determine, for example, whether college students learn better by reading material on printed pages or on a computer screen, you would need to gather information about students' study habits and their academic performance. When researchers finish the task of gathering information, they typically find themselves with pages and pages of measurements such as IQ scores, personality scores, exam scores, and so on. In this book, we present the statistics that researchers use to analyze and interpret the information that they gather. Specifically, statistics serve two general purposes:

1. Statistics are used to organize and summarize the information so that the researcher can see what happened in the research study and can communicate the results to others.

2. Statistics help the researcher to answer the questions that initiated the research by determining exactly what general conclusions are justified based on the specific results that were obtained.

DEFINITION

> The term **statistics** refers to a set of mathematical procedures for organizing, summarizing, and interpreting information.

Statistical procedures help to ensure that the information or observations are presented and interpreted in an accurate and informative way. In somewhat grandiose terms, statistics help researchers bring order out of chaos. Statistics also provide researchers with a set of standardized techniques that are recognized and understood throughout the scientific community. Thus, the statistical methods used by one researcher are familiar to other researchers, who can accurately interpret the statistical analyses with a full understanding of how the analysis was done and what the results signify.

1.2   POPULATIONS AND SAMPLES

Research in the behavioral sciences typically begins with a general question about a specific group (or groups) of individuals. For example, a researcher may want to know what factors are associated with academic dishonesty among college students. Or a researcher may want to examine the amount of time spent in the bathroom for men compared to women. In the first example, the researcher is interested in the group of *college students.* In the second example, the researcher wants to compare the group of *men* with the group of *women.* In statistical terminology, the entire group that a researcher wishes to study is called a *population.*

DEFINITION

> A **population** is the entire set of the individuals of interest for a particular research question.

As you can well imagine, a population can be quite large—for example, the entire set of men on the planet Earth. A researcher might be more specific, limiting the population for study to retired men who live in the United States. Perhaps the investigator would like to study the population consisting of men who are professional basketball players. Populations can obviously vary in size from extremely large to very small, depending on how the researcher defines the population. The population being studied should always be identified by the researcher. In addition, the population need not consist of people—it could be a population of rats, corporations, parts produced in a factory, or anything else a researcher wants to study. In practice, populations are typically very large, such as the population of college sophomores in the United States or the population of small businesses.

Because populations tend to be very large, it usually is impossible for a researcher to examine every individual in the population of interest. Therefore, researchers typically select a smaller, more manageable group from the population and limit their studies to the individuals in the selected group. In statistical terms, a set of individuals selected from a population is called a *sample*. A sample is intended to be representative of its population, and a sample should always be identified in terms of the population from which it was selected.

DEFINITION

> A **sample** is a set of individuals selected from a population, usually intended to represent the population in a research study.

Just as we saw with populations, samples can vary in size. For example, one study might examine a sample of only 10 autistic children, and another study might use a sample of more than 10,000 people who take a specific cholesterol medication.

So far we have talked about a sample being selected from a population. However, this is actually only half of the full relationship between a sample and its population. Specifically, when a researcher finishes examining the sample, the goal is to generalize the results back to the entire population. Remember that the research started with a general question about the population. To answer the question, a researcher studies a sample and then generalizes the results from the sample to the population. The full relationship between a sample and a population is shown in Figure 1.1.

VARIABLES AND DATA Typically, researchers are interested in specific characteristics of the individuals in the population (and in the sample), or they are interested in outside factors that may influence the individuals. For example, a researcher may be interested in the influence

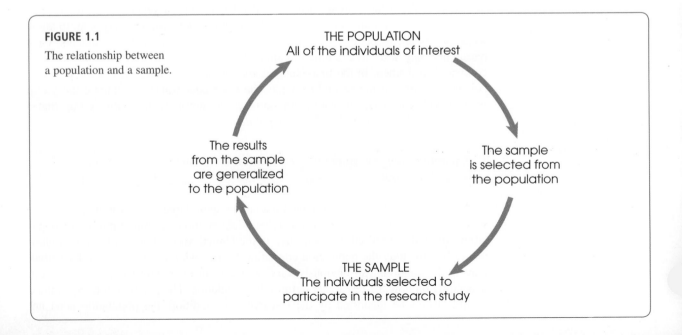

FIGURE 1.1

The relationship between a population and a sample.

THE POPULATION
All of the individuals of interest

The sample is selected from the population

THE SAMPLE
The individuals selected to participate in the research study

The results from the sample are generalized to the population of the weather on people's moods. As the weather changes, do people's moods also change? Something that can change or have different values is called a *variable*.

DEFINITION

> A **variable** is a characteristic or condition that changes or has different values for different individuals.

Once again, variables can be characteristics that differ from one individual to another, such as height, weight, gender, or personality. Also, variables can be environmental conditions that change such as temperature, time of day, or the size of the room in which the research is being conducted.

To demonstrate changes in variables, it is necessary to make measurements of the variables being examined. The measurement obtained for each individual is called a *datum* or, more commonly, a *score* or *raw score*. The complete set of scores is called the *data set,* or simply the *data*.

DEFINITIONS

> **Data** (plural) are measurements or observations. A **data set** is a collection of measurements or observations. A **datum** (singular) is a single measurement or observation and is commonly called a **score** or **raw score.**

Before we move on, we should make one more point about samples, populations, and data. Earlier, we defined populations and samples in terms of *individuals*. For example, we discussed a population of college students and a sample of autistic children. Be fore-warned, however, that we will also refer to populations or samples of *scores*. Because research typically involves measuring each individual to obtain a score, every sample (or population) of individuals produces a corresponding sample (or population) of scores.

PARAMETERS AND STATISTICS

When describing data, it is necessary to distinguish whether the data come from a population or a sample. A characteristic that describes a population—for example, the average score for the population—is called a *parameter*. A characteristic that describes a sample is called a *statistic*. Thus, the average score for a sample is an example of a statistic. Typically, the research process begins with a question about a population parameter. However, the actual data come from a sample and are used to compute sample statistics.

DEFINITIONS

> A **parameter** is a value, usually a numerical value, that describes a population. A parameter is usually derived from measurements of the individuals in the population.
>
> A **statistic** is a value, usually a numerical value, that describes a sample. A statistic is usually derived from measurements of the individuals in the sample.

Every population parameter has a corresponding sample statistic, and most research studies involve using statistics from samples as the basis for answering questions about population parameters. As a result, much of this book is concerned with the relationship between sample statistics and the corresponding population parameters. In Chapter 7, for example, we examine the relationship between the mean obtained for a sample and the mean for the population from which the sample was obtained.

DESCRIPTIVE AND INFERENTIAL STATISTICAL METHODS

Although researchers have developed a variety of different statistical procedures to organize and interpret data, these different procedures can be classified into two general categories. The first category, *descriptive statistics,* consists of statistical procedures that are used to simplify and summarize data.

DEFINITION

> **Descriptive statistics** are statistical procedures used to summarize, organize, and simplify data.

Descriptive statistics are techniques that take raw scores and organize or summarize them in a form that is more manageable. Often the scores are organized in a table or a graph so that it is possible to see the entire set of scores. Another common technique is to summarize a set of scores by computing an average. Note that even if the data set has hundreds of scores, the average provides a single descriptive value for the entire set.

The second general category of statistical techniques is called *inferential statistics*. Inferential statistics are methods that use sample data to make general statements about a population.

DEFINITION

> **Inferential statistics** consist of techniques that allow us to study samples and then make generalizations about the populations from which they were selected.

Because populations are typically very large, it usually is not possible to measure everyone in the population. Therefore, a sample is selected to represent the population. By analyzing the results from the sample, we hope to answer general questions about the population. Typically, researchers use sample statistics as the basis for drawing conclusions about population parameters.

One problem with using samples, however, is that a sample provides only limited information about the population. Although samples are generally *representative* of their populations, a sample is not expected to give a perfectly accurate picture of the whole population. Thus, there typically is some discrepancy between a sample statistic and the corresponding population parameter. This discrepancy is called *sampling error*, and it creates the fundamental problem that inferential statistics must always address (Box 1.1).

DEFINITION

> **Sampling error** is the naturally occurring discrepancy, or error, that exists between a sample statistic and the corresponding population parameter.

The concept of sampling error is illustrated in Figure 1.2. The figure shows a population of 1,000 college students and two samples, each with 5 students, who have been selected from the population. Notice that each sample contains different individuals who have different characteristics. Because the characteristics of each sample depend on the specific people in the sample, statistics vary from one

---

BOX 1.1   **THE MARGIN OF ERROR BETWEEN STATISTICS AND PARAMETERS**

One common example of sampling error is the error associated with a sample proportion. For example, in newspaper articles reporting results from political polls, you frequently find statements such as this:

Candidate Brown leads the poll with 51% of the vote. Candidate Jones has 42% approval, and the remaining 7% are undecided. This poll was taken from a sample of registered voters and has a margin of error of plus-or-minus 4 percentage points.

The *margin of error* is the sampling error. In this case, the percentages that are reported were obtained from a sample and are being generalized to the whole population. As always, you do not expect the statistics from a sample to be perfect. There is always some margin of error when sample statistics are used to represent population parameters.

FIGURE 1.2

A demonstration of sampling error. Two samples are selected from the same population. Notice that the sample statistics are different from one sample to another, and all of the sample statistics are different from the corresponding population parameters. The natural differences that exist, by chance, between a sample statistic and a population parameter are called sampling error.

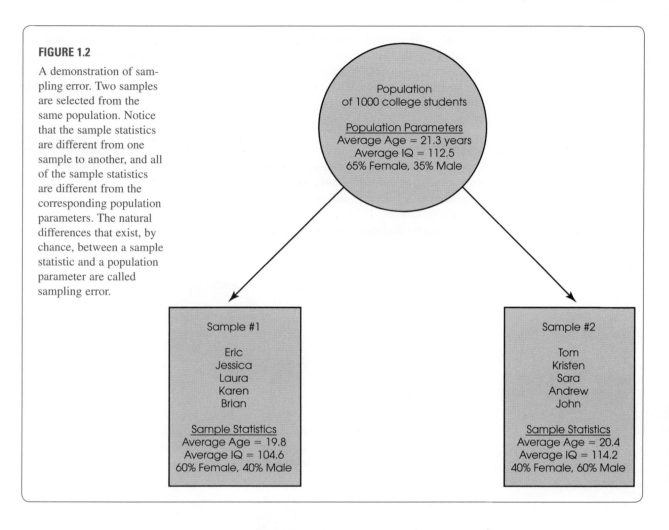

Population
of 1000 college students

Population Parameters
Average Age = 21.3 years
Average IQ = 112.5
65% Female, 35% Male

Sample #1

Eric
Jessica
Laura
Karen
Brian

Sample Statistics
Average Age = 19.8
Average IQ = 104.6
60% Female, 40% Male

Sample #2

Tom
Kristen
Sara
Andrew
John

Sample Statistics
Average Age = 20.4
Average IQ = 114.2
40% Female, 60% Male

sample to another. For example, the five students in sample 1 have an average age of 19.8 years and the students in sample 2 have an average age of 20.4 years.

Also note that the statistics obtained for a sample are not identical to the parameters for the entire population. In Figure 1.2, for example, neither sample has statistics that are exactly the same as the population parameters. You should also realize that Figure 1.2 shows only two of the hundreds of possible samples. Each sample would contain different individuals and would produce different statistics. This is the basic concept of sampling error: sample statistics vary from one sample to another and typically are different from the corresponding population parameters.

As a further demonstration of sampling error, imagine that your statistics class is separated into two groups by drawing a line from front to back through the middle of the room. Now imagine that you compute the average age (or height, or IQ) for each group. Will the two groups have exactly the same average? Almost certainly they will not. No matter what you chose to measure, you will probably find some difference between the two groups. However, the difference you obtain does not necessarily mean that there is a systematic difference between the two groups. For example, if the average age for students on the right-hand side of the room is higher than the average for students on the left, it is unlikely that some mysterious force has caused the older people to gravitate to the right side of the room. Instead, the difference is probably the result of random factors such as chance. The unpredictable, unsystematic differences that exist from one sample to another are an example of sampling error.

STATISTICS IN THE CONTEXT OF RESEARCH

The following example shows the general stages of a research study and demonstrates how descriptive statistics and inferential statistics are used to organize and interpret the data. At the end of the example, note how sampling error can affect the interpretation of experimental results, and consider why inferential statistical methods are needed to deal with this problem.

EXAMPLE 1.1

Figure 1.3 shows an overview of a general research situation and demonstrates the roles that descriptive and inferential statistics play. The purpose of the research study is to address a question that we posed earlier: Do college students learn better by studying text on printed pages or on a computer screen? Two samples are selected from the population of college students. The students in sample A are given printed pages of text to study for 30 minutes and the students in sample B study the same text on a computer screen.

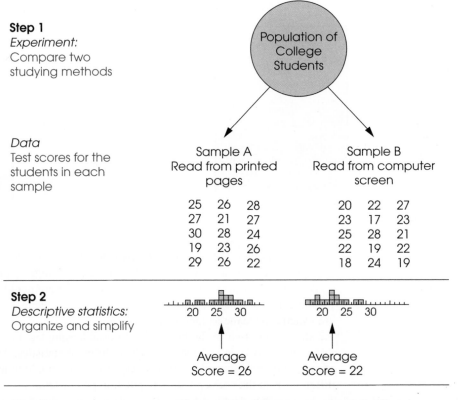

Step 1
Experiment:
Compare two studying methods

Population of College Students

Data
Test scores for the students in each sample

Sample A
Read from printed pages

25	26	28
27	21	27
30	28	24
19	23	26
29	26	22

Sample B
Read from computer screen

20	22	27
23	17	23
25	28	21
22	19	22
18	24	19

Step 2
Descriptive statistics:
Organize and simplify

20   25   30

Average Score = 26

20   25   30

Average Score = 22

Step 3
Inferential statistics:
Interpret results

The sample data show a 4-point difference between the two methods of studying. However, there are two ways to interpret the results.
1. There actually is no difference between the two studying methods, and the sample difference is due to chance (sampling error).
2. There really is a difference between the two methods, and the sample data accurately reflect this difference.
The goal of inferential statistics is to help researchers decide between the two interpretations.

FIGURE 1.3

The role of statistics in research.

Next, all of the students are given a multiple-choice test to evaluate their knowledge of the material. At this point, the researcher has two sets of data: the scores for sample A and the scores for sample B (see Figure 1.3). Now is the time to begin using statistics.

First, descriptive statistics are used to simplify the pages of data. For example, the researcher could draw a graph showing the scores for each sample or compute the average score for each sample. Note that descriptive methods provide a simplified, organized description of the scores. In this example, the students who studied printed pages had an average score of 26 on the test, and the students who studied text on the computer averaged 22.

Once the researcher has described the results, the next step is to interpret the outcome. This is the role of inferential statistics. In this example, the researcher has found a difference of 4 points between the two samples (sample A averaged 26 and sample B averaged 22). The problem for inferential statistics is to differentiate between the following two interpretations:

1. There is no real difference between the two study methods, and the 4-point difference between the samples is just an example of sampling error (like the samples in Figure 1.2).

2. There really is a difference between the two study methods, and the 4-point difference between the samples was caused by the different methods of studying.

In simple English, does the 4-point difference between samples provide convincing evidence of a difference between the two studying methods, or is the 4-point difference just chance? The purpose of inferential statistics is to answer this question.

LEARNING CHECK

1. A researcher is interested in the texting habits of high school students in the United States. If the researcher measures the number of text messages that each individual sends each day and calculates the average number for the entire group of high school students, the average number would be an example of a _____.

2. A researcher is interested in how watching a reality television show featuring fashion models influences the eating behavior of 13-year-old girls.

    a. A group of 30 13-year-old girls is selected to participate in a research study. The group of 30 13-year-old girls is an example of a _____.

    b. In the same study, the amount of food eaten in one day is measured for each girl and the researcher computes the average score for the 30 13-year-old girls. The average score is an example of a _____.

3. Statistical techniques are classified into two general categories. What are the two categories called, and what is the general purpose for the techniques in each category?

4. Briefly define the concept of sampling error.

ANSWERS

1. parameter

2. a. sample

    b. statistic

3. The two categories are descriptive statistics and inferential statistics. Descriptive techniques are intended to organize, simplify, and summarize data. Inferential techniques use sample data to reach general conclusions about populations.

4. Sampling error is the error, or discrepancy, between the value obtained for a sample statistic and the value for the corresponding population parameter.

DATA STRUCTURES, RESEARCH METHODS, AND STATISTICS

INDIVIDUAL VARIABLES

Some research studies are conducted simply to describe individual variables as they exist naturally. For example, a college official may conduct a survey to describe the eating, sleeping, and studying habits of a group of college students. When the results consist of numerical scores, such as the number of hours spent studying each day, they are typically described by the statistical techniques that are presented in Chapters 3 and 4. Non-numerical scores are typically described by computing the proportion or percentage in each category. For example, a recent newspaper article reported that 61% of the adults in the United States drink alcohol.

RELATIONSHIPS BETWEEN VARIABLES

Most research, however, is intended to examine relationships between two or more variables. For example, is there a relationship between the amount of violence that children see on television and the amount of aggressive behavior they display? Is there a relationship between the quality of breakfast and level of academic performance for elementary school children? Is there a relationship between the number of hours of sleep and grade point average for college students? To establish the existence of a relationship, researchers must make observations—that is, measurements of the two variables. The resulting measurements can be classified into two distinct data structures that also help to classify different research methods and different statistical techniques. In the following section we identify and discuss these two data structures.

Data structure I. Measuring two variables for each individual: The correlational method   One method for examining the relationship between variables is to observe the two variables as they exist naturally for a set of individuals. That is, simply measure the two variables for each individual. For example, research has demonstrated a relationship between sleep habits, especially wake-up time, and academic performance for college students (Trockel, Barnes, and Egget, 2000). The researchers used a survey to measure wake-up time and school records to measure academic performance for each student. Figure 1.4 shows an example of the kind of data obtained in the study. The researchers then look for consistent patterns in the data to provide evidence for a relationship between variables. For example, as wake-up time changes from one student to another, is there also a tendency for academic performance to change?

Patterns in the data are often easier to see if the scores are presented in a graph. Figure 1.4 also shows the scores for the eight students in a graph called a scatter plot. In the scatter plot, each individual is represented by a point so that the horizontal position corresponds to the student's wake-up time and the vertical position corresponds to the student's academic performance score. The scatter plot shows a clear relationship between wake-up time and academic performance: as wake-up time increases, academic performance decreases.

A research study that simply measures two different variables for each individual and produces the kind of data shown in Figure 1.4 is an example of the *correlational method,* or the *correlational research strategy.*

DEFINITION

In the **correlational method,** two different variables are observed to determine whether there is a relationship between them.

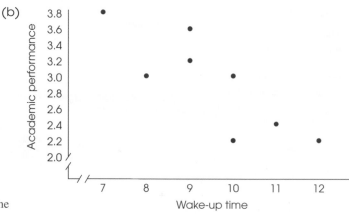

(a)

Student	Wake-up Time	Academic Performance
A	11	2.4
B	9	3.6
C	9	3.2
D	12	2.2
E	7	3.8
F	10	2.2
G	10	3.0
H	8	3.0

FIGURE 1.4

One of two data structures for studies evaluating the relationship between variables. Note that there are two separate measurements for each individual (wake-up time and academic performance). The same scores are shown in a table (a) and a graph (b).

Limitations of the correlational method   The results from a correlational study can demonstrate the existence of a relationship between two variables, but they do not provide an explanation for the relationship. In particular, a correlational study cannot demonstrate a cause-and-effect relationship. For example, the data in Figure 1.4 show a systematic relationship between wake-up time and academic performance for a group of college students; those who sleep late tend to have lower performance scores than those who wake early. However, there are many possible explanations for the relationship and we do not know exactly what factor (or factors) is responsible for late sleepers having lower grades. In particular, we cannot conclude that waking students up earlier would cause their academic performance to improve, or that studying more would cause students to wake up earlier. To demonstrate a cause-and-effect relationship between two variables, researchers must use the experimental method, which is discussed next.

Data structure II. Comparing two (or more) groups of scores: Experimental and nonexperimental methods   The second method for examining the relationship between two variables involves the comparison of two or more groups of scores. In this situation, the relationship between variables is examined by using one of the variables to define the groups, and then measuring the second variable to obtain scores for each group. For example, one group of elementary school children is shown a 30-minute action/adventure television program involving numerous instances of violence, and a second group is shown a 30-minute comedy that includes no violence. Both groups are then observed on the playground and a researcher records the number of aggressive acts committed by each child. An example of the resulting data is shown in Figure 1.5. The researcher compares the scores for the violence group with the scores for the no-violence group. A systematic difference between the two groups provides evidence for a relationship between viewing television violence and aggressive behavior for elementary school children.

THE EXPERIMENTAL METHOD   One specific research method that involves comparing groups of scores is known as the *experimental method* or the *experimental research strategy*. The goal of an experimental study is to demonstrate a cause-and-effect relationship between two variables.

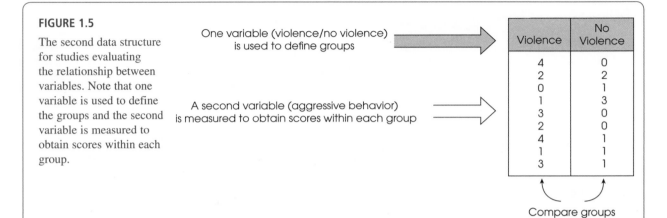

FIGURE 1.5

The second data structure for studies evaluating the relationship between variables. Note that one variable is used to define the groups and the second variable is measured to obtain scores within each group.

Specifically, an experiment attempts to show that changing the value of one variable causes changes to occur in the second variable. To accomplish this goal, the experimental method has two characteristics that differentiate experiments from other types of research studies:

1. **Manipulation** The researcher manipulates one variable by changing its value from one level to another. A second variable is observed (measured) to determine whether the manipulation causes changes to occur.

2. **Control** The researcher must exercise control over the research situation to ensure that other, extraneous variables do not influence the relationship being examined.

In more complex experiments, a researcher may systematically manipulate more than one variable and may observe more than one variable. Here we are considering the simplest case, in which only one variable is manipulated and only one variable is observed.

To demonstrate these two characteristics, consider an experiment in which researchers demonstrate the pain-killing effects of handling money (Zhou & Vohs, 2009). In the experiment, a group of college students was told that they were participating in a manual dexterity study. The researchers then created two treatment conditions by manipulating the kind of material that each participant would be handling. Half of the students were given a stack of money to count and the other half got a stack of blank pieces of paper. After the counting task, the participants were asked to dip their hands into bowls of painfully hot water (122° F) and rate how uncomfortable it was. Participants who had counted money rated the pain significantly lower than those who had counted paper. The structure of the experiment is shown in Figure 1.6.

To be able to say that the difference in pain perception is caused by the money, the researcher must rule out any other possible explanation for the difference. That is, the researchers must control any other variables that might affect pain tolerance. There are two general categories of variables that researchers must consider:

1. **Participant Variables** These are characteristics such as age, gender, and intelligence that vary from one individual to another.

   In the money-counting experiment, for example, suppose that the participants in the money condition were primarily females and those in the paper condition were primarily males. In this case, there is an alternative explanation for any difference in the pain ratings that exists between the two groups. Specifically, it is possible that the difference was caused by the money, but it also is possible that the difference was caused by the participants' gender (females can tolerate

FIGURE 1.6

The structure of an experiment. Participants are randomly assigned to one of two treatment conditions: counting money or counting blank pieces of paper. Later, each participant is tested by placing one hand in a bowl of hot (122° F) water and rating the level of pain. A difference between the ratings for the two groups is attributed to the treatment (paper versus money).

Variable #1: Counting money or blank paper (the independent variable) Manipulated to create two treatment conditions.

Variable #2: Pain rating (the dependent variable) Measured in each of the treatment conditions.

Money	Paper
7	8
4	10
5	8
6	9
6	8
8	10
6	7
5	8
5	8
6	7

Compare groups of scores

more pain than males can). Whenever a research study allows more than one explanation for the results, the study is said to be *confounded* because it is impossible to reach an unambiguous conclusion.

2. **Environmental Variables** These are characteristics of the environment such as lighting, time of day, and weather conditions. Using the money-counting experiment (see Figure 1.6) as an example, suppose that the individuals in the money condition were all tested in the morning and the individuals in the paper condition were all tested in the evening. Again, this would produce a confounded experiment because the researcher could not determine whether the differences in the pain ratings were caused by the money or caused by the time of day.

Researchers typically use three basic techniques to control other variables. First, the researcher could use *random assignment,* which means that each participant has an equal chance of being assigned to each of the treatment conditions. The goal of random assignment is to distribute the participant characteristics evenly between the two groups so that neither group is noticeably smarter (or older, or faster) than the other. Random assignment can also be used to control environmental variables. For example, participants could be assigned randomly for testing either in the morning or in the afternoon. Second, the researcher can use *matching* to ensure equivalent groups or equivalent environments. For example, the researcher could match groups by ensuring that every group has exactly 60% females and 40% males. Finally, the researcher can control variables by *holding them constant.* For example, if an experiment uses only 10-year-old children as participants (holding age constant), then the researcher can be certain that one group is not noticeably older than another.

DEFINITION

In the **experimental method**, one variable is manipulated while another variable is observed and measured. To establish a cause-and-effect relationship between the two variables, an experiment attempts to control all other variables to prevent them from influencing the results.

Terminology in the experimental method Specific names are used for the two variables that are studied by the experimental method. The variable that is manipulated by the experimenter is called the *independent variable.* It can be identified as the treatment conditions to which participants are assigned. For the example in Figure 1.6, money versus blank paper is the independent variable. The variable that is observed and measured to obtain scores within each condition is the *dependent variable.* For the example in Figure 1.6, the level of pain is the dependent variable.

DEFINITIONS

> The **independent variable** is the variable that is manipulated by the researcher. In behavioral research, the independent variable usually consists of the two (or more) treatment conditions to which subjects are exposed. The independent variable consists of the *antecedent* conditions that are manipulated *prior* to observing the dependent variable.

> The **dependent variable** is the variable that is observed to assess the effect of the treatment.

An experimental study evaluates the relationship between two variables by manipulating one variable (the independent variable) and measuring one variable (the dependent variable). Note that in an experiment only one variable is actually measured. You should realize that this is different from a correlational study, in which both variables are measured and the data consist of two separate scores for each individual.

Control Conditions in an Experiment   Often an experiment will include a condition in which the participants do not receive any treatment. The scores from these individuals are then compared with scores from participants who do receive the treatment. The goal of this type of study is to demonstrate that the treatment has an effect by showing that the scores in the treatment condition are substantially different from the scores in the no-treatment condition. In this kind of research, the no-treatment condition is called the *control condition,* and the treatment condition is called the *experimental condition.*

DEFINITIONS

> Individuals in a **control condition** do not receive the experimental treatment. Instead, they either receive no treatment or they receive a neutral, placebo treatment. The purpose of a control condition is to provide a baseline for comparison with the experimental condition. The individuals in the control condition are often called the **control group.**

> Individuals in the **experimental condition** do receive the experimental treatment and are often called the **experimental group.**

Note that the independent variable always consists of at least two values. (Something must have at least two different values before you can say that it is "variable.") For the money-counting experiment (see Figure 1.6), the independent variable is money versus plain paper. For an experiment with an experimental group and a control group, the independent variable is treatment versus no treatment.

NONEXPERIMENTAL METHODS: NONEQUIVALENT GROUPS AND PRE–POST STUDIES   In informal conversation, there is a tendency for people to use the term *experiment* to refer to any kind of research study. You should realize, however, that the term only applies to studies that satisfy the specific requirements outlined earlier. In particular, a real experiment must include manipulation of an independent variable and rigorous control of other, extraneous variables. As a result, there are a number of other research designs that compare groups of scores but are not true experiments. Two examples are shown in Figure 1.7 and are discussed in the following paragraphs. This type of research study is classified as nonexperimental.

FIGURE 1.7

Two examples of nonexperimental studies that involve comparing two groups of scores. In (a), a participant variable (gender) is used to create groups, and then the dependent variable (verbal score) is measured in each group. In (b), time is the variable used to define the two groups, and the dependent variable (depression) is measured at each of the two times.

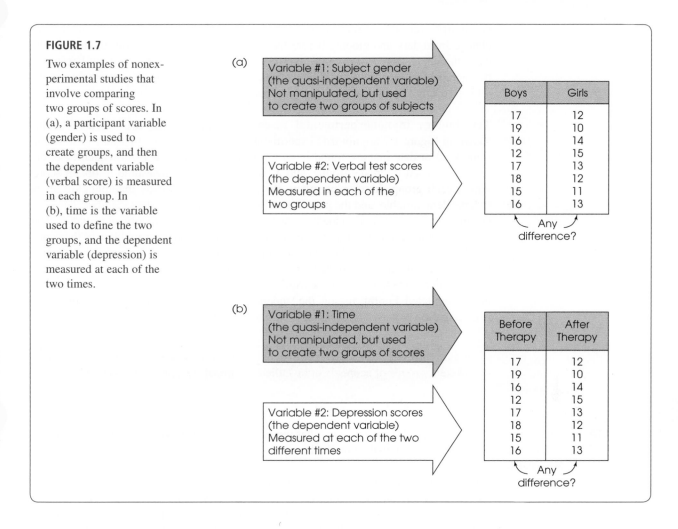

(a)

Variable #1: Subject gender (the quasi-independent variable) Not manipulated, but used to create two groups of subjects

Variable #2: Verbal test scores (the dependent variable) Measured in each of the two groups

Boys	Girls
17	12
19	10
16	14
12	15
17	13
18	12
15	11
16	13

Any difference?

(b)

Variable #1: Time (the quasi-independent variable) Not manipulated, but used to create two groups of scores

Variable #2: Depression scores (the dependent variable) Measured at each of the two different times

Before Therapy	After Therapy
17	12
19	10
16	14
12	15
17	13
18	12
15	11
16	13

Any difference?

The top part of Figure 1.7 shows an example of a *nonequivalent groups* study comparing boys and girls. Notice that this study involves comparing two groups of scores (like an experiment). However, the researcher has no ability to control the assignment of participants to groups—the males automatically go in the boy group and the females go in the girl group. Because this type of research compares preexisting groups, the researcher cannot control the assignment of participants to groups and cannot ensure equivalent groups. Other examples of nonequivalent group studies include comparing 8-year-old children and 10-year-old children or comparing people with an eating disorder and those with no disorder. Because it is impossible to use techniques like random assignment to control participant variables and ensure equivalent groups, this type of research is not a true experiment.

Correlational studies are also examples of nonexperimental research. In this section, however, we are discussing nonexperimental studies that compare two or more groups of scores.

The bottom part of Figure 1.7 shows an example of a *pre–post* study comparing depression scores before therapy and after therapy. The two groups of scores are obtained by measuring the same variable (depression) twice for each participant; once before therapy and again after therapy. In a pre–post study, however, the researcher has no control over the passage of time. The "before" scores are always measured earlier than the "after" scores. Although a difference between the two groups of scores may be caused by the treatment, it is always possible that the scores simply change as time goes by. For example, the depression scores may decrease over time in the same way that the symptoms of a cold disappear over time. In a pre–post study, the researcher also has no control over other variables that change with time. For example, the weather could change from dark and gloomy before therapy to bright and sunny after therapy. In this case, the depression scores could improve because of the weather and not because of the therapy. Because the researcher cannot control the passage of time or other variables related to time, this study is not a true experiment.

Terminology in nonexperimental research   Although the two research studies shown in Figure 1.7 are not true experiments, you should notice that they produce the same kind of data that are found in an experiment (see Figure 1.6). In each case, one variable is used to create groups, and a second variable is measured to obtain scores within each group. In an experiment, the groups are created by manipulation of the independent variable, and the participants' scores are the dependent variable. The same terminology is often used to identify the two variables in nonexperimental studies. That is, the variable that is used to create groups is the independent variable and the scores are the dependent variable. For example, the top part of Figure 1.7, gender (boy/girl), is the independent variable and the verbal test scores are the dependent variable. However, you should realize that gender (boy/girl) is not a true independent variable because it is not manipulated. For this reason, the "independent variable" in a nonexperimental study is often called a *quasi-independent variable.*

DEFINITION

> In a nonexperimental study, the "independent" variable that is used to create the different groups of scores is often called the **quasi-independent variable**.

DATA STRUCTURES AND STATISTICAL METHODS

The two general data structures that we used to classify research methods can also be used to classify statistical methods.

I. One group with two variables measured for each individual   Recall that the data from a correlational study consist of two scores, representing two different variables, for each individual. The scores can be listed in a table or displayed in a scatter plot as in Figure 1.5. The relationship between the two variables is usually measured and described using a statistic called a *correlation*. Correlations and the correlational method are discussed in detail in Chapter 14.

Occasionally, the measurement process used for a correlational study simply classifies individuals into categories that do not correspond to numerical values. For example, Greitemeyer and Osswald (2010) examine the effect of prosocial video games on prosocial behavior. One group of participants played a prosocial game and a second group played a neutral game. After the game was finished, the experimenter accidentally knocked a cup of pencils onto the floor and recorded whether the participants helped to pick them up. Note that the researcher has two scores for each individual (type of game and helping behavior) but neither of the scores is a numerical value. This type of data is typically summarized in a table showing how many individuals are classified into each of the possible categories. Table 1.1 is an example of this kind of summary table showing results similar to those obtained in the study. The table shows, for example, that 12 of the 18 participants playing the prosocial game helped to pick up pencils. This type of data can be coded with numbers (for example, neutral = 0 and prosocial = 1) so that it is possible to compute a correlation. However, the relationship between variables for non-numerical data, such as the data in Table 1.1, is usually evaluated using a statistical technique known as a *chi-square test*. Chi-square tests are presented in Chapter 15.

TABLE 1.1

Correlational data consisting of non-numerical scores. Note that there are two measurements for each individual: type of game played and helping behavior. The numbers indicate how many people are in each category. For example, out of the 18 participants who played a prosocial game, 12 helped the researcher.

	Type of Video Game	
	Prosocial	Neutral
Helped	12	6
Did not Help	6	12

II. Comparing two or more groups of scores   Most of the statistical procedures presented in this book are designed for research studies that compare groups of scores, like the experimental study in Figure 1.6 and the nonexperimental studies in Figure 1.7. Specifically, we examine descriptive statistics that summarize and describe the scores in each group, and we examine inferential statistics that allow us to use the groups, or samples, to generalize to the entire population.

When the measurement procedure produces numerical scores, the statistical evaluation typically involves computing the average score for each group and then comparing the averages. The process of computing averages is presented in Chapter 3, and a variety of statistical techniques for comparing averages are presented in Chapters 8–13. If the measurement process simply classifies individuals into non-numerical categories, the statistical evaluation usually consists of computing proportions for each group and then comparing proportions. Previously, in Table 1.1, we presented an example of non-numerical data examining the relationship between type of video game and helping behavior. The same data can be used to compare the proportions for prosocial game players with the proportions for neutral game players. For example, 67% of those who played the prosocial game helped the researcher compared to 33% of those who played the neutral game. As mentioned before, these data are evaluated using a chi-square test, which is presented in Chapter 15.

LEARNING CHECK

1. A research study comparing alcohol use for college students in the United States and Canada reports that more Canadian students drink but American students drink more (Kuo, Adlaf, Lee, Gliksman, Demers, and Wechsler, 2002). Is this study an example of an experiment? Explain why or why not.

2. What two elements are necessary for a research study to be an experiment?

3. Stephens, Atkins, and Kingston (2009) conducted an experiment in which participants were able to tolerate more pain when they shouted their favorite swear words over and over than when they shouted neutral words. Identify the independent and dependent variables for this study.

ANSWERS

1. This study is nonexperimental. The researcher is simply observing, not manipulating, two nonequivalent groups of participants.

2. First, the researcher must manipulate one of the two variables being studied. Second, all other variables that might influence the results must be controlled.

3. The independent variable is the type of word being shouted and the dependent variable is the amount of pain tolerated by each participant.

1.4   VARIABLES AND MEASUREMENT

The scores that are obtained in a research study are the result of observing and measuring variables. For example, a researcher may finish a study with a set of IQ scores, personality scores, or reaction-time scores. In this section, we take a closer look at the variables that are being measured and the process of measurement.

CONSTRUCTS AND OPERATIONAL DEFINITIONS

Some variables, such as height, weight, and eye color are well-defined, concrete entities that can be observed and measured directly. On the other hand, many variables studied by behavioral scientists are internal characteristics that cannot be observed or measured directly. However, we all assume that these variables exist and we use them to help describe and explain behavior. For example, we say that a student does well in school because he or she is *intelligent.* Or we say that someone is *anxious* in social situations, or that someone seems to be *hungry.* Variables like intelligence, anxiety, and hunger are called *constructs,* and because they are intangible and cannot be directly observed, they are often called *hypothetical constructs.*

Although constructs such as intelligence are internal characteristics that cannot be directly observed, it is possible to observe and measure behaviors that are representative of the construct. For example, we cannot "see" intelligence but we can see examples of intelligent behavior. The external behaviors can then be used to create an *operational definition* for the construct. An operational definition measures and defines a construct in terms of external behaviors. For example, we can measure performance on an IQ test and then use the test scores as a definition of intelligence. Or hunger can be measured and defined by the number of hours since last eating.

DEFINITIONS

> **Constructs,** also known as **hypothetical constructs,** are internal attributes or characteristics that cannot be directly observed but are useful for describing and explaining behavior.

> An **operational definition** identifies a measurement procedure (a set of operations) for measuring an external behavior and uses the resulting measurements as a definition and a measurement of an internal construct. Note that an operational definition has two components: First, it describes a set of operations for measuring a construct. Second, it defines the construct in terms of the resulting measurements.

DISCRETE AND CONTINUOUS VARIABLES

The variables in a study can be characterized by the type of values that can be assigned to them. A *discrete variable* consists of separate, indivisible categories. For this type of variable, there are no intermediate values between two adjacent categories. Consider the values displayed when dice are rolled. Between neighboring values—for example, five dots and six dots—no other values can ever be observed.

DEFINITION

> A **discrete variable** consists of separate, indivisible categories. No values can exist between two neighboring categories.

Discrete variables are commonly restricted to whole, countable numbers—for example, the number of children in a family or the number of students attending class. If you observe class attendance from day to day, you may count 18 students one day and 19 students the next day. However, it is impossible ever to observe a value between 18 and 19. A discrete variable may also consist of observations that differ qualitatively. For example, people can be classified by gender (male or female), by occupation (nurse, teacher, lawyer, and so on), and college students can be classified by academic major (art, biology, chemistry, and so on). In each case, the variable is discrete because it consists of separate, indivisible categories.

On the other hand, many variables are not discrete. Variables such as time, height, and weight are not limited to a fixed set of separate, indivisible categories. You can measure time, for example, in hours, minutes, seconds, or fractions of seconds. These variables are called *continuous* because they can be divided into an infinite number of fractional parts.

DEFINITION

> For a **continuous variable,** there are an infinite number of possible values that fall between any two observed values. A continuous variable is divisible into an infinite number of fractional parts.

Note that the terms *continuous* and *discrete* apply to the variables that are being measured and not to the scores that are obtained from the measurement. For example, people's heights can be measured by simply classifying individuals into three broad categories: tall, average, and short. Note that there is no measurement category between tall and average. Thus, it may appear that we are measuring a discrete variable. However, the underlying variable, height, is continuous. In this example, we chose to limit the measurement scale to three categories. We could have decided to measure height to the nearest inch, or the nearest half inch, and so on. The key to determining whether a variable is continuous or discrete is that a continuous variable can be divided into any number of fractional parts. Height can be measured to the nearest inch, the nearest 0.1 inch, or the nearest 0.01 inch. Similarly, a professor evaluating students' knowledge could use a pass/fail system that classifies students into two broad categories. However, the professor could choose to use a 10-point quiz that divides student knowledge into 11 categories corresponding to quiz scores from 0 to 10. Or the professor could use a 100-point exam that potentially divides student knowledge into 101 categories from 0 to 100. Whenever you are free to choose the degree of precision or the number of categories for measuring a variable, the variable must be continuous.

Measuring a continuous variable   Any continuous variable, for example, weight, can be pictured as a continuous line (Figure 1.8). Note that there are an infinite number of possible points on the line without any gaps or separations between neighboring points. For any two different points on the line, it is always possible to find a third value that is between the two points.

FIGURE 1.8

When measuring weight to the nearest whole pound, 149.6 and 150.3 are assigned the value of 150 (top). Any value in the interval between 149.5 and 150.5 is given the value of 150.

Two other factors apply to continuous variables:

1. When measuring a continuous variable, it should be very rare to obtain identical measurements for two different individuals. Because a continuous variable has an infinite number of possible values, it should be almost impossible for two people to have exactly the same score. If the data show a substantial number of tied scores, then you should suspect that the measurement procedure is relatively crude or that the variable is not really continuous.

2. When measuring a continuous variable, each measurement category is actually an *interval* that must be defined by boundaries. For example, two people who both claim to weigh 150 pounds are probably not *exactly* the same weight. However, they are both around 150 pounds. One person may actually weigh 149.6 and the other 150.3. Thus, a score of 150 is not a specific point on the scale but instead is an interval (see Figure 1.8). To differentiate a score of 150 from a score of 149 or 151, we must set up boundaries on the scale of measurement. These boundaries are called *real limits* and are positioned exactly halfway between adjacent scores. Thus, a score of $X = 150$ pounds is actually an interval bounded by a lower real limit of 149.5 at the bottom and an upper real limit of 150.5 at the top. Any individual whose weight falls between these real limits is assigned a score of $X = 150$.

DEFINITIONS

> **Real limits** are the boundaries of intervals for scores that are represented on a continuous number line. The real limit separating two adjacent scores is located exactly halfway between the scores. Each score has two real limits. The **upper real limit** is at the top of the interval, and the **lower real limit** is at the bottom.

The concept of real limits applies to any measurement of a continuous variable, even when the score categories are not whole numbers. For example, if you were measuring time to the nearest tenth of a second, the measurement categories would be 31.0, 31.1, 31.2, and so on. Each of these categories represents an interval on the scale that is bounded by real limits. For example, a score of $X = 31.1$ seconds indicates that the actual measurement is in an interval bounded by a lower real limit of 31.05 and an upper real limit of 31.15. Remember that the real limits are always halfway between adjacent categories.

Later in this book, real limits are used for constructing graphs and for various calculations with continuous scales. For now, however, you should realize that real limits are a necessity whenever you make measurements of a continuous variable.

SCALES OF MEASUREMENT

It should be obvious by now that data collection requires that we make measurements of our observations. Measurement involves assigning individuals or events to categories. The categories can simply be names such as male/female or employed/unemployed, or they can be numerical values such as 68 inches or 175 pounds. The set of categories makes up a *scale of measurement,* and the relationships between the categories determine different types of scales. The distinctions among the scales are important because they identify the limitations of certain types of measurements and because certain statistical procedures are appropriate for scores that have been measured on some scales but not on others. If you were interested in people's heights, for example, you could measure a group of individuals by simply classifying them into three categories: tall, medium, and short. However, this simple classification would not tell you much about the actual heights of the individuals, and these measurements would not give you enough information to calculate an average height for the group. Although the simple classification would be adequate for some purposes, you would need more sophisticated measurements before you could answer more detailed questions. In this section, we examine four different scales of measurement, beginning with the simplest and moving to the most sophisticated.

THE NOMINAL SCALE

The word *nominal* means "having to do with names." Measurement on a nominal scale involves classifying individuals into categories that have different names but are not related to each other in any systematic way. For example, if you were measuring the academic majors for a group of college students, the categories would be art, biology, business, chemistry, and so on. Each student would be classified in one category according to his or her major. The measurements from a nominal scale allow us to determine whether two individuals are different, but they do not identify either the direction or the size of the difference. If one student is an art major and another is a biology major, we can say that they are different, but we cannot say that art is "more than" or "less than" biology and we cannot specify how much difference there is between art and biology. Other examples of nominal scales include classifying people by race, gender, or occupation.

DEFINITION

> A **nominal scale** consists of a set of categories that have different names. Measurements on a nominal scale label and categorize observations, but do not make any quantitative distinctions between observations.

Although the categories on a nominal scale are not quantitative values, they are occasionally represented by numbers. For example, the rooms or offices in a building may be identified by numbers. You should realize that the room numbers are simply names and do not reflect any quantitative information. Room 109 is not necessarily bigger than Room 100 and certainly not 9 points bigger. It also is fairly common to use numerical values as a code for nominal categories when data are entered into computer programs. For example, the data from a survey may code males with a 0 and females with a 1. Again, the numerical values are simply names and do not represent any quantitative difference. The scales that follow do reflect an attempt to make quantitative distinctions.

THE ORDINAL SCALE

The categories that make up an *ordinal scale* not only have different names (as in a nominal scale) but also are organized in a fixed order corresponding to differences of magnitude.

DEFINITION

> An **ordinal scale** consists of a set of categories that are organized in an ordered sequence. Measurements on an ordinal scale rank observations in terms of size or magnitude.

Often, an ordinal scale consists of a series of ranks (first, second, third, and so on) like the order of finish in a horse race. Occasionally, the categories are identified by verbal labels like small, medium, and large drink sizes at a fast-food restaurant. In either case, the fact that the categories form an ordered sequence means that there is a directional relationship between categories. With measurements from an ordinal scale, you can determine whether two individuals are different and you can determine the direction of difference. However, ordinal measurements do not allow you to determine the size of the difference between two individuals. In a NASCAR race, for example, the first-place car finished faster than the second-place car, but the ranks don't tell you how much faster. Other examples of ordinal scales include socioeconomic class (upper, middle, lower) and T-shirt sizes (small, medium, large). In addition, ordinal scales are often used to measure variables for which it is difficult to assign numerical scores. For example, people can rank their food preferences but might have trouble explaining "how much" they prefer chocolate ice cream to steak.

THE INTERVAL AND RATIO SCALES

Both an *interval scale* and a *ratio scale* consist of a series of ordered categories (like an ordinal scale) with the additional requirement that the categories form a series of intervals that are all exactly the same size. Thus, the scale of measurement consists of a series of equal intervals, such as inches on a ruler. Other examples of interval and ratio scales are the measurement of time in seconds, weight in pounds, and temperature in degrees Fahrenheit. Note that, in each case, one interval (1 inch, 1 second, 1 pound, 1 degree) is the same size, no matter where it is located on the scale. The fact that the intervals are all the same size makes it possible to determine both the size and the direction of the difference between two measurements. For example, you know that a measurement of 80° Fahrenheit is higher than a measure of 60°, and you know that it is exactly 20° higher.

The factor that differentiates an interval scale from a ratio scale is the nature of the zero point. An interval scale has an arbitrary zero point. That is, the value 0 is assigned to a particular location on the scale simply as a matter of convenience or reference. In particular, a value of zero does not indicate a total absence of the variable being measured. For example, a temperature of 0 degrees Fahrenheit does not mean that there is no temperature, and it does not prohibit the temperature from going even lower. Interval scales with an arbitrary zero point are relatively rare. The two most common examples are the Fahrenheit and Celsius temperature scales. Other examples include golf scores (above and below par) and relative measures such as above and below average rainfall.

A ratio scale is anchored by a zero point that is not arbitrary but rather is a meaningful value representing none (a complete absence) of the variable being measured. The existence of an absolute, nonarbitrary zero point means that we can measure the absolute amount of the variable; that is, we can measure the distance from 0. This makes it possible to compare measurements in terms of ratios. For example, a gas tank with 10 gallons (10 more than 0) has twice as much gas as a tank with only 5 gallons (5 more than 0). Also note that a completely empty tank has 0 gallons. With a ratio scale, we can measure the direction and the size of the difference between two measurements and we can describe the difference in terms of a ratio. Ratio scales are quite common and include physical measures such as height and weight, as well as variables such as reaction time or the number of errors on a test. The distinction between an interval scale and a ratio scale is demonstrated in Example 1.2.

DEFINITIONS

An **interval scale** consists of ordered categories that are all intervals of exactly the same size. Equal differences between numbers on the scale reflect equal differences in magnitude. However, the zero point on an interval scale is arbitrary and does not indicate a zero amount of the variable being measured.

A **ratio scale** is an interval scale with the additional feature of an absolute zero point. With a ratio scale, ratios of numbers do reflect ratios of magnitude.

EXAMPLE 1.2

A researcher obtains measurements of height for a group of 8-year-old boys. Initially, the researcher simply records each child's height in inches, obtaining values such as 44, 51, 49, and so on. These initial measurements constitute a ratio scale. A value of zero represents no height (absolute zero). Also, it is possible to use these measurements to form ratios. For example, a child who is 60 inches tall is one-and-a-half times taller than a child who is 40 inches tall.

Now suppose that the researcher converts the initial measurement into a new scale by calculating the difference between each child's actual height and the average height for this age group. A child who is 1 inch taller than average now gets a score of +1; a child who is 4 inches taller than average gets a score of +4. Similarly, a child who is 2 inches shorter than average gets a score of –2. On this scale, a score of zero is a convenient reference point corresponding to the average height. Because zero no longer indicates a complete absence of height, the new scores constitute an interval scale of measurement.

Notice that original scores and the converted scores both involve measurement in inches, and you can compute differences, or distances, on either scale. For example, there is a 6-inch difference in height between two boys who measure 57 and 51 inches tall on the first scale. Likewise, there is a 6-inch difference between two boys who measure +9 and +3 on the second scale. However, you should also notice that ratio comparisons are not possible on the second scale. For example, a boy who measures +9 is not three times taller than a boy who measures +3.

STATISTICS AND SCALES OF MEASUREMENT

For our purposes, scales of measurement are important because they influence the kind of statistics that can and cannot be used. For example, if you measure IQ scores for a group of students, it is possible to add the scores together and calculate a mean score for the group. On the other hand, if you measure the academic major for each student, you

LEARNING CHECK

1. A tax form asks people to identify their annual income, number of dependents, and social security number. For each of these three variables, identify the scale of measurement that probably is used and identify whether the variable is continuous or discrete.

2. An English professor uses letter grades (A, B, C, D, and F) to evaluate a set of student essays. What kind of scale is being used to measure the quality of the essays?

3. The teacher in a communications class asks students to identify their favorite reality television show. The different television shows make up a _____ scale of measurement.

4. A researcher studies the factors that determine the number of children that couples decide to have. The variable, number of children, is a _____ (discrete/ continuous) variable.

5. **a.** When measuring height to the nearest inch, what are the real limits for a score of 68 inches?

   b. When measuring height to the nearest half inch, what are the real limits for a score of 68 inches?

ANSWERS

1. Annual income and number of dependents are measured on ratio scales, and income is a continuous variable. Social security number is measured on a nominal scale and is a discrete variable. The number of dependents is also discrete.

2. ordinal

3. nominal

4. discrete

5. **a.** 67.5 and 68.5

   b. 67.75 and 68.25

cannot compute the mean. (What is the mean of three psychology majors, an English major, and two chemistry majors?) The vast majority of the statistical techniques presented in this book are designed for numerical scores from an interval or a ratio scale. For most statistical applications, the distinction between an interval scale and a ratio scale is not important because both scales produce numerical values that permit us to compute differences between scores, to add scores, and to calculate mean scores. On the other hand, measurements from nominal or ordinal scales are typically not numerical values and are not compatible with many basic arithmetic operations. Therefore, alternative statistical techniques are necessary for data from nominal or ordinal scales of measurement (for example, the median and the mode in Chapter 3, the Spearman correlation in Chapter 14, and the chi-square tests in Chapter 15).

1.5   STATISTICAL NOTATION

The measurements obtained in research studies provide the data for statistical analysis. Most statistical techniques use the same general mathematical operations, notation, and basic arithmetic that you have learned during previous years of school. In case you are unsure of your mathematical skills, there is a mathematics review section in Appendix A at the back of this book. The appendix also includes a skills-assessment exam (p. 550) to help you determine whether you need the basic mathematics review. In this section, we introduce some of the specialized notation that is used for statistical calculations. In later chapters, additional statistical notation is introduced as it is needed.

SCORES   Measuring a variable in a research study typically yields a value or a score for each individual. Raw scores are the original, unchanged scores obtained in the study. Scores for a particular variable are represented by the letter X. For example, if performance in your statistics course is measured by tests and you obtain a 35 on the first test, then we could state that $X = 35$. A set of scores can be presented in a column that is headed by X. For example, a list of quiz scores from your class might be presented as shown in the margin (the single column on the left).

Score		
X	X	Y
37	72	165
35	68	151
35	67	160
30	67	160
25	68	146
17	70	160
16	66	133

When two variables are measured for each individual, the data can be presented as two lists labeled X and Y. For example, measurements of people's height in inches (variable X) and weight in pounds (variable Y) can be presented as shown in the double column in the margin. Each pair X, Y represents the observations made of a single participant.

The letter N is used to specify how many scores are in a set. An uppercase letter N identifies the number of scores in a population and a lowercase letter n identifies the number of scores in a sample. Throughout the remainder of the book you will notice that we often use notational differences to distinguish between samples and populations. For the height and weight data in the preceding table, $n = 7$ for both variables. Note that by using a lowercase letter n, we are indicating that these scores come from a sample.

SUMMATION NOTATION   Many of the computations required in statistics involve adding a set of scores. Because this procedure is used so frequently, a special notation is used to refer to the sum of a set of scores. The Greek letter *sigma,* or Σ, is used to stand for summation. The expression ΣX means to add all the scores for variable X. The summation sign, Σ, can be read as "the sum of." Thus, ΣX is read "the sum of the scores." For the following set of quiz scores,

10, 6, 7, 4

$\Sigma X = 27$ and $N = 4$.

To use summation notation correctly, keep in mind the following two points:

1. The summation sign, Σ, is always followed by a symbol or mathematical expression. The symbol or expression identifies exactly which values are to be added. To compute ΣX, for example, the symbol following the summation sign is X, and the task is to find the sum of the X values. On the other hand, to compute $\Sigma(X - 1)^2$, the summation sign is followed by a relatively complex mathematical expression, so your first task is to calculate all of the $(X - 1)^2$ values and then add the results.

2. The summation process is often included with several other mathematical operations, such as multiplication or squaring. To obtain the correct answer, it is essential that the different operations be done in the correct sequence. Following is a list showing the correct *order of operations* for performing mathematical operations. Most of this list should be familiar, but you should note that we have inserted the summation process as the fourth operation in the list.

Order of Mathematical Operations

1. Any calculation contained within parentheses is done first.

2. Squaring (or raising to other exponents) is done second.

3. Multiplying and/or dividing is done third. A series of multiplication and/or division operations should be done in order from left to right.

More information on the order of operations for mathematics is available in the Math Review appendix, page 551.

4. Summation using the Σ notation is done next.

5. Finally, any other addition and/or subtraction is done.

The following examples demonstrate how summation notation is used in most of the calculations and formulas we present in this book.

EXAMPLE 1.3

A set of four scores consists of values 3, 1, 7, and 4. We will compute ΣX, ΣX^2, and $(\Sigma X)^2$ for these scores. To help demonstrate the calculations, we will use a computational table showing the original scores (the X values) in the first column. Additional columns can then be added to show additional steps in the series of operations. You should notice that the first three operations in the list (parentheses, squaring, and multiplying) all create a new column of values. The last two operations, however, produce a single value corresponding to the sum.

X	X^2
3	9
1	1
7	49
4	16

The table to the left shows the original scores (the X values) and the squared scores (the X^2 values) that are needed to compute ΣX^2.

The first calculation, ΣX, does not include any parentheses, squaring, or multiplication, so we go directly to the summation operation. The X values are listed in the first column of the table, and we simply add the values in this column:

$$\Sigma X = 3 + 1 + 7 + 4 = 15$$

To compute ΣX^2, the correct order of operations is to square each score and then find the sum of the squared values. The computational table shows the original scores and the results obtained from squaring (the first step in the calculation). The second step is to find the sum of the squared values, so we simply add the numbers in the X^2 column.

$$\Sigma X^2 = 9 + 1 + 49 + 16 = 75$$

The final calculation, $(\Sigma X)^2$, includes parentheses, so the first step is to perform the calculation inside the parentheses. Thus, we first find ΣX and then square this sum. Earlier, we computed $\Sigma X = 15$, so

$$(\Sigma X)^2 = (15)^2 = 225$$

E X A M P L E   1 . 4

Next, we use the same set of four scores from Example 1.3 and compute $\Sigma(X - 1)$ and $\Sigma(X - 1)^2$. The following computational table will help demonstrate the calculations.

X	(X − 1)	(X − 1)²	
3	2	4	The first column lists the original scores. A second column lists the (X − 1) values, and a third column shows the (X − 1)² values.
1	0	0	
7	6	36	
4	3	9	

To compute $\Sigma(X - 1)$, the first step is to perform the operation inside the parentheses. Thus, we begin by subtracting one point from each of the X values. The resulting values are listed in the middle column of the table. The next step is to add the $(X - 1)$ values.

$$\Sigma(X - 1) = 2 + 0 + 6 + 3 + = 11$$

The calculation of $\Sigma(X - 1)^2$ requires three steps. The first step (inside parentheses) is to subtract 1 point from each X value. The results from this step are shown in the middle column of the computational table. The second step is to square each of the $(X - 1)$ values. The results from this step are shown in the third column of the table. The final step is to add the $(X - 1)^2$ values to obtain

$$\Sigma(X - 1)^2 = 4 + 0 + 36 + 9 = 49$$

Notice that this calculation requires squaring before adding. A common mistake is to add the $(X - 1)$ values and then square the total. Be careful!

E X A M P L E   1 . 5

In both of the preceding examples, and in many other situations, the summation operation is the last step in the calculation. According to the order of operations, parentheses, exponents, and multiplication all come before summation. However, there are situations in which extra addition and subtraction are completed after the summation. For this example, use the same scores that appeared in the previous two examples, and compute $\Sigma X - 1$.

With no parentheses, exponents, or multiplication, the first step is the summation. Thus, we begin by computing ΣX. Earlier we found $\Sigma X = 15$. The next step is to subtract one point from the total. For these data,

$$\Sigma X - 1 = 15 - 1 = 14$$

EXAMPLE 1.6   For this example, each individual has two scores. The first score is identified as X, and the second score is Y. With the help of the following computational table, we compute ΣX, ΣY, and ΣXY.

To find ΣX, simply add the values in the X column.

Person	X	Y	XY
A	3	5	15
B	1	3	3
C	7	4	28
D	4	2	8

$$\Sigma X = 3 + 1 + 7 + 4 = 15$$

Similarly, ΣY is the sum of the Y values.

$$\Sigma Y = 5 + 3 + 4 + 2 = 14$$

To compute ΣXY, the first step is to multiply X by Y for each individual. The resulting products (XY values) are listed in the third column of the table. Finally, we add the products to obtain

$$\Sigma XY = 15 + 3 + 28 + 8 = 54$$

LEARNING CHECK

1. Calculate each value requested for the following scores: 4, 3, 7, 1.

   a. ΣX **d.** $\Sigma X - 1$

   b. ΣX^2 **e.** $\Sigma(X - 1)$

   c. $(\Sigma X)^2$ **f.** $\Sigma(X - 1)^2$

2. Identify the first step in each of the following calculations.

   a. ΣX^2 **c.** $\Sigma(X - 2)^2$

   b. $(\Sigma X)^2$

3. Use summation notation to express each of the following.

   a. Subtract 2 points from each score and then add the resulting values.

   b. Subtract 2 points from each score, square the resulting values, and then add the squared numbers.

   c. Add the scores and then square the total.

ANSWERS

1. **a.** 15   **d.** 14

   b. 75   **e.** 11

   c. 225   **f.** 49

2. **a.** Square each score.

   b. Add the scores.

   c. Subtract 2 points from each score.

3. **a.** $\Sigma(X - 2)$ **c.** $(\Sigma X)^2$

   b. $\Sigma(X - 2)^2$

SUMMARY

1. The term *statistics* is used to refer to methods for organizing, summarizing, and interpreting data.

2. Scientific questions usually concern a population, which is the entire set of individuals one wishes to study. Usually, populations are so large that it is impossible to examine every individual, so most research is conducted with samples. A sample is a group selected from a population, usually for purposes of a research study.

3. A characteristic that describes a sample is called a statistic, and a characteristic that describes a population is called a parameter. Although sample statistics are usually representative of corresponding population parameters, there is typically some discrepancy between a statistic and a parameter. The naturally occurring difference between a statistic and a parameter is called sampling error.

4. Statistical methods can be classified into two broad categories: descriptive statistics, which organize and summarize data, and inferential statistics, which use sample data to draw inferences about populations.

5. The correlational method examines relationships between variables by measuring two different variables for each individual. This method allows researchers to measure and describe relationships, but cannot produce a cause-and-effect explanation for the relationship.

6. The experimental method examines relationships between variables by manipulating an independent variable to create different treatment conditions and then measuring a dependent variable to obtain a group of scores in each condition. The groups of scores are then compared. A systematic difference between groups provides evidence that changing the independent variable from one condition to another also caused a change in the dependent variable. All other variables are controlled to prevent them from influencing the relationship. The intent of the experimental method is to demonstrate a cause-and-effect relationship between variables.

7. Nonexperimental studies also examine relationships between variables by comparing groups of scores, but they do not have the rigor of true experiments and cannot produce cause-and-effect explanations. Instead of manipulating a variable to create different groups, a nonexperimental study uses a preexisting participant characteristic (such as male/female) or the passage of time (before/after) to create the groups being compared.

8. A discrete variable consists of indivisible categories, often whole numbers that vary in countable steps. A continuous variable consists of categories that are infinitely divisible and each score corresponds to an interval on the scale. The boundaries that separate intervals are called real limits and are located exactly halfway between adjacent scores.

9. A measurement scale consists of a set of categories that are used to classify individuals. A nominal scale consists of categories that differ only in name and are not differentiated in terms of magnitude or direction. In an ordinal scale, the categories are differentiated in terms of direction, forming an ordered series. An interval scale consists of an ordered series of categories that are all equal-sized intervals. With an interval scale, it is possible to differentiate direction and magnitude (or distance) between categories. Finally, a ratio scale is an interval scale for which the zero point indicates none of the variable being measured. With a ratio scale, ratios of measurements reflect ratios of magnitude.

10. The letter X is used to represent scores for a variable. If a second variable is used, Y represents its scores. The letter N is used as the symbol for the number of scores in a population; n is the symbol for the number of scores in a sample.

11. The Greek letter sigma (Σ) is used to stand for summation. Therefore, the expression ΣX is read "the sum of the scores." Summation is a mathematical operation (like addition or multiplication) and must be performed in its proper place in the order of operations; summation occurs after operations in parentheses, exponents, and multiplication/division have been completed.

KEY TERMS

statistics (5)
population (5)
sample (6)
variable (7)
datum (7)
raw score (7)
data (7)
data set (7)
parameter (7)
statistic (7)
descriptive statistics (8)
inferential statistics (8)
sampling error (8)
correlational method (12)
correlational research strategy (12)
experimental method (15)

confounded (15)
random assignment (15)
matching (15)
independent variable (16)
dependent variable (16)
control condition or control
    group (16)
experimental condition or
    experimental group (16)
nonequivalent groups study (17)
pre–post study (17)
quasi-independent variable (18)
construct or hypothetical
    construct (20)
operational definition (20)
discrete variable (20)

continuous variable (21)
real limits (22)
lower real limit (22)
upper real limit (22)
nominal scale (23)
ordinal scale (23)
interval scale (24)
ratio scale (24)
sigma (26)
order of operations (27)

RESOURCES

 Go to CengageBrain.com to access Psychology CourseMate, where you will find an interactive eBook, glossaries, flashcards, quizzes, statistics workshops, and more.

aplia

If your professor has assigned Aplia:

1. Sign in to your account.
2. Complete the corresponding exercises as required by your professor.
3. When finished, click "Grade It Now" to see which areas you have mastered, which areas need more work, and detailed explanations of every answer.

The Statistical Package for the Social Sciences, known as SPSS, is a computer program that performs most of the statistical calculations that are presented in this book, and is commonly available on college and university computer systems. Appendix D contains a general introduction to SPSS. In the Resources section at the end of each chapter for which SPSS is applicable, there are step-by-step instructions for using SPSS to perform the statistical operations presented in the chapter.

FOCUS ON PROBLEM SOLVING

It may help to simplify summation notation if you observe that the summation sign is always followed by a symbol or symbolic expression—for example, ΣX or $\Sigma(X + 3)$. This symbol specifies which values you are to add. If you use the symbol as a column heading and list all the appropriate values in the column, your task is simply to add up the numbers in the column. To find $\Sigma(X + 3)$ for example, start a column headed with $(X + 3)$ next to the column of Xs. List all the $(X + 3)$ values; then find the total for the column.

Often, summation notation is part of a relatively complex mathematical expression that requires several steps of calculation. The series of steps must be performed according to the order of mathematical operations (see page 27). The best procedure is to use a computational table that begins with the original X values listed in the first column. Except for summation, each step in the calculation creates a new column of values. For example, computing $\Sigma(X + 1)^2$ involves three steps and produces a computational table with three columns. The final step is to add the values in the third column (see Example 1.4).

DEMONSTRATION 1.1

SUMMATION NOTATION

A set of scores consists of the following values:

7   3   9   5   4

For these scores, compute each of the following:

ΣX
$(\Sigma X)^2$
ΣX^2
$\Sigma X + 5$
$\Sigma(X - 2)$

Compute ΣX To compute ΣX, we simply add all of the scores in the group.

$$\Sigma X = 7 + 3 + 9 + 5 + 4 = 28$$

Compute $(\Sigma X)^2$ The first step, inside the parentheses, is to compute ΣX. The second step is to square the value for ΣX.

X	X^2
7	49
3	9
9	81
5	25
4	16

$$\Sigma X = 28 \text{ and } (\Sigma X)^2 = (28)^2 = 784$$

Compute ΣX^2 The first step is to square each score. The second step is to add the squared scores. The computational table shows the scores and squared scores. To compute ΣX^2 we add the values in the X^2 column.

$$\Sigma X^2 = 49 + 9 + 81 + 25 + 16 = 180$$

X	X − 2
7	5
3	1
9	7
5	3
4	2

Compute $\Sigma X + 5$ The first step is to compute ΣX. The second step is to add 5 points to the total.

$$\Sigma X = 28 \text{ and } \Sigma X + 5 = 28 + 5 = 33$$

Compute $\Sigma(X − 2)$ The first step, inside parentheses, is to subtract 2 points from each score. The second step is to add the resulting values. The computational table shows the scores and the $(X − 2)$ values. To compute $\Sigma(X − 2)$, add the values in the $(X − 2)$ column

$$\Sigma(X − 2) = 5 + 1 + 7 + 3 + 2 = 18$$

PROBLEMS

*1. A researcher is investigating the effectiveness of a treatment for adolescent boys who are taking medication for depression. A group of 30 boys is selected and half receive the new treatment in addition to their medication and the other half continue to take their medication without any treatment. For this study,
   a. Identify the population.
   b. Identify the sample.

2. Define the terms *population, sample, parameter,* and *statistic.*

3. Statistical methods are classified into two major categories: descriptive and inferential. Describe the general purpose for the statistical methods in each category.

4. Define the concept of sampling error and explain why this phenomenon creates a problem to be addressed by inferential statistics.

5. Describe the data for a correlational research study. Explain how these data are different from the data obtained in experimental and nonexperimental studies, which also evaluate relationships between two variables.

6. What is the goal for an experimental research study? Identify the two elements that are necessary for an experiment to achieve its goal.

7. Knight and Haslam (2010) found that office workers who had some input into the design of their office space were more productive and had higher well-being compared to workers for whom the office design was completely controlled by an office manager. For this study, identify the independent variable and the dependent variable.

8. Judge and Cable (2010) found that thin women had higher incomes than heavier women. Is this an example of an experimental or a nonexperimental study?

9. Two researchers are both interested in determining whether large doses of vitamin C can help prevent

the common cold. Each obtains a sample of $n = 20$ college students.
   a. The first researcher interviews each student to determine whether they routinely take a vitamin C supplement. The researcher then records the number of colds each individual gets during the winter. Is this an experimental or a nonexperimental study? Explain your answer.
   b. The second researcher separates the students into two roughly equivalent groups. The students in one group are given a daily multivitamin containing a large amount of vitamin C, and the other group gets a multivitamin with no vitamin C. The researcher then records the number of colds each individual gets during the winter. Is this an experimental or a nonexperimental study? Explain your answer.

10. Weinstein, McDermott, and Roediger (2010) conducted an experiment to evaluate the effectiveness of different study strategies. One part of the study asked students to prepare for a test by reading a passage. In one condition, students generated and answered questions after reading the passage. In a second condition, students simply read the passage a second time. All students were then given a test on the passage material and the researchers recorded the number of correct answers.
   a. Identify the dependent variable for this study.
   b. Is the dependent variable discrete or continuous?
   c. What scale of measurement (nominal, ordinal, interval, or ratio) is used to measure the dependent variable?

11. A research study reports that alcohol consumption is significantly higher for students at a state university than for students at a religious college (Wells, 2010). Is this study an example of an experiment? Explain why or why not.

12. Oxytocin is a naturally occurring brain chemical that is nicknamed the "love hormone" because it seems to play a role in the formation of social relationships such as mating pairs and parent–child bonding. A recent study demonstrated that oxytocin appears to

increase people's tendency to trust others (Kosfeld, Heinrichs, Zak, Fischbacher, and Fehr, 2005). Using an investment game, the study demonstrated that people who inhaled oxytocin were more likely to give their money to a trustee compared to people who inhaled an inactive placebo. For this experimental study, identify the independent variable and the dependent variable.

13. For each of the following, determine whether the variable being measured is discrete or continuous and explain your answer.
    a. Social networking (number of daily minutes on Facebook)
    b. Family size (number of siblings)
    c. Preference between digital or analog watch
    d. Number of correct answers on a statistics quiz

14. Four scales of measurement were introduced in this chapter: nominal, ordinal, interval, and ratio.
    a. What additional information is obtained from measurements on an ordinal scale compared to measurements on a nominal scale?
    b. What additional information is obtained from measurements on an interval scale compared to measurements on an ordinal scale?
    c. What additional information is obtained from measurements on a ratio scale compared to measurements on an interval scale?

15. In an experiment examining the effects Tai Chi on arthritis pain, Callahan (2009) selected a large sample of individuals with doctor-diagnosed arthritis. Half of the participants immediately began a Tai Chi course and the other half (the control group) waited 8 weeks before beginning the program. At the end of 8 weeks, the individuals who had experienced Tai Chi had less arthritis pain that those who had not participated in the course.
    a. Identify the independent variable for this study.
    b. What scale of measurement is used for the independent variable?
    c. Identify the dependent variable for this study.
    d. What scale of measurement is used for the dependent variable?

16. Explain why *shyness* is a hypothetical construct instead of a concrete variable. Describe how shyness might be measured and defined using an operational definition.

17. Ford and Torok (2008) found that motivational signs were effective in increasing physical activity on a college campus. Signs such as "Step up to a healthier lifestyle" and "An average person burns 10 calories a minute walking up the stairs" were posted by the elevators and stairs in a college building. Students and faculty increased their use of the stairs during times that the signs were posted compared to times when there were no signs.
    a. Identify the independent and dependent variables for this study.
    b. What scale of measurement is used for the independent variable?

18. For the following scores, find the value of each expression:
    a. ΣX
    b. ΣX^2
    c. $\Sigma X + 1$
    d. $\Sigma(X + 1)$

X
3
5
0
2

19. For the following set of scores, find the value of each expression:
    a. ΣX^2
    b. $(\Sigma X)^2$
    c. $\Sigma(X - 1)$
    d. $\Sigma(X - 1)^2$

X
3
2
5
1
3

20. For the following set of scores, find the value of each expression:
    a. ΣX
    b. ΣX^2
    c. $\Sigma(X + 3)$

X
6
−2
0
−3
−1

21. Two scores, X and Y, are recorded for each of $n = 4$ subjects. For these scores, find the value of each expression.
    a. ΣX
    b. ΣY
    c. ΣXY

Subject	X	Y
A	3	4
B	0	7
C	−1	5
D	2	2

22. Use summation notation to express each of the following calculations:
    a. Add 1 point to each score, and then add the resulting values.

b. Add 1 point to each score and square the result. Then add the squared values.

c. Add the scores and square the sum. Then subtract 3 points from the squared value.

23. For the set of scores at the right, find the value of each expression:

X
1
6
2
3

a. ΣX^2

b. $(\Sigma X)^2$

c. $\Sigma(X - 3)$

d. $\Sigma(X - 3)^2$

C H A P T E R

2

Frequency Distributions

Tools You Will Need

The following items are considered essential background material for this chapter. If you doubt your knowledge of any of these items, you should review the appropriate chapter or section before proceeding.

- Proportions (math review, Appendix A)
  - Fractions
  - Decimals
  - Percentages

- Scales of measurement (Chapter 1): Nominal, ordinal, interval, and ratio
- Continuous and discrete variables (Chapter 1)
- Real limits (Chapter 1)

aplia

Aplia for *Essentials of Statistics for the Behavioral Sciences*
After reading, go to "Resources" at the end of this chapter for an introduction on how to use Aplia's homework and learning resources.

2.1 INTRODUCTION TO FREQUENCY DISTRIBUTIONS

The results from a research study usually consist of pages of numbers corresponding to the measurements, or scores, collected during the study. The immediate problem for the researcher is to organize the scores into some comprehensible form so that any patterns in the data can be seen easily and communicated to others. This is the job of descriptive statistics: to simplify the organization and presentation of data. One of the most common procedures for organizing a set of data is to place the scores in a *frequency distribution*.

DEFINITION

> A **frequency distribution** is an organized tabulation of the number of individuals located in each category on the scale of measurement.

A frequency distribution takes a disorganized set of scores and places them in order from highest to lowest, grouping together individuals who all have the same score. If the highest score is $X = 10$, for example, the frequency distribution groups together all the 10s, then all the 9s, then the 8s, and so on. Thus, a frequency distribution allows the researcher to see "at a glance" the entire set of scores. It shows whether the scores are generally high or low, whether they are concentrated in one area or spread out across the entire scale, and generally provides an organized picture of the data. In addition to providing a picture of the entire set of scores, a frequency distribution allows you to see the location of any individual score relative to all of the other scores in the set.

A frequency distribution can be structured either as a table or as a graph, but in either case, the distribution presents the same two elements:

1. The set of categories that make up the original measurement scale.

2. A record of the frequency, or number of individuals in each category.

Thus, a frequency distribution presents a picture of how the individual scores are distributed on the measurement scale—hence the name *frequency distribution*.

2.2 FREQUENCY DISTRIBUTION TABLES

It is customary to list categories from highest to lowest, but this is an arbitrary arrangement. Many computer programs list categories from lowest to highest.

The simplest frequency distribution table presents the measurement scale by listing the different measurement categories (*X* values) in a column from highest to lowest. Beside each *X* value, we indicate the frequency, or the number of times that particular measurement occurred in the data. It is customary to use an *X* as the column heading for the scores and an *f* as the column heading for the frequencies. An example of a frequency distribution table follows.

EXAMPLE 2.1

The following set of $N = 20$ scores was obtained from a 10-point statistics quiz. We organize these scores by constructing a frequency distribution table. Scores:

8	9	8	7	10	9	6	4	9	8
7	8	10	9	8	6	9	7	8	9

1. The highest score is $X = 10$, and the lowest score is $X = 4$. Therefore, the first column of the table lists the categories that make up the scale of measurement

X	f
10	2
9	5
8	7
7	3
6	2
5	0
4	1

(X values) from 10 down to 4. Notice that all of the possible values are listed in the table. For example, no one had a score of $X = 5$, but this value is included. With an ordinal, interval, or ratio scale, the categories are listed in order (usually highest to lowest). For a nominal scale, the categories can be listed in any order.

2. The frequency associated with each score is recorded in the second column. For example, two people had scores of $X = 10$, so there is a 2 in the f column beside $X = 10$.

Because the table organizes the scores, it is possible to see the general quiz results very quickly. For example, there were only two perfect scores, but most of the class had high grades (8s and 9s). With one exception (the score of $X = 4$), it appears that the class has learned the material fairly well.

Notice that the X values in a frequency distribution table represent the scale of measurement, *not* the actual set of scores. For example, the X column lists the value 10 only one time, but the frequency column indicates that there are actually two values of $X = 10$. Also, the X column lists a value of $X = 5$, but the frequency column indicates that no one actually had a score of $X = 5$.

You also should notice that the frequencies can be used to find the total number of scores in the distribution. By adding up the frequencies, you obtain the total number of individuals:

$$\Sigma f = N$$

OBTAINING ΣX FROM A FREQUENCY DISTRIBUTION TABLE

There may be times when you need to compute the sum of the scores, ΣX, or perform other computations for a set of scores that has been organized into a frequency distribution table. To complete these calculations correctly, you must use all of the information presented in the table. That is, it is essential to use the information in the f column as well as that in the X column to obtain the full set of scores.

When it is necessary to perform calculations for scores that have been organized into a frequency distribution table, the safest procedure is to take the individual scores out of the table before you begin any computations. This process is demonstrated in the following example.

EXAMPLE 2.2

X	f
5	1
4	2
3	3
2	3
1	1

Consider the frequency distribution table shown in the margin. The table shows that the distribution has one 5, two 4s, three 3s, three 2s, and one 1, for a total of 10 scores. If you simply list all 10 scores, you can safely proceed with calculations such as finding ΣX or ΣX^2. For example, to compute ΣX you must add all 10 scores:

$$\Sigma X = 5 + 4 + 4 + 3 + 3 + 3 + 2 + 2 + 2 + 1$$

For the distribution in this table, you should obtain $\Sigma X = 29$. Try it yourself. Similarly, to compute ΣX^2 you square each of the 10 scores and then add the squared values.

$$\Sigma X^2 = 5^2 + 4^2 + 4^2 + 3^2 + 3^2 + 3^2 + 2^2 + 2^2 + 2^2 + 1^2$$

This time you should obtain $\Sigma X^2 = 97$.

An alternative way to get ΣX from a frequency distribution table is to multiply each X value by its frequency and then add these products. This sum may be expressed in symbols as ΣfX. The computation is summarized as follows for the data in Example 2.2:

Caution: Doing calculations within the table works well for ΣX but can lead to errors for more complex formulas.

X	f	fX	
5	1	5	(the one 5 totals 5)
4	2	8	(the two 4s total 8)
3	3	9	(the three 3s total 9)
2	3	6	(the three 2s total 6)
1	1	1	(the one 1 totals 1)
		$\Sigma X = 29$	

No matter which method you use to find ΣX, the important point is that you must use the information given in the frequency column as well as the information in the X column.

PROPORTIONS AND PERCENTAGES

In addition to the two basic columns of a frequency distribution table, there are other measures that describe the distribution of scores and can be incorporated into the table. The two most common are proportion and percentage.

Proportion measures the fraction of the total group that is associated with each score. In Example 2.2, there were two individuals with $X = 4$. Thus, 2 out of 10 people had $X = 4$, so the proportion would be $\frac{2}{10} = 0.20$. In general, the proportion associated with each score is

$$\text{proportion} = p = \frac{f}{N}$$

Because proportions describe the frequency (f) in relation to the total number (N), they often are called *relative frequencies*. Although proportions can be expressed as fractions (for example, $\frac{2}{10}$), they more commonly appear as decimals. A column of proportions, headed with a p, can be added to the basic frequency distribution table (see Example 2.3).

In addition to using frequencies (f) and proportions (p), researchers often describe a distribution of scores with percentages. For example, an instructor might describe the results of an exam by saying that 15% of the class earned As, 23% earned Bs, and so on. To compute the percentage associated with each score, you first find the proportion (p) and then multiply by 100:

$$\text{percentage} = p(100) = \frac{f}{N}(100)$$

Percentages can be included in a frequency distribution table by adding a column headed with % (see Example 2.3).

EXAMPLE 2.3   The frequency distribution table from Example 2.2 is repeated here. This time we have added columns showing the proportion (p) and the percentage (%) associated with each score.

X	f	$p = f/N$	$\% = p(100)$
5	1	1/10 = 0.10	10%
4	2	2/10 = 0.20	20%
3	3	3/10 = 0.30	30%
2	3	3/10 = 0.30	30%
1	1	1/10 = 0.10	10%

1. Construct a frequency distribution table for the following set of scores.

   Scores: 3, 2, 3, 2, 4, 1, 3, 3, 5

2. Find each of the following values for the sample in the following frequency distribution table.

   a. n

   b. ΣX

   c. ΣX^2

X	f
5	1
4	2
3	2
2	4
1	1

ANSWERS

1.

X	f
5	1
4	1
3	4
2	2
1	1

2. **a.** $n = 10$ **b.** $\Sigma X = 28$ **c.** $\Sigma X^2 = 92$ (square then add all 10 scores)

GROUPED FREQUENCY DISTRIBUTION TABLES

When the scores are whole numbers, the total number of rows for a regular table can be obtained by finding the difference between the highest and the lowest scores and adding 1:

rows = highest – lowest + 1

When a set of data covers a wide range of values, it is unreasonable to list all of the individual scores in a frequency distribution table. Consider, for example, a set of exam scores that range from a low of $X = 41$ to a high of $X = 96$. These scores cover a *range* of more than 50 points.

If we were to list all of the individual scores from $X = 96$ down to $X = 41$, it would take 56 rows to complete the frequency distribution table. Although this would organize the data, the table would be long and cumbersome. Remember: The purpose for constructing a table is to obtain a relatively simple, organized picture of the data. This can be accomplished by grouping the scores into intervals and then listing the intervals in the table instead of listing each individual score. For example, we could construct a table showing the number of students who had scores in the 90s, the number with scores in the 80s, and so on. The result is called a *grouped frequency distribution table* because we are presenting groups of scores rather than individual values. The groups, or intervals, are called *class intervals.*

There are several guidelines that help guide you in the construction of a grouped frequency distribution table. Note that these are simply guidelines, rather than absolute requirements, but they do help to produce a simple, well-organized, and easily understood table.

Guideline 1   The grouped frequency distribution table should have about 10 class intervals. If a table has many more than 10 intervals, it becomes cumbersome and defeats the purpose of a frequency distribution table. On the other hand, if you have too few intervals, you begin to lose information about the distribution of the scores. At the extreme, with only one interval, the table would not tell you anything about how the scores are distributed. Remember that the purpose of a frequency distribution is to help a researcher see the data. With too few or too many intervals, the table will not provide a clear picture. You should note that 10 intervals is a general guide. If you are constructing a table on a blackboard, for example, you probably want only 5 or 6 intervals. If the table is to be printed in a scientific report, you may want 12 or 15 intervals. In each case, your goal is to present a table that is relatively easy to see and understand.

Guideline 2   The width of each interval should be a relatively simple number. For example, 2, 5, 10, or 20 would be a good choice for the interval width. Notice that it is easy to count by 5s or 10s. These numbers are easy to understand and make it possible for someone to see quickly how you have divided the range of scores.

Guideline 3   The bottom score in each class interval should be a multiple of the width. If you are using a width of 10 points, for example, the intervals should start with 10, 20, 30, 40, and so on. Again, this makes it easier for someone to understand how the table has been constructed.

Guideline 4   All intervals should be the same width. They should cover the range of scores completely with no gaps and no overlaps, so that any particular score belongs in exactly one interval.

The application of these rules is demonstrated in Example 2.4.

EXAMPLE 2.4

An instructor has obtained the set of $N = 25$ exam scores shown here. To help organize these scores, we will place them in a frequency distribution table. The scores are:

82	75	88	93	53	84	87	58	72	94	69	84	61
91	64	87	84	70	76	89	75	80	73	78	60	

Remember, when the scores are whole numbers, the number of rows is determined by

highest − lowest + 1

The first step is to determine the range of scores. For these data, the smallest score is $X = 53$ and the largest score is $X = 94$, so a total of 42 rows would be needed for a table that lists each individual score. Because 42 rows would not provide a simple table, we have to group the scores into class intervals.

The best method for finding a good interval width is a systematic trial-and-error approach that uses guidelines 1 and 2 simultaneously. The goal is to find an interval width that is an easy number and produces a table with around 10 intervals. For this example, the scores cover a range of 42 points, so we will try several different interval widths to see how many intervals are needed to cover the range. For example, if each interval is 2 points wide, it would take 21 intervals to cover a range of 42 points. This is too many, so we move on to an interval width of 5 or 10 points. The following table shows how many intervals would be needed for these possible widths:

Width	Number of Intervals Needed to Cover a Range of 42 Points
2	21 (too many)
5	9 (OK)
10	5 (too few)

Note that the computed number of intervals is just an estimate of the actual number needed for the final table. Because the bottom interval usually extends below the lowest score and the top interval extends above the highest score, you may need slightly more than the computed number of intervals. Also notice that an interval width of 5 points will produce a table with about 10 intervals, which is exactly what we want.

The next step is to identify the actual intervals. The lowest score for these data is $X = 53$, so the lowest interval should contain this value. Because the interval should have a multiple of 5 as its bottom score, the interval should begin at 50. The interval has a width of 5, so it should contain 5 values: 50, 51, 52, 53, and 54. Thus, the bottom interval is 50–54. The next interval would start at 55 and go to 59. Note that this interval also has a bottom score that is a multiple of 5, and contains exactly 5 scores (55, 56, 57, 58, and 59). The complete frequency distribution table showing all of the class intervals is presented in Table 2.1.

Once the class intervals are listed, you complete the table by adding a column of frequencies. The values in the frequency column indicate the number of individuals who have scores located in that class interval. For this example, there were three students with scores in the 60–64 interval, so the frequency for this class interval is $f = 3$ (see Table 2.1). The basic table can be extended by adding columns showing the proportion and percentage associated with each class interval.

Finally, you should note that, after the scores have been placed in a grouped table, you lose information about the specific value for any individual score. For example, Table 2.1 shows that one person had a score between 65 and 69, but the table does not identify the exact value for the score. In general, the wider the class intervals are, the more information is lost. In Table 2.1, the interval width is 5 points, and the table shows that there are three people with scores in the lower 60s and one person with a score in the upper 60s. This information would be lost if the interval width were increased to 10 points. With an interval width of 10, all of the 60s would be grouped together into one interval labeled 60–69. The table would show a frequency of four people in the 60–69 interval, but it would not tell whether the scores were in the upper 60s or the lower 60s.

REAL LIMITS AND FREQUENCY DISTRIBUTIONS

Recall from Chapter 1 that a continuous variable has an infinite number of possible values and can be represented by a number line that is continuous and contains an infinite number of points. However, when a continuous variable is measured, the resulting measurements correspond to *intervals* on the number line rather than single points. If you are measuring time in seconds, for example, a score of $X = 8$ seconds actually represents an interval bounded by the real limits 7.5 seconds and 8.5 seconds. Thus,

TABLE 2.1

This grouped frequency distribution table shows the data from Example 2.4. The original scores range from a high of $X = 94$ to a low of $X = 53$. This range has been divided into 9 intervals with each interval exactly 5 points wide. The frequency column (f) lists the number of individuals with scores in each of the class intervals.

X	f
90–94	3
85–89	4
80–84	5
75–79	4
70–74	3
65–69	1
60–64	3
55–59	1
50–54	1

a frequency distribution table showing a frequency of $f = 3$ individuals all assigned a score of $X = 8$ does not mean that all three individuals had exactly the same measurement. Instead, you should realize that the three measurements are simply located in the same interval between 7.5 and 8.5.

The concept of real limits also applies to the class intervals of a grouped frequency distribution table. For example, a class interval of 40–49 contains scores from $X = 40$ to $X = 49$. These values are called the *apparent limits* of the interval because it appears that they form the upper and lower boundaries for the class interval. If you are measuring a continuous variable, however, a score of $X = 40$ is actually an interval from 39.5 to 40.5. Similarly, $X = 49$ is an interval from 48.5 to 49.5. Therefore, the real limits of the interval are 39.5 (the lower real limit) and 49.5 (the upper real limit). Notice that the next higher class interval is 50–59, which has a lower real limit of 49.5. Thus, the two intervals meet at the real limit 49.5, so there are no gaps in the scale. You also should notice that the width of each class interval becomes easier to understand when you consider the real limits of an interval. For example, the interval 50–59 has real limits of 49.5 and 59.5. The distance between these two real limits is 10 points, which is the width of the interval.

LEARNING CHECK

1. Place the following scores in a grouped frequency distribution table using an interval width of 10 points.

   Scores: 39 41 37 16 44 20 34 39 42
            24 51 22 35 18 46 53 19 26

2. If the scores in the previous question were placed in a grouped table with an interval width of 5 points, what are the apparent limits and the real limits for the bottom interval?

3. Using only the frequency distribution table you constructed for Exercise 1, how many individuals had a score of $X = 53$?

ANSWERS

1.

X	f
50–59	2
40–49	4
30–39	5
20–29	4
10–19	3

2. The apparent limits are 15–19 and the real limits are 14.5–19.5.

3. After a set of scores has been summarized in a grouped table, you cannot determine the frequency for any specific score. There is no way to determine how many individuals had $X = 53$ from the table alone. (You can say that *at most* two people had $X = 53$.)

2.3   FREQUENCY DISTRIBUTION GRAPHS

A frequency distribution graph is basically a picture of the information available in a frequency distribution table. We consider several different types of graphs, but all start with two perpendicular lines called *axes*. The horizontal line is the X-axis, or the abscissa (ab-SIS-uh). The vertical line is the Y-axis, or the ordinate. The measurement scale (set of *X* values) is listed along the *X*-axis with values increasing from left to right. The frequencies are listed on the *Y*-axis with values increasing from bottom to top. As a general rule, the point where the two axes intersect should have a value of zero for both the scores and the frequencies. A final general rule is that the graph should be constructed so that its height (*Y*-axis) is approximately two-thirds to three-quarters of its length (*X*-axis). Violating these guidelines can result in graphs that give a misleading picture of the data (see Box 2.1).

GRAPHS FOR INTERVAL OR RATIO DATA

When the data consist of numerical scores that have been measured on an interval or a ratio scale, there are two options for constructing a frequency distribution graph. The two types of graphs are called *histograms* and *polygons*.

Histograms   To construct a histogram, you first list the numerical scores (the categories of measurement) along the *X*-axis. Then you draw a bar above each *X* value so that

a. The height of the bar corresponds to the frequency for that category.

b. For continuous variables, the width of the bar extends to the real limits of the category. For discrete variables, each bar extends exactly half the distance to the adjacent category on each side.

For both continuous and discrete variables, each bar in a histogram extends to the midpoint between adjacent categories. As a result, adjacent bars touch and there are no spaces or gaps between bars. An example of a histogram is shown in Figure 2.1.

When data have been grouped into class intervals, you can construct a frequency distribution histogram by drawing a bar above each interval so that the width of the bar extends exactly half the distance to the adjacent category on each side. This process is demonstrated in Figure 2.2.

For the two histograms shown in Figures 2.1 and 2.2, notice that the values on both the vertical and horizontal axes are clearly marked and that both axes are labeled. Also note that, whenever possible, the units of measurement are specified; for example, Figure 2.2 shows a distribution of heights measured in inches. Finally, notice that the horizontal axis in Figure 2.2 does not list all of the possible heights starting from zero and going up to 48 inches. Instead, the graph clearly shows a break between zero and 30, indicating that some scores have been omitted.

A modified histogram   A slight modification to the traditional histogram produces a very easy to draw and simple to understand sketch of a frequency distribution. Instead

FIGURE 2.1

An example of a frequency distribution histogram. The same set of quiz scores is presented in a frequency distribution table and in a histogram.

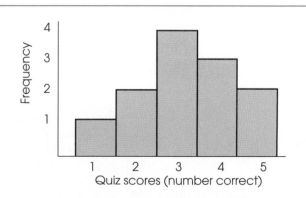

X	f
5	2
4	3
3	4
2	2
1	1

FIGURE 2.2

An example of a frequency distribution histogram for grouped data. The same set of children's heights is presented in a frequency distribution table and in a histogram.

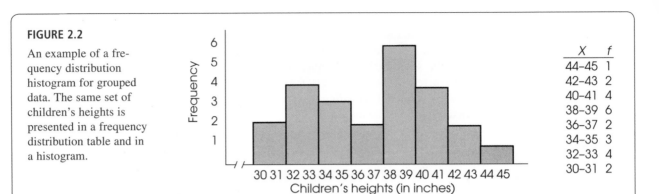

X	f
44–45	1
42–43	2
40–41	4
38–39	6
36–37	2
34–35	3
32–33	4
30–31	2

of drawing a bar above each score, the modification consists of drawing a stack of blocks. Each block represents one individual, so the number of blocks above each score corresponds to the frequency for that score. An example is shown in Figure 2.3.

Note that the number of blocks in each stack makes it very easy to see the absolute frequency for each category. In addition, it is easy to see the exact difference in frequency from one category to another. In Figure 2.3, for example, there are exactly two more people with scores of $X = 2$ than with scores of $X = 1$. Because the frequencies are clearly displayed by the number of blocks, this type of display eliminates the need for a vertical line (the Y-axis) showing frequencies. In general, this kind of graph provides a simple and concrete picture of the distribution for a sample of scores. Note that we often use this kind of graph to show sample data throughout the rest of the book. You should also note, however, that this kind of display simply provides a sketch of the distribution and is not a substitute for an accurately drawn histogram with two labeled axes.

Polygons   The second option for graphing a distribution of numerical scores from an interval or a ratio scale of measurement is called a polygon. To construct a polygon, you begin by listing the numerical scores (the categories of measurement) along the X-axis. Then,

   a. A dot is centered above each score so that the vertical position of the dot corresponds to the frequency for the category.

   b. A continuous line is drawn from dot to dot to connect the series of dots.

   c. The graph is completed by drawing a line down to the X-axis (zero frequency) at each end of the range of scores. The final lines are usually drawn so that they reach the X-axis at a point that is one category below the lowest score on the

FIGURE 2.3

A frequency distribution in which each individual is represented by a block placed directly above the individual's score. For example, three people had scores of $X = 2$.

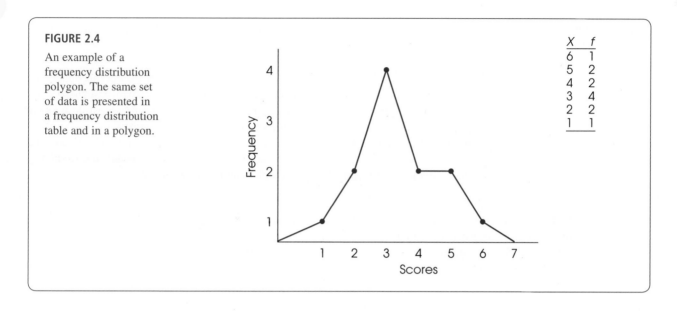

FIGURE 2.4

An example of a frequency distribution polygon. The same set of data is presented in a frequency distribution table and in a polygon.

X	f
6	1
5	2
4	2
3	4
2	2
1	1

left side and one category above the highest score on the right side. An example of a polygon is shown in Figure 2.4.

A polygon also can be used with data that have been grouped into class intervals. For a grouped distribution, you position each dot directly above the midpoint of the class interval. The midpoint can be found by averaging the highest and the lowest scores in the interval. For example, a class interval that is listed as 20–29 would have a midpoint of 24.5.

$$\text{midpoint} = \frac{20 + 29}{2} = \frac{49}{2} = 24.5$$

An example of a frequency distribution polygon with grouped data is shown in Figure 2.5.

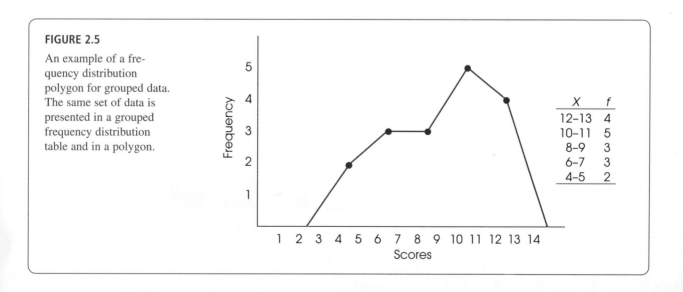

FIGURE 2.5

An example of a frequency distribution polygon for grouped data. The same set of data is presented in a grouped frequency distribution table and in a polygon.

X	f
12–13	4
10–11	5
8–9	3
6–7	3
4–5	2

GRAPHS FOR NOMINAL OR ORDINAL DATA

When the scores are measured on a nominal or ordinal scale (usually non-numerical values), the frequency distribution can be displayed in a *bar graph*.

Bar graphs A bar graph is essentially the same as a histogram, except that spaces are left between adjacent bars. For a nominal scale, the space between bars emphasizes that the scale consists of separate, distinct categories. For ordinal scales, separate bars are used because you cannot assume that the categories are all the same size.

To construct a bar graph, list the categories of measurement along the *X*-axis and then draw a bar above each category so that the height of the bar equals the frequency for the category. An example of a bar graph is shown in Figure 2.6.

GRAPHS FOR POPULATION DISTRIBUTIONS

When you can obtain an exact frequency for each score in a population, you can construct frequency distribution graphs that are exactly the same as the histograms, polygons, and bar graphs that are typically used for samples. For example, if a population is defined as a specific group of $N = 50$ people, we could easily determine how many have IQs of $X = 110$. However, if we are interested in the entire population of adults in the United States, it would be impossible to obtain an exact count of the number of people with an IQ of 110. Although it is still possible to construct graphs showing frequency distributions for extremely large populations, the graphs usually involve two special features: relative frequencies and smooth curves.

Relative frequencies Although you usually cannot find the absolute frequency for each score in a population, you very often can obtain *relative frequencies*. For example, you may not know exactly how many fish are in the lake, but after years of fishing you do know that there are twice as many bluegill as there are bass. You can represent these relative frequencies in a bar graph by making the bar above bluegill two times taller than the bar above bass (Figure 2.7). Notice that the graph does not show the absolute number of fish. Instead, it shows the relative number of bluegill and bass.

Smooth curves When a population consists of numerical scores from an interval or a ratio scale, it is customary to draw the distribution with a smooth curve instead of the jagged, step-wise shapes that occur with histograms and polygons. The smooth curve indicates that you are not connecting a series of dots (real frequencies) but instead are showing

---

FIGURE 2.6

A bar graph showing the distribution of personality types in a sample of college students. Because personality type is a discrete variable measured on a nominal scale, the graph is drawn with space between the bars.

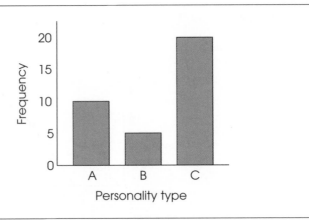

FIGURE 2.7

A frequency distribution showing the relative frequency for two types of fish. Notice that the exact number of fish is not reported; the graph simply says that there are twice as many bluegill as there are bass.

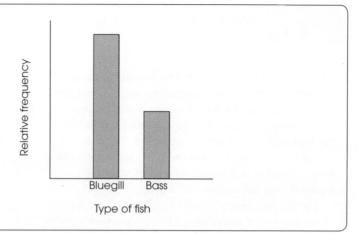

the relative changes that occur from one score to the next. One commonly occurring population distribution is the normal curve. The word *normal* refers to a specific shape that can be precisely defined by an equation. Less precisely, we can describe a normal distribution as being symmetrical, with the greatest frequency in the middle and relatively smaller frequencies as you move toward either extreme. A good example of a normal distribution is the population distribution for IQ scores shown in Figure 2.8. Because normal-shaped distributions occur commonly and because this shape is mathematically guaranteed in certain situations, we give it extensive attention throughout this book.

In the future, we will be referring to *distributions of scores*. Whenever the term *distribution* appears, you should conjure up an image of a frequency distribution graph. The graph provides a picture showing exactly where the individual scores are located. To make this concept more concrete, you might find it useful to think of the graph as showing a pile of individuals just like we showed a pile of blocks in Figure 2.3. For the population of IQ scores shown in Figure 2.8, the pile is highest at an IQ score around 100 because most people have average IQs. There are only a few individuals piled up at an IQ of 130; it must be lonely at the top.

FIGURE 2.8

The population distribution of IQ scores: an example of a normal distribution.

BOX 2.1   THE USE AND MISUSE OF GRAPHS

Although graphs are intended to provide an accurate picture of a set of data, they can be used to exaggerate or misrepresent a set of scores. These misrepresentations generally result from failing to follow the basic rules for graph construction. The following example demonstrates how the same set of data can be presented in two entirely different ways by manipulating the structure of a graph.

For the past several years, the city has kept records of the number of homicides. The data are summarized as follows:

Year	Number of Homicides
2007	42
2008	44
2009	47
2010	49

These data are shown in two different graphs in Figure 2.9. In the first graph, we have exaggerated the height and started numbering the Y-axis at 40 rather than at zero. As a result, the graph seems to indicate a rapid rise in the number of homicides over the 4-year period. In the second graph, we have stretched out the X-axis and used zero as the starting point for the Y-axis. The result is a graph that shows little change in the homicide rate over the 4-year period.

Which graph is correct? The answer is that neither one is very good. Remember that the purpose of a graph is to provide an accurate display of the data. The first graph in Figure 2.9 exaggerates the differences between years, and the second graph conceals the differences. Some compromise is needed. Also note that in some cases a graph may not be the best way to display information. For these data, for example, showing the numbers in a table would be better than either graph.

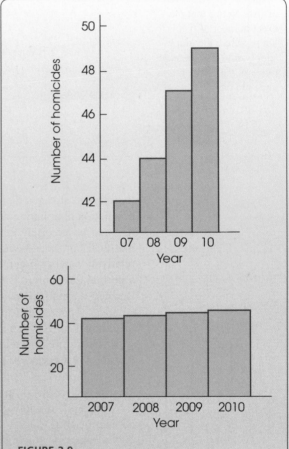

FIGURE 2.9

Two graphs showing the number of homicides in a city over a 4-year period. Both graphs show exactly the same data. However, the first graph gives the appearance that the homicide rate is high and rising rapidly. The second graph gives the impression that the homicide rate is low and has not changed over the 4-year period.

2.4   THE SHAPE OF A FREQUENCY DISTRIBUTION

Rather than drawing a complete frequency distribution graph, researchers often simply describe a distribution by listing its characteristics. There are three characteristics that completely describe any distribution: shape, central tendency, and variability. In simple terms, central tendency measures where the center of the distribution is located. Variability tells whether the scores are spread over a wide range or are clustered together.

FIGURE 2.10

Examples of different
shapes for distributions.

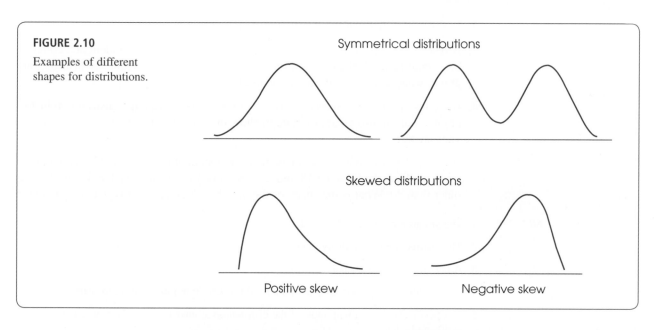

Central tendency and variability will be covered in detail in Chapters 3 and 4. Technically, the shape of a distribution is defined by an equation that prescribes the exact relationship between each X and Y value on the graph. However, we rely on a few less-precise terms that serve to describe the shape of most distributions.

Nearly all distributions can be classified as being either *symmetrical* or *skewed*.

DEFINITIONS

In a **symmetrical distribution,** it is possible to draw a vertical line through the middle so that one side of the distribution is a mirror image of the other (Figure 2.10).

In a **skewed distribution,** the scores tend to pile up toward one end of the scale and taper off gradually at the other end (see Figure 2.10).

The section where the scores taper off is called the **tail** of the distribution.

A skewed distribution with the tail on the right-hand side is **positively skewed** because the tail points toward the positive (above-zero) end of the X-axis. If the tail points to the left, the distribution is **negatively skewed** (see Figure 2.10).

For a very difficult exam, most scores tend to be low, with only a few individuals earning high scores. This produces a positively skewed distribution. Similarly, a very easy exam tends to produce a negatively skewed distribution, with most of the students earning high scores and only a few with low values.

LEARNING CHECK

1. Sketch a frequency distribution histogram and a frequency distribution polygon for the data in the following table:

X	f
5	4
4	6
3	3
2	1
1	1

2. Describe the shape of the distribution in Exercise 1.

3. A researcher records the gender and academic major for each student at a college basketball game. If the distribution of majors is shown in a frequency distribution graph, what type of graph should be used?

4. If the results from a research study are presented in a frequency distribution histogram, would it also be appropriate to show the same results in a polygon? Explain your answer.

5. A college reports that the youngest registered student is 17 years old, the majority of students are between 18 and 25, and only 10% of the registered students are older than 30. What is the shape of the distribution of ages for registered students?

ANSWERS 1. The graphs are shown in Figure 2.11.

2. The distribution is negatively skewed.

3. A bar graph is used for nominal data.

4. Yes. Histograms and polygons are both used for data from interval or ratio scales.

5. It is positively skewed with most of the distribution around 17–25 and a few scores scattered at 30 and higher.

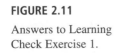

FIGURE 2.11

Answers to Learning Check Exercise 1.

SUMMARY

1. The goal of descriptive statistics is to simplify the organization and presentation of data. One descriptive technique is to place the data in a frequency distribution table or graph that shows exactly how many individuals (or scores) are located in each category on the scale of measurement.

2. A frequency distribution table lists the categories that make up the scale of measurement (the X values) in one column. Beside each X value, in a second column, is the frequency of, or number of individuals in, that category. The table may include a proportion column showing the relative frequency for each category:

$$\text{proportion} = p = \frac{f}{n}$$

The table may include a percentage column showing the percentage associated with each X value:

$$\text{percentage} = p(100) = \frac{f}{n}(100)$$

3. It is recommended that a frequency distribution table have a maximum of 15 rows to keep it simple. If the scores cover a range that is wider than this suggested maximum, it is customary to divide the range into sections called *class intervals*. These intervals are then listed in the frequency distribution table along with the frequency, or number of individuals with scores in each interval. The result is called a *grouped frequency distribution*. The guidelines for

constructing a grouped frequency distribution table are as follows:

a. There should be about 10 intervals.

b. The width of each interval should be a simple number (e.g., 2, 5, or 10).

c. The bottom score in each interval should be a multiple of the width.

d. All intervals should be the same width, and they should cover the range of scores with no gaps.

4. A frequency distribution graph lists scores on the horizontal axis and frequencies on the vertical axis. The type of graph used to display a distribution depends on the scale of measurement used. For interval or ratio scales, you should use a histogram or a polygon. For a histogram, a bar is drawn above each score so that the height of the bar corresponds to the frequency. Each bar extends to the real limits of the score, so that adjacent bars touch. For a polygon, a dot is placed above the midpoint of each score or class interval so that the height of the dot corresponds to the frequency; then lines are drawn to connect the dots. Bar graphs are used with nominal or ordinal scales. Bar graphs are similar to histograms except that gaps are left between adjacent bars.

5. Shape is one of the basic characteristics used to describe a distribution of scores. Most distributions can be classified as either symmetrical or skewed. A skewed distribution with the tail on the right is said to be positively skewed. If it has the tail on the left, it is negatively skewed.

KEY TERMS

frequency distribution (38)

range (41)

grouped frequency distribution (41)

class interval (41)

apparent limits (44)

axes (44)

histogram (45)

polygon (46)

bar graph (48)

relative frequency (48)

distribution of scores (49)

symmetrical distribution (51)

tail(s) of a distribution (51)

positively skewed distribution (51)

negatively skewed distribution (51)

RESOURCES

 Go to CengageBrain.com to access Psychology CourseMate, where you will find an interactive eBook, glossaries, flashcards, quizzes, statistics workshops, and more.

If your professor has assigned Aplia:

1. Sign in to your account.

2. Complete the corresponding exercises as required by your professor.

3. When finished, click "Grade It Now" to see which areas you have mastered, which areas need more work, and detailed explanations of every answer.

General instructions for using SPSS are presented in Appendix D. Following are detailed instructions for using SPSS to produce **Frequency Distribution Tables or Graphs.**

Frequency Distribution Tables

Data Entry

Enter all the scores in one column of the data editor, probably VAR00001.

Data Analysis

1. Click **Analyze** on the tool bar, select **Descriptive Statistics,** and click on **Frequencies.**

2. Highlight the column label for the set of scores (VAR00001) in the left box and click the arrow to move it into the **Variable** box.

3. Be sure that the option to **Display Frequency Table** is selected.

4. Click **OK.**

SPSS Output

The frequency distribution table lists the score values in a column from smallest to largest, with the percentage and cumulative percentage also listed for each score. Score values that do not occur (zero frequencies) are not included in the table, and the program does not group scores into class intervals (all values are listed).

Frequency Distribution Histograms or Bar Graphs

Data Entry

Enter all the scores in one column of the data editor, probably VAR00001.

Data Analysis

1. Click **Analyze** on the tool bar, select **Descriptive Statistics,** and click on **Frequencies.**

2. Highlight the column label for the set of scores (VAR00001) in the left box and click the arrow to move it into the **Variable** box.

3. Click **Charts.**

4. Select either **Bar Graphs** or **Histogram.**

5. Click **Continue.**

6. Click **OK.**

SPSS Output

SPSS displays a frequency distribution table and a graph. Note that SPSS often produces a histogram that groups the scores in unpredictable intervals. A bar graph usually produces a clearer picture of the actual frequency associated with each score.

FOCUS ON PROBLEM SOLVING

1. The reason for constructing frequency distributions is to put a disorganized set of raw data into a comprehensible, organized format. Because several different types of frequency distribution tables and graphs are available, one problem is deciding which type to use. Tables have the advantage of being easier to construct, but graphs generally give a better picture of the data and are easier to understand.

To help you decide which type of frequency distribution is best, consider the following points:

a. What is the range of scores? With a wide range, you need to group the scores into class intervals.

b. What is the scale of measurement? With an interval or a ratio scale, you can use a polygon or a histogram. With a nominal or an ordinal scale, you must use a bar graph.

2. When using a grouped frequency distribution table, a common mistake is to calculate the interval width by using the highest and lowest values that define each interval. For example, some students are tricked into thinking that an interval identified as 20–24 is only 4 points wide. To determine the correct interval width, you can:

a. Count the individual scores in the interval. For this example, the scores are 20, 21, 22, 23, and 24, for a total of 5 values. Thus, the interval width is 5 points.

b. Use the real limits to determine the real width of the interval. For example, an interval identified as 20–24 has a lower real limit of 19.5 and an upper real limit of 24.5 (halfway to the next score). Using the real limits, the interval width is

$$24.5 - 19.5 = 5 \text{ points}$$

DEMONSTRATION 2.1

A GROUPED FREQUENCY DISTRIBUTION TABLE

For the following set of $N = 20$ scores, construct a grouped frequency distribution table using an interval width of 5 points. The scores are:

14	8	27	16	10	22	9	13	16	12
10	9	15	17	6	14	11	18	14	11

STEP 1 Set up the class intervals.

The largest score in this distribution is $X = 27$, and the lowest is $X = 6$. Therefore, a frequency distribution table for these data would have 22 rows and would be too large. A grouped frequency distribution table would be better. We have asked specifically for an interval width of 5 points, and the resulting table has five rows.

X
25–29
20–24
15–19
10–14
5–9

Remember that the interval width is determined by the real limits of the interval. For example, the class interval 25–29 has an upper real limit of 29.5 and a lower real limit of 24.5. The difference between these two values is the width of the interval—namely, 5.

STEP 2   Determine the frequencies for each interval.

Examine the scores, and count how many fall into the class interval of 25–29. Cross out each score that you have already counted. Record the frequency for this class interval. Now repeat this process for the remaining intervals. The result is the following table:

X	f
25–29	1 (the score X = 27)
20–24	1 (X = 22)
15–19	5 (the scores X = 16, 16, 15, 17, and 18)
10–14	9 (X = 14, 10, 13, 12, 10, 14, 11, 14, and 11)
5–9	4 (X = 8, 9, 9, and 6)

PROBLEMS

1. Place the following set of $n = 20$ scores in a frequency distribution table.

6	2	2	1	3	2	4	7	1	2
5	3	1	6	2	6	3	3	7	2

2. Construct a frequency distribution table for the following set of scores. Include columns for proportion and percentage in your tables.

Scores: 5 7 8 4 7 9 6 6 5 3
          9 6 4 7 7 8 6 7 8 5

3. Find each value requested for the distribution of scores in the following table.
   a. n
   b. ΣX
   c. ΣX^2

X	f
5	2
4	3
3	5
2	1
1	1

4. Find each value requested for the distribution of scores in the following table.
   a. n
   b. ΣX
   c. ΣX^2

X	f
5	1
4	2
3	3
2	5
1	3

5. For the following scores, the smallest value is $X = 17$ and the largest value is $X = 53$. Place the scores in a grouped frequency distribution table
   a. using an interval width of 5 points.
   b. using an interval width of 10 points.

44	19	23	17	25	47	32	26
25	30	18	24	49	51	24	19
43	27	34	18	52	18	36	25

6. The following scores are the ages for a random sample of $n = 30$ drivers who were issued speeding tickets in New York during 2008. Determine the best interval width and place the scores in a grouped frequency distribution table. From looking at your table, does it appear that tickets are issued equally across age groups?

17	30	45	20	39	53	28	19
24	21	34	38	22	29	64	
22	44	36	16	56	20	23	58
32	25	28	22	51	26	43	

7. For each of the following samples, determine the interval width that is most appropriate for a grouped frequency distribution and identify the approximate number of intervals needed to cover the range of scores.
   a. Sample scores range from $X = 8$ to $X = 41$.
   b. Sample scores range from $X = 16$ to $X = 33$.
   c. Sample scores range from $X = 26$ to $X = 98$.

8. What information can you obtain about the scores in a regular frequency distribution table that is not available from a grouped table?

9. Describe the difference in appearance between a bar graph and a histogram and identify the circumstances in which each type of graph is used.

10. For the following set of scores:

8	5	9	6	8	7	4	10	6	7
9	7	9	9	5	8	8	6	7	10

a. Construct a frequency distribution table to organize the scores.
b. Draw a frequency distribution histogram for these data.

11. Sketch a histogram and a polygon showing the distribution of scores presented in the following table:

X	f
7	1
6	1
5	3
4	6
3	4
2	1

12. Sketch a histogram showing the distribution of scores shown in the following table:

X	f
45–49	4
40–44	6
35–39	10
30–34	5
25–29	3
20–24	2

13. A survey given to a sample of college students contained questions about the following variables. For each variable, identify the kind of graph that should be used to display the distribution of scores (histogram, polygon, or bar graph).
   a. number of brothers and sisters
   b. birth-order position among siblings (oldest = 1st)
   c. gender (male/female)
   d. favorite television show during the previous year

14. Each year the college gives away T-shirts to new students during freshman orientation. The students are allowed to pick the shirt sizes that they want. To determine how many of each size shirt they should order, college officials look at the distribution from last year. The following table shows the distribution of shirt sizes selected last year.

Size	f
S	27
M	48
L	136
XL	120
XXL	39

   a. What kind of graph would be appropriate for showing this distribution?
   b. Sketch the frequency distribution graph.

15. Gaucher, Friesen, and Kay (2011) found that masculine-themed words (such as competitive, independent, analyze, strong) are commonly used in job recruitment materials, especially for job advertisements in male-dominated areas. In a similar study, a researcher counted the number of masculine-themed words in job advertisements for job areas, and obtained the following data.

Area	Number of Masculine Words
Plumber	14
Electrician	12
Security guard	17
Bookkeeper	9
Nurse	6
Early-childhood educator	7

Determine what kind of graph would be appropriate for showing this distribution and sketch the frequency distribution graph.

16. Find each of the following values for the distribution shown in the following polygon.
   a. n
   b. ΣX
   c. ΣX^2

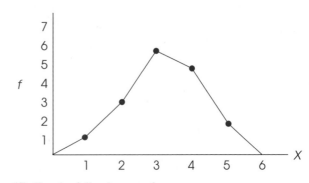

17. For the following set of scores:

   Scores: 5 8 5 7 6 6 5 7 4 6
            6 9 5 5 4 6 7 5 7 5

   a. Place the scores in a frequency distribution table.
   b. Identify the shape of the distribution.

18. Place the following scores in a frequency distribution table. Based on the frequencies, what is the shape of the distribution?

   13 14 12 15 15 14 15 11 13 14
   11 13 15 12 14 14 10 14 13 15

19. For the following set of scores:

   8 6 7 5 4 10 8 9 5 7 2 9
   9 10 7 8 8 7 4 6 3 8 9 6

a. Construct a frequency distribution table.
b. Sketch a histogram showing the distribution.
c. Describe the distribution using the following characteristics:
  (1) What is the shape of the distribution?
  (2) What score best identifies the center (average) for the distribution?
  (3) Are the scores clustered together, or are they spread out across the scale?

20. Fowler and Christakis (2008) report that personal happiness tends to be associated with having a social network including many other happy friends. To test this claim, a researcher obtains a sample of $n = 16$ adults who claim to be happy people and a similar sample of $n = 16$ adults who describe themselves as neutral or unhappy. Each individual is then asked to identify the number of their close friends whom they consider to be happy people. The scores are as follows:

Happy: 8 7 4 10 6 6 8 9 8 8
           7 5 6 9 8 9
Unhappy: 5 8 4 6 6 7 9 6 2 8
           5 6 4 7 5 6

Sketch a polygon showing the frequency distribution for the happy people. In the same graph, sketch a polygon for the unhappy people. (Use two different colors, or use a solid line for one polygon and a dashed line for the other.) Does one group seem to have more happy friends?

21. Recent research suggests that the amount of time that parents spend talking about numbers can have a big effect on the mathematical development of their children (Levine, Suriyakham, Rowe, Huttenlocher, & Gunderson, 2010). In the study, the researchers visited the children's homes between the ages of 14 and 30 months and recorded the amount of "number talk" they heard from the children's parents. The researchers then tested the children's knowledge of the meaning of numbers at 46 months. The following data are similar to the results obtained in the study.

Children's Knowledge-of-Numbers Scores for Two Groups of Parents	
Low Number-Talk Parents	*High Number-Talk Parents*
2, 1, 2, 3, 4	3, 4, 5, 4, 5
3, 3, 2, 2, 1	4, 2, 3, 5, 4
5, 3, 4, 1, 2	5, 3, 4, 5, 4

Sketch a polygon showing the frequency distribution for children with low number-talk parents. In the same graph, sketch a polygon showing the scores for the children with high number-talk parents. (Use two different colors or use a solid line for one polygon and a dashed line for the other.) Does it appear that there is a difference between the two groups?

CHAPTER

3

Measures of Central Tendency

Tools You Will Need

The following items are considered essential background material for this chapter. If you doubt your knowledge of any of these items, you should review the appropriate chapter or section before proceeding.

- Summation notation (Chapter 1)
- Frequency distributions (Chapter 2)

aplia

Aplia for *Essentials of Statistics for the Behavioral Sciences*
After reading, go to "Resources" at the end of this chapter for an introduction on how to use Aplia's homework and learning resources.

3.1   DEFINING CENTRAL TENDENCY

The general purpose of descriptive statistical methods is to organize and summarize a set of scores. Perhaps the most common method for summarizing and describing a distribution is to find a single value that defines the average score and can serve as a representative for the entire distribution. In statistics, the concept of an average, or representative, score is called *central tendency*. The goal in measuring central tendency is to describe a distribution of scores by determining a single value that identifies the center of the distribution. Ideally, this central value is the score that is the best representative value for all of the individuals in the distribution.

DEFINITION

> **Central tendency** is a statistical measure that attempts to determine the single value, usually located in the center of a distribution, that is most typical or most representative of the entire set of scores.

In everyday language, central tendency attempts to identify the "average," or "typical," individual. This average value can then be used to provide a simple description of an entire population or a sample. In addition to describing an entire distribution, measures of central tendency are also useful for making comparisons between groups of individuals or between sets of figures. For example, weather data indicate that for Seattle, Washington, the average yearly temperature is 53° and the average annual precipitation is 34 inches. By comparison, the average temperature in Phoenix, Arizona, is 71° and the average precipitation is 7.4 inches. The point of these examples is to demonstrate the great advantage of being able to describe a large set of data with a single, representative number. Central tendency characterizes what is typical for a large population and, in doing so, makes large amounts of data more digestible. Statisticians sometimes use the expression *number crunching* to illustrate this aspect of data description. That is, we take a distribution consisting of many scores and "crunch" them down to a single value that describes them all.

Unfortunately, there is no single, standard procedure for determining central tendency. The problem is that no single measure produces a central, representative value in every situation. The three distributions shown in Figure 3.1 should help demonstrate this fact. Before we discuss the three distributions, take a moment to look at the figure and try to identify the center or the most representative score for each distribution.

1. The first distribution [Figure 3.1(a)] is symmetrical, with the scores forming a distinct pile centered around $X = 5$. For this type of distribution, it is easy to identify the center, and most people would agree that the value $X = 5$ is an appropriate measure of central tendency.

2. In the second distribution [Figure 3.1(b)], however, problems begin to appear. Now the scores form a *negatively skewed* distribution, piling up at the high end of the scale around $X = 8$, but tapering off to the left all the way down to $X = 1$. Where is the center in this case? Some people might select $X = 8$ as the center because more individuals had this score than any other single value. However, $X = 8$ is clearly not in the middle of the distribution. In fact, the majority of the scores (10 out of 16) have values less than 8, so it seems reasonable that the center should be defined by a value that is less than 8.

3. Now consider the third distribution [Figure 3.1(c)]. Again, the distribution is symmetrical, but now there are two distinct piles of scores. Because the distribution is symmetrical with $X = 5$ as the midpoint, you may choose $X = 5$ as the center. However, none of the scores is located at $X = 5$ (or even close), so this value is not particularly good as a representative score. On the other hand,

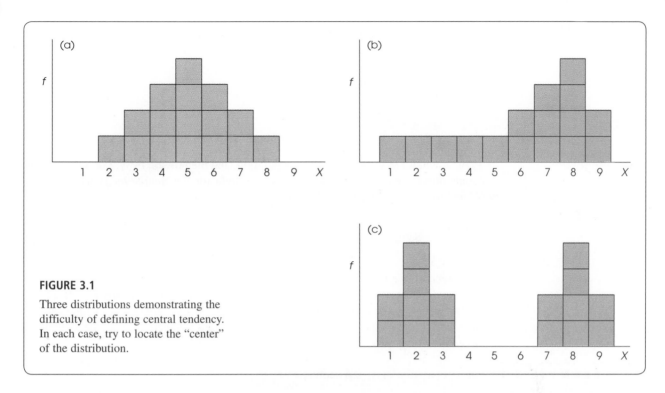

FIGURE 3.1

Three distributions demonstrating the difficulty of defining central tendency. In each case, try to locate the "center" of the distribution.

because there are two separate piles of scores with one group centered at $X = 2$ and the other centered at $X = 8$, it is tempting to say that this distribution has two centers. But can one distribution have two centers?

THREE MEASURES OF CENTRAL TENDENCY

Clearly, there can be problems defining the center of a distribution. Occasionally, you will find a nice, neat distribution like the one shown in Figure 3.1(a), for which everyone agrees on the center. But you should realize that other distributions are possible and that there may be different opinions concerning the definition of the center. To deal with these problems, statisticians have developed three different methods for measuring central tendency: the mean, the median, and the mode. They are computed differently and have different characteristics. To decide which of the three measures is best for any particular distribution, you should keep in mind that the general purpose of central tendency is to find the single most representative score. Each of the three measures we present has been developed to work best in a specific situation. We examine this issue in more detail after we introduce the three measures.

3.2   THE MEAN

The *mean,* also known as the arithmetic average, is computed by adding all the scores in the distribution and dividing by the number of scores. The mean for a population is identified by the Greek letter mu, μ (pronounced "mew"), and the mean for a sample is identified by M or $\overline{X}$ (read "x-bar").

The convention in many statistics textbooks is to use $\overline{X}$ to represent the mean for a sample. However, in manuscripts and in published research reports the letter M is the standard notation for a sample mean. Because you will encounter the letter M when reading research reports and because you should use the letter M when writing research reports, we have decided to use the same notation in this text. Keep in mind that the $\overline{X}$ notation is still appropriate for identifying a sample mean, and you may find it used on occasion, especially in textbooks.

DEFINITION

The **mean** for a distribution is the sum of the scores divided by the number of scores.

The formula for the *population mean* is

$$\mu = \frac{\Sigma X}{N} \tag{3.1}$$

First, add all of the scores in the population, and then divide by N. For a sample, the computation is exactly the same, but the formula for the *sample mean* uses symbols (M and n) that signify sample values:

$$\text{Sample mean} = M = \frac{\Sigma X}{N} \tag{3.2}$$

In general, we use Greek letters to identify characteristics of a population (parameters) and letters of our own alphabet to stand for sample values (statistics). If a mean is identified with the symbol M, you should realize that we are dealing with a sample. Also note that the equation for the sample mean uses a lowercase n as the symbol for the number of scores in the sample.

EXAMPLE 3.1

For a population of $N = 4$ scores,

3 7 4 6

the mean is

$$\mu = \frac{\Sigma X}{N} = \frac{20}{4} = 5$$

ALTERNATIVE
DEFINITIONS
FOR THE MEAN

Although the procedure of adding the scores and dividing by the number of scores provides a useful definition of the mean, there are two alternative definitions that may give you a better understanding of this important measure of central tendency.

Dividing the total equally   The first alternative is to think of the mean as the amount each individual receives when the total (ΣX) is divided equally among all of the individuals (N) in the distribution. This somewhat socialistic viewpoint is particularly useful in problems for which you know the mean and must find the total. Consider the following example.

EXAMPLE 3.2

A group of $n = 6$ boys buys a box of baseball cards at a garage sale and discovers that the box contains a total of 180 cards. If the boys divide the cards equally among themselves, how many cards will each boy get? You should recognize that this problem represents the standard procedure for computing the mean. Specifically, the total (ΣX) is divided by the number (n) to produce the mean, $\frac{180}{6} = 30$ cards for each boy.

The previous example demonstrates that it is possible to define the mean as the amount that each individual gets when the total is distributed equally. This new definition can be useful for some problems involving the mean. Consider the following example.

EXAMPLE 3.3   Now suppose that the 6 boys from Example 3.2 decide to sell their baseball cards on eBay. If they make an average of $M = \$5$ per boy, what is the total amount of money for the whole group? Although you do not know exactly how much money each boy has, the new definition of the mean tells you that if they pool their money together and then distribute the total equally, each boy will get $5. For each of $n = 6$ boys to get $5, the total must be 6($5) = $30. To check this answer, use the formula for the mean:

$$M = \frac{\Sigma X}{n} = \frac{\$30}{6} = \$5$$

The mean as a balance point   The second alternative definition of the mean describes the mean as a balance point for the distribution. Consider a population consisting of $N = 5$ scores (1, 2, 6, 6, 10). For this population, $\Sigma X = 25$ and $\mu = \frac{25}{5} = 5$. Figure 3.2 shows this population drawn as a histogram, with each score represented as a box that is sitting on a seesaw. If the seesaw is positioned so that it pivots at a point equal to the mean, then it will be balanced and will rest level.

The reason that the seesaw is balanced over the mean becomes clear when we measure the distance of each box (score) from the mean:

Score	Distance from the Mean
$X = 1$	4 points below the mean
$X = 2$	3 points below the mean
$X = 6$	1 point above the mean
$X = 6$	1 point above the mean
$X = 10$	5 points above the mean

Notice that the mean balances the distances. That is, the total distance below the mean is the same as the total distance above the mean:

below the mean: 4 + 3 = 7 points

above the mean: 1 + 1 + 5 = 7 points

Because the mean serves as a balance point, the value of the mean is always located somewhere between the highest score and the lowest score; that is, the mean can never be outside the range of scores. If the lowest score in a distribution is $X = 8$ and the

FIGURE 3.2

The frequency distribution shown as a seesaw balanced at the mean.

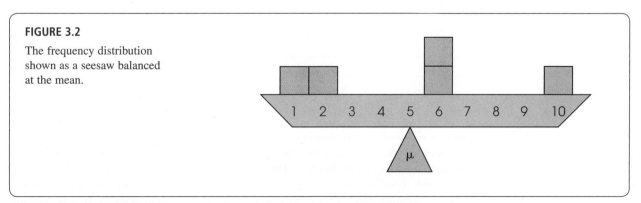

Based on Weinberg, G. A., Schumaker, J. A., & Oltman, D. (1981). *Statistics: An Intuitive Approach* (p. 14). Belmont, CA: Wadsworth.

highest is $X = 15$, then the mean *must* be between 8 and 15. If you calculate a value that is outside this range, then you have made an error.

The image of a seesaw with the mean at the balance point is also useful for determining how a distribution is affected if a new score is added or if an existing score is removed. For the distribution in Figure 3.2, for example, what would happen to the mean (balance point) if a new score were added at $X = 10$?

THE WEIGHTED MEAN

Often it is necessary to combine two sets of scores and then find the overall mean for the combined group. Suppose that we begin with two separate samples. The first sample has $n = 12$ scores and a mean of $M = 6$. The second sample has $n = 8$ and $M = 7$. If the two samples are combined, what is the mean for the total group?

To calculate the overall mean, we need two values:

1. the overall sum of the scores for the combined group (ΣX), and

2. the total number of scores in the combined group (n).

The total number of scores in the combined group can be found easily by adding the number of scores in the first sample (n_1) and the number in the second sample (n_2). In this case, there are $12 + 8 = 20$ scores in the combined group. Similarly, the overall sum for the combined group can be found by adding the sum for the first sample (ΣX_1) and the sum for the second sample (ΣX_2). With these two values, we can compute the mean using the basic equation

$$\text{overall mean} = M = \frac{\Sigma X \text{ (overall sum for the combined group)}}{n \text{ (total number in the combined group)}}$$

$$= \frac{\Sigma X_1 + \Sigma X_2}{n_1 + n_2}$$

To find the sum of the scores for each sample, remember that the mean can be defined as the amount each person receives when the total (ΣX) is distributed equally. The first sample has $n = 12$ and $M = 6$. (Expressed in dollars instead of scores, this sample has $n = 12$ people and each person gets \$6 when the total is divided equally.) For each of 12 people to get $M = 6$, the total must be $\Sigma X = 12 \times 6 = 72$. In the same way, the second sample has $n = 8$ and $M = 7$ so the total must be $\Sigma X = 8 \times 7 = 56$. Using these values, we obtain an overall mean of

$$\text{overall mean} = M = \frac{\Sigma X_1 + \Sigma X_2}{n_1 + n_2} = \frac{72 + 56}{12 + 8} = \frac{128}{20} = 6.4$$

The following table summarizes the calculations.

First Sample	Second Sample	Combined Sample
$n = 12$	$n = 8$	$n = 20$ $(12 + 8)$
$\Sigma X = 72$	$\Sigma X = 56$	$\Sigma X = 128$ $(72 + 56)$
$M = 6$	$M = 7$	$M = 6.4$

Note that the overall mean is not halfway between the original two sample means. Because the samples are not the same size, one makes a larger contribution to the total group and, therefore, carries more weight in determining the overall mean. For this reason, the overall mean we have calculated is called the *weighted mean*. In this example, the overall mean of $M = 6.4$ is closer to the value of $M = 6$ (the larger sample) than it is to $M = 7$ (the smaller sample).

COMPUTING THE MEAN FROM A FREQUENCY DISTRIBUTION TABLE

When a set of scores has been organized in a frequency distribution table, the calculation of the mean is usually easier if you first remove the individual scores from the table. Table 3.1 shows a distribution of scores organized in a frequency distribution table. To compute the mean for this distribution you must be careful to use both the X values in the first column and the frequencies in the second column. The values in the table show that the distribution consists of one 10, two 9s, four 8s, and one 6, for a total of $n = 8$ scores. Remember that you can determine the number of scores by adding the frequencies, $n = \Sigma f$. To find the sum of the scores, you must be careful to add all eight scores:

TABLE 3.1

Statistics quiz scores for a sample of $n = 8$ students.

Quiz Score (X)	f	fX
10	1	10
9	2	18
8	4	32
7	0	0
6	1	6

$$\Sigma X = 10 + 9 + 9 + 8 + 8 + 8 + 8 + 6 = 66$$

Note that you can also find the sum of the scores by computing ΣfX as we demonstrated in Chapter 2 (pp. 39–40). Once you have found ΣX and n, you compute the mean as usual. For these data,

$$M = \frac{\Sigma X}{n} = \frac{66}{8} = 8.25$$

LEARNING CHECK

1. Find the mean for the following sample of $n = 5$ scores: 1, 8, 7, 5, 9.

2. A sample of $n = 6$ scores has a mean of $M = 8$. What is the value of ΣX for this sample?

3. One sample has $n = 5$ scores with a mean of $M = 4$. A second sample has $n = 3$ scores with a mean of $M = 10$. If the two samples are combined, what is the mean for the combined sample?

4. A sample of $n = 6$ scores has a mean of $M = 40$. One new score is added to the sample and the new mean is found to be $M = 35$. What can you conclude about the value of the new score?

   a. It must be greater 40.
   b. It must be less than 40.

5. Find the values for n, ΣX, and M for the sample that is summarized in the following frequency distribution table.

X	f
5	1
4	2
3	3
2	5
1	1

ANSWERS   1. $\Sigma X = 30$ and $M = 6$

2. $\Sigma X = 48$

3. The combined sample has $n = 8$ scores that total $\Sigma X = 50$. The mean is $M = 6.25$.

4. b

5. For this sample $n = 12$, $\Sigma X = 33$, and $M = 33/12 = 2.75$.

CHARACTERISTICS OF THE MEAN

The mean has many characteristics that will be important in future discussions. In general, these characteristics result from the fact that every score in the distribution contributes to the value of the mean. Specifically, every score adds to the total (ΣX) and every score contributes one point to the number of scores (n). These two values (ΣX and n) determine the value of the mean. Also note that any factor that influences a population mean will have exactly the same influence on a sample mean. Therefore, the characteristics of the sample mean are the same as the characteristics of the population mean. We now discuss four of the more important characteristics of the mean.

Changing a score   Changing the value of any score changes the mean. For example, a sample of quiz scores for a psychology lab section consists of 9, 8, 7, 5, and 1. Note that the sample consists of $n = 5$ scores with $\Sigma X = 30$. The mean for this sample is

$$M = \frac{\Sigma X}{n} = \frac{30}{5} = 6.00$$

Now suppose that the score of $X = 1$ is changed to $X = 8$. Note that we have added 7 points to this individual's score, which also adds 7 points to the total (ΣX). After changing the score, the new distribution consists of

9   8   7   5   8

There are still $n = 5$ scores, but now the total is $\Sigma X = 37$. Thus, the new mean is

$$M = \frac{\Sigma X}{n} = \frac{37}{5} = 7.40$$

Notice that changing a single score in the sample has produced a new mean. You should recognize that changing any score also changes the value of ΣX (the sum of the scores), and, thus, always changes the value of the mean.

Introducing a new score or removing a score   Adding a new score to a distribution, or removing an existing score, usually changes the mean. The exception is when the new score (or the removed score) is exactly equal to the mean. It is easy to visualize the effect of adding or removing a score if you remember that the mean is defined as the balance point for the distribution. Figure 3.3 shows a distribution of scores represented as boxes on a seesaw that is balanced at the mean, $\mu = 7$. Imagine what would happen if we added a new score (a new box) at $X = 10$. Clearly, the seesaw would tip to the right and we would need to move the pivot point (the mean) to the right to restore balance.

Now imagine what would happen if we removed the score (the box) at $X = 9$. This time the seesaw would tip to the left and, once again, we would need to change the mean to restore balance.

Finally, consider what would happen if we added a new score of $X = 7$, exactly equal to the mean. It should be clear that the seesaw would not tilt in either direction, so the mean would stay in exactly the same place. Also note that if we removed the new

FIGURE 3.3

A distribution of $N = 5$ scores that is balanced with a mean of $\mu = 7$.

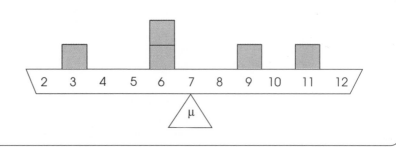

score at $X = 7$, the seesaw would remain balanced and the mean would not change. In general, adding a new score or removing an existing score causes the mean to change unless that score is located exactly at the mean.

The following example demonstrates exactly how the new mean is computed when a new score is added to an existing sample.

EXAMPLE 3.4

Adding a score (or removing a score) has the same effect on the mean whether the original set of scores is a sample or a population. To demonstrate the calculation of the new mean, we will use the set of scores that is shown in Figure 3.3. This time, however, we will treat the scores as a sample with $n = 5$ and $M = 7$. Note that this sample must have $\Sigma X = 35$. What happens to the mean if a new score of $X = 13$ is added to the sample?

To find the new sample mean, we must determine how the values for n and ΣX are changed by a new score. We begin with the original sample and then consider the effect of adding the new score. The original sample had $n = 5$ scores, so adding one new score produces $n = 6$. Similarly, the original sample had $\Sigma X = 35$. Adding a score of $X = 13$ increases the sum by 13 points, producing a new sum of $\Sigma X = 35 + 13 = 48$. Finally, the new mean is computed using the new values for n and ΣX.

$$M = \frac{\Sigma X}{n} = \frac{48}{6} = 8$$

The entire process can be summarized as follows:

Original Sample	New Sample, Adding X = 13
$n = 5$	$n = 6$
$\Sigma X = 35$	$\Sigma X = 48$
$M = \frac{35}{5} = 7$	$M = \frac{48}{6} = 8$

Adding or subtracting a constant from each score If a constant value is added to every score in a distribution, the same constant is added to the mean. Similarly, if you subtract a constant from every score, the same constant is subtracted from the mean.

To demonstrate this characteristic of the mean, we use a study that confirms what you already suspected to be true—alcohol consumption increases the attractiveness of opposite-sex individuals (Jones, Jones, Thomas, & Piper, 2003). Participants in the study were shown photographs of male and female faces and asked to rate the attractiveness of each face. Table 3.2 shows results for a sample of $n = 6$ male participants who are rating a specific female face. The first column shows the ratings

TABLE 3.2

Attractiveness ratings of a female face for a sample of $n = 6$ males.

Participant	Sober	Moderate Alcohol
A	4	6
B	2	4
C	3	5
D	3	5
E	2	4
F	3	5
	$\Sigma X = 17$	$\Sigma X = 29$
	$M = 2.83$	$M = 4.83$

when the participants are sober. Note that the total for this column is $\Sigma X = 17$ for a sample of $n = 6$ participants, so the mean is $M = \frac{17}{6} = 2.83$. Now suppose that the effect of alcohol is to add a constant amount (2 points) to each individual's rating score. The resulting scores, after moderate alcohol consumption, are shown in the second column of the table. For these scores, the total is $\Sigma X = 29$, so the mean is $M = \frac{29}{6} = 4.83$. Adding 2 points to each rating score has also added 2 points to the mean, from $M = 2.83$ to $M = 4.83$. (It is important to note that treatment effects are usually not as simple as adding or subtracting a constant amount. Nonetheless, the concept of adding a constant to every score is important and will be addressed in later chapters when we are using statistics to evaluate mean differences.)

Multiplying or dividing each score by a constant   If every score in a distribution is multiplied by (or divided by) a constant value, the mean changes in the same way.

Multiplying (or dividing) each score by a constant value is a common method for changing the unit of measurement. To change a set of measurements from minutes to seconds, for example, you multiply by 60; to change from inches to feet, you divide by 12. One common task for researchers is converting measurements into metric units to conform to international standards. For example, publication guidelines of the American Psychological Association call for metric equivalents to be reported in parentheses when most nonmetric units are used. Table 3.3 shows how a sample of $n = 5$ scores measured in inches would be transformed to a set of scores measured in centimeters. (Note that 1 inch equals 2.54 centimeters.) The first column shows the original scores that total $\Sigma X = 50$, with $M = 10$ inches. In the second column, each of the original scores has been multiplied by 2.54 (to convert from inches to centimeters) and the resulting values total $\Sigma X = 127$, with $M = 25.4$. Multiplying each score by 2.54 has also caused the mean to be multiplied by 2.54. You should realize, however, that although the numerical values for the individual scores and the sample mean have changed, the actual measurements have not changed.

TABLE 3.3

Measurements converted from inches to centimeters.

Original Measurement in Inches	Conversion to Centimeters (Multiply by 2.54)
10	25.40
9	22.86
12	30.48
8	20.32
11	27.94
$\Sigma X = 50$	$\Sigma X = 127.00$
$M = 10$	$M = 25.40$

1. Adding a new score to a distribution always changes the mean. (True or false?)

2. Changing the value of a score in a distribution always changes the mean. (True or false?)

3. A population has a mean of $\mu = 40$.

   a. If 5 points were added to every score, what would be the value for the new mean?

   b. If every score were multiplied by 3, what would be the value for the new mean?

4. A sample of $n = 4$ scores has a mean of 9. If one person with a score of $X = 3$ is removed from the sample, what is the value for the new sample mean?

ANSWERS

1. False. If the score is equal to the mean, it does not change the mean.

2. True.

3. **a.** The new mean would be 45.

   b. The new mean would be 120.

4. The original sample has $n = 4$ and $\Sigma X = 36$. The new sample has $n = 3$ scores that total $\Sigma X = 33$. The new mean is $M = 11$.

3.3 THE MEDIAN

The second measure of central tendency we consider is called the *median*. The goal of the median is to locate the midpoint of the distribution. Unlike the mean, there are no specific symbols or notation to identify the median. Instead, the median is simply identified by the word *median*. In addition, the definition and the computations for the median are identical for a sample and for a population.

DEFINITION

> If the scores in a distribution are listed in order from smallest to largest, the **median** is the midpoint of the list. More specifically, the median is the point on the measurement scale below which 50% of the scores in the distribution are located.

FINDING THE MEDIAN FOR MOST DISTRIBUTIONS

Defining the median as the *midpoint* of a distribution means that the scores are divided into two equal-sized groups. We are not locating the midpoint between the highest and lowest X values. To find the median, list the scores in order from smallest to largest. Begin with the smallest score and count the scores as you move up the list. The median is the first point you reach that is greater than 50% of the scores in the distribution. The median can be equal to a score in the list or it can be a point between two scores. Notice that the median is not algebraically defined (there is no equation for computing the median), which means that there is a degree of subjectivity in determining the exact value. However, the following two examples demonstrate the process of finding the median for most distributions.

EXAMPLE 3.5

This example demonstrates the calculation of the median when n is an odd number. With an odd number of scores, you list the scores in order (lowest to highest), and the median is the middle score in the list. Consider the following set of $N = 5$ scores, which have been listed in order:

3   5   8   10   11

The middle score is $X = 8$, so the median is equal to 8. Using the counting method, with $N = 5$ scores, the 50% point would be $2\frac{1}{2}$ scores. Starting with the smallest scores, we must count the 3, the 5, and the 8 before we reach the target of at least 50%. Again, for this distribution, the median is the middle score, $X = 8$.

EXAMPLE 3.6

This example demonstrates the calculation of the median when n is an even number. With an even number of scores in the distribution, you list the scores in order (lowest to highest) and then locate the median by finding the average of the middle two scores. Consider the following population:

   1   1   4   5   7   8

Now we select the middle pair of scores (4 and 5), add them together, and divide by 2:

$$\text{median} = \frac{4+5}{2} = \frac{9}{2} = 4.5$$

Using the counting procedure, with $N = 6$ scores, the 50% point is 3 scores. Starting with the smallest scores, we must count the first 1, the second 1, and the 4 before we reach the target of at least 50%. Again, the median for this distribution is 4.5, which is the first point on the scale beyond $X = 4$. For this distribution, exactly 3 scores (50%) are located below 4.5. Note: If there is a gap between the middle two scores, the convention is to define the median as the midpoint between the two scores. For example, if the middle two scores are $X = 4$ and $X = 6$, the median would be defined as 5.

The simple technique of listing and counting scores is sufficient to determine the median for most distributions and is always appropriate for discrete variables. Notice that this technique always produces a median that either is a whole number or is halfway between two whole numbers. With a continuous variable, however, it is possible to divide a distribution precisely in half so that *exactly* 50% of the distribution is located below (and above) a specific point. The procedure for locating the precise median is discussed in the following section.

FINDING THE PRECISE MEDIAN FOR A CONTINUOUS VARIABLE

Recall from Chapter 1 that a continuous variable consists of categories that can be split into an infinite number of fractional parts. For example, time can be measured in seconds, tenths of a second, hundredths of a second, and so on. When the scores in a distribution are measurements of a continuous variable, it is possible to split one of the categories into fractional parts and find the median by locating the precise point that separates the bottom 50% of the distribution from the top 50%. The following example demonstrates this process.

EXAMPLE 3.7

For this example, we will find the precise median for the following sample of $n = 8$ scores: 1, 2, 3, 4, 4, 4, 4, 6

The frequency distribution for this sample is shown in Figure 3.4(a). With an even number of scores, you normally would compute the average of the middle two scores to find the median. This process produces a median of $X = 4$. For a discrete variable, $X = 4$ is the correct value for the median. Recall from Chapter 1 that a discrete variable consists of indivisible categories, such as the number of children in a family. Some families have 4 children and some have 5, but none have 4.31 children. For a discrete variable, the category $X = 4$ cannot be divided and the whole number 4 is the median.

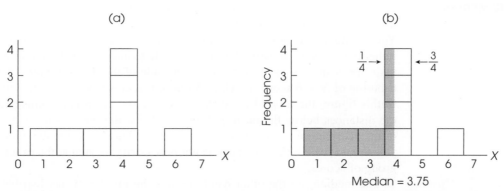

FIGURE 3.4

A distribution with several scores clustered at the median. The median for this distribution is positioned so that each of the four boxes above $X = 4$ is divided into two sections, with $\frac{1}{4}$ of each box below the median (to the left) and $\frac{3}{4}$ of each box above the median (to the right). As a result, there are exactly four boxes, 50% of the distribution, on each side of the median.

However, if you look at the distribution histogram, the value $X = 4$ does not appear to be the exact midpoint. The problem comes from the tendency to interpret a score of $X = 4$ as meaning exactly 4.00. However, if the scores are measurements of a continuous variable, then the score $X = 4$ actually corresponds to an interval from 3.5 to 4.5, and the median corresponds to a point within this interval.

To find the precise median, we first observe that the distribution contains $n = 8$ scores represented by 8 boxes in the graph. The median is the point that has exactly 4 boxes (50%) on each side. Starting at the left-hand side and moving up the scale of measurement, we accumulate a total of 3 boxes when we reach a value of 3.5 on the X-axis [see Figure 3.4(a)]. What is needed is 1 more box to reach the goal of 4 boxes (50%). The problem is that the next interval contains four boxes. The solution is to take a fraction of each box so that the fractions combine to give you one box. For this example, if we take $\frac{1}{4}$ of each box, the four quarters will combine to make one whole box. This solution is shown in Figure 3.4(b). The fraction is determined by the number of boxes needed to reach 50% and the number of boxes in the interval.

$$\text{fraction} = \frac{\text{number needed to reach 50\%}}{\text{number in the interval}}$$

For this example, we needed 1 out of the 4 boxes in the interval, so the fraction is $\frac{1}{4}$. To obtain one-fourth of each box, the median is the point that is located exactly one-fourth of the way into the interval. The interval for $X = 4$ extends from 3.5 to 4.5. The interval width is 1 point, so one-fourth of the interval corresponds to 0.25 points. Starting at the bottom of the interval and moving up 0.25 points produces a value of $3.50 + 0.25 = 3.75$. This is the median, with exactly 50% of the distribution (4 boxes) on each side.

Remember, finding the precise midpoint by dividing scores into fractional parts is sensible for a continuous variable, however; it is not appropriate for a discrete variable. For example, a median time of 3.75 seconds is reasonable, but a median family size of 3.75 children is not.

THE MEDIAN, THE MEAN, AND THE MIDDLE

Earlier, we defined the mean as the "balance point" for a distribution because the distances above the mean must have the same total as the distances below the mean. You should notice, however, that the concept of a balance point focuses on distances rather than scores. In particular, it is possible to have a distribution in which the vast majority of the scores are located on one side of the mean. Figure 3.5 shows a distribution of $N = 6$ scores in which 5 out of 6 scores have values less than the mean. In this figure, the total of the distances above the mean is 8 points and the total of the distances below the mean is 8 points. Thus, the mean is located in the middle of the distribution if you use the concept of distance to define the middle. However, you should realize that the mean is not necessarily located at the exact center of the group of scores.

The median, on the other hand, defines the middle of the distribution in terms of scores. In particular, the median is located so that half of the scores are on one side and half are on the other side. For the distribution in Figure 3.5, for example, the median is located at $X = 2.5$, with exactly 3 scores above this value and exactly 3 scores below. Thus, it is possible to claim that the median is located in the middle of the distribution, provided that the term *middle* is defined by the number of scores.

In summary, the mean and the median are both methods for defining and measuring central tendency. Although they both define the middle of the distribution, they use different definitions of the term *middle*.

LEARNING CHECK

1. Find the median for each distribution of scores:

   a. 3, 4, 6, 7, 9, 10, 11

   b. 8, 10, 11, 12, 14, 15

2. If you have a score of 52 on an 80-point exam, then you definitely scored above the median. (True or false?)

3. The following is a distribution of measurements for a continuous variable. Find the precise median that divides the distribution exactly in half.

   Scores: 1, 2, 2, 3, 4, 4, 4, 4, 4, 5

ANSWERS

1. **a.** The median is $X = 7$.   **b.** The median is $X = 11.5$.

2. False. The value of the median would depend on where all of the scores are located.

3. The median is 3.70 (one-fifth of the way into the interval from 3.5 to 4.5).

FIGURE 3.5

A population of $N = 6$ scores with a mean of $\mu = 4$. Notice that the mean does not necessarily divide the scores into two equal groups. In this example, 5 out of the 6 scores have values less than the mean.

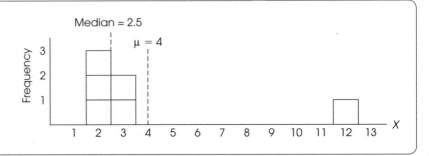

3.4 THE MODE

The final measure of central tendency that we consider is called the *mode*. In its common usage, the word *mode* means "the customary fashion" or "a popular style." The statistical definition is similar in that the mode is the most common observation among a group of scores.

DEFINITION

In a frequency distribution, the **mode** is the score or category that has the greatest frequency.

As with the median, there are no symbols or special notation used to identify the mode or to differentiate between a sample mode and a population mode. In addition, the definition of the mode is the same for a population and for a sample distribution.

The mode is a useful measure of central tendency because it can be used to determine the typical or average value for any scale of measurement, including a nominal scale (see Chapter 1). Consider, for example, the data shown in Table 3.4. These data were obtained by asking a sample of 100 students to name their favorite restaurants in town. The result is a sample of $n = 100$ scores with each score corresponding to the restaurant that the student named.

For these data, the mode is Luigi's, the restaurant (score) that was named most frequently as a favorite place. Although we can identify a modal response for these data, you

TABLE 3.4

Favorite restaurants named by a sample of $n = 100$ students. *Caution:* The mode is a score or category, not a frequency. For this example, the mode is Luigi's, not $f = 42$.

Restaurant	f
College Grill	5
George & Harry's	16
Luigi's	42
Oasis Diner	18
Roxbury Inn	7
Sutter's Mill	12

should notice that it would be impossible to compute a mean or a median. For example, you cannot add the scores to determine a mean (How much is 5 College Grills plus 42 Luigi's?). Also, it is impossible to list the scores in order because the restaurants do not form any natural order. For example, the College Grill is not "more than" or "less than" the Oasis Diner, they are simply two different restaurants. Thus, it is impossible to obtain the median by finding the midpoint of the list. In general, the mode is the only measure of central tendency that can be used with data from a nominal scale of measurement.

The mode also can be useful because it is the only measure of central tendency that corresponds to an actual score in the data; by definition, the mode is the most frequently occurring score. The mean and the median, on the other hand, are both calculated values and often produce an answer that does not equal any score in the distribution. For example, in Figure 3.5 on the previous page we presented a distribution with a mean of 4 and a median of 2.5. Note that none of the scores is equal to 4 and none of the scores is equal to 2.5. However, the mode for this distribution is $X = 2$ and there are three individuals who actually have scores of $X = 2$.

In a frequency distribution graph, the greatest frequency appears as the tallest part of the figure. To find the mode, you simply identify the score located directly beneath the highest point in the distribution.

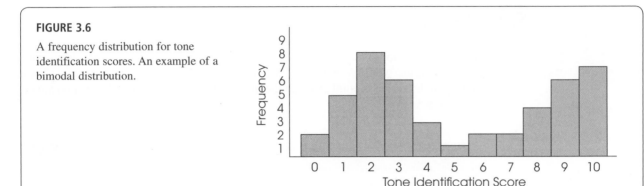

FIGURE 3.6

A frequency distribution for tone identification scores. An example of a bimodal distribution.

Although a distribution has only one mean and only one median, it is possible to have more than one mode. Specifically, it is possible to have two or more scores that have the same highest frequency. In a frequency distribution graph, the different modes correspond to distinct, equally high peaks. A distribution with two modes is said to be *bimodal,* and a distribution with more than two modes is called *multimodal.* Occasionally, a distribution with several equally high points is said to have no mode.

Incidentally, a bimodal distribution is often an indication that two separate and distinct groups of individuals exist within the same population (or sample). For example, if you measured height for each person in a set of 100 college students, the resulting distribution would probably have two modes, one corresponding primarily to the males in the group and one corresponding primarily to the females.

Technically, the mode is the score with the absolute highest frequency. However, the term *mode* is often used more casually to refer to scores with relatively high frequencies— that is, scores that correspond to peaks in a distribution even though the peaks are not the absolute highest points. For example, Athos, et al. (2007) asked people to identify the pitch for both pure tones and piano tones. Participants were presented with a series of tones and had to name the note corresponding to each tone. Nearly half the participants (44%) had extraordinary pitch-naming ability (absolute pitch), and were able to identify most of the tones correctly. Most of the other participants performed around chance level, apparently guessing the pitch names randomly. Figure 3.6 shows a distribution of scores that is consistent with the results of the study. There are two distinct peaks in the distribution, one located at $X = 2$ (chance performance) and the other located at $X = 10$ (perfect performance). Each of these values is a mode in the distribution. Note, however, that the two modes do not have identical frequencies. Eight people scored at $X = 2$ and only seven had scores of $X = 10$. Nonetheless, both of these points are called modes. When two modes have unequal frequencies, researchers occasionally differentiate the two values by calling the taller peak the *major mode,* and the shorter one the *minor mode.*

3.5   SELECTING A MEASURE OF CENTRAL TENDENCY

Deciding which measure of central tendency is best to use depends on several factors. Before we discuss these factors, however, note that the mean is usually the preferred measure of central tendency whenever the data consist of numerical scores. Because the mean uses every score in the distribution, it typically produces a good representative value. Remember that the goal of central tendency is to find the single value that best represents the entire distribution. Besides being a good representative, the mean has the added advantage of being closely related to variance and standard deviation,

LEARNING CHECK

1. During the month of October, an instructor recorded the number of absences for each student in a class of $n = 20$ and obtained the following distribution.

Number of Absences	f
5	1
4	2
3	7
2	5
1	3
0	2

a. Using the mean, what is the average number of absences for the class?
b. Using the median, what is the average number of absences for the class?
c. Using the mode, what is the average number of absences for the class?

ANSWERS

1.

a. The mean is $\frac{47}{20} = 2.35$.

b. The median is 2.5.

c. The mode is 3.

the most common measures of variability (see Chapter 4). This relationship makes the mean a valuable measure for purposes of inferential statistics. For these reasons, and others, the mean generally is considered to be the best of the three measures of central tendency. But there are specific situations in which it is impossible to compute a mean or in which the mean is not particularly representative. It is in these situations that the mode and the median are used.

WHEN TO USE THE MEDIAN

We consider four situations in which the median serves as a valuable alternative to the mean. In the first three cases, the data consist of numerical values (interval or ratio scales) for which you would normally compute the mean. However, each case also involves a special problem so that either it is impossible to compute the mean, or the calculation of the mean produces a value that is not central or not representative. The fourth situation involves measuring central tendency for ordinal data.

Extreme scores or skewed distributions   When a distribution has a few extreme scores, scores that are very different in value from most of the others, then the mean may not be a good representative of the majority of the distribution. The problem comes from the fact that one or two extreme values can have a large influence and cause the mean to be displaced. In this situation, the fact that the mean uses all of the scores equally can be a disadvantage. Consider, for example, the distribution of $n = 10$ scores in Figure 3.7. For this sample, the mean is

$$M = \frac{\Sigma X}{n} = \frac{203}{10} = 20.3$$

Notice that the mean is not very representative of any score in this distribution. Although most of the scores are clustered between 10 and 13, the extreme score of $X = 100$ inflates the value of ΣX and distorts the mean.

The median, on the other hand, usually is not affected by extreme scores. For this sample, $n = 10$, so there should be five scores on either side of the median. The median is 11.50. Notice that this is a very representative value. Also note that the median would

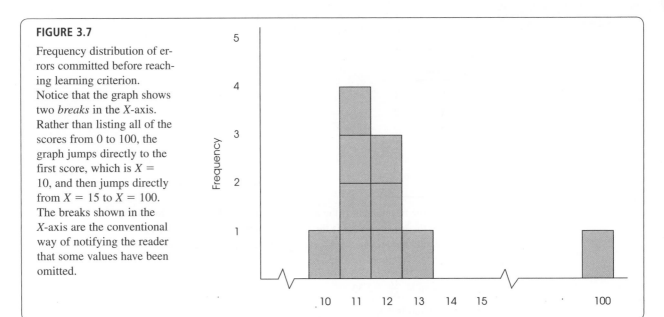

FIGURE 3.7

Frequency distribution of errors committed before reaching learning criterion. Notice that the graph shows two *breaks* in the *X*-axis. Rather than listing all of the scores from 0 to 100, the graph jumps directly to the first score, which is $X = 10$, and then jumps directly from $X = 15$ to $X = 100$. The breaks shown in the *X*-axis are the conventional way of notifying the reader that some values have been omitted.

be unchanged even if the extreme score were 1000 instead of only 100. Because it is relatively unaffected by extreme scores, the median commonly is used when reporting the average value for a skewed distribution. For example, the distribution of personal incomes is very skewed, with a small segment of the population earning incomes that are astronomical. These extreme values distort the mean, so that it is not very representative of the salaries that most of us earn. The median is the preferred measure of central tendency when extreme scores exist.

Undetermined values   Occasionally, you encounter a situation in which an individual has an unknown or undetermined score. This often occurs when you are measuring the number of errors or the amount of time required for an individual to complete a task. For example, suppose that preschool children are asked to assemble a wooden puzzle as quickly as possible. The experimenter records how long (in minutes) it takes each child to arrange all of the pieces to complete the puzzle. Table 3.5 presents results for a sample of $n = 6$ children.

Notice that one child never completed the puzzle. After an hour, this child still showed no sign of solving the puzzle, so the experimenter stopped him or her. This participant has an undetermined score. (There are two important points to be noted. First, the experimenter should not throw out this individual's score. The whole purpose for using a sample is to gain a picture of the population, and this child tells us that part of the population cannot solve the puzzle. Second, this child should not be given a score of

TABLE 3.5

Number of minutes needed to assemble a wooden puzzle.

Child	Time (Min.)
1	8
2	11
3	12
4	13
5	17
6	Never finished

$X = 60$ minutes. Even though the experimenter stopped the individual after 1 hour, the child did not finish the puzzle. The score that is recorded is the amount of time needed to finish. For this individual, we do not know how long this is.)

It is impossible to compute the mean for these data because of the undetermined value. We cannot calculate the ΣX part of the formula for the mean. However, it is possible to determine the median. For these data, the median is 12.5. Three scores are below the median, and three scores (including the undetermined value) are above the median.

Number of Pizzas (X)	f
5 or more	3
4	2
3	2
2	3
1	6
0	4

Open-ended distributions   A distribution is said to be *open-ended* when there is no upper limit (or lower limit) for one of the categories. The table in the margin provides an example of an open-ended distribution, showing the number of pizzas eaten during a 1-month period for a sample of $n = 20$ high school students. The top category in this distribution shows that three of the students consumed "5 or more" pizzas. This is an open-ended category. Notice that it is impossible to compute a mean for these data because you cannot find ΣX (the total number of pizzas for all 20 students). However, you can find the median. Listing the 20 scores in order produces $X = 1$ and $X = 2$ as the middle two scores. For these data, the median is 1.5.

Ordinal scale   Many researchers believe that it is not appropriate to use the mean to describe central tendency for ordinal data. When scores are measured on an ordinal scale, the median is always appropriate and is usually the preferred measure of central tendency.

You should recall that ordinal measurements allow you to determine direction (greater than or less than) but do not allow you to determine distance. The median is compatible with this type of measurement because it is defined by direction: half of the scores are above the median and half are below the median. The mean, on the other hand, defines central tendency in terms of distance. Remember that the mean is the balance point for the distribution, so that the distances above the mean are exactly balanced by the distances below the mean. Because the mean is defined in terms of distances, and because ordinal scales do not measure distance, it is not appropriate to compute a mean for scores from an ordinal scale.

WHEN TO USE THE MODE

We consider three situations in which the mode is commonly used as an alternative to the mean, or is used in conjunction with the mean to describe central tendency.

Nominal scales   The primary advantage of the mode is that it can be used to measure and describe central tendency for data that are measured on a nominal scale. Recall that the categories that make up a nominal scale are differentiated only by name. Because nominal scales do not measure quantity (distance or direction), it is impossible to compute a mean or a median for data from a nominal scale. Therefore, the mode is the only option for describing central tendency for nominal data.

Discrete variables   Recall that discrete variables are those that exist only in whole, indivisible categories. Often, discrete variables are numerical values, such as the number of children in a family or the number of rooms in a house. When these variables produce numerical scores, it is possible to calculate means. In this situation, the calculated means are usually fractional values that cannot actually exist. For example, computing means generates results such as "the average family has 2.4 children and a house with 5.33 rooms." On the other hand, the mode always identifies the most typical case and, therefore, it produces more sensible measures of central tendency. Using the mode, our conclusion would be "the typical, or modal, family has 2 children and a house with 5 rooms." In many situations, especially with discrete variables, people are more comfortable using the realistic, whole-number values produced by the mode.

Describing shape   Because the mode requires little or no calculation, it is often included as a supplementary measure along with the mean or median as a no-cost extra. The value of the mode (or modes) in this situation is that it gives an indication of the shape of the distribution as well as a measure of central tendency. Remember that the mode identifies the location of the peak (or peaks) in the frequency distribution graph. For example, if you are told that a set of exam scores has a mean of 72 and a mode of 80, you should have a better picture of the distribution than would be available from the mean alone (see Section 3.6).

IN THE LITERATURE
REPORTING MEASURES OF CENTRAL TENDENCY

Measures of central tendency are commonly used in the behavioral sciences to summarize and describe the results of a research study. For example, a researcher may report the sample means from two different treatments or the median score for a large sample. These values may be reported in verbal descriptions of the results, in tables, or in graphs.

In reporting results, many behavioral science journals use guidelines adopted by the American Psychological Association (APA), as outlined in the *Publication Manual of the American Psychological Association* (2010). We refer to the APA manual from time to time in describing how data and research results are reported in the scientific literature. The APA style uses the letter *M* as the symbol for the sample mean. Thus, a study might state:

> The treatment group showed fewer errors ($M = 2.56$) on the task than the control group ($M = 11.76$).

When there are many means to report, tables with headings provide an organized and more easily understood presentation. Table 3.6 illustrates this point.

The median can be reported using the abbreviation *Mdn,* as in "Mdn = 8.5 errors," or it can simply be reported in narrative text, as follows:

> The median number of errors for the treatment group was 8.5, compared to a median of 13 for the control group.

There is no special symbol or convention for reporting the mode. If mentioned at all, the mode is usually just reported in narrative text.

PRESENTING MEANS AND MEDIANS IN GRAPHS

Graphs also can be used to report and compare measures of central tendency. Usually, graphs are used to display values obtained for sample means, but occasionally sample medians are reported in graphs (modes are rarely, if ever, shown in a graph). The value of a graph is that it allows several means (or medians) to be shown simultaneously, so it is possible to make quick comparisons between groups or treatment conditions. When preparing a graph, it is customary to list the different groups or treatment conditions on the horizontal axis. Typically, these are the different values that make up the

TABLE 3.6

The mean number of errors made on the task for treatment and control groups, divided by gender.

	Treatment	Control
Females	1.45	8.36
Males	3.83	14.77

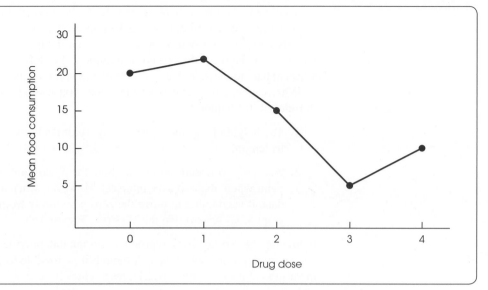

FIGURE 3.8

FIGURE 3.8

The relationship between an independent variable (drug dose) and a dependent variable (food consumption). Because drug dose is a continuous variable, a continuous line is used to connect the different dose levels.

independent variable or the quasi-independent variable. Values for the dependent variable (the scores) are listed on the vertical axis. The means (or medians) are then displayed using a *line graph,* a *histogram,* or a *bar graph,* depending on the scale of measurement used for the independent variable.

Figure 3.8 shows an example of a *line graph* displaying the relationship between drug dose (the independent variable) and food consumption (the dependent variable). In this study, there were five different drug doses (treatment conditions) and they are listed along the horizontal axis. The five means appear as points in the graph. To construct this graph, a point was placed above each treatment condition so that the vertical position of the point corresponds to the mean score for the treatment condition. The points are then connected with straight lines. A line graph is used when the values on the horizontal axis are measured on an interval or a ratio scale. An alternative to the line graph is a *histogram.* For this example, the histogram would show a bar above each drug dose so that the height of each bar corresponds to the mean food consumption for that group, with no space between adjacent bars.

Figure 3.9 shows a bar graph displaying the median selling price for single-family homes in different regions of the United States. Bar graphs are used to present means

FIGURE 3.9

Median cost of a new, single-family home by region.

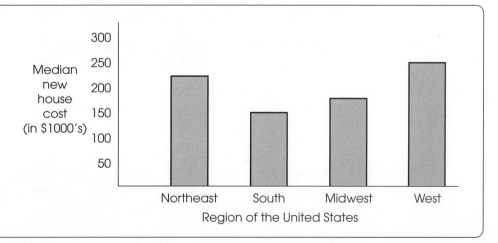

(or medians) when the groups or treatments shown on the horizontal axis are measured on a nominal or an ordinal scale. To construct a bar graph, you simply draw a bar directly above each group or treatment so that the height of the bar corresponds to the mean (or median) for that group or treatment. For a bar graph, a space is left between adjacent bars to indicate that the scale of measurement is nominal or ordinal.

When constructing graphs of any type, you should recall the basic rules that we introduced in Chapter 2:

1. The height of a graph should be approximately two-thirds to three-quarters of its length.

2. Normally, you start numbering both the *X*-axis and the *Y*-axis with zero at the point where the two axes intersect. However, when a value of zero is part of the data, it is common to move the zero point away from the intersection so that the graph does not overlap the axes (see Figure 3.8).

Following these rules helps to produce a graph that provides an accurate presentation of the information in a set of data. Although it is possible to construct graphs that distort the results of a study (see Box 2.1), researchers have an ethical responsibility to present an honest and accurate report of their research results.

3.6 CENTRAL TENDENCY AND THE SHAPE OF THE DISTRIBUTION

We have identified three different measures of central tendency, and often a researcher calculates all three for a single set of data. Because the mean, the median, and the mode are all trying to measure the same thing, it is reasonable to expect that these three values should be related. In fact, there are some consistent and predictable relationships among the three measures of central tendency. Specifically, there are situations in which all three measures have exactly the same value. On the other hand, there are situations in which the three measures are guaranteed to be different. In part, the relationships among the mean, median, and mode are determined by the shape of the distribution. We consider two general types of distributions.

SYMMETRICAL DISTRIBUTIONS

For a *symmetrical distribution,* the right-hand side of the graph is a mirror image of the left-hand side. If a distribution is perfectly symmetrical, the median is exactly at the center because exactly half of the area in the graph is on either side of the center. The mean also is exactly at the center of a perfectly symmetrical distribution because each score on the left side of the distribution is balanced by a corresponding score (the mirror image) on the right side. As a result, the mean (the balance point) is located at the center of the distribution. Thus, for a perfectly symmetrical distribution, the mean and the median are the same (Figure 3.10). If a distribution is roughly symmetrical, but not perfect, the mean and median are close together in the center of the distribution.

If a symmetrical distribution has only one mode, then it is also in the center of the distribution. Thus, for a perfectly symmetrical distribution with one mode, all three measures of central tendency—the mean, the median, and the mode—have the same value. For a roughly symmetrical distribution, the three measures are clustered together in the center of the distribution. On the other hand, a bimodal distribution that is symmetrical [see Figure 3.10(b)] has the mean and median together in the center with the modes on each side. A rectangular distribution [see Figure 3.10(c)] has no mode

FIGURE 3.10

Measures of central tendency for three symmetrical distributions: normal, bimodal, and rectangular.

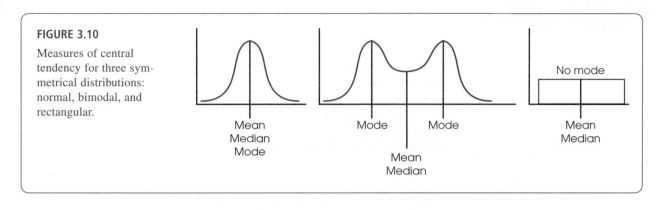

because all X values occur with the same frequency. Still, the mean and the median are in the center of the distribution.

SKEWED DISTRIBUTIONS

The positions of the mean, median, and mode are not as consistently predictable in distributions of discrete variables (see Von Hippel, 2005).

In *skewed distributions,* especially distributions for continuous variables, there is a strong tendency for the mean, median, and mode to be located in predictably different positions. Figure 3.11(a), for example, shows a *positively skewed* distribution with the peak (highest frequency) on the left-hand side. This is the position of the mode. However, it should be clear that the vertical line drawn at the mode does not divide the distribution into two equal parts. To have exactly 50% of the distribution on each side, the median must be located to the right of the mode. Finally, the mean is located to the right of the median because it is the measure of central tendency that is influenced most by the extreme scores in the tail and, therefore, tends to be displaced toward the tail of the distribution. Thus, in a positively skewed distribution, the typical order of the three measures of central tendency from smallest to largest (left to right) is the mode, the median, and the mean.

Negatively skewed distributions are lopsided in the opposite direction, with the scores piling up on the right-hand side and the tail tapering off to the left. The grades on an easy exam, for example, tend to form a negatively skewed distribution [see Figure 3.11(b)]. For a distribution with negative skew, the mode is on the right-hand side (with the peak), whereas the mean is displaced toward the left by the extreme scores in the tail. As before, the median is usually located between the mean and the mode. Therefore, in a *negatively skewed* distribution, the most probable order for the three measures of central tendency from smallest value to largest value (left to right), is the mean, the median, and the mode.

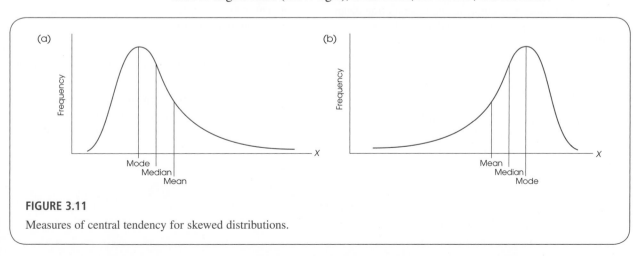

FIGURE 3.11

Measures of central tendency for skewed distributions.

LEARNING CHECK

1. Which measure of central tendency is most affected if one extremely large score is added to a distribution? (mean, median, mode)

2. Why is it usually considered inappropriate to compute a mean for scores measured on an ordinal scale?

3. In a perfectly symmetrical distribution, the mean, the median, and the mode will all have the same value. (True or false?)

4. A distribution with a mean of 70 and a median of 75 is probably positively skewed. (True or false?)

ANSWERS

1. mean

2. The definition of the mean is based on distances (the mean balances the distances) and ordinal scales do not measure distance.

3. False, if the distribution is bimodal.

4. False. The mean is displaced toward the tail on the left-hand side.

SUMMARY

1. The goal of central tendency is to determine the single value that identifies the center of the distribution and best represents the entire set of scores. The three standard measures of central tendency are the mode, the median, and the mean.

2. The mean is the arithmetic average. It is computed by adding all of the scores and then dividing by the number of scores. Conceptually, the mean is obtained by dividing the total (ΣX) equally among the number of individuals (N or n). The mean can also be defined as the balance point for the distribution. The distances above the mean are exactly balanced by the distances below the mean. Although the calculation is the same for a population or a sample mean, a population mean is identified by the symbol μ, and a sample mean is identified by M. In most situations with numerical scores from an interval or a ratio scale, the mean is the preferred measure of central tendency.

3. Changing any score in the distribution causes the mean to be changed. When a constant value is added to (or subtracted from) every score in a distribution, the same constant value is added to (or subtracted from) the mean. If every score is multiplied by a constant, the mean is multiplied by the same constant.

4. The median is the midpoint of a distribution of scores. The median is the preferred measure of central tendency when a distribution has a few extreme scores that displace the value of the mean. The median also is used for open-ended distributions or when there are undetermined (infinite) scores that make it impossible to compute a mean. Finally, the median is the preferred measure of central tendency for data from an ordinal scale.

5. The mode is the most frequently occurring score in a distribution. It is easily located by finding the peak in a frequency distribution graph. For data measured on a nominal scale, the mode is the appropriate measure of central tendency. It is possible for a distribution to have more than one mode.

6. For symmetrical distributions, the mean is equal to the median. If there is only one mode, then it has the same value, too.

7. For skewed distributions, the mode is located toward the side where the scores pile up, and the mean tends to be pulled toward the extreme scores in the tail. The median is usually located between these two values.

KEY TERMS

central tendency (60)	mode (73)	line graph (79)
population mean (μ) (62)	bimodal (74)	symmetrical distribution (80)
sample mean (*M*) (62)	multimodal (74)	skewed distribution (81)
weighted mean (64)	major mode (74)	positively skewed (81)
median (69)	minor mode (74)	negatively skewed (81)

RESOURCES

 Go to CengageBrain.com to access Psychology CourseMate, where you will find an interactive eBook, glossaries, flashcards, quizzes, statistics workshops, and more.

If your professor has assigned Aplia:

1. Sign in to your account.

2. Complete the corresponding exercises as required by your professor.

3. When finished, click "Grade It Now" to see which areas you have mastered, which areas need more work, and detailed explanations of every answer.

General instructions for using SPSS are presented in Appendix D. Following are detailed instructions for using SPSS to compute the **Mean** and ΣX for a set of scores.

Data Entry

Enter all of the scores in one column of the data editor, probably VAR00001.

Data Analysis

1. Click **Analyze** on the tool bar, select **Descriptive Statistics,** and click on **Descriptives.**

2. Highlight the column label for the set of scores (VAR00001) in the left box and click the arrow to move it into the **Variable** box.

3. If you want ΣX as well as the mean, click on the **Options** box, select **Sum,** then click **Continue.**

4. Click **OK.**

SPSS Output

SPSS produces a summary table listing the number of scores (*N*), the maximum and minimum scores, the sum of the scores (if you selected this option), the mean, and the standard deviation. Note: The standard deviation is a measure of variability that is presented in Chapter 4.

FOCUS ON PROBLEM SOLVING

1. Although the three measures of central tendency appear to be very simple to calculate, there is always a chance for errors. The most common sources of error are listed next.

X	f
4	1
3	4
2	3
1	2

  a. Many students find it very difficult to compute the mean for data presented in a frequency distribution table. They tend to ignore the frequencies in the table and simply average the score values listed in the X column. You must use the frequencies *and* the scores! Remember that the number of scores is found by $N = \Sigma f$, and the sum of all N scores is found by ΣfX. For the distribution shown in the margin, the mean is $\frac{24}{10} = 2.40$.

  b. The median is the midpoint of the distribution of scores, not the midpoint of the scale of measurement. For a 100-point test, for example, many students incorrectly assume that the median must be X = 50. To find the median, you must have the *complete set* of individual scores. The median separates the individuals into two equal-sized groups.

  c. The most common error with the mode is for students to report the highest frequency in a distribution rather than the *score* with the highest frequency. Remember that the purpose of central tendency is to find the most representative score. For the distribution in the margin, the mode is X = 3, not f = 4.

DEMONSTRATION 3.1

COMPUTING MEASURES OF CENTRAL TENDENCY

For the following sample, find the mean, the median, and the mode. The scores are:

$$5 \quad 6 \quad 9 \quad 11 \quad 5 \quad 11 \quad 8 \quad 14 \quad 2 \quad 11$$

Compute the mean   The calculation of the mean requires two pieces of information; the sum of the scores, ΣX; and the number of scores, n. For this sample, $n = 10$ and

$$\Sigma X = 5 + 6 + 9 + 11 + 5 + 11 + 8 + 14 + 2 + 11 = 82$$

Therefore, the sample mean is

$$M = \frac{\Sigma X}{n} = \frac{82}{10} = 8.2$$

Find the median   To find the median, first list the scores in order from smallest to largest. With an even number of scores, the median is the average of the middle two scores in the list. Listed in order, the scores are:

$$2 \quad 5 \quad 5 \quad 6 \quad 8 \quad 9 \quad 11 \quad 11 \quad 11 \quad 14$$

The middle two scores are 8 and 9, and the median is 8.5.

Find the mode   For this sample, X = 11 is the score that occurs most frequently. The mode is X = 11.

PROBLEMS

1. Why is it necessary to have more than one method for measuring central tendency?

2. Find the mean, median, and mode for the following sample of scores:

$$5 \quad 4 \quad 5 \quad 2 \quad 7 \quad 1 \quad 3 \quad 5$$

3. Find the mean, median, and mode for the following sample of scores:

$$3 \quad 6 \quad 7 \quad 3 \quad 9 \quad 8 \quad 3 \quad 7 \quad 5$$

4. Find the mean, median, and mode for the scores in the following frequency distribution table:

X	f
6	1
5	2
4	2
3	2
2	2
1	5

5. Find the mean, median, and mode for the scores in the following frequency distribution table:

X	f
8	1
7	1
6	2
5	5
4	2
3	2

6. For the following sample:

   a. Assume that the scores are measurements of a continuous variable and find the median by locating the precise midpoint of the distribution.

   b. Assume that the scores are measurements of a discrete variable and find the median.

   Scores: 1   2   3   3   3   4

7. A population of $N = 15$ scores has $\Sigma X = 120$. What is the population mean?

8. A sample of $n = 8$ scores has a mean of $M = 12$. What is the value of ΣX for this sample?

9. A population with a mean of $\mu = 8$ has $\Sigma X = 40$. How many scores are in the population?

10. A sample of $n = 7$ scores has a mean of $M = 9$. If one new person with a score of $X = 1$ is added to the sample, what is the value for the new mean?

11. A sample of $n = 6$ scores has a mean of $M = 13$. If one person with a score of $X = 3$ is removed from the sample, what is the value for the new mean?

12. A sample of $n = 15$ scores has a mean of $M = 6$. One person with a score of $X = 22$ is added to the sample. What is the value for the new sample mean?

13. A sample of $n = 10$ scores has a mean of $M = 9$. One person with a score of $X = 0$ is removed from the sample. What is the value for the new sample mean?

14. A population of $N = 15$ scores has a mean of $\mu = 8$. One score in the population is changed from $X = 20$ to $X = 5$. What is the value for the new population mean?

15. A sample of $n = 7$ scores has a mean of $M = 16$. One score in the sample is changed from $X = 6$ to $X = 20$. What is the value for the new sample mean?

16. A sample of $n = 7$ scores has a mean of $M = 5$. After one new score is added to the sample, the new mean is found to be $M = 6$. What is the value of the new score? (Hint: Compare the values for ΣX before and after the score was added.)

17. A population of $N = 8$ scores has a mean of $\mu = 16$. After one score is removed from the population, the new mean is found to be $\mu = 15$. What is the value of the score that was removed? (Hint: Compare the values for ΣX before and after the score was removed.)

18. A sample of $n = 9$ scores has a mean of $M = 13$. After one score is added to the sample, the mean is found to be $M = 12$. What is the value of the score that was added?

19. A sample of $n = 9$ scores has a mean of $M = 20$. One of the scores is changed and the new mean is found to be $M = 22$. If the changed score was originally $X = 7$, what is its new value?

20. One sample of $n = 12$ scores has a mean of $M = 7$ and a second sample of $n = 8$ scores has a mean of $M = 12$. If the two samples are combined, what is the mean for the combined sample?

21. One sample has a mean of $M = 8$ and a second sample has a mean of $M = 16$. The two samples are combined into a single set of scores.

   a. What is the mean for the combined set if both of the original samples have $n = 4$ scores?

   b. What is the mean for the combined set if the first sample has $n = 3$ and the second sample has $n = 5$?

c. What is the mean for the combined set if the first sample has $n = 5$ and the second sample has $n = 3$?

22. One sample has a mean of $M = 5$ and a second sample has a mean of $M = 10$. The two samples are combined into a single set of scores.

    a. What is the mean for the combined set if both of the original samples have $n = 5$ scores?

    b. What is the mean for the combined set if the first sample has $n = 4$ scores and the second sample has $n = 6$?

    c. What is the mean for the combined set if the first sample has $n = 6$ scores and the second sample has $n = 4$?

23. Explain why the mean is often not a good measure of central tendency for a skewed distribution.

24. A researcher conducts a study comparing two different treatments with a sample of $n = 16$ participants in each treatment. The study produced the following data:

    Treatment 1:   6   7   11   4   19   17   2   5
    9   13   6   23   11   4   6   1

    Treatment 2:   10   9   6   6   1   11   8   6   3
    2   11   1   12   7   10   9

    a. Calculate the mean for each treatment. Based on the two means, which treatment produces the higher scores?

    b. Calculate the median for each treatment. Based on the two medians, which treatment produces the higher scores?

    c. Calculate the mode for each treatment. Based on the two modes, which treatment produces the higher scores?

25. Schmidt (1994) conducted a series of experiments examining the effects of humor on memory. In one study, participants were shown a list of sentences, of which half were humorous and half were non-humorous. A humorous example is, "If at first you don't succeed, you are probably not related to the boss." Other participants would see a nonhumorous version of this sentence, such as "People who are related to the boss often succeed the very first time."
Schmidt then measured the number of each type of sentence recalled by each participant. The following scores are similar to the results obtained in the study.

Number of Sentences Recalled	
Humorous Sentences	*Nonhumorous Sentences*
4 5 2 4	5 2 4 2
6 7 6 6	2 3 1 6
2 5 4 3	3 2 3 3
1 3 5 5	4 1 5 3

Calculate the mean number of sentences recalled for each of the two conditions. Do the data suggest that humor helps memory?

26. Stephens, Atkins, and Kingston (2009) conducted a research study demonstrating that swearing can help reduce pain. In the study, each participant was asked to plunge a hand into icy water and keep it there as long as the pain would allow. In one condition, the participants repeatedly yelled their favorite curse words while their hands were in the water. In the other condition the participants repeated a neutral word. Data similar to the results obtained in the study are shown in the following table. Calculate the mean number of seconds that the participants could tolerate the pain for each of the two treatment conditions. Does it appear that swearing helped with pain tolerance?

Amount of Time (in seconds)		
Participant	*Swear Words*	*Neutral Words*
1	94	59
2	70	61
3	52	47
4	83	60
5	46	35
6	117	92
7	69	53
8	39	30
9	51	56
10	73	61

27. Earlier in this chapter (p. 67), we mentioned a research study demonstrating that alcohol consumption increases attractiveness ratings for members of the opposite sex (Jones, Jones, Thomas, & Piper, 2003). In the actual study, college-age participants were recruited from bars and restaurants near campus and asked to participate in a "market research" study. During the introductory conversation, they were asked to report their alcohol consumption for the day and were told that moderate consumption would not prevent them from taking part in the study. Participants were then shown a series of photographs of male and female faces and asked to rate the attractiveness of each face

on a 1–7 scale. The following data duplicate the general pattern of results obtained in the study. The two sets of scores are attractiveness ratings for one female obtained from two groups of males: those who had no alcohol and those with moderate alcohol consumption. Calculate the mean for each group. Does it appear from these data that alcohol has an effect on judgments of attractiveness?

Group 1 No Alcohol	Group 2 Moderate Alcohol
3 4 5 1 2	5 3 5 2 4
4 2 3 4 4	6 5 6 5 4
5 6 3 4 3	7 5 6 5 6

CHAPTER

4

Measures of Variability

Tools You Will Need

The following items are considered essential background material for this chapter. If you doubt your knowledge of any of these items, you should review the appropriate chapter or section before proceeding.

- Summation notation (Chapter 1)
- Central tendency (Chapter 3)
  - Mean
  - Median

aplia

Aplia for *Essentials of Statistics for the Behavioral Sciences*
After reading, go to "Resources" at the end of this chapter for an introduction on how to use Aplia's homework and learning resources.

4.1   DEFINING VARIABILITY

The term *variability* has much the same meaning in statistics as it has in everyday language; to say that things are variable means that they are not all the same. In statistics, our goal is to measure the amount of variability for a particular set of scores: a distribution. In simple terms, if the scores in a distribution are all the same, then there is no variability. If there are small differences between scores, then the variability is small, and if there are large differences between scores, then the variability is large.

DEFINITION

Variability provides a quantitative measure of the differences between scores in a distribution and describes the degree to which the scores are spread out or clustered together.

Figure 4.1 shows two distributions of familiar values for the population of adult males: Part (a) shows the distribution of men's heights (in inches), and part (b) shows the distribution of men's weights (in pounds). Notice that the two distributions differ in terms of central tendency. The mean height is 70 inches (5 feet, 10 inches) and the mean weight is 170 pounds. In addition, notice that the distributions differ in terms of variability. For example, most heights are clustered close together, within 5 or 6 inches of the mean. On the other hand, weights are spread over a much wider range. In the weight distribution it is not unusual to find individuals who are located more than 30 pounds away from the mean, and it would not be surprising to find two individuals whose weights differ by more than 30 or 40 pounds. The purpose for measuring variability is to obtain an objective measure of how the scores are spread out in a distribution. In general, a good measure of variability serves two purposes:

1. Variability describes the distribution. Specifically, it tells whether the scores are clustered close together or are spread out over a large distance. Usually, variability is defined in terms of *distance*. It tells how much distance to expect between one score and another, or how much distance to expect between an individual score and the mean. For example, we know that the heights for most adult males are clustered close together, within 5 or 6 inches of the average. Although more extreme heights exist, they are relatively rare.

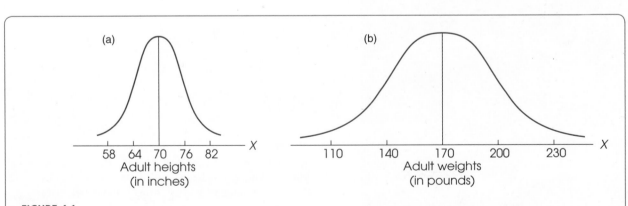

FIGURE 4.1

Population distribution of adult heights and adult weights.

2. Variability measures how well an individual score (or group of scores) represents the entire distribution. This aspect of variability is very important for inferential statistics, in which relatively small samples are used to answer questions about populations. For example, suppose that you selected one person to represent the entire population. Because most adult males have heights that are within a few inches of the population average (the distances are small), there is a very good chance that you would select someone whose height is within 6 inches of the population mean. On the other hand, the scores are much more spread out (greater distances) in the distribution of weights. In this case, you probably would *not* obtain someone whose weight was within 6 pounds of the population mean. Thus, variability provides information about how much error to expect if you are using a sample to represent a population.

In this chapter, we consider three different measures of variability: the range, standard deviation, and the variance. Of these three, the standard deviation and the related measure of variance are by far the most important.

4.2 **THE RANGE**

The *range* is the distance covered by the scores in a distribution, from the smallest score to the largest score. When the scores are measurements of a continuous variable, the range can be defined as the difference between the upper real limit (URL) for the largest score (X_{max}) and the lower real limit (LRL) for the smallest score (X_{min}).

$$\text{range} = \text{URL for } X_{max} - \text{LRL for } X_{min}$$

If the scores have values from 1 to 5, for example, the range is $5.5 - 0.5 = 5$ points. When the scores are whole numbers, this definition of the range is also a measure of the number of measurement categories. If every individual is classified as either 1, 2, 3, 4, or 5, then there are five measurement categories and the range is 5 points.

Continuous and discrete variables were discussed in Chapter 1 on pages 20-22.

Defining the range as the number of measurement categories also works for discrete variables that are measured with numerical scores. For example, if you are measuring the number of children in a family and the data produce values from 0 to 4, then there are five measurement categories (0, 1, 2, 3, and 4) and the range is 5 points. By this definition, when the scores are all whole numbers, the range can be obtained by

$$X_{max} - X_{min} + 1.$$

A commonly used alternative definition of the range simply measures the distance between the largest score (X_{max}) and the smallest score (X_{min}), without any reference to real limits.

$$\text{range} = X_{max} - X_{max}$$

By this definition, scores having values from 1 to 5 cover a range of only 4 points. Many computer programs, such as SPSS, use this definition. For discrete variables, which do not have real limits, this definition is often considered more appropriate. Also, this definition works well for variables with precisely defined upper and lower boundaries. For example, if you are measuring proportions of an object, like pieces of a pizza, you can obtain values such as $\frac{1}{8}$, $\frac{1}{4}$, $\frac{1}{2}$, $\frac{3}{4}$, and so on. Expressed as decimal values, the proportions range from 0 to 1. You can never have a value less than 0 (none of the pizza) and you can never have a value greater than 1 (all of the pizza). Thus, the complete set of proportions is bounded by 0 at one end and by 1 at the other. As a result, the proportions cover a range of 1 point.

Using either definition, the range is probably the most obvious way to describe how spread out the scores are—simply find the distance between the maximum and the minimum scores. The problem with using the range as a measure of variability is that it is completely determined by the two extreme values and ignores the other scores in the distribution. Thus, a distribution with one unusually large (or small) score has a large range even if the other scores are all clustered close together.

Because the range does not consider all of the scores in the distribution, it often does not give an accurate description of the variability for the entire distribution. For this reason, the range is considered to be a crude and unreliable measure of variability. Therefore, in most situations, it does not matter which definition you use to determine the range.

4.3 STANDARD DEVIATION AND VARIANCE FOR A POPULATION

The standard deviation is the most commonly used and the most important measure of variability. Standard deviation uses the mean of the distribution as a reference point and measures variability by considering the distance between each score and the mean.

In simple terms, the standard deviation provides a measure of the standard, or average, distance from the mean, and describes whether the scores are clustered closely around the mean or are widely scattered. The fundamental definition of the standard deviation is the same for both samples and populations, but the calculations differ slightly. We look first at the standard deviation as it is computed for a population, and then turn our attention to samples in Section 4.4.

THE PROCESS OF COMPUTING STANDARD DEVIATION

Although the concept of standard deviation is straightforward, the actual equations appear complex. Therefore, we begin by looking at the logic that leads to these equations. If you remember that our goal is to measure the standard, or typical, distance from the mean, then this logic and the equations that follow should be easier to remember.

Step 1   The first step in finding the standard distance from the mean is to determine the *deviation*, or distance from the mean, for each individual score. By definition, the deviation for each score is the difference between the score and the mean.

DEFINITION

> **Deviation** is distance from the mean:
>
> deviation score = $X - \mu$

A deviation score is often represented by a lowercase letter *x*.

For a distribution of scores with $\mu = 50$, if your score is $X = 53$, then your *deviation score* is

$$X - \mu = 53 - 50 = 3$$

If your score is $X = 45$, then your deviation score is

$$X - \mu = 45 - 50 = -5$$

Notice that there are two parts to a deviation score: the sign (+ or −) and the number. The sign tells the direction from the mean—that is, whether the score is located above (+) or below (−) the mean. The number gives the actual distance from the mean.

For example, a deviation score of -6 corresponds to a score that is below the mean by a distance of 6 points.

Step 2   Because our goal is to compute a measure of the standard distance from the mean, the obvious next step is to calculate the mean of the deviation scores. To compute this mean, you first add up the deviation scores and then divide by N. This process is demonstrated in the following example.

E X A M P L E   4 . 1   We start with the following set of $N = 4$ scores. These scores add up to $\Sigma X = 12$, so the mean is $\mu = \frac{12}{4} = 3$. For each score, we have computed the deviation.

X	$X - \mu$
8	+5
1	-2
3	0
0	-3
	$0 = \Sigma(X - \mu)$

Note that the deviation scores add up to zero. This should not be surprising if you remember that the mean serves as a balance point for the distribution. The total of the distances above the mean is exactly equal to the total of the distances below the mean (see page 63). Thus, the total for the positive deviations is exactly equal to the total for the negative deviations, and the complete set of deviations always adds up to zero.

Because the sum of the deviations is always zero, the mean of the deviations is also zero and is of no value as a measure of variability. Specifically, it is zero if the scores are closely clustered and it is zero if the scores are widely scattered. You should note, however, that the constant value of zero can be useful in other ways. Whenever you are working with deviation scores, you can check your calculations by making sure that the deviation scores add up to zero.

Step 3   The average of the deviation scores does not work as a measure of variability because it is always zero. Clearly, this problem results from the positive and negative values canceling each other out. The solution is to get rid of the signs ($+$ and $-$). The standard procedure for accomplishing this is to square each deviation score. Using the squared values, you then compute the *mean squared deviation*, which is called *population variance*.

D E F I N I T I O N   **Population variance** equals the mean squared deviation. Variance is the average squared distance from the mean.

Note that the process of squaring deviation scores does more than simply get rid of plus and minus signs. It results in a measure of variability based on *squared* distances. Although variance is valuable for some of the *inferential* statistical methods covered later, the concept of squared distance is not an intuitive or easy to understand *descriptive* measure. For example, it is not particularly useful to know that the squared distance from New York City to Boston is 26,244 miles squared. The squared value becomes meaningful, however, if you take the square root. For example, the distance from New York City to Boston is $\sqrt{26,244} = 162$ miles. Therefore, we continue the process with one more step.

Step 4   Remember that our goal is to compute a measure of the standard distance from the mean. Variance, which measures the average squared distance from the mean, is not exactly what we want. The final step simply takes the square root of the variance to obtain the *standard deviation*, which measures the standard distance from the mean.

DEFINITION

> **Standard deviation** is the square root of the variance and provides a measure of the standard, or average, distance from the mean.
>
> $$\text{Standard deviation} = \sqrt{\text{variance}}$$

Figure 4.2 shows the overall process of computing variance and standard deviation. Remember that our goal is to measure variability by finding the standard distance from the mean. However, we cannot simply calculate the average of the distances because this value will always be zero. Therefore, we begin by squaring each distance, then we find the average of the squared distances, and finally we take the square root to obtain a measure of the standard distance. Technically, the standard deviation is the square root of the average squared deviation. Conceptually, however, the standard deviation provides a measure of the average distance from the mean.

Because the standard deviation and variance are defined in terms of distance from the mean, these measures of variability are used only with numerical scores that are obtained from measurements on an interval or a ratio scale. Recall from Chapter 1 (page 24) that these two scales are the only ones that provide information about distance; nominal and ordinal scales do not. Also, recall from Chapter 3 (page 77) that it is inappropriate to compute the mean for ordinal data and impossible to compute the mean for nominal data. Because the mean is a critical component in the calculation of standard deviation and

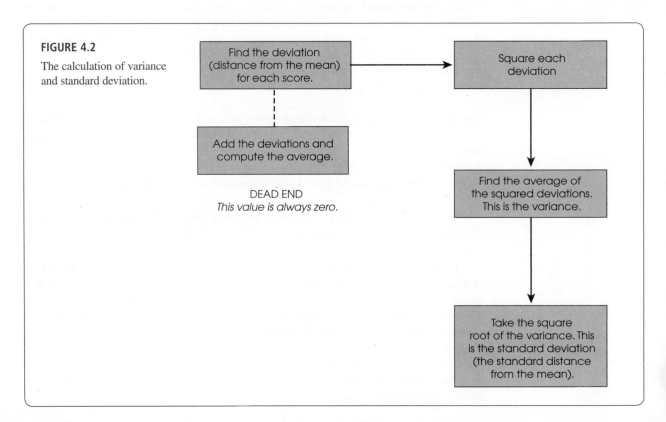

FIGURE 4.2

The calculation of variance and standard deviation.

variance, the same restrictions that apply to the mean also apply to these two measures of variability. Specifically, the mean, the standard deviation, and the variance should be used only with numerical scores from interval or ordinal scales of measurement.

Although we still have not presented any formulas for variance or standard deviation, you should be able to compute these two statistical values from their definitions. The following example demonstrates this process.

EXAMPLE 4.2   We will calculate the variance and standard deviation for the following population of $N = 5$ scores:

$$1 \quad 9 \quad 5 \quad 8 \quad 7$$

Remember that the purpose of standard deviation is to measure the standard distance from the mean, so we begin by computing the population mean. These five scores add up to $\Sigma X = 30$ so the mean is $\mu = \frac{30}{5} = 6$. Next, we find the deviation (distance from the mean) for each score and then square the deviations. Using the population mean $\mu = 6$, these calculations are shown in the following table.

Score X	Deviation $X - \mu$	Squared Deviation $(X - \mu)^2$
1	-5	25
9	3	9
5	-1	1
8	2	4
7	1	1

$40 =$ the sum of the squared deviations

For this set of $N = 5$ scores, the squared deviations add up to 40. The mean of the squared deviations, the variance, is $\frac{40}{5} = 8$, and the standard deviation is $\sqrt{8} = 2.83$.

You should note that a standard deviation of 2.83 is a sensible answer for this distribution. The five scores in the population are shown in a histogram in Figure 4.3 so that you can see the distances more clearly. Note that the scores closest to the mean are only 1 point away. Also, the score farthest from the mean is 5 points away. For this distribution,

FIGURE 4.3

A frequency distribution histogram for a population of $N = 5$ scores. The mean for this population is $\mu = 6$. The smallest distance from the mean is 1 point, and the largest distance is 5 points. The standard distance (or standard deviation) should be between 1 and 5 points.

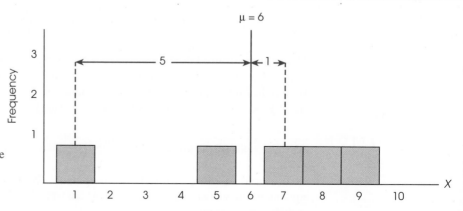

the largest distance from the mean is 5 points and the smallest distance is 1 point. Thus, the standard distance should be somewhere between 1 and 5. By looking at a distribution in this way, you should be able to make a rough estimate of the standard deviation. In this case, the standard deviation should be between 1 and 5, probably around 3 points. The value we calculated for the standard deviation is in excellent agreement with this estimate.

Making a quick estimate of the standard deviation can help you avoid errors in calculation. For example, if you calculated the standard deviation for the scores in Figure 4.3 and obtained a value of 12, you should realize immediately that you have made an error. If the biggest deviation is only 5 points, then it is impossible for the standard deviation to be 12.

LEARNING CHECK	**1.** Briefly explain what is measured by the standard deviation and what is measured by the variance.
	2. The deviation scores are calculated for each individual in a population of $N = 4$. The first three individuals have deviations of $+2$, $+4$, and -1. What is the deviation for the fourth individual?
	3. What is the standard deviation for the following set of $N = 5$ scores: 10, 10, 10, 10, and 10? (*Note:* You should be able to answer this question directly from the definition of standard deviation, without doing any calculations.)
	4. Calculate the variance for the following population of $N = 5$ scores: 4, 0, 7, 1, 3.
ANSWERS	**1.** Standard deviation measures the standard distance from the mean, and variance measures the average squared distance from the mean.
	2. The deviation scores for the entire set must add up to zero. The first three deviations add to $+5$ so the fourth deviation must be -5.
	3. Because there is no variability (the scores are all the same), the standard deviation is zero.
	4. For these scores, the sum of the squared deviations is 30 and the variance is $\frac{30}{5} = 6$.

FORMULAS FOR POPULATION VARIANCE AND STANDARD DEVIATION

The concepts of standard deviation and variance are the same for both samples and populations. However, the details of the calculations differ slightly, depending on whether you have data from a sample or from a complete population. We first consider the formulas for populations and then look at samples in Section 4.4.

Recall that variance is defined as the mean of the squared deviations. This mean is computed in exactly the same way you compute any mean: First find the sum, and then divide by the number of scores.

$$\text{variance} = \text{mean squared deviation} = \frac{\text{sum of squared deviations}}{\text{number of scores}}$$

The sum of squared deviations (*SS*)   The value in the numerator of this equation, the sum of the squared deviations, is a basic component of variability, and we focus on it. To simplify things, it is identified by the notation *SS* (for sum of squared deviations), and it generally is referred to as the *sum of squares*.

DEFINITION

SS, or sum of squares, is the sum of the squared deviation scores.

You need to know two formulas to compute *SS*. These formulas are algebraically equivalent (they always produce the same answer), but they look different and are used in different situations.

The Definitional Formula for SS   The first of these formulas is called the definitional formula because the symbols in the formula literally define the process of adding up the squared deviations:

$$\text{Definitional Formula: } SS = \Sigma(X - \mu)^2 \tag{4.1}$$

To find the sum of the squared deviations, the formula instructs you to perform the following sequence of calculations:

1. Find each deviation score $(X - \mu)$.

2. Square each deviation score $(X - \mu)^2$.

3. Add the squared deviations.

The result is SS, the sum of the squared deviations. Note that this is the process we used (without a formula) to compute the sum of the squared deviations in Example 4.2. The following example demonstrates the formula.

EXAMPLE 4.3   We compute SS for the following set of $N = 4$ scores. These scores have a sum of $\Sigma X = 8$, so the mean is $\mu = \frac{8}{4} = 2$. The following table shows the deviation and the squared deviation for each score. The sum of the squared deviation is $SS = 22$.

Score X	Deviation $X - \mu$	Squared Deviation $(X - \mu)^2$	
1	−1	1	$\Sigma X = 8$
0	−2	4	$\mu = 2$
6	+4	16	$\Sigma(X - \mu)^2 = 22$
1	−1	1	

The Computational Formula for SS   Although the definitional formula is the most direct method for computing SS, it can be awkward to use. In particular, when the mean is not a whole number, the deviations all contain decimals or fractions, and the calculations become difficult. In addition, calculations with decimal values introduce the opportunity for rounding error, which can make the result less accurate. For these reasons, an alternative formula has been developed for computing SS. The alternative, known as the computational formula, performs calculations with the scores (not the deviations) and therefore minimizes the complications of decimals and fractions.

$$\text{Computational formula: } SS = \Sigma X^2 - \frac{(\Sigma X)^2}{N} \tag{4.2}$$

The first part of this formula directs you to square each score and then add the squared values, ΣX^2. In the second part of the formula, you find the sum of the scores, ΣX, then square this total and divide the result by N. Finally, subtract the second part from the first. The use of this formula is shown in Example 4.4 with the same scores that we used to demonstrate the definitional formula.

EXAMPLE 4.4   The computational formula can be used to calculate SS for the same set of $N = 4$ scores we used in Example 4.3. Note that the formula requires the calculation of two sums: first, compute ΣX, and then square each score and compute ΣX^2. These calculations are shown in the following table. The two sums are used in the formula to compute SS.

X	X^2
1	1
0	0
6	36
1	1
$\Sigma X = 8$	$\Sigma X^2 = 38$

$$SS = \Sigma X^2 - \frac{(\Sigma X)^2}{N}$$

$$= 38 - \frac{(8)^2}{4}$$

$$= 38 - \frac{64}{4}$$

$$= 38 - 16$$

$$= 22$$

Note that the two formulas produce exactly the same value for SS. Although the formulas look different, they are in fact equivalent. The definitional formula provides the most direct representation of the concept of SS; however, this formula can be awkward to use, especially if the mean includes a fraction or decimal value. If you have a small group of scores and the mean is a whole number, then the definitional formula is fine; otherwise the computational formula is usually easier to use.

FINAL FORMULAS AND NOTATION   With the definition and calculation of SS behind you, the equations for variance and standard deviation become relatively simple. Remember that variance is defined as the mean squared deviation. The mean is the sum of the squared deviations divided by N, so the equation for the *population variance* is

$$\text{variance} = \frac{SS}{N}$$

In the same way that sum of squares, or SS, is used to refer to the sum of squared deviations, the term *mean square,* or MS, is often used to refer to variance, which is the mean squared deviation.

Standard deviation is the square root of variance, so the equation for the *population standard deviation* is

$$\text{standard deviation} = \sqrt{\frac{SS}{N}}$$

There is one final bit of notation before we work completely through an example computing SS, variance, and standard deviation. Like the mean (μ), variance and standard deviation are parameters of a population and are identified by Greek letters. To identify the standard deviation, we use the Greek letter sigma (the Greek letter *s,* standing for standard deviation). The capital letter sigma (Σ) has been used already, so we now use the lowercase sigma, σ, as the symbol for the population standard deviation. To emphasize the relationship between standard deviation and variance, we use σ^2 as the symbol for population variance (standard deviation is the square root of the variance). Thus,

$$\text{population standard deviation} = \sigma = \sqrt{\sigma^2} = \sqrt{\frac{SS}{N}} \tag{4.3}$$

$$\text{population variance} = \sigma^2 = \frac{SS}{N} \tag{4.4}$$

Earlier, in Examples 4.3 and 4.4, we computed the sum of squared deviations for a population of $N = 4$ scores (1, 0, 6, 1) and obtained $SS = 22$. For this population, the variance is

$$\sigma^2 = \frac{SS}{N} = \frac{22}{4} = 5.50$$

and the standard deviation is $\sigma = \sqrt{5.50} = 2.345$

LEARNING CHECK

1. Find the sum of the squared deviations, SS, for each of the following populations. Note that the definitional formula works well for one population but the computational formula is better for the other.

    Population 1:   3   1   5   1
    Population 2:   6   4   2   0   9   3

2. **a.** Sketch a histogram showing the frequency distribution for the following population of $N = 6$ scores: 12, 0, 1, 7, 4, 6. Locate the mean in your sketch, and estimate the value of the standard deviation.

    b. Calculate SS, variance, and the standard deviation for these scores. How well does your estimate compare with the actual standard deviation?

ANSWERS

1. For population 1, the mean is not a whole number ($M = 2.5$) and the computational formula is better and produces $SS = 11$. The mean is a whole number ($M = 4$) and definitional formula works well for population 2, which has $SS = 50$.

2. **a.** Your sketch should show a mean of $\mu = 5$. The scores closest to the mean are $X = 4$ and $X = 6$, both of which are only 1 point away. The score farthest from the mean is $X = 12$, which is 7 points away. The standard deviation should have a value between 1 and 7, probably around 4 points.

    b. For these scores, $SS = 96$, the variance is $\frac{96}{6} = 16$, and the standard deviation is $\sigma = 4$.

4.4   STANDARD DEVIATION AND VARIANCE FOR A SAMPLE

The goal of inferential statistics is to use the limited information from samples to draw general conclusions about populations. The basic assumption of this process is that samples should be representative of the populations from which they come. This assumption poses a special problem for variability because samples consistently tend to be less variable than their populations. An example of this general tendency is shown in Figure 4.4. Notice that a few extreme scores in the population tend to make the population variability relatively large. However, these extreme values are unlikely to be obtained when you are selecting a sample, which means that the sample variability is relatively small. The fact that a sample tends to be less variable than its population means that sample variability gives a *biased* estimate of population variability. This bias is in the direction of underestimating the population value rather than being right on the mark. (The concept of a biased statistic is discussed in more detail in Section 4.5.)

Fortunately, the bias in sample variability is consistent and predictable, which means it can be corrected. For example, if the speedometer in your car consistently shows speeds that are 5 mph slower than you are actually going, it does not mean that

FIGURE 4.4

The population of adult heights forms a normal distribution. If you select a sample from this population, you are most likely to obtain individuals who are near average in height. As a result, the scores in the sample will be less variable (spread out) than the scores in the population.

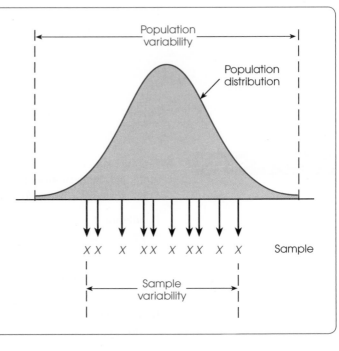

A sample statistic is said to be *biased* if, on average, it consistently overestimates or underestimates the corresponding population parameter.

the speedometer is useless. It simply means that you must make an adjustment to the speedometer reading to get an accurate speed. In the same way, we make an adjustment in the calculation of sample variance. The purpose of the adjustment is to make the resulting value for sample variance an accurate and unbiased representative of the population variance.

The calculations of variance and standard deviation for a sample follow the same steps that were used to find population variance and standard deviation. First, calculate the sum of squared deviations (*SS*). Second, calculate the variance. Third, find the square root of the variance, which is the standard deviation.

The sum of squared deviations for a sample   Except for minor changes in notation, calculating the sum of the squared deviations, *SS*, is the same for a sample as it is for a population. The changes in notation involve using *M* for the sample mean instead of μ, and using *n* (instead of *N*) for the number of scores. For example, the definitional formula for *SS* for a sample is

$$\text{Definitional formula: } SS = \Sigma (X - M)^2 \tag{4.5}$$

Note that the sample formula has exactly the same structure as the population formula (Equation 4.1 on p. 97) and instructs you to find the sum of the squared deviations using the following sequence of three steps:

1. Find the deviation from the mean for each score: deviation = $X - M$

2. Square each deviation: squared deviation = $(X - M)^2$

3. Add the squared deviations: $SS = \Sigma(X - M)^2$

The value of SS also can be obtained using a computational formula. Except for one minor difference in notation (using n in place of N), the computational formula for SS is the same for a sample as it was for a population (see Equation 4.2). Using sample notation, this formula is:

$$\text{Computational formula: } SS = \Sigma X^2 - \frac{(\Sigma X)^2}{n} \tag{4.6}$$

Formulas for sample variance and sample standard deviation   Again, calculating SS for a sample is exactly the same as for a population, except for minor changes in notation. After you compute SS, however, it becomes critical to differentiate between samples and populations. To correct for the bias in sample variability, it is necessary to make an adjustment in the formulas for sample variance and standard deviation. With this in mind, *sample variance* (identified by the symbol s^2) is defined as

$$\text{sample variance} = s^2 = \frac{SS}{n-1} \tag{4.7}$$

Sample standard deviation (identified by the symbol s) is simply the square root of the variance.

$$\text{sample standard deviation} = s = \sqrt{s^2} = \sqrt{\frac{SS}{n-1}} \tag{4.8}$$

Remember, sample variability tends to underestimate population variability unless some correction is made.

Notice that the sample formulas divide by $n - 1$, unlike the population formulas, which divide by N (see Equations 4.3 and 4.4). This is the adjustment that is necessary to correct for the bias in sample variability. The effect of the adjustment is to increase the value that you obtain. Dividing by a smaller number ($n - 1$ instead of n) produces a larger result and makes sample variance an accurate and unbiased estimator of population variance. The following example demonstrates the calculation of variance and standard deviation for a sample.

EXAMPLE 4.5   We have selected a sample of $n = 8$ scores from a population. The scores are 4, 6, 5, 11, 7, 9, 7, 3. The frequency distribution histogram for this sample is shown in Figure 4.5. Before we begin any calculations, you should be able to look at the sample distribution and make a preliminary estimate of the outcome. Remember that standard deviation measures the standard distance from the mean. For this sample the mean is $M = \frac{52}{8} = 6.5$. The scores closest to the mean are $X = 6$ and $X = 7$, both of which are exactly 0.5 points away. The score farthest from the mean is $X = 2$, which is 4.5 points away. With the smallest distance from the mean equal to 0.5 and the largest distance equal to 4.5, we should obtain a standard distance somewhere between 0.5 and 4.5, probably around 2.5.

We begin the calculations by finding the value of SS for this sample. Because the mean is not a whole number ($M = 6.5$), the computational formula is easier to use. The scores, and the squared scores, needed for this formula are shown in the following table.

Scores X	Squared Scores X^2
4	16
6	36
5	25
11	121
7	49
9	81
7	49
3	9
$\Sigma X = 52$	$\Sigma X^2 = 386$

Using the two sums,

$$SS = \Sigma X^2 - \frac{(\Sigma X)^2}{n} = 386 - \frac{(52)^2}{8}$$
$$= 386 - 338$$
$$= 48$$

The sum of squared deviations for this sample is $SS = 48$. Continuing the calculations,

$$\text{sample variance} = s^2 = \frac{SS}{n-1} = \frac{48}{8-1} = 6.86$$

Finally, the standard deviation is

$$s = \sqrt{s^2} = \sqrt{6.86} = 2.62$$

Note that the value we obtained is in excellent agreement with our preliminary prediction (see Figure 4.5).

Remember that the formulas for sample variance and standard deviation were constructed so that the sample variability would provide a good estimate of population variability. For this reason, the sample variance is often called *estimated population*

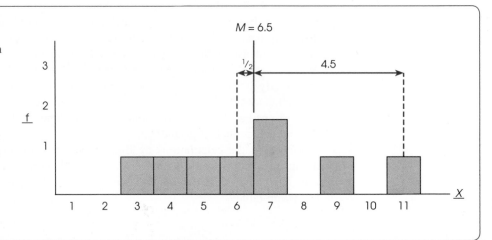

FIGURE 4.5

The frequency distribution histogram for a sample of $n = 8$ scores. The sample mean is $M = 6.5$. The smallest distance from the mean is 0.5 points, and the largest distance from the mean is 4.5 points. The standard distance (standard deviation) should be between 0.5 and 4.5 points, or about 2.5.

variance, and the sample standard deviation is called *estimated population standard deviation.* When you have only a sample to work with, the variance and standard deviation for the sample provide the best possible estimates of the population variability.

SAMPLE VARIABILITY AND DEGREES OF FREEDOM

Although the concept of a deviation score and the calculation of SS are almost exactly the same for samples and populations, the minor differences in notation are really very important. Specifically, with a population, you find the deviation for each score by measuring its distance from the population mean, μ. With a sample, on the other hand, the value of μ is unknown and you must measure distances from the sample mean. Because the value of the sample mean varies from one sample to another, you must first compute the sample mean before you can begin to compute deviations. However, calculating the value of M places a restriction on the variability of the scores in the sample. This restriction is demonstrated in the following example.

EXAMPLE 4.6

Suppose we select a sample of $n = 3$ scores and compute a mean of $M = 5$. The first two scores in the sample have no restrictions; they are independent of each other and they can have any values. For this demonstration, we assume that we obtained $X = 2$ for the first score and $X = 9$ for the second. At this point, however, the third score in the sample is restricted.

X	A sample of $n = 3$ scores with a mean of $M = 5$.
2	
9	
—	← What is the third score?

For this example, the third score must be $X = 4$. The reason that the third score is restricted to $X = 4$ is that the sample has a mean of $M = 5$. For $n = 3$ scores to have a mean of 5, the scores must have a total of $\Sigma X = 15$. Because the first two scores add up to 11 (9 + 2), the third score must be $X = 4$.

In Example 4.6, the first two out of three scores were free to have any values, but the final score was dependent on the values chosen for the first two. In general, with a sample of n scores, the first $n - 1$ scores are free to vary, but the final score is restricted. As a result, the sample is said to have $n - 1$ *degrees of freedom.*

DEFINITION

> For a sample of n scores, the **degrees of freedom,** or *df,* for the sample variance are defined as $df = n - 1$. The degrees of freedom determine the number of scores in the sample that are independent and free to vary.

The $n - 1$ degrees of freedom for a sample is the same $n - 1$ that is used in the formulas for sample variance and standard deviation. Remember that variance is defined as the mean squared deviation. As always, this mean is computed by finding the sum and dividing by the number of scores:

$$\text{mean} = \frac{\text{sum}}{\text{number}}$$

To calculate sample variance (mean squared deviation), we find the sum of the squared deviations (SS) and divide by the number of scores that are free to vary. This number is $n - 1 = df$. Thus, the formula for sample variance is

$$s^2 = \frac{\text{sum of squared deviations}}{\text{number of scores free to vary}} = \frac{SS}{df} = \frac{SS}{n-1}$$

Later in this book, we use the concept of degrees of freedom in other situations. For now, remember that knowing the sample mean places a restriction on sample variability. Only $n - 1$ of the scores are free to vary; $df = n - 1$.

LEARNING CHECK

1. a. Sketch a histogram showing the frequency distribution for the following sample of $n = 5$ scores: 3, 1, 9, 4, 3. Locate the mean in your sketch, and estimate the value of the sample standard deviation.

   b. Calculate *SS*, variance, and standard deviation for this sample. How well does your estimate from part a compare with the real standard deviation?

2. For the following set of scores: 1, 5, 7, 3, 4

   a. Assume that this is a population of $N = 5$ scores and compute *SS* and variance for the population.

   b. Assume that this is a sample of $n = 5$ scores and compute SS and variance for the sample.

3. Explain why the formula for sample variance divides *SS* by $n - 1$ instead of dividing by n.

ANSWERS

1. a. Your graph should show a sample mean of $M = 4$. The score farthest from the mean is $X = 9$ (which is 5 points away), and the closest score is $X = 3$ (which is 1 point away). You should estimate the standard deviation to be between 1 and 5 points, probably around 3 points.

   b. For this sample, $SS = 36$; the sample variance is $\frac{36}{4} = 9$; the sample standard deviation is $\sqrt{9} = 3$.

2. a. $SS = 20$ and the population variance is $\frac{20}{5} = 4$.

   b. $SS = 20$ and the sample variance is $\frac{20}{4} = 5$.

3. Without some correction, sample variability consistently underestimates the population variability. Dividing by a smaller number ($n - 1$ instead of n) increases the value of the sample variance and makes it an unbiased estimate of the population variance.

4.5   MORE ABOUT VARIANCE AND STANDARD DEVIATION

PRESENTING THE MEAN AND STANDARD DEVIATION IN A FREQUENCY DISTRIBUTION GRAPH

In frequency distribution graphs, we identify the position of the mean by drawing a vertical line and labeling it with μ or *M*. Because the standard deviation measures distance from the mean, it is represented by a line or an arrow drawn from the mean outward for a distance equal to the standard deviation and labeled with a σ or an *s*. Figure 4.6(a) shows an example of a population distribution with a mean of μ = 80 and a standard deviation of σ = 8, and Figure 4.6(b) shows the frequency distribution for a sample with a mean of $M = 16$ and a standard deviation of $s = 2$. For rough sketches, you can identify the mean with a vertical line in the middle of the distribution. The standard deviation line should extend approximately halfway from the mean to the most extreme score. [*Note:* In Figure 4.6(a) we show the standard deviation as a line to the right of the

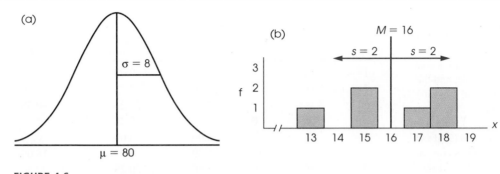

FIGURE 4.6

Showing means and standard deviations in frequency distribution graphs. (a) A population distribution with a mean of $\mu = 80$ and a standard deviation of $\sigma = 8$. (b) A sample with a mean of $M = 16$ and a standard deviation of $s = 2$.

mean. You should realize that we could have drawn the line pointing to the left, or we could have drawn two lines (or arrows), with one pointing to the right and one pointing to the left, as in Figure 4.6(b). In each case, the goal is to show the standard distance from the mean.]

SAMPLE VARIANCE AS AN UNBIASED STATISTIC

Earlier we noted that sample variability tends to underestimate the variability in the corresponding population. To correct for this problem we adjusted the formula for sample variance by dividing by $n - 1$ instead of dividing by n. The result of the adjustment is that sample variance provides a much more accurate representation of the population variance. Specifically, dividing by $n - 1$ produces a sample variance that provides an *unbiased* estimate of the corresponding population variance. This does not mean that each individual sample variance is exactly equal to its population variance. In fact, some sample variances overestimate the population value and some underestimate it. However, the average of all the sample variances produces an accurate estimate of the population variance. This is the idea behind the concept of an unbiased statistic.

D E F I N I T I O N S

A sample statistic is **unbiased** if the average value of the statistic is equal to the population parameter. (The average value of the statistic is obtained from all the possible samples for a specific sample size, n.)

A sample statistic is **biased** if the average value of the statistic either underestimates or overestimates the corresponding population parameter.

The following example demonstrates the concept of biased and unbiased statistics.

E X A M P L E   4 . 7

We have structured this example to mimic "sampling with replacement," which is covered in Chapter 6.

We begin with a population that consists of exactly $N = 6$ scores: 0, 0, 3, 3, 9, 9. With a few calculations you should be able to verify that this population has a mean of $\mu = 4$ and a variance of $\sigma^2 = 14$.

Next, we select samples of $n = 2$ scores from this population. In fact, we obtain every single possible sample with $n = 2$. The complete set of samples is listed in Table 4.1. Notice that the samples are listed systematically to ensure that every possible sample is included. We begin by listing all the samples that have $X = 0$ as the first score, then all

TABLE 4.1

The set of all the possible samples for $n = 2$ selected from the population described in Example 4.7. The mean is computed for each sample, and the variance is computed two different ways: (1) dividing by n, which is incorrect and produces a biased statistic; and (2) dividing by $n - 1$, which is correct and produces an unbiased statistic.

				Sample Statistics	
Sample	First Score	Second Score	Mean M	Biased Variance (Using n)	Unbiased Variance (Using n − 1)
1	0	0	0.00	0.00	0.00
2	0	3	1.50	2.25	4.50
3	0	9	4.50	20.25	40.50
4	3	0	1.50	2.25	4.50
5	3	3	3.00	0.00	0.00
6	3	9	6.00	9.00	18.00
7	9	0	4.50	20.25	40.50
8	9	3	6.00	9.00	18.00
9	9	9	9.00	0.00	0.00
		Totals	36.00	63.00	126.00

the samples with $X = 3$ as the first score, and so on. Notice that the table shows a total of 9 samples.

Finally, we have computed the mean and the variance for each sample. Note that the sample variance has been computed two different ways. First, we examine what happens if the sample variance is computed as the mean squared deviation (SS divided by n) without any correction for bias. Second, we examine the correct sample variance for which SS is divided by $n - 1$ to produce an unbiased measure of variance. You should verify our calculations by computing one or two of the values for yourself. The complete set of sample means and sample variances is presented in Table 4.1.

First, consider the column of biased sample variances, which were calculated by dividing by n. These 9 sample variances add up to a total of 63, which produces an average value of $\frac{63}{9} = 7$. The original population variance, however, is $\sigma^2 = 14$. Note that the average of the sample variances is *not* equal to the population variance. If the sample variance is computed by dividing by n, the resulting values do not produce an accurate estimate of the population variance. On average, these sample variances underestimate the population variance and, therefore, are biased statistics.

Next, consider the column of sample variances that are computed using $n - 1$. Although the population has a variance of $\sigma^2 = 14$, you should notice that none of the samples has a variance exactly equal to 14. However, if you consider the complete set of sample variances, you will find that the 9 values add up to a total of 126, which produces an average value of $\frac{126}{9} = 14$. Thus, the average of the sample variances is exactly equal to the original population variance. On average, the sample variance (computed using $n - 1$) produces an accurate, unbiased estimate of the population variance.

Finally, direct your attention to the column of sample means. For this example, the original population has a mean of $\mu = 4$. Although none of the samples has a mean exactly equal to 4, if you consider the complete set of sample means, you will find that the 9 sample means add up to a total of 36, so the average of the sample means is $\frac{36}{9} = 4$. Note that the average of the sample means is exactly equal to the population mean. Again, this is what is meant by the concept of an unbiased statistic. On average, the sample values provide an accurate representation of the population. In this example, the average of the 9 sample means is exactly equal to the population mean.

In summary, both the sample mean and the sample variance (using $n - 1$) are examples of unbiased statistics. This fact makes the sample mean and sample variance extremely valuable for use as inferential statistics. Although no individual sample is likely to have a mean and variance exactly equal to the population values, both the sample mean and the sample variance, on average, do provide accurate estimates of the corresponding population values.

STANDARD DEVIATION AND DESCRIPTIVE STATISTICS

Because standard deviation requires extensive calculations, there is a tendency to get lost in the arithmetic and forget what standard deviation is and why it is important. Standard deviation is primarily a descriptive measure; it describes how variable, or how spread out, the scores are in a distribution. Behavioral scientists must deal with the variability that comes from studying people and animals. People are not all the same; they have different attitudes, opinions, talents, IQs, and personalities. Although we can calculate the average value for any of these variables, it is equally important to describe the variability. Standard deviation describes variability by measuring *distance from the mean*. In any distribution, some individuals are close to the mean, and others are relatively far from the mean. Standard deviation provides a measure of the typical, or standard, distance from the mean.

Describing an entire distribution   Rather than listing all of the individual scores in a distribution, research reports typically summarize the data by reporting only the mean and the standard deviation. When you are given these two descriptive statistics, however, you should be able to visualize the entire set of data. For example, consider a sample with a mean of $M = 36$ and a standard deviation of $s = 4$. Although there are several different ways to picture the data, one simple technique is to imagine (or sketch) a histogram in which each score is represented by a box in the graph. For this sample, the data can be pictured as a pile of boxes (scores) with the center of the pile located at a value of $M = 36$. The individual scores, or boxes, are scattered on both sides of the mean with some of the boxes relatively close to the mean and some farther away. As a rule of thumb, roughly 70% of the scores in a distribution are located within a distance of one standard deviation from the mean, and almost all of the scores (roughly 95%) are within two standard deviations of the mean. In this example, the standard distance from the mean is $s = 4$ points, so your image should have most of the boxes within 4 points of the mean, and nearly all of the boxes within 8 points. One possibility for the resulting image is shown in Figure 4.7.

Describing the location of individual scores   Notice that Figure 4.7 not only shows the mean and the standard deviation, but also uses these two values to reconstruct the underlying scale of measurement (the X values along the horizontal line). The scale of

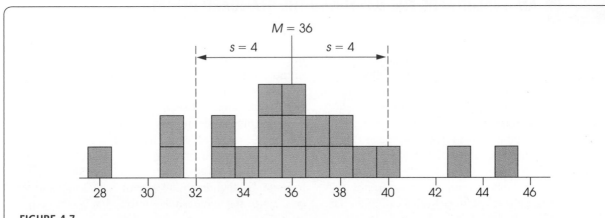

FIGURE 4.7

A sample of $n = 20$ scores with a mean of $M = 36$ and a standard deviation of $s = 4$.

measurement helps to complete the picture of the entire distribution and relate each individual score to the rest of the group. In this example, you should realize that a score of $X = 34$ is located near the center of the distribution, only slightly below the mean. On the other hand, a score of $X = 45$ is an extremely high score, located far out in the right-hand tail of the distribution.

Notice that the relative position of a score depends in part on the size of the standard deviation. In Figure 4.6 (p. 105), for example, we show a population distribution with a mean of $\mu = 80$ and a standard deviation of $\sigma = 8$, and a sample distribution with a mean of $M = 16$ and a standard deviation of $s = 2$. In the population distribution, a score that is 4 points above the mean is slightly above average but is certainly not an extreme value. In the sample distribution, however, a score that is 4 points above the mean is an extremely high score. In each case, the relative position of the score depends on the size of the standard deviation. For the population, a deviation of 4 points from the mean is relatively small, corresponding to only half of the standard deviation. For the sample, on the other hand, a 4-point deviation is very large, twice the size of the standard deviation.

The general point of this discussion is that the mean and standard deviation are not simply abstract concepts or mathematical equations. Instead, these two values should be concrete and meaningful, especially in the context of a set of scores. The mean and standard deviation are central concepts for most of the statistics that are presented in the following chapters. A good understanding of these two statistics will help you with the more complex procedures that follow (see Box 4.1).

TRANSFORMATIONS OF SCALE

Occasionally a set of scores is transformed by adding a constant to each score or by multiplying each score by a constant value. This happens, for example, when exposure to a treatment adds a fixed amount to each participant's score or when you want to change the unit of measurement (to convert from minutes to seconds, multiply each score by 60). What happens to the standard deviation when the scores are transformed in this manner?

The easiest way to determine the effect of a transformation is to remember that the standard deviation is a measure of distance. If you select any two scores and see what happens to the distance between them, you also find out what happens to the standard deviation.

1. Adding a constant to each score does not change the standard deviation If you begin with a distribution that has a mean of $\mu = 40$ and a standard deviation of $\sigma = 10$, what

---

| **BOX 4.1** | **AN ANALOGY FOR THE MEAN AND THE STANDARD DEVIATION** |

Although the basic concepts of the mean and the standard deviation are not overly complex, the following analogy often helps students gain a more complete understanding of these two statistical measures.

In our local community, the site for a new high school was selected because it provides a central location. An alternative site on the western edge of the community was considered, but this site was rejected because it would require extensive busing for students living on the east side. In this example, the location of the high school is analogous to the concept of the mean; just as the high school is located in the center of the community, the mean is located in the center of the distribution of scores. For each student in the community, it is possible to measure the distance between home and the new high school. Some students live only a few blocks from the new school and others live as much as 3 miles away. The average distance that a student must travel to school was calculated to be 0.80 miles. The average distance from the school is analogous to the concept of the standard deviation; that is, the standard deviation measures the standard distance from an individual score to the mean.

happens to σ if you add 5 points to every score? Consider any two scores in this distribution: Suppose, for example, that these are exam scores and that you had a score of $X = 41$ and your friend had $X = 43$. The distance between these two scores is $43 - 41 = 2$ points. After adding the constant, 5 points, to each score, your score would be $X = 46$, and your friend would have $X = 48$. The distance between scores is still 2 points. Adding a constant to every score does not affect any of the distances and, therefore, does not change the standard deviation. This fact can be seen clearly if you imagine a frequency distribution graph. If, for example, you add 5 points to each score, then every score in the graph is moved 5 points to the right. The result is that the entire distribution is shifted to a new position 5 points up the scale. Note that the mean moves along with the scores and is increased by 5 points. However, the variability does not change because each of the deviation scores $(X - \mu)$ does not change.

2. Multiplying each score by a constant causes the standard deviation to be multiplied by the same constant Consider the same distribution of exam scores we looked at earlier. If $\mu = 40$ and $\sigma = 10$, what would happen to σ if each score were multiplied by 2? Again, we look at two scores, $X = 41$ and $X = 43$, with a distance between them equal to 2 points. After the scores have been multiplied by 2, these two scores become $X = 82$ and $X = 86$. Now the distance between scores is 4 points, twice the original distance. Multiplying each score causes each distance to be multiplied, so the standard deviation also is multiplied by the same amount.

IN THE LITERATURE

REPORTING THE STANDARD DEVIATION

In reporting the results of a study, the researcher often provides descriptive information for both central tendency and variability. The dependent variables in psychology research are often numerical values obtained from measurements on interval or ratio scales. With numerical scores, the most common descriptive statistics are the mean (central tendency) and the standard deviation (variability), which are usually reported together. In many journals, especially those following APA style, the symbol *SD* is used for the sample standard deviation. For example, the results might state:

Children who viewed the violent cartoon displayed more aggressive responses $(M = 12.45, SD = 3.7)$ than those who viewed the control cartoon $(M = 4.22, SD = 1.04)$.

When reporting the descriptive measures for several groups, the findings may be summarized in a table. Table 4.2 illustrates the results of hypothetical data.

Sometimes the table also indicates the sample size, *n*, for each group. You should remember that the purpose of the table is to present the data in an organized, concise, and accurate manner.

TABLE 4.2

The number of aggressive responses in male and female children after viewing cartoons.

		Type of Cartoon	
		Violent	Control
Males		$M = 15.72$	$M = 6.94$
		$SD = 4.43$	$SD = 2.26$
Females		$M = 3.47$	$M = 2.61$
		$SD = 1.12$	$SD = 0.98$

VARIANCE AND INFERENTIAL STATISTICS

In very general terms, the goal of inferential statistics is to detect meaningful and significant patterns in research results. The basic question is whether the patterns observed in the sample data reflect corresponding patterns that exist in the population, or are simply random fluctuations that occur by chance. Variability plays an important role in the inferential process because the variability in the data influences how easy it is to see patterns. In general, low variability means that existing patterns can be seen clearly, whereas high variability tends to obscure any patterns that might exist. The following example provides a simple demonstration of how variance can influence the perception of patterns.

EXAMPLE 4.8

In most research studies the goal is to compare means for two (or more) sets of data. For example:

Is the mean level of depression lower after therapy than it was before therapy?

Is the mean attitude score for men different from the mean score for women?

Is the mean reading achievement score higher for students in a special program than for students in regular classrooms?

In each of these situations, the goal is to find a clear difference between two means that would demonstrate a significant, meaningful pattern in the results. Variability plays an important role in determining whether a clear pattern exists. Consider the following data representing hypothetical results from two experiments, each comparing two treatment conditions. For both experiments, your task is to determine whether there appears to be any consistent difference between the scores in treatment 1 and the scores in treatment 2.

Experiment A		Experiment B	
Treatment 1	*Treatment 2*	*Treatment 1*	*Treatment 2*
35	39	31	46
34	40	15	21
36	41	57	61
35	40	37	32

For each experiment, the data have been constructed so that there is a 5-point mean difference between the two treatments: On average, the scores in treatment 2 are 5 points higher than the scores in treatment 1. The 5-point difference is relatively easy to see in experiment A, where the variability is low, but the same 5-point difference is difficult to see in experiment B, where the variability is large. Again, high variability tends to obscure any patterns in the data. This general fact is perhaps even more convincing when the data are presented in a graph. Figure 4.8 shows the two sets of data from experiments A and B. Notice that the results from experiment A clearly show the 5-point difference between treatments. One group of scores piles up around 35 and the second group piles up around 40. On the other hand, the scores from experiment B [Figure 4.8(b)] seem to be mixed together randomly with no clear difference between the two treatments.

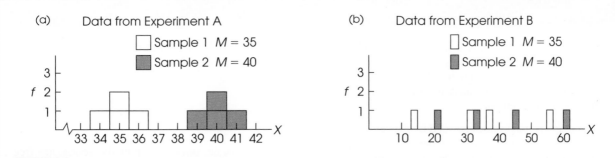

FIGURE 4.8

Graphs showing the results from two experiments. In experiment A, the variability is small and it is easy to see the 5-point mean difference between the two treatments. In experiment B, however, the 5-point mean difference between treatments is obscured by the large variability.

In the context of inferential statistics, the variance that exists in a set of sample data is often classified as *error variance*. This term is used to indicate that the sample variance represents unexplained and uncontrolled differences between scores. As the error variance increases, it becomes more difficult to see any systematic differences or patterns that might exist in the data. An analogy is to think of variance as the static that appears on a radio station or a cell phone when you enter an area of poor reception. In general, variance makes it difficult to get a clear signal from the data. High variance can make it difficult or impossible to see a mean difference between two sets of scores, or to see any other meaningful patterns in the results from a research study.

LEARNING CHECK

1. Explain the difference between a biased and an unbiased statistic.

2. In a population with a mean of $\mu = 50$ and a standard deviation of $\sigma = 10$, would a score of $X = 58$ be considered an extreme value (far out in the tail of the distribution)? What if the standard deviation were $\sigma = 3$?

3. A population has a mean of $\mu = 70$ and a standard deviation of $\sigma = 5$.

   a. If 10 points were added to every score in the population, what would be the new values for the population mean and standard deviation?

   b. If every score in the population were multiplied by 2, what would be the new values for the population mean and standard deviation?

ANSWERS

1. If a statistic is biased, it means that the average value of the statistic does not accurately represent the corresponding population parameter. Instead, the average value of the statistic either overestimates or underestimates the parameter. If a statistic is unbiased, it means that the average value of the statistic is an accurate representation of the corresponding population parameter.

2. With $\sigma = 10$, a score of $X = 58$ would be located in the central section of the distribution (within one standard deviation). With $\sigma = 3$, a score of $X = 58$ would be an extreme value, located more than two standard deviations above the mean.

3. **a.** The new mean would be $\mu = 80$ but the standard deviation would still be $\sigma = 5$.

   b. The new mean would be $\mu = 140$ and the new standard deviation would be $\sigma = 10$.

SUMMARY

1. The purpose of variability is to measure and describe the degree to which the scores in a distribution are spread out or clustered together. There are three basic measures of variability: the range, the variance, and the standard deviation.

   The range is the distance covered by the set of scores, from the smallest score to the largest score. The range is completely determined by the two extreme scores and is considered to be a relatively crude measure of variability.

   Standard deviation and variance are the most commonly used measures of variability. Both of these measures are based on the idea that each score can be described in terms of its deviation, or distance, from the mean. The variance is the mean of the squared deviations. The standard deviation is the square root of the variance and provides a measure of the standard distance from the mean.

2. To calculate variance or standard deviation, you first need to find the sum of the squared deviations, SS. Except for minor changes in notation, the calculation of SS is identical for samples and populations. There are two methods for calculating SS:

   I. By definition, you can find SS using the following steps:
   a. Find the deviation $(X - \mu)$ for each score.
   b. Square each deviation.
   c. Add the squared deviations.
   This process can be summarized in a formula as follows:

   Definitional Formula: $SS = \Sigma(X - \mu)^2$

   II. The sum of the squared deviations can also be found using a computational formula, which is especially useful when the mean is not a whole number:

   Computational formula: $SS = \Sigma X^2 - \dfrac{(\Sigma X)^2}{N}$

3. Variance is the mean squared deviation and is obtained by finding the sum of the squared deviations and then dividing by the number of scores. For a population, variance is

$$\sigma^2 = \frac{SS}{N}$$

For a sample, only $n - 1$ of the scores are free to vary (degrees of freedom or $df = n - 1$), so sample variance is

$$s^2 = \frac{SS}{n-1} = \frac{SS}{df}$$

Using $n - 1$ in the sample formula makes the sample variance an accurate and unbiased estimate of the population variance.

4. Standard deviation is the square root of the variance. For a population, this is

$$\sigma = \sqrt{\frac{SS}{N}}$$

Sample standard deviation is

$$s = \sqrt{\frac{SS}{n-1}} = \sqrt{\frac{SS}{df}}$$

5. Adding a constant value to every score in a distribution does not change the standard deviation. Multiplying every score by a constant, however, causes the standard deviation to be multiplied by the same constant.

KEY TERMS

variability (90)

range (91)

deviation (92)

deviation score (92)

sum of squares (*SS*) (96)

mean squared deviation (93)

population variance (σ^2) (93)

population standard deviation (σ) (94)

sample variance (s^2) (101)

sample standard deviation (s) (101)

degrees of freedom (*df*) (103)

unbiased statistic (105)

biased statistic (105)

error variance (111)

RESOURCES

 Go to CengageBrain.com to access Psychology CourseMate, where you will find an interactive eBook, glossaries, flashcards, quizzes, statistics workshops, and more.

If your professor has assigned Aplia:

1. Sign in to your account.
2. Complete the corresponding exercises as required by your professor.
3. When finished, click "Grade It Now" to see which areas you have mastered, which areas need more work, and detailed explanations of every answer.

General instructions for using SPSS are presented in Appendix D. Following are detailed instructions for using SPSS to compute the **Range, Standard Deviation,** and **Variance** for a sample of scores.

Data Entry

Enter all of the scores in one column of the data editor, probably VAR00001.

Data Analysis

1. Click **Analyze** on the tool bar, select **Descriptive Statistics,** and click on **Descriptives.**

2. Highlight the column label for the set of scores (VAR00001) in the left box and click the arrow to move it into the **Variable** box.

3. If you want the variance and/or the range reported along with the standard deviation, click on the **Options** box, select **Variance** and/or **Range,** then click **Continue.**

4. Click **OK.**

SPSS Output

We used SPSS to find the variance and standard deviation for the sample of $n = 8$ scores from Example 4.5 (p. 101), and the SPSS output is shown in Figure 4.9. The summary table lists the number of scores, the maximum and minimum scores, the mean, the range, the standard deviation, and the variance. Note that the range and variance are included because these values were selected using the Options box during data analysis. Caution: SPSS computes the *sample* standard deviation and *sample* variance using $n - 1$. If your scores are intended to be a population, you can multiply the sample standard deviation by the square root of $(n - 1)/n$ to obtain the population standard deviation.

Note: You can also obtain the mean and standard deviation for a sample if you use SPSS to display the scores in a frequency distribution histogram (see the SPSS section at the end of Chapter 2). The mean and standard deviation are displayed beside the graph.

FOCUS ON PROBLEM SOLVING

1. The purpose of variability is to provide a measure of how spread out the scores in a distribution are. Usually this is described by the standard deviation. Because the calculations are relatively complicated, it is wise to make a preliminary estimate of the standard deviation before you begin. Remember that standard deviation provides a measure of the typical, or standard, distance from the mean. Therefore, the standard deviation must have a value somewhere between the largest and the smallest deviation scores. As a rule of thumb, the standard deviation should be about one-fourth of the range.

2. Rather than trying to memorize all of the formulas for *SS*, variance, and standard deviation, you should focus on the definitions of these values and the logic that relates them to each other:

   SS is the sum of squared deviations.

   Variance is the mean squared deviation.

   Standard deviation is the square root of variance.

   The only formula you should need to memorize is the computational formula for *SS*.

3. A common error is to use $n - 1$ in the computational formula for *SS* when you have scores from a sample. Remember that the *SS* formula always uses n (or N). After you compute *SS* for a sample, you must correct for the sample bias by using $n - 1$ in the formulas for variance and standard deviation.

	N	Range	Minimum	Maximum	Mean	Std. Deviation	Variance
VAR00001	8	8.00	3.00	11.00	6.5000	2.61861	6.85714
Valid N (listwise)	8						

FIGURE 4.9

The SPSS summary table showing descriptive statistics for the sample of $n = 8$ scores from Example 4.5.

DEMONSTRATION 4.1

COMPUTING MEASURES OF VARIABILITY

For the following sample data, compute the variance and standard deviation. The scores are:

10   7   6   10   6   15

STEP 1   Compute SS, the sum of squared deviations

We use the computational formula. For this sample, $n = 6$ and

$$\Sigma X = 10 + 7 + 6 + 10 + 6 + 15 = 54$$

$$\Sigma X^2 = 10^2 + 7^2 + 6^2 + 10^2 + 6^2 + 15^2 = 546$$

$$SS = \Sigma X^2 - \frac{(\Sigma X)^2}{N} = 546 - \frac{(54)^2}{6}$$

$$= 546 - 486$$

$$= 60$$

STEP 2   Compute the sample variance

For sample variance, SS is divided by the degrees of freedom, $df = n - 1$.

$$s^2 = \frac{SS}{n-1} = \frac{60}{5} = 12$$

STEP 3   Compute the sample standard deviation

Standard deviation is simply the square root of the variance.

$$s = \sqrt{12} = 3.46$$

PROBLEMS

1. In words, explain what is measured by each of the following:
   a. SS
   b. Variance
   c. Standard deviation

2. Can SS ever have a value less than zero? Explain your answer.

3. Is it possible to obtain a negative value for the variance or the standard deviation?

4. What does it mean for a sample to have a standard deviation of zero? Describe the scores in such a sample.

5. Explain why the formulas for sample variance and population variance are different.

6. A population has a mean of $\mu = 80$ and a standard deviation of $\sigma = 20$.
   a. Would a score of $X = 70$ be considered an extreme value (out in the tail) in this sample?
   b. If the standard deviation were $\sigma = 5$, would a score of $X = 70$ be considered an extreme value?

7. On an exam with a mean of $M = 78$, you obtain a score of $X = 84$.
   a. Would you prefer a standard deviation of $s = 2$ or $s = 10$? (*Hint:* Sketch each distribution and find the location of your score.)
   b. If your score were $X = 72$, would you prefer $s = 2$ or $s = 10$? Explain your answer.

8. Calculate the mean and SS (sum of squared deviations) for each of the following samples. Based on the value for the mean, you should be able to decide which SS formula is better to use.

   Sample A: 1   4   8   5

   Sample B: 3   0   9   4

9. For the following population of $N = 6$ scores:

   3   1   4   3   3   4

   a. Sketch a histogram showing the population distribution.
   b. Locate the value of the population mean in your sketch, and make an estimate of the standard deviation (as done in Example 4.2).
   c. Compute SS, variance, and standard deviation for the population. (How well does your estimate compare with the actual value of σ?)

10. For the following sample of $n = 7$ scores:

   8   6   5   2   6   3   5

   a. Sketch a histogram showing the sample distribution.
   b. Locate the value of the sample mean in your sketch, and make an estimate of the standard deviation (as done in Example 4.5).
   c. Compute SS, variance, and standard deviation for the sample. (How well does your estimate compare with the actual value of s?)

11. For the following population of $N = 6$ scores:

   11   0   2   9   9   5

   a. Calculate the range and the standard deviation. (Use either definition for the range.)
   b. Add 2 points to each score and compute the range and standard deviation again. Describe how adding a constant to each score influences measures of variability.

12. The range is completely determined by the two extreme scores in a distribution. The standard deviation, on the other hand, uses every score.
   a. Compute the range (choose either definition) and the standard deviation for the following sample of $n = 5$ scores. Note that there are three scores clustered around the mean in the center of the distribution, and two extreme values.

   Scores: 0   6   7   8   14

   b. Now we break up the cluster in the center of the distribution by moving two of the central scores out to the extremes. Once again compute the range and the standard deviation.

   New scores: 0   0   7   14   14

   c. According to the range, how do the two distributions compare in variability? How do they compare according to the standard deviation?

13. A population has a mean of $\mu = 30$ and a standard deviation of $\sigma = 5$.
   a. If 5 points were added to every score in the population, what would be the new values for the mean and standard deviation?
   b. If every score in the population were multiplied by 3, what would be the new values for the mean and standard deviation?

14. a. After 3 points have been added to every score in a sample, the mean is found to be $M = 83$ and the standard deviation is $s = 8$. What were the values for the mean and standard deviation for the original sample?
   b. After every score in a sample has been multiplied by 4, the mean is found to be $M = 48$ and the standard deviation is $s = 12$. What were the values for the mean and standard deviation for the original sample?

15. For the following sample of $n = 4$ scores: 82, 88, 82, and 86:
   a. Simplify the arithmetic by first subtracting 80 points from each score to obtain a new sample of 2, 8, 2, and 6. Then, compute the mean and standard deviation for the new sample.
   b. Using the values you obtained in part a, what are the values for the mean and standard deviation for the original sample?

16. For the following sample of $n = 8$ scores: 0, 1, $\frac{1}{2}$, 0, 3, $\frac{1}{2}$, 0, and 1:
   a. Simplify the arithmetic by first multiplying each score by 2 to obtain a new sample of 0, 2, 1, 0, 6, 1, 0, and 2. Then, compute the mean and standard deviation for the new sample.
   b. Using the values you obtained in part a, what are the values for the mean and standard deviation for the original sample?

17. For the data in the following sample:

   8   1   5   1   5

   a. Find the mean and the standard deviation.
   b. Now change the score of $X = 8$ to $X = 18$, and find the new mean and standard deviation.
   c. Describe how one extreme score influences the mean and standard deviation.

18. Calculate SS, variance, and standard deviation for the following sample of $n = 4$ scores: 7, 4, 2, 1. (*Note:* The computational formula for SS works well with these scores.)

19. Calculate SS, variance, and standard deviation for the following population of $N = 8$ scores: 0, 0, 5, 0, 3, 0, 0, 4. (*Note:* The computational formula for SS works well with these scores.)

20. Calculate SS, variance, and standard deviation for the following population of $N = 6$ scores: 1, 6, 10, 9, 4, 6. (*Note:* The definitional formula for SS works well with these scores.)

21. Calculate SS, variance, and standard deviation for the following sample of $n = 5$ scores: 10, 4, 8, 5, 8. (Note: The definitional formula for SS works well with these scores.)

22. In an extensive study involving thousands of British children, Arden and Plomin (2006) found significantly higher variance in the intelligence scores for males than for females. Following are hypothetical data, similar to the results obtained in the study. Note that the scores are not regular IQ scores but have been standardized so that the entire sample has a mean of $M = 10$ and a standard deviation of $s = 2$.
   a. Calculate the mean and the standard deviation for the sample of $n = 8$ females and for the sample of $n = 8$ males.
   b. Based on the means and the standard deviations, describe the differences in intelligence scores for males and females.

Female	Male
9	8
11	10
10	11
13	12
8	6
9	10
11	14
9	9

23. Within a population, the differences that exist from one person to another are often called diversity. Researchers comparing cognitive skills for younger adults and older adults, typically find greater differences (greater diversity) in the older population (Morse, 1993). Following are typical data showing problem-solving scores for two groups of participants.

Older Adults (average age 72)	Younger Adults (average age 31)
9 4 7 3 8	7 9 6 7 8
6 2 8 4 5	6 7 6 6 8
7 5 2 6 6	9 7 8 6 9

   a. Compute the mean, the variance, and the standard deviation for each group.
   b. Is one group of scores noticeably more variable (more diverse) than the other?

24. In the previous problem we noted that the differences in cognitive skills tend to be bigger among older people than among younger people. These differences are often called diversity. Similarly, the differences in performance from trial to trial for the same person are often called consistency. Research in this area suggests that consistency of performance seems to decline as people age. A study by Wegesin and Stern (2004) found lower consistency (more variability) in the memory performance scores for older women than for younger women. The following data represent memory scores obtained for two women, one older and one younger, over a series of memory trials.
   a. Calculate the variance of the scores for each woman.
   b. Are the scores for the younger woman more consistent (less variable)?

Younger	Older
8	7
6	5
6	8
7	5
8	7
7	6
8	8
8	5

By completing this part, you should understand and be able to perform basic descriptive statistical procedures. These include:

1. Familiarity with statistical terminology and notation (Chapter 1).
2. The ability to organize a set of scores in a frequency distribution table or a frequency distribution graph (Chapter 2).
3. The ability to summarize and describe a distribution of scores by computing a measure of central tendency (Chapter 3).
4. The ability to summarize and describe a distribution of scores by computing a measure of variability (Chapter 4).

The general goal of descriptive statistics is to simplify a set of data by organizing or summarizing a large set of scores. A frequency distribution table or graph organizes the entire set of scores so that it is possible to see the complete distribution all at once. Measures of central tendency describe the distribution by identifying its center. They also summarize the distribution by condensing all of the individual scores into one value that represents the entire group. Measures of variability describe whether the scores in a distribution are widely scattered or closely clustered. Variability also provides an indication of how accurately a measure of central tendency represents the entire group.

Of the basic skills presented in this part, the most commonly used are calculating the mean and standard deviation for a sample of numerical scores. The following exercises should provide an opportunity to use and reinforce these statistical skills.

REVIEW EXERCISES

1. **a.** What is the general goal for descriptive statistics?
   b. How is the goal served by putting scores in a frequency distribution?
   c. How is the goal served by computing a measure of central tendency?
   d. How is the goal served by computing a measure of variability?

2. In Example 1.1, we proposed an experiment in which one group of students prepared for an exam by studying text on printed pages and a second group studied the same text on a computer screen. The goal is to determine whether one study technique leads to better exam scores than the other. This same experiment was actually conducted by Ackerman and Goldsmith (2011). In one part of the experiment, the students were allowed to control the amount of time that they spent studying. Data similar to the results obtained from this condition are presented in the following table. The data are the test scores obtained from the students in the two conditions.

Number Correct on a 20-Question Multiple-Choice Exam					
Text Studied on Printed Pages			Text Studied on a Computer Screen		
16	17	18	16	14	17
18	19	15	13	18	17
19	14	18	10	17	12
18	18	19	16	15	18
14	17	17	15	19	16
20	15	19	14	12	15
16	17	13	11	13	17

   a. Sketch a polygon showing the distribution of test scores for the students who read printed pages. On the same graph, sketch a polygon for the students who read the computer screen. (Use two different colors or use a dashed line for one group and a solid line for the other.) Based on the appearance of your graph, describe the differences between the two groups.
   b. Calculate the mean test score for each sample. Does the mean difference support your description from part a?
   c. Calculate the variance and standard deviation for each sample. Based on the measures of variability, is one group of scores more widely scattered than the other?

P A R T

Foundations of Inferential Statistics

You should recall from Chapter 1 that statistical methods are classified into two general categories: descriptive statistics, which attempt to organize and summarize data, and inferential statistics, which use the limited information from samples to answer general questions about populations. In most research situations, both kinds of statistics are used to gain a complete understanding of the research results. In Part I of this book we introduced the techniques of descriptive statistics. We now are ready to turn our attention to inferential statistics.

Before we proceed with inferential statistics, however, it is necessary to present some additional information about samples. We know that it is possible to obtain hundreds or even thousands of different samples from the same population. We need to determine how all the different samples are related to each other and how individual samples are related to the population from which they were obtained. Finally, we need a system for designating which samples are representative of their populations and which are not.

In the next four chapters we develop the concepts and skills that form the foundation for inferential statistics. In general, these chapters establish formal, quantitative relationships between samples and populations and introduce a standardized procedure for determining whether the data from a sample justify a conclusion about the population. After we have developed this foundation, we can begin inferential statistics. That is, we can begin to look at statistical techniques that use the sample data obtained in research studies as the basis for answering questions about populations.

CHAPTER

5

z-Scores: Location of Scores and Standardized Distributions

Tools You Will Need
The following items are considered essential background material for this chapter. If you doubt your knowledge of any of these items, you should review the appropriate chapter or section before proceeding.

- The mean (Chapter 3)
- The standard deviation (Chapter 4)
- Basic algebra (math review, Appendix A)

aplia

Aplia for *Essentials of Statistics for the Behavioral Sciences*
After reading, go to "Resources" at the end of this chapter for an introduction on how to use Aplia's homework and learning resources.

5.1   INTRODUCTION TO z-SCORES

In the previous two chapters, we introduced the concepts of the mean and the standard deviation as methods for describing an entire distribution of scores. Now we shift attention to the individual scores within a distribution. In this chapter, we introduce a statistical technique that uses the mean and the standard deviation to transform each score (*X* value) into a *z-score,* or a *standard score.* The purpose of *z*-scores, or standard scores, is to identify and describe the exact location of each score in a distribution.

The following example demonstrates why *z*-scores are useful and introduces the general concept of transforming *X* values into *z*-scores.

EXAMPLE 5.1   Suppose you received a score of $X = 76$ on a statistics exam. How did you do? It should be clear that you need more information to predict your grade. Your score of $X = 76$ could be one of the best scores in the class, or it might be the lowest score in the distribution. To find the location of your score, you must have information about the other scores in the distribution. It would be useful, for example, to know the mean for the class. If the mean were $\mu = 70$, you would be in a much better position than if the mean were $\mu = 85$. Obviously, your position relative to the rest of the class depends on the mean. However, the mean by itself is not sufficient to tell you the exact location of your score. Suppose you know that the mean for the statistics exam is $\mu = 70$ and your score is $X = 76$. At this point, you know that your score is 6 points above the mean, but you still do not know exactly where it is located. Six points may be a relatively big distance and you may have one of the highest scores in the class, or 6 points may be a relatively small distance and you may be only slightly above the average. Figure 5.1 shows two possible distributions of exam scores. Both distributions have a mean of $\mu = 70$, but for one distribution, the standard deviation is $\sigma = 3$, and for the other, $\sigma = 12$. The location of $X = 76$ is highlighted in each of the two distributions. When the standard deviation is $\sigma = 3$, your score of $X = 76$ is in the extreme right-hand tail, the highest score in the distribution. However, in the other distribution, where $\sigma = 12$, your score is only slightly above average. Thus, the relative location of your score within the distribution depends on the standard deviation as well as the mean.

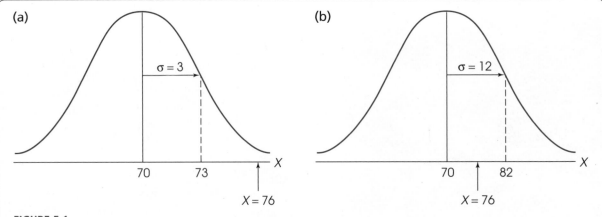

FIGURE 5.1

Two distributions of exam scores. For both distributions, $\mu = 70$, but for one distribution, $\sigma = 3$, and for the other, $\sigma = 12$. The relative position of $X = 76$ is very different for the two distributions.

The purpose of the preceding example is to demonstrate that a score *by itself* does not necessarily provide much information about its position within a distribution. These original, unchanged scores that are the direct result of measurement are called *raw scores*. To make raw scores more meaningful, they are often transformed into new values that contain more information. This transformation is one purpose for *z*-scores. In particular, we transform *X* values into *z*-scores so that the resulting *z*-scores tell exactly where the original scores are located.

A second purpose for *z*-scores is to *standardize* an entire distribution. A common example of a standardized distribution is the distribution of IQ scores. Although there are several different tests for measuring IQ, the tests usually are standardized so that they have a mean of 100 and a standard deviation of 15. Because all the different tests are standardized, it is possible to understand and compare IQ scores even though they come from different tests. For example, we all understand that an IQ score of 95 is a little below average, *no matter which IQ test was used.* Similarly, an IQ of 145 is extremely high, *no matter which IQ test was used.* In general terms, the process of standardizing takes different distributions and makes them equivalent. The advantage of this process is that it is possible to compare distributions even though they may have been quite different before standardization.

In summary, the process of transforming *X* values into *z*-scores serves two useful purposes:

1. Each *z*-score tells the exact location of the original *X* value within the distribution.

2. The *z*-scores form a standardized distribution that can be directly compared to other distributions that also have been transformed into *z*-scores.

Each of these purposes is discussed in the following sections.

5.2   *z*-SCORES AND LOCATION IN A DISTRIBUTION

One of the primary purposes of a *z*-score is to describe the exact location of a score within a distribution. The *z*-score accomplishes this goal by transforming each *X* value into a signed number (+ or −) so that

1. The *sign* tells whether the score is located above (+) or below (−) the mean, and

2. The *number* tells the distance between the score and the mean in terms of the number of standard deviations.

In Figure 5.1(a), for example, we show a distribution with a mean of $\mu = 70$ and $\sigma = 3$. In this distribution, a score of $X = 76$ would be transformed into $z = +2.00$. The *z* value indicates that the score is located above the mean (+) by a distance equal to 2 standard deviations (6 points). For the distribution in Figure 5.1(b), $\mu = 70$ and $\sigma = 12$. In this distribution, a score of $X = 76$ would be transformed into $z = +\frac{1}{2}$ or $z = +0.50$. In this case, the score is above the mean (+) by a distance of only $\frac{1}{2}$ of a standard deviation (6 points).

DEFINITION

> A ***z*-score** specifies the precise location of each *X* value within a distribution. The sign of the *z*-score (+ or −) signifies whether the score is above the mean (positive) or below the mean (negative). The numerical value of the *z*-score specifies the distance from the mean by counting the number of standard deviations between *X* and μ.

Notice that a z-score always consists of two parts: a sign ($+$ or $-$) and a magnitude. Both parts are necessary to describe completely where a raw score is located within a distribution.

Figure 5.2 shows a population distribution with various positions identified by their z-score values. Notice that all z-scores above the mean are positive and all z-scores below the mean are negative. The sign of a z-score tells you immediately whether the score is located above or below the mean. Also, note that a z-score of $z = +1.00$ corresponds to a position exactly 1 standard deviation above the mean. A z-score of $z = +2.00$ is always located exactly 2 standard deviations above the mean. The numerical value of the z-score tells you the number of standard deviations it is from the mean. Finally, you should notice that Figure 5.2 does not give any specific values for the population mean or the standard deviation. The locations identified by z-scores are the same for *all distributions,* no matter what mean or standard deviation the distributions may have.

Whenever you are working with z-scores, you should imagine or draw a picture similar to Figure 5.2. Although you should realize that not all distributions are normal, we use the normal shape as an example when showing z-scores for populations.

LEARNING CHECK

1. Identify the z-score value corresponding to each of the following locations in a distribution.

   a. Below the mean by 2 standard deviations.

   b. Above the mean by $\frac{1}{2}$ standard deviation.

   c. Below the mean by 1.50 standard deviations.

2. Describe the location in the distribution for each of the following z-scores. (For example, $z = +1.00$ is located above the mean by 1 standard deviation.)

   a. $z = -1.50$ **b.** $z = 0.25$ **c.** $z = -2.50$ **d.** $z = 0.50$

3. For a population with $\mu = 30$ and $\sigma = 8$, find the z-score for each of the following scores:

   a. $X = 32$ **b.** $X = 26$ **c.** $X = 42$

4. For a population with $\mu = 50$ and $\sigma = 12$, find the X value corresponding to each of the following z-scores:

   a. $z = -0.25$ **b.** $z = 2.00$ **c.** $z = 0.50$

ANSWERS

1. **a.** $z = -2.00$ **b.** $z = +0.50$ **c.** $z = -1.50$

2. **a.** Below the mean by $1\frac{1}{2}$ standard deviations.

   b. Above the mean by $\frac{1}{4}$ standard deviation.

   c. Below the mean by $2\frac{1}{2}$ standard deviations.

   d. Above the mean by $\frac{1}{2}$ standard deviation.

3. **a.** $z = +0.25$ **b.** $z = -0.50$ **c.** $z = +1.50$

4. **a.** $X = 47$ **b.** $X = 74$ **c.** $X = 56$

THE z-SCORE FORMULA

The z-score definition is adequate for transforming back and forth from X values to z-scores as long as the arithmetic is easy to do in your head. For more complicated values, it is best to have an equation to help structure the calculations. Fortunately, the relationship between X values and z-scores is easily expressed in a formula. The formula for transforming scores into z-scores is

$$z = \frac{X - \mu}{\sigma} \tag{5.1}$$

FIGURE 5.2

The relationship between
z-score values and locations
in a population distribution.

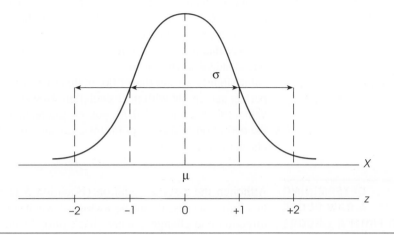

The numerator of the equation, $X - \mu$, is a *deviation score* (Chapter 4, page 92), which measures the distance in points between X and μ and indicates whether X is located above or below the mean. The deviation score is then divided by σ because we want the z-score to measure distance in terms of standard deviation units. The formula performs exactly the same arithmetic that is used with the z-score definition, and it provides a structured equation to organize the calculations when the numbers are more difficult. The following examples demonstrate the use of the z-score formula.

EXAMPLE 5.2   A distribution of scores has a mean of $\mu = 100$ and a standard deviation of $\sigma = 10$.

What z-score corresponds to a score of $X = 130$ in this distribution?

According to the definition, the z-score has a value of $+3$ because the score is located above the mean by exactly 3 standard deviations. Using the z-score formula, we obtain

$$z = \frac{X - \mu}{\sigma} = \frac{130 - 100}{10} = \frac{30}{10} = 3.00$$

The formula produces exactly the same result that is obtained using the z-score definition.

EXAMPLE 5.3   A distribution of scores has a mean of $\mu = 86$ and a standard deviation of $\sigma = 7$. What z-score corresponds to a score of $X = 95$ in this distribution?

Note that this problem is not particularly easy, especially if you try to use the z-score definition and perform the calculations in your head. However, the z-score formula organizes the numbers and allows you to finish the final arithmetic with a calculator. Using the formula, we obtain

$$z = \frac{X - \mu}{\sigma} = \frac{95 - 86}{7} = \frac{9}{7} = 1.29$$

According to the formula, a score of $X = 95$ corresponds to $z = 1.29$. The z-score indicates a location that is above the mean (positive) by slightly more than 1 standard deviation.

When you use the z-score formula, it can be useful to pay attention to the definition of a z-score as well. For example, we used the formula in Example 5.3 to calculate the z-score corresponding to $X = 95$, and obtained $z = 1.29$. Using the z-score definition, we note that $X = 95$ is located above the mean by 9 points, which is slightly more than one standard deviation ($\sigma = 7$). Therefore, the z-score should be positive and have a value slightly greater than 1.00. In this case, the answer predicted by the definition is in perfect agreement with the calculation. However, if the calculations produce a different value, for example $z = 0.78$, you should realize that this answer is not consistent with the definition of a z-score. In this case, an error has been made and you should double check the calculations.

DETERMINING A RAW SCORE (X) FROM A z-SCORE

Although the z-score equation (Equation 5.1) works well for transforming X values into z-scores, it can be awkward when you are trying to work in the opposite direction and change z-scores back into X values. In general, it is easier to use the definition of a z-score, rather than a formula, when you are changing z-scores into X values. Remember, the z-score describes exactly where the score is located by identifying the direction and distance from the mean. It is possible, however, to express this definition as a formula, and we use a sample problem to demonstrate how the formula can be created.

For a distribution with a mean of $\mu = 60$ and $s = 5$, what X value corresponds to a z-score of $z = -3.00$?

To solve this problem, we use the z-score definition and carefully monitor the step-by-step process. The value of the z-score indicates that X is located below the mean by a distance equal to 3 standard deviations. Thus, the first step in the calculation is to determine the distance corresponding to 3 standard deviations. For this problem, the standard deviation is $\sigma = 5$ points, so 3 standard deviations is $3(5) = 15$ points. The next step is to find the value of X that is located below the mean by 15 points. With a mean of $\mu = 60$, the score is

$$X = \mu - 15 = 60 - 15 = 45$$

The two steps can be combined to form a single formula:

$$X = \mu + z\sigma \tag{5.2}$$

In the formula, the value of $z\sigma$ is the *deviation* of X and determines both the direction and the size of the distance from the mean. In this problem, $z\sigma = (-3)(5) = -15$, or 15 points below the mean. Equation 5.2 simply combines the mean and the deviation from the mean to determine the exact value of X.

Finally, you should realize that Equation 5.1 and Equation 5.2 are actually two different versions of the same equation. If you begin with either formula and use algebra to shuffle the terms around, you soon end up with the other formula. We leave this as an exercise for those who want to try it.

OTHER RELATIONSHIPS BETWEEN z, X, μ, AND σ

In most cases, we simply transform scores (X values) into z-scores, or change z-scores back into X values. However, you should realize that a z-score establishes a relationship between the score, the mean, and the standard deviation. This relationship can be used to answer a variety of different questions about scores and the distributions in which they are located. The following examples demonstrate some possibilities.

EXAMPLE 5.4   In a population with a mean of $\mu = 65$, a score of $X = 59$ corresponds to $z = -2.00$. What is the standard deviation for the population?

To answer the question, we begin with the *z*-score value. A *z*-score of -2.00 indicates that the corresponding score is located below the mean by a distance of 2 standard deviations. You also can determine that the score ($X = 59$) is located below the mean ($\mu = 65$) by a distance of 6 points. Thus, 2 standard deviations correspond to a distance of 6 points, which means that 1 standard deviation must be $\sigma = 3$ points.

EXAMPLE 5.5   In a population with a standard deviation of $\sigma = 6$, a score of $X = 33$ corresponds to $z = +1.50$. What is the mean for the population?

Again, we begin with the *z*-score value. In this case, a *z*-score of $+1.50$ indicates that the score is located above the mean by a distance corresponding to 1.50 standard deviations. With a standard deviation of $\sigma = 6$, this distance is $(1.50)(6) = 9$ points. Thus, the score is located 6 points above the mean. The score is $X = 33$, so the mean must be $\mu = 24$.

Many students find problems like those in Examples 5.4 and 5.5 easier to understand if they draw a picture showing all of the information presented in the problem. For the problem in Example 5.4, the picture would begin with a distribution that has a mean of $\mu = 65$ (we use a normal distribution, which is shown in Figure 5.3). The value of the standard deviation is unknown, but you can add arrows to the sketch pointing outward from the mean for a distance corresponding to 1 standard deviation. Finally, use standard deviation arrows to identify the location of $z = -2.00$ (2 standard deviations below the mean) and add $X = 59$ at that location. All of these factors are shown in Figure 5.3. In the figure, it is easy to see that $X = 59$ is located 6 points below the mean, and that the 6-point distance corresponds to exactly 2 standard deviations. Again, if 2 standard deviations equal 6 points, then 1 standard deviation must be $\sigma = 3$ points.

A slight variation on Examples 5.4 and 5.5 is demonstrated in the following example. This time you must use the *z*-score information to find both the population mean and the standard deviation.

FIGURE 5.3

A visual presentation of the question in Example 5.4. If 2 standard deviations correspond to a 6-point distance, then one standard deviation must equal 3 points.

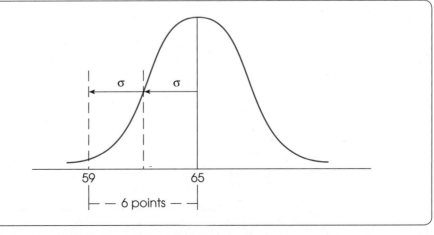

EXAMPLE 5.6

In a population distribution, a score of $X = 54$ corresponds to $z = +2.00$ and a score of $X = 42$ corresponds to $z = -1.00$. What are the values for the mean and the standard deviation for the population?

The key to solving this kind of problem is to focus on the distance between the two scores. By subtraction, the distance between $X = 54$ and $X = 42$ is 12 points. The two z-scores also provide information about the distance between the scores. A z-score of $+2.00$ indicates that $X = 52$ is above the mean by 2.00 standard deviations, and $z = -1.00$ indicates that $X = 44$ is below the mean by 1.00 standard deviation. Thus, the total distance between the scores is equal to $2.00 + 1.00 = 3$ standard deviations. At this point, you know that the distance between the scores is 12 points and the distance is equal to 3 standard deviations. If a distance of 12 points is equal to 3 standard deviations, then the standard deviation must be $\sigma = 4$. Now, you can pick either score and use the standard deviation to find the value of the mean. For example, $X = 42$ is below the mean by 1.00 standard deviation. One standard deviation is 4 points, so the mean must be $\mu = 46$. Thus, the population has $\mu = 46$ and $\sigma = 4$.

Once again, solving problems like the one is Example 5.6 can be easier if you sketch a picture showing the information. Figure 5.4 shows a generic distribution (similar to the one in Figure 5.2), for which the mean and the standard deviation are shown with lines and arrows but are not assigned specific values. Next, we locate the two scores in the distribution; $X = 42$ is placed one standard deviation below the mean ($z = -1.00$) and $X = 54$ is located two standard deviations above the mean ($z = +2.00$). At this point, you can see that the distance between the scores is 12 points, and that this 12-point distance corresponds to 3 standard deviations. Therefore, one standard deviation is $\sigma = 4$. With a standard deviation of 4 points, you can see that $X = 42$ is below the mean by 4 points, so the mean must be $\mu = 46$. Again, we conclude that the population has $\mu = 46$ and $\sigma = 4$.

LEARNING CHECK

1. For a distribution with $\mu = 40$ and $s = 12$, find the z-score for each of the following scores.

   a. $X = 36$ **b.** $X = 46$ **c.** $X = 56$

2. For a distribution with $\mu = 40$ and $\sigma = 12$, find the X value corresponding to each of the following z-scores.

   a. $z = 1.50$ **b.** $z = -1.25$ **c.** $z = \frac{1}{3}$

3. In a distribution with $\mu = 50$, a score of $X = 42$ corresponds to $z = -2.00$. What is the standard deviation for this distribution?

4. In a distribution with $\sigma = 12$, a score of $X = 56$ corresponds to $z = -0.25$. What is the mean for this distribution?

ANSWERS

1. **a.** $z = -0.33$ (or $-\frac{1}{3}$)   **b.** $z = 0.50$ **c.** $z = 1.33$ ($+1\frac{1}{3}$)

2. **a.** $X = 58$ **b.** $X = 25$ **c.** $X = 44$

3. $\sigma = 4$

4. $\mu = 59$

FIGURE 5.4

A visual presentation of the question in Example 5.6. The 12-point distance from 42 to 54 corresponds to 3 standard deviations. Therefore, the standard deviation must be $\sigma = 4$. Also, the score $X = 42$ is below the mean by one standard deviation, so the mean must be $\mu = 46$.

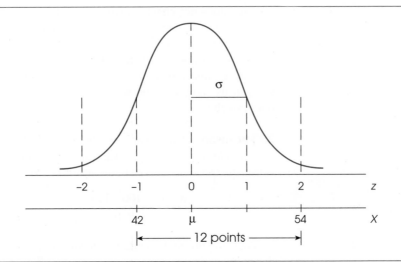

5.3   USING *z*-SCORES TO STANDARDIZE A DISTRIBUTION

It is possible to transform every X value in a distribution into a corresponding z-score. The result of this process is that the entire distribution of X values is transformed into a distribution of z-scores (Figure 5.5). The new distribution of z-scores has characteristics that make the *z-score transformation* a very useful tool. Specifically, if every X value is transformed into a z-score, then the distribution of z-scores will have the following properties:

1. Shape   The distribution of z-scores will have exactly the same shape as the original distribution of scores. If the original distribution is negatively skewed, for example, then the z-score distribution will also be negatively skewed. If the original distribution is normal, the distribution of z-scores will also be normal. Transforming raw scores into

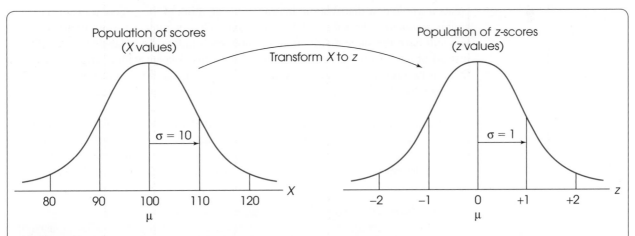

FIGURE 5.5

An entire population of scores is transformed into z-scores. The transformation does not change the shape of the population, but the mean is transformed into a value of 0 and the standard deviation is transformed to a value of 1.

z-scores does not change anyone's position in the distribution. For example, any raw score that is above the mean by 1 standard deviation will be transformed to a *z*-score of +1.00, which is still above the mean by 1 standard deviation. Transforming a distribution from *X* values to *z* values does not move scores from one position to another; the procedure simply relabels each score (see Figure 5.5). Because each individual score stays in its same position within the distribution, the overall shape of the distribution does not change.

2. The mean   The *z*-score distribution will *always* have a mean of zero. In Figure 5.5, the original distribution of *X* values has a mean of $\mu = 100$. When this value, $X = 100$, is transformed into a *z*-score, the result is

$$z = \frac{X - \mu}{\sigma} = \frac{100 - 100}{10} = 0$$

Thus, the original population mean is transformed into a value of zero in the *z*-score distribution. The fact that the *z*-score distribution has a mean of zero makes the mean a convenient reference point. Recall from the definition of *z*-scores that all positive *z*-scores are above the mean and all negative *z*-scores are below the mean. In other words, for *z*-scores, $\mu = 0$.

3. The standard deviation   The distribution of *z*-scores will *always* have a standard deviation of 1. In Figure 5.5, the original distribution of *X* values has $\mu = 100$ and $\sigma = 10$. In this distribution, a value of $X = 110$ is above the mean by exactly 10 points or 1 standard deviation. When $X = 110$ is transformed, it becomes $z = +1.00$, which is above the mean by exactly 1 point in the *z*-score distribution. Thus, the standard deviation corresponds to a 10-point distance in the *X* distribution and is transformed into a 1-point distance in the *z*-score distribution. The advantage of having a standard deviation of 1 is that the numerical value of a *z*-score is exactly the same as the number of standard deviations from the mean. For example, a *z*-score of $z = 1.50$ is exactly 1.50 standard deviations from the mean.

In Figure 5.5, we showed the *z*-score transformation as a process that changed a distribution of *X* values into a new distribution of *z*-scores. In fact, there is no need to create a whole new distribution. Instead, you can think of the *z*-score transformation as simply *relabeling* the values along the *X*-axis. That is, after a *z*-score transformation, you still have the same distribution, but now each individual is labeled with a *z*-score instead of an *X* value. Figure 5.6 demonstrates this concept with a single distribution that has two sets of labels: the *X* values along one line and the corresponding *z*-scores along another line. Notice that the mean for the distribution of *z*-scores is zero and the standard deviation is 1.

When *any* distribution (with any mean or standard deviation) is transformed into *z*-scores, the resulting distribution will always have a mean of $\mu = 0$ and a standard deviation of $\sigma = 1$. Because all *z*-score distributions have the same mean and the same standard deviation, the *z*-score distribution is called a *standardized distribution*.

D E F I N I T I O N

> A **standardized distribution** is composed of scores that have been transformed to create predetermined values for μ and σ. Standardized distributions are used to make dissimilar distributions comparable.

A *z*-score distribution is an example of a standardized distribution with $\mu = 0$ and $\sigma = 1$. That is, when any distribution (with any mean or standard deviation) is transformed into *z*-scores, the transformed distribution will always have $\mu = 0$ and $\sigma = 1$.

FIGURE 5.6

Following a z-score transformation, the X-axis is relabeled in z-score units. The distance that is equivalent to 1 standard deviation on the X-axis ($\sigma = 10$ points in this example) corresponds to 1 point on the z-score scale.

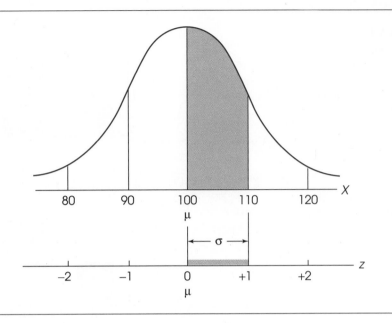

DEMONSTRATION OF A z-SCORE TRANSFORMATION

Although the basic characteristics of a z-score distribution have been explained logically, the following example provides a concrete demonstration that a z-score transformation creates a new distribution with a mean of zero, a standard deviation of 1, and the same shape as the original population.

EXAMPLE 5.7

We begin with a population of $N = 6$ scores consisting of the following values: 0, 6, 5, 2, 3, 2. This population has a mean of $\mu = \frac{18}{6} = 3$ and a standard deviation of $\sigma = 2$ (check the calculations for yourself).

Each of the X values in the original population is then transformed into a z-score as summarized in the following table.

$X = 0$	Below the mean by $1\frac{1}{2}$ standard deviations	$z = -1.50$
$X = 6$	Above the mean by $1\frac{1}{2}$ standard deviations	$z = +1.50$
$X = 5$	Above the mean by 1 standard deviation	$z = +1.00$
$X = 2$	Below the mean by $\frac{1}{2}$ standard deviation	$z = -0.50$
$X = 3$	Exactly equal to the mean—zero deviation	$z = 0$
$X = 2$	Below the mean by $\frac{1}{2}$ standard deviation	$z = -0.50$

The frequency distribution for the original population of X values is shown in Figure 5.7(a) and the corresponding distribution for the z-scores is shown in Figure 5.7(b). A simple comparison of the two distributions demonstrates the results of a z-score transformation.

1. The two distributions have exactly the same shape. Each individual has exactly the same relative position in the X distribution and in the z-score distribution.

2. After the transformation to z-scores, the mean of the distribution becomes $\mu = 0$. For these z-scores values, $N = 6$ and $\Sigma z = -1.50 + 1.50 + 1.00 + -0.50 + 0 + -0.50 = 0$. Thus, the mean for the z-scores is $\mu = \frac{\Sigma z}{N} = \frac{0}{6} = 0$.

FIGURE 5.7

Transforming a distribution of raw scores
(a) into z-scores (b) will not change the shape of the distribution.

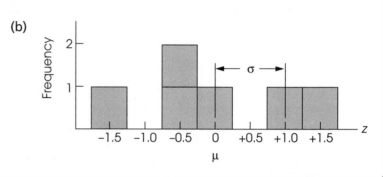

Note that the individual with a score of $X = 3$ is located exactly at the mean in the X distribution and this individual is transformed into $z = 0$, exactly at the mean in the z-distribution.

3. After the transformation, the standard deviation becomes $\sigma = 1$. For these z-scores, $\Sigma z = 0$ and

$$\Sigma z^2 = (-1.50)^2 + (1.50)^2 + (1.00)^2 + (-0.50)^2 + (0)^2 + (-0.50)^2$$

$$= 2.25 + 2.25 + 1.00 + 0.25 + 0 + 0.25$$

$$= 6.00$$

Using the computational formula for SS, substituting z in place of X, we obtain

$$SS = \Sigma z^2 - \frac{(\Sigma z)^2}{N} = 6 - \frac{(0)^2}{6} = 6.00$$

For these z-scores, the variance is $\sigma^2 = \dfrac{SS}{N} = \dfrac{6}{6} = 1.00$ and the standard deviation is

$$\sigma = \sqrt{1.00} = 1.00$$

Note that the individual with $X = 5$ is located above the mean by 2 points, which is exactly one standard deviation in the X distribution. After transformation, this individual has a z-score that is located above the mean by 1 point, which is exactly one standard deviation in the z-score distribution.

USING z-SCORES TO MAKE COMPARISONS   One advantage of standardizing distributions is that it makes it possible to compare different scores or different individuals even though they come from completely different distributions. Normally, if two scores come from different distributions, it is impossible to make any direct comparison between them. Suppose, for example, Dave received a score of $X = 60$ on a psychology exam and a score of $X = 56$ on a biology test. For which course should Dave expect the better grade?

Because the scores come from two different distributions, you cannot make any direct comparison. Without additional information, it is even impossible to determine whether Dave is above or below the mean in either distribution. Before you can begin to make comparisons, you must know the values for the mean and standard deviation for each distribution. Suppose the psychology scores had $\mu = 50$ and $\sigma = 10$, and the biology scores had $\mu = 48$ and $\sigma = 4$. With this new information, you could sketch the two distributions, locate Dave's score in each distribution, and compare the two locations.

Instead of drawing the two distributions to compare Dave's two scores, we simply can compute the corresponding z-scores to determine the two locations. For psychology, Dave's z-score is

> Be sure to use the μ and σ values for the distribution to which X belongs.

$$z = \frac{X - \mu}{\sigma} = \frac{60 - 50}{10} = \frac{10}{10} = +1.0$$

For biology, Dave's z-score is

$$z = \frac{56 - 48}{4} = \frac{8}{4} = +2.0$$

Note that Dave's z-score for biology is $+2.0$, which means that his test score is 2 standard deviations above the class mean. On the other hand, his z-score is $+1.0$ for psychology, or 1 standard deviation above the mean. In terms of relative class standing, Dave is doing much better in the biology class.

Notice that we cannot compare Dave's two exam scores ($X = 60$ and $X = 56$) because the scores come from different distributions with different means and standard deviations. However, we can compare the two z-scores because all distributions of z-scores have the same mean ($\mu = 0$) and the same standard deviation ($\sigma = 1$).

LEARNING CHECK

1. A normal-shaped distribution with $\mu = 40$ and $\sigma = 8$ is transformed into z-scores. Describe the shape, the mean, and the standard deviation for the resulting distribution of z-scores.

2. What is the advantage of having a mean of $\mu = 0$ for a distribution of z-scores?

3. A distribution of English exam scores has $\mu = 70$ and $\sigma = 4$. A distribution of history exam scores has $\mu = 60$ and $\sigma = 20$. For which exam would a score of $X = 78$ have a higher standing? Explain your answer.

4. A distribution of English exam scores has $\mu = 50$ and $\sigma = 12$. A distribution of history exam scores has $\mu = 58$ and $\sigma = 4$. For which exam would a score of $X = 62$ have a higher standing? Explain your answer.

ANSWERS

1. The z-score distribution would be normal with a mean of 0 and a standard deviation of 1.

2. With a mean of zero, all positive scores are above the mean and all negative scores are below the mean.

3. For the English exam, $X = 78$ corresponds to $z = 2.00$, which is a higher standing than $z = 0.90$ for the history exam.

4. The score $X = 62$ corresponds to $z = +1.00$ in both distributions. The score has exactly the same standing for both exams.

5.4   OTHER STANDARDIZED DISTRIBUTIONS BASED ON *z*-SCORES

TRANSFORMING
***z*-SCORES TO**
A DISTRIBUTION WITH
A PREDETERMINED
μ AND σ

Although *z*-score distributions have distinct advantages, many people find them cumbersome because they contain negative values and decimals. For this reason, it is common to standardize a distribution by transforming the scores into a new distribution with a predetermined mean and standard deviation that are whole round numbers. The goal is to create a new (standardized) distribution that has "simple" values for the mean and standard deviation but does not change any individual's location within the distribution. Standardized scores of this type are frequently used in psychological or educational testing. For example, raw scores of the Scholastic Aptitude Test (SAT) are transformed to a standardized distribution that has μ = 500 and σ = 100. For intelligence tests, raw scores are frequently converted to standard scores that have a mean of 100 and a standard deviation of 15. Because most IQ tests are standardized so that they have the same mean and standard deviation, it is possible to compare IQ scores even though they may come from different tests.

The procedure for standardizing a distribution to create new values for μ and σ involves two steps:

1. The original raw scores are transformed into *z*-scores.

2. The *z*-scores are then transformed into new *X* values so that the specific μ and σ are attained.

This procedure ensures that each individual has exactly the same *z*-score location in the new distribution as in the original distribution. The following example demonstrates the standardization procedure.

EXAMPLE 5.8

A distribution of exam scores has a mean of μ = 57 with σ = 14. The instructor would like to simplify the distribution by transforming all scores into a new, standardized distribution with μ = 50 and σ = 10. To demonstrate this process, we consider what happens to two specific students: Maria, who has a score of *X* = 64 in the original distribution; and Joe, whose original score is *X* = 43.

Step 1   Transform each of the original scores into *z*-scores. Maria started with *X* = 64, so her *z*-score is

$$z = \frac{X - \mu}{\sigma} = \frac{64 - 57}{14} = +0.5$$

For Joe, *X* = 43, and his *z*-score is

$$z = \frac{X - \mu}{\sigma} = \frac{43 - 57}{14} = -1.0$$

Remember: The values of μ and σ are for the distribution from which *X* was taken.

Step 2   Change each *z*-score into an *X* value in the new standardized distribution that has a mean of μ = 50 and a standard deviation of σ = 10.

Maria's *z*-score, *z* = +0.50, indicates that she is located above the mean by $\frac{1}{2}$ standard deviation. In the new, standardized distribution, this location corresponds to *X* = 55 (above the mean by 5 points).

TABLE 5.1

A demonstration of how two individual scores are changed when a distribution is standardized. See Example 5.8.

	Original Scores $\mu = 57$ and $\sigma = 14$		z-Score Location		Standardized Scores $\mu = 50$ and $\sigma = 10$
Maria	$X = 64$	$\rightarrow$	$z = +0.50$	$\rightarrow$	$X = 55$
Joe	$X = 43$	$\rightarrow$	$z = -1.00$	$\rightarrow$	$X = 40$

Joe's z-score, $z = -1.00$, indicates that he is located below the mean by exactly 1 standard deviation. In the new distribution, this location corresponds to $X = 40$ (below the mean by 10 points).

The results of this two-step transformation process are summarized in Table 5.1. Note that Joe, for example, has exactly the same z-score ($z = -1.00$) in both the original distribution and the new standardized distribution. This means that Joe's position relative to the other students in the class has not changed.

Figure 5.8 provides another demonstration of the concept that standardizing a distribution does not change the individual positions within the distribution. The figure shows the original exam scores from Example 5.7, with a mean of $\mu = 57$ and a standard deviation of $\sigma = 14$. In the original distribution, Joe is located at a score of $X = 43$. In addition to the original scores, we have included a second scale showing the z-score value for each location in the distribution. In terms of z-scores, Joe is located at a value of $z = -1.00$. Finally, we have added a third scale showing the *standardized scores,* for which the mean is $\mu = 50$ and the standard deviation is $\sigma = 10$. For the standardized scores, Joe is located at $X = 40$. Note that Joe is always in the same place in the distribution. The only thing that changes is the number that is assigned to Joe: For the original scores, Joe is at 43; for the z-scores, Joe is at -1.00; and for the standardized scores, Joe is at 40.

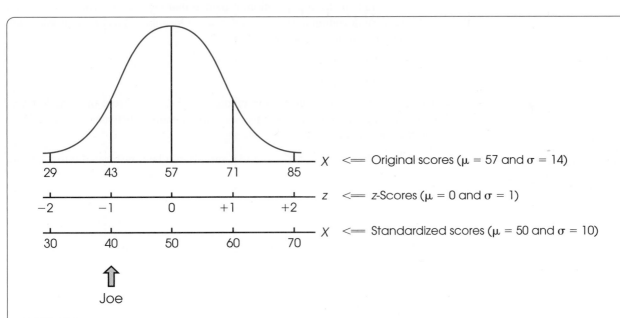

FIGURE 5.8

The distribution of exam scores from Example 5.7. The original distribution was standardized to produce a new distribution with $\mu = 50$ and $\sigma = 10$. Note that each individual is identified by an original score, a z-score, and a new, standardized score. For example, Joe has an original score of 43, a z-score of -100, and a standardized score of 40.

1. A population of scores has μ = 73 and σ = 8. If the distribution is standardized to create a new distribution with μ = 100 and σ = 20, what are the new values for each of the following scores from the original distribution?

    a. *X* = 65   **b.** *X* = 71   **c.** *X* = 81   **d.** *X* = 83

2. A population with a mean of μ = 44 and a standard deviation of σ = 6 is standardized to create a new distribution with μ = 50 and σ = 10.

    a. What is the new standardized value for a score of *X* = 47 from the original distribution?

    b. One individual has a new standardized score of *X* = 65. What was this person's score in the original distribution?

ANSWERS
1. **a.** *z* = −1.00, *X* = 80   **b.** *z* = −0.25, *X* = 95
   c. *z* = 1.00, *X* = 120   **d.** *z* = 1.25, *X* = 125

2. **a.** *X* = 47 corresponds to z = +0.50 in the original distribution. In the new distribution, the corresponding score is *X* = 55.

   b. In the new distribution, *X* = 65 corresponds to z = +1.50. The corresponding score in the original distribution is *X* = 53.

5.5   COMPUTING *z*-SCORES FOR A SAMPLE

Although *z*-scores have been presented in the context of a population, the same principles can be used to compute *z*-scores within a sample. The definition of a *z*-score is the same for a sample as for a population, provided that you use the sample mean and the sample standard deviation to specify each *z*-score location. Thus, for a sample, each *X* value is transformed into a *z*-score so that

1. The sign of the *z*-score indicates whether the *X* value is above (+) or below (−) the sample mean, and

2. The numerical value of the *z*-score identifies the distance from the sample mean by measuring the number of sample standard deviations between the score (*X*) and the sample mean (*M*).

See the population equations (5.1 and 5.2) on pages 126 and 128 for comparison.

Expressed as a formula, each *X* value in a sample can be transformed into a *z*-score as follows:

$$z = \frac{X - M}{s}$$

(5.3)

Similarly, each *z*-score can be transformed back into an *X* value, as follows:

$$X = M + zs$$

(5.4)

EXAMPLE 5.9

In a sample with a mean of *M* = 40 and a standard deviation of *s* = 10, what is the *z*-score corresponding to *X* = 35 and what is the *X* value corresponding to *z* = +2.00?

The score, *X* = 35, is located below the mean by 5 points, which is exactly half of the standard deviation. Therefore, the corresponding *z*-score is *z* = −0.50. The *z*-score, *z* = +2.00, corresponds to a location above the mean by 2 standard deviations. With a standard deviation of $s = 10$, this is a distance of 20 points. The score that is located 20 points above the mean is $X = 60$. Note that it is possible to find these answers using either the z-score definition or one of the equations (5.3 or 5.4).

STANDARDIZING A SAMPLE DISTRIBUTION

If all the scores in a sample are transformed into z-scores, the result is a sample of z-scores. The transformed distribution of z-scores will have the same properties that exist when a population of X values is transformed into z-scores. Specifically,

1. The sample of z-scores will have the same shape as the original sample of scores.

2. The sample of z-scores will have a mean of $M_z = 0$.

3. The sample of z-scores will have a standard deviation of $s_z = 1$.

Note that the set of z-scores is still considered to be a sample (just like the set of X values) and the sample formulas must be used to compute variance and standard deviation. The following example demonstrates the process of transforming the scores from a sample into z-scores.

EXAMPLE 5.10

We begin with a sample of $n = 5$ scores: 0, 2, 4, 4, 5. With a few simple calculations, you should be able to verify that the sample mean is $M = 3$, the sample variance is $s^2 = 4$, and the sample standard deviation is $s = 2$. Using the sample mean and sample standard deviation, we can convert each X value into a z-score. For example, $X = 5$ is located above the mean by 2 points. Thus, $X = 5$ is above the mean by exactly 1 standard deviation and has a z-score of $z = +1.00$. The z-scores for the entire sample are shown in the following table.

X	z
0	-1.50
2	-0.50
4	$+0.50$
4	$+0.50$
5	$+1.00$

Again, a few simple calculations demonstrate that the sum of the z-score values is $\Sigma z = 0$, so the mean is $M_z = 0$.

Because the mean is zero, each z-score value is its own deviation from the mean. Therefore, the sum of the squared z-scores is also the sum of the squared deviations. For this sample of z-scores,

$$SS = \Sigma z^2 = (-1.50)^2 + (-0.50)^2 + (+0.50)^2 + (0.50)^2 + (+1.00)^2$$

$$= 2.25 + 0.25 + 0.25 + 0.25 + 1.00$$

$$= 4.00$$

The variance for the sample of *z*-scores is

Notice that the set of *z*-scores is considered to be a sample and the variance is computed using the sample formula with $df = n - 1$.

$$s_z^2 = \frac{SS}{n-1} = \frac{4}{4} = 1.00$$

Finally, the standard deviation for the sample of *z*-scores is $s_z = \sqrt{1.00} = 1.00$. As always, the distribution of *z*-scores has a mean of 0 and a standard deviation of 1.

5.6 LOOKING AHEAD TO INFERENTIAL STATISTICS

Recall that inferential statistics are techniques that use the information from samples to answer questions about populations. In later chapters, we use inferential statistics to help interpret the results from research studies. A typical research study begins with a question about how a treatment will affect the individuals in a population. Because it is usually impossible to study an entire population, the researcher selects a sample and administers the treatment to the individuals in the sample. This general research situation is shown in Figure 5.9. To evaluate the effect of the treatment, the researcher simply compares the treated sample with the original population. If the individuals in the sample are noticeably different from the individuals in the original population, the researcher has evidence that the treatment has had an effect. On the other hand, if the sample is not noticeably different from the original population, it would appear that the treatment has had no effect.

Notice that the interpretation of the research results depends on whether the sample is *noticeably different* from the population. One technique for deciding whether a sample is noticeably different is to use *z*-scores. For example, an individual with a *z*-score near 0 is located in the center of the population and would be considered to be a fairly typical or representative individual. However, an individual with an extreme *z*-score, beyond

FIGURE 5.9

A diagram of a research study. The goal of the study is to evaluate the effect of a treatment. A sample is selected from the population, and the treatment is administered to the sample. If, after treatment, the individuals in the sample are noticeably different from the individuals in the original population, then we have evidence that the treatment does have an effect.

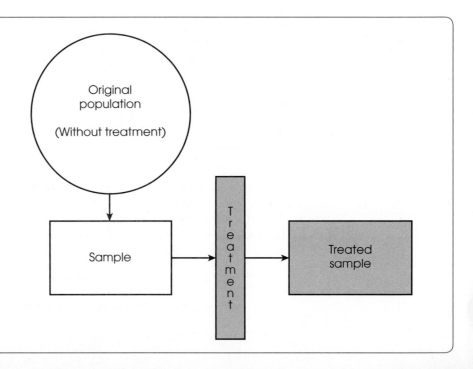

+2.00 or −2.00 for example, would be considered noticeably different from most of the individuals in the population. Thus, we can use z-scores to help decide whether the treatment has caused a change. Specifically, if the individuals who receive the treatment in a research study tend to have extreme z-scores, we can conclude that the treatment does appear to have an effect. The following example demonstrates this process.

EXAMPLE 5.11   A researcher is evaluating the effect of a new growth hormone. It is known that regular adult rats weigh an average of $\mu = 400$ grams. The weights vary from rat to rat, and the distribution of weights is normal with a standard deviation of $\sigma = 20$ grams. The population distribution is shown in Figure 5.10. The researcher selects one newborn rat and injects the rat with the growth hormone. When the rat reaches maturity, it is weighed to determine whether there is any evidence that the hormone has an effect.

First, assume that the hormone-injected rat weighs $X = 418$ grams. Although this is more than the average nontreated rat ($\mu = 400$ grams), is it convincing evidence that the hormone has an effect? If you look at the distribution in Figure 5.10, you should realize that a rat weighing 418 grams is not noticeably different from the regular rats that did not receive any hormone injection. Specifically, our injected rat would be located near the center of the distribution for regular rats with a z-score of

$$z = \frac{X - \mu}{\sigma} = \frac{418 - 400}{20} = \frac{18}{20} = 0.90$$

Because the injected rat still looks the same as a regular, nontreated rat, the conclusion is that the hormone does not appear to have an effect.

Now, assume that our injected rat weighs $X = 450$ grams. In the distribution of regular rats (see Figure 5.10), this animal would have a z-score of

$$z = \frac{X - \mu}{\sigma} = \frac{450 - 400}{20} = \frac{50}{20} = 2.50$$

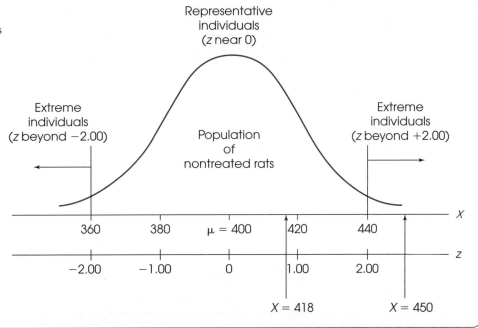

FIGURE 5.10

The distribution of weights for the population of adult rats. Note that individuals with z-scores near 0 are typical or representative. However, individuals with z-scores beyond +2.00 or –2.00 are extreme and noticeably different from most of the others in the distribution.

Representative individuals
(z near 0)

Extreme individuals
(z beyond −2.00)

Population of nontreated rats

Extreme individuals
(z beyond +2.00)

360   380 $\mu = 400$ 420   440 X

−2.00   −1.00   0   1.00   2.00 z

$X = 418$ $X = 450$

In this case, the hormone-injected rat is substantially bigger than most ordinary rats, and it would be reasonable to conclude that the hormone does have an effect on weight.

In the preceding example, we used z-scores to help interpret the results obtained from a sample. Specifically, if the individuals who receive the treatment in a research study have extreme z-scores compared to those who do not receive the treatment, we can conclude that the treatment does appear to have an effect. The example, however, used an arbitrary definition to determine which z-score values are noticeably different. Although it is reasonable to describe individuals with z-scores near 0 as "highly representative" of the population, and individuals with z-scores beyond ± 2.00 as "extreme," you should realize that these z-score boundaries were not determined by any mathematical rule. In the following chapter we introduce *probability,* which gives us a rationale for deciding exactly where to set the boundaries.

LEARNING CHECK

1. For a sample with a mean of $M = 40$ and a standard deviation of $s = 12$, find the z-score corresponding to each of the following X values.

$X = 43$	$X = 58$	$X = 49$
$X = 34$	$X = 28$	$X = 16$

2. For a sample with a mean of $M = 80$ and a standard deviation of $s = 20$, find the X value corresponding to each of the following z-scores.

$z = -1.00$	$z = -0.50$	$z = -0.20$
$z = 1.50$	$z = 0.80$	$z = 1.40$

3. For a sample with a mean of $M = 85$, a score of $X = 80$ corresponds to $z = -0.50$. What is the standard deviation for the sample?

4. For a sample with a standard deviation of $s = 12$, a score of $X = 83$ corresponds to $z = 0.50$. What is the mean for the sample?

5. A sample has a mean of $M = 30$ and a standard deviation of $s = 8$.

   a. Would a score of $X = 36$ be considered a central score or an extreme score in the sample?

   b. If the standard deviation were $s = 2$, would $X = 36$ be central or extreme?

ANSWERS

1. | | | |
   |---|---|---|
   | $z = 0.25$ | $z = 1.50$ | $z = 0.75$ |
   | $z = -0.50$ | $z = -1.00$ | $z = -2.00$ |

2. | | | |
   |---|---|---|
   | $X = 60$ | $X = 70$ | $X = 76$ |
   | $X = 110$ | $X = 96$ | $X = 108$ |

3. $s = 10$

4. $M = 77$

5. a. $X = 36$ is a central score corresponding to $z = 0.75$.

   b. $X = 36$ would be an extreme score corresponding to $z = 3.00$.

SUMMARY

1. Each X value can be transformed into a z-score that specifies the exact location of X within the distribution. The sign of the z-score indicates whether the location is above the mean (positive) or below the mean (negative). The numerical value of the z-score specifies the number of standard deviations between X and μ.

2. The z-score formula is used to transform X values into z-scores. For a population:

$$z = \frac{X - \mu}{\sigma}$$

   For a sample:

$$z = \frac{X - M}{s}$$

3. To transform z-scores back into X values, it usually is easier to use the z-score definition rather than a formula. However, the z-score formula can be transformed into a new equation.

   For a population: $X = \mu + z\sigma$

   For a sample: $X = M + zs$

4. When an entire distribution of X values is transformed into z-scores, the result is a distribution of z-scores.

   The z-score distribution will have the same shape as the distribution of raw scores, and it always will have a mean of 0 and a standard deviation of 1.

5. One method for comparing scores from different distributions is to standardize the distributions with a z-score transformation. The distributions will then be comparable because they will have the same parameters ($\mu = 0$, $\sigma = 1$). In practice, it is necessary to transform only those raw scores that are being compared.

6. A distribution also can be standardized by converting the original X values into z-scores and then converting the z-scores into a new distribution of scores with predetermined values for the mean and the standard deviation.

7. In inferential statistics, z-scores provide an objective method for determining how well a specific score represents its population. A z-score near 0 indicates that the score is close to the population mean and, therefore, is representative. A z-score beyond $+2.00$ (or -2.00) indicates that the score is extreme and is noticeably different from the other scores in the distribution.

KEY TERMS

raw score (125)
z-score (125)

deviation score (127)
z-score transformation (131)

standardized distribution (132)
standardized score (137)

RESOURCES

 Go to CengageBrain.com to access Psychology CourseMate, where you will find an interactive eBook, glossaries, flashcards, quizzes, statistics workshops, and more.

aplia

If your professor has assigned Aplia:

1. Sign in to your account.
2. Complete the corresponding exercises as required by your professor.
3. When finished, click "Grade It Now" to see which areas you have mastered, which areas need more work, and detailed explanations of every answer.

General instructions for using SPSS are presented in Appendix D. Following are detailed instructions for using SPSS to **Transform *X* Values into *z*-Scores for a Sample.**

Data Entry

Enter all of the scores in one column of the data editor, probably VAR00001.

Data Analysis

1. Click **Analyze** on the tool bar, select **Descriptive Statistics,** and click on **Descriptives.**

2. Highlight the column label for the set of scores (VAR0001) in the left box and click the arrow to move it into the **Variable** box.

3. Click the box to **Save standardized values as variables** at the bottom of the **Descriptives** screen.

4. Click **OK.**

SPSS Output

The program produces the usual output display listing the number of scores (*N*), the maximum and minimum scores, the mean, and the standard deviation. However, if you go back to the Data Editor (use the tool bar at the bottom of the screen), you can see that SPSS has produced a new column showing the *z*-score corresponding to each of the original *X* values.

Caution: The SPSS program computes the *z*-scores using the sample standard deviation instead of the population standard deviation. If your set of scores is intended to be a population, SPSS does not produce the correct *z*-score values. You can convert the SPSS values into population *z*-scores by multiplying each *z*-score value by the square root of $\frac{n}{(n-1)}$.

FOCUS ON PROBLEM SOLVING

1. When you are converting an *X* value to a *z*-score (or vice versa), do not rely entirely on the formula. You can avoid careless mistakes if you use the definition of a *z*-score (sign and numerical value) to make a preliminary estimate of the answer before you begin computations. For example, a *z*-score of $z = -0.85$ identifies a score located below the mean by almost 1 standard deviation. When computing the *X* value for this *z*-score, be sure that your answer is smaller than the mean, and check that the distance between *X* and μ is slightly less than the standard deviation.

2. When comparing scores from distributions that have different standard deviations, it is important to be sure that you use the correct values for μ and σ in the *z*-score formula. Use the values for the distribution from which the score was taken.

3. Remember that a *z*-score specifies a relative position within the context of a specific distribution. A *z*-score is a relative value, not an absolute value. For

example, a z-score of $z = -2.0$ does not necessarily suggest a very low raw score—it simply means that the raw score is among the lowest within that specific group.

DEMONSTRATION 5.1

TRANSFORMING X VALUES INTO z-SCORES

A distribution of scores has a mean of $\mu = 60$ with $\sigma = 12$. Find the z-score for $X = 75$.

STEP 1   Determine the sign of the z-score.

First, determine whether X is above or below the mean. This determines the sign of the z-score. For this demonstration, X is larger than (above) μ, so the z-score is positive.

STEP 2   Convert the distance between X and μ into standard deviation units.

For $X = 75$ and $\mu = 60$, the distance between X and μ is 15 points. With $\sigma = 12$ points, this distance corresponds to $\frac{15}{12} = 1.25$ standard deviations.

STEP 3   Combine the sign from step 1 with the numerical value from step 2.

The score is above the mean $(+)$ by a distance of 1.25 standard deviations. Thus, $z = +1.25$.

STEP 4   Confirm the answer using the z-score formula.

For this example, $X = 75$, $\mu = 60$, and $\sigma = 12$.

$$z = \frac{X - \mu}{\sigma} = \frac{75 - 60}{12} = \frac{+15}{12} = +1.25$$

DEMONSTRATION 5.2

CONVERTING z-SCORES TO X VALUES

For a population with $\mu = 60$ and $\sigma = 12$, what is the X value corresponding to $z = -0.50$?

STEP 1   Locate X in relation to the mean.

A z-score of -0.50 indicates a location below the mean by half of a standard deviation.

STEP 2   Convert the distance from standard deviation units to points.

With $\sigma = 12$, half of a standard deviation is 6 points.

STEP 3   Identify the X value.

The value we want is located below the mean by 6 points. The mean is $\mu = 60$, so the score must be $X = 54$.

PROBLEMS

1. What information is provided by the sign (+/−) of a z-score? What information is provided by the numerical value of the z-score?

2. A distribution has a standard deviation of $\sigma = 10$. Find the z-score for each of the following locations in the distribution.
   a. Above the mean by 5 points.
   b. Above the mean by 2 points.
   c. Below the mean by 20 points.
   d. Below the mean by 15 points.

3. For a distribution with a standard deviation of $\sigma = 20$, describe the location of each of the following z-scores in terms of its position relative to the mean. For example, $z = +1.00$ is a location that is 20 points above the mean.
   a. $z = +2.00$
   b. $z = +0.50$
   c. $z = -1.00$
   d. $z = -0.25$

4. For a population with $\mu = 80$ and $\sigma = 10$,
   a. Find the z-score for each of the following X values. (*Note:* You should be able to find these values using the definition of a z-score. You should not need to use a formula or do any serious calculations.)

$X = 75$	$X = 100$	$X = 60$
$X = 95$	$X = 50$	$X = 85$

   b. Find the score (X value) that corresponds to each of the following z-scores. (Again, you should not need a formula or any serious calculations.)

$z = 1.00$	$z = 0.20$	$z = 1.50$
$z = -0.50$	$z = -2.00$	$z = -1.50$

5. For a population with $\mu = 40$ and $\sigma = 11$, find the z-score for each of the following X values. (*Note:* You probably will need to use a formula and a calculator to find these values.)

$X = 45$	$X = 52$	$X = 41$
$X = 30$	$X = 25$	$X = 38$

6. For a population with a mean of $\mu = 100$ and a standard deviation of $\sigma = 20$,
   a. Find the z-score for each of the following X values.

$X = 108$	$X = 115$	$X = 130$
$X = 90$	$X = 88$	$X = 95$

   b. Find the score (X value) that corresponds to each of the following z-scores.

$z = -0.40$	$z = -0.50$	$z = 1.80$
$z = 0.75$	$z = 1.50$	$z = -1.25$

7. A population has a mean of $\mu = 60$ and a standard deviation of $\sigma = 12$.
   a. For this population, find the z-score for each of the following X values.

$X = 69$	$X = 84$	$X = 63$
$X = 54$	$X = 48$	$X = 45$

   b. For the same population, find the score (X value) that corresponds to each of the following z-scores.

$z = 0.50$	$z = 1.50$	$z = -2.50$
$z = -0.25$	$z = -0.50$	$z = 1.25$

8. A sample has a mean of $M = 30$ and a standard deviation of $s = 8$. Find the z-score for each of the following X values from this sample.

$X = 32$	$X = 34$	$X = 36$
$X = 28$	$X = 20$	$X = 18$

9. A sample has a mean of $M = 25$ and a standard deviation of $s = 5$. For this sample, find the X value corresponding to each of the following z-scores.

$z = 0.40$	$z = 1.20$	$z = 2.00$
$z = -0.80$	$z = -0.60$	$z = -1.40$

10. Find the z-score corresponding to a score of $X = 45$ for each of the following distributions.
    a. $\mu = 40$ and $\sigma = 20$
    b. $\mu = 40$ and $\sigma = 10$
    c. $\mu = 40$ and $\sigma = 5$
    d. $\mu = 40$ and $\sigma = 2$

11. Find the X value corresponding to $z = 0.25$ for each of the following distributions.
    a. $\mu = 40$ and $\sigma = 4$
    b. $\mu = 40$ and $\sigma = 8$
    c. $\mu = 40$ and $\sigma = 16$
    d. $\mu = 40$ and $\sigma = 32$

12. A score that is 6 points below the mean corresponds to a z-score of $z = -2.00$. What is the population standard deviation?

13. A score that is 9 points above the mean corresponds to a z-score of $z = 1.50$. What is the population standard deviation?

14. For a population with a standard deviation of $\sigma = 12$, a score of $X = 44$ corresponds to $z = -0.50$. What is the population mean?

15. For a sample with a standard deviation of $s = 8$, a score of $X = 65$ corresponds to $z = 1.50$. What is the sample mean?

16. For a sample with a mean of $M = 51$, a score of $X = 59$ corresponds to $z = 2.00$. What is the sample standard deviation?

17. For a population with a mean of $\mu = 70$, a score of $X = 64$ corresponds to $z = -1.50$. What is the population standard deviation?

18. In a population distribution, a score of $X = 28$ corresponds to $z = -1.00$ and a score of $X = 34$ corresponds to $z = -0.50$. Find the mean and standard deviation for the population. (*Hint:* Sketch the distribution and locate the two scores on your sketch.)

19. In a sample distribution, $X = 56$ corresponds to $z = 1.00$, and $X = 47$ corresponds to $z = -0.50$. Find the mean and standard deviation for the sample.

20. For each of the following populations, would a score of $X = 50$ be considered a central score (near the middle of the distribution) or an extreme score (far out in the tail of the distribution)?
   a. $\mu = 45$ and $\sigma = 10$
   b. $\mu = 45$ and $\sigma = 2$
   c. $\mu = 90$ and $\sigma = 20$
   d. $\mu = 60$ and $\sigma = 20$

21. A distribution of exam scores has a mean of $\mu = 78$.
   a. If your score is $X = 70$, which standard deviation would give you a better grade: $\sigma = 4$ or $\sigma = 8$?
   b. If your score is $X = 80$, which standard deviation would give you a better grade: $\sigma = 4$ or $\sigma = 8$?

22. For each of the following, identify the exam score that should lead to the better grade. In each case, explain your answer.
   a. A score of $X = 74$ on an exam with $M = 82$ and $\sigma = 8$; or a score of $X = 40$ on an exam with $\mu = 50$ and $\sigma = 20$.
   b. A score of $X = 51$ on an exam with $\mu = 45$ and $\sigma = 2$; or a score of $X = 90$ on an exam with $\mu = 70$ and $\sigma = 20$.
   c. A score of $X = 62$ on an exam with $\mu = 50$ and $\sigma = 8$; or a score of $X = 23$ on an exam with $\mu = 20$ and $\sigma = 2$.

23. A distribution with a mean of $\mu = 38$ and a standard deviation of $\sigma = 5$ is transformed into a standardized distribution with $\mu = 50$ and $\sigma = 10$. Find the new, standardized score for each of the following values from the original population.
   a. $X = 39$
   b. $X = 43$
   c. $X = 35$
   d. $X = 28$

24. A distribution with a mean of $\mu = 76$ and a standard deviation of $\sigma = 12$ is transformed into a standardized distribution with $\mu = 100$ and $\sigma = 20$. Find the new, standardized score for each of the following values from the original population.
   a. $X = 61$
   b. $X = 70$
   c. $X = 85$
   d. $X = 94$

25. A population consists of the following $N = 5$ scores: 0, 6, 4, 3, and 12.
   a. Compute μ and σ for the population.
   b. Find the z-score for each score in the population.
   c. Transform the original population into a new population of $N = 5$ scores with a mean of $\mu = 100$ and a standard deviation of $\sigma = 20$.

26. A sample consists of the following $n = 7$ scores: 5, 0, 4, 5, 1, 2, and 4.
   a. Compute the mean and standard deviation for the sample.
   b. Find the z-score for each score in the sample.
   c. Transform the original sample into a new sample with a mean of $M = 50$ and $s = 10$.

CHAPTER

6

Probability

Tools You Will Need

The following items are considered
essential background material for this
chapter. If you doubt your knowledge
of any of these items, you should
review the appropriate chapter or
section before proceeding.

- Proportions (math review,
  Appendix A)
- Fractions
- Decimals
- Percentages
- Basic algebra (math review,
  Appendix A)
- z-Scores (Chapter 5)

aplia

Aplia for *Essentials of Statistics for the Behavioral Sciences*
After reading, go to "Resources" at the end of this chapter for
an introduction on how to use Aplia's homework and learning
resources.

6.1   INTRODUCTION TO PROBABILITY

In Chapter 1, we introduced the idea that research studies begin with a general question about an entire population, but the actual research is conducted using a sample. In this situation, the role of inferential statistics is to use the sample data as the basis for answering questions about the population. To accomplish this goal, inferential procedures are typically built around the concept of probability. Specifically, the relationships between samples and populations are usually defined in terms of probability.

Suppose, for example, that you are selecting a single marble from a jar that contains 50 black and 50 white marbles. (In this example, the jar of marbles is the *population* and the single marble to be selected is the *sample*.) Although you cannot guarantee the exact outcome of your sample, it is possible to talk about the potential outcomes in terms of probabilities. In this case, you have a 50-50 chance of getting either color. Now consider another jar (population) that has 90 black and only 10 white marbles. Again, you cannot predict the exact outcome of a sample, but now you know that the sample probably will be a black marble. By knowing the makeup of a population, we can determine the probability of obtaining specific samples. In this way, probability gives us a connection between populations and samples, and this connection is the foundation for the inferential statistics that are presented in the chapters that follow.

You may have noticed that the preceding examples begin with a population and then use probability to describe the samples that could be obtained. This is exactly backward from what we want to do with inferential statistics. Remember that the goal of inferential statistics is to begin with a sample and then answer a general question about the population. We reach this goal in a two-stage process. In the first stage, we develop probability as a bridge from populations to samples. This stage involves identifying the types of samples that probably would be obtained from a specific population. Once this bridge is established, we simply reverse the probability rules to allow us to move from samples to populations (Figure 6.1). The process of reversing the probability relationship can be demonstrated by considering again the two jars of marbles we looked at earlier. (Jar 1 has 50 black and 50 white marbles; jar 2 has 90 black and only 10 white marbles.) This time, suppose you are blindfolded when the sample is selected, so you do not know which jar is being used.

FIGURE 6.1

The role of probability in inferential statistics. Probability is used to predict what kind of samples are likely to be obtained from a population. Thus, probability establishes a connection between samples and populations. Inferential statistics rely on this connection when they use sample data as the basis for making conclusions about populations.

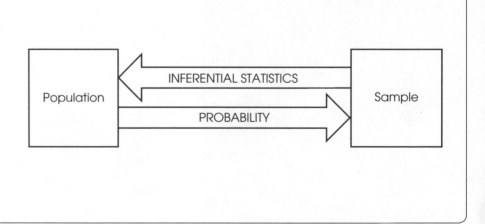

Your task is to look at the sample that you obtain and then decide which jar is most likely. If you select a sample of $n = 4$ marbles and all are black, which jar would you choose? It should be clear that it would be relatively unlikely (low probability) to obtain this sample from jar 1; in four draws, you almost certainly would get at least 1 white marble. On the other hand, this sample would have a high probability of coming from jar 2, where nearly all of the marbles are black. Your decision, therefore, is that the sample probably came from jar 2. Note that you now are using the sample to make an inference about the population.

DEFINING PROBABILITY   Probability is a huge topic that extends far beyond the limits of introductory statistics, and we do not attempt to examine it all here. Instead, we concentrate on the few concepts and definitions that are needed for an introduction to inferential statistics. We begin with a relatively simple definition of probability.

DEFINITION

> For a situation in which several different outcomes are possible, the **probability** for any specific outcome is defined as a fraction or a proportion of all the possible outcomes. If the possible outcomes are identified as A, B, C, D, and so on, then
>
> $$\text{probability of } A = \frac{\text{number of outcomes classified as } A}{\text{total number of possible outcomes}}$$

For example, if you are selecting a card from a complete deck, there are 52 possible outcomes. The probability of selecting the king of hearts is $p = \frac{1}{52}$. The probability of selecting an ace is $p = \frac{4}{52}$ because there are 4 aces in the deck.

To simplify the discussion of probability, we use a notation system that eliminates a lot of the words. The probability of a specific outcome is expressed with a p (for probability) followed by the specific outcome in parentheses. For example, the probability of selecting a king from a deck of cards is written as $p(\text{king})$. The probability of obtaining heads for a coin toss is written as $p(\text{heads})$.

Note that probability is defined as a proportion, or a part of the whole. This definition makes it possible to restate any probability problem as a proportion problem. For example, the probability problem "What is the probability of selecting a king from a deck of cards?" can be restated as "What proportion of the whole deck consists of kings?" In each case, the answer is $\frac{4}{52}$, or "4 out of 52." This translation from probability to proportion may seem trivial now, but it is a great aid when the probability problems become more complex. In most situations, we are concerned with the probability of obtaining a particular sample from a population. The terminology of *sample* and *population* do change the basic definition of probability. For example, the whole deck of cards can be considered as a population, and the single card we select is the sample.

Probability values   The definition we are using identifies probability as a fraction or a proportion. If you work directly from this definition, the probability values you obtain are expressed as fractions. For example, if you are selecting a card at random,

$$p(\text{spade}) = \frac{13}{52} = \frac{1}{4}$$

Or, if you are tossing a coin,

$$p(\text{heads}) = \frac{1}{2}$$

You should be aware that these fractions can be expressed equally well as either decimals or percentages:

$$p = \frac{1}{4} = 0.25 = 25\%$$

$$p = \frac{1}{2} = 0.50 = 50\%$$

If you are unsure of how to convert from fractions to decimals or percentages, you should review the section on proportions in the math review, Appendix A.

By convention, probability values most often are expressed as decimal values. But you should realize that any of these three forms is acceptable.

You also should note that all of the possible probability values are contained in a limited range. At one extreme, when an event never occurs, the probability is zero, or 0%. At the other extreme, when an event always occurs, the probability is 1, or 100%. Thus, all probability values are contained in a range from 0 to 1. For example, suppose that you have a jar containing 10 white marbles. The probability of randomly selecting a black marble is

$$p(\text{black}) = \frac{0}{10} = 0$$

The probability of selecting a white marble is

$$p(\text{white}) = \frac{10}{10} = 1$$

RANDOM SAMPLING

For the preceding definition of probability to be accurate, it is necessary that the outcomes be obtained by a process called *random sampling*.

DEFINITION

> A **simple random sample** requires that each individual in the population has an equal chance of being selected.

A second requirement, necessary for many statistical applications, states that if more than one individual is being selected, the probabilities must stay constant from one selection to the next. Adding this second requirement produces what technically is called *independent random sampling*. The term *independent* refers to the fact that the probability of selecting any particular individual is independent of those individuals who have already been selected for the sample. For example, the probability that you will be selected is constant and does not change even when other individuals are selected before you are.

Because independent random sampling is a fundamental requirement for many statistical applications, we always assume that this is the sampling method being used. To simplify discussion, we typically omit the word "independent" and simply refer to this sampling technique as *random sampling*.

DEFINITIONS

> **Random sampling** requires that each individual has an equal chance of being selected and that the probability of being selected stays constant from one selection to the next if more than one individual is selected. A sample produced by this technique is known as a **random sample**.

Each of the two requirements for random sampling has some interesting consequences. The first ensures that there is no bias in the selection process. For a population with N individuals, each individual must have the same probability, $p = \frac{1}{N}$, of being selected. This means, for example, that you would not get a random sample of people in your city by selecting names from a yacht-club membership list. Similarly, you would not get a random sample of college students by selecting individuals from your psychology classes. You also should note that the first requirement of random sampling prohibits you from applying the definition of probability to situations in which the possible outcomes are not equally likely. Consider, for example, the question of whether you will win a million dollars in the lottery tomorrow. There are only two possible alternatives.

1. You will win.

2. You will not win.

According to our simple definition, the probability of winning would be one out of two, or $p = \frac{1}{2}$. However, the two alternatives are not equally likely, so the simple definition of probability does not apply.

The second requirement also is more interesting than may be apparent at first glance. Consider, for example, the selection of $n = 2$ cards from a complete deck. For the first draw, the probability of obtaining the jack of diamonds is

$$p(\text{jack of diamonds}) = \frac{1}{52}$$

After selecting one card for the sample, you are ready to draw the second card. What is the probability of obtaining the jack of diamonds this time? Assuming that you still are holding the first card, there are two possibilities:

$$p(\text{jack of diamonds}) = \frac{1}{51} \text{ if the first card was not the jack of diamonds}$$

or

$$p(\text{jack of diamonds}) = 0 \text{ if the first card was the jack of diamonds}$$

In either case, the probability is different from its value for the first draw. This contradicts the requirement for random sampling, which says that the probability must stay constant. To keep the probabilities from changing from one selection to the next, it is necessary to return each individual to the population before you make the next selection. This process is called *sampling with replacement.* The second requirement for random samples (constant probability) demands that you sample with replacement.

(*Note:* We are using a definition of random sampling that requires equal chance of selection and constant probabilities. This kind of sampling often is called *random sampling with replacement.* Many of the statistics we encounter later are founded on this kind of sampling. However, you should realize that other definitions exist for the concept of random sampling. In particular, it is very common to define random sampling without the requirement of constant probabilities—that is, *random sampling without replacement.* In addition, there are many different sampling techniques that are used when researchers are selecting individuals to participate in research studies.)

**PROBABILITY
AND FREQUENCY
DISTRIBUTIONS**

The situations in which we are concerned with probability usually involve a population of scores that can be displayed in a frequency distribution graph. If you think of the graph as representing the entire population, then different proportions of the graph represent different proportions of the population. Because probabilities and proportions are equivalent, a particular proportion of the graph corresponds to a particular probability in the population. Thus, whenever a population is presented in a frequency distribution graph, it is possible to represent probabilities as proportions of the graph. The relationship between graphs and probabilities is demonstrated in the following example.

EXAMPLE 6.1   We use a very simple population that contains only $N = 10$ scores with values 1, 1, 2, 3, 3, 4, 4, 4, 5, 6. This population is shown in the frequency distribution graph in Figure 6.2. If you take a random sample of $n = 1$ score from this population, what is the probability of obtaining an individual with a score greater than 4? In probability notation,

$$p(X > 4) = ?$$

Using the definition of probability, there are 2 scores that meet this criterion out of the total group of $N = 10$ scores, so the answer would be $p = \frac{2}{10}$. This answer can be obtained directly from the frequency distribution graph if you recall that probability and proportion measure the same thing. Looking at the graph (see Figure 6.2), what proportion of the population consists of scores greater than 4? The answer is the shaded part of the distribution—that is, 2 squares out of the total of 10 squares in the distribution. Notice that we now are defining probability as a proportion of *area* in the frequency distribution graph. This provides a very concrete and graphic way of representing probability.

Using the same population once again, what is the probability of selecting an individual with a score less than 5? In symbols,

$$p(X < 5) = ?$$

Going directly to the distribution in Figure 6.2, we now want to know what part of the graph is not shaded. The unshaded portion consists of 8 out of the 10 blocks (eight-tenths of the area of the graph), so the answer is $p = \frac{8}{10}$.

FIGURE 6.2

A frequency distribution histogram for a population that consists of $N = 10$ scores. The shaded part of the figure indicates the portion of the whole population that corresponds to scores greater than $X = 4$. The shaded portion is two-tenths ($p = \frac{2}{10}$) of the whole distribution.

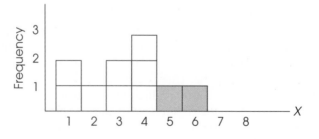

LEARNING CHECK

1. A survey of the students in a psychology class revealed that there were 19 females and 8 males. Of the 19 females, only 4 had no brothers or sisters, and 3 of the males were also the only child in the household. If a student is randomly selected from this class,

   a. What is the probability of obtaining a male?

   b. What is the probability of selecting a student who has at least one brother or sister?

   c. What is the probability of selecting a female who has no siblings?

2. A jar contains 10 red marbles and 30 blue marbles.

   a. If you randomly select 1 marble from the jar, what is the probability of obtaining a red marble?

   b. If you take a *random sample* of $n = 3$ marbles from the jar and the first two marbles are both blue, what is the probability that the third marble will be red?

3. Suppose that you are going to select a random sample of $n = 1$ score from the distribution in Figure 6.2. Find the following probabilities:

   a. $p(X > 2)$ **b.** $p(X > 5)$ **c.** $p(X < 3)$

ANSWERS   1. **a.** $p = \frac{8}{27}$ **b.** $p = \frac{20}{27}$ **c.** $p = \frac{4}{27}$

2. **a.** $p = \frac{10}{40} = 0.25$

   b. $p = \frac{10}{40} = 0.25$. Remember that random sampling requires sampling with replacement.

3. **a.** $p = \frac{7}{10} = 0.70$ **b.** $p = \frac{1}{10} = 0.10$ **c.** $p = \frac{3}{10} = 0.30$

6.2   PROBABILITY AND THE NORMAL DISTRIBUTION

The normal distribution was first introduced in Chapter 2 as an example of a commonly occurring shape for population distributions. An example of a normal distribution is shown in Figure 6.3.

Note that the normal distribution is symmetrical, with the highest frequency in the middle and frequencies tapering off as you move toward either extreme. Although the exact shape for the normal distribution is defined by an equation (see Figure 6.3), the normal shape can also be described by the proportions of area contained in each section of the distribution. Statisticians often identify sections of a normal distribution by using z-scores. Figure 6.4 shows a normal distribution with several sections marked in z-score units. You should recall that z-scores identify locations in a distribution in terms of standard deviations from the mean. For example, $z = +1$ is 1 standard deviation above the mean, $z = +2$ is 2 standard deviations above the mean, and so on. Figure 6.4 shows the percentage of scores that fall in each of these sections for a normal distribution. For example, the section between the mean ($z = 0$) and the point that is 1 standard deviation above the mean ($z = 1$) contains 34.13% of the scores. Similarly, 13.59% of the scores are located in the section between 1 and 2 standard deviations above the mean. In this way it is possible to define a normal distribution in terms of its proportions; that is, a distribution is normal if and only if it has all the right proportions.

There are two additional points to be made about the distribution shown in Figure 6.4. First, you should realize that the sections on the left side of the distribution

FIGURE 6.3

The normal distribution. The exact shape of the normal distribution is specified by an equation relating to each X value (score) with each Y value (frequency). The equation is

$$Y = \frac{1}{\sqrt{2\pi\sigma^2}}\, e^{-(X-\mu)^2/2\sigma^2}$$

(π and e are mathematical constants.) In simpler terms, the normal distribution is symmetrical with a single mode in the middle. The frequency tapers off as you move farther from the middle in either direction.

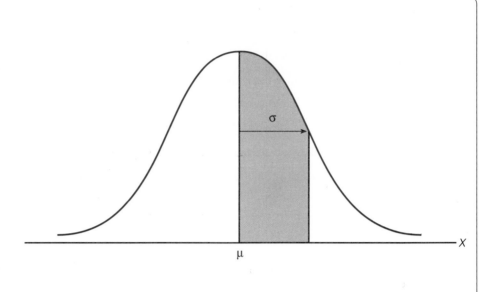

FIGURE 6.4

The normal distribution following a z-score transformation.

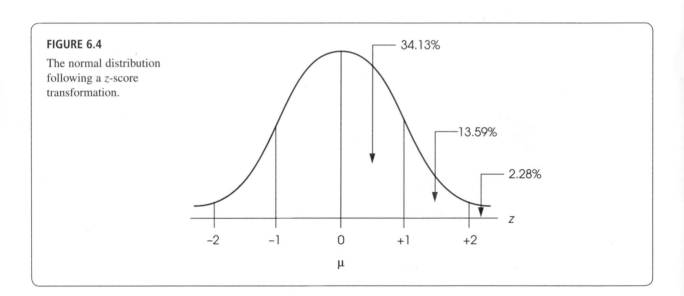

have exactly the same areas as the corresponding sections on the right side because the normal distribution is symmetrical. Second, because the locations in the distribution are identified by z-scores, the percentages shown in the figure apply to *any normal distribution* regardless of the values for the mean and the standard deviation. Remember: When any distribution is transformed into z-scores, the mean becomes zero and the standard deviation becomes one.

Because the normal distribution is a good model for many naturally occurring distributions and because this shape is guaranteed in some circumstances (as we see in Chapter 7), we devote considerable attention to this particular distribution. The process of answering probability questions about a normal distribution is introduced in the following example.

EXAMPLE 6.2 The population distribution of SAT scores is normal with a mean of $\mu = 500$ and a standard deviation of $\sigma = 100$. Given this information about the population and the known proportions for a normal distribution (see Figure 6.4), we can determine the probabilities associated with specific samples. For example, what is the probability of randomly selecting an individual from this population who has an SAT score greater than 700?

Restating this question in probability notation, we get

$$p(X > 700) = ?$$

We follow a step-by-step process to find the answer to this question.

1. First, the probability question is translated into a proportion question: Out of all possible SAT scores, what proportion corresponds to scores greater than 700?

2. The set of "all possible SAT scores" is simply the population distribution. This population is shown in Figure 6.5. The mean is $\mu = 500$, so the score $X = 700$ is to the right of the mean. Because we are interested in all scores greater than 700, we shade in the area to the right of 700. This area represents the proportion we are trying to determine.

3. Identify the exact position of $X = 700$ by computing a z-score. For this example,

$$z = \frac{X - \mu}{\sigma} = \frac{700 - 500}{100} = \frac{200}{100} = 2.00$$

That is, an SAT score of $X = 700$ is exactly 2 standard deviations above the mean and corresponds to a z-score of $z = +2.00$. We have also located this z-score in Figure 6.5.

4. The proportion we are trying to determine may now be expressed in terms of its z-score:

$$p(z > 2.00) = ?$$

FIGURE 6.5

The distribution of SAT scores described in Example 6.2.

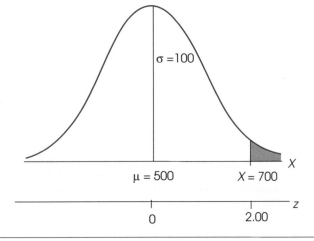

According to the proportions shown in Figure 6.4, all normal distributions, regardless of the values for μ and σ, have 2.28% of the scores in the tail beyond $z = +2.00$. Thus, for the population of SAT scores,

$$p(X > 700) = p(z > +2.00) = 2.28\%$$

THE UNIT NORMAL TABLE

Before we attempt any more probability questions, we must introduce a more useful tool than the graph of the normal distribution shown in Figure 6.4. The graph shows proportions for only a few selected z-score values. A more complete listing of z-scores and proportions is provided in the *unit normal table*. This table lists proportions of the normal distribution for a full range of possible z-score values.

The complete unit normal table is provided in Appendix B Table B.1, and part of the table is reproduced in Figure 6.6. Notice that the table is structured in a four-column format. The first column (A) lists z-score values corresponding to different locations in a

(A) z	(B) Proportion in body	(C) Proportion in tail	(D) Proportion between mean and z	
0.00	.5000	.5000	.0000	
0.01	.5040	.4960	.0040	
0.02	.5080	.4920	.0080	
0.03	.5120	.4880	.0120	
0.21	.5832	.4168	.0832	
0.22	.5871	.4129	.0871	
0.23	.5910	.4090	.0910	
0.24	.5948	.4052	.0948	
0.25	.5987	.4013	.0987	
0.26	.6026	.3974	.1026	
0.27	.6064	.3936	.1064	
0.28	.6103	.3897	.1103	
0.29	.6141	.3859	.1141	
0.30	.6179	.3821	.1179	
0.31	.6217	.3783	.1217	
0.32	.6255	.3745	.1255	
0.33	.6293	.3707	.1293	
0.34	.6331	.3669	.1331	

FIGURE 6.6

A portion of the unit normal table. This table lists proportions of the normal distribution corresponding to each z-score value. Column A of the table lists z-scores. Column B lists the proportion in the body of the normal distribution up to the z-score value. Column C lists the proportion of the normal distribution that is located in the tail of the distribution beyond the z-score value. Column D lists the proportion between the mean and the z-score value.

normal distribution. If you imagine a vertical line drawn through a normal distribution, then the exact location of the line can be described by one of the z-score values listed in column A. You should also realize that a vertical line separates the distribution into two sections: a larger section called the *body* and a smaller section called the *tail*. Columns B and C in the table identify the proportion of the distribution in each of the two sections. Column B presents the proportion in the body (the larger portion), and column C presents the proportion in the tail. Finally, we have added a fourth column, column D, that identifies the proportion of the distribution that is located *between* the mean and the z-score.

We use the distribution in Figure 6.7(a) to demonstrate how the unit normal table can be used to find specific proportions of a normal distribution. The figure shows a normal distribution with a vertical line drawn at z = +0.25. Using the portion of the table shown in Figure 6.6, find the row in the table that contains z = 0.25 in column A. Reading across the row, you should find that the line drawn at z = + 0.25 separates the distribution into two sections with the larger section containing 0.5987 (59.87%) of the distribution and the smaller section containing 0.4013 (40.13%) of the distribution. Also, there is exactly 0.0987 (9.87%) of the distribution between the mean and z = +0.25.

To make full use of the unit normal table, there are a few facts to keep in mind:

1. The *body* always corresponds to the larger part of the distribution whether it is on the right-hand side or the left-hand side. Similarly, the *tail* is always the smaller section whether it is on the right or the left.

2. Because the normal distribution is symmetrical, the proportions on the right-hand side are exactly the same as the corresponding proportions on the left-hand side. Earlier, for example, we used the unit normal table to obtain proportions for z = +0.25. Figure 6.7(b) shows the same proportions for z = −0.25. For a negative z-score, however, notice that the tail of the distribution is on the left side and the body is on the right. For a positive z-score [Figure 6.7(a)], the positions are reversed. However, the proportions in each section are exactly the same, with 0.55987 in the body and 0.4013 in the tail. Once again, the table does not list negative z-score values. To find proportions for negative z-scores, you must look up the corresponding proportions for the positive value of z.

3. Although the z-score values change signs (+ and −) from one side to the other, the proportions are always positive. Thus, column C in the table always lists the proportion in the tail whether it is the right-hand tail or the left-hand tail.

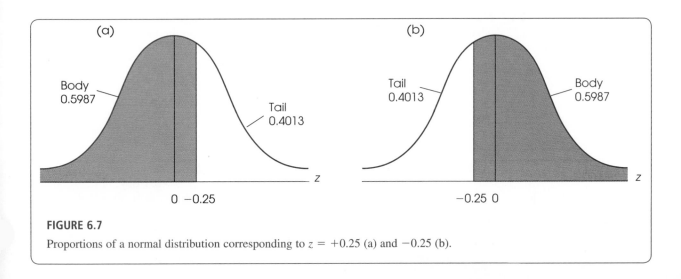

FIGURE 6.7

Proportions of a normal distribution corresponding to z = +0.25 (a) and −0.25 (b).

PROBABILITIES, PROPORTIONS, AND Z-SCORES

The unit normal table lists relationships between z-score locations and proportions in a normal distribution. For any z-score location, you can use the table to look up the corresponding proportions. Similarly, if you know the proportions, you can use the table to find the specific z-score location. Because we have defined probability as equivalent to proportion, you can also use the unit normal table to look up probabilities for normal distributions. The following examples demonstrate a variety of different ways that the unit normal table can be used.

Finding proportions or probabilities for specific z-score values   For each of the following examples, we begin with a specific z-score value and then use the unit normal table to find probabilities or proportions associated with the z-score.

EXAMPLE 6.3A

What proportion of the normal distribution corresponds to z-score values greater than $z = 1.00$? First, you should sketch the distribution and shade in the area you are trying to determine. This is shown in Figure 6.8(a). In this case, the shaded portion is the tail of the distribution beyond $z = 1.00$. To find this shaded area, you simply look for $z = 1.00$ in column A to find the appropriate row in the unit normal table. Then scan across the row to column C (tail) to find the proportion. Using the table in Appendix B, you should find that the answer is 0.1587.

You also should notice that this same problem could have been phrased as a probability question. Specifically, we could have asked, "For a normal distribution, what is the probability of selecting a z-score value greater than $z = +1.00$?" Again, the answer is $p(z > 1.00) = 0.1587$ (or 15.87%).

EXAMPLE 6.3B

For a normal distribution, what is the probability of selecting a z-score less than $z = 1.50$? In symbols, $p(z < 1.50) = ?$ Our goal is to determine what proportion of the normal distribution corresponds to z-scores less than 1.50. A normal distribution is shown in Figure 6.8(b) and $z = 1.50$ is marked in the distribution. Notice that we have shaded all of the values to the left of (less than) $z = 1.50$. This is the portion we are trying to find. Clearly the shaded portion is more than 50%, so it corresponds to the body of the distribution. Therefore, find $z = 1.50$ in column A of the unit normal table and read across the row to obtain the proportion from column B. The answer is $p(z < 1.50) = 0.9332$ (or 93.32%).

EXAMPLE 6.3C

Many problems require that you find proportions for negative z-scores. For example, what proportion of the normal distribution is contained in the tail beyond $z = -0.50$?

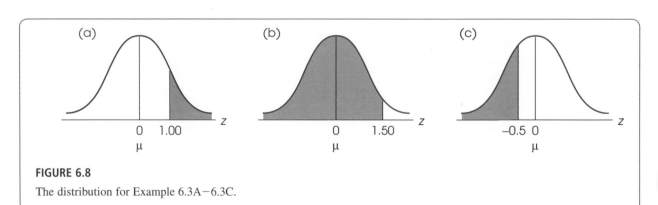

FIGURE 6.8

The distribution for Example 6.3A–6.3C.

Moving to the left on the X-axis results in smaller X values and smaller z-scores. Thus, a z-score of −3.00 reflects a smaller value than a z-score of −1.

That is, $p(z < -0.50)$. This portion has been shaded in Figure 6.8(c). To answer questions with negative z-scores, simply remember that the normal distribution is symmetrical with a z-score of zero at the mean, positive values to the right, and negative values to the left. The proportion in the left tail beyond $z = -0.50$ is identical to the proportion in the right tail beyond $z = +0.50$. To find this proportion, look up $z = 0.50$ in column A, and read across the row to find the proportion in column C (tail). You should get an answer of 0.3085 (30.85%).

Finding the z-score location that corresponds to specific proportions   The preceding examples all involved using a z-score value in column A to look up proportions in column B or C. You should realize, however, that the table also allows you to begin with a known proportion and then look up the corresponding z-score. The following examples demonstrate this process.

EXAMPLE 6.4A   For a normal distribution, what z-score separates the top 10% from the remainder of the distribution? To answer this question, we have sketched a normal distribution [Figure 6.9(a)] and drawn a vertical line that separates the highest 10% (approximately) from the rest. The problem is to find the exact location of this line. For this distribution, we know that the tail contains 0.1000 (10%) and the body contains 0.9000 (90%). To find the z-score value, you simply locate the row in the unit normal table that has 0.1000 in column C or 0.9000 in column B. For example, you can scan down the values in column C (tail) until you find a proportion of 0.1000. Note that you probably will not find the exact proportion, but you can use the closest value listed in the table. For this example, a proportion of 0.1000 is not listed in column C but you can use 0.1003, which is listed. Once you have found the correct proportion in the table, simply read across the row to find the corresponding z-score value in column A.

For this example, the z-score that separates the extreme 10% in the tail is $z = 1.28$. At this point you must be careful because the table does not differentiate between the right-hand tail and the left-hand tail of the distribution. Specifically, the final answer could be either $z = +1.28$, which separates 10% in the right-hand tail, or $z = -1.28$, which separates 10% in the left-hand tail. For this problem, we want the right-hand tail (the highest 10%), so the z-score value is $z = +1.28$.

EXAMPLE 6.4B   For a normal distribution, what z-score values form the boundaries that separate the middle 60% of the distribution from the rest of the scores?

Again, we have sketched a normal distribution [Figure 6.9(b)] and drawn vertical lines so that roughly 60% of the distribution in the central section, with the remainder

FIGURE 6.9

The distributions for Examples 6.4A and 6.4B.

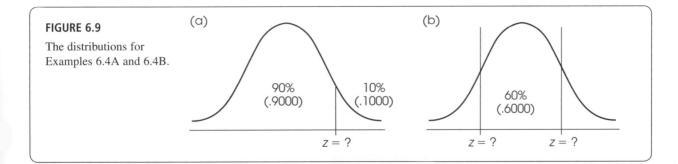

split equally between the two tails. The problem is to find the z-score values that define the exact locations for the lines. To find the z-score values, we begin with the known proportions: 0.6000 in the center and 0.4000 divided equally between the two tails. Although these proportions can be used in several different ways, this example provides an opportunity to demonstrate how column D in the table can be used to solve problems. For this problem, the 0.6000 in the center can be divided in half with exactly 0.3000 to the right of the mean and exactly 0.3000 to the left. Each of these sections corresponds to the proportion listed in column D. Begin by scanning down column D, looking for a value of 0.3000. Again, this exact proportion is not in the table, but the closest value is 0.2995. Reading across the row to column A, you should find a z-score value of $z = 0.84$. Looking again at the sketch [see Figure 6.9(b)], the right-hand line is located at $z = +0.84$ and the left-hand line is located at $z = -0.84$.

You may have noticed that we sketched distributions for each of the preceding problems. As a general rule, you should always sketch a distribution, locate the mean with a vertical line, and shade in the portion that you are trying to determine. Look at your sketch. It will help you to determine which columns to use in the unit normal table. If you make a habit of drawing sketches, you will avoid careless errors when using the table.

LEARNING CHECK

1. Find the proportion of a normal distribution that corresponds to each of the following sections:

   a. $z < 0.25$ **b.** $z > 0.80$ **c.** $z < -1.50$ **d.** $z > -0.75$

2. For a normal distribution, find the z-score location that divides the distribution as follows:

   a. Separate the top 20% from the rest.

   b. Separate the top 60% from the rest.

   c. Separate the middle 70% from the rest.

3. The tail will be on the right-hand side of a normal distribution for any positive z-score. (True or false?)

ANSWERS

1. **a.** $p = 0.5987$ **b.** $p = 0.2119$ **c.** $p = 0.0668$ **d.** $p = 0.7734$

2. **a.** $z = 0.84$ **b.** $z = -0.25$ **c.** $z = -1.04$ and $+1.04$.

3. True

6.3 PROBABILITIES AND PROPORTIONS FOR SCORES FROM A NORMAL DISTRIBUTION

In the preceding section, we used the unit normal table to find probabilities and proportions corresponding to specific z-score values. In most situations, however, it is necessary to find probabilities for specific X values. Consider the following example:

It is known that IQ scores form a normal distribution with $\mu = 100$ and $\sigma = 15$. Given this information, what is the probability of randomly selecting an individual with an IQ score that is less than 120?

This problem is asking for a specific probability or proportion of a normal distribution. However, before we can look up the answer in the unit normal table, we must first transform the IQ scores (X values) into z-scores. Thus, to solve this new kind of probability problem, we must add one new step to the process. Specifically, to answer probability questions about scores (X values) from a normal distribution, you must use the following two-step procedure:

1. Transform the X values into z-scores.

2. Use the unit normal table to look up the proportions corresponding to the z-score values.

Caution: The unit normal table can be used only with normal-shaped distributions. If a distribution is not normal, transforming raw scores to z-scores does not make it normal.

This process is demonstrated in the following examples. Once again, we suggest that you sketch the distribution and shade the portion you are trying to find to avoid careless mistakes.

EXAMPLE 6.5   We now answer the probability question about IQ scores that we presented earlier. Specifically, what is the probability of randomly selecting an individual with an IQ score that is less than 120? Restated in terms of proportions, we want to find the proportion of the IQ distribution that corresponds to scores less than 120. The distribution is drawn in Figure 6.10, and the portion we want has been shaded.

The first step is to change the X values into z-scores. In particular, the score of $X = 120$ is changed to

$$z = \frac{X - \mu}{\sigma} = \frac{120 - 100}{15} = \frac{20}{15} = 1.33$$

Thus, an IQ score of $X = 120$ corresponds to a z-score of $z = 1.33$, and IQ scores less than 120 correspond to z-scores less than 1.33.

Next, look up the z-score value in the unit normal table. Because we want the proportion of the distribution in the body to the left of $X = 120$ (see Figure 6.10), the answer is in column B. First, locate $z = 1.33$ in column A, and then read across the row to find $p = 0.9082$ in column B. Thus, the probability of randomly selecting an individual with an IQ less than 120 is $p = 0.9082$. In symbols,

$$p(X < 120) = p(z < 1.33) = 0.9082 \text{ (or 90.82\%)}$$

FIGURE 6.10

The distribution of IQ scores. The problem is to find the probability or proportion of the distribution corresponding to scores less than 120.

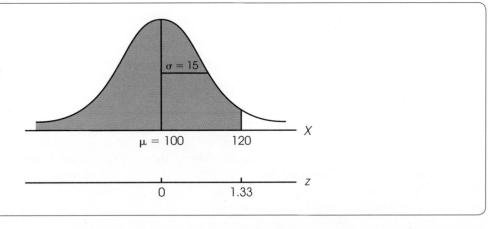

Finally, notice that we phrased this question in terms of a *probability.* Specifically, we asked, "What is the probability of selecting an individual with an IQ less than 120?" However, the same question can be phrased in terms of a *proportion:* "What proportion of all of the individuals in the population have IQ scores that are less than 120?" Both versions ask exactly the same question and produce exactly the same answer. A third alternative for presenting the same question is introduced in Box 6.1.

Finding proportions/probabilities located between two scores   The next example demonstrates the process of finding the probability of selecting a score that is located *between* two specific values. Although these problems can be solved using the proportions of columns B and C (body and tail), they are often easier to solve with the proportions listed in column D.

EXAMPLE 6.6   The highway department conducted a study measuring driving speeds on a local section of interstate highway. They found an average speed of $\mu = 58$ miles per hour with a standard deviation of $\sigma = 10$. The distribution was approximately normal. Given this information, what proportion of the cars are traveling between 55 and 65 miles per hour? Using probability notation, we can express the problem as

$$p(55 < X < 65) = ?$$

The distribution of driving speeds is shown in Figure 6.11 with the appropriate area shaded. The first step is to determine the z-score corresponding to the X value at each end of the interval.

$$\text{For } X = 55: z = \frac{X - \mu}{\sigma} = \frac{55 - 58}{10} = \frac{-3}{10} = -0.30$$

$$\text{For } X = 65: z = \frac{X - \mu}{\sigma} = \frac{65 - 58}{10} = \frac{7}{10} = 0.70$$

BOX 6.1   **PROBABILITIES, PROPORTIONS, AND PERCENTILE RANKS**

Thus far we have discussed parts of distributions in terms of proportions and probabilities. However, there is another set of terminology that deals with many of the same concepts. Specifically, the *percentile rank* for a specific score is defined as the percentage of the individuals in the distribution who have scores that are less than or equal to the specific score. For example, if 70% of the individuals have scores of $X = 45$ or lower, then $X = 45$ has a percentile rank of 70%. When a score is referred to by its percentile rank, the score is called a *percentile.* For example, a score with a percentile rank of 70% is called the 70th percentile.

Using this terminology, it is possible to rephrase some of the probability problems that we have been working. In Example 6.5, the problem is presented as "What is the probability of randomly selecting an individual with an IQ of less than 120?" Exactly the same question could be phrased as "What is the percentile rank for an IQ score of 120?" In each case, we are drawing a line at $X = 120$ and looking for the proportion of the distribution on the left-hand side of the line. Similarly, Example 6.8 asks "How much time do you have to spend commuting each day to be in the highest 10% nationwide?" Because this score separates the top 10% from the bottom 90%, the same question could be rephrased as "What is the 90th percentile for the distribution of commuting times?"

FIGURE 6.11

The distribution for
Example 6.6.

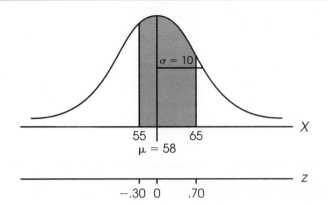

Looking again at Figure 6.11, we see that the proportion we are seeking can be divided into two sections: (1) the area left of the mean, and (2) the area right of the mean. The first area is the proportion between the mean and $z = -0.30$, and the second is the proportion between the mean and $z = +0.70$. Using column D of the unit normal table, these two proportions are 0.1179 and 0.2580. The total proportion is obtained by adding these two sections:

$$p(55 < X < 65) = p(-0.30 < z < +0.70) = 0.1179 + 0.2580 = 0.3759$$

EXAMPLE 6.7 Using the same distribution of driving speeds from the previous example, what proportion of cars are traveling between 65 and 75 miles per hour?

$$p(65 < X < 75) = ?$$

The distribution is shown in Figure 6.12 with the appropriate area shaded. Again, we start by determining the z-score corresponding to each end of the interval.

$$\text{For } X = 65: z = \frac{X - \mu}{\sigma} = \frac{65 - 58}{10} = \frac{7}{10} = 0.70$$

$$\text{For } X = 75: z = \frac{X - \mu}{\sigma} = \frac{75 - 58}{10} = \frac{17}{10} = 1.70$$

FIGURE 6.12

The distribution for
Example 6.7.

There are several different ways to use the unit normal table to find the proportion between these two z-scores. For this example, we use the proportions in the tail of the distribution (column C). According to column C in the unit normal table, the proportion in the tail beyond $z = 0.70$ is $p = 0.2420$. Note that this proportion includes the section that we want, but it also includes an extra, unwanted section located in the tail beyond $z = 1.70$. Locating $z = 1.70$ in the table, and reading across the row to column C, we see that the unwanted section is $p = 0.0446$. To obtain the correct answer, we subtract the unwanted portion from the total proportion in the tail beyond $z = 0.70$.

$$p(65 < X < 75) = p(0.70 < z < 1.70) = 0.2420 - 0.0446 = 0.1974$$

Finding scores corresponding to specific proportions or probabilities   In the previous three examples, the problem was to find the proportion or probability corresponding to specific X values. The two-step process for finding these proportions is shown in Figure 6.13. Thus far, we have only considered examples that move in a clockwise direction around the triangle shown in the figure; that is, we start with an X value that is transformed into a z-score, and then we use the unit normal table to look up the appropriate proportion. You should realize, however, that it is possible to reverse this two-step process so that we move counterclockwise around the triangle. This reverse process allows us to find the score (X value) corresponding to a specific proportion in the distribution. Following the lines in Figure 6.13, we begin with a specific proportion, use the unit normal table to look up the corresponding z-score, and then transform the z-score into an X value. The following example demonstrates this process.

EXAMPLE   6.8   The U.S. Census Bureau (2005) reports that Americans spend an average of $\mu = 24.3$ minutes commuting to work each day. Assuming that the distribution of commuting times is normal with a standard deviation of $\sigma = 10$ minutes, how much time do you have to spend commuting each day to be in the highest 10% nationwide? (An alternative form of the same question is presented in Box 6.1.) The distribution is shown in Figure 6.14 with a portion representing approximately 10% shaded in the right-hand tail.

In this problem, we begin with a proportion (10% or 0.10), and we are looking for a score. According to the map in Figure 6.13, we can move from p (proportion) to X (score) via z-scores. The first step is to use the unit normal table to

---

FIGURE 6.13

Determining probabilities or proportions for a normal distribution is shown as a two-step process with z-scores as an intermediate stop along the way. Note that you cannot move directly along the dashed line between X values and probabilities or proportions. Instead, you must follow the solid lines around the corner.

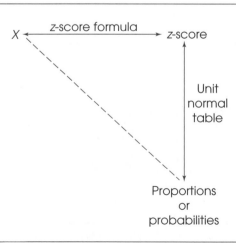

FIGURE 6.14

The distribution of commuting times for American workers. The problem is to find the score that separates the highest 10% of commuting times from the rest.

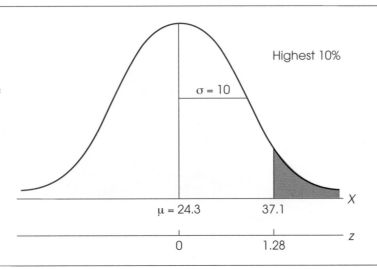

find the z-score that corresponds to a proportion of 0.10 in the tail. First, scan the values in column C to locate the row that has a proportion of 0.10 in the tail of the distribution. Note that you will not find 0.1000 exactly, but locate the closest value possible. In this case, the closest value is 0.1003. Reading across the row, we find $z = 1.28$ in column A.

The next step is to determine whether the z-score is positive or negative. Remember that the table does not specify the sign of the z-score. Looking at the distribution in Figure 6.14, you should realize that the score we want is above the mean, so the z-score is positive, $z = +1.28$.

The final step is to transform the z-score into an X value. By definition, a z-score of $+1.28$ corresponds to a score that is located above the mean by 1.28 standard deviations. One standard deviation is equal to 10 points ($\sigma = 10$), so 1.28 standard deviations is

$$1.28\sigma = 1.28(10) = 12.8 \text{ points}$$

Thus, our score is located above the mean ($\mu = 24.3$) by a distance of 12.8 points. Therefore,

$$X = 24.3 + 12.8 = 37.1$$

The answer for our original question is that you must commute at least 37.1 minutes a day to be in the top 10% of American commuters.

EXAMPLE 6.9   Again, the distribution of commuting time for American workers is normal with a mean of $\mu = 24.3$ minutes and a standard deviation of $\sigma = 10$ minutes. For this example, we find the range of values that defines the middle 90% of the distribution. The entire distribution is shown in Figure 6.15 with the middle portion shaded.

The 90% (0.9000) in the middle of the distribution can be split in half with 45% (0.4500) on each side of the mean. Looking up 0.4500, in column D of the unit normal table, you will find that the exact proportion is not listed. However, you will find 0.4495 and 0.4505, which are equally close. Technically, either value is acceptable, but we use

FIGURE 6.15

The distribution of commuting times for American workers. The problem is to find the middle 90% of the distribution.

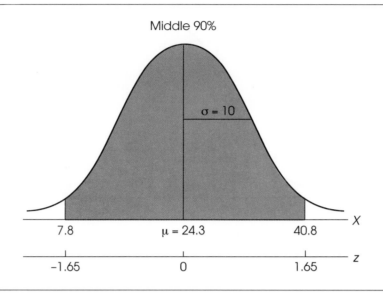

0.4505 so that the total area in the middle is at least 90%. Reading across the row, you should find a z-score of $z = 1.65$ in column A. Thus, the z-score at the right boundary is $z = +1.65$ and the z-score at the left boundary is $z = -1.65$. In either case, a z-score of 1.65 indicates a location that is 1.65 standard deviations away from the mean. For the distribution of commuting times, one standard deviation is $\sigma = 10$, so 1.65 standard deviations is a distance of

$$1.65\sigma = 1.65(10) = 16.5 \text{ points}$$

Therefore, the score at the right-hand boundary is located above the mean by 16.5 points and corresponds to $X = 24.3 + 16.5 = 40.8$. Similarly, the score at the left-hand boundary is below the mean by 16.5 points and corresponds to $X = 24.3 - 16.5 = 7.8$. The middle 90% of the distribution corresponds to values between 7.8 and 40.8. Thus, 90% of American commuters spend between 7.8 and 40.8 minutes commuting to work each day. Only 10% of commuters spend either more time or less time.

LEARNING CHECK

1. For a normal distribution with a mean of $\mu = 60$ and a standard deviation of $\sigma = 12$, find each probability value requested.

   a. $p(X > 66)$ **b.** $p(X < 75)$ **c.** $p(X < 57)$ **d.** $p(48 < X < 72)$

2. Scores on the Mathematics section of the SAT Reasoning Test form a normal distribution with a mean of $\mu = 500$ and a standard deviation of $\sigma = 100$.

   a. If the state college only accepts students who score in the top 60% on this test, what is the minimum score needed for admission?

   b. What is the minimum score necessary to be in the top 10% of the distribution?

   c. What scores form the boundaries for the middle 50% of the distribution?

3. What is the probability of selecting a score greater than 45 from a positively skewed distribution with $\mu = 40$ and $\sigma = 10$? (Be careful.)

ANSWERS   **1. a.** $p = 0.3085$ **b.** $p = 0.8944$ **c.** $p = 0.4013$ **d.** $p = 0.6826$

   2. a. $z = -0.25; X = 475$

   b. $z = 1.28; X = 628$

   c. $z = \pm 0.67; X = 433$ and $X = 567$

   3. You cannot obtain the answer. The unit normal table cannot be used to answer this question because the distribution is not normal.

6.4   LOOKING AHEAD TO INFERENTIAL STATISTICS

Probability forms a direct link between samples and the populations from which they come. As we noted at the beginning of this chapter, this link is the foundation for the inferential statistics in future chapters. The following example provides a brief preview of how probability is used in the context of inferential statistics.

We ended Chapter 5 with a demonstration of how inferential statistics are used to help interpret the results of a research study. A general research situation was shown in Figure 5.9 and is repeated here in Figure 6.16. The research begins with a population that forms a normal distribution with a mean of $\mu = 400$ and a standard deviation of $\sigma = 20$. A sample is selected from the population and a treatment is administered to the sample. The goal for the study is to evaluate the effect of the treatment.

To determine whether the treatment has an effect, the researcher simply compares the treated sample with the original population. If the individuals in the sample have scores around 400 (the original population mean), then we must conclude that the treatment appears to have no effect. On the other hand, if the treated individuals have scores that are noticeably different from 400, then the researcher has evidence that the treatment does have an effect. Notice that the study is using

FIGURE 6.16

A diagram of a research study. A sample is selected from the population and receives a treatment. The goal is to determine whether the treatment has an effect.

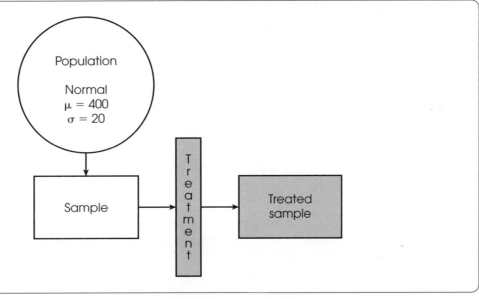

a sample to help answer a question about a population; this is the essence of inferential statistics.

The problem for the researcher is determining exactly what is meant by "noticeably different" from 400. If a treated individual has a score of $X = 415$, is that enough to say that the treatment has an effect? What about $X = 420$ or $X = 450$? In Chapter 5, we suggested that z-scores provide one method for solving this problem. Specifically, we suggested that a z-score value beyond $z = 2.00$ (or -2.00) was an extreme value and, therefore, noticeably different. However, the choice of $z = \pm2.00$ was purely arbitrary. Now we have another tool, *probability,* to help us decide exactly where to set the boundaries. Specifically, we can determine exactly which samples have a high probability of being selected and which are extremely unlikely. For example, we can set the boundaries to separate the most likely 95% of the samples in the middle of the distribution from the extremely unlikely 5% in the tails.

Figure 6.17 shows the original population from our hypothetical research study. Note that most of the scores are located close to $\mu = 400$. Also note that we have added boundaries separating the middle 95% of the distribution from the extreme 5%, or 0.0500, in the two tails. Dividing the 0.0500 in half produces proportions of 0.0250 in the right-hand tail and 0.0250 in the left-hand tail. Using column C of the unit normal table, the z-score boundaries for the right and left tails are $z = +1.96$ and $z = -1.96$, respectively.

The boundaries set at $z = \pm1.96$ provide objective criteria for deciding whether the treated sample is noticeably different from the original population. Specifically, any sample that is beyond the ±1.96 boundaries is an extreme value and is extremely unlikely to occur ($p = 0.05$ or less) if the treatment has no effect. Therefore, this kind of sample provides convincing evidence that the treatment really does have an effect.

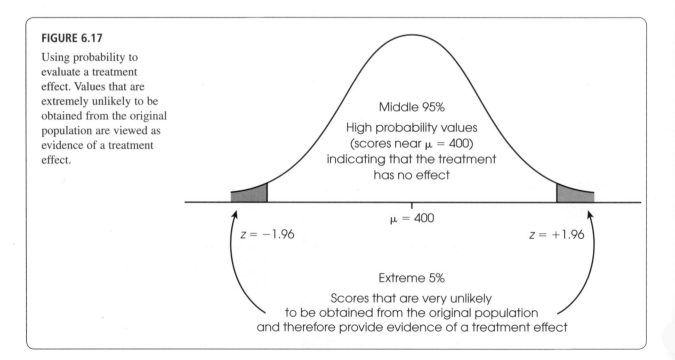

FIGURE 6.17

Using probability to evaluate a treatment effect. Values that are extremely unlikely to be obtained from the original population are viewed as evidence of a treatment effect.

Middle 95%
High probability values
(scores near $\mu = 400$)
indicating that the treatment
has no effect

$\mu = 400$

$z = -1.96$

$z = +1.96$

Extreme 5%
Scores that are very unlikely
to be obtained from the original population
and therefore provide evidence of a treatment effect

SUMMARY

1. The probability of a particular event A is defined as a fraction or proportion:

$$p(A) = \frac{\text{number of outcomes classified as } A}{\text{total number of possible outcomes}}$$

2. Our definition of probability is accurate only for random samples. There are two requirements that must be satisfied for a random sample:
   a. Every individual in the population has an equal chance of being selected.
   b. When more than one individual is being selected, the probabilities must stay constant. This means that there must be sampling with replacement.

3. All probability problems can be restated as proportion problems. The "probability of selecting a king from a deck of cards" is equivalent to the "proportion of the deck that consists of kings." For frequency distributions, probability questions can be answered by determining proportions of area. The "probability of selecting an individual with an IQ greater than 108" is equivalent to the "proportion of the whole population that consists of IQs greater than 108."

4. For normal distributions, probabilities (proportions) can be found in the unit normal table. The table provides a listing of the proportions of a normal distribution that correspond to each z-score value. With the table, it is possible to move between X values and probabilities using a two-step procedure:
   a. The z-score formula (Chapter 5) allows you to transform X to z or to change z back to X.
   b. The unit normal table allows you to look up the probability (proportion) corresponding to each z-score or the z-score corresponding to each probability.

5. Percentiles and percentile ranks measure the relative standing of a score within a distribution (see Box 6.1). Percentile rank is the percentage of individuals with scores at or below a particular X value. A percentile is an X value that is identified by its rank. The percentile rank always corresponds to the proportion to the left of the score in question.

KEY TERMS

probability (151)

random sample (152)

independent random sample (152)

sampling with replacement (153)

unit normal table (158)

percentile rank (164)

percentile (164)

RESOURCES

 Go to CengageBrain.com to access Psychology CourseMate, where you will find an interactive eBook, glossaries, flashcards, quizzes, statistics workshops, and more.

aplia

If your professor has assigned Aplia:
1. Sign in to your account.
2. Complete the corresponding exercises as required by your professor.
3. When finished, click "Grade It Now" to see which areas you have mastered, which areas need more work, and detailed explanations of every answer.

The statistics computer package SPSS is not structured to compute probabilities. However, the program does report probability values as part of the inferential statistics that we examine later in this book. In the context of inferential statistics, the probabilities are called *significance levels,* and they warn researchers about the probability of misinterpreting their research results.

FOCUS ON PROBLEM SOLVING

1. We have defined probability as being equivalent to a proportion, which means that you can restate every probability problem as a proportion problem. This definition is particularly useful when you are working with frequency distribution graphs in which the population is represented by the whole graph and probabilities (proportions) are represented by portions of the graph. When working problems with the normal distribution, you always should start with a sketch of the distribution. You should shade the portion of the graph that reflects the proportion you are looking for.

2. Remember that the unit normal table shows only positive z-scores in column A. However, because the normal distribution is symmetrical, the proportions in the table apply to both positive and negative z-score values.

3. A common error for students is to use negative values for proportions on the left-hand side of the normal distribution. Proportions (or probabilities) are always positive: 10% is 10% whether it is in the left or right tail of the distribution.

4. The proportions in the unit normal table are accurate only for normal distributions. If a distribution is not normal, you cannot use the table.

DEMONSTRATION 6.1

FINDING PROBABILITY FROM THE UNIT NORMAL TABLE

A population is normally distributed with a mean of $\mu = 45$ and a standard deviation of $\sigma = 4$. What is the probability of randomly selecting a score that is greater than 43? In other words, what proportion of the distribution consists of scores greater than 43?

STEP 1 Sketch the distribution.   For this demonstration, the distribution is normal with $\mu = 45$ and $\sigma = 4$. The score of $X = 43$ is lower than the mean and therefore is placed to the left of the mean. The question asks for the proportion corresponding to scores greater than 43, so shade in the area to the right of this score. Figure 6.18 shows the sketch.

STEP 2 Transform the X value to a z-score.

$$z = \frac{X - \mu}{\sigma} = \frac{43 - 45}{4} = \frac{-2}{4} = -0.5$$

FIGURE 6.18

A sketch of the distribution for Demonstration 6.1.

STEP 3   Find the appropriate proportion in the unit normal table. Ignoring the negative size, locate $z = -0.50$ in column A. In this case, the proportion we want corresponds to the body of the distribution and the value is found in column B. For this example,

$$p(X > 43) = p(z > -0.50) = 0.6915$$

PROBLEMS

1. A local hardware store has a "Savings Wheel" at the checkout. Customers get to spin the wheel and, when the wheel stops, a pointer indicates how much they will save. The wheel can stop in any one of 50 sections. Of the sections, 10 produce 0% off, 20 sections are for 10% off, 10 sections for 20%, 5 for 30%, 3 for 40%, 1 for 50%, and 1 for 100% off. Assuming that all 50 sections are equally likely,
   a. What is the probability that a customer's purchase will be free (100% off)?
   b. What is the probability that a customer will get no savings from the wheel (0% off)?
   c. What is the probability that a customer will get at least 20% off?

2. A psychology class consists of 14 males and 36 females. If the professor selects names from the class list using *random sampling,*
   a. What is the probability that the first student selected will be a female?
   b. If a random sample of $n = 3$ students is selected and the first two are both females, what is the probability that the third student selected will be a male?

3. What are the two requirements that must be satisfied for a random sample?

4. Draw a vertical line through a normal distribution for each of the following z-score locations. Determine whether the tail is on the right or left side of the line and find the proportion in the tail.
   a. $z = 1.00$
   b. $z = 0.50$
   c. $z = -1.25$
   d. $z = -0.40$

5. Draw a vertical line through a normal distribution for each of the following z-score locations. Determine whether the body is on the right or left side of the line and find the proportion in the body.
   a. $z = 2.50$
   b. $z = 0.80$
   c. $z = -0.50$
   d. $z = -0.77$

6. Find each of the following probabilities for a normal distribution.
   a. $p(z > 1.25)$
   b. $p(z > -0.60)$
   c. $p(z < 0.70)$
   d. $p(z < -1.30)$

7. What proportion of a normal distribution is located between each of the following z-score boundaries?
   a. $z = -0.25$ and $z = +0.25$
   b. $z = -0.67$ and $z = +0.67$
   c. $z = -1.20$ and $z = +1.20$

8. Find each of the following probabilities for a normal distribution.
   a. $p(-0.80 < z < 0.80)$
   b. $p(-0.50 < z < 1.00)$
   c. $p(0.20 < z < 1.50)$
   d. $p(-1.20 < z < -0.80)$

9. Find the z-score location of a vertical line that separates a normal distribution as described in each of the following.
   a. 5% in the tail on the left
   b. 30% in the tail on the right
   c. 65% in the body on the left
   d. 80% in the body on the right

10. Find the z-score boundaries that separate a normal distribution as described in each of the following.
   a. The middle 30% from the 70% in the tails.
   b. The middle 40% from the 60% in the tails.
   c. The middle 50% from the 50% in the tails.
   d. The middle 60% from the 40% in the tails.

11. A normal distribution has a mean of $\mu = 70$ and a standard deviation of $\sigma = 8$. For each of the following scores, indicate whether the tail is to the right or left of the score and find the proportion of the distribution located in the tail.
   a. $X = 72$
   b. $X = 76$
   c. $X = 66$
   d. $X = 60$

12. A normal distribution has a mean of $\mu = 30$ and a standard deviation of $\sigma = 12$. For each of the following scores, indicate whether the body is to the right or left of the score and find the proportion of the distribution located in the body.
   a. $X = 33$
   b. $X = 18$
   c. $X = 24$
   d. $X = 39$

13. For a normal distribution with a mean of $\mu = 60$ and a standard deviation of $\sigma = 10$, find the proportion of the population corresponding to each of the following.
   a. Scores greater than 65.
   b. Scores less than 68.
   c. Scores between 50 and 70.

14. IQ test scores are standardized to produce a normal distribution with a mean of $\mu = 100$ and a standard deviation of $\sigma = 15$. Find the proportion of the population in each of the following IQ categories.
   a. Genius or near genius: IQ greater than 140
   b. Very superior intelligence: IQ between 120 and 140
   c. Average or normal intelligence: IQ between 90 and 109

15. The distribution of SAT scores is normal with $\mu = 500$ and $\sigma = 100$.
   a. What SAT score, X value, separates the top 15% of the distribution from the rest?
   b. What SAT score, X value, separates the top 10% of the distribution from the rest?
   c. What SAT score, X value, separates the top 2% of the distribution from the rest?

16. According to a recent report, people smile an average of $\mu = 62$ time per day. Assuming that the distribution of smiles is approximately normal with a standard deviation of $\sigma = 18$, find each of the following values.
   a. What proportion of people smile more than 80 times a day?
   b. What proportion of people smile at least 50 times a day?

17. A recent newspaper article reported the results of a survey of well-educated suburban parents. The responses to one question indicated that by age 2, children were watching an average of $\mu = 60$ minutes of television each day. Assuming that the distribution of television-watching times is normal with a standard deviation of $\sigma = 25$ minutes, find each of the following proportions.
   a. What proportion of 2-year-old children watch more than 90 minutes of television each day?
   b. What proportion of 2-year-old children watch less than 20 minutes a day?

18. Information from the Department of Motor Vehicles indicates that the average age of licensed drivers is $\mu = 45.7$ years with a standard deviation of $\sigma = 12.5$ years. Assuming that the distribution of drivers' ages is approximately normal,
   a. What proportion of licensed drivers are older than 50 years old?
   b. What proportion of licensed drivers are younger than 30 years old?

19. A consumer survey indicates that the average household spends $\mu = \$185$ on groceries each week. The distribution of spending amounts is approximately normal with a standard deviation of $\sigma = \$25$. Based on this distribution,
   a. What proportion of the population spends more than $200 per week on groceries?
   b. What is the probability of randomly selecting a family that spends less than $150 per week on groceries?
   c. How much money do you need to spend on groceries each week to be in the top 20% of the distribution?

20. A report in 2010 indicates that Americans between the ages of 8 and 18 spend an average of $\mu = 7.5$ hours per day using some sort of electronic device such as smart phones, computers, or tablets. Assume that the distribution of times is normal with a standard deviation of $\sigma = 2.5$ hours and find the following values.
   a. What is the probability of selecting an individual who uses electronic devices more than 12 hours a day?
   b. What proportion of 8- to 18-year-old Americans spend between 5 and 10 hours per day using electronic devices? In symbols, $p(5 < X < 10) = ?$

21. Rochester, New York, averages $\mu = 21.9$ inches of snow for the month of December. The distribution of snowfall amounts is approximately normal with a standard deviation of $\sigma = 6.5$ inches. This year, a local jewelry store is advertising a refund of 50% off of all purchases made in December, if Rochester finishes the month with more than 3 feet (36 inches) of total snowfall. What is the probability that the jewelry store will have to pay off on its promise?

CHAPTER

7

Tools You Will Need

The following items are considered essential background material for this chapter. If you doubt your knowledge of any of these items, you should review the appropriate chapter or section before proceeding.

- Random sampling (Chapter 6)
- Probability and the normal distribution (Chapter 6)
- z-Scores (Chapter 5)

Probability and Samples: The Distribution of Sample Means

aplia

Aplia for *Essentials of Statistics for the Behavioral Sciences*
After reading, go to "Resources" at the end of this chapter for an introduction on how to use Aplia's homework and learning resources.

7.1   SAMPLES AND POPULATIONS

The preceding two chapters presented the topics of z-scores and probability. Whenever a score is selected from a population, you should be able to compute a z-score that describes exactly where the score is located in the distribution. If the population is normal, you also should be able to determine the probability value for obtaining any individual score. In a normal distribution, for example, any score located in the tail of the distribution beyond $z = +2.00$ is an extreme value, and a score this large has a probability of only $p = 0.0228$.

However, the z-scores and probabilities that we have considered so far are limited to situations in which the sample consists of a single score. Most research studies involve much larger samples, such as $n = 25$ preschool children or $n = 100$ American Idol contestants. In these situations, the sample mean, rather than a single score, is used to answer questions about the population. In this chapter, we extend the concepts of z-scores and probability to cover situations with larger samples. In particular, we introduce a procedure for transforming a sample mean into a z-score. Thus, a researcher is able to compute a z-score that describes an entire sample. As always, a z-score near zero indicates a central, representative sample; a z-score beyond $+2.00$ or -2.00 indicates an extreme sample. Thus, it is possible to describe how any specific sample is related to all the other possible samples. In addition, we can use the z-scores to look up probabilities for obtaining certain samples, no matter how many scores the sample contains.

In general, the difficulty of working with samples is that a sample provides an incomplete picture of the population. Suppose, for example, a researcher randomly selects a sample of $n = 25$ students from the state college. Although the sample should be representative of the entire student population, there are almost certainly some segments of the population that are not included in the sample. In addition, any statistics that are computed for the sample are not identical to the corresponding parameters for the entire population. For example, the average IQ for the sample of 25 students is not the same as the overall mean IQ for the entire population. This difference, or *error,* between sample statistics and the corresponding population parameters is called *sampling error* and was illustrated in Figure 1.2 (p. 9).

D E F I N I T I O N

Sampling error is the natural discrepancy, or amount of error, between a sample statistic and its corresponding population parameter.

Furthermore, samples are variable; they are not all the same. If you take two separate samples from the same population, the samples are different. They contain different individuals, they have different scores, and they have different sample means. How can you tell which sample gives the best description of the population? Can you even predict how well a sample describes its population? What is the probability of selecting a sample with specific characteristics? These questions can be answered once we establish the rules that relate samples and populations.

7.2   THE DISTRIBUTION OF SAMPLE MEANS

As noted, two separate samples probably are different even though they are taken from the same population. The samples have different individuals, different scores, different means, and so on. In most cases, it is possible to obtain thousands of different samples from one population. With all these different samples coming from the same population, it may seem hopeless to try to establish some simple rules for the relationships between samples and populations. Fortunately, however, the huge set of possible samples forms a relatively simple and orderly pattern that makes it possible to predict the characteristics of a sample with some accuracy. The ability to predict sample characteristics is based on the *distribution of sample means*.

DEFINITION

> The **distribution of sample means** is the collection of sample means for all of the possible random samples of a particular size (n) that can be obtained from a population.

Notice that the distribution of sample means contains *all of the possible samples*. It is necessary to have all of the possible values to compute probabilities. For example, if the entire set contains exactly 100 samples, then the probability of obtaining any specific sample is 1 out of 100: $p = \frac{1}{100}$ (Box 7.1).

Also, you should notice that the distribution of sample means is different from the distributions that we have considered before. Until now we always have discussed distributions of scores; now the values in the distribution are not scores, but statistics (sample means). Because statistics are obtained from samples, a distribution of statistics is referred to as a *sampling distribution*.

DEFINITION

> A **sampling distribution** is a distribution of statistics obtained by selecting all of the possible samples of a specific size from a population.

Thus, the distribution of sample means is an example of a sampling distribution. In fact, it often is called the sampling distribution of M.

If you actually wanted to construct the distribution of sample means, you would first select a random sample of a specific size (n) from a population, calculate the sample mean, and place the sample mean in a frequency distribution. Then you would select another random sample with the same number of scores. Again, you would calculate the sample mean and add it to your distribution. You would continue selecting samples and calculating means, over and over, until you had the complete set of all the possible

---

BOX 7.1   **PROBABILITY AND THE DISTRIBUTION OF SAMPLE MEANS**

I have a bad habit of losing playing cards. This habit is compounded by the fact that I always save the old deck in the hope that someday I will find the missing cards. As a result, I have a drawer filled with partial decks of playing cards. Suppose that I take one of these almost-complete decks, shuffle the cards carefully, and then randomly select one card. What is the probability that I will draw a king?

You should realize that it is impossible to answer this probability question. To find the probability of selecting a king, you must know how many cards are in the deck and exactly which cards are missing. (It is crucial that you know whether any kings are missing.) The point of this simple example is that any probability question requires that you have complete information about the population from which the sample is being selected. In this case, you must know all of the possible cards in the deck before you can find the probability for selecting any specific card.

In this chapter, we are examining probability and sample means. To find the probability for any specific sample mean, you first must know *all of the possible sample means*. Therefore, we begin by defining and describing the set of all possible sample means that can be obtained from a particular population. Once we have specified the complete set of all possible sample means (i.e., the distribution of sample means), we can find the probability of selecting any specific sample mean.

random samples. At this point, your frequency distribution would show the distribution of sample means.

We demonstrate the process of constructing a distribution of sample means in Example 7.1, but first we use common sense and a little logic to predict the general characteristics of the distribution.

1. The sample means should pile up around the population mean. Samples are not expected to be perfect but they are representative of the population. As a result, most of the sample means should be relatively close to the population mean.

2. The pile of sample means should tend to form a normal-shaped distribution. Logically, most of the samples should have means close to μ, and it should be relatively rare to find sample means that are substantially different from μ. As a result, the sample means should pile up in the center of the distribution (around μ) and the frequencies should taper off as the distance between M and μ increases. This describes a normal-shaped distribution.

3. In general, the larger the sample size, the closer the sample means should be to the population mean, μ. Logically, a large sample should be a better representative than a small sample. Thus, the sample means obtained with a large sample size should cluster relatively close to the population mean; the means obtained from small samples should be more widely scattered.

As you will see, each of these three commonsense characteristics is an accurate description of the distribution of sample means. The following example demonstrates the process of constructing the distribution of sample means by repeatedly selecting samples from a population.

EXAMPLE 7.1

Remember that random sampling requires sampling with replacement.

Consider a population that consists of only 4 scores: 2, 4, 6, 8. This population is pictured in the frequency distribution histogram in Figure 7.1.

We are going to use this population as the basis for constructing the distribution of sample means for $n = 2$. Remember: This distribution is the collection of sample means from all of the possible random samples of $n = 2$ from this population. We begin by looking at all of the possible samples. For this example, there are 16 different samples, and they are all listed in Table 7.1. Notice that the samples are listed systematically. First, we list all of the possible samples with $X = 2$ as the first score, then all of the possible samples with $X = 4$ as the first score, and so on. In this way, we can be sure that we have all of the possible random samples.

Next, we compute the mean, M, for each of the 16 samples (see the last column of Table 7.1). The 16 means are then placed in a frequency distribution histogram in Figure 7.2.

FIGURE 7.1

Frequency distribution histogram for a population of 4 scores: 2, 4, 6, 8.

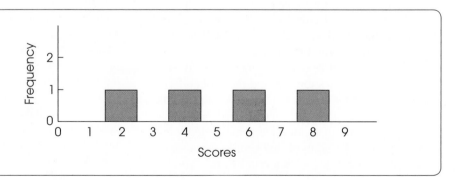

TABLE 7.1

All the possible samples of $n = 2$ scores that can be obtained from the population presented in Figure 7.1. Notice that the table lists *random samples*. This requires sampling with replacement, so it is possible to select the same score twice.

| Sample | Scores | | Sample Mean |
	First	Second	(M)
1	2	2	2
2	2	4	3
3	2	6	4
4	2	8	5
5	4	2	3
6	4	4	4
7	4	6	5
8	4	8	6
9	6	2	4
10	6	4	5
11	6	6	6
12	6	8	7
13	8	2	5
14	8	4	6
15	8	6	7
16	8	8	8

FIGURE 7.2

The distribution of sample means for $n = 2$. The distribution shows the 16 sample means from Table 7.1.

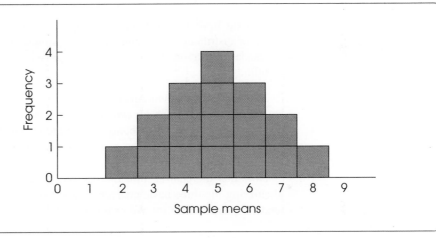

This is the distribution of sample means. Note that the distribution in Figure 7.2 demonstrates two of the characteristics that we predicted for the distribution of sample means.

1. The sample means pile up around the population mean. For this example, the population mean is $\mu = 5$, and the sample means are clustered around a value of 5. It should not surprise you that the sample means tend to approximate the population mean. After all, samples are supposed to be representative of the population.

2. The distribution of sample means is roughly normal in shape. This is a characteristic that is discussed in detail later and is extremely useful because we already know a great deal about probabilities and the normal distribution (Chapter 6).

Remember that our goal in this chapter is to answer probability questions about samples with $n > 1$.

Finally, you should notice that we can use the distribution of sample means to answer probability questions about sample means. For example, if you take a sample of $n = 2$ scores from the original population, what is the probability of obtaining a sample mean greater than 7? In symbols,

$$p(M > 7) = ?$$

Because probability is equivalent to proportion, the probability question can be restated as follows: Of all of the possible sample means, what proportion have values greater than 7? In this form, the question is easily answered by looking at the distribution of sample means. All of the possible sample means are pictured (see Figure 7.2), and only 1 out of the 16 means has a value greater than 7. The answer, therefore, is 1 out of 16, or $p = \frac{1}{16}$.

THE CENTRAL LIMIT THEOREM

Example 7.1 demonstrated the construction of the distribution of sample means for an overly simplified situation with a very small population and samples that each contain only $n = 2$ scores. In more realistic circumstances, with larger populations and larger samples, the number of possible samples increases dramatically and it is virtually impossible to actually obtain every possible random sample. Fortunately, it is possible to determine exactly what the distribution of sample means looks like without taking hundreds or thousands of samples. Specifically, a mathematical proposition known as the *central limit theorem* provides a precise description of the distribution that would be obtained if you selected every possible sample, calculated every sample mean, and constructed the distribution of the sample mean. This important and useful theorem serves as a cornerstone for much of inferential statistics. Following is the essence of the theorem.

> **Central limit theorem:** For any population with mean μ and standard deviation σ, the distribution of sample means for sample size n will have a mean of μ and a standard deviation of $\sigma/\sqrt{n}$ and will approach a normal distribution as n approaches infinity.

The value of this theorem comes from two simple facts. First, it describes the distribution of sample means for *any population,* no matter what shape, mean, or standard deviation. Second, the distribution of sample means "approaches" a normal distribution very rapidly. By the time the sample size reaches $n = 30$, the distribution is almost perfectly normal.

Note that the central limit theorem describes the distribution of sample means by identifying the three basic characteristics that describe any distribution: shape, central tendency, and variability. We examine each of these.

THE SHAPE OF THE DISTRIBUTION OF SAMPLE MEANS

It has been observed that the distribution of sample means tends to be a normal distribution. In fact, this distribution is almost perfectly normal if either of the following two conditions is satisfied:

1. The population from which the samples are selected is a normal distribution.

2. The number of scores (n) in each sample is relatively large, around 30 or more.

(As n gets larger, the distribution of sample means more closely approximates a normal distribution. When $n > 30$, the distribution is almost normal, regardless of the shape of the original population.)

As we noted earlier, the fact that the distribution of sample means tends to be normal is not surprising. Whenever you take a sample from a population, you expect the sample mean to be near to the population mean. When you take lots of different samples, you expect the sample means to "pile up" around μ, resulting in a normal-shaped distribution. You can see this tendency emerging (although it is not yet normal) in Figure 7.2.

THE MEAN OF THE DISTRIBUTION OF SAMPLE MEANS: THE EXPECTED VALUE OF *M*

In Example 7.1, the distribution of sample means is centered around the mean of the population from which the samples were obtained. In fact, the average value of all of the sample means is exactly equal to the value of the population mean. This fact should be intuitively reasonable; the sample means are expected to be close to the population mean, and they do tend to pile up around μ. The formal statement of this phenomenon is that the mean of the distribution of sample means always is identical to the population mean. This mean value is called the *expected value of* M. In commonsense terms, a sample mean is "expected" to be near its population mean. When all of the possible sample means are obtained, the average value is identical to μ.

The fact that the average value of *M* is equal to μ was first introduced in Chapter 4 (p. 106) in the context of *biased* versus *unbiased* statistics. The sample mean is an example of an unbiased statistic, which means that, on average, the sample statistic produces a value that is exactly equal to the corresponding population parameter. In this case, the average value of all of the sample means is exactly equal to μ.

DEFINITION

> The mean of the distribution of sample means is equal to the mean of the population of scores, μ, and is called the **expected value of *M***.

THE STANDARD ERROR OF *M*

So far, we have considered the shape and the central tendency of the distribution of sample means. To completely describe this distribution, we need one more characteristic: variability. The value we will be working with is the standard deviation for the distribution of sample means. This standard deviation is identified by the symbol σ_M and is called the *standard error of* M.

When the standard deviation was first introduced in Chapter 4, we noted that this measure of variability serves two general purposes. First, the standard deviation describes the distribution by telling whether the individual scores are clustered close together or scattered over a wide range. Second, the standard deviation measures how well any individual score represents the population by providing a measure of how much distance is reasonable to expect between a score and the population mean. The standard error serves the same two purposes for the distribution of sample means.

1. The standard error describes the distribution of sample means. It provides a measure of how much difference is expected from one sample to another. When the standard error is small, then all of the sample means are close together and have similar values. If the standard error is large, then the sample means are scattered over a wide range and there are big differences from one sample to another.

2. Standard error measures how well an individual sample mean represents the entire distribution. Specifically, it provides a measure of how much distance is reasonable to expect between a sample mean and the overall mean for the distribution of sample means. However, because the overall mean is equal to μ, the standard error also provides a measure of how much distance to expect between a sample mean (*M*) and the population mean (μ).

Remember that a sample is not expected to provide a perfectly accurate reflection of its population. Although a sample mean should be representative of the population mean, there typically is some error between the sample and the population. The standard error measures exactly how much difference is expected on average between a sample mean, *M,* and the population mean, μ.

DEFINITION

> The standard deviation of the distribution of sample means, σ_M, is called the **standard error of M**. The standard error provides a measure of how much distance is expected on average between a sample mean (M) and the population mean (μ).

Once again, the symbol for the standard error is σ_M. The σ indicates that this value is a standard deviation, and the subscript M indicates that it is the standard deviation for the distribution of sample means. Similarly, it is common to use the symbol μ_M to represent the mean of the distribution of sample means. However, μ_M is always equal to μ and our primary interest in inferential statistics is to compare sample means (M) with their population means (μ). Therefore, we simply use the symbol μ to refer to the mean of the distribution of sample means.

The standard error is an extremely valuable measure because it specifies precisely how well a sample mean estimates its population mean—that is, how much error you should expect, on the average, between M and μ. Remember that one basic reason for taking samples is to use the sample data to answer questions about the population. However, you do not expect a sample to provide a perfectly accurate picture of the population. There always is some discrepancy, or error, between a sample statistic and the corresponding population parameter. Now we are able to calculate exactly how much error to expect. For any sample size (n), we can compute the standard error, which measures the average distance between a sample mean and the population mean.

The magnitude of the standard error is determined by two factors: (1) the size of the sample and (2) the standard deviation of the population from which the sample is selected. We examine each of these factors.

The sample size   Earlier we predicted, based on common sense, that the size of a sample should influence how accurately the sample represents its population. Specifically, a large sample should be more accurate than a small sample. In general, as the sample size increases, the error between the sample mean and the population mean should decrease. This rule is also known as the *law of large numbers*.

DEFINITION

> The **law of large numbers** states that the larger the sample size (n), the more probable it is that the sample mean is close to the population mean.

The population standard deviation   As we noted earlier, there is an inverse relationship between the sample size and the standard error: bigger samples have smaller error, and smaller samples have bigger error. At the extreme, the smallest possible sample (and the largest standard error) occurs when the sample consists of $n = 1$ score. At this extreme, each sample is a single score and the distribution of sample means is identical to the original distribution of scores. In this case, the standard deviation for the distribution of sample means, which is the standard error, is identical to the standard deviation for the distribution of scores. In other words, when $n = 1$, the standard error = σ_M is identical to the standard deviation = σ.

When $n = 1$, $\sigma_M = \sigma$ (standard error = standard deviation).

You can think of the standard deviation as the "starting point" for standard error. When $n = 1$, the standard error and the standard deviation are the same: $\sigma_M = \sigma$. As sample size increases beyond $n = 1$, the sample becomes a more accurate representative of the population, and the standard error decreases. The formula for standard error expresses this relationship between standard deviation and sample size (n).

This formula is contained in the central limit theorem.

$$\text{standard error} = \sigma_M = \frac{\sigma}{\sqrt{n}}$$

(7.1)

Note that the formula satisfies all of the requirements for the standard error. Specifically,

a. As sample size (*n*) increases, the size of the standard error decreases. (Larger samples are more accurate.)

b. When the sample consists of a single score (*n* = 1), the standard error is the same as the standard deviation ($\sigma_M = \sigma$).

In Equation 7.1 and in most of the preceding discussion, we defined standard error in terms of the population standard deviation. However, the population standard deviation (σ) and the population variance (σ^2) are directly related, and it is easy to substitute variance into the equation for standard error. Using the simple equality $\sigma = \sqrt{\sigma^2}$, the equation for standard error can be rewritten as follows:

$$\text{standard error} = \sigma_M = \frac{\sigma}{\sqrt{n}} = \frac{\sqrt{\sigma^2}}{\sqrt{n}} = \sqrt{\frac{\sigma^2}{n}} \tag{7.2}$$

Throughout the rest of this chapter (and in Chapter 8), we continue to define standard error in terms of the standard deviation (Equation 7.1). However, in later chapters (starting in Chapter 9), the formula based on variance (Equation 7.2) will become more useful.

Figure 7.3 illustrates the general relationship between standard error and sample size. (The calculations for the data points in Figure 7.3 are presented in Table 7.2.) Again, the basic concept is that the larger a sample is, the more accurately it represents its population. Also note that the standard error decreases in relation to the *square root* of the sample size. As a result, researchers can substantially reduce error by increasing sample size up to around *n* = 30. However, increasing sample size beyond *n* = 30 does not produce much additional improvement in how well the sample represents the population.

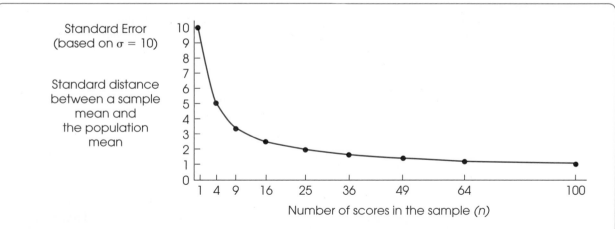

FIGURE 7.3

The relationship between standard error and sample size. As the sample size is increased, there is less error between the sample mean and the population mean.

TABLE 7.2

Calculations for the points shown in Figure 7.3. Again, notice that the size of the standard error decreases as the size of the sample increases.

Sample Size (n)	Standard Error	
1	$\sigma_M = \dfrac{10}{\sqrt{1}}$	$= 10.00$
4	$\sigma_M = \dfrac{10}{\sqrt{4}}$	$= 5.00$
9	$\sigma_M = \dfrac{10}{\sqrt{9}}$	$= 3.33$
16	$\sigma_M = \dfrac{10}{\sqrt{16}}$	$= 2.50$
25	$\sigma_M = \dfrac{10}{\sqrt{25}}$	$= 2.00$
49	$\sigma_M = \dfrac{10}{\sqrt{49}}$	$= 1.43$
64	$\sigma_M = \dfrac{10}{\sqrt{64}}$	$= 1.25$
100	$\sigma_M = \dfrac{10}{\sqrt{100}}$	$= 1.00$

THREE DIFFERENT DISTRIBUTIONS

Before we move forward with our discussion of the distribution of sample means, we pause for a moment to emphasize the idea that we are now dealing with three different but interrelated distributions.

1. First, we have the original population of scores. This population contains the scores for thousands or millions of individual people, and it has its own shape, mean, and standard deviation. For example, the population of IQ scores consists of millions of individual IQ scores that form a normal distribution with a mean of $\mu = 100$ and a standard deviation of $\sigma = 15$. An example of a population is shown in Figure 7.4(a).

2. Next, we have a sample that is selected from the population. The sample consists of a small set of scores for a few people who have been selected to represent the entire population. For example, we could select a sample of $n = 25$ people and measure each individual's IQ score. The 25 scores could be organized in a frequency distribution and we could calculate the sample mean and the sample standard deviation. Note that the sample also has its own shape, mean, and standard deviation. An example of a sample is shown in Figure 7.4(b).

3. The third distribution is the distribution of sample means. This is a theoretical distribution consisting of the sample means obtained from all of the possible random samples of a specific size. For example, the distribution of sample means for samples of $n = 25$ IQ scores would be normal with a mean (expected value) of $\mu = 100$ and a standard deviation (standard error) of $\sigma_M = \frac{15}{\sqrt{25}} = 3$. This distribution, shown in Figure 7.4(c), also has its own shape, mean, and standard deviation.

FIGURE 7.4

Three distributions. Part (a) shows the population of IQ scores. Part (b) shows a sample of $n = 25$ IQ scores. Part (c) shows the distribution of sample means for samples of $n = 100$ scores. Note that the sample mean from part (b) is one of the thousands of sample means in the part (c) distribution.

(a) Original population of IQ scores.

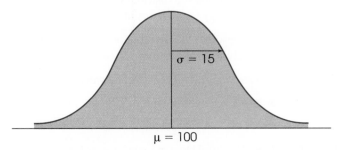

(b) A sample of $n = 25$ IQ scores.

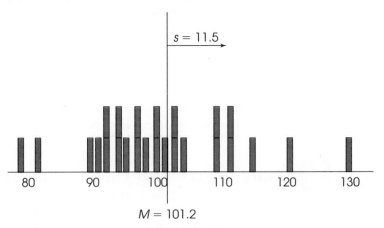

(c) The distribution of sample means. Sample means for all the possible random samples of $n = 25$ IQ scores.

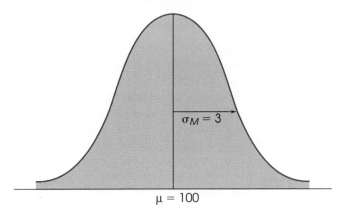

Note that the scores for the sample [Figure 7.4(b)] were taken from the original population [Figure 7.4(a)] and that the mean for the sample is one of the values contained in the distribution of sample means [Figure 7.4(c)]. Thus, the three distributions are all connected, but they are all distinct.

LEARNING CHECK

1. A population has a mean of $\mu = 65$ and a standard deviation of $\sigma = 16$.

    a. Describe the distribution of sample means (shape, central tendency, and variability) for samples of size $n = 4$ selected from this population.

    b. Describe the distribution of sample means (shape, central tendency, and variability) for samples of size $n = 64$ selected from this population.

2. Describe the relationship between the sample size and the standard error of M.

3. For a population with of $\mu = 40$ and a standard deviation of $\sigma = 8$, the standard error for a sample mean can never be larger than 8. (True or false.)

ANSWERS

1. **a** The distribution of sample means has an expected value of $\mu = 65$ and a standard error of $\sigma_M = \frac{16}{\sqrt{4}} = 8$. The shape of the distribution is unknown because the sample is not large enough to guarantee a normal distribution and the population shape is not known.

    b. The distribution of sample means has an expected value of $\mu = 65$ and a standard error of $\sigma_M = \frac{16}{\sqrt{64}} = 2$. The shape of the distribution is normal because the sample is large enough to guarantee a normal distribution.

2. The standard error decreases as sample size increases.

3. True. If each sample has $n = 1$ score, then the standard error is 8. For any other sample size, the standard error is smaller than 8.

7.3 PROBABILITY AND THE DISTRIBUTION OF SAMPLE MEANS

The primary use of the distribution of sample means is to find the probability associated with any specific sample. Recall that probability is equivalent to proportion. Because the distribution of sample means presents the entire set of all possible sample means, we can use proportions of this distribution to determine probabilities. The following example demonstrates this process.

EXAMPLE 7.2

Caution: Whenever you have a probability question about a sample mean, you must use the distribution of sample means.

The population of scores on the SAT forms a normal distribution with $\mu = 500$ and $\sigma = 100$. If you take a random sample of $n = 25$ students, what is the probability that the sample mean will be greater than $M = 540$?

First, you can restate this probability question as a proportion question: Out of all of the possible sample means, what proportion have values greater than 540? You know about "all of the possible sample means"; this is the distribution of sample means. The problem is to find a specific portion of this distribution.

Although we cannot construct the distribution of sample means by repeatedly taking samples and calculating means (as in Example 7.1), we know exactly what the distribution looks like based on the information from the central limit theorem. Specifically, the distribution of sample means has the following characteristics:

a. The distribution is normal because the population of SAT scores is normal.

b. The distribution has a mean of 500 because the population mean is $\mu = 500$.

c. For $n = 25$, the distribution has a standard error of $\sigma_M = 20$:

$$\sigma_M = \frac{\sigma}{\sqrt{n}} = \frac{100}{\sqrt{25}} = \frac{100}{5} = 20$$

This distribution of sample means is shown in Figure 7.5.

We are interested in sample means greater than 540 (the shaded area in Figure 7.5), so the next step is to use a z-score to locate the exact position of $M = 540$ in the distribution. The value 540 is located above the mean by 40 points, which is exactly 2 standard deviations (in this case, exactly 2 standard errors). Thus, the z-score for $M = 540$ is $z = +2.00$.

Because this distribution of sample means is normal, you can use the unit normal table to find the probability associated with $z = +2.00$. The table indicates that 0.0228 of the distribution is located in the tail of the distribution beyond $z = +2.00$. Our conclusion is that it is very unlikely, $p = 0.0228$ (2.28%), to obtain a random sample of $n = 25$ students with an average SAT score greater than 540.

A *Z*-SCORE FOR SAMPLE MEANS

As demonstrated in Example 7.2, it is possible to use a z-score to describe the exact location of any specific sample mean within the distribution of sample means. The z-score tells exactly where the sample mean is located in relation to all of the other possible sample means that could have been obtained. As defined in Chapter 5, a z-score identifies the location with a signed number so that

1. The sign tells whether the location is above ($+$) or below ($-$) the mean.

2. The number tells the distance between the location and the mean in terms of the number of standard deviations.

However, we are now finding a location within the distribution of sample means. Therefore, we must use the notation and terminology appropriate for this distribution. First, we are finding the location for a sample mean (M) rather than a score (X). Second, the standard deviation for the distribution of sample means is the standard error, σ_M. With these changes, the z-score formula for locating a sample mean is

$$z = \frac{M - \mu}{\sigma_M} \tag{7.3}$$

FIGURE 7.5

The distribution of sample means for $n = 25$. Samples were selected from a normal population with $\mu = 500$ and $\sigma = 100$.

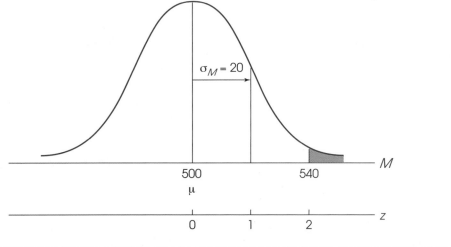

Caution: When computing z for a single score, use the standard deviation, σ. When computing z for a sample mean, you must use the standard error, σ_M (see Box 7.2).

Just as every score (X) has a z-score that describes its position in the distribution of scores, every sample mean (M) has a z-score that describes its position in the distribution of sample means. When the distribution of sample means is normal, it is possible to use z-scores and the unit normal table to find the probability associated with any specific sample mean (as in Example 7.2). The following example demonstrates that it also is possible to make quantitative predictions about the kinds of samples that should be obtained from any population.

EXAMPLE 7.3

Once again, the distribution of SAT scores forms a normal distribution with a mean of $\mu = 500$ and a standard deviation of $\sigma = 100$. For this example, we are going to determine what kind of sample mean is likely to be obtained as the average SAT score for a random sample of $n = 25$ students. Specifically, we determine the exact range of values that is expected for the sample mean 80% of the time.

We begin with the distribution of sample means for $n = 25$. As demonstrated in Example 7.2, this distribution is normal with an expected value of $\mu = 500$ and a standard error of $\sigma_M = 20$ (Figure 7.6). Our goal is to find the range of values that make up the middle 80% of the distribution. Because the distribution is normal, we can use the unit normal table. First, the 80% in the middle is split in half, with 40% (0.4000) on each side of the mean. Looking up 0.4000 in column D (the proportion between the mean and z), we find a corresponding z-score of $z = 1.28$. Thus, the z-score boundaries for the middle 80% are $z = +1.28$ and $z = -1.28$. By definition, a z-score of 1.28 represents a location that is 1.28 standard deviations (or standard errors) from the mean. With a standard error of 20 points, the distance from the mean is $1.28(20) = 25.6$ points. The mean is $\mu = 500$, so a distance of 25.6 in both directions produces a range of values from 474.4 to 525.6.

Thus, 80% of all the possible sample means are contained in a range between 474.4 and 525.6. If we select a sample of $n = 25$ students, we can be 80% confident that the mean SAT score for the sample will be in this range.

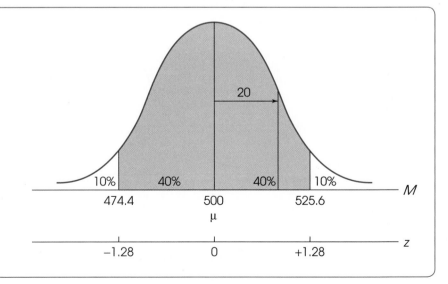

FIGURE 7.6

The middle 80% of the distribution of sample means for $n = 25$. Samples were selected from a normal population with $\mu = 500$ and $\sigma = 100$.

BOX 7.2	THE DIFFERENCE BETWEEN STANDARD DEVIATION AND STANDARD ERROR

A constant source of confusion for many students is the difference between standard deviation and standard error. Remember that standard deviation measures the standard distance between a *score* and the population mean, $X - \mu$. If you are working with a distribution of scores, the standard deviation is the appropriate measure of variability. Standard error, on the other hand, measures the standard distance between a *sample mean* and the population mean, $M - \mu$. Whenever you have a question concerning a sample, the standard error is the appropriate measure of variability.

If you still find the distinction confusing, there is a simple solution. Namely, if you always use standard error, you always will be right. Consider the formula for standard error:

$$\text{standard error} = \sigma_M = \frac{\sigma}{\sqrt{n}}$$

If you are working with a single score, then $n = 1$, and the standard error becomes

$$\text{standard error} = \sigma_M = \frac{\sigma}{\sqrt{n}} = \frac{\sigma}{\sqrt{1}} = \sigma = \text{standard deviation}$$

Thus, standard error always measures the standard distance from the population mean for any sample size, including $n = 1$.

The point of Example 7.3 is that the distribution of sample means makes it possible to predict the value that ought to be obtained for a sample mean. We know, for example, that a sample of $n = 25$ students ought to have a mean SAT score around 500. More specifically, we are 80% confident that the value of the sample mean will be between 474.4 and 525.6. The ability to predict sample means in this way is a valuable tool for the inferential statistics that follow.

LEARNING CHECK

1. A sample is selected from a population with a mean of $\mu = 90$ and a standard deviation of $\sigma = 15$. Find the z-score for the sample mean for each of the following samples.

   a. $n = 9$ scores with $M = 100$

   b. $n = 25$ scores with $M = 89$

2. What is the probability of obtaining a sample mean greater than $M = 60$ for a random sample of $n = 16$ scores selected from a normal population with a mean of $\mu = 65$ and a standard deviation of $\sigma = 20$?

3. What are the boundaries for the middle 50% of all possible random samples of $n = 25$ scores selected from a normal population with $\mu = 80$ and $\sigma = 10$?

ANSWERS

1. **a.** The standard error is $\sigma_M = 5$, and $z = 2.00$.

   b. The standard error is $\sigma_M = 3$, and $z = -0.33$.

2. The standard error is $\sigma_M = 5$, and $M = 60$ corresponds to $z = -1.00$, $p(M > 60) = p(z > -1.00) = 0.8413$ (or 84.13%).

3. The standard error is $\sigma_M = 2$, and the z-score boundaries for the middle 50% are $z = -0.67$ and $z = +0.67$. The boundaries are 78.66 and 81.34.

7.4 MORE ABOUT STANDARD ERROR

At the beginning of this chapter, we introduced the idea that it is possible to obtain thousands of different samples from a single population. Each sample has its own individuals, its own scores, and its own sample mean. The distribution of sample means provides a method for organizing all of the different sample means into a single picture. Figure 7.7 shows a prototypical distribution of sample means. To emphasize the fact that the distribution contains many different samples, we have constructed this figure so that the distribution is made up of hundreds of small boxes, each box representing a single sample mean. Also notice that the sample means tend to pile up around the population mean (μ), forming a normal-shaped distribution as predicted by the central limit theorem.

The distribution shown in Figure 7.7 provides a concrete example for reviewing the general concepts of sampling error and standard error. Although the following points may seem obvious, they are intended to provide you with a better understanding of these two statistical concepts.

1. **Sampling Error.** The general concept of sampling error is that a sample typically does not provide a perfectly accurate representation of its population. More specifically, there typically is some discrepancy (or error) between a statistic computed for a sample and the corresponding parameter for the population. As you look at Figure 7.7, notice that the individual sample means are not exactly equal to the population mean. In fact, 50% of the samples have means that are smaller than μ (the entire left-hand side of the distribution). Similarly, 50% of the samples produce means that overestimate the true population mean. In general, there is some discrepancy, or *sampling error,* between the mean for a sample and the mean for the population from which the sample was obtained.

2. **Standard Error.** Again looking at Figure 7.7, notice that most of the sample means are relatively close to the population mean (those in the center of the distribution). These samples provide a fairly accurate representation of the population.

FIGURE 7.7

An example of a typical distribution of sample means. Each of the small boxes represents the mean obtained for one sample.

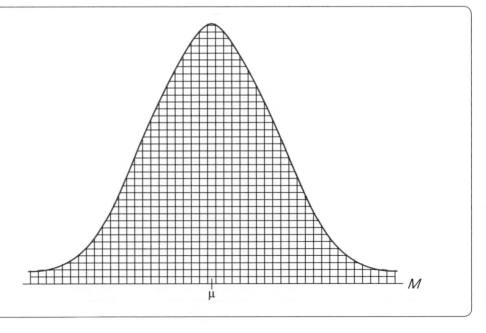

On the other hand, some samples produce means that are out in the tails of the distribution, relatively far from the population mean. These extreme sample means do not accurately represent the population. For each individual sample, you can measure the error (or distance) between the sample mean and the population mean. For some samples, the error is relatively small, but for other samples, the error is relatively large. The *standard error* provides a way to measure the "average," or standard, distance between a sample mean and the population mean.

Thus, the standard error provides a method for defining and measuring sampling error. Knowing the standard error gives researchers a good indication of how accurately their sample data represent the populations that they are studying. In most research situations, for example, the population mean is unknown, and the researcher selects a sample to help obtain information about the unknown population. Specifically, the sample mean provides information about the value of the unknown population mean. The sample mean is not expected to give a perfectly accurate representation of the population mean; there will be some error, and the standard error tells *exactly how much error,* on average, should exist between the sample mean and the unknown population mean. The following example demonstrates the use of standard error and provides additional information about the relationship between standard error and standard deviation.

EXAMPLE 7.4   A recent survey of students at a local college included the following question: How many minutes do you spend each day watching electronic video (e.g., online, TV, cell phone, iPad, etc.). The average response was $\mu = 80$ minutes, and the distribution of viewing times was approximately normal with a standard deviation of $\sigma = 20$ minutes. Next, we take a sample from this population and examine how accurately the sample mean represents the population mean. More specifically, we will examine how sample size affects accuracy by considering three different samples: one with $n = 1$ student, one with $n = 4$ students, and one with $n = 100$ students.

Figure 7.8 shows the distributions of sample means based on samples of $n = 1$, $n = 4$, and $n = 100$. Each distribution shows the collection of all possible sample means that could be obtained for that particular sample size. Notice that all three sampling

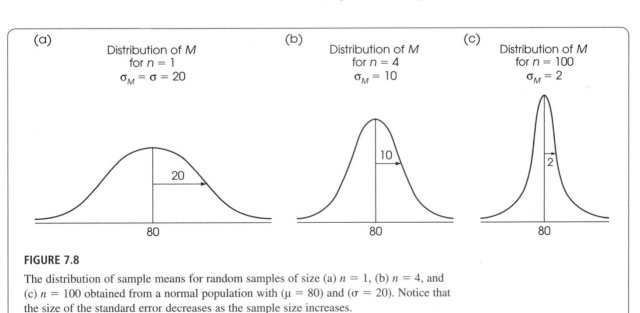

FIGURE 7.8

The distribution of sample means for random samples of size (a) $n = 1$, (b) $n = 4$, and (c) $n = 100$ obtained from a normal population with ($\mu = 80$) and ($\sigma = 20$). Notice that the size of the standard error decreases as the sample size increases.

distributions are normal (because the original population is normal), and all three have the same mean, $\mu = 80$, which is the expected value of M. However, the three distributions differ greatly with respect to variability. We will consider each one separately.

The smallest sample size is $n = 1$. When a sample consists of a single student, the mean for the sample equals the score for the student, $M = X$. Thus, when $n = 1$, the distribution of sample means is identical to the original population of scores. In this case, the standard error for the distribution of sample means is equal to the standard deviation for the original population. Equation 7.1 confirms this observation.

$$\sigma_M = \frac{\sigma}{\sqrt{n}} = \frac{20}{\sqrt{1}} = 20$$

When the sample consists of a single student, you expect, on average, a 20-point difference between the sample mean and the mean for the population. As we noted earlier, the population standard deviation is the "starting point" for the standard error. With the smallest possible sample, $n = 1$, the standard error is equal to the standard deviation [see Figure 7.8(a)].

As the sample size increases, however, the standard error gets smaller. For a sample of $n = 4$ students, the standard error is

$$\sigma_M = \frac{\sigma}{\sqrt{n}} = \frac{20}{\sqrt{4}} = \frac{20}{2} = 10$$

That is, the typical (or standard) distance between M and μ is 10 points. Figure 7.8(b) illustrates this distribution. Notice that the sample means in this distribution approximate the population mean more closely than in the previous distribution where $n = 1$.

With a sample of $n = 100$, the standard error is still smaller.

$$\sigma_M = \frac{\sigma}{\sqrt{n}} = \frac{20}{\sqrt{100}} = \frac{20}{10} = 2$$

A sample of $n = 100$ students should produce a sample mean that represents the population much more accurately than a sample of $n = 4$ or $n = 1$. As shown in Figure 7.8(c), there is very little error between M and μ when $n = 100$. Specifically, you would expect, on average, only a 2-point difference between the population mean and the sample mean.

In summary, this example illustrates that with the smallest possible sample ($n = 1$), the standard error and the population standard deviation are the same. When sample size is increased, the standard error gets smaller, and the sample means tend to approximate μ more closely. Thus, standard error defines the relationship between sample size and the accuracy with which M represents μ.

IN THE LITERATURE
REPORTING STANDARD ERROR

As we will see later, standard error plays a very important role in inferential statistics. Because of its crucial role, the standard error for a sample mean, rather than the sample standard deviation, is often reported in scientific papers. Scientific journals vary in how they refer to the standard error, but frequently the symbols *SE* and *SEM* (for standard error of the mean) are used. The standard error is reported in

TABLE 7.3

The mean self-consciousness scores for participants who were working in front of a video camera and those who were not (controls).

	n	Mean	SE
Control	17	32.23	2.31
Camera	15	45.17	2.78

two ways. Much like the standard deviation, it may be reported in a table along with the sample means (Table 7.3). Alternatively, the standard error may be reported in graphs.

Figure 7.9 illustrates the use of a bar graph to display information about the sample mean and the standard error. In this experiment, two samples (groups A and B) are given different treatments, and then the subjects' scores on a dependent variable are recorded. The mean for group A is $M = 15$, and for group B, it is $M = 30$. For both samples, the standard error of M is $\sigma_M = 5$. Note that the mean is represented by the height of the bar, and the standard error is depicted by brackets at the top of each bar. Each bracket extends 1 standard error above and 1 standard error below the sample mean. Thus, the graph illustrates the mean for each group plus or minus 1 standard error ($M \pm SE$). When you glance at Figure 7.9, not only do you get a "picture" of the sample means, but you also get an idea of how much error you should expect for those means.

Figure 7.10 shows how sample means and standard error are displayed in a line graph. In this study, two samples representing different age groups are tested on a

FIGURE 7.9

The mean ($\pm SE$) score for treatment groups A and B.

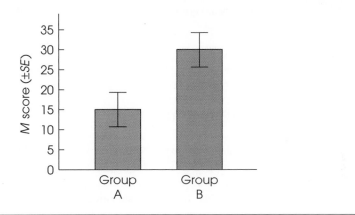

FIGURE 7.10

The mean ($\pm SE$) number of mistakes made for groups A and B on each trial.

task for four trials. The number of errors committed on each trial is recorded for all participants. The graph shows the mean (M) number of errors committed for each group on each trial. The brackets show the size of the standard error for each sample mean. Again, the brackets extend 1 standard error above and below the value of the mean.

LEARNING CHECK

1. If a sample is selected from a population with a mean of $\mu = 120$ and a standard deviation of $\sigma = 20$, then, on average, how much difference should there be between the sample mean and the population mean

   a. for a sample of $n = 25$ scores?

   b. for a sample of $n = 100$ scores?

2. Can the value of the standard error ever be larger than the value of the population standard deviation? Explain your answer.

3. If a random sample is selected from a population with a standard deviation of $\sigma = 40$, then how large a sample is needed to have a standard error of 2 points or less?

4. A sample of $n = 25$ scores is selected from a population. If the sample mean has a standard error of 4 points, then what is the population standard deviation?

ANSWERS

1. **a.** $\sigma_M = 4$ points

   b. $\sigma_M = 2$ points

2. No. The standard error is computed by dividing the standard deviation by the square root of n. The standard error is always less than or equal to the standard deviation.

3. A sample of $n = 400$ or larger.

4. $\sigma = 20$

7.5 LOOKING AHEAD TO INFERENTIAL STATISTICS

Inferential statistics are methods that use sample data as the basis for drawing general conclusions about populations. However, we have noted that a sample is not expected to give a perfectly accurate reflection of its population. In particular, there will be some error or discrepancy between a sample statistic and the corresponding population parameter. In this chapter, we have observed that a sample mean is not exactly equal to the population mean. The standard error of M specifies how much difference is expected on average between the mean for a sample and the mean for the population.

The natural differences that exist between samples and populations introduce a degree of uncertainty and error into all inferential processes. Specifically, there is always a margin of error that must be considered whenever a researcher uses a sample mean as the basis for drawing a conclusion about a population mean. Remember that the sample mean is not perfect. In the next seven chapters we introduce a variety of statistical methods that all use sample means to draw inferences about population means.

In each case, the distribution of sample means and the standard error are critical elements in the inferential process. Before we begin this series of chapters, we pause briefly to demonstrate how the distribution of sample means, along with z-scores and probability, can help us use sample means to draw inferences about population means.

EXAMPLE 7.5

We ended Chapters 5 and 6 with a demonstration of how inferential statistics are used to help interpret the results of a research study. A general research situation was shown in Figures 5.9 and 6.16, and is repeated here in Figure 7.11. The research begins with a population that forms a normal distribution with a mean of $\mu = 400$ and a standard deviation of $\sigma = 20$. A sample is selected from the population and a treatment is administered to the sample. The goal for the study is to evaluate the effect of the treatment. In the previous two chapters, however, we were limited to using a sample of $n = 1$ individual. Now, we can use any sample size and have selected $n = 25$ for this example.

The psychologist makes a decision about the effect of the treatment by comparing the treated sample with the original population. If the scores in the sample are noticeably different from the scores in the population, then the researcher has evidence that the treatment has an effect. The problem is to determine exactly how much difference is necessary before we can say that the sample is *noticeably different.*

The distribution of sample means and the standard error can help researchers make this decision. In particular, the distribution of sample means can be used to show exactly what would be expected for samples that do not receive any treatment. This allows researchers to make a simple comparison between

   a. The treated sample (from the research study)

   b. Untreated samples (from the distribution of sample means)

If our treated sample is noticeably different from the untreated samples, then we have evidence that the treatment has an effect. On the other hand, if our treated sample still looks like one of the untreated samples, then we must conclude that the treatment does not appear to have any effect.

We begin with the original population and consider the distribution of sample means for all of the possible samples of $n = 25$. The distribution of sample means has the following characteristics:

   1. It is a normal distribution, because the original population is normal.

   2. It has an expected value of 400, because the population mean is $\mu = 400$.

   3. It has a standard error of $\sigma_M = \dfrac{20}{\sqrt{25}} = \dfrac{20}{5} = 4$, because the population standard deviation is $\sigma = 20$ and the sample size is $n = 25$.

FIGURE 7.11

The structure of the research study described in Example 7.5. The purpose of the study is to determine whether the treatment has an effect.

FIGURE 7.12

The distribution of sample means for samples of $n = 25$ untreated rats (from Example 7.5).

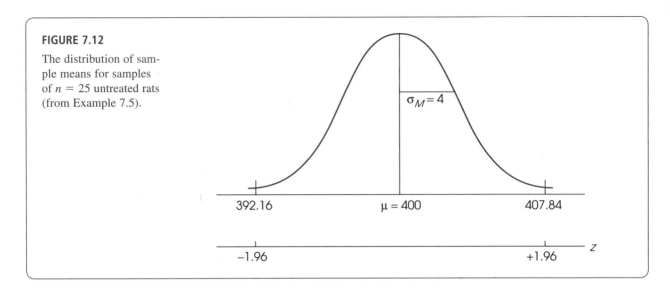

The distribution of sample means is shown in Figure 7.12. Notice that an untreated sample of $n = 25$ should have a mean around $\mu = 400$. To be more precise, we can use z-scores to determine the middle 95% of all the possible sample means. As demonstrated in Chapter 6 (p. 170), the middle 95% of a normal distribution is located between z-score boundaries of $z = +1.96$ and $z = -1.96$ (check the unit normal table). These z-score boundaries are shown in Figure 7.12. With a standard error of $\sigma = 4$ points, a z-score of 1.96 corresponds to a distance of $1.96(4) = 7.84$ points from the mean. Thus, the z-score boundaries of ± 1.96 correspond to sample means of 392.16 and 407.84.

We have demonstrated that an untreated sample is almost guaranteed (95% probability) to have a sample mean between 392.16 and 407.84. If our sample has a mean within this range, then we must conclude that our sample of is not noticeably different from untreated samples. In this case, we conclude that the treatment does not appear to have any effect.

On the other hand, if the mean for the treated sample is outside the 95% range, then we can conclude that our sample is noticeably different from the samples that would be obtained without any treatment. In this case, the research results provide evidence that the treatment has an effect.

In Example 7.5 we used the distribution of sample means, together with z-scores and probability, to provide a description of what is reasonable to expect for an untreated sample. Then, we evaluated the effect of a treatment by determining whether the treated sample was noticeably different from an untreated sample. This procedure forms the foundation for the inferential technique known as *hypothesis testing,* which is introduced in Chapter 8 and repeated throughout the remainder of this book.

LEARNING CHECK

1. A population forms a normal distribution with a mean of $\mu = 80$ and a standard deviation of $\sigma = 20$.

    a. If single score is selected from this population, how much distance would you expect, on average, between the score and the population mean?

    b. If a sample of $n = 100$ scores is selected from this population, how much distance would you expect, on average, between the sample mean and the population mean?

2. A population forms a normal shaped distribution with $\mu = 40$ and $\sigma = 8$.

    a. A sample of $n = 16$ scores from this population has a mean of $M = 36$. Would you describe this as a relatively typical sample, or is the sample mean an extreme value? Explain your answer.

    b. If the sample from part a had $n = 4$ scores, would it be considered typical or extreme?

3. The SAT scores for the entering freshman class at a local college form a normal distribution with a mean of $\mu = 530$ and a standard deviation of $\sigma = 80$.

    a. For a random sample of $n = 16$ students, what range of values for the sample mean would be expected 95% of the time?

    b. What range of values would be expected 95% of the time if the sample size were $n = 100$?

4. A sample of $n = 16$ individuals is selected from a normal population with a mean of $\mu = 50$ with $\sigma = 12$. After a treatment is administered to the sample, the sample mean is found to be $M = 57$. Is this sample mean likely to occur if the treatment has no effect? Specifically, is the sample mean within the range of values that would be expected 95% of the time?

ANSWERS

1. **a.** For a single score, the standard distance from the mean is the standard deviation, $\sigma = 20$.

    b. For a sample of $n = 100$ scores, the average distance between the sample mean and the population mean is the standard error, $\sigma_M = \frac{20}{\sqrt{100}} = 2$.

2. **a.** With $n = 16$, the standard error is 2, and the sample mean corresponds to $z = -2.00$. This is an extreme value.

    b. With $n = 4$, the standard error is 4, and the sample mean corresponds to $z = -1.00$. This is a relatively typical value.

3. **a.** With $n = 16$, the standard error is $\sigma_M = 20$ points. Using $z = \pm 1.96$, the 95% range extends from 490.8 to 569.2.

    b. With $n = 100$, the standard error is only 8 points and the range extends from 514.32 to 545.68.

4. With $n = 16$, the standard error is $\sigma_M = 3$. If the treatment has no effect, then the population mean is still $\mu = 50$ and 95% of all the possible sample means should be within $1.96(3) = 5.88$ points of $\mu = 50$. This is a range of values from 44.12 to 55.88. Our sample mean is outside this range, so it is not the kind of sample that ought to be obtained if the treatment has no effect.

SUMMARY

1. The distribution of sample means is defined as the set of *M*s for all of the possible random samples for a specific sample size (*n*) that can be obtained from a given population. According to the *central limit theorem,* the parameters of the distribution of sample means are as follows:

   a. *Shape.* The distribution of sample means is normal if either one of the following two conditions is satisfied:

      (1) The population from which the samples are selected is normal.

      (2) The size of the samples is relatively large (*n* = 30 or more).

   b. *Central Tendency.* The mean of the distribution of sample means is identical to the mean of the population from which the samples are selected. The mean of the distribution of sample means is called the expected value of *M.*

   c. *Variability.* The standard deviation of the distribution of sample means is called the standard error of *M* and is defined by the formula

   $$\sigma_M = \frac{\sigma}{\sqrt{n}} \text{ or } \sigma_M = \sqrt{\frac{\sigma^2}{n}}$$

   Standard error measures the standard distance between a sample mean (*M*) and the population mean (μ).

2. One of the most important concepts in this chapter is standard error. The standard error is the standard deviation of the distribution of sample means. It measures the standard distance between a sample mean (*M*) and the population mean (μ). The standard error tells how much error to expect if you are using a sample mean to represent a population mean.

3. The location of each *M* in the distribution of sample means can be specified by a *z*-score:

   $$z = \frac{M - \mu}{\sigma_M}$$

   Because the distribution of sample means tends to be normal, we can use these *z*-scores and the unit normal table to find probabilities for specific sample means. In particular, we can identify which sample means are likely and which are very unlikely to be obtained from any given population. This ability to find probabilities for samples is the basis for the inferential statistics in the chapters ahead.

4. In general terms, the standard error measures how much discrepancy you should expect between a sample statistic and a population parameter. Statistical inference involves using sample statistics to make a general conclusion about a population parameter. Thus, standard error plays a crucial role in inferential statistics.

KEY TERMS

sampling error (176)

distribution of sample means (177)

sampling distribution (177)

central limit theorem (180)

expected value of *M* (181)

standard error of *M* (181)

law of large numbers (182)

RESOURCES

Go to CengageBrain.com to access Psychology CourseMate, where you will find an interactive eBook, glossaries, flashcards, quizzes, statistics workshops, and more.

aplia

If your professor has assigned Aplia:

1. Sign in to your account.

2. Complete the corresponding exercises as required by your professor.

3. When finished, click "Grade It Now" to see which areas you have mastered, which areas need more work, and detailed explanations of every answer.

SPSS

The statistical computer package SPSS is not structured to compute the standard error or a z-score for a sample mean. In later chapters, however, we introduce new inferential statistics that are included in SPSS. When these new statistics are computed, SPSS typically includes a report of standard error that describes how accurately, on average, the sample represents its population.

FOCUS ON PROBLEM SOLVING

1. Whenever you are working probability questions about sample means, you must use the distribution of sample means. Remember that every probability question can be restated as a proportion question. Probabilities for sample means are equivalent to proportions of the distribution of sample means.

2. When computing probabilities for sample means, the most common error is to use standard deviation (σ) instead of standard error (σ_M) in the z-score formula. Standard deviation measures the typical deviation (or error) for a single score. Standard error measures the typical deviation (or error) for a sample. Remember: The larger the sample is, the more accurately the sample represents the population. Thus, sample size (n) is a critical part of the standard error.

$$\text{Standard error} = \sigma_M = \frac{\sigma}{\sqrt{n}}$$

3. Although the distribution of sample means is often normal, it is not always a normal distribution. Check the criteria to be certain that the distribution is normal before you use the unit normal table to find probabilities (see item 1a of the Summary). Remember that all probability problems with a normal distribution are easier to solve if you sketch the distribution and shade in the area of interest.

DEMONSTRATION 7.1

PROBABILITY AND THE DISTRIBUTION OF SAMPLE MEANS

A population forms a normal distribution with a mean of $\mu = 60$ and a standard deviation of $\sigma = 12$. For a sample of $n = 36$ scores from this population, what is the probability of obtaining a sample mean greater than 64?

$$p(M > 64) = ?$$

STEP 1 Rephrase the probability question as a proportion question.   Out of all of the possible sample means for $n = 36$, what proportion has values greater than 64? *All of the possible sample means* is simply the distribution of sample means, which is normal, with a mean of $\mu = 60$ and a standard error of

$$\sigma_M = \frac{\sigma}{\sqrt{n}} = \frac{12}{\sqrt{36}} = \frac{12}{6} = 2$$

The distribution is shown in Figure 7.13(a). Because the problem is asking for the proportion greater than $M = 64$, this portion of the distribution is shaded in Figure 7.13(b).

STEP 2 Compute the z-score for the sample mean.   A sample mean of $M = 64$ corresponds to a z-score of

$$z = \frac{M - \mu}{\sigma_M} = \frac{64 - 60}{2} = \frac{4}{2} = 2.00$$

Therefore, $p(M > 64) = p(z > 2.00)$

STEP 3 Look up the proportion in the unit normal table.   Find $z = 2.00$ in column A and read across the row to find $p = 0.0228$ in column C. This is the answer as shown in Figure 7.13(c).

$$p(M > 64) = p(z > 2.00) = 0.0228 \text{ (or } 2.28\%)$$

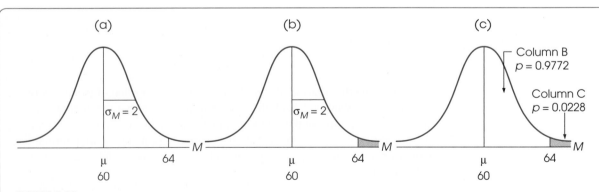

FIGURE 7.13

Sketches of the distribution for Demonstration 7.1.

PROBLEMS

1. Describe the distribution of sample means (shape, expected value, and standard error) for samples of $n = 100$ selected from a population with a mean of $\mu = 40$ and a standard deviation of $\sigma = 10$.

2. A sample is selected from a population with a mean of $\mu = 40$ and a standard deviation of $\sigma = 8$.
   a. If the sample has $n = 4$ scores, what is the expected value of M and the standard error of M?
   b. If the sample has $n = 16$ scores, what is the expected value of M and the standard error of M?

3. The distribution of sample means is not always a normal distribution. Under what circumstances is the distribution of sample means *not* normal?

4. A population has a standard deviation of $\sigma = 24$.
   a. On average, how much difference should exist between the population mean and the sample mean for $n = 4$ scores randomly selected from the population?
   b. On average, how much difference should exist for a sample of $n = 9$ scores?
   c. On average, how much difference should exist for a sample of $n = 16$ scores?

5. For a population with a mean of $\mu = 70$ and a standard deviation of $\sigma = 20$, how much error, on average, would you expect between the sample mean (M) and the population mean for each of the following sample sizes?
   a. $n = 4$ scores
   b. $n = 16$ scores
   c. $n = 25$ scores

6. For a population with a standard deviation of $\sigma = 20$, how large a sample is necessary to have a standard error that is:
   a. less than or equal to 5 points?
   b. less than or equal to 2 points?
   c. less than or equal to 1 point?

7. For a population with $\sigma = 12$, how large a sample is necessary to have a standard error that is:
   a. less than 4 points?
   b. less than 3 points?
   c. less than 2 point?

8. For a sample of $n = 25$ scores, what is the value of the population standard deviation (σ) necessary to produce each of the following a standard error values?
   a. $\sigma_M = 10$ points?
   b. $\sigma_M = 5$ points?
   c. $\sigma_M = 2$ points?

9. For a population with a mean of $\mu = 80$ and a standard deviation of $\sigma = 12$, find the z-score corresponding to each of the following samples.
   a. $M = 83$ for a sample of $n = 4$ scores
   b. $M = 83$ for a sample of $n = 16$ scores
   c. $M = 83$ for a sample of $n = 36$ scores

10. A sample of $n = 4$ scores has a mean of $M = 75$. Find the z-score for this sample:
    a. If it was obtained from a population with $\mu = 80$ and $\sigma = 10$.
    b. If it was obtained from a population with $\mu = 80$ and $\sigma = 20$.
    c. If it was obtained from a population with $\mu = 80$ and $\sigma = 40$.

11. A normal distribution has a mean of $\mu = 60$ and a standard deviation of $\sigma = 18$. For each of the following samples, compute the z-score for the sample mean and determine whether the sample mean is a typical, representative value or an extreme value for a sample of this size.
    a. $M = 67$ for $n = 4$ scores
    b. $M = 67$ for $n = 36$ scores

12. A random sample is obtained from a normal population with a mean of $\mu = 95$ and a standard deviation of $\sigma = 40$. The sample mean is $M = 86$.
    a. Is this a representative sample mean or an extreme value for a sample of $n = 16$ scores?
    b. Is this a representative sample mean or an extreme value for a sample of $n = 100$ scores?

13. The population of IQ scores forms a normal distribution with a mean of $\mu = 100$ and a standard deviation of $\sigma = 15$. What is the probability of obtaining a sample mean greater than $M = 97$,
    a. for a random sample of $n = 9$ people?
    b. for a random sample of $n = 25$ people?

14. The scores on a standardized mathematics test for 8th-grade children in New York State form a normal distribution with a mean of $\mu = 70$ and a standard deviation of $\sigma = 10$.
    a. What proportion of the students in the state have scores less than $X = 75$?
    b. If samples of $n = 4$ are selected from the population, what proportion of the samples will have means less than $M = 75$?
    c. If samples of $n = 25$ are selected from the population, what proportion of the samples will have means less than $M = 75$?

15. A normal distribution has a mean of $\mu = 54$ and a standard deviation of $\sigma = 6$.
    a. What is the probability of randomly selecting a score less than $X = 51$?
    b. What is the probability of selecting a sample of $n = 4$ scores with a mean less than $M = 51$?
    c. What is the probability of selecting a sample of $n = 36$ scores with a mean less than $M = 51$?

16. A population of scores forms a normal distribution with a mean of $\mu = 80$ and a standard deviation of $\sigma = 10$.
    a. What proportion of the scores have values between 75 and 85?
    b. For samples of $n = 4$, what proportion of the samples will have means between 75 and 85?

c. For samples of $n = 16$, what proportion of the samples will have means between 75 and 85?

17. For random samples of size $n = 25$ selected from a normal distribution with a mean of $\mu = 50$ and a standard deviation of $\sigma = 20$, find each of the following:
  a. The range of sample means that defines the middle 95% of the distribution of sample means.
  b. The range of sample means that defines the middle 99% of the distribution of sample means.

18. The distribution ages for students at the state college is positively skewed with a mean of $\mu = 21.5$ and a standard deviation of $\sigma = 3$.
  a. What is the probability of selecting a random sample of $n = 4$ students with an average age greater than 23? (Careful: This is a trick question.)
  b. What is the probability of selecting a random sample of $n = 36$ students with an average age greater than 23?
  c. For a sample of $n = 36$ students, what is the probability that the average age is between 21 and 22?

19. At the end of the spring semester, the Dean of Students sent a survey to the entire freshman class. One question asked the students how much weight they had gained or lost since the beginning of the school year. The average was a gain of $\mu = 9$ pounds with a standard deviation of $\sigma = 6$. The distribution of scores was approximately normal. A sample of $n = 4$ students is selected and the average weight change is computed for the sample.
  a. What is the probability that the sample mean will be greater than $M = 10$ pounds? In symbols, what is $p(M > 10)$?
  b. Of all of the possible samples, what proportion will show an average weight loss? In symbols, what is $p(M < 0)$?
  c. What is the probability that the sample mean will be a gain of between $M = 9$ and $M = 12$ pounds? In symbols, what is $p(9 < M < 12)$?

20. Jumbo shrimp are those that require 10 to 15 shrimp to make a pound. Suppose that the number of jumbo shrimp in a 1-pound bag averages $\mu = 12.5$ with a standard deviation of $s = 1$, and forms a normal distribution. What is the probability of randomly picking a sample of $n = 25$ 1-pound bags that average more than $M = 13$ shrimp per bag?

21. The average age for licensed drivers in the county is $\mu = 40.3$ years with a standard deviation of $\sigma = 13.2$ years.
  a. A researcher obtained a random sample of $n = 16$ parking tickets and computed an average age of $M = 38.9$ years for the drivers. Compute the z-score for the sample mean and find the probability of obtaining an average age this young or younger for a random sample of licensed drivers. Is it reasonable to conclude that this set of $n = 16$ people is a representative sample of licensed drivers?
  b. The same researcher obtained a random sample of $n = 36$ speeding tickets and computed an average age of $M = 36.2$ years for the drivers. Compute the z-score for the sample mean and find the probability of obtaining an average age this young or younger for a random sample of licensed drivers. Is it reasonable to conclude that this set of $n = 36$ people is a representative sample of licensed drivers?

22. Callahan (2009) conducted a study to evaluate the effectiveness of physical exercise programs for individuals with chronic arthritis. Participants with doctor-diagnosed arthritis either received a Tai Chi course immediately or were placed in a control group to begin the course 8 weeks later. At the end of the 8-week period, self-reports of pain were obtained for both groups. Data similar to the results obtained in the study are shown in the following table.

Self-Reported Level of Pain		
	Mean	*SE*
Tai Chi course	3.7	1.2
No Tai Chi course	7.6	1.7

  a. Construct a bar graph that incorporates all of the information in the table.
  b. Looking at your graph, do you think that participation in the Tai Chi course reduces arthritis pain?

23. Xu and Garcia (2008) conducted a research study demonstrating that 8-month-old infants appear to recognize which samples are likely to be obtained from a population and which are not. In the study, the infants watched as a sample of $n = 5$ ping-pong balls was selected from a large box. In one condition, the sample consisted of 1 red ball and 4 white balls. After the sample was selected, the front panel of the box was removed to reveal the contents. In the *expected* condition, the box contained primarily white balls like the sample, and the infants looked at it for an average of $M = 7.5$ seconds. In the *unexpected* condition, the box had primarily red balls, unlike the sample, and the infants looked at it for $M = 9.9$ seconds. The researchers interpreted the results as demonstrating that the infants found the unexpected result surprising and, therefore, more interesting than the expected result. Assuming that the standard error for both means is $\sigma_M = 1$ second, draw a bar graph showing the two sample means using brackets to show the size of the standard error for each mean.

C H A P T E R

8

Introduction to Hypothesis Testing

Tools You Will Need

The following items are considered essential background material for this chapter. If you doubt your knowledge of any of these items, you should review the appropriate chapter or section before proceeding.

- *z*-Scores (Chapter 5)
- Distribution of sample means (Chapter 7)
- Expected value
- Standard error
- Probability and sample means

aplia

Aplia for *Essentials of Statistics for the Behavioral Sciences*
After reading, go to "Resources" at the end of this chapter for an introduction on how to use Aplia's homework and learning resources.

8.1   THE LOGIC OF HYPOTHESIS TESTING

It usually is impossible or impractical for a researcher to observe every individual in a population. Therefore, researchers usually collect data from a sample and then use the sample data to help answer questions about the population. Hypothesis testing is a statistical procedure that allows researchers to use sample data to draw inferences about the population of interest.

Hypothesis testing is one of the most commonly used inferential procedures. In fact, most of the remainder of this book examines hypothesis testing in a variety of different situations and applications. Although the details of a hypothesis test change from one situation to another, the general process remains constant. In this chapter, we introduce the general procedure for a hypothesis test. You should notice that we use the statistical techniques that have been developed in the preceding three chapters—that is, we combine the concepts of z-scores, probability, and the distribution of sample means to create a new statistical procedure known as a *hypothesis test*.

DEFINITION

> A **hypothesis test** is a statistical method that uses sample data to evaluate a hypothesis about a population.

In very simple terms, the logic underlying the hypothesis-testing procedure is as follows:

1. First, we state a hypothesis about a population. Usually the hypothesis concerns the value of a population parameter. For example, we might hypothesize that American adults gain an average of $\mu = 7$ pounds between Thanksgiving and New Year's Day each year.

2. Before we select a sample, we use the hypothesis to predict the characteristics that the sample should have. For example, if we predict that the average weight gain for the population is $\mu = 7$ pounds, then we would predict that our sample should have a mean *around* 7 pounds. Remember: The sample should be similar to the population, but you always expect a certain amount of error.

3. Next, we obtain a random sample from the population. For example, we might select a sample of $n = 200$ American adults and measure the average weight change for the sample between Thanksgiving and New Year's Day.

4. Finally, we compare the obtained sample data with the prediction that was made from the hypothesis. If the sample mean is consistent with the prediction, then we conclude that the hypothesis is reasonable. But if there is a big discrepancy between the data and the prediction, then we decide that the hypothesis is wrong.

A hypothesis test is typically used in the context of a research study. That is, a researcher completes a research study and then uses a hypothesis test to evaluate the results. Depending on the type of research and the type of data, the details of the hypothesis test change from one research situation to another. In later chapters, we examine different versions of hypothesis testing that are used for different kinds of research. For now, however, we focus on the basic elements that are common to all hypothesis tests. To accomplish this general goal, we examine a hypothesis test as it applies to the simplest possible situation—using a sample mean to test a hypothesis about a population mean.

In the five chapters that follow, we consider hypothesis testing in more complex research situations involving sample means and mean differences. In Chapter 14, we look at correlational research and examine how the relationships obtained for sample data are used to evaluate hypotheses about relationships in the population. In Chapter 15, we examine how the proportions that exist in a sample are used to test hypotheses about the corresponding proportions in the population.

Once again, we introduce hypothesis testing with a situation in which a researcher is using one sample mean to evaluate a hypothesis about one unknown population mean.

The unknown population   Figure 8.1 shows the general research situation that we use to introduce the process of hypothesis testing. Notice that the researcher begins with a known population. This is the set of individuals as they exist *before treatment*. For this example, we are assuming that the original set of scores forms a normal distribution with $\mu = 80$ and $\sigma = 20$. The purpose of the research is to determine the effect of a treatment on the individuals in the population.

To simplify the hypothesis-testing situation, one basic assumption is made about the effect of the treatment: If the treatment has any effect, it is simply to add a constant amount to (or subtract a constant amount from) each individual's score. You should recall from Chapters 3 and 4 that adding (or subtracting) a constant to each score causes the mean to change but does not change the shape of the distribution, nor does it change the standard deviation. Thus, we assume that the population after treatment has the same shape as the original population and the same standard deviation as the original population. This assumption is incorporated into the situation shown in Figure 8.1.

Note that the unknown population, after treatment, is the focus of the research question. Specifically, the purpose of the research is to determine what would happen if the treatment were administered to every individual in the population.

The sample in the research study   The goal of the hypothesis test is to determine whether the treatment has any effect on the individuals in the population (see Figure 8.1). Usually, however, we cannot administer the treatment to the entire population, so the actual research study is conducted using a sample. Figure 8.2 shows the structure of the research study from the point of view of the hypothesis test. The original population, before treatment, is shown on the left-hand side. The unknown population, after treatment, is shown on the right-hand side. Note that the unknown population is actually *hypothetical* (the treatment is never administered to the entire population). Instead, we are asking *what would happen if* the treatment were administered to the entire population. The research study involves selecting a sample from the original population, administering the treatment to the sample, and then recording scores for the individuals in the treated sample. Notice that the research study produces a treated

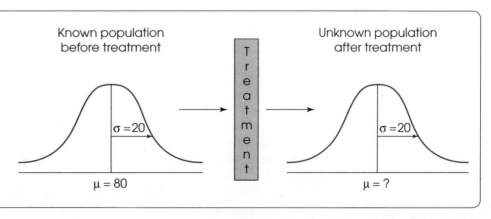

FIGURE 8.1

The basic experimental situation for hypothesis testing. It is assumed that the parameter μ is known for the population before treatment. The purpose of the experiment is to determine whether the treatment has an effect on the population mean.

Known population before treatment

Unknown population after treatment

Treatment

$\sigma = 20$

$\mu = 80$

$\sigma = 20$

$\mu = ?$

FIGURE 8.2

From the point of view of the hypothesis test, the entire population receives the treatment and then a sample is selected from the treated population. In the actual research study, a sample is selected from the original population and the treatment is administered to the sample. From either perspective, the result is a treated sample that represents the treated population.

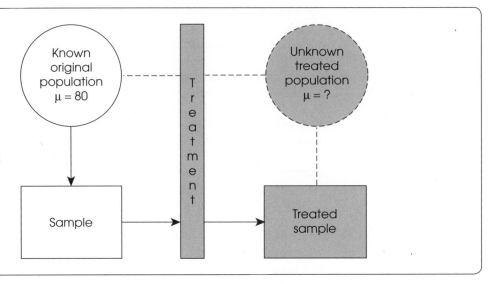

sample. Although this sample was obtained indirectly, it is equivalent to a sample that is obtained directly from the unknown treated population. The hypothesis test uses the treated sample on the right-hand side of Figure 8.2 to evaluate a hypothesis about the unknown treated population on the right side of the figure.

A hypothesis test is a formalized procedure that follows a standard series of operations. In this way, researchers have a standardized method for evaluating the results of their research studies. Other researchers recognize and understand exactly how the data were evaluated and how conclusions were reached. To emphasize the formal structure of a hypothesis test, we present hypothesis testing as a four-step process that is used throughout the rest of the book. The following example provides a concrete foundation for introducing the hypothesis-testing procedure.

EXAMPLE 8.1 Researchers have demonstrated that it is possible to improve mathematics skills using mild electrical brain stimulation (Kadosh, Soskic, Iuculano, Kanai, & Walsh, 2010). In the study, participants were taught artificial number symbols while researchers applied mild electrical current across their skulls near the parietal lobes, a part of the brain that is important for mathematical skill. Other participants learned the same number symbols with current applied in a different brain location. After six study sessions, the parietal-lobe group performed significantly better on a test evaluating their knowledge of the number symbols.

Suppose that a researcher is testing the same kind of brain stimulation on students who are studying for a standardized mathematics exam. For the general population, scores on this exam form a normal distribution with a mean of $\mu = 80$ and a standard deviation of $\sigma = 20$. The researcher's plan is to obtain a sample of $n = 25$ students who are scheduled to take the exam, and have each student study for 30 minutes each day while current is applied near the parietal lobe. After 4 weeks, the participants are given the standardized exam. If the mean score for the sample is noticeably different from the mean for the general population of students, then the researcher can conclude that the electric stimulation does appear to have an effect on mathematical skill. On the other hand, if the sample mean is around 80 (the same as the general population mean), the researcher must conclude that the stimulation does not appear to have any effect.

THE FOUR STEPS OF A HYPOTHESIS TEST

Figure 8.2 depicts the research situation that was described in the preceding example. Notice that the population after treatment is unknown. Specifically, we do not know what will happen to the mean score if the entire population of students is given the brain stimulation while studying. However, we do have a sample of $n = 25$ participants who have received the stimulation and we can use this sample to help draw inferences about the unknown population. The following four steps outline the hypothesis-testing procedure that allows us to use sample data to answer questions about an unknown population.

STEP 1: STATE THE HYPOTHESIS

The goal of inferential statistics is to make general statements about the population by using sample data. Therefore, when testing hypotheses, we make our predictions about the population parameters.

As the name implies, the process of hypothesis testing begins by stating a hypothesis about the unknown population. Actually, we state two opposing hypotheses. Notice that both hypotheses are stated in terms of population parameters.

The first, and most important, of the two hypotheses is called the *null hypothesis*. The null hypothesis states that the treatment has no effect. In general, the null hypothesis states that there is no change, no effect, no difference—nothing happened, hence the name *null*. The null hypothesis is identified by the symbol H_0. (The H stands for *hypothesis*, and the zero subscript indicates that this is the *zero-effect* hypothesis.) For the study in Example 8.1, the null hypothesis states that the brain stimulation has no effect on mathematical skill for the population of students. In symbols, this hypothesis is

$$H_0 : \mu_{\text{with stimulation}} = 80 \qquad \text{(Even with the stimulation, the mean test score is still 80.)}$$

DEFINITION

> The **null hypothesis** (H_0) states that in the general population there is no change, no difference, or no relationship. In the context of an experiment, H_0 predicts that the independent variable (treatment) *has no effect* on the dependent variable (scores) for the population.

The second hypothesis is the opposite of the null hypothesis, and it is called the *scientific,* or *alternative, hypothesis* (H_1). This hypothesis states that the treatment has an effect on the dependent variable.

DEFINITION

> The **alternative hypothesis** (H_1) states that there is a change, a difference, or a relationship for the general population. In the context of an experiment, H_1 predicts that the independent variable (treatment) *does have an effect* on the dependent variable.

The null hypothesis and the alternative hypothesis are mutually exclusive and exhaustive. They cannot both be true, and one of them must be true. The data determine which one should be rejected.

For this example, the alternative hypothesis states that the stimulation does have an effect on mathematical skill for the population and will cause a change in the mean score. In symbols, the alternative hypothesis is represented as

$$H_1 : \mu_{\text{with stimulation}} \neq 80 \qquad \text{(With the stimulation, the mean test score is different from 80.)}$$

Notice that the alternative hypothesis simply states that there will be some type of change. It does not specify whether the effect will be increased or decreased test scores. In some circumstances, it is appropriate for the alternative hypothesis to specify the direction of the effect. For example, the researcher might hypothesize that the stimulation will increase test scores ($\mu > 80$). This type of hypothesis results in a directional hypothesis test, which is examined in detail later in this chapter. For now we concentrate on nondirectional tests, for which the hypotheses simply state that the treatment has no effect (H_0) or has some effect (H_1).

STEP 2: SET THE CRITERIA FOR A DECISION

Eventually the researcher uses the data from the sample to evaluate the credibility of the null hypothesis. The data either provide support for the null hypothesis or tend to refute the null hypothesis. In particular, if there is a big discrepancy between the data and the null hypothesis, then we conclude that the null hypothesis is wrong.

To formalize the decision process, we use the null hypothesis to predict the kind of sample mean that ought to be obtained. Specifically, we determine exactly which sample means are consistent with the null hypothesis and which sample means are at odds with the null hypothesis.

For our example, the null hypothesis states that the brain stimulation has no effect and the population mean is still $\mu = 80$. If this is true, then the sample mean should have a value around 80. Therefore, a sample mean near 80 is consistent with the null hypothesis. On the other hand, a sample mean that is very different from 80 is not consistent with the null hypothesis. To determine exactly which values are "near" 80 and which values are "very different from" 80, we examine all of the possible sample means that could be obtained if the null hypothesis is true. For our example, this is the distribution of sample means for $n = 25$. According to the null hypothesis, this distribution is centered at $\mu = 80$. The distribution of sample means is then divided into two sections:

1. Sample means that are likely to be obtained if H_0 is true; that is, sample means that are close to the null hypothesis

2. Sample means that are very unlikely to be obtained if H_0 is true; that is, sample means that are very different from the null hypothesis

Figure 8.3 shows the distribution of sample means divided into these two sections. Notice that the high-probability samples are located in the center of the distribution

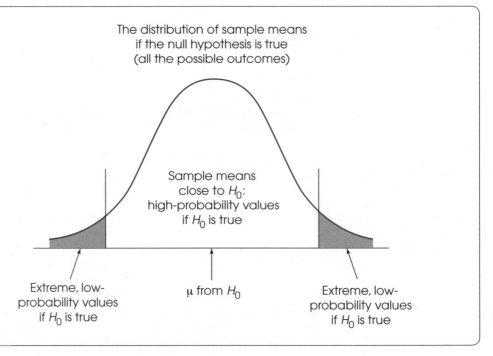

FIGURE 8.3

The set of potential samples is divided into those that are likely to be obtained and those that are very unlikely to be obtained if the null hypothesis is true.

The distribution of sample means
if the null hypothesis is true
(all the possible outcomes)

Sample means
close to H_0:
high-probability values
if H_0 is true

Extreme, low-
probability values
if H_0 is true

μ from H_0

Extreme, low-
probability values
if H_0 is true

and have sample means close to the value specified in the null hypothesis. On the other hand, the low-probability samples are located in the extreme tails of the distribution. After the distribution has been divided in this way, we can compare our sample data with the values in the distribution. Specifically, we can determine whether our sample mean is consistent with the null hypothesis (like the values in the center of the distribution) or whether our sample mean is very different from the null hypothesis (like the values in the extreme tails).

The alpha level   To find the boundaries that separate the high-probability samples from the low-probability samples, we must define exactly what is meant by "low" probability and "high" probability. This is accomplished by selecting a specific probability value, which is known as the *level of significance,* or the *alpha level,* for the hypothesis test. The alpha (α) value is a small probability that is used to identify the low-probability samples. By convention, commonly used alpha levels are $\alpha = .05$ (5%), $\alpha = .01$ (1%), and $\alpha = .001$ (0.1%). For example, with $\alpha = .05$, we separate the most unlikely 5% of the sample means (the extreme values) from the most likely 95% of the sample means (the central values).

> With rare exceptions, an alpha level is never larger than .05.

The extremely unlikely values, as defined by the alpha level, make up what is called the *critical region.* These extreme values in the tails of the distribution define outcomes that are not consistent with the null hypothesis; that is, they are very unlikely to occur if the null hypothesis is true. Whenever the data from a research study produce a sample mean that is located in the critical region, we conclude that the data are not consistent with the null hypothesis, and we reject the null hypothesis.

DEFINITIONS

> The **alpha level,** or the **level of significance,** is a probability value that is used to define the concept of "very unlikely" in a hypothesis test.

> The **critical region** is composed of the extreme sample values that are very unlikely (as defined by the alpha level) to be obtained if the null hypothesis is true. The boundaries for the critical region are determined by the alpha level. If sample data fall in the critical region, the null hypothesis is rejected.

Technically, the critical region is defined by sample outcomes that are *very unlikely* to occur if the treatment has no effect (that is, if the null hypothesis is true). Reversing the point of view, we can also define the critical region as sample values that provide *convincing evidence* that the treatment really does have an effect. For our example, the regular population of students has a mean test score of $\mu = 80$. We selected a sample from this population and administered a treatment (the brain stimulation) to the individuals in the sample. What kind of sample mean would convince you that the treatment has an effect? It should be obvious that the most convincing evidence would be a sample mean that is really different from $\mu = 80$. In a hypothesis test, the critical region is determined by sample values that are "really different" from the original population.

The boundaries for the critical region   To determine the exact location for the boundaries that define the critical region, we use the alpha-level probability and the unit normal table. In most cases, the distribution of sample means is normal, and the unit normal table provides the precise z-score location for the critical region boundaries. With $\alpha = .05$, for example, the boundaries separate the extreme 5% from the middle 95%. Because the extreme 5% is split between two tails of the distribution, there is exactly 2.5% (or 0.0250) in each tail. In the unit normal table, you can look up a proportion of 0.0250 in column C (the tail) and find that the z-score boundary is $z = 1.96$. Thus,

FIGURE 8.4

The critical region (very unlikely outcomes) for $\alpha = .05$.

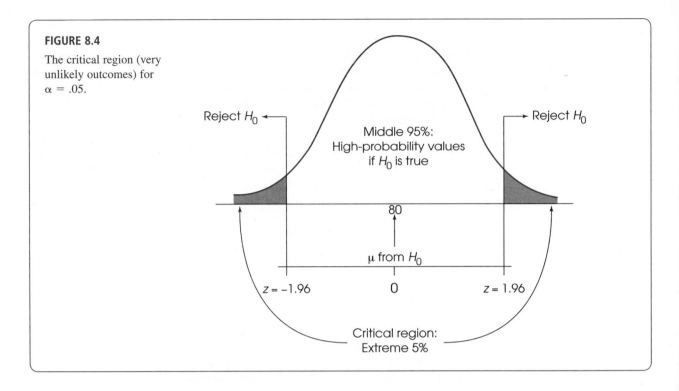

Reject H_0 ← ⟶ Reject H_0

Middle 95%:
High-probability values
if H_0 is true

80

μ from H_0

$z = -1.96$ 0 $z = 1.96$

Critical region:
Extreme 5%

for any normal distribution, the extreme 5% is in the tails of the distribution beyond $z = +1.96$ and $z = -1.96$. These values define the boundaries of the critical region for a hypothesis test using $\alpha = .05$ (Figure 8.4).

Similarly, an alpha level of $\alpha = .01$ means that 1%, or .0100, is split between the two tails. In this case, the proportion in each tail is .0050, and the corresponding z-score boundaries are $z = \pm2.58$ (±2.57 is equally good). For $\alpha = .001$, the boundaries are located at $z = \pm3.30$. You should verify these values in the unit normal table and be sure that you understand exactly how they are obtained.

LEARNING CHECK

1. The city school district is considering increasing class size in the elementary schools. However, some members of the school board are concerned that larger classes may have a negative effect on student learning. In words, what would the null hypothesis say about the effect of class size on student learning?

2. If the alpha level is increased from $\alpha = .01$ to $\alpha = .05$, then the boundaries for the critical region move farther away from the center of the distribution. (True or false?)

3. If a researcher conducted a hypothesis test with an alpha level of $\alpha = .02$, what z-score values would form the boundaries for the critical region?

ANSWERS

1. The null hypothesis would say that class size has no effect on student learning.

2. False. A larger alpha means that the boundaries for the critical region move closer to the center of the distribution.

3. The .02 would be split between the two tails, with .01 in each tail. The z-score boundaries would be $z = +2.33$ and $z = -2.33$.

STEP 3: COLLECT DATA AND COMPUTE SAMPLE STATISTICS

At this time, we select a sample of students and give them 30 minutes of brain stimulation each day while they study for the mathematics exam. After 4 weeks, the students take the standardized mathematics test. Notice that the data are collected *after* the researcher has stated the hypotheses and established the criteria for a decision. This sequence of events helps to ensure that a researcher makes an honest, objective evaluation of the data and does not tamper with the decision criteria after the experimental outcome is known.

Next, the raw data from the sample are summarized with the appropriate statistics: For this example, the researcher would compute the sample mean. Now it is possible for the researcher to compare the sample mean (the data) with the null hypothesis. This is the heart of the hypothesis test: comparing the data with the hypothesis.

The comparison is accomplished by computing a z-score that describes exactly where the sample mean is located relative to the hypothesized population mean from H_0. In step 2, we constructed the distribution of sample means that would be expected if the null hypothesis were true—that is, the entire set of sample means that could be obtained if the treatment has no effect (see Figure 8.4). Now we calculate a z-score that identifies where our sample mean is located in this hypothesized distribution. The z-score formula for a sample mean is

$$z = \frac{M - \mu}{\sigma_M}$$

In the formula, the value of the sample mean (M) is obtained from the sample data, and the value of μ is obtained from the null hypothesis. Thus, the z-score formula can be expressed in words as follows:

$$z = \frac{\text{sample mean} - \text{hypothesized population mean}}{\text{standard error between } M \text{ and } \mu}$$

Notice that the top of the z-score formula measures how much difference there is between the data and the hypothesis. The bottom of the formula measures the standard distance that ought to exist between a sample mean and the population mean.

STEP 4: MAKE A DECISION

In the final step, the researcher uses the z-score value obtained in step 3 to make a decision about the null hypothesis according to the criteria established in step 2. There are two possible outcomes:

1. The sample data are located in the critical region. By definition, a sample value in the critical region is very unlikely to occur if the null hypothesis is true. Therefore, we conclude that the sample is not consistent with H_0 and our decision is to *reject the null hypothesis*. Remember, the null hypothesis states that there is no treatment effect, so rejecting H_0 means that we are concluding that the treatment did have an effect.

   For the example we have been considering, suppose that the sample produced a mean of $M = 89$ after receiving brain stimulation while studying. The null hypothesis states that the population mean is $\mu = 80$ and, with $n = 25$ and $\sigma = 20$, the standard error for the sample mean is

$$\sigma_M = \frac{\sigma}{\sqrt{n}} = \frac{20}{\sqrt{25}} = \frac{20}{5} = 4$$

Thus, a sample mean of $M = 89$ produces a z-score of

$$z = \frac{M - \mu}{\sigma_M} = \frac{89 - 80}{4} = \frac{9}{4} = 2.25$$

With an alpha level of $\alpha = .05$, this z-score is beyond the boundary of 1.96. Because the sample z-score is in the critical region, we reject the null hypothesis and conclude that the brain stimulation did have an effect on mathematics skill.

2. The second possibility is that the sample data are not in the critical region. In this case, the sample mean is reasonably close to the population mean specified in the null hypothesis (in the center of the distribution). Because the data do not provide strong evidence that the null hypothesis is wrong, our conclusion is to *fail to reject the null hypothesis*. This conclusion means that the treatment does not appear to have an effect.

For the research study examining the brain stimulation, if our sample produced a mean test score of $M = 84$, then we would obtain a z-score of

$$z = \frac{M - \mu}{\sigma_M} = \frac{84 - 80}{4} = \frac{4}{4} = 1.00$$

The z-score of 1.00 is not in the critical region. Therefore, we would fail to reject the null hypothesis and conclude that the brain stimulation does not appear to have an effect on mathematical skill.

In general, the final decision is made by comparing our treated sample with the distribution of sample means that would be obtained for untreated samples. If our treated sample looks much the same as samples that do not receive the brain stimulation, then we conclude that the treatment does not appear to have any effect. On the other hand, if the treated sample is noticeably different from the majority of untreated samples, then we conclude that the treatment does have an effect.

An analogy for hypothesis testing It may seem awkward to phrase both of the two possible decisions in terms of rejecting the null hypothesis; either we reject H_0 or we fail to reject H_0. These two decisions may be easier to understand if you think of a research study as an attempt to gather evidence to prove that a treatment works. From this perspective, the process of conducting a hypothesis test is similar to the process that takes place during a jury trial. For example,

1. The test begins with a null hypothesis stating that there is no treatment effect. The trial begins with a null hypothesis that the defendant did not commit a crime (innocent until proven guilty).

2. The research study gathers evidence to show that the treatment actually does have an effect, and the police gather evidence to show that the defendant really did commit a crime. Note that both are trying to refute the null hypothesis.

3. If there is enough evidence, the researcher rejects the null hypothesis and concludes that there really is a treatment effect. If there is enough evidence, the jury rejects the hypothesis and concludes that the defendant is guilty of a crime.

4. If there is not enough evidence, the researcher fails to reject the null hypothesis. Note that the researcher does not conclude that there is no treatment effect, simply that there is not enough evidence to conclude that there is an effect. Similarly, if there is not enough evidence, the jury fails to find the defendant guilty. Note that the jury does not conclude that the defendant is innocent, simply that there is not enough evidence for a guilty verdict.

LEARNING CHECK

1. A researcher selects a sample of $n = 16$ individuals from a normal population with a mean of $\mu = 40$ and $\sigma = 8$. A treatment is administered to the sample and, after treatment, the sample mean is $M = 43$. If the researcher uses a hypothesis test to evaluate the treatment effect, what z-score would be obtained for this sample?

2. A small value (near zero) for the z-score statistic is evidence that the sample data are consistent with the null hypothesis. (True or false?)

3. A z-score value in the critical region means that you should reject the null hypothesis. (True or false?)

ANSWERS

1. The standard error is 2 points and $z = \frac{3}{2} = 1.50$.

2. True. A z-score near zero indicates that the data support the null hypothesis.

3. True. A z-score value in the critical region means that the sample is not consistent with the null hypothesis.

8.2 UNCERTAINTY AND ERRORS IN HYPOTHESIS TESTING

Hypothesis testing is an *inferential process*, which means that it uses limited information as the basis for reaching a general conclusion. Specifically, a sample provides only limited or incomplete information about the whole population, and yet a hypothesis test uses a sample to draw a conclusion about the population. In this situation, there is always the possibility that an incorrect conclusion will be made. Although sample data are usually representative of the population, there is always a chance that the sample is misleading and will cause a researcher to make the wrong decision about the research results. In a hypothesis test, there are two different kinds of errors that can be made.

TYPE I ERRORS

It is possible that the data will lead you to reject the null hypothesis when in fact the treatment has no effect. Remember: Samples are not expected to be identical to their populations, and some extreme samples can be very different from the populations that they are supposed to represent. If a researcher selects one of these extreme samples by chance, then the data from the sample may give the appearance of a strong treatment effect, even though there is no real effect. In the previous section, for example, we discussed a research study examining how brain stimulation near the parietal lobe affects the learning of new mathematical skills. Suppose that the researcher selects a sample of $n = 25$ students who already have mathematical skills that are well above average. Even if the stimulation (the treatment) has no effect at all, these people will still score higher than average on the standardized test. In this case, the researcher is likely to conclude that the treatment does have an effect, when in fact it really does not. This is an example of what is called a *Type I error.*

DEFINITION

> A **Type I error** occurs when a researcher rejects a null hypothesis that is actually true. In a typical research situation, a Type I error means that the researcher concludes that a treatment does have an effect when, in fact, it has no effect.

You should realize that a Type I error is not a stupid mistake in the sense that a researcher is overlooking something that should be perfectly obvious. On the contrary, the researcher is looking at sample data that appear to show a clear treatment effect. The researcher then makes a careful decision based on the available information. The problem is that the information from the sample is misleading.

In most research situations, the consequences of a Type I error can be very serious. Because the researcher has rejected the null hypothesis and believes that the treatment has a real effect, it is likely that the researcher will report or even publish the research results. A Type I error, however, means that this is a false report. Thus, Type I errors lead to false reports in the scientific literature. Other researchers may try to build theories or develop other experiments based on the false results. A lot of precious time and resources may be wasted.

The probability of a Type I error   A Type I error occurs when a researcher unknowingly obtains an extreme, nonrepresentative sample. Fortunately, the hypothesis test is structured to minimize the risk that this will occur. Figure 8.4 shows the distribution of sample means and the critical region for the research study we have been discussing. This distribution contains all of the possible sample means for samples of $n = 25$ if the null hypothesis is true. Notice that most of the sample means are near the hypothesized population mean, $\mu = 80$, and that means in the critical region are very unlikely to occur.

With an alpha level of $\alpha = .05$, only 5% of the samples have means in the critical region. Therefore, there is only a 5% probability ($p = .05$) that one of these samples will be obtained. Thus, the alpha level determines the probability of obtaining a sample mean in the critical region when the null hypothesis is true. In other words, the *alpha level* determines the probability of a Type I error.

DEFINITION

> The **alpha level** for a hypothesis test is the probability that the test will lead to a Type I error if the null hypothesis is true. That is, the alpha level determines the probability of obtaining sample data in the critical region even though there is no treatment effect.

In summary, whenever the sample data are in the critical region, the appropriate decision for a hypothesis test is to reject the null hypothesis. Normally this is the correct decision because the treatment has caused the sample to be different from the original population. In this case, the hypothesis test has correctly identified a real treatment effect. Occasionally, however, sample data are in the critical region just by chance, without any treatment effect. When this occurs, the researcher makes a Type I error; that is, the researcher concludes that a treatment effect exists when in fact it does not. Fortunately, the risk of a Type I error is small and is under the control of the researcher. Specifically, the probability of a Type I error is equal to the alpha level.

TYPE II ERRORS   Whenever a researcher rejects the null hypothesis, there is a risk of a Type I error. Similarly, whenever a researcher fails to reject the null hypothesis, there is a risk of a *Type II error.* By definition, a Type II error is the failure to reject a false null hypothesis. In more straightforward English, a Type II error means that a treatment effect really exists, but the hypothesis test fails to detect it.

DEFINITION

> A **Type II error** occurs when a researcher fails to reject a null hypothesis that is really false. In a typical research situation, a Type II error means that the hypothesis test has failed to detect a real treatment effect.

A Type II error occurs when the sample mean is not in the critical region even though the treatment has had an effect on the sample. Often this happens when the effect of the treatment is relatively small. In this case, the treatment does influence the sample, but the magnitude of the effect is not big enough to move the sample mean into the critical region. Because the sample is not substantially different from the original population (it is not in the critical region), the statistical decision is to fail to reject the null hypothesis and to conclude that there is not enough evidence to say that there is a treatment effect.

The consequences of a Type II error are usually not as serious as those of a Type I error. In general terms, a Type II error means that the research data do not show the results that the researcher had hoped to obtain. The researcher can accept this outcome and conclude that the treatment either has no effect or has only a small effect that is not worth pursuing, or the researcher can repeat the experiment (usually with some improvement, such as a larger sample) and try to demonstrate that the treatment really does work.

Unlike a Type I error, it is impossible to determine a single, exact probability for a Type II error. Instead, the probability of a Type II error depends on a variety of factors and therefore is a function, rather than a specific number. Nonetheless, the probability of a Type II error is represented by the symbol β, the Greek letter *beta*.

In summary, a hypothesis test always leads to one of two decisions:

1. The sample data provide sufficient evidence to reject the null hypothesis and conclude that the treatment has an effect.

2. The sample data do not provide enough evidence to reject the null hypothesis. In this case, you fail to reject H_0 and conclude that the treatment does not appear to have an effect.

In either case, there is a chance that the data are misleading and the decision is wrong. The complete set of decisions and outcomes is shown in Table 8.1. The risk of an error is especially important in the case of a Type I error, which can lead to a false report. Fortunately, the alpha level, which is completely under the control of the researcher, defines the probability of a Type I error if the null hypothesis is true. At the beginning of a hypothesis test, the researcher states the hypotheses and selects the alpha level, which immediately determines the risk that a Type I error will be made.

SELECTING AN ALPHA LEVEL

As you have seen, the alpha level for a hypothesis test serves two very important functions. First, the alpha level helps to determine the boundaries for the critical region by defining the concept of "very unlikely" outcomes. At the same time, the alpha level determines the probability of a Type I error if the null hypothesis is true. When you select a value for alpha at the beginning of a hypothesis test, your decision influences both of these functions.

The primary concern when selecting an alpha level is to minimize the risk of a Type I error. Thus, alpha levels tend to be very small probability values. By convention, the largest permissible value is $\alpha = .05$. When there is no treatment effect, an alpha level of .05 means that there is a 5% risk, or a 1-in-20 probability, of rejecting the null hypothesis and committing a Type I error. Because the consequences of a Type I error can be relatively serious, many individual researchers and many scientific publications

TABLE 8.1

Possible outcomes of a statistical decision.

		Actual Situation	
		No Effect, H_0 True	Effect Exists, H_0 False
Experimenter's Decision	Reject H_0	Type I error	Decision correct
	Retain H_0	Decision correct	Type II error

prefer to use a more conservative alpha level such as .01 or .001 to reduce the risk that a false report is published and becomes part of the scientific literature. (For more information on the origins of the .05 level of significance, see the excellent short article by Cowles and Davis, 1982.)

At this point, it may appear that the best strategy for selecting an alpha level is to choose the smallest possible value to minimize the risk of a Type I error. However, there is a different kind of risk that develops as the alpha level is lowered. Specifically, a lower alpha level means less risk of a Type I error, but it also means that the hypothesis test demands more evidence from the research results.

The trade-off between the demands of the test and the risk of a Type I error is controlled by the boundaries of the critical region. For the hypothesis test to conclude that the treatment does have an effect, the sample data must be in the critical region. If the treatment really has an effect, it should cause the sample to be different from the original population; essentially, the treatment should push the sample into the critical region. However, as the alpha level is lowered, the boundaries for the critical region move farther out and become more difficult to reach. Figure 8.5 shows how the boundaries for the critical region move farther into the tails as the alpha level decreases. Notice that $z = 0$, in the center of the distribution, corresponds to the value of μ specified in the null hypothesis. The boundaries for the critical region determine how much distance between the sample mean and μ is needed to reject the null hypothesis. As the alpha level gets smaller, this distance gets larger.

Thus, an extremely small alpha level, such as .000001 (one in a million), would mean almost no risk of a Type I error but would push the critical region so far out that it would become essentially impossible to ever reject the null hypothesis; that is, it would require an enormous treatment effect before the sample data would reach the critical boundaries.

In general, researchers try to maintain a balance between the risk of a Type I error and the demands of the hypothesis test. Alpha levels of .05, .01, and .001 are considered reasonably good values because they provide a low risk of error without placing excessive demands on the research results.

FIGURE 8.5

The locations of the critical region boundaries for three different levels of significance: $\alpha = .05$, $\alpha = .01$, and $\alpha = .001$.

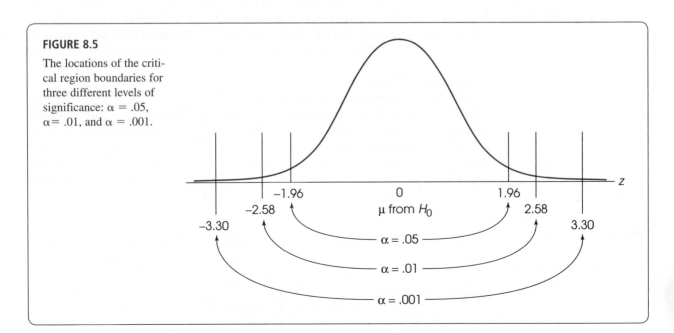

LEARNING CHECK

1. Define a Type I error.

2. Define a Type II error.

3. Under what circumstances is a Type II error likely to occur?

4. If a sample mean is in the critical region with $\alpha = .05$, it would still (always) be in the critical region if alpha were changed to $\alpha = .01$. (True or false?)

5. If a sample mean is in the critical region with $\alpha = .01$, it would still (always) be in the critical region if alpha were changed to $\alpha = .05$. (True or false?)

ANSWERS

1. A Type I error is rejecting a true null hypothesis—that is, saying that the treatment has an effect when, in fact, it does not.

2. A Type II error is the failure to reject a false null hypothesis. In terms of a research study, a Type II error occurs when a study fails to detect a treatment effect that really exists.

3. A Type II error is likely to occur when the treatment effect is very small. In this case, a research study is more likely to fail to detect the effect.

4. False. With $\alpha = .01$, the boundaries for the critical region move farther out into the tails of the distribution. It is possible that a sample mean could be beyond the .05 boundary but not beyond the .01 boundary.

5. True. With $\alpha = .01$, the boundaries for the critical region are farther out into the tails of the distribution than for $\alpha = .05$. If a sample mean is beyond the .01 boundary it is definitely beyond the .05 boundary.

8.3   MORE ABOUT HYPOTHESIS TESTS

A SUMMARY OF THE HYPOTHESIS TEST

In section 8.1, we presented a complete example of a hypothesis test evaluating the effect of brain stimulation on students' mathematical test scores. The 4-step process for that hypothesis test is summarized as follows:

STEP 1   *State the hypotheses and select an alpha level.* For this example, the general population, without treatment, has an average test score of $\mu = 80$ with $\sigma = 20$. Therefore, the hypotheses are:

$$H_0: \mu_{\text{with stimulation}} = 80 \qquad \text{(the brain stimulation has no effect)}$$

$$H_1: \mu_{\text{with stimulation}} \neq 80 \qquad \text{(the brain stimulation does have an effect)}$$

We set $\alpha = .05$.

STEP 2   *Locate the critical region.* For a normal distribution with $\alpha = .05$, the critical region consists of sample means that produce z-scores in the extreme tails of the distribution beyond $z = \pm 1.96$.

STEP 3   *Compute the test statistic (the z-score).* We obtained a sample mean of $M = 89$ for $n = 25$ participants. With a standard error of $\sigma_M = 4$, we obtain

$$z = \frac{M - \mu}{\sigma_M} = \frac{89 - 80}{4} = \frac{9}{4} = 2.25$$

STEP 4   *Make a decision.* The *z*-score is in the critical region, which means that this sample mean is very unlikely if the null hypothesis is true. Therefore, we reject the null hypothesis and conclude that the brain stimulation did have an effect on the students' test scores.

IN THE LITERATURE
REPORTING THE RESULTS OF THE STATISTICAL TEST

A special jargon and notational system are used in published reports of hypothesis tests. When you are reading a scientific journal, for example, you typically are not told explicitly that the researcher evaluated the data using a *z*-score as a test statistic with an alpha level of .05. Nor are you told that "the null hypothesis is rejected." Instead, you see a statement such as:

> Electrical stimulation of the scalp near the parietal lobe had a significant effect on the mathematics test scores for the students, $z = 2.25$, $p < .05$.

Let us examine this statement, piece by piece. First, what is meant by the word *significant?* In statistical tests, a *significant* result means that the null hypothesis has been rejected, which means that the result is very unlikely to have occurred merely by chance. For this example, the null hypothesis stated that the brain stimulation has no effect; however, the data clearly indicate that it did have an effect. Specifically, it is very unlikely that the sample mean, $M = 89$, would have been obtained if the stimulation did not have an effect.

DEFINITION

> A result is said to be **significant,** or **statistically significant,** if it is very unlikely to occur when the null hypothesis is true. That is, the result is sufficient to reject the null hypothesis. Thus, a treatment has a significant effect if the decision from the hypothesis test is to reject H_0.

Next, what is the meaning of $z = 2.25$? The *z* indicates that a *z*-score was used as the test statistic to evaluate the sample data and that its value is 2.25. Finally, what is meant by $p < .05$? This part of the statement is a conventional way of specifying the alpha level that was used for the hypothesis test. It also acknowledges the possibility (and the probability) of a Type I error. Specifically, the researcher is reporting that the treatment had an effect but admits that this could be a false report. That is, it is possible that the sample mean was in the critical region even though the brain stimulation had no effect. However, the probability (p) of obtaining a sample mean in the critical region is extremely small (less than .05) if there is no treatment effect.

In circumstances in which the statistical decision is to *fail to reject H_0*, the report might state that.

> The sample did not provide sufficient evidence to conclude that the brain stimulation had an effect on mathematics test scores, $z = 1.30$, $p > .05$.

The APA style does not use a leading zero in a probability value that refers to a level of significance.

In that case, we would be saying that the obtained result, $z = 1.30$, is not unusual (not in the critical region) and that it has a relatively high probability of occurring (greater than .05) even if the null hypothesis is true.

Sometimes students become confused trying to differentiate between $p < .05$ and $p > .05$. Remember that you reject the null hypothesis with extreme, low-probability values, located in the critical region in the tails of the distribution. Thus, a significant result that rejects the null hypothesis corresponds to $p < .05$ (Figure 8.6).

When a hypothesis test is conducted using a computer program, the printout often includes not only a *z*-score value but also an exact value for p, the probability

FIGURE 8.6

Sample means that fall in the critical region (shaded areas) have a probability *less than* alpha ($p < \alpha$). In this case, H_0 should be rejected. Sample means that do not fall in the critical region have a probability *greater than* alpha ($p > \alpha$).

that the result occurred without any treatment effect. In this case, researchers are encouraged to report the exact p value instead of using the less-than or greater-than notation. For example, a research report might state that the treatment effect was significant, with $z = 2.45$, $p = .0142$. When using exact values for p, however, you must still satisfy the traditional criterion for significance; specifically, the p value must be smaller than .05 to be considered statistically significant. Remember: The p value is the probability that the result would occur if H_0 were true (there is no treatment effect), which is also the probability of a Type I error. It is essential that this probability be very small.

ASSUMPTIONS FOR HYPOTHESIS TESTS WITH z-SCORES

The mathematics used for a hypothesis test are based on a set of assumptions. When these assumptions are satisfied, you can be confident that the test produces a justified conclusion. However, if the assumptions are not satisfied, then the hypothesis test may be compromised. In practice, researchers are not overly concerned with the assumptions underlying a hypothesis test because the tests usually work well even when the assumptions are violated. However, you should be aware of the fundamental conditions that are associated with each type of statistical test to ensure that the test is being used appropriately. The assumptions for hypothesis tests with z-scores are summarized as follows.

Random sampling   It is assumed that the participants used in the study were selected randomly. Remember, we wish to generalize our findings from the sample to the population. Therefore, the sample must be representative of the population from which it has been drawn. Random sampling helps to ensure that it is representative.

Independent observations   The values in the sample must consist of *independent* observations. In everyday terms, two observations are independent if there is no consistent, predictable relationship between the first observation and the second. More precisely, two events (or observations) are independent if the occurrence of the first event has no effect on the probability of the second event. Specific examples of independence and non-independence are examined in Box 8.1. Usually, this assumption is satisfied by using a *random* sample, which also helps to ensure that the sample is representative of the population and that the results can be generalized to the population.

The value of σ is unchanged by the treatment   A critical part of the z-score formula in a hypothesis test is the standard error, σ_M. To compute the value for the

BOX 8.1   INDEPENDENT OBSERVATIONS

Independent observations are a basic requirement for nearly all hypothesis tests. The critical concern is that each observation or measurement is not influenced by any other observation or measurement. An example of independent observations is the set of outcomes obtained in a series of coin tosses. Assuming that the coin is balanced, each toss has a 50–50 chance of coming up either heads or tails. More important, each toss is *independent* of the tosses that came before. On the fifth toss, for example, there is a 50% chance of heads no matter what happened on the previous four tosses; the coin does not remember what happened earlier and is not influenced by the past. (*Note:* Many people fail to believe in the independence of events. For example, after a series of four tails in a row, it is tempting to think that the probability of heads must increase because the coin is overdue to come up heads. This is a mistake, called the "gambler's fallacy." Remember that the coin does not know what happened on the preceding tosses and cannot be influenced by previous outcomes.)

In most research situations, the requirement for independent observations is satisfied by using a random sample of separate, unrelated individuals. Thus, the measurement obtained for each individual is not influenced by other participants in the study. The following two situations demonstrate circumstances in which the observations are *not* independent.

1. A researcher is interested in examining television preferences for children. To obtain a sample of $n = 20$ children, the researcher selects 4 children from family A, 3 children from family B, 5 children from family C, 2 children from family D, and 6 children from family E.

    It should be obvious that the researcher does *not* have 20 independent observations. Within each family, the children probably share television preference (at least, they watch the same shows). Thus, the response for each child is likely to be related to the responses of his or her siblings.

2. The principle of independent observations is violated if the sample is obtained using *sampling without replacement*. For example, if you are selecting from a group of 20 potential participants, each individual has a 1 in 20 chance of being selected first. After the first person is selected, however, there are only 19 people remaining and the probability of being selected changes to 1 in 19. Because the probability of the second selection depends on the first, the two selections are not independent.

---

standard error, we must know the sample size (n) and the population standard deviation (σ). In a hypothesis test, however, the sample comes from an *unknown* population (see Figure 8.2). If the population is really unknown, it would suggest that we do not know the standard deviation and, therefore, we cannot calculate the standard error. To solve this dilemma, we have made an assumption. Specifically, we assume that the standard deviation for the unknown population (after treatment) is the same as it was for the population before treatment.

Actually, this assumption is the consequence of a more general assumption that is part of many statistical procedures. This general assumption states that the effect of the treatment is to add a constant amount to (or subtract a constant amount from) every score in the population. You should recall that adding (or subtracting) a constant changes the mean but has no effect on the standard deviation. You also should note that this assumption is a theoretical ideal. In actual experiments, a treatment generally does not show a perfect and consistent additive effect.

Normal sampling distribution   To evaluate hypotheses with z-scores, we have used the unit normal table to identify the critical region. This table can be used only if the distribution of sample means is normal.

A CLOSER LOOK AT THE z-SCORE IN A HYPOTHESIS TEST

The z-score statistic that is used in the hypothesis test is the first specific example of what is called a *test statistic*. The term *test statistic* simply indicates that the sample data are converted into a single, specific statistic that is used to test the hypotheses. In the chapters that follow, we introduce several other test statistics that are used in a variety of different research situations. However, most of the new test statistics have the same basic structure and serve the same purpose as the z-score. We have already described the z-score equation as a formal method for comparing the sample data and the population hypothesis. In this section, we discuss the z-score from two other perspectives that may give you a better understanding of hypothesis testing and the role that z-scores play in this inferential technique. In each case, keep in mind that the z-score serves as a general model for other test statistics that come in future chapters.

The z-score formula as a recipe   The z-score formula, like any formula, can be viewed as a recipe. If you follow instructions and use all of the right ingredients, the formula produces a z-score. In the hypothesis-testing situation, however, you do not have all of the necessary ingredients. Specifically, you do not know the value for the population mean (μ), which is one component, or ingredient, in the formula.

This situation is similar to trying to follow a cake recipe in which one of the ingredients is not clearly listed. For example, the recipe may call for flour but there is a grease stain that makes it impossible to read how much flour. Faced with this situation, you might try the following steps:

1. Make a hypothesis about the amount of flour. For example, hypothesize that the correct amount is 2 cups.

2. To test your hypothesis, add the rest of the ingredients along with the hypothesized amount of flour and bake the cake.

3. If the cake turns out to be good, you can reasonably conclude that your hypothesis was correct. But if the cake is terrible, you conclude that your hypothesis was wrong.

In a hypothesis test with z-scores, we do essentially the same thing. We have a formula (recipe) for z-scores, but one ingredient (the population mean) is missing. Therefore, we try the following steps:

1. Make a hypothesis about the value of μ. This is the null hypothesis.

2. Plug the hypothesized value in the formula along with the other values (ingredients).

3. If the formula produces a z-score near zero (which is where z-scores are supposed to be), we conclude that the hypothesis was correct. On the other hand, if the formula produces an extreme value (a very unlikely result), we conclude that the hypothesis was wrong.

The z-score formula as a ratio   In the context of a hypothesis test, the z-score formula has the following structure:

$$z = \frac{M - \mu}{\sigma_M} = \frac{\text{sample mean} - \text{hypothesized population mean}}{\text{standard error between } M \text{ and } \mu}$$

Notice that the numerator of the formula measures the obtained difference between the sample mean and the hypothesized population mean. The standard error in the denominator measures the standard amount of distance that exists naturally between a sample mean and the population mean without any treatment effect causing the sample to be different. Thus, the z-score formula (and most other test statistics) forms a ratio

$$z = \frac{\text{actual difference between the sample } (M) \text{ and the hypothesis } (\mu)}{\text{standard difference between } M \text{ and } \mu \text{ with no treatment effect}}$$

Thus, for example, a z-score of $z = 3.00$ means that the obtained difference between the sample and the hypothesis is 3 times bigger than would be expected if the treatment had no effect. A discrepancy this large is a strong indication that the hypothesis is probably wrong.

FACTORS THAT INFLUENCE A HYPOTHESIS TEST

The final decision in a hypothesis test is determined by the value obtained for the z-score statistic. If the z-score is large enough to be in the critical region, then we reject the null hypothesis and conclude that there is a significant treatment effect. Otherwise, we fail to reject H_0 and conclude that the treatment does not have a significant effect. The most obvious factor influencing the size of the z-score is the difference between the sample mean and the hypothesized population mean from H_0. A big mean difference indicates that the treated sample is noticeably different from the untreated population and usually supports a conclusion that the treatment effect is significant. In addition to the mean difference, however, there are other factors that help determine whether the z-score is large enough to reject H_0. In this section, we examine two factors that can influence the outcome of a hypothesis test.

1. The variability of the scores, which is measured by either the standard deviation or the variance. The variability influences the size of the standard error in the denominator of the z-score.

2. The number of scores in the sample. This value also influences the size of the standard error in the denominator.

We use the research study from Example 8.1 to examine each of these factors. The study used a sample of $n = 25$ students and produced a mean test score of $M = 89$. Based on these results, the hypothesis test concluded that brain stimulation near the parietal lobe has a significant effect on the ability to learn new mathematical skills.

The variability of the scores   In Chapter 4 (p. 110), we noted that high variability can make it very difficult to see any clear patterns in the results from a research study. In a hypothesis test, higher variability can reduce the chances of finding a significant treatment effect. For the study in Example 8.1, the standard deviation is $\sigma = 20$. With a sample of $n = 25$, this produced a standard error of $\sigma_M = 4$ points and a significant z-score of $z = 2.25$. Now consider what happens if the standard deviation is increased to $\sigma = 30$. With the increased variability, the standard error becomes $\sigma_M = \frac{30}{\sqrt{25}} = 6$ points. Using the same sample mean from the original example, the new z-score becomes

$$z = \frac{M - \mu}{\sigma_M} = \frac{89 - 80}{6} = \frac{9}{6} = 1.50$$

The z-score is no longer beyond the critical boundary of 1.96, so the statistical decision is to fail to reject the null hypothesis. The increased variability means that the sample data are no longer sufficient to conclude that the treatment has a significant effect. In general, increasing the variability of the scores produces a larger standard error and a smaller value (closer to zero) for the z-score. If other factors are held constant, then the larger the variability, the lower the likelihood of finding a significant treatment effect.

The number of scores in the sample   The second factor that influences the outcome of a hypothesis test is the number of scores in the sample. The study in Example 8.1 used a sample of $n = 25$ students obtained a standard error of $\sigma_M = \frac{20}{\sqrt{25}} = 4$ points and a significant z-score of $z = 2.25$. Now consider what happens if we increase the sample size to $n = 100$ students. With $n = 100$, the standard error becomes $\sigma_M = \frac{20}{\sqrt{100}} = 2$ points, and the z-score becomes

$$z = \frac{M - \mu}{\sigma_M} = \frac{89 - 80}{2} = \frac{9}{2} = 4.50$$

Increasing the sample size from $n = 25$ to $n = 100$ has doubled the size of the z-score. In general, increasing the number of scores in the sample produces a smaller standard error and a larger value for the z-score. If all other factors are held constant, the larger the sample size, the greater the likelihood of finding a significant treatment effect. In simple terms, finding a 9-point treatment effect with a large sample is more convincing than finding a 9-point effect with a small sample.

LEARNING CHECK

1. A researcher conducts a hypothesis test with $\alpha = .05$ to evaluate the effectiveness of a treatment. Assume that the sample mean produces a z-score of $z = 2.17$.

   a. Do the data indicate that the treatment has a significant effect?

   b. Write a sentence describing the outcome of the hypothesis test as it would appear in a research report.

2. In a research report, the term *significant* is used when the null hypothesis is rejected. (True or false?)

3. In a research report, the results of a hypothesis test include the phrase "$z = 1.63$, $p > .05$." This means that the test failed to reject the null hypothesis. (True or false?)

4. If other factors are held constant, increasing the size of the sample increases the likelihood of rejecting the null hypothesis. (True or false?)

5. If other factors are held constant, are you more likely to reject the null hypothesis with a standard deviation of $\sigma = 2$ or with $\sigma = 10$?

ANSWERS

1. **a.** With $\alpha = .05$, the critical region consists of z-scores in the tails beyond $z = \pm1.96$. Reject the null hypothesis.

   b. The data indicate that the treatment had a significant effect, $z = 2.17$, $p < .05$.

2. True.

3. True. The probability is *greater than* .05, which means there is a reasonable likelihood that the result occurred without any treatment effect.

4. True. A larger sample produces a smaller standard error, which leads to a larger z-score.

5. $\sigma = 2$. A smaller standard deviation produces a smaller standard error, which leads to a larger z-score.

8.4   DIRECTIONAL (ONE-TAILED) HYPOTHESIS TESTS

The hypothesis-testing procedure presented in Section 8.1 is the standard, or *two-tailed,* test format. The term *two-tailed* comes from the fact that the critical region is divided between the two tails of the distribution. This format is by far the most widely accepted procedure for hypothesis testing. Nonetheless, there is an alternative that is discussed in this section.

Usually a researcher begins an experiment with a specific prediction about the direction of the treatment effect. For example, a special training program is expected to *increase* student performance, or alcohol consumption is expected to *slow* reaction times. In these situations, it is possible to state the statistical hypotheses in a manner that incorporates the directional prediction into the statement of H_0 and H_1. The result is a *directional test,* or what commonly is called a *one-tailed test.*

DEFINITION

> In a **directional hypothesis test,** or a **one-tailed test,** the statistical hypotheses (H_0 and H_1) specify either an increase or a decrease in the population mean. That is, they make a statement about the direction of the effect.

The following example demonstrates the elements of a one-tailed hypothesis test.

EXAMPLE 8.2   Earlier, in Example 8.1, we discussed a research study that examined the effect of electrical stimulation near the parietal lobe on the mathematical skills of students. In the study, each participant in a sample of $n = 25$ received electrical current near the parietal lobe for 30 minutes each day while studying for a standardized mathematics exam. For the general population of students (without any brain stimulation), the test scores form a normal distribution with a mean of $\mu = 80$ and a standard deviation of $\sigma = 20$. For this example, the expected effect is that the parietal lobe stimulation will improve test performance. If the researcher obtains a sample mean of $M = 87$ for the $n = 25$ participants, is the result sufficient to conclude that the stimulation really works?

THE HYPOTHESIS FOR A DIRECTIONAL TEST   Because a specific direction is expected for the treatment effect, it is possible for the researcher to perform a directional test. The first step (and the most critical step) is to incorporate the directional prediction into the statement of the statistical hypotheses. Remember that the null hypothesis states that there is no treatment effect and that the alternative hypothesis says that there is an effect. For this example, the predicted effect is that the electrical stimulation will increase test scores. Thus, the two hypotheses would state:

H_0: Test scores are not increased. (The treatment does not work.)

H_1: Test scores are increased. (The treatment works as predicted.)

To express directional hypotheses in symbols, it usually is easier to begin with the alternative hypothesis (H_1). Again, we know that the general population has an average test score of $\mu = 80$, and H_1 states that test scores will be increased by the brain stimulation. Therefore, expressed in symbols, H_1 states,

H_1: $\mu > 80$ (With the stimulation, the average score is greater than 80.)

The null hypothesis states that the stimulation does not increase scores. In symbols,

H_0: $\mu \leq 80$ (With the stimulation, the average score is not greater than 80.)

Note again that the two hypotheses are mutually exclusive and cover all of the possibilities.

THE CRITICAL REGION FOR DIRECTIONAL TESTS

The critical region is defined by sample outcomes that are very unlikely to occur if the null hypothesis is true (that is, if the treatment has no effect). Earlier (p. 209), we noted that the critical region can also be defined in terms of sample values that provide *convincing evidence* that the treatment really does have an effect. For a directional test, the concept of "convincing evidence" is the simplest way to determine the location of the critical region. We begin with all of the possible sample means that could be obtained if the null hypothesis is true. This is the distribution of sample means, and it is normal (because the population of test scores is normal), has an expected value of $\mu = 80$ (from H_0), and, for a sample of $n = 25$, has a standard error of $\mu_M = \frac{20}{\sqrt{25}} = 4$. The distribution is shown in Figure 8.7.

For this example, the treatment is expected to increase test scores. If untreated students average $\mu = 80$ on the test, then a sample mean that is substantially more than 80 would provide convincing evidence that the treatment worked. Thus, the critical region is located entirely in the right-hand tail of the distribution corresponding to sample means much greater than $\mu = 80$ (see Figure 8.7). Because the critical region is contained in one tail of the distribution, a directional test is commonly called a *one-tailed* test. Also note that the proportion specified by the alpha level is not divided between two tails, but rather is contained entirely in one tail. Using $\alpha = .05$, for example, the whole 5% is located in one tail. In this case, the z-score boundary for the critical region is $z = 1.65$, which is obtained by looking up a proportion of .05 in column C (the tail) of the unit normal table.

Notice that a directional (one-tailed) test requires changes in the first two steps of the step-by-step hypothesis-testing procedure.

> If the prediction is that the treatment will produce a *decrease* in scores, then the critical region is located entirely in the left-hand tail of the distribution.

1. In the first step, the directional prediction is included in the statement of the hypotheses.

2. In the second step of the process, the critical region is located entirely in one tail of the distribution.

After these two changes, the remainder of a one-tailed test proceeds exactly the same as a regular two-tailed test. Specifically, you calculate the z-score statistic and then make a decision about H_0 depending on whether the z-score is in the critical region.

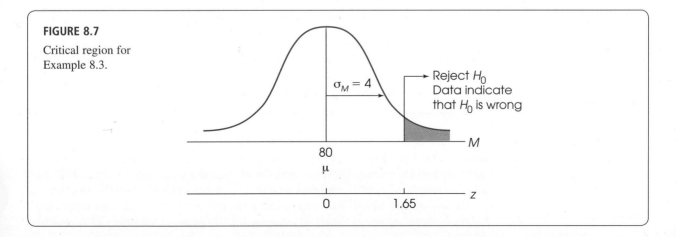

FIGURE 8.7

Critical region for Example 8.3.

For this example, the researcher obtained a mean of $M = 87$ for the 25 participants who received the brain stimulation. This sample mean corresponds to a z-score of

$$z = \frac{M - \mu}{\sigma_M} = \frac{87 - 80}{4} = \frac{7}{4} = 1.75$$

A z-score of $z = 1.75$ is in the critical region for a one-tailed test (see Figure 8.7). This is a very unlikely outcome if H_0 is true. Therefore, we reject the null hypothesis and conclude that the electrical stimulation produces a significant increase in mathematics test scores. In the literature, this result would be reported as follows:

The stimulation produced a significant increase in scores, $z = 1.75$, p < .05, one tailed.

Note that the report clearly acknowledges that a one-tailed test was used.

COMPARISON OF ONE-TAILED VERSUS TWO-TAILED TESTS

The general goal of hypothesis testing is to determine whether a particular treatment has any effect on a population. The test is performed by selecting a sample, administering the treatment to the sample, and then comparing the result with the original population. If the treated sample is noticeably different from the original population, then we conclude that the treatment has an effect, and we reject H_0. On the other hand, if the treated sample is still similar to the original population, then we conclude that there is no convincing evidence for a treatment effect, and we fail to reject H_0. The critical factor in this decision is the *size of the difference* between the treated sample and the original population. A large difference is evidence that the treatment worked; a small difference is not sufficient to say that the treatment had any effect.

The major distinction between one-tailed and two-tailed tests is the criteria that they use for rejecting H_0. A one-tailed test allows you to reject the null hypothesis when the difference between the sample and the population is relatively small, provided that the difference is in the specified direction. A two-tailed test, on the other hand, requires a relatively large difference independent of direction. This point is illustrated in the following example.

EXAMPLE 8.3

Consider again the one-tailed test evaluating the effect of parietal lobe stimulation. If we had used a standard two-tailed test, the hypotheses would be

H_0: $\mu = 80$ (The stimulation has no effect on test scores.)

H_1: $\mu \neq 80$ (The stimulation does have an effect on test scores.)

For a two-tailed test with $\alpha = .05$, the critical region consists of z-scores beyond ± 1.96. The data from Example 8.3 produced a sample mean of $M = 87$ and $z = 1.75$. For the two-tailed test, this z-score is not in the critical region, and we conclude that the supplement does not have a significant effect.

With the two-tailed test in Example 8.3, the 7-point difference between the sample mean and the hypothesized population mean ($M = 87$ and $\mu = 80$) is not big enough to reject the null hypothesis. However, with the one-tailed test, the same 7-point difference is large enough to reject H_0 and conclude that the treatment had a significant effect.

All researchers agree that one-tailed tests are different from two-tailed tests. However, there are several ways to interpret the difference. One group of researchers contends that a two-tailed test is more rigorous and, therefore, more convincing than a one-tailed test. Remember that the two-tailed test demands more evidence to reject H_0 and thus provides a stronger demonstration that a treatment effect has occurred.

Other researchers feel that one-tailed tests are preferable because they are more sensitive. That is, a relatively small treatment effect may be significant with a one-tailed test but fail to reach significance with a two-tailed test. Also, there is the argument that one-tailed tests are more precise because they test hypotheses about a specific directional effect instead of an indefinite hypothesis about a general effect.

In general, two-tailed tests should be used in research situations when there is no strong directional expectation or when there are two competing predictions. For example, a two-tailed test would be appropriate for a study in which one theory predicts an increase in scores but another theory predicts a decrease. One-tailed tests should be used only in situations in which the directional prediction is made before the research is conducted and there is a strong justification for making the directional prediction. In particular, if a two-tailed test fails to reach significance, you should never follow up with a one-tailed test as a second attempt to salvage a significant result for the same data.

LEARNING CHECK

1. A researcher selects a sample from a population with a mean of $\mu = 60$ and administers a treatment to the individuals in the sample. If the researcher predicts that the treatment will increase scores, then

   a. Using symbols, state the hypotheses for a one-tailed test.

   b. For the one-tailed test, would the critical region be located in the right-hand tail or the left-hand tail of the distribution?

2. If a sample is sufficient to reject the null hypothesis for a one-tailed test, then the same sample would also reject H_0 for a two-tailed test. (True or false?)

3. A researcher obtains $z = 2.43$ for a hypothesis test. Using $\alpha = .01$, the researcher should reject the null hypothesis for a one-tailed test but fail to reject for a two-tailed test. (True or false?)

ANSWERS

1. **a.** H_0: $\mu \leq 60$ and H_1: $\mu > 60$

   b. A large sample mean, in the right-hand tail, would indicate that the treatment worked as predicted.

2. False. Because a two-tailed test requires a larger mean difference, it is possible for a sample to be significant for a one-tailed test but not for a two-tailed test.

3. True. The one-tailed critical value is $z = 2.33$ and the two-tailed value is $z = 2.58$.

8.5 **CONCERNS ABOUT HYPOTHESIS TESTING: MEASURING EFFECT SIZE**

Although hypothesis testing is the most commonly used technique for evaluating and interpreting research data, a number of scientists have expressed a variety of concerns about the hypothesis testing procedure (for example, see Loftus, 1996; Hunter, 1997; and Killeen, 2005).

There are two serious limitations with using a hypothesis test to establish the significance of a treatment effect. The first concern is that the focus of a hypothesis test is on the data rather than the hypothesis. Specifically, when the null hypothesis is rejected, we are actually making a strong probability statement about the sample data, not about the null hypothesis. A significant result permits the following conclusion: "This specific sample mean is very unlikely ($p < .05$) if the null hypothesis is true." Note that the conclusion does not make any definite statement about the probability of the null hypothesis being true or false. The fact that the sample is very unlikely *suggests* that the null hypothesis is also very unlikely, but we do not have any solid grounds for making a probability statement about the null hypothesis. Specifically, you cannot conclude that the probability of the null hypothesis being true is less than 5% simply because you rejected the null hypothesis with $\alpha = .05$ (see Box 8.2).

A second concern is that demonstrating a *significant* treatment effect does not necessarily indicate a *substantial* treatment effect. In particular, statistical significance does

---

BOX 8.2   A FLAW IN THE LOGIC OF HYPOTHESIS TESTING

Suppose that you do a hypothesis test and reject the null hypothesis with $\alpha = .05$. Can you conclude that there is a 5% probability that you are making a Type I error? Can you also conclude that there is a 95% probability that your decision is correct and the treatment does have an effect? For both questions, the answer is no.

The problem is that the probabilities for a hypothesis test are well defined only when the null hypothesis is true. Specifically, a hypothesis test using $\alpha = .05$ is structured so that the error rate is $p < .05$ and the accuracy rate is $p \geq .95$ *if the null hypothesis is true*. If H_0 is false, however, these probabilities start to fall apart. When there is a treatment effect (H_0 is false), the probability that a hypothesis test will detect it and reject H_0 depends on a variety of factors. For example, if the treatment effect is very small, then a hypothesis test is unlikely to detect it. With a large treatment effect, the hypothesis test is more likely to detect it and the probability of rejecting H_0 increases. Thus, whenever there is a treatment effect (H_0 is false), it becomes impossible to define precisely the probability of rejecting the null hypothesis.

Most researchers begin research studies believing that there is a good likelihood that the null hypothesis is false and there really is a treatment effect. They are hoping that the study will provide evidence of the effect so they can convince their colleagues. Thus, most research begins with some probability that the null hypothesis is false. For the sake of argument, let's assume that there is an 80% probability that the null hypothesis is true.

p(there is no treatment effect— H_0 is true) = 0.80 and
p(there is a treatment effect— H_0 is false) = 0.20

In this situation, suppose that 125 researchers are all doing hypothesis tests with $\alpha = .05$. Of these researchers, 80% ($n = 100$) are testing a true H_0. For these researchers, the probability of rejecting the null hypothesis (and making a Type I error) is $\alpha = .05$. Therefore, the 100 hypothesis tests for this group should produce, on average, 5 tests that reject H_0.

Meanwhile, the other 20% of the researchers ($n = 25$) are testing a false null hypothesis. For this group, the probability of rejecting the null hypothesis is unknown. For the sake of argument, however, let's assume that the probability of detecting the treatment effect and correctly rejecting H_0 is 60%. This means that the 25 hypothesis tests should result in 15 tests (60%) that reject H_0 and 10 that fail to reject H_0.

Notice that there should be 20 hypothesis tests that reject the null hypothesis (5 from the first group and 15 from the second group). Thus, a total of 20 researchers will find a statistically significant effect. Of these 20 "significant" results, however, the 5 from the first group are making a Type I error. Thus, when the null hypothesis is rejected, the actually likelihood of a Type I error is 5 out of 20, or $p = \frac{5}{20} = .25$, which is five times greater than the alpha level of .05.

Based on this kind of argument, many scientists suspect that a large number of the results and conclusions published in research journals are simply wrong. Specifically, the Type I error rate in published research is almost certainly higher than the alpha levels used in the hypothesis tests that support the results (Siegfried, 2010).

not provide any real information about the absolute size of a treatment effect. Instead, the hypothesis test has simply established that the results obtained in the research study are very unlikely to have occurred if there is no treatment effect. The hypothesis test reaches this conclusion by (1) calculating the standard error, which measures how much difference is reasonable to expect between M and μ, and (2) demonstrating that the obtained mean difference is substantially bigger than the standard error.

Notice that the test is making a *relative* comparison: the size of the treatment effect is being evaluated relative to the standard error. If the standard error is very small, then the treatment effect can also be very small and still be large enough to be significant. Thus, a significant effect does not necessarily mean a big effect. The idea that a hypothesis test evaluates the relative size of a treatment effect, rather than the absolute size, is illustrated in the following example.

EXAMPLE 8.4   We begin with a population of scores that forms a normal distribution with $\mu = 50$ and $\sigma = 10$. A sample is selected from the population and a treatment is administered to the sample. After treatment, the sample mean is found to be $M = 51$. Does this sample provide evidence of a statistically significant treatment effect?

Although there is only a 1-point difference between the sample mean and the original population mean, the difference may be enough to be significant. In particular, the outcome of the hypothesis test depends on the sample size. For example, with a sample of $n = 25$ the standard error is

$$\sigma_M = \frac{\sigma}{\sqrt{n}} = \frac{10}{\sqrt{25}} = \frac{10}{5} = 2.00$$

and the z-score for $M = 51$ is

$$z = \frac{M - \mu}{\sigma_M} = \frac{51 - 50}{2} = \frac{1}{2} = 0.50$$

This z-score fails to reach the critical boundary of $z = 1.96$, so we fail to reject the null hypothesis. In this case, the 1-point difference between M and μ is not significant because it is being evaluated relative to a standard error of 2 points.

Now consider the outcome with a sample of $n = 400$. With a larger sample, the standard error is

$$\sigma_M = \frac{\sigma}{\sqrt{n}} = \frac{10}{\sqrt{400}} = \frac{10}{20} = 0.50$$

and the z-score for $M = 51$ is

$$z = \frac{M - \mu}{\sigma_M} = \frac{51 - 50}{0.5} = \frac{1}{0.5} = 2.00$$

Now the z-score is beyond the 1.96 boundary, so we reject the null hypothesis and conclude that there is a significant effect. In this case, the 1-point difference between M and μ is considered statistically significant because it is being evaluated relative to a standard error of only 0.5 points.

The purpose of Example 8.4 is to demonstrate that a small treatment effect can still be statistically significant. If the sample size is large enough, any treatment effect, no matter how small, can be large enough to reject the null hypothesis.

MEASURING EFFECT SIZE

As noted in the previous section, one concern with hypothesis testing is that a hypothesis test does not really evaluate the absolute size of a treatment effect. To correct this problem, it is recommended that whenever researchers report a statistically significant effect, they also provide a report of the effect size (see the guidelines presented by L. Wilkinson and the APA Task Force on Statistical Inference, 1999). Therefore, as we present different hypothesis tests, we also present different options for measuring and reporting *effect size*.

DEFINITION

A measure of **effect size** is intended to provide a measurement of the absolute magnitude of a treatment effect, independent of the size of the sample(s) being used.

One of the simplest and most direct methods for measuring effect size is *Cohen's d*. Cohen (1988) recommended that effect size can be standardized by measuring the mean difference in terms of the standard deviation. The resulting measure of effect size is computed as

$$\text{Cohen's } d = \frac{\text{mean difference}}{\text{standard deviation}} = \frac{\mu_{\text{treatment}} - \mu_{\text{no treatment}}}{\sigma} \tag{8.1}$$

For the *z*-score hypothesis test, the mean difference is determined by the difference between the population mean before treatment and the population mean after treatment. However, the population mean after treatment is unknown. Therefore, we must use the mean for the treated sample in its place. Remember, the sample mean is expected to be representative of the population mean and provides the best measure of the treatment effect. Thus, the actual calculations are really estimating the value of Cohen's *d* as follows

$$\text{estimated Cohen's } d = \frac{\text{mean difference}}{\text{standard deviation}} = \frac{M_{\text{treatment}} - \mu_{\text{no treatment}}}{\sigma} \tag{8.2}$$

Cohen's *d* measures the distance between two means and is typically reported as a positive number even when the formula produces a negative value.

The standard deviation is included in the calculation to standardize the size of the mean difference in much the same way that *z*-scores standardize locations in a distribution. For example, a 15-point mean difference can be a relatively large treatment effect or a relatively small effect depending on the size of the standard deviation. This phenomenon is demonstrated in Figure 8.8. The top portion of the figure [part (a)] shows the results of a treatment that produces a 15-point mean difference in SAT scores; before treatment, the average SAT score is $\mu = 500$, and after treatment the average is 515. Notice that the standard deviation for SAT scores is $\sigma = 100$, so the 15-point difference appears to be small. For this example, Cohen's *d* is

$$\text{Cohen's } d = \frac{\text{mean difference}}{\text{standard deviation}} = \frac{15}{100} = 0.15$$

Now consider the treatment effect shown in Figure 8.8(b). This time, the treatment produces a 15-point mean difference in IQ scores; before treatment the average IQ is 100, and after treatment the average is 115. Because IQ scores have a standard deviation of $\sigma = 15$, the 15-point mean difference now appears to be large. For this example, Cohen's *d* is

$$\text{Cohen's } d = \frac{\text{mean difference}}{\text{standard deviation}} = \frac{15}{15} = 1.00$$

Notice that Cohen's *d* measures the size of the treatment effect in terms of the standard deviation. For example, a value of $d = 0.50$ indicates that the treatment changed the mean by half of a standard deviation; similarly, a value of $d = 1.00$ indicates that the

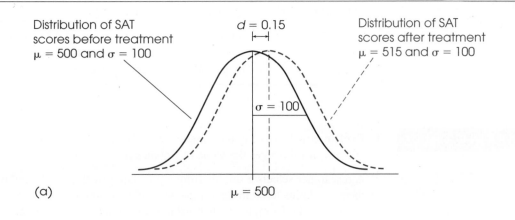

Distribution of SAT
scores before treatment
$\mu = 500$ and $\sigma = 100$

$d = 0.15$

Distribution of SAT
scores after treatment
$\mu = 515$ and $\sigma = 100$

$\sigma = 100$

(a)

$\mu = 500$

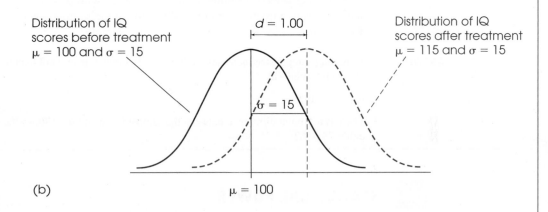

Distribution of IQ
scores before treatment
$\mu = 100$ and $\sigma = 15$

$d = 1.00$

Distribution of IQ
scores after treatment
$\mu = 115$ and $\sigma = 15$

$\sigma = 15$

(b)

$\mu = 100$

FIGURE 8.8

The appearance of a 15-point treatment effect in two different situations. In part (a), the standard deviation is $\sigma = 100$ and the 15-point effect is relatively small. In part (b), the standard deviation is $\sigma = 15$ and the 15-point effect is relatively large. Cohen's d uses the standard deviation to help measure effect size.

size of the treatment effect is equal to one whole standard deviation. Cohen (1988) also suggested criteria for evaluating the size of a treatment effect as shown in Table 8.2.

As one final demonstration of Cohen's d, consider the two hypothesis tests in Example 8.4. For each test, the original population had a mean of $\mu = 50$ with a standard deviation of $\sigma = 10$. For each test, the mean for the treated sample was $M = 51$. Although one test used a sample of $n = 25$ and the other test used a sample of $n = 400$, the sample size is not considered when computing Cohen's d. Therefore, both of the hypothesis tests would produce the same value:

$$\text{Cohen's } d = \frac{\text{mean difference}}{\text{standard deviation}} = \frac{1}{10} = 0.10$$

Notice that Cohen's d simply describes the size of the treatment effect and is not influenced by the number of scores in the sample. For both hypothesis tests, the original population mean was $\mu = 50$ and, after treatment, the sample mean was $M = 51$. Thus, treatment appears to have increased the scores by 1 point, which is equal to one-tenth of a standard deviation (Cohen's $d = 0.1$).

TABLE 8.2

Evaluating effect size with
Cohen's *d*.

Magnitude of *d*	Evaluation of Effect Size
d = 0.2	Small effect (mean difference around 0.2 standard deviation)
d = 0.5	Medium effect (mean difference around 0.5 standard deviation)
d = 0.8	Large effect (mean difference around 0.8 standard deviation)

LEARNING CHECK

1. Explain how increasing the sample size influences the outcome of a hypothesis test and how it influences the value of Cohen's *d*.

2. A researcher selects a sample from a population with $\mu = 45$ and $\sigma = 8$. A treatment is administered to the sample and, after treatment, the sample mean is found to be $M = 47$. Compute Cohen's *d* to measure the size of the treatment effect.

3. A researcher selects a sample from a population with $\mu = 70$ and $\sigma = 12$. After administering a treatment to the individuals in the sample, the researcher computes Cohen's $d = 0.25$. What is the mean for the sample?

ANSWERS

1. Increasing sample size increases the likelihood of rejecting the null hypothesis but has no effect on Cohen's *d*.

2. $d = \frac{2}{8} = 0.25$

3. There is a 3-point difference between the sample mean and $\mu = 70$, so the sample mean is either 73 or 67.

8.6   STATISTICAL POWER

Instead of measuring effect size directly, an alternative approach to determining the size or strength of a treatment effect is to measure the power of the statistical test. The *power* of a test is defined as the probability that the test will reject the null hypothesis if the treatment really has an effect.

DEFINITION

> The **power** of a statistical test is the probability that the test will correctly reject a false null hypothesis. That is, power is the probability that the test will identify a treatment effect if one really exists.

Whenever a treatment has an effect, there are only two possible outcomes for a hypothesis test: either fail to reject H_0 or reject H_0. Because there are only two possible outcomes, the probability for the first and the probability for the second must add up to 1.00. The first outcome, failing to reject H_0 when there is a real effect, was defined earlier (p. 214) as a Type II error with a probability identified as $p = \beta$. Therefore, the second outcome must have a probability of $1 - \beta$. However, the second outcome, rejecting H_0 when there is a real effect, is the power of the test. Thus, the power of a hypothesis test is equal to $1 - \beta$. In the examples that follow, we demonstrate the calculation of power for a hypothesis test; that is, the probability that the test will correctly reject the null hypothesis. At the same time, however, we are computing the probability that the test will result in a Type II error. For example, if the power of the test is 70% ($1 - \beta$), then the probability of a Type II error must be 30% (β).

Researchers typically calculate power as a means of determining whether a research study is likely to be successful. Thus, researchers usually calculate the power of a hypothesis test *before* they actually conduct the research study. In this way, they can determine the probability that the results will be significant (reject H_0) before investing time and effort in the actual research. To calculate power, however, it is first necessary to make assumptions about a variety of factors that influence the outcome of a hypothesis test. Factors such as the sample size, the size of the treatment effect, and the value chosen for the alpha level can all influence a hypothesis test. The following example demonstrates the calculation of power for a specific research situation.

EXAMPLE 8.5   We start with a normal-shaped population with a mean of $\mu = 80$ and a standard deviation of $\sigma = 10$. A researcher plans to select a sample of $n = 25$ individuals from this population and administer a treatment to each individual. It is expected that the treatment will have an 8-point effect; that is, the treatment will add 8 points to each individual's score.

Figure 8.9 shows the original population distribution and two possible outcomes:

1. If the null hypothesis is true and there is no treatment effect.

2. If the researcher's expectation is correct and there is an 8-point effect.

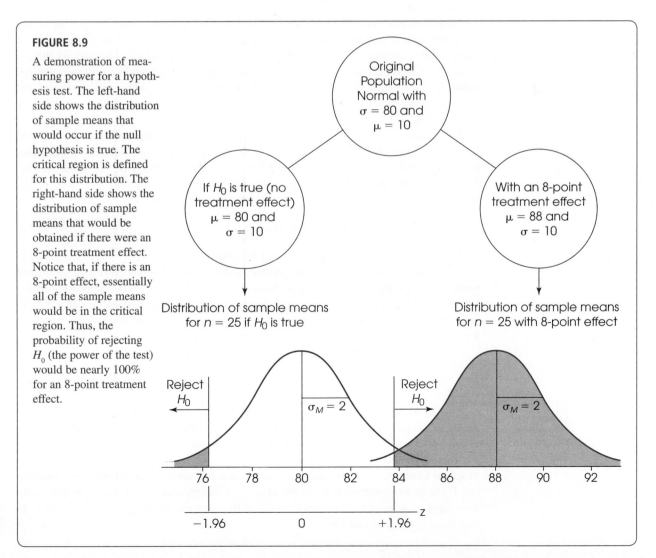

FIGURE 8.9

A demonstration of measuring power for a hypothesis test. The left-hand side shows the distribution of sample means that would occur if the null hypothesis is true. The critical region is defined for this distribution. The right-hand side shows the distribution of sample means that would be obtained if there were an 8-point treatment effect. Notice that, if there is an 8-point effect, essentially all of the sample means would be in the critical region. Thus, the probability of rejecting H_0 (the power of the test) would be nearly 100% for an 8-point treatment effect.

The left-hand side of the figure shows what should happen according to the null hypothesis. In this case, the treatment has no effect and the population mean is still $\mu = 80$. On the right-hand side of the figure we show what would happen if the treatment has an 8-point effect. If the treatment adds 8 points to each person's score, then the population mean after treatment increases to $\mu = 88$.

Beneath each of the two populations, Figure 8.9 shows the distribution of sample means for $n = 25$. According to the null hypothesis, the sample means are centered around $\mu = 80$. With an 8-point treatment effect, the sample means are centered around $\mu = 88$. Both distributions have a standard error of

$$\sigma_M = \frac{\sigma}{\sqrt{n}} = \frac{10}{\sqrt{25}} = \frac{10}{5} = 2$$

Notice that the distribution on the left shows all of the possible sample means if the null hypothesis is true. This is the distribution we use to locate the critical region for the hypothesis test. Using $\alpha = .05$, the critical region consists of extreme values in this distribution, specifically sample means beyond $z = 1.96$ or $z = -1.96$. These values are shown in Figure 8.9, and we have shaded all of the sample means located in the critical region.

Now turn your attention to the distribution on the right, which shows all of the possible sample means if there is an 8-point treatment effect. Notice that most of these sample means are located beyond the $z = 1.96$ boundary. This means that, if there is an 8-point treatment effect, you are almost guaranteed to obtain a sample mean in the critical region and reject the null hypothesis. Thus, the power of the test (the probability of rejecting H_0) is close to 100% if there is an 8-point treatment effect.

To calculate the exact value for the power of the test we must determine what portion of the distribution on the right-hand side is shaded. Thus, we must locate the exact boundary for the critical region, then find the probability value in the unit normal table. For the distribution on the left-hand side, the critical boundary of $z = +1.96$ corresponds to a location that is above $\mu = 80$ by a distance equal to

$$1.96\sigma_M = 1.96(2) = 3.92 \text{ points}$$

Thus, the critical boundary of $z = +1.96$ corresponds to a sample mean of $M = 80 + 3.92 = 83.92$. Any sample mean greater than $M = 83.92$ is in the critical region and would lead to rejecting the null hypothesis. Next, we determine what proportion of the treated samples are greater than $M = 83.92$. For the treated distribution (right-hand side), the population mean is $\mu = 88$ and a sample mean of $M = 83.92$ corresponds to a z-score of

$$z = \frac{M - \mu}{\sigma_M} = \frac{83.92 - 88}{2} = \frac{-4.08}{2} = -2.04$$

Finally, look up $z = -2.04$ in the unit normal table and determine that the shaded area ($z > -2.04$) corresponds to $p = 0.9793$ (or 97.93%). Thus, if the treatment has an 8-point effect, 97.93% of all the possible sample means will be in the critical region and we will reject the null hypothesis. In other words, the power of the test is 97.93%. In practical terms, this means that the research study is almost guaranteed to be successful. If the researcher selects a sample of $n = 25$ individuals, and if the treatment really does have an 8-point effect, then 97.93% of the time the hypothesis test will conclude that there is a significant effect.

POWER AND EFFECT SIZE

Logically, it should be clear that power and effect size are related. Figure 8.9 shows the calculation of power for an 8-point treatment effect. Now consider what would happen if the treatment effect were only 4 points. With a 4-point treatment effect, the distribution on the right-hand side would shift to the left so that it is centered at $\mu = 84$. In this new position, only about 50% of the treated sample means would be beyond the $z = 1.96$ boundary. Thus, with a 4-point treatment effect, there is only a 50% probability of selecting a sample that leads to rejecting the null hypothesis. In other words, the power of the test is only about 50% for a 4-point effect compared to nearly 98% with an 8-point effect (see Example 8.5). Again, it is possible to find the z-score corresponding to the exact location of the critical boundary and to look up the probability value for power in the unit normal table. In this case, you should obtain $z = -0.04$ and the exact power of the test is $p = 0.5160$, or 51.60%.

In general, as the effect size increases, the distribution of sample means on the right-hand side moves even farther to the right so that more and more of the samples are beyond the $z = 1.96$ boundary. Thus, as the effect size increases, the probability of rejecting H_0 also increases, which means that the power of the test increases. Thus, measures of effect size such as Cohen's d and measures of power both provide an indication of the strength or magnitude of a treatment effect.

OTHER FACTORS THAT AFFECT POWER

Although the power of a hypothesis test is directly influenced by the size of the treatment effect, power is not meant to be a pure measure of effect size. Instead, power is influenced by several factors, other than effect size, that are related to the hypothesis test. Some of these factors are considered in the following sections.

Sample size   One factor that has a huge influence on power is the size of the sample. In Example 8.5, we demonstrated power for an 8-point treatment effect using a sample of $n = 25$. If the researcher decided to conduct the study using a sample of $n = 4$, then the power would be dramatically different. With $n = 4$, the standard error for the sample means would be

$$\sigma_M = \frac{\sigma}{\sqrt{n}} = \frac{10}{\sqrt{4}} = \frac{10}{2} = 5$$

Figure 8.10 shows the two distributions of sample means with $n = 4$ and a standard error of $\sigma_M = 5$ points. Again, the distribution on the left is centered at $\mu = 80$ and shows all of the possible sample means if H_0 is true. As always, this distribution is used to locate the critical boundaries for the hypothesis test, $z = -1.96$ and $z = +1.96$. The distribution on the right is centered at $\mu = 88$ and shows all of the possible sample means if there is an 8-point treatment effect. Note that less than half of the treated sample means in the right-hand distribution are now located beyond the 1.96 boundary. Thus, with a sample of $n = 4$, there is less than a 50% probability that the hypothesis test would reject H_0, even though the treatment has an 8-point effect. Earlier, in Example 8.5, we found power equal to 97.93% for a sample of $n = 25$. However, when the sample size is reduced to $n = 4$, power decreases to less than 50%. In general, a larger sample produces greater power for a hypothesis test.

Because power is directly related to sample size, one of the primary reasons for computing power is to determine what sample size is necessary to achieve a reasonable probability for a successful research study. Before a study is conducted, researchers can compute power to determine the probability that their research will successfully reject the null hypothesis. If the probability (power) is too small, they always have the option of increasing sample size to increase power.

FIGURE 8.10

A demonstration of how sample size affects the power of a hypothesis test. As in Figure 8.9, the left-hand side shows the distribution of sample means if the null hypothesis were true. The critical region is defined for this distribution. The right-hand side shows the distribution of sample means that would be obtained if there were an 8-point treatment effect. Notice that reducing the size to $n = 4$ has reduced the power of the test to less than 50% compared to a power of nearly 100% with a sample of $n = 25$ in Figure 8.9.

Alpha level Reducing the alpha level for a hypothesis test also reduces the power of the test. For example, lowering α from .05 to .01 lowers the power of the hypothesis test. The effect of reducing the alpha level can be seen by referring again to Figure 8.10. In this figure, the boundaries for the critical region are drawn using $\alpha = .05$. Specifically, the critical region on the right-hand side begins at $z = 1.96$. If α were changed to .01, the boundary would be moved farther to the right, out to $z = 2.58$. It should be clear that moving the critical boundary to the right means that a smaller portion of the treatment distribution (the distribution on the right-hand side) will be in the critical region. Thus, there would be a lower probability of rejecting the null hypothesis and a lower value for the power of the test.

One-tailed versus two-tailed tests Changing from a regular two-tailed test to a one-tailed test increases the power of the hypothesis test. Again, this effect can be seen by referring to Figure 8.10. The figure shows the boundaries for the critical region using a two-tailed test with $\alpha = .05$ so that the critical region on the right-hand side begins at $z = 1.96$. Changing to a one-tailed test would move the critical boundary to the left to a value of $z = 1.65$. Moving the boundary to the left would cause a larger proportion of the treatment distribution to be in the critical region and, therefore, would increase the power of the test.

1. As the power of a test increases, what happens to the probability of a Type II error?

2. For a 5-point treatment effect, a researcher computes power of $p = 0.50$ for a two-tailed hypothesis test with $\alpha = .05$.

   a. Will the power increase or decrease for a 10-point treatment effect?

   b. Will the power increase or decrease if alpha is changed to $\alpha = .01$?

   c. Will the power increase or decrease if the researcher changes to a one-tailed test?

3. How does sample size influence the power of a hypothesis test?

4. A researcher administers a treatment to a sample of $n = 16$ individuals selected from a normal population with $\mu = 60$ and $\sigma = 12$. If the treatment increases scores by 4 points, what is the power of a two-tailed hypothesis test with $\alpha = .05$?

ANSWERS

1. As power increases, the probability of a Type II error decreases.

2. a. The hypothesis test is more likely to detect a 10-point effect, so power will be greater.

   b. Decreasing the alpha level also decreases the power of the test.

   c. Switching to a one-tailed test will increase the power.

3. Increasing sample size increases the power of a test

4. With standard error of 3 points, the critical boundary of $z = 1.96$ corresponds to a sample mean of $M = 65.88$. With a 4-point effect, the distribution of sample means has $\mu = 64$ and a sample mean of $M = 65.88$ corresponds to $z = 0.63$. Power $= p(z > 0.63) = 0.2643$.

SUMMARY

1. Hypothesis testing is an inferential procedure that uses the data from a sample to draw a general conclusion about a population. The procedure begins with a hypothesis about an unknown population. Then a sample is selected, and the sample data provide evidence that either supports or refutes the hypothesis.

2. In this chapter, we introduced hypothesis testing using the simple situation in which a sample mean is used to test a hypothesis about an unknown population mean; usually the mean for a population that has received a treatment. The question is to determine whether the treatment has an effect on the population mean (see Figure 8.1).

3. Hypothesis testing is structured as a four-step process that is used throughout the remainder of the book.

   a. State the null hypothesis (H_0), and select an alpha level. The null hypothesis states that there is no effect or no change. In this case, H_0 states that the mean for the treated population is the same as the mean before treatment. The alpha level, usually $\alpha = .05$ or $\alpha = .01$, provides a definition of the term *very unlikely* and determines the risk of a Type I error when H_0 is true. Also state an

   alternative hypothesis (H_1), which is the exact opposite of the null hypothesis.

   b. Locate the critical region. The critical region is defined as extreme sample outcomes that would be very unlikely to occur if the null hypothesis is true. The alpha level defines "very unlikely."

   c. Collect the data, and compute the test statistic. The sample mean is transformed into a z-score by the formula

   $$z = \frac{M - \mu}{\sigma_M}$$

   The value of μ is obtained from the null hypothesis. The z-score test statistic identifies the location of the sample mean in the distribution of sample means.

   d. Make a decision. If the obtained z-score is in the critical region, reject H_0 because it is very unlikely that these data would be obtained if H_0 were true. In this case, conclude that the treatment has changed the population mean. If the z-score is not in the critical region, fail to reject H_0 because the data are not significantly different from the null hypothesis. In this case, the data do not provide sufficient evidence to indicate that the treatment has had an effect.

4. Whatever decision is reached in a hypothesis test, there is always a risk of making the incorrect decision. There are two types of errors that can be committed.

A Type I error is defined as rejecting a true H_0. This is a serious error because it results in falsely reporting a treatment effect. The risk of a Type I error is determined by the alpha level and, therefore, is under the experimenter's control.

A Type II error is defined as the failure to reject a false H_0. In this case, the experiment fails to detect an effect that actually occurred. The probability of a Type II error cannot be specified as a single value and depends in part on the size of the treatment effect. It is identified by the symbol β (beta).

5. When a researcher expects that a treatment will change scores in a particular direction (increase or decrease), it is possible to do a directional, or one-tailed, test. The first step in this procedure is to incorporate the directional prediction into the hypotheses. For example, if the prediction is that a treatment will increase scores, the null hypothesis says that there is no increase and the alternative hypothesis states that there is an increase. To locate the critical region, you must determine what kind of data would refute the null hypothesis by demonstrating that the treatment worked as predicted. These outcomes are located entirely in one tail of the distribution, so the entire critical region (5%, 1%, or 0.1% depending on α) is in one tail.

6. In addition to using a hypothesis test to evaluate the *significance* of a treatment effect, it is recommended that you also measure and report the *effect size*. One measure of effect size is Cohen's *d*, which is a standardized measure of the mean difference. Cohen's *d* is computed as

$$\text{Cohen's } d = \frac{\text{mean difference}}{\text{standard deviation}}$$

7. The power of a hypothesis test is defined as the probability that the test will correctly reject the null hypothesis.

8. To determine the power for a hypothesis test, you must first identify the treatment and null distributions. Also, you must specify the magnitude of the treatment effect. Next, you sketch the distribution of sample means predicted by the null hypothesis and the distribution predicted by the specified treatment effect. Locate the critical region in the null hypothesis distribution and then determine the proportion of the treated distribution that is beyond the critical boundaries. This proportion is the power of the hypothesis test.

9. As the size of the treatment effect increases, statistical power increases. Also, power is influenced by several factors that can be controlled by the experimenter:
   a. A large sample results in more power than a small sample.
   b. Increasing the alpha level increases power.
   c. A one-tailed test has greater power than a two-tailed test.

KEY TERMS

RESOURCES

 Go to CengageBrain.com to access Psychology CourseMate, where you will find an interactive eBook, glossaries, flashcards, quizzes, statistics workshops, and more.

aplia

If your professor has assigned Aplia:

1. Sign in to your account.
2. Complete the corresponding exercises as required by your professor.
3. When finished, click "Grade It Now" to see which areas you have mastered, which areas need more work, and detailed explanations of every answer.

SPSS

The statistical computer package SPSS is not structured to conduct hypothesis tests using z-scores. In truth, the z-score test presented in this chapter is rarely used in actual research situations. The problem with the z-score test is that it requires that you know the value of the population standard deviation, and this information is usually not available. Researchers rarely have detailed information about the populations that they wish to study. Instead, they must obtain information entirely from samples. In the following chapters, we introduce new hypothesis-testing techniques that are based entirely on sample data. These new techniques are included in SPSS.

FOCUS ON PROBLEM SOLVING

1. Hypothesis testing involves a set of logical procedures and rules that enable us to make general conclusions about a population based on data from a sample. This process is reflected in the four steps that have been used throughout this chapter.

   STEP 1   State the hypotheses and set the alpha level.

   STEP 2   Locate the critical region.

   STEP 3   Compute the test statistic (in this case, the z-score) for the sample.

   STEP 4   Make a decision about H_0 based on the result of step 3.

2. Take time to consider the implications of your decision about the null hypothesis. The null hypothesis states that the treatment has no effect. If your decision is to reject H_0, then you are concluding that the sample data provide evidence that a treatment effect exists. However, when you fail to reject the null hypothesis, the results are inconclusive. In this case, all you can state is that there is not sufficient evidence to support the existence of a treatment effect.

3. When you are doing a directional hypothesis test, read the problem carefully, and watch for key words (such as increase or decrease, raise or lower, and more or less) that tell you which direction the researcher is predicting. The predicted direction determines the alternative hypothesis (H_1) and the critical region. For example, if a treatment is expected to *increase* scores, H_1 would contain a *greater than* symbol, and the critical region would be in the tail associated with high scores.

DEMONSTRATION 8.1

HYPOTHESIS TEST WITH *z*

A researcher begins with a known population—in this case, scores on a standardized test that are normally distributed with $\mu = 65$ and $\sigma = 15$. The researcher suspects that special training in reading skills will produce a change in the scores for the individuals in the population. Because it is not feasible to administer the treatment (the special training) to everyone in the population, a sample of $n = 25$ individuals is selected, and the treatment is given to this sample. Following treatment, the average score for this sample is $M = 70$. Is there evidence that the training has an effect on test scores?

STEP 1   State the hypothesis and select an alpha level.   The null hypothesis states that the special training has no effect. In symbols,

H_0: $\mu = 65$ (After special training, the mean is still 65.)

The alternative hypothesis states that the treatment does have an effect.

H_1: $\mu \neq 65$ (After training, the mean is different from 65.)

At this time you also select the alpha level. For this demonstration, we will use $\alpha = .05$. Thus, there is a 5% risk of committing a Type I error if we reject H_0.

STEP 2   Locate the critical region.   With $\alpha = .05$, the critical region consists of sample means that correspond to z-scores beyond the critical boundaries of $z = \pm 1.96$.

STEP 3   Obtain the sample data, and compute the test statistic.   For this example, the distribution of sample means, according to the null hypothesis, is normal with an expected value of $\mu = 65$ and a standard error of

$$\sigma_M = \frac{\sigma}{\sqrt{n}} = \frac{15}{\sqrt{25}} = \frac{15}{5} = 3$$

In this distribution, our sample mean of $M = 70$ corresponds to a z-score of

$$z = \frac{M - \mu}{\sigma_M} = \frac{70 - 65}{3} = \frac{5}{3} = +1.67$$

STEP 4   Make a decision about H_0, and state the conclusion.   The z-score we obtained is not in the critical region. This indicates that our sample mean of $M = 70$ is not an extreme or unusual value to be obtained from a population with $\mu = 65$. Therefore, our statistical decision is to *fail to reject H_0*. Our conclusion for the study is that the data do not provide sufficient evidence that the special training changes test scores.

DEMONSTRATION 8.2

EFFECT SIZE USING COHEN'S *d*

We will compute Cohen's *d* using the research situation and the data from Demonstration 8.1. Again, the original population mean was $\mu = 65$ and, after treatment (special training), the sample mean was $M = 70$. Thus, there is a 5-point mean difference. Using the population standard deviation, $\sigma = 15$, we obtain an effect size of

$$\text{Cohen's } d = \frac{\text{mean difference}}{\text{standard deviation}} = \frac{5}{15} = 0.33$$

According to Cohen's evaluation standards (see Table 8.2), this is a medium treatment effect.

PROBLEMS

1. The value of the z-score in a hypothesis test is influenced by a variety of factors. Assuming that all other variables are held constant, explain how the value of z is influenced by each of the following:
   a. An increase in the difference between the sample mean and the original population mean.
   b. An increase in the population standard deviation.
   c. An increase in the number of scores in the sample.

2. Define the alpha level and the critical region, and explain how they are related.

3. Although there is a popular belief that herbal remedies such as Ginkgo biloba and Ginseng may improve learning and memory in healthy adults, these effects are usually not supported by well-controlled research (Persson, Bringlov, Nilsson, & Nyberg, 2004). In a typical study, a researcher obtains a sample of $n = 16$ participants and has each person take the herbal supplements every day for 90 days. At the end of the 90 days, each person takes a standardized memory test. For the general population, scores from the test form a normal distribution with a mean of $\mu = 50$ and a standard deviation of $\sigma = 12$. The sample of research participants had an average of $M = 54$.
   a. Assuming a two-tailed test, state the null hypothesis in a sentence that includes the two variables being examined.
   b. Using the standard 4-step procedure, conduct a two-tailed hypothesis test with $\alpha = .05$ to evaluate the effect of the supplements.

4. Childhood participation in sports, cultural groups, and youth groups appears to be related to improved self-esteem for adolescents (McGee, Williams, Howden-Chapman, Martin, & Kawachi, 2006). In a representative study, a sample of $n = 100$ adolescents with a history of group participation is given a standardized self-esteem questionnaire. For the general population of adolescents, scores on this questionnaire form a normal distribution with a mean of $\mu = 50$ and a standard deviation of $\sigma = 15$. The sample of group-participation adolescents had an average of $M = 53.8$.
   a. Does this sample provide enough evidence to conclude that self-esteem scores for these adolescents are significantly different from those of the general population? Use a two-tailed test with $\alpha = .05$.
   b. Compute Cohen's d to measure the size of the difference.
   c. Write a sentence describing the outcome of the hypothesis test and the measure of effect size as it would appear in a research report.

5. A local college requires an English composition course for all freshmen. This year they are evaluating a new online version of the course. A random sample of $n = 16$ freshmen is selected and the students are placed in the online course. At the end of the semester, all freshmen take the same English composition exam. The average score for the sample is $M = 76$. For the general population of freshmen who took the traditional lecture class, the exam scores form a normal distribution with a mean of $\mu = 80$.
   a. If the final exam scores for the population have a standard deviation of $\sigma = 12$, does the sample provide enough evidence to conclude that the new online course is significantly different from the traditional class? Assume a two-tailed test with $\alpha = .05$.
   b. If the population standard deviation is $\sigma = 6$, is the sample sufficient to demonstrate a significant difference? Again, assume a two-tailed test with $\alpha = .05$.
   c. Comparing your answers for parts a and b, explain how the magnitude of the standard deviation influences the outcome of a hypothesis test.

6. A random sample is selected from a normal population with a mean of $\mu = 30$ and a standard deviation of $\sigma = 8$. After a treatment is administered to the individuals in the sample, the sample mean is found to be $M = 33$.
   a. If the sample consists of $n = 16$ scores, is the sample mean sufficient to conclude that the treatment has a significant effect? Use a two-tailed test with $\alpha = .05$.

b. If the sample consists of $n = 64$ scores, is the sample mean sufficient to conclude that the treatment has a significant effect? Use a two-tailed test with $\alpha = .05$.

c. Comparing your answers for parts a and b, explain how the size of the sample influences the outcome of a hypothesis test.

7. A random sample of $n = 25$ scores is selected from a normal population with a mean of $\mu = 40$. After a treatment is administered to the individuals in the sample, the sample mean is found to be $M = 44$.

a. If the population standard deviation is $\sigma = 5$, is the sample mean sufficient to conclude that the treatment has a significant effect? Use a two-tailed test with $\alpha = .05$.

b. If the population standard deviation is $\sigma = 15$, is the sample mean sufficient to conclude that the treatment has a significant effect? Use a two-tailed test with $\alpha = .05$.

c. Comparing your answers for parts a and b, explain how the magnitude of the standard deviation influences the outcome of a hypothesis test.

8. Brunt, Rhee, and Zhong (2008) surveyed 557 undergraduate college students to examine their weight status, health behaviors, and diet. Using body mass index (BMI), they classified the students into four categories: underweight, healthy weight, overweight, and obese. They also measured dietary variety by counting the number of different foods each student ate from several food groups. Note that the researchers are not measuring the amount of food eaten, but rather the number of different foods eaten (variety, not quantity). Nonetheless, it was somewhat surprising that the results showed no differences among the four weight categories that were related to eating fatty and/or sugary snacks.

Suppose a researcher conducting a follow up study obtains a sample of $n = 25$ students classified as healthy weight and a sample of $n = 36$ students classified as overweight. Each student completes the food variety questionnaire, and the healthy-weight group produces a mean of $M = 4.01$ for the fatty, sugary snack category compared to a mean of $M = 4.48$ for the overweight group. The results from the Brunt, Rhee, and Zhong study showed an overall mean variety score of $\mu = 4.22$ for the discretionary sweets or fats food group. Assume that the distribution of scores is approximately normal with a standard deviation of $\sigma = 0.60$.

a. Does the sample of $n = 36$ indicate that the number of fatty, sugary snacks eaten by overweight students is significantly different from the overall population mean? Use a two-tailed test with $\alpha = .05$.

b. Based on the sample of $n = 25$ healthy-weight students, can you conclude that healthy-weight students eat significantly fewer fatty, sugary snacks than the overall population? Use a one-tailed test with $\alpha = .05$.

9. A random sample is selected from a normal population with a mean of $\mu = 100$ and a standard deviation of $\sigma = 20$. After a treatment is administered to the individuals in the sample, the sample mean is found to be $M = 96$.

a. How large a sample is necessary for this sample mean to be statistically significant? Assume a two-tailed test with $\alpha = .05$.

b. If the sample mean were $M = 98$, what sample size would be needed to be significant for a two-tailed test with $\alpha = .05$?

10. In a study examining the effect of alcohol on reaction time, Liguori and Robinson (2001) found that even moderate alcohol consumption significantly slowed response time to an emergency situation in a driving simulation. In a similar study, researchers measured reaction time 30 minutes after participants consumed one 6-ounce glass of wine. Again, they used a standardized driving simulation task for which the regular population averages $\mu = 400$ msec. The distribution of reaction times is approximately normal with $\sigma = 40$. Assume that the researcher obtained a sample mean of $M = 422$ for the $n = 25$ participants in the study.

a. Are the data sufficient to conclude that the alcohol has a significant effect on reaction time? Use a two-tailed test with $\alpha = .01$.

b. Do the data provide evidence that the alcohol significantly increased (slowed) reaction time? Use a one-tailed test with $\alpha = .05$.

c. Compute Cohen's d to estimate the size of the effect.

11. The researchers cited in the previous problem (Liguori & Robinson, 2001) also examined the effect of caffeine on response time in the driving simulator. In a similar study, researchers measured reaction time 30 minutes after participants consumed one 6-ounce cup of coffee. Using the same driving simulation task, for which the distribution of reaction times is normal with $\mu = 400$ msec. and $\sigma = 40$, they obtained a mean of $M = 392$ for a sample of $n = 36$ participants.

a. Are the data sufficient to conclude that caffeine has a significant effect on reaction time? Use a two-tailed test with $\alpha = .05$.

b. Compute Cohen's d to estimate the size of the effect.

c. Write a sentence describing the outcome of the hypothesis test and the measure of effect size as it would appear in a research report.

12. There is some evidence indicating that people with visible tattoos are viewed more negatively than people without visible tattoos (Resenhoeft, Villa, & Wiseman, 2008). In a similar study, a researcher first obtained overall ratings of attractiveness for a woman with no tattoos shown in a color photograph. On a 7-point scale, the woman received an average rating of $\mu = 4.9$, and the distribution of ratings was normal with a standard deviation of $\sigma = 0.84$. The researcher then modified the photo by adding a tattoo of a butterfly on the woman's left arm. The modified photo was then shown to a sample of $n = 16$ students at a local community college and the students used the same 7-point scale to rate the attractiveness of the woman. The average score for the photo with the tattoo was $M = 4.2$.

  a. Do the data indicate a significant difference in rated attractiveness when the woman appeared to have a tattoo? Use a two-tailed test with $\alpha = .05$.

  b. Compute Cohen's d to measure the size of the effect.

  c. Write a sentence describing the outcome of the hypothesis test and the measure of effect size as it would appear in a research report.

13. Researchers at a National Weather Center in the northeastern United States recorded the number of 90° days each year since records first started in 1875. The numbers form a normal shaped distribution with a mean of $\mu = 9.6$ and a standard deviation of $\sigma = 1.9$. To see if the data showed any evidence of global warming, they also computed the mean number of 90° days for the most recent $n = 4$ years and obtained $M = 11.85$. Do the data indicate that the past four years have had significantly more 90° days than would be expected for a random sample from this population? Use a one-tailed test with $\alpha = .05$.

14. Montarello and Martens (2005) found that fifth-grade students completed more mathematics problems correctly when simple problems were mixed in with their regular math assignments. To further explore this phenomenon, suppose that a researcher selects a standardized mathematics achievement test that produces a normal distribution of scores with a mean of $\mu = 100$ and a standard deviation of $\sigma = 18$. The researcher modifies the test by inserting a set of very easy problems among the standardized questions, and gives the modified test to a sample of $n = 36$ students. If the average test score for the sample is $M = 104$, is this result sufficient to conclude that inserting the easy questions improves student performance? Use a one-tailed test with $\alpha = .01$.

15. Researchers have noted a decline in cognitive functioning as people age (Bartus, 1990). However, the results from other research suggest that the antioxidants in foods such as blueberries can reduce and even reverse these age-related declines, at least in laboratory rats (Joseph et al., 1999). Based on these results, one might theorize that the same antioxidants might also benefit elderly humans. Suppose a researcher is interested in testing this theory. The researcher obtains a sample of $n = 16$ adults who are older than 65, and gives each participant a daily dose of a blueberry supplement that is very high in antioxidants. After taking the supplement for 6 months, the participants are given a standardized cognitive skills test and produce a mean score of $M = 50.2$. For the general population of elderly adults, scores on the test average $\mu = 45$ and form a normal distribution with $\sigma = 9$.

  a. Can the researcher conclude that the supplement has a significant effect on cognitive skill? Use a two-tailed test with $\alpha = .05$.

  b. Compute Cohen's d for this study.

  c. Write a sentence demonstrating how the outcome of the hypothesis test and the measure of effect size would appear in a research report.

16. A researcher plans to conduct an experiment evaluating the effect of a treatment. A sample of $n = 9$ participants is selected and each person receives the treatment before being tested on a standardized dexterity task. The treatment is expected to lower scores on the test by an average of 30 points. For the regular population, scores on the dexterity task form a normal distribution with $\mu = 240$ and $\sigma = 30$.

  a. If the researcher uses a two-tailed test with $\alpha = .05$, what is the power of the hypothesis test?

  b. Again assuming a two-tailed test with $\alpha = .05$, what is the power of the hypothesis test if the sample size is increased to $n = 25$?

17. A sample of $n = 40$ is selected from a normal population with $\mu = 75$ msec. and $\sigma = 12$, and a treatment is administered to the sample. The treatment is expected to increase scores by an average of 4 msec.

  a. If the treatment effect is evaluated with a two-tailed hypothesis test using $\alpha = .05$, what is the power of the test?

  b. What is the power of the test if the researcher uses a one-tailed test with $\alpha = .05$?

18. Briefly explain how increasing sample size influences each of the following. Assume that all other factors are held constant.

  a. The size of the z-score in a hypothesis test.

  b. The size of Cohen's d.

  c. The power of a hypothesis test.

19. Explain how the power of a hypothesis test is influenced by each of the following. Assume that all other factors are held constant.

  a. Increasing the alpha level from .01 to .05.

  b. Changing from a one-tailed test to a two-tailed test.

20. A researcher is investigating the effectiveness of a new medication for lowering blood pressure for individuals with systolic pressure greater than 140. For this population, systolic scores average $\mu = 160$ with a standard deviation of $\sigma = 20$, and the scores form a normal-shaped distribution. The researcher plans to select a sample of $n = 25$ individuals, and measure their systolic blood pressure after they take the medication for 60 days. If the researcher uses a two-tailed test with $\alpha = .05$,

    a. What is the power of the test if the medication has a 5-point effect?

b. What is the power of the test if the medication has a 10-point effect?

21. A researcher is evaluating the influence of a treatment using a sample selected from a normally distributed population with a mean of $\mu = 80$ and a standard deviation of $\sigma = 20$. The researcher expects a 12-point treatment effect and plans to use a two-tailed hypothesis test with $\alpha = .05$.

    a. Compute the power of the test if the researcher uses a sample of $n = 16$ individuals.

    b. Compute the power of the test if the researcher uses a sample of $n = 25$ individuals.

After completing this part, you should understand the basic procedures that form the foundation of inferential statistics. These include:

1. The ability to transform scores into z-scores to describe locations within a distribution and to standardize entire distributions (Chapter 5).
2. The ability to determine probabilities associated with individual scores selected from a distribution, especially for scores from normal distributions (Chapter 6).
3. The ability to transform sample means into z-scores and to determine the probabilities associated with sample means (Chapter 7).
4. The ability to use a sample mean to evaluate a hypothesis about an unknown population mean (Chapter 8).

The general goal of inferential statistics is to use the limited information from a sample to answer general questions about an unknown population. In Chapter 8, we introduced hypothesis testing, one of the most commonly used inferential procedures. The hypothesis test presented in Chapter 8 integrates z-scores from Chapter 5, probability from Chapter 6, and the distribution of sample means from Chapter 7 into a single procedure that allows researchers to use a sample from an unknown population to evaluate a hypothesis about the population mean. The researcher first obtains a sample from the unknown population and computes the sample mean. The sample mean and a hypothesized value for the population mean are then used to compute a z-score. If the resulting z-score is a high-probability value, near the center of the distribution of sample means, then the researcher concludes that the sample data fit the hypothesis and the decision is to fail to reject the hypothesis. On the other hand, if the resulting z-score is a low-probability value, out in the tails of the distribution of sample means, then the researcher concludes that the sample data do not fit the hypothesis and the decision is to reject the hypothesis.

REVIEW EXERCISES

1. Find each of the requested values for a population with a mean of $\mu = 50$ and a standard deviation of $\sigma = 20$.
   a. What is the z-score corresponding to $X = 52$?
   b. What is the X value corresponding to $z = -0.50$?

   c. If all of the scores in the population are transformed into z-scores, what will be the values for the mean and standard deviation for the complete set of z-scores?
   d. What is the z-score corresponding to a sample mean of $M = 42$ for a sample of $n = 4$ scores?
   e. What is the z-score corresponding to a sample mean of $M = 42$ for a sample of $n = 16$ scores?

2. A survey of high school seniors shows that the average wake-up time the previous Saturday morning was $\mu = 9:45$. Assume that the distribution of times is approximately normal with a standard deviation of $\sigma = 65$ minutes, and find each of the requested values.
   a. What proportion of high school seniors wake up later than 11:00?
   b. What is the probability of randomly selecting a high school senior who woke up before 9:00?
   c. What is the probability of obtaining a mean wake-up time earlier than $M = 9:30$ for a sample of $n = 25$ high school students?

3. Miller (2008) examined the energy drink consumption of college undergraduates and found that males use energy drinks significantly more often than females. To further investigate this phenomenon, suppose that a researcher selects a random sample of $n = 36$ male undergraduates and a sample of $n = 25$ females. On average, the males reported consuming $M = 2.45$ drinks per month and females had an average of $M = 1.28$. Assume that the overall level of consumption for college undergraduates averages $\mu = 1.85$ energy drinks per month, and that the distribution of monthly consumption scores is approximately normal with a standard deviation of $\sigma = 1.2$.
   a. Did this sample of males consume significantly more energy drinks than the overall population average? Use a one-tailed test with $\alpha = .01$.
   b. Did this sample of females consume significantly fewer energy drinks than the overall population average? Use a one-tailed test with $\alpha = .01$.

PART

III

Using *t* Statistics for Inferences About Population Means and Mean Differences

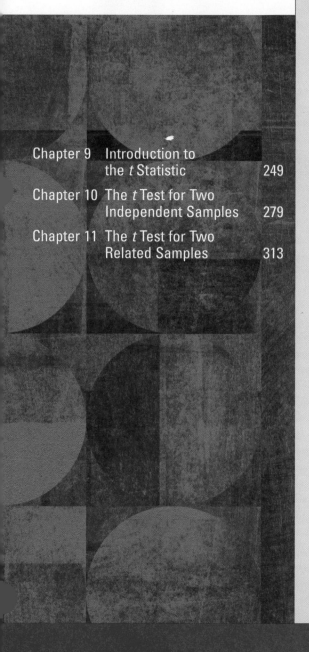

In Part II, we presented the foundation for inferential statistics. In this part, we begin to introduce some of the inferential procedures that are actually used in behavioral science research. Specifically, we look at a family of *t* statistics that use sample means and mean differences to draw inferences about the corresponding population means and mean differences. The *t* statistics are all modeled after the *z*-score for sample means that was introduced in Chapter 7 and used for hypothesis testing in Chapter 8. However, the *t* statistics do not require any prior knowledge about the population being evaluated. The three *t* statistics introduced in this part apply to three distinct research situations:

1. Using a single sample to draw an inference about the unknown mean for a single population.

2. Using two separate samples to draw an inference about the mean difference between two unknown populations.

3. Using one sample, with each individual tested in two different treatment conditions, to draw an inference about the population mean difference between the two conditions.

In addition to the hypothesis testing procedure introduced in Chapter 8, this part introduces a new inferential technique known as *confidence intervals*. Confidence intervals allow researchers to use sample data to estimate population means or mean differences by computing a range of values that is highly likely to contain the unknown parameter.

247

C H A P T E R

9

Introduction to the *t* Statistic

Tools You Will Need

The following items are considered essential background material for this chapter. If you doubt your knowledge of any of these items, you should review the appropriate chapter or section before proceeding.

- Sample variance and standard deviation (Chapter 4)
- Standard error (Chapter 7)
- Hypothesis testing (Chapter 8)

aplia

Aplia for *Essentials of Statistics for the Behavioral Sciences*
After reading, go to "Resources" at the end of this chapter for an introduction on how to use Aplia's homework and learning resources.

9.1 THE *t* STATISTIC: AN ALTERNATIVE TO *z*

Remember that the expected value of the distribution of sample means is μ, the population mean.

In the previous chapter, we presented the statistical procedures that permit researchers to use a sample mean to test hypotheses about an unknown population mean. These statistical procedures were based on a few basic concepts, which we summarize as follows:

1. A sample mean (M) is expected to approximate its population mean (μ). This permits us to use the sample mean to test a hypothesis about the population mean.

2. The standard error provides a measure of how well a sample mean approximates the population mean. Specifically, the standard error determines how much difference is reasonable to expect between a sample mean (M) and the population mean (μ).

$$\sigma_M = \frac{\sigma}{\sqrt{n}} \quad \text{or} \quad \sigma_M = \sqrt{\frac{\sigma^2}{n}}$$

3. To quantify our inferences about the population, we compare the obtained sample mean (M) with the hypothesized population mean (μ) by computing a z-score test statistic.

$$z = \frac{M - \mu}{\sigma_M} = \frac{\text{obtained difference between data and hypothesis}}{\text{standard distance between } M \text{ and } \mu}$$

The goal of the hypothesis test is to determine whether the obtained difference between the data and the hypothesis is significantly greater than would be expected by chance. When the z-scores form a normal distribution, we are able to use the unit normal table (in Appendix B) to find the critical region for the hypothesis test.

THE PROBLEM WITH *z*-SCORES

The shortcoming of using a z-score for hypothesis testing is that the z-score formula requires more information than is usually available. Specifically, a z-score requires that we know the value of the population standard deviation (or variance), which is needed to compute the standard error. In most situations, however, the standard deviation for the population is not known. In fact, the whole reason for conducting a hypothesis test is to gain knowledge about an *unknown* population. This situation appears to create a paradox: You want to use a z-score to find out about an unknown population, but you must know about the population before you can compute a z-score. Fortunately, there is a relatively simple solution to this problem. When the variance for the population is not known, we use the corresponding sample value in its place.

INTRODUCING THE *t* STATISTIC

In Chapter 4, the sample variance was developed specifically to provide an unbiased estimate of the corresponding population variance. Recall that the formulas for sample variance and sample standard deviation are as follows:

$$\text{sample variance} = s^2 = \frac{SS}{n-1} = \frac{SS}{df}$$

$$\text{sample standard deviation} = s = \sqrt{\frac{SS}{n-1}} = \sqrt{\frac{SS}{df}}$$

The concept of degrees of freedom, $df = n - 1$, was introduced in Chapter 4 (p. 103) and is discussed later in this chapter (p. 252).

Using the sample values, we can now *estimate* the standard error. Recall from Chapters 7 and 8 that the value of the standard error can be computed using either standard deviation or variance:

$$\text{standard error} = \sigma_M = \frac{\sigma}{\sqrt{n}} \quad \text{or} \quad \sigma_M = \sqrt{\frac{\sigma^2}{n}}$$

Now we estimate the standard error by simply substituting the sample variance or standard deviation in place of the unknown population value:

$$\text{estimated standard error} = s_M = \frac{s}{\sqrt{n}} \quad \text{or} \quad s_M = \sqrt{\frac{s^2}{n}} \tag{9.1}$$

Notice that the symbol for the *estimated standard error of* M is s_M instead of σ_M, indicating that the estimated value is computed from sample data rather than from the actual population parameter.

DEFINITION

> The **estimated standard error** (s_M) is used as an estimate of the real standard error, σ_M, when the value of σ is unknown. It is computed using the sample variance or sample standard deviation and provides an estimate of the standard distance between a sample mean, *M*, and the population mean, μ.

Finally, you should recognize that we have shown formulas for standard error (actual or estimated) using both the standard deviation and the variance. In the past (Chapters 7 and 8), we concentrated on the formula using the standard deviation. At this point, however, we shift our focus to the formula based on variance. Thus, throughout the remainder of this chapter, and in following chapters, the estimated standard error of *M* typically is presented and computed using

$$s_M = \sqrt{\frac{s^2}{n}}$$

There are two reasons for making this shift from standard deviation to variance:

1. In Chapter 4 (p. 105), we saw that the sample variance is an *unbiased* statistic; on average, the sample variance (s^2) provides an accurate and unbiased estimate of the population variance (σ^2). Therefore, the most accurate way to estimate the standard error is to use the sample variance to estimate the population variance.

2. In future chapters, we encounter other versions of the *t* statistic that require variance (instead of standard deviation) in the formulas for estimated standard error. To maximize the similarity from one version to another, we use variance in the formula for *all* of the different *t* statistics. Thus, whenever we present a *t* statistic, the estimated standard error is computed as

$$\text{estimated standard error} = \sqrt{\frac{\text{sample variance}}{\text{sample size}}}$$

Now we can substitute the estimated standard error in the denominator of the *z*-score formula. The result is a new test statistic called a *t* statistic:

$$t = \frac{M - \mu}{s_M} \tag{9.2}$$

D E F I N I T I O N

> The *t* **statistic** is used to test hypotheses about an unknown population mean, μ, when the value of σ is unknown. The formula for the *t* statistic has the same structure as the *z*-score formula, except that the *t* statistic uses the estimated standard error in the denominator.

The only difference between the *t* formula and the *z*-score formula is that the *z*-score uses the actual population variance, σ^2 (or the standard deviation), and the *t* formula uses the corresponding sample variance (or standard deviation) when the population value is not known.

$$z = \frac{M - \mu}{\sigma_M} = \frac{M - \mu}{\sqrt{\sigma^2 / n}} \qquad t = \frac{M - \mu}{s_M} = \frac{M - \mu}{\sqrt{s^2 / n}}$$

DEGREES OF FREEDOM AND THE *t* STATISTIC

In this chapter, we have introduced the *t* statistic as a substitute for a *z*-score. The basic difference between these two is that the *t* statistic uses sample variance (s^2) and the *z*-score uses the population variance (σ^2). To determine how well a *t* statistic approximates a *z*-score, we must determine how well the sample variance approximates the population variance.

In Chapter 4, we introduced the concept of degrees of freedom (p. 103). Reviewing briefly, you must know the sample mean before you can compute sample variance. This places a restriction on sample variability such that only $n - 1$ scores in a sample are independent and free to vary. The value $n - 1$ is called the *degrees of freedom* (or *df*) for the sample variance.

$$\text{degrees of freedom} = df = n - 1 \tag{9.3}$$

D E F I N I T I O N

> **Degrees of freedom** describe the number of scores in a sample that are independent and free to vary. Because the sample mean places a restriction on the value of one score in the sample, there are $n - 1$ degrees of freedom for a sample with n scores (see Chapter 4).

As the value of *df* for a sample increases, the better the sample variance, s^2, represents the population variance, σ^2, and the better the *t* statistic approximates the *z*-score. This should make sense because the larger the sample (n) is, the better the sample represents its population. Thus, the degrees of freedom associated with s^2 also describe how well *t* represents *z*.

THE *t* DISTRIBUTION

Every sample from a population can be used to compute a *z*-score or a *t* statistic. If you select all of the possible samples of a particular size (n), and compute the *z*-score for each sample mean, then the entire set of *z*-scores form a *z*-score distribution. In the same way, you can compute the *t* statistic for every sample and the entire set of *t* values form a *t* *distribution*. As we saw in Chapter 7, the distribution of *z*-scores for sample means tends to be a normal distribution. Specifically, if the sample size is large (around $n = 30$ or more) or if the sample is selected from a normal population, then the distribution of sample means is a nearly perfect normal distribution. In these same situations, the *t* distribution approximates a normal distribution, just as a *t* statistic approximates a *z*-score. How well a *t* distribution approximates a normal distribution is determined by degrees of freedom. In general, as the sample size (n) increases, the degrees of freedom ($n - 1$) also increase, and the better the *t* distribution approximates the normal distribution (Figure 9.1).

FIGURE 9.1

Distributions of the *t* statistic for different values of degrees of freedom are compared to a normal *z*-score distribution. Like the normal distribution, *t* distributions are bell-shaped and symmetrical and have a mean of zero. However, *t* distributions have more variability, indicated by the flatter and more spread-out shape. The larger the value of *df* is, the more closely the *t* distribution approximates a normal distribution.

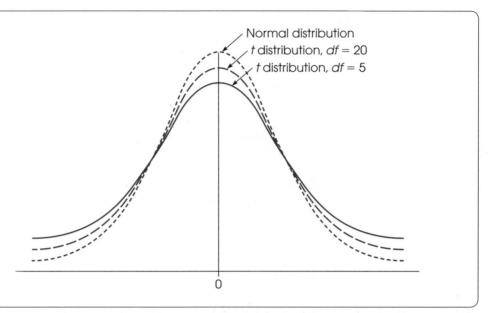

DEFINITION

A *t* **distribution** is the complete set of *t* values computed for every possible random sample for a specific sample size (*n*) or a specific degrees of freedom (*df*). The *t* distribution approximates the shape of a normal distribution, especially for large samples or samples from a normal population.

THE SHAPE OF THE *t* DISTRIBUTION

The exact shape of a *t* distribution changes with degrees of freedom. In fact, statisticians speak of a "family" of *t* distributions. That is, there is a different sampling distribution of *t* for each possible number of degrees of freedom. As *df* gets very large, the *t* distribution gets closer in shape to a normal *z*-score distribution. Figure 9.1 shows that distributions of *t* are bell-shaped and symmetrical and have a mean of zero. However, the *t* distribution has more variability than a normal *z* distribution, especially when *df* values are small (see Figure 9.1). The *t* distribution tends to be flatter and more spread out, whereas the normal *z* distribution has more of a central peak.

The reason that the *t* distribution is flatter and more variable than the normal *z*-score distribution becomes clear if you look at the structure of the formulas for *z* and *t*. For both formulas, *z* and *t*, the top of the formula, $M - \mu$, can take on different values because the sample mean (*M*) varies from one sample to another. For *z*-scores, however, the bottom of the formula does not vary, provided that all of the samples are the same size and are selected from the same population. Specifically, all of the *z*-scores have the same standard error in the denominator, $\sigma_M = \sqrt{\sigma^2 / n}$, because the population variance and the sample size are the same for every sample. For *t* statistics, on the other hand, the bottom of the formula varies from one sample to another. Specifically, the sample variance (s^2) changes from one sample to the next, so the estimated standard error also varies, $s_M = \sqrt{s^2 / n}$. Thus, only the numerator of the *z*-score formula varies, but both the numerator and the denominator of the *t* statistic vary. As a result, *t* statistics are more variable than are *z*-scores, and the *t* distribution is flatter and more spread out. As sample size and *df* increase, however, the variability in the *t* distribution decreases, and it more closely resembles a normal distribution.

DETERMINING
PROPORTIONS
AND PROBABILITIES
FOR *t* DISTRIBUTIONS

Just as we used the unit normal table to locate proportions associated with z-scores, we use a t distribution table to find proportions for t statistics. The complete t distribution table is presented in Appendix B, page 575, and a portion of this table is reproduced in Table 9.1. The two rows at the top of the table show proportions of the t distribution contained in either one or two tails, depending on which row is used. The first column of the table lists degrees of freedom for the t statistic. Finally, the numbers in the body of the table are the t values that mark the boundary between the tails and the rest of the t distribution.

For example, to find proportions for the t distribution with $df = 3$, you begin by locating $df = 3$ in the first column. Then, use the top two rows of the table to identify a proportion in either one tail or two tails. For example, to find the t value that separates 5% in the tail from the rest of the distribution, locate a proportion of 0.05 in the one-tail row at the top of the table. When you line up the 0.05 proportion in the top row with $df = 3$ in the first column, you find a value of $t = 2.352$ in the body of the table (see highlight in Table 9.1). Because the t distribution is symmetrical, 5% of the distribution is also located in the tail beyond $t = -2.353$ (see Figure 9.2). Finally, notice that a total of 10% (or 0.10) is contained in the two tails beyond $t = \pm2.353$ (check the proportion value in the "two-tails combined" row at the top of the table).

A close inspection of the t distribution table in Appendix B demonstrates a point we made earlier: As the value for df increases, the t distribution becomes more similar to a normal distribution. For example, examine the column containing t values for a 0.05 proportion in two tails. You will find that when $df = 1$, the t values that separate the extreme 5% (0.05) from the rest of the distribution are $t = \pm12.706$. As you read down the column, however, you will find that the critical t values become smaller and smaller, ultimately reaching ±1.96. You should recognize ±1.96 as the z-score values that separate the extreme 5% in a normal distribution. Thus, as df increases, the proportions in a t distribution become more like the proportions in a normal distribution. When the sample size (and degrees of freedom) is sufficiently large, the difference between a t distribution and the normal distribution becomes negligible.

Caution: The t distribution table printed in this book has been abridged and does not include entries for every possible df value. For example, the table lists t values for $df = 40$ and for $df = 60$, but does not list any entries for df values between 40 and 60. Occasionally, you will encounter a situation in which your t statistic has a df value that is not listed in the table. In these situations, you should look up the critical t for both of the surrounding df values listed and then use the *larger* value for t. If, for example, you have $df = 53$ (not listed), look up the critical t value for both $df = 40$ and $df = 60$ and *then use the larger* t *value*. If your sample t statistic is greater than the larger value listed, then you can be certain that the data are in the critical region, and you can confidently reject the null hypothesis.

TABLE 9.1

A portion of the *t*-distribution table. The numbers in the table are the values of *t* that separate the tail from the main body of the distribution. Proportions for one or two tails are listed at the top of the table, and *df* values for *t* are listed in the first column.

	Proportion in One Tail					
	0.25	*0.10*	*0.05*	*0.025*	*0.01*	*0.005*
	Proportion in Two Tails Combined					
df	*0.50*	*0.20*	*0.10*	*0.05*	*0.02*	*0.01*
1	1.000	3.078	6.314	12.706	31.821	63.657
2	0.816	1.886	2.920	4.303	6.965	9.925
3	0.765	1.638	2.353	3.182	4.541	5.841
4	0.741	1.533	2.132	2.776	3.747	4.604
5	0.727	1.476	2.015	2.571	3.365	4.032
6	0.718	1.440	1.943	2.447	3.143	3.707

FIGURE 9.2

The *t* distribution with $df = 3$. Note that 5% of the distribution is located in the tail beyond $t = 2.353$. Also, 5% is in the tail beyond $t = -2.353$. Thus, a total proportion of 10% (0.10) is in the two tails beyond $t = \pm2.353$.

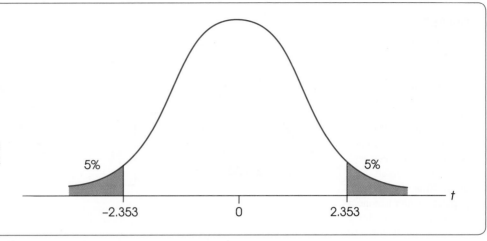

5%   5%

−2.353   0   2.353   *t*

1. Under what circumstances is a *t* statistic used instead of a *z*-score for a hypothesis test?

2. A sample of $n = 9$ scores has $SS = 288$.

   a. Compute the variance for the sample.

   b. Compute the estimated standard error for the sample mean.

3. In general, a distribution of *t* statistics is flatter and more spread out than the standard normal distribution. (True or false?)

4. A researcher reports a *t* statistic with $df = 20$. How many individuals participated in the study?

5. For $df = 15$, find the value(s) of *t* associated with each of the following:

   a. The top 5% of the distribution.

   b. The middle 95% of the distribution.

   c. The middle 99% of the distribution.

ANSWERS

1. A *t* statistic is used instead of a *z*-score when the population standard deviation and variance are not known.

2. a. $s^2 = 36$ b. $s_M = 2$

3. True.

4. $n = 21$

5. a. $t = +1.753$ b. $t = \pm2.131$ c. $t = \pm2.947$

9.2 HYPOTHESIS TESTS WITH THE *t* STATISTIC

In the hypothesis-testing situation, we begin with a population with an unknown mean and an unknown variance, often a population that has received some treatment (Figure 9.3). The goal is to use a sample from the treated population (a treated sample) as the basis for determining whether the treatment has any effect.

FIGURE 9.3

The basic experimental situation for using the *t* statistic or the *z*-score is presented. It is assumed that the parameter μ is known for the population before treatment. The purpose of the experiment is to determine whether the treatment has an effect. Note that the population after treatment has unknown values for the mean and the variance. We will use a sample to test a hypothesis about the population mean.

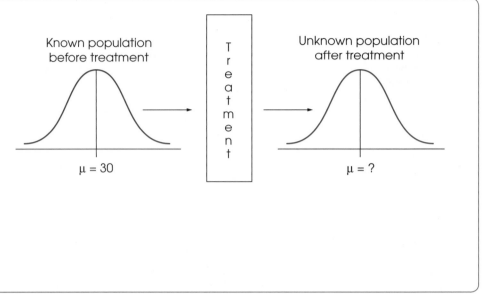

Known population before treatment

$\mu = 30$

Treatment

Unknown population after treatment

$\mu = ?$

As always, the null hypothesis states that the treatment has no effect; specifically, H_0 states that the population mean is unchanged. Thus, the null hypothesis provides a specific value for the unknown population mean. The sample data provide a value for the sample mean. Finally, the variance and estimated standard error are computed from the sample data. When these values are used in the *t* formula, the result becomes

$$t = \frac{\underset{\text{(from the data)}}{\text{sample mean}} - \underset{\text{(hypothesized from } H_0)}{\text{population mean}}}{\underset{\text{(computed from the sample data)}}{\text{estimated standard error}}}$$

As with the *z*-score formula, the *t* statistic forms a ratio. The numerator measures the actual difference between the sample data (*M*) and the population hypothesis (μ). The estimated standard error in the denominator measures how much difference is reasonable to expect between a sample mean and the population mean. When the obtained difference between the data and the hypothesis (numerator) is much greater than expected (denominator), we obtain a large value for *t* (either large positive or large negative). In this case, we conclude that the data are not consistent with the hypothesis, and our decision is to "reject H_0." On the other hand, when the difference between the data and the hypothesis is small relative to the standard error, we obtain a *t* statistic near zero, and our decision is "fail to reject H_0."

The unknown population   As mentioned earlier, the hypothesis test often concerns a population that has received a treatment. This situation is shown in Figure 9.3. Note that the value of the mean is known for the population before treatment. The question is whether the treatment influences the scores and causes the mean to change. In this case, the unknown population is the one that exists after the treatment is administered, and the null hypothesis simply states that the value of the mean is not changed by the treatment.

Although the *t* statistic can be used in the "before and after" type of research shown in Figure 9.3, it also permits hypothesis testing in situations for which you do not have a known population mean to serve as a standard. Specifically, the *t* test does not require any prior knowledge about the population mean or the population variance. All you need to compute a *t* statistic is a null hypothesis and a sample from the unknown population. Thus, a *t* test can be used in situations for which the null hypothesis is obtained from a theory, a logical prediction, or just wishful thinking. For example, many surveys contain rating-scale questions to determine how people feel about controversial issues. Participants are presented with a statement and asked to express their opinion on a scale from 1 to 7, with 1 indicating "strongly agree" and 7 indicating "strongly disagree." A score of 4 indicates a neutral position, with no strong opinion one way or the other. In this situation, the null hypothesis would state that there is no preference in the population, H_0: $\mu = 4$. The data from a sample are then used to evaluate the hypothesis. Note that the researcher has no prior knowledge about the population mean and states a hypothesis that is based on logic.

HYPOTHESIS TESTING EXAMPLE

The following research situation demonstrates the procedures of hypothesis testing with the *t* statistic. Note that this is another example of a null hypothesis that is founded in logic rather than prior knowledge of a population mean.

EXAMPLE 9.1

Infants, even newborns, prefer to look at attractive faces compared to less attractive faces (Slater, et al., 1998). In the study, infants from 1 to 6 days old were shown two photographs of women's faces. Previously, a group of adults had rated one of the faces as significantly more attractive than the other. The babies were positioned in front of a screen on which the photographs were presented. The pair of faces remained on the screen until the baby accumulated a total of 20 seconds of looking at one or the other. The number of seconds looking at the attractive face was recorded for each infant. Suppose that the study used a sample of $n = 9$ infants and the data produced an average of $M = 13$ seconds for the attractive face with $SS = 72$. Note that all of the available information comes from the sample. Specifically, we do not know the population mean or the population standard deviation.

Step 1 State the hypotheses and select an alpha level. Although we have no information about the population of scores, it is possible to form a logical hypothesis about the value of μ. In this case, the null hypothesis states that the infants have no preference for either face. That is, they should average half of the 20 seconds looking at each of the two faces. In symbols, the null hypothesis states

$$H_0: \mu_{\text{attractive}} = 10 \text{ seconds}$$

The alternative hypothesis states that there is a preference and one of the faces is preferred over the other. A directional, one-tailed test would specify which of the two faces is preferred, but the nondirectional alternative hypothesis is expressed as follows:

$$H_1: \mu_{\text{attractive}} \neq 10 \text{ seconds}$$

We set the level of significance at $\alpha = .05$ for two tails.

Step 2 Locate the critical region. The test statistic is a *t* statistic because the population variance is not known. Therefore, the value for degrees of freedom must be determined before the critical region can be located. For this sample

$$df = n - 1 = 9 - 1 = 8$$

Consulting the *t* distribution table or a two-tailed test with $\alpha = .05$ and $df = 8$, you should find that the critical region consists of *t* values greater than $+2.306$ or less than -2.306. Figure 9.4 depicts the critical region in this *t* distribution.

Step 3   Calculate the test statistic. The *t* statistic typically requires much more computation than is necessary for a *z*-score. Therefore, we recommend that you divide the calculations into a three-stage process as follows:

a. First, calculate the sample variance. Remember that the population variance is unknown, and you must use the sample value in its place. (This is why we are using a *t* statistic instead of a *z*-score.)

$$s^2 = \frac{SS}{n-1} = \frac{SS}{df} = \frac{72}{8} = 9$$

b. Next, use the sample variance (s^2) and the sample size (n) to compute the estimated standard error. This value is the denominator of the *t* statistic and measures how much difference is reasonable to expect by chance between a sample mean and the corresponding population mean if there is no treatment effect.

$$s_M = \sqrt{\frac{s^2}{n}} = \sqrt{\frac{9}{9}} = \sqrt{1} = 1$$

Finally, compute the *t* statistic for the sample data.

$$t = \frac{M - \mu}{s_M} = \frac{13 - 10}{1} = 3.00$$

Step 4   Make a decision regarding H_0. The obtained *t* statistic of 3.00 falls into the critical region on the right-hand side of the *t* distribution (see Figure 9.4). Our statistical decision is to reject H_0 and conclude that babies do show a preference when given a choice between an attractive and an unattractive face. Specifically, the average amount of time that the babies spent looking at the attractive face was significantly different from the 10 seconds that would be expected if there were no preference. As indicated by the sample mean, there is a tendency for the babies to spend more time looking at the attractive face.

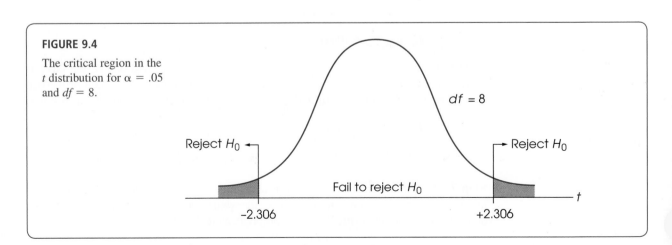

FIGURE 9.4

The critical region in the *t* distribution for $\alpha = .05$ and $df = 8$.

ASSUMPTIONS OF THE *t* TEST

Two basic assumptions are necessary for hypothesis tests with the *t* statistic.

1. The values in the sample must consist of *independent* observations.

In everyday terms, two observations are independent if there is no consistent, predictable relationship between the first observation and the second. More precisely, two events (or observations) are independent if the occurrence of the first event has no effect on the probability of the second event. We examined specific examples of independence and non-independence in Box 8.1 (p. 220).

2. The population that is sampled must be normal.

This assumption is a necessary part of the mathematics underlying the development of the *t* statistic and the *t* distribution table. However, violating this assumption has little practical effect on the results obtained for a *t* statistic, especially when the sample size is relatively large. With very small samples, a normal population distribution is important. With larger samples, this assumption can be violated without affecting the validity of the hypothesis test. If you have reason to suspect that the population distribution is not normal, use a large sample to be safe.

THE INFLUENCE OF SAMPLE SIZE AND SAMPLE VARIANCE

As we noted in Chapter 8 (p. 222), a variety of factors can influence the outcome of a hypothesis test. In particular, the number of scores in the sample and the magnitude of the sample variance both have a large effect on the *t* statistic and, thereby, influence the statistical decision. The structure of the *t* formula makes these factors easier to understand.

$$t = \frac{M - \mu}{s_M} \quad \text{where} \quad s_M = \sqrt{\frac{s^2}{n}}$$

Because the estimated standard error, s_M, appears in the denominator of the formula, a larger value for s_M produces a smaller value (closer to zero) for *t*. Thus, any factor that influences the standard error also affects the likelihood of rejecting the null hypothesis and finding a significant treatment effect. The two factors that determine the size of the standard error are the sample variance, s^2, and the sample size, *n*.

The estimated standard error is directly related to the sample variance so that the larger the variance, the larger the error. Thus, large variance means that you are less likely to obtain a significant treatment effect. In general, large variance is bad for inferential statistics. Large variance means that the scores are widely scattered, which makes it difficult to see any consistent patterns or trends in the data. In general, high variance reduces the likelihood of rejecting the null hypothesis.

On the other hand, the estimated standard error is inversely related to the number of scores in the sample. The larger the sample is, the smaller the error is. If all other factors are held constant, large samples tend to produce bigger *t* statistics and therefore are more likely to produce significant results. For example, a 2-point mean difference with a sample of *n* = 4 may not be convincing evidence of a treatment effect. However, the same 2-point difference with a sample of *n* = 100 is much more compelling.

1. A sample of $n = 4$ individuals is selected from a population with a mean of $\mu = 40$. A treatment is administered to the individuals in the sample and, after treatment, the sample has a mean of $M = 44$ and a variance of $s^2 = 16$.

   a. Is this sample sufficient to conclude that the treatment has a significant effect? Use a two-tailed test with $\alpha = .05$.

   b. If all other factors are held constant and the sample size is increased to $n = 16$, is the sample sufficient to conclude that the treatment has a significant effect? Again, use a two-tailed test with $\alpha = .05$.

ANSWERS

1. **a.** H_0: $\mu = 40$ even after the treatment. With $n = 4$, the estimated standard error is 2, and $t = \frac{4}{2} = 2.00$. With $df = 3$, the critical boundaries are set at $t = \pm 3.182$. Fail to reject H_0 and conclude that the treatment does not have a significant effect.

   b. With $n = 16$, the estimated standard error is 1 and $t = 4.00$. With $df = 15$, the critical boundary is ± 2.131. The t value is beyond the critical boundary, so we reject H_0 and conclude that the treatment does have a significant effect.

9.3 MEASURING EFFECT SIZE FOR THE *t* STATISTIC

In Chapter 8, we noted that one criticism of a hypothesis test is that it does not really evaluate the size of the treatment effect. Instead, a hypothesis test simply determines whether the treatment effect is greater than chance, where "chance" is determined by the standard error and the alpha level. In particular, it is possible for a very small treatment effect to be "statistically significant," especially when the sample size is very large. To correct for this problem, it is recommended that the results from a hypothesis test be accompanied by a report of effect size, such as Cohen's *d*.

ESTIMATED COHEN'S *d*

When Cohen's *d* was originally introduced (p. 230), the formula was presented as

$$\text{Cohen's } d = \frac{\text{mean difference}}{\text{standard deviation}} = \frac{\mu_{\text{treatment}} - \mu_{\text{no treatment}}}{\sigma}$$

Cohen defined this measure of effect size in terms of the population mean difference and the population standard deviation. However, in most situations the population values are not known and you must substitute the corresponding sample values in their place. When this is done, many researchers prefer to identify the calculated value as an "*estimated* d" or name the value after one of the statisticians who first substituted sample statistics into Cohen's formula (e.g., Glass's *g* or Hedges's *g*). For hypothesis tests using the *t* statistic, the population mean with no treatment is the value specified by the null hypothesis. However, the population mean with treatment and the standard deviation are both unknown. Therefore, we use the mean for the treated sample and the standard deviation for the sample after treatment as estimates of the unknown parameters. With these substitutions, the formula for estimating Cohen's *d* becomes

$$\text{estimated } d = \frac{\text{mean difference}}{\text{sample standard deviation}} = \frac{M - \mu}{s} \tag{9.4}$$

The numerator measures that magnitude of the treatment effect by finding the difference between the mean for the treated sample and the mean for the untreated population (μ from H_0). The sample standard deviation in the denominator standardizes the mean difference into standard deviation units. Thus, an estimated *d* of 1.00 indicates that the size of the treatment effect is equivalent to one standard deviation. The following example demonstrates how the estimated *d* is used to measure effect size for a hypothesis test using a *t* statistic.

EXAMPLE 9.2   For the infant face-preference study in Example 9.1, the babies averaged $M = 13$ out of 20 seconds looking at the attractive face. If there were no preference (as stated by the null hypothesis), the population mean would be $\mu = 10$ seconds. Thus, the results show a 3-second difference between the mean for the sample ($M = 13$) and the mean that would be expected if there were no preference between the two faces ($\mu = 10$). Also, for this study the sample standard deviation is

$$s = \sqrt{\frac{SS}{df}} = \sqrt{\frac{72}{8}} = \sqrt{9} = 3$$

Thus, Cohen's *d* for this example is estimated to be

$$\text{Cohen's } d = \frac{M - \mu}{s} = \frac{13 - 10}{3} = 1.00$$

According to the standards suggested by Cohen (Table 8.2, p. 232), this is a large treatment effect.

To help you visualize what is measured by Cohen's *d,* we have constructed a set of $n = 9$ scores with a mean of $M = 13$ and a standard deviation of $s = 3$ (the same values as in Examples 9.1 and 9.2). The set of scores is shown in Figure 9.5. Notice that the figure also includes an arrow that locates $\mu = 10$. Recall that $\mu = 10$ is the value specified by the null hypothesis and identifies what the mean ought to be if the treatment has no effect. Clearly, our sample is not centered around $\mu = 10$. Instead, the scores have been shifted to the right so that the sample mean is $M = 13$. This shift, from 10 to 13, is the 3-point mean difference that was caused by the treatment effect. Also notice that

FIGURE 9.5

The sample distribution for the scores that were used in Examples 9.1 and 9.2. The population mean, $\mu = 10$ seconds, is the value that would be expected if attractiveness has no effect on the infants' behavior. Note that the sample mean is displaced away from $\mu = 10$ by a distance equal to one standard deviation.

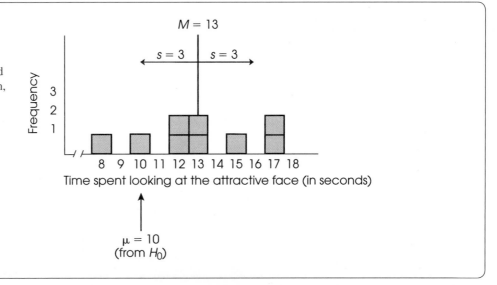

the 3-point mean difference is exactly equal to the standard deviation. Thus, the size of the treatment effect is equal to 1 standard deviation. In other words, Cohen's $d = 1.00$.

MEASURING THE PERCENTAGE OF VARIANCE EXPLAINED, r^2

An alternative method for measuring effect size is to determine how much of the variability in the scores is explained by the treatment effect. The concept behind this measure is that the treatment causes the scores to increase (or decrease), which means that the treatment is causing the scores to vary. If we can measure how much of the variability is explained by the treatment, we can obtain a measure of the size of the treatment effect.

To demonstrate this concept, we use the data from the hypothesis test in Example 9.1. Recall that the null hypothesis stated that the treatment (the attractiveness of the faces) has no effect on the infants' behavior. According to the null hypothesis, the infants should show no preference between the two photographs, and therefore should spend an average of $\mu = 10$ out of 20 seconds looking at the attractive face.

However, if you look at the data in Figure 9.5, the scores are not centered around $\mu = 10$. Instead, the scores are shifted to the right so that they are centered around the sample mean, $M = 13$. This shift is the treatment effect. To measure the size of the treatment effect, we calculate deviations from the mean and the sum of squared deviations, SS, in two different ways.

Figure 9.6(a) shows the original set of scores. For each score, the deviation from $\mu = 10$ is shown as a colored line. Recall that $\mu = 10$ comes from the null hypothesis and represents the population mean if the treatment has no effect. Note that almost all of the scores are located on the right-hand side of $\mu = 10$. This shift to the right is the treatment effect. Specifically, the preference for the attractive face has caused the infants to spend more time looking at the attractive photograph, which means that their

---

FIGURE 9.6

Deviations from $\mu = 10$ (no treatment effect) for the scores in Example 9.1. The colored lines in part (a) show the deviations for the original scores, including the treatment effect. In part (b) the colored lines show the deviations for the adjusted scores after the treatment effect has been removed.

(a) Original scores, including the treatment effect

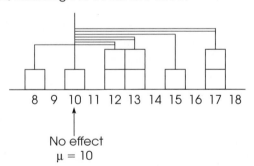

(b) Adjusted scores with the treatment effect removed

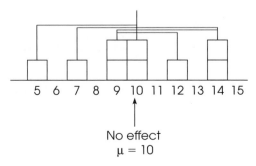

scores are generally greater than 10. Thus, the treatment has pushed the scores away from $\mu = 10$ and has increased the size of the deviations.

Next, we see what happens if the treatment effect is removed. In this example, the treatment has a 3-point effect (the average increases from $\mu = 10$ to $M = 13$). To remove the treatment effect, we simply subtract 3 points from each score. The adjusted scores are shown in Figure 9.6(b) and, once again, the deviations from $\mu = 10$ are shown as colored lines. First, notice that the adjusted scores are centered at $\mu = 10$, indicating that there is no treatment effect. Also notice that the deviations, the colored lines, are noticeably smaller when the treatment effect is removed.

To measure how much the variability is reduced when the treatment effect is removed, we compute the sum of squared deviations, SS, for each set of scores. The left-hand columns of Table 9.2 show the calculations for the original scores [Figure 9.6(a)], and the right-hand columns show the calculations for the adjusted scores [Figure 9.6(b)]. Note that the total variability, including the treatment effect, is $SS = 153$. However, when the treatment effect is removed, the variability is reduced to $SS = 72$. The difference between these two values, $153 - 72 = 81$ points, is the amount of variability that is accounted for by the treatment effect. This value is usually reported as a proportion or percentage of the total variability:

$$\frac{\text{variability accounted for}}{\text{total variability}} = \frac{81}{153} = 0.5294 \quad (52.94\%)$$

Thus, removing the treatment effect reduces the variability by 52.94%. This value is called the *percentage of variance accounted for by the treatment* and is identified as r^2.

Rather than computing r^2 directly by comparing two different calculations for SS, the value can be found from a single equation based on the outcome of the t test.

$$r^2 = \frac{t^2}{t^2 + df} \tag{9.5}$$

The letter r is the traditional symbol used for a correlation, and the concept of r^2 is discussed again when we consider correlations in Chapter 14. Also, in the context of t statistics, the percentage of variance that we are calling r^2 is often identified by the Greek letter omega, squared (ω^2).

TABLE 9.2

Calculation of SS, the sum of squared deviations, for the data in Figure 9.6. The first three columns show the calculations for the original scores, including the treatment effect. The last three columns show the calculations for the adjusted scores after the treatment effect has been removed.

	Calculation of SS including the treatment effect			Calculation of SS after the treatment effect is removed		
Score	Deviation from $\mu = 10$	Squared Deviation		Adjusted Score	Deviation from $\mu = 10$	Squared Deviation
8	−2	4		8 − 3 = 5	−5	25
10	0	0		10 − 3 = 7	−3	9
12	2	4		12 − 3 = 9	−1	1
12	2	4		12 − 3 = 9	−1	1
13	3	9		13 − 3 = 10	0	0
13	3	9		13 − 3 = 10	0	0
15	5	25		15 − 3 = 12	2	4
17	7	49		17 − 3 = 14	4	16
17	7	49		17 − 3 = 14	4	16
		$SS = 153$				$SS = 72$

For the hypothesis test in Example 9.1, we obtained $t = 3.00$ with $df = 8$. These values produce

$$r^2 = \frac{3^2}{3^2 + 8} = \frac{9}{17} = 0.5294 \quad (52.94\%)$$

Note that this is exactly the same as the value we obtained with the direct calculation of the percentage of variability accounted for by the treatment.

Interpreting r^2 In addition to developing the Cohen's d measure of effect size, Cohen (1988) also proposed criteria for evaluating the size of a treatment effect that is measured by r^2. The criteria were actually suggested for evaluating the size of a correlation, r, but are easily extended to apply to r^2. Cohen's standards for interpreting r^2 are shown in Table 9.3.

According to these standards, the data we constructed for Examples 9.1 and 9.2 show a very large effect size with $r^2 = 0.5294$.

As a final note, we should remind you that, although sample size affects the hypothesis test, this factor has little or no effect on measures of effect size. In particular, estimates of Cohen's d are not influenced at all by sample size, and measures of r^2 are only slightly affected by changes in the size of the sample. The sample variance, on the other hand, influences hypothesis tests and measures of effect size. Specifically, high variance reduces both the likelihood of rejecting the null hypothesis and measures of effect size.

CONFIDENCE INTERVALS FOR ESTIMATING μ

An alternative technique for describing the size of a treatment effect is to compute an estimate of the population mean after treatment. For example, if the mean before treatment is known to be $\mu = 80$ and the mean after treatment is estimated to be $\mu = 86$, then we can conclude that the size of the treatment effect is around 6 points.

Estimating an unknown population mean involves constructing a *confidence interval*. A confidence interval is based on the observation that a sample mean tends to provide a reasonably accurate estimate of the population mean. The fact that a sample mean tends to be near to the population mean implies that the population mean should be near to the sample mean. For example, if we obtain a sample mean of $M = 86$, we can be reasonably confident that the population mean is around 86. Thus, a confidence interval consists of an interval of values around a sample mean, and we can be reasonably confident that the unknown population mean is located somewhere in the interval.

D E F I N I T I O N

A **confidence interval** is an interval, or range of values, centered around a sample statistic. The logic behind a confidence interval is that a sample statistic, such as a sample mean, should be relatively near to the corresponding population parameter. Therefore, we can confidently estimate that the value of the parameter should be located in the interval.

TABLE 9.3

Criteria for interpreting the value of r^2 as proposed by Cohen (1988).

Percentage of Variance Explained, r^2	
$r^2 = 0.01$	Small effect
$r^2 = 0.09$	Medium effect
$r^2 = 0.25$	Large effect

CONSTRUCTING A CONFIDENCE INTERVAL

The construction of a confidence interval begins with the observation that every sample mean has a corresponding *t* value defined by the equation

$$t = \frac{M - \mu}{s_M}$$

Although the values for M and s_M are available from the sample data, we cannot use the equation to calculate t because the value for μ is unknown. Instead of calculating the t value, for a confidence interval we *estimate* the t value. For example, if the sample has $n = 9$ scores, then the t statistic has $df = 8$, and the distribution of all possible t values can be pictured as in Figure 9.7. Notice that the t values pile up around $t = 0$, so we can estimate that the t value for our sample should have a value around 0. Furthermore, the t distribution table lists a variety of different t values that correspond to specific proportions of the t distribution. With $df = 8$, for example, 80% of the t values are located between $t = +1.397$ and $t = -1.397$. To obtain these values, simply look up a two-tailed proportion of 0.20 (20%) for $df = 8$. Because 80% of all of the possible t values are located between ± 1.397, we can be 80% confident that our sample mean corresponds to a t value in this interval. Similarly, we can be 95% confident that the mean for a sample of $n = 9$ scores corresponds to a t value between $+2.306$ and -2.306. Notice that we are able to estimate the value of t with a specific level of confidence. To construct a confidence interval for μ, we plug the estimated t value into the t equation, and then we can calculate the value of μ.

Before we demonstrate the process of constructing a confidence interval for an unknown population mean, we simplify the calculations by regrouping the terms in the t equation. Because the goal is to compute the value of μ, we use simple algebra to solve the equation for μ. The result is

$$\mu = M \pm t s_M \tag{9.5}$$

The process of using this equation to construct a confidence interval is demonstrated in the following example.

EXAMPLE 9.3

Example 9.1 describes a study in which infants displayed a preference for the more attractive face by looking at it, instead of the less attractive face, for the majority of a 20-second viewing period. Specifically, a sample of $n = 9$ infants spent an average

FIGURE 9.7

The distribution of *t* statistics with $df = 8$. The *t* values pile up around $t = 0$ and 80% of all of the possible values are located between $t = -1.397$ and $t = +1.397$.

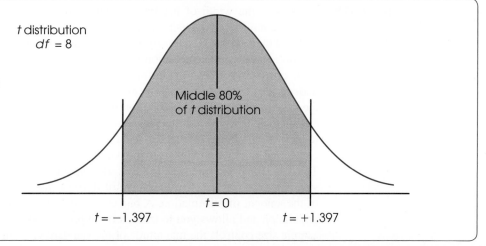

t distribution
df = 8

Middle 80%
of *t* distribution

$t = 0$

$t = -1.397$ $t = +1.397$

of $M = 13$ seconds out of a 20-second period looking at the more attractive face. The data produced an estimated standard error of $s_M = 1$. We use this sample to construct a confidence interval to estimate the mean amount of time that the population of infants spends looking at the more attractive face. That is, we construct an interval of values that is likely to contain the unknown population mean.

Again, the estimation formula is

$$\mu = M \pm t(s_M)$$

To have 80% in the middle, there must be 20% (or .20) in the tails. To find the *t* values, look under two tails, .20 in the *t* table.

In the equation, the value of $M = 13$ and $s_M = 1$ are obtained from the sample data. The next step is to select a level of confidence that determines the value of *t* in the equation. The most commonly used confidence level is probably 95%, but values of 80%, 90%, and 99% are also common. For this example, we use a confidence level of 80%, which means that we construct the confidence interval so that we are 80% confident that the population mean is actually contained in the interval. Because we are using a confidence level of 80%, the resulting interval is called the *80% confidence interval for* μ.

To obtain the value for *t* in the equation, we simply estimate that the *t* statistic for our sample is located somewhere in the middle 80% of the *t* distribution. With *df* $= n - 1 = 8$, the middle 80% of the distribution is bounded by *t* values of $+1.397$ and -1.397 (see Figure 9.7). Using the sample data and the estimated range of *t* values, we obtain

$$\mu = M \pm t(s_M) = 13 \pm 1.397(1.00) = 13 \pm 1.397$$

At one end of the interval, we obtain $\mu = 13 + 1.397 = 14.397$, and at the other end we obtain $\mu = 13 - 1.397 = 11.603$. Our conclusion is that the average time looking at the more attractive face for the population of infants is between $\mu = 11.603$ seconds and $\mu = 14.397$ seconds, and we are 80% confident that the true population mean is located within this interval. The confidence comes from the fact that the calculation was based on only one assumption. Specifically, we assumed that the *t* statistic was located between $+1.397$ and -1.397, and we are 80% confident that this assumption is correct because 80% of all of the possible *t* values are located in this interval. Finally, note that the confidence interval is constructed around the sample mean. As a result, the sample mean, $M = 13$, is located exactly in the center of the interval.

FACTORS AFFECTING THE WIDTH OF A CONFIDENCE INTERVAL

Two characteristics of the confidence interval should be mentioned. First, notice what happens to the width of the interval when you change the level of confidence (the percent confidence). To gain more confidence in your estimate, you must increase the width of the interval. Conversely, to have a smaller, more precise interval, you must give up confidence. In the estimation formula, the percentage of confidence influences the value of *t*. A larger level of confidence (the percentage) produces a larger *t* value and a wider interval. This relationship can be seen in Figure 9.7. In the figure, we identified the middle 80% of the *t* distribution to find an 80% confidence interval. It should be obvious that if we were to increase the confidence level to 95%, it would be necessary to increase the range of *t* values, and thereby increase the width of the interval.

Second, note what happens to the width of the interval if you change the sample size. This time the basic rule is as follows: The bigger the sample (n), the smaller the interval. This relationship is straightforward if you consider the sample size as a measure of the amount of information. A bigger sample gives you more information about the population and allows you to make a more precise estimate (a narrower interval). The sample size controls the magnitude of the standard error in the estimation formula. As the sample size increases, the standard error decreases, and the interval gets smaller. Finally, we should also note that the width of the confidence interval is also related to the sample variance. The variance contributes directly to the magnitude of the standard error so that an increase in variance produces an increase in the standard error and, thereby, increases the width of the confidence interval.

Because confidence intervals are influenced by sample size, they do not provide an unqualified measure of absolute effect size and are not an adequate substitute for Cohen's *d* or r^2. Nonetheless, they can be used in a research report to provide a description of the size of the treatment effect.

LEARNING CHECK

1. If all other factors are held constant, an 80% confidence interval is wider than a 90% confidence interval. (True or false?)

2. If all other factors are held constant, a confidence interval computed from a sample of $n = 25$ is wider than a confidence interval computed from a sample of n = 100. (True or false?)

ANSWERS

1. False. Greater confidence requires a wider interval.

2. True. The smaller sample produces a wider interval.

IN THE LITERATURE
REPORTING THE RESULTS OF A *t* TEST

In Chapter 8, we noted the conventional style for reporting the results of a hypothesis test, according to APA format. First, recall that a scientific report typically uses the term *significant* to indicate that the null hypothesis has been rejected and the term *not significant* to indicate failure to reject H_0. Additionally, there is a prescribed format for reporting the calculated value of the test statistic, degrees of freedom, and alpha level for a *t* test. This format parallels the style introduced in Chapter 8 (p. 218).

In Example 9.1 we calculated a *t* statistic of 3.00 with $df = 8$, and we decided to reject H_0 with alpha set at .05. Using the same data, we obtained $r^2 = 0.5294$ (52.94%) for the percentage of variance explained by the treatment effect. In a scientific report, this information is conveyed in a concise statement, as follows:

> The infants spent an average of $M = 13$ out of 20 seconds looking at the attractive face, with $SD = 3.00$. Statistical analysis indicates that the time spent looking at the attractive face was significantly greater than would be expected if there were no preference, $t(8) = 3.00, p < .05, r^2 = 0.5294$.

The first statement reports the descriptive statistics, the mean ($M = 13$) and the standard deviation ($SD = 3$), as previously described (Chapter 4, p. 109). The next statement provides the results of the inferential statistical analysis. Note that the degrees of freedom are reported in parentheses immediately after the symbol *t*. The value for the obtained *t* statistic follows (3.00), and next is the probability of committing a Type I error (less than 5%). Finally, the effect size is reported, $r^2 = 52.94\%$. If the 80% confidence interval from Example 9.3 were included in the report as a description of effect size, it would be added after the results of the hypothesis test as follows:

$$t(8) = 3.00, p < .05, 80\% \text{ CI } [11.603, 14.397].$$

The statement $p < .05$ was explained in Chapter 8, page 218.

Often, researchers use a computer to perform a hypothesis test like the one in Example 9.1. In addition to calculating the mean, standard deviation, and the *t* statistic for the data, the computer usually calculates and reports the *exact probability* (or a level) associated with the *t* value. In Example 9.1, we determined that any *t* value beyond ± 2.306 has a probability of less than .05 (see Figure 9.4). Thus, the obtained *t* value, $t = 3.00$, is reported as being very unlikely, $p < .05$. A computer printout, however, would have included an exact probability for our specific *t* value.

Whenever a specific probability value is available, you are encouraged to use it in a research report. For example, the computer analysis of these data reports an exact *p* value of $p = .017$, and the research report would state "$t(8) = 3.00$, $p = .017$" instead of using the less specific "$p < .05$." As one final caution, we note that occasionally a *t* value is so extreme that the computer reports $p = 0.000$. The zero value does not mean that the probability is literally zero; instead, it means that the computer has rounded off the probability value to three decimal places and obtained a result of 0.000. In this situation, you do not know the exact probability value, but you can report $p < .001$.

LEARNING CHECK

1. A sample of $n = 16$ individuals is selected from a population with a mean of $\mu = 80$. A treatment is administered to the sample and, after treatment, the sample mean is found to be $M = 86$ with a standard deviation of $s = 8$.

   a. Does the sample provide sufficient evidence to conclude that the treatment has a significant effect? Test with $\alpha = .05$.

   b. Compute Cohen's *d* and r^2 to measure the effect size.

   c. Find the 95% confidence interval for the population mean after treatment.

2. How does sample size influence the outcome of a hypothesis test and measures of effect size? How does the standard deviation influence the outcome of a hypothesis test and measures of effect size?

ANSWERS

1. **a.** The estimated standard error is 2 points and the data produce $t = \frac{6}{2} = 3.00$. With $df = 15$, the critical values are $t = \pm 2.131$, so the decision is to reject H_0 and conclude that there is a significant treatment effect.

   b. For these data, $d = \frac{6}{8} = 0.75$ and $r^2 = \frac{9}{24} = 0.375$ or 37.5%.

   c. For 95% confidence and $df = 15$, use $t = \pm 2.131$. The confidence interval is $\mu = 86 \pm 2.131(2)$ and extends from 81.738 to 90.262.

2. Increasing sample size increases the likelihood of rejecting the null hypothesis but has little or no effect on measures of effect size. Increasing the sample variance reduces the likelihood of rejecting the null hypothesis and reduces measures of effect size.

9.4 DIRECTIONAL HYPOTHESES AND ONE-TAILED TESTS

As noted in Chapter 8, the nondirectional (two-tailed) test is more commonly used than the directional (one-tailed) alternative. On the other hand, a directional test may be used in some research situations, such as exploratory investigations or pilot studies or when there is *a priori* justification (for example, a theory or previous findings). The following example demonstrates a directional hypothesis test with a *t* statistic, using the same experimental situation presented in Example 9.1.

EXAMPLE 9.4   The research question is whether attractiveness affects the behavior of infants looking at photographs of women's faces. The researcher is expecting the infants to prefer the more attractive face. Therefore, the researcher predicts that the infants will spend more than half of the 20-second period looking at the attractive face. For this example, we use the same sample data that were used in the original hypothesis test in Example 9.1. Specifically, the researcher tested a sample of $n = 9$ infants and obtained a mean of $M = 13$ seconds looking at the attractive face with $SS = 72$.

Step 1   State the hypotheses, and select an alpha level. With most directional tests, it is usually easier to state the hypothesis in words, including the directional prediction, and then convert the words into symbols. For this example, the researcher is predicting that attractiveness will cause the infants to increase the amount of time they spend looking at the attractive face; that is, more than half of the 20 seconds should be spent looking at the attractive face. In general, the null hypothesis states that the predicted effect will not happen. For this study, the null hypothesis states that the infants will not spend more than half of the 20 seconds looking at the attractive face. In symbols,

$$H_0: \mu_{attractive} \leq 10 \text{ seconds} \qquad \text{(Not more than half of the 20 seconds looking at the attractive face)}$$

Similarly, the alternative states that the treatment will work. In this case, H_1 states that the infants will spend more than half of the time looking at the attractive face. In symbols,

$$H_1: \mu_{attractive} > 10 \text{ seconds} \qquad \text{(More than half of the 20 seconds looking at the attractive face)}$$

This time, we set the level of significance at $\alpha = .01$.

Step 2   Locate the critical region. In this example, the researcher is predicting that the sample mean (M) will be greater than 10 seconds. Thus, if the infants average more than 10 seconds looking at the attractive face, the data will provide support for the researcher's prediction and will tend to refute the null hypothesis. Also note that a sample mean greater than 10 will produce a positive value for the t statistic. Thus, the critical region for the one-tailed test will consist of positive t values located in the right-hand tail of the distribution. To find the critical value, you must look in the t distribution table using the one-tail proportions. With a sample of $n = 9$, the t statistic has $df = 8$; using $\alpha = .01$, you should find a critical value of $t = 2.896$. Therefore, if we obtain a t statistic greater than 2.896, we will reject the null hypothesis and conclude that the infants show a significant preference for the attractive face. Figure 9.8 shows the one-tailed critical region for this test.

Step 3   Calculate the test statistic. The computation of the t statistic is the same for either a one-tailed or a two-tailed test. Earlier (in Example 9.1), we found that the data for this experiment produce a test statistic of $t = 3.00$.

Step 4   Make a decision. The test statistic is in the critical region, so we reject H_0. In terms of the experimental variables, we have decided that the infants show a preference and spend significantly more time looking at the attractive face than they do looking at the unattractive face. In a research report, the results would be presented as follows:

> The time spent looking at the attractive face was significantly greater than would be expected if there were no preference, $t(8) = 3.00$, $p < .01$, one tailed.

Note that the report clearly acknowledges that a one-tailed test was used.

FIGURE 9.8

The one-tailed critical region for the hypothesis test in Example 9.4 with $df = 8$ and $\alpha = .01$.

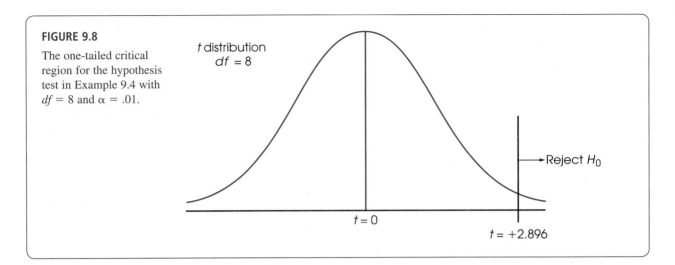

THE CRITICAL REGION
FOR A ONE-TAILED TEST

In step 2 of Example 9.4, we determined that the critical region is in the right-hand tail of the distribution. However, it is possible to divide this step into two stages that eliminate the need to determine which tail (right or left) should contain the critical region. The first stage in this process is simply to determine whether the sample mean is in the direction predicted by the original research question. For this example, the researcher predicted that the infants would prefer the attractive face and spend more time looking at it. Specifically, the researcher expects the infants to spend more than 10 out of 20 seconds focused on the attractive face. The obtained sample mean, $M = 13$ seconds, is in the correct direction. This first stage eliminates the need to determine whether the critical region is in the left- or right-hand tail. Because we already have determined that the effect is in the correct direction, the sign of the t statistic ($+$ or $-$) no longer matters. The second stage of the process is to determine whether the effect is large enough to be significant. For this example, the requirement is that the sample produces a t statistic greater than 2.896. If the magnitude of the t statistic, independent of its sign, is greater than 2.896, then the result is significant and H_0 is rejected.

LEARNING CHECK

1. A new over-the-counter cold medication includes a warning label stating that it "may cause drowsiness." A researcher would like to evaluate this effect. It is known that under regular circumstances the distribution of reaction times is normal with $\mu = 200$. A sample of $n = 9$ participants is obtained. Each person is given the new cold medication, and, 1 hour later, reaction time is measured for each individual. The average reaction time for this sample is $M = 206$ with $SS = 648$. The researcher would like to use a hypothesis test with $\alpha = .05$ to evaluate the effect of the medication.

   a. Use a two-tailed test with $\alpha = .05$ to determine whether the medication has a significant effect on reaction time.

   b. Write a sentence that demonstrates how the outcome of the hypothesis test would appear in a research report.

   c. Use a one-tailed test with $\alpha = .05$ to determine whether the medication produces a significant increase in reaction time.

   d. Write a sentence that demonstrates how the outcome of the one-tailed hypothesis test would appear in a research report.

SUMMARY

1. The t statistic is used instead of a z-score for hypothesis testing when the population standard deviation (or variance) is unknown.

2. To compute the t statistic, you must first calculate the sample variance (or standard deviation) as a substitute for the unknown population value.

$$\text{sample variance} = s^2 = \frac{SS}{df}$$

Next, the standard error is *estimated* by using s^2, instead of σ^2, in the formula for standard error. The estimated standard error is calculated in the following manner:

$$\text{estimated standard error} = s_M = \sqrt{\frac{s^2}{n}}$$

Finally, a t statistic is computed using the estimated standard error. The t statistic is used as a substitute for a z-score, which cannot be computed when the population variance or standard deviation is unknown.

$$t = \frac{M - \mu}{s_M}$$

3. The structure of the t formula is similar to that of the z-score in that

$$z \text{ or } t = \frac{\text{sample mean} - \text{population mean}}{\text{(estimated) standard error}}$$

For a hypothesis test, you hypothesize a value for the unknown population mean and plug the hypothesized value into the equation along with the sample mean and the estimated standard error, which are computed from the sample data. If the hypothesized mean produces an extreme value for t, then you conclude that the hypothesis was wrong.

4. There is a family of t distributions, with the exact shape of a particular distribution of t values depending on degrees of freedom $(n - 1)$. Therefore, the critical t values depend on the value for df associated with the t test. As df increases, the shape of the t distribution approaches a normal distribution.

5. When a t statistic is used for a hypothesis test, Cohen's d can be computed to measure effect size. In this situation, the sample standard deviation is used in the formula to obtain an estimated value for d:

$$\text{estimated } d = \frac{\text{mean difference}}{\text{standard deviation}} = \frac{M - \mu}{s}$$

6. A second measure of effect size is r^2, which measures the percentage of the variability that is accounted for by the treatment effect. This value is computed as follows:

$$r^2 = \frac{t^2}{t^2 + df}$$

7. An alternative method for describing the size of a treatment effect is to use a confidence interval for μ. A confidence interval is a range of values that estimates the unknown population mean. The confidence interval uses the t equation, solved for the unknown mean:

$$\mu = M \pm t(s_M)$$

First, select a level of confidence and then look up the corresponding t values to use in the equation. For example, for 95% confidence, use the range of t values that determine the middle 95% of the distribution.

KEY TERMS

estimated standard error (251)

t statistic (252)

degrees of freedom (252)

t distribution (252)

estimated *d* (260)

percentage of variance accounted for by the treatment (r^2) (263)

confidence interval (264)

RESOURCES

 Go to CengageBrain.com to access Psychology CourseMate, where you will find an interactive eBook, glossaries, flashcards, quizzes, statistics workshops, and more.

aplia

If your professor has assigned Aplia:

1. Sign in to your account.
2. Complete the corresponding exercises as required by your professor.
3. When finished, click "Grade It Now" to see which areas you have mastered, which areas need more work, and detailed explanations of every answer.

SPSS

General instructions for using SPSS are presented in Appendix D. Following are detailed instructions for using SPSS to perform the *t* **Test** presented in this chapter.

Data Entry

Enter all of the scores from the sample in one column of the data editor, probably VAR00001.

Data Analysis

1. Click Analyze on the tool bar, select **Compare Means,** and click on **One-Sample t Test.**

2. Highlight the column label for the set of scores (VAR0001) in the left box and click the arrow to move it into the **Test Variable(s)** box.

3. In the **Test Value** box at the bottom of the One-Sample *t* Test window, enter the hypothesized value for the population mean from the null hypothesis. *Note:* The value is automatically set at zero until you type in a new value.

4. In addition to performing the hypothesis test, the program computes a confidence interval for the population mean difference. The confidence level is automatically set at 95%, but you can select **Options** and change the percentage.

5. Click **OK.**

SPSS Output

We used the SPSS program to analyze the data from the infants-and-attractive-faces study in Example 9.1, and the program output is shown in Figure 9.9. The output includes a table of sample statistics with the mean, standard deviation, and standard error for the sample mean. A second table shows the results of the hypothesis test, including the values for t, df, and the level of significance (the p value for the test), as well as the mean difference from the hypothesized value of $\mu = 10$ and a 95% confidence interval for the mean difference. To obtain a 95% confidence interval for the mean, simply add $\mu = 10$ points to the values in the table.

FOCUS ON PROBLEM SOLVING

1. The first problem we confront in analyzing data is determining the appropriate statistical test. Remember that you can use a z-score for the test statistic only when the value for σ is known. If the value for σ is not provided, then you must use the t statistic.

2. For the t test, the sample variance is used to find the value for the estimated standard error. Remember to use $n - 1$ in the denominator when computing the sample variance (see Chapter 4). When computing estimated standard error, use n in the denominator.

DEMONSTRATION 9.1

A HYPOTHESIS TEST WITH THE t STATISTIC

A psychologist has prepared an "Optimism Test" that is administered yearly to graduating college seniors. The test measures how each graduating class feels about

One-Sample Statistics

	N	Mean	Std. Deviation	Std. Error Mean
VAR00001	9	13.0000	3.00000	1.00000

One-Sample Test

	Test Value = 10					
					95% Confidence Interval of the Difference	
	t	df	Sig. (2-tailed)	Mean Difference	Lower	Upper
VAR00001	3.000	8	.017	3.00000	.6940	5.3060

FIGURE 9.9

The SPSS output for the hypothesis test presented in Example 9.1.

its future—the higher the score, the more optimistic the class. Last year's class had a mean score of $\mu = 15$. A sample of $n = 9$ seniors from this year's class was selected and tested. The scores for these seniors are 7, 12, 11, 15, 7, 8, 15, 9, and 6, which produce a sample mean of $M = 10$ with $SS = 94$.

On the basis of this sample, can the psychologist conclude that this year's class has a different level of optimism than last year's class?

Note that this hypothesis test uses a t statistic because the population variance (σ^2) is not known.

STEP 1   State the hypotheses, and select an alpha level.   The null hypothesis states that the mean optimism score for this year's class is the same as the mean for last year's class.

$H_0: \mu = 15$ (There is no change.)

$H_1: \mu \neq 15$ (This year's mean is different.)

For this demonstration, we use $\alpha = .05$, two tails.

STEP 2   Locate the critical region.   With a sample of $n = 9$ students, the t statistic has $df = n - 1 = 8$. For a two-tailed test with $\alpha = .05$ and $df = 8$, the critical t values are $t = \pm 2.306$. These critical t values define the boundaries of the critical region.

STEP 3   Compute the test statistic.   As we have noted, it is easier to separate the calculation of the t statistic into three stages.

Sample variance.

$$s^2 = \frac{SS}{n-1} = \frac{94}{8} = 11.75$$

Estimated standard error. The estimated standard error for these data is

$$s_M = \sqrt{\frac{s^2}{n}} = \sqrt{\frac{11.75}{9}} = 1.14$$

The t statistic. Now that we have the estimated standard error and the sample mean, we can compute the t statistic. For this demonstration,

$$t = \frac{M - \mu}{s_M} = \frac{10 - 15}{1.14} = \frac{-5}{1.14} = -4.39$$

STEP 4   Make a decision about H_0, and state a conclusion.   The t statistic we obtained ($t = -4.39$) is in the critical region. Thus, our sample data are unusual enough to reject the null hypothesis at the .05 level of significance. We can conclude that there is a significant difference in level of optimism between this year's and last year's graduating classes, $t(8) = -4.39$, $p < .05$, two-tailed.

DEMONSTRATION 9.2

EFFECT SIZE: ESTIMATING COHEN'S *d* AND COMPUTING r^2

We estimate Cohen's d for the same data used for the hypothesis test in Demonstration 9.1. The mean optimism score for the sample from this year's class was 5 points lower than the mean from last year ($M = 10$ versus $\mu = 15$).

In Demonstration 9.1, we computed a sample variance of $s^2 = 11.75$, so the standard deviation is $\sqrt{11.75} = 3.43$. With these values,

$$\text{estimated } d = \frac{\text{mean difference}}{\text{standard deviation}} = \frac{5}{3.43} = 1.46$$

To calculate the percentage of variance explained by the treatment effect, r^2, we need the value of t and the df value from the hypothesis test. In Demonstration 9.1, we obtained $t = -4.39$ with $df = 8$. Using these values in Equation 9.5, we obtain

$$r^2 = \frac{t^2}{t^2 + df} = \frac{(-4.39)^2}{(-4.39)^2 + 8} = \frac{19.27}{27.27} = 0.71$$

PROBLEMS

1. Under what circumstances is a t statistic used instead of a z-score for a hypothesis test?

2. A sample of $n = 25$ scores has a mean of $M = 83$ and a standard deviation of $s = 15$.
   a. Explain what is measured by the sample standard deviation.
   b. Compute the estimated standard error for the sample mean and explain what is measured by the standard error.

3. Find the estimated standard error for the sample mean for each of the following samples.
   a. $n = 4$ with $SS = 48$
   b. $n = 6$ with $SS = 270$
   c. $n = 12$ with $SS = 132$

4. Explain why t distributions tend to be flatter and more spread out than the normal distribution.

5. Find the t values that form the boundaries of the critical region for a two-tailed test with $\alpha = .05$ for each of the following sample sizes:
   a. $n = 6$
   b. $n = 12$
   c. $n = 24$

6. The following sample of $n = 6$ scores was obtained from a population with unknown parameters.

   Scores: 7, 1, 6, 3, 6, 7

   a. Compute the sample mean and standard deviation. (Note that these are descriptive values that summarize the sample data.)
   b. Compute the estimated standard error for M. (Note that this is an inferential value that describes how accurately the sample mean represents the unknown population mean.)

7. The following sample was obtained from a population with unknown parameters.

   Scores: 6, 12, 0, 13, 4, 7

   a. Compute the sample mean and standard deviation. (Note that these are descriptive values that summarize the sample data.)
   b. Compute the estimated standard error for M. (Note that this is an inferential value that describes how accurately the sample mean represents the unknown population mean.)

8. A random sample of $n = 25$ individuals is selected from a population with $\mu = 20$, and a treatment is administered to each individual in the sample. After treatment, the sample mean is found to be $M = 22.2$ with $SS = 384$.
   a. How much difference is there between the mean for the treated sample and the mean for the original population? (Note: In a hypothesis test, this value forms the numerator of the t statistic.)
   b. If there is no treatment effect, how much difference is expected between the sample mean and its population mean? That is, find the standard error for M. (Note: In a hypothesis test, this value is the denominator of the t statistic.)
   c. Based on the sample data, does the treatment have a significant effect? Use a two-tailed test with $\alpha = .05$.

9. To evaluate the effect of a treatment, a sample is obtained from a population with a mean of $\mu = 30$, and the treatment is administered to the individuals in the sample. After treatment, the sample mean is found to be $M = 31.3$ with a standard deviation of $s = 3$.
   a. If the sample consists of $n = 16$ individuals, are the data sufficient to conclude that the treatment has a significant effect using a two-tailed test with $\alpha = .05$?
   b. If the sample consists of $n = 36$ individuals, are the data sufficient to conclude that the treatment has a significant effect using a two-tailed test with $\alpha = .05$?
   c. Comparing your answer for parts a and b, how does the size of the sample influence the outcome of a hypothesis test?

10. To evaluate the effect of a treatment, a sample of $n = 8$ is obtained from a population with a mean of $\mu = 40$, and the treatment is administered to the individuals in the sample. After treatment, the sample mean is found to be $M = 35$.
    a. If the sample variance is $s^2 = 32$, are the data sufficient to conclude that the treatment has a significant effect using a two-tailed test with $\alpha = .05$?
    b. If the sample variance is $s^2 = 72$, are the data sufficient to conclude that the treatment has a significant effect using a two-tailed test with $\alpha = .05$?
    c. Comparing your answer for parts a and b, how does the variability of the scores in the sample influence the outcome of a hypothesis test?

11. The spotlight effect refers to overestimating the extent to which others notice your appearance or behavior, especially when you commit a social faux pas. Effectively, you feel as if you are suddenly standing in a spotlight with everyone looking. In one demonstration of this phenomenon, Gilovich, Medvec, and Savitsky (2000) asked college students to put on a Barry Manilow T-shirt that fellow students had previously judged to be embarrassing. The participants were then led into a room in which other students were already participating in an experiment. After a few minutes, the participant was led back out of the room and was allowed to remove the shirt. Later, each participant was asked to estimate how many people in the room had noticed the shirt. The individuals who were in the room were also asked whether they noticed the shirt. In the study, the participants significantly overestimated the actual number of people who had noticed.
    a. In a similar study using a sample of $n = 9$ participants, the individuals who wore the shirt produced an average estimate of $M = 6.4$ with $SS = 162$. The average number who said they noticed was 3.1. Is the estimate from the participants significantly different from the actual number? Test the null hypothesis that the true mean is $\mu = 3.1$ using a two-tailed test with $\alpha = .05$.
    b. Is the estimate from the participants significantly higher than the actual number ($\mu = 3.1$)? Use a one-tailed test with $\alpha = .05$.

12. Many animals, including humans, tend to avoid direct eye contact and even patterns that look like eyes. Some insects, including moths, have evolved eye-spot patterns on their wings to help ward off predators. Scaife (1976) reports a study examining how eye-spot patterns affect the behavior of birds. In the study, the birds were tested in a box with two chambers and were free to move from one chamber to another. In one chamber, two large eye-spots were painted on one wall. The other chamber had plain walls. The researcher recorded the amount of time each bird spent in the plain chamber during a 60-minute session. Suppose the study produced a mean of $M = 37$ minutes in the plain chamber with $SS = 288$ for a sample of $n = 9$ birds. (*Note:* If the eye spots have no effect, then the birds should spend an average of $\mu = 30$ minutes in each chamber.)
    a. Is this sample sufficient to conclude that the eye-spots have a significant influence on the birds' behavior? Use a two-tailed test with $\alpha = .05$.
    b. Compute the estimated Cohen's *d* to measure the size of the treatment effect.
    c. Construct the 95% confidence interval to estimate the mean amount of time spent on the plain side for the population of birds.

13. Standardized measures seem to indicate that the average level of anxiety has increased gradually over the past 50 years (Twenge, 2000). In the 1950s, the average score on the Child Manifest Anxiety Scale was $\mu = 15.1$. A sample of $n = 16$ of today's children produces a mean score of $M = 23.3$ with $SS = 240$.
    a. Based on the sample, has there been a significant change in the average level of anxiety since the 1950s? Use a two-tailed test with $\alpha = .01$.
    b. Make a 90% confidence interval estimate of today's population mean level of anxiety.
    c. Write a sentence that demonstrates how the outcome of the hypothesis test and the confidence interval would appear in a research report.

14. The librarian at the local elementary school claims that, on average, the books in the library are more than 20 years old. To test this claim, a student takes a sample of $n = 30$ books and records the publication date for each. The sample produces an average age of $M = 23.8$ years with a variance of $s^2 = 67.5$. Use this sample to conduct a one-tailed test with $\alpha = .01$ to determine whether the average age of the library books is significantly greater than 20 years ($\mu > 20$).

15. For several years researchers have noticed that there appears to be a regular, year-by-year increase in the average IQ for the general population. This phenomenon is called the Flynn effect after the researcher who first reported it (Flynn, 1984, 1999), and it means that psychologists must continuously update IQ tests to keep the population mean at $\mu = 100$. To evaluate the size of the effect, a researcher obtained a 10-year-old IQ test that was standardized to produce a mean IQ of $\mu = 100$ for the population 10 years ago. The test was then given to a sample of $n = 64$ of today's 20-year-old adults. The average score for the sample was $M = 107$ with a standard deviation of $s = 12$.
    a. Based on the sample, is the average IQ for today's population significantly different from the average 10 years ago, when the test would have produced

a mean of $\mu = 100$? Use a two-tailed test with $\alpha = .01$.

b. Make an 80% confidence interval estimate of to-day's population mean IQ for the 10-year-old test.

16. Weinstein, McDermott, and Roediger (2010) report that students who were given questions to be answered while studying new material had better scores when tested on the material compared to students who were simply given an opportunity to reread the material. In a similar study, an instructor in a large psychology class gave one group of students questions to be answered while studying for the final exam. The overall average for the exam was $\mu = 73.4$, but the $n = 16$ students who answered questions had a mean of $M = 78.3$ with a standard deviation of $s = 8.4$. For this study, did answering questions while studying produce significantly higher exam scores? Use a one-tailed test with $\alpha = .01$.

17. Ackerman and Goldsmith (2011) found that students who studied text from printed hardcopy had better test scores than students who studied from text presented on a screen. In a related study, a professor noticed that several students in a large class had purchased the e-book version of the course textbook. For the final exam, the overall average for the entire class was $\mu = 81.7$, but the $n = 9$ students who used e-books had a mean of $M = 77.2$ with a standard deviation of $s = 5.7$.

a. Is the sample sufficient to conclude that scores for students using e-books were significantly different from scores for the regular class? Use a two-tailed test with $\alpha = .05$.

b. Construct the 90% confidence interval to estimate the mean exam score if the entire population used e-books.

c. Write a sentence demonstrating how the results from the hypothesis test and the confidence interval would appear in a research report.

18. A random sample of $n = 16$ scores is obtained from a population with a mean of $\mu = 45$. After a treatment is administered to the individuals in the sample, the sample mean is found to be $M = 49.2$.

a. Assuming that the sample standard deviation is $s = 8$, compute r^2 and the estimated Cohen's d to measure the size of the treatment effect.

b. Assuming that the sample standard deviation is $s = 20$, compute r^2 and the estimated Cohen's d to measure the size of the treatment effect.

c. Comparing your answers from parts a and b, how does the variability of the scores in the sample influence the measures of effect size?

19. A random sample is obtained from a population with a mean of $\mu = 45$. After a treatment is administered

to the individuals in the sample, the sample mean is $M = 49$ with a standard deviation of $s = 12$.

a. Assuming that the sample consists of $n = 9$ scores, compute r^2 and the estimated Cohen's d to measure the size of treatment effect.

b. Assuming that the sample consists of $n = 16$ scores, compute r^2 and the estimated Cohen's d to measure the size of treatment effect.

c. Comparing your answers from parts a and b, how does the number of scores in the sample influence the measures of effect size?

20. An example of the vertical-horizontal illusion is shown in the figure. Although the two lines are exactly the same length, the vertical line appears to be much longer. To examine the strength of this illusion, a researcher prepared an example in which both lines were exactly 10 inches long. The example was shown to individual participants who were told that the horizontal line was 10 inches long and then were asked to estimate the length of the vertical line. For a sample of $n = 25$ participants, the average estimate was $M = 12.2$ inches with a standard deviation of $s = 1.00$.

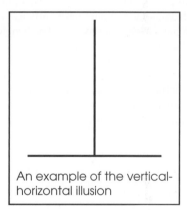

An example of the vertical-horizontal illusion

a. Use a one-tailed hypothesis test with $\alpha = .01$ to demonstrate that the individuals in the sample significantly overestimate the true length of the line. (*Note:* Accurate estimation would produce a mean of $\mu = 10$ inches.)

b. Calculate the estimated d and r^2, the percentage of variance accounted for, to measure the size of this effect.

c. Construct a 95% confidence interval for the population mean estimated length of the vertical line.

21. In studies examining the effect of humor on interpersonal attractions, McGee and Shevlin (2009) found that an individual's sense of humor had a significant effect on how the individual was perceived by others. In one part of the study, female college students were given brief descriptions of a potential romantic

partner. The fictitious male was described positively as being single, ambitious, and having good job prospects. For one group of participants, the description also said that he had a great sense of humor. For another group, it said that he had no sense of humor. After reading the description, each participant was asked to rate the attractiveness of the man on a seven-point scale from 1 (very attractive) to 7 (very unattractive). A score of 4 indicates a neutral rating.

   a. The females who read the "great sense of humor" description gave the potential partner an average attractiveness score of $M = 4.53$ with a standard deviation of $s = 1.04$. If the sample consisted of $n = 16$ participants, is the average rating significantly higher than neutral ($\mu = 4$)? Use a one-tailed test with $\alpha = .05$.

   b. The females who read the description saying "no sense of humor" gave the potential partner an average attractiveness score of $M = 3.30$ with a standard deviation of $s = 1.18$. If the sample consisted of $n = 16$ participants, is the average rating significantly lower than neutral ($\mu = 4$)? Use a one-tailed test with $\alpha = .05$.

22. Oishi and Shigehiro (2010) report that people who move from home to home frequently as children tend to have lower than average levels of well-being as adults. To further examine this relationship, a psychologist obtains a sample of $n = 12$ young adults who each experienced 5 or more different homes before they were 16 years old. These participants were given a standardized well-being questionnaire for which the general population has an average score of $\mu = 40$. The well-being scores for this sample are as follows: 38, 37, 41, 35, 42, 40, 33, 33, 36, 38, 32, 39.

   a. On the basis of this sample, is well-being for frequent movers significantly different from well-being in the general population? Use a two-tailed test with $\alpha = .05$.

   b. Compute the estimated Cohen's *d* to measure the size of the difference.

   c. Write a sentence showing how the outcome of the hypothesis test and the measure of effect size would appear in a research report.

23. Research examining the effects of preschool child-care has found that children who spent time in day care, especially high-quality day care, perform better on math and language tests than children who stay home with their mothers (Broberg, Wessels, Lamb, & Hwang, 1997). In a typical study, a researcher obtains a sample of $n = 10$ children who attended day care before starting school. The children are given a standardized math test for which the population mean is $\mu = 50$. The scores for the sample are as follows: 53, 57, 61, 49, 52, 56, 58, 62, 51, 56.

   a. Is this sample sufficient to conclude that the children with a history of preschool day care are significantly different from the general population? Use a two-tailed test with $\alpha = .01$.

   b. Compute Cohen's *d* to measure the size of the preschool effect.

   c. Write a sentence showing how the outcome of the hypothesis test and the measure of effect size would appear in a research report.

C H A P T E R

10

Tools You Will Need

The following items are considered essential background material for this chapter. If you doubt your knowledge of any of these items, you should review the appropriate chapter or section before proceeding.

- Sample variance (Chapter 4)
- Standard error formulas (Chapter 7)
- The *t* statistic (Chapter 9)
  - Distribution of *t* values
  - *df* for the *t* statistic
  - Estimated standard error

The *t* Test for Two Independent Samples

aplia

Aplia for *Essentials of Statistics for the Behavioral Sciences*
After reading, go to "Resources" at the end of this chapter for an introduction on how to use Aplia's homework and learning resources.

10.1 INTRODUCTION TO THE INDEPENDENT-MEASURES DESIGN

Until this point, all of the inferential statistics we have considered involve using one sample as the basis for drawing conclusions about one population. Although these *single-sample* techniques are used occasionally in real research, most research studies require the comparison of two (or more) sets of data. For example, a social psychologist may want to compare men and women in terms of their political attitudes, an educational psychologist may want to compare two methods for teaching mathematics, or a clinical psychologist may want to evaluate a therapy technique by comparing depression scores for patients before therapy with their scores after therapy. In each case, the research question concerns a mean difference between two sets of data.

There are two general research designs that can be used to obtain the two sets of data to be compared:

1. The two sets of data could come from two completely separate groups of participants. For example, the study could involve a sample of men compared with a sample of women. Or the study could compare grades for one group of freshmen who are given laptop computers with grades for a second group who are not given computers.

2. The two sets of data could come from the same group of participants. For example, the researcher could obtain one set of scores by measuring depression for a sample of patients before they begin therapy and then obtain a second set of data by measuring the same individuals after 6 weeks of therapy.

The first research strategy, using completely separate groups, is called an *independent-measures* research design or a *between-subjects* design. These terms emphasize the fact that the design involves separate and independent samples and makes a comparison between two groups of individuals. The structure of an independent-measures research design is shown in Figure 10.1. Notice that the research study uses two separate samples to represent the two different populations (or two different treatments) being compared.

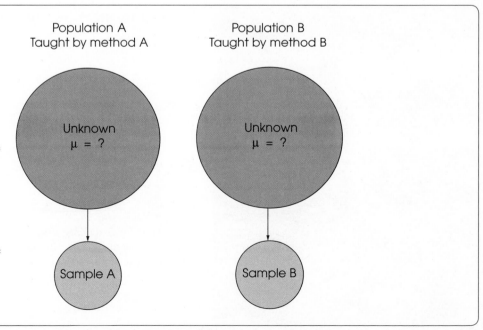

FIGURE 10.1

Do the achievement scores for children taught by method A differ from the scores for children taught by method B? In statistical terms, are the two population means the same or different? Because neither of the two population means is known, it will be necessary to take two samples, one from each population. The first sample provides information about the mean for the first population, and the second sample provides information about the second population.

Population A
Taught by method A

Unknown
$\mu = ?$

Sample A

Population B
Taught by method B

Unknown
$\mu = ?$

Sample B

DEFINITION

> A research design that uses a separate group of participants for each treatment condition (or for each population) is called an **independent-measures research design** or a **between-subjects research design.**

In this chapter, we examine the statistical techniques used to evaluate the data from an independent-measures design. More precisely, we introduce the hypothesis test that allows researchers to use the data from two separate samples to evaluate the mean difference between two populations or between two treatment conditions.

The second research strategy, in which the two sets of data are obtained from the same group of participants, is called a *repeated-measures* research design or a *within-subjects* design. The statistics for evaluating the results from a repeated-measures design are introduced in Chapter 11. Also, at the end of Chapter 11, we discuss some of the advantages and disadvantages of independent-measures and repeated-measures designs.

10.2 THE *t* STATISTIC FOR AN INDEPENDENT-MEASURES RESEARCH DESIGN

Because an independent-measures study involves two separate samples, we need some special notation to help specify which data go with which sample. This notation involves the use of subscripts, which are small numbers written beside a sample statistic. For example, the number of scores in the first sample is identified by n_1; for the second sample, the number of scores is n_2. The sample means are identified by M_1 and M_2. The sums of squares are SS_1 and SS_2.

THE HYPOTHESIS FOR AN INDEPENDENT-MEASURES TEST

The goal of an independent-measures research study is to evaluate the mean difference between two populations (or between two treatment conditions). Using subscripts to differentiate the two populations, the mean for the first population is μ_1, and the second population mean is μ_2. The difference between means is simply $\mu_1 - \mu_2$. As always, the null hypothesis states that there is no change, no effect, or, in this case, no difference. Thus, in symbols, the null hypothesis for the independent-measures test is

$$H_0: \mu_1 - \mu_2 = 0 \text{ (No difference between the population means)}$$

You should notice that the null hypothesis could also be stated as $\mu_1 = \mu_2$. However, the first version of H_0 produces a specific numerical value (zero) that is used in the calculation of the *t* statistic. Therefore, we prefer to phrase the null hypothesis in terms of the difference between the two population means.

The alternative hypothesis states that there is a mean difference between the two populations,

$$H_1: \mu_1 - \mu_2 \neq 0 \text{ (There is a mean difference.)}$$

Equivalently, the alternative hypothesis can simply state that the two population means are not equal: $\mu_1 \neq \mu_2$.

THE FORMULAS FOR AN INDEPENDENT-MEASURES HYPOTHESIS TEST

The independent-measures hypothesis test uses another version of the *t* statistic. The formula for this new *t* statistic has the same general structure as the *t* statistic formula that was introduced in Chapter 9. To help distinguish between the two *t* formulas, we refer to the original formula (Chapter 9) as the *single-sample* t *statistic* and we refer to the new formula as the *independent-measures* t *statistic*. Because the new independent-measures *t* includes data from two separate samples and hypotheses about two populations, the formulas may appear to be a bit overpowering. However, the new formulas are easier to understand if you view them in relation to the single-sample *t* formulas from Chapter 9. In particular, there are two points to remember:

1. The basic structure of the *t* statistic is the same for both the independent-measures and the single-sample hypothesis tests. In both cases,

$$t = \frac{\text{sample statistic} - \text{hypothesized population parameter}}{\text{estimated standard error}}$$

2. The independent-measures *t* is basically a *two-sample* t *that doubles all the elements of the single-sample* t *formulas*.

To demonstrate the second point, we examine the two *t* formulas piece by piece.

The overall *t* formula   The single-sample *t* uses one sample mean to test a hypothesis about one population mean. The sample mean and the population mean appear in the numerator of the *t* formula, which measures how much difference there is between the sample data and the population hypothesis.

$$t = \frac{\text{sample mean} - \text{population mean}}{\text{estimated standard error}} = \frac{M - \mu}{s_M}$$

The independent-measures *t* uses the difference between *two* sample means to evaluate a hypothesis about the difference between *two* population means. Thus, the independent-measures *t* formula is

$$t = \frac{\substack{\text{sample mean} - \text{population mean} \\ \text{difference} \quad\quad \text{difference}}}{\text{estimated standard error}} = \frac{(M_1 - M_2) - (\mu_1 - \mu_2)}{s_{(M_1 - M_2)}}$$

In this formula, the value of $M_1 - M_2$ is obtained from the sample data and the value for $\mu_1 - \mu_2$ comes from the null hypothesis.

The estimated standard error   In each of the *t*-score formulas, the standard error in the denominator measures how accurately the sample statistic represents the population parameter. In the single-sample *t* formula, the standard error measures the amount of error expected for a sample mean and is represented by the symbol s_M. For the independent-measures *t* formula, the standard error measures the amount of error that is expected when you use a sample mean difference $(M_1 - M_2)$ to represent a population mean difference $(\mu_1 - \mu_2)$. The standard error for the sample mean difference is represented by the symbol $s_{(M_1 - M_2)}$.

Caution: Do not let the notation for standard error confuse you. In general, standard error measures how accurately a statistic represents a parameter. The symbol for standard error takes the form $s_{\text{statistic}}$. When the statistic is a sample mean, M, the symbol for standard error is s_M. For the independent-measures test, the statistic is a sample mean difference $(M_1 - M_2)$, and the symbol for standard error is $s_{(M_1 - M_2)}$. In each case, the standard error tells how much discrepancy is reasonable to expect between the sample statistic and the corresponding population parameter.

Interpreting the estimated standard error   The *estimated standard error of* $M_1 - M_2$ that appears in the bottom of the independent-measures t statistic can be interpreted in two ways. First, the standard error is defined as a measure of the standard, or average, distance between a sample statistic ($M_1 - M_2$) and the corresponding population parameter ($\mu_1 - \mu_2$). As always, samples are not expected to be perfectly accurate and the standard error measures how much difference is reasonable to expect between a sample statistic and the population parameter.

Sample mean
difference
$(M_1 - M_2)$
   ←——— estimated standard error ———→
   (average distance)
   Population mean
difference
$(\mu_1 - \mu_2)$

When the null hypothesis is true, however, the population mean difference is zero.

Sample mean
difference
$(M_1 - M_2)$
   ←——— estimated standard error ———→
   (average distance)
   0 (If H_0 is true)

The standard error is measuring how close the sample mean difference is to zero, which is equivalent to measuring how much difference there is between the two sample means.

M_1 ←——— estimated standard error ———→ M_2
        (average distance)

This produces a second interpretation for the estimated standard error. Specifically, the standard error can be viewed as a measure of how much difference is reasonable to expect between two sample means if the null hypothesis is true.

The second interpretation of the estimated standard error produces a simplified version of the independent-measures t statistic.

$$t = \frac{\text{sample mean difference}}{\text{estimated standard error}}$$

$$= \frac{\text{actual difference between } M_1 \text{ and } M_2}{\text{standard difference (If } H_0 \text{ is true) between } M_1 \text{ and } M_2}$$

In this version, the numerator of the t statistic measures how much difference *actually exists* between the two sample means, including any difference that is caused by the different treatments. The denominator measures how much difference *should exist* between the two sample means if there is no treatment effect that causes them to be different. A large value for the t statistic is evidence for the existence of a treatment effect.

**CALCULATING THE
ESTIMATED STANDARD
ERROR**

To develop the formula for $s_{(M_1 - M_2)}$ we consider the following three points:

1. Each of the two sample means represents it own population mean, but in each case there is some error.

   M_1 approximates μ_1 with some error

   M_2 approximates μ_2 with some error

Thus, there are two sources of error.

2. The amount of error associated with each sample mean is measured by the estimated standard error of *M*. Using Equation 9.1 (p. 251), the estimated standard error for each sample mean is computed as follows:

$$\text{For } M_1 \ s_M = \sqrt{\frac{s_1^2}{n_1}} \qquad \text{For } M_2 \ s_M = \sqrt{\frac{s_2^2}{n_2}}$$

3. For the independent-measures *t* statistic, we want to know the total amount of error involved in using *two* sample means to approximate *two* population means. To do this, we find the error from each sample separately and then add the two errors together. The resulting formula for standard error is

$$s_{(M_1-M_2)} = \sqrt{\frac{s_1^2}{n_1} + \frac{s_2^2}{n_2}} \tag{10.1}$$

Because the independent-measures *t* statistic uses two sample means, the formula for the estimated standard error simply combines the error for the first sample mean and the error for the second sample mean (Box 10.1).

POOLED VARIANCE   Although Equation 10.1 accurately presents the concept of standard error for the independent-measures *t* statistic, this formula is limited to situations in which the two samples are exactly the same size (that is, $n_1 = n_2$). For situations in which the two sample sizes are different, the formula is *biased* and, therefore, inappropriate. The bias comes from the fact that Equation 10.1 treats the two sample

---

BOX 10.1   THE VARIABILITY OF DIFFERENCE SCORES

It may seem odd that the independent-measures *t* statistic *adds* together the two sample errors when it *subtracts* to find the difference between the two sample means. The logic behind this apparently unusual procedure is demonstrated here.

We begin with two populations, I and II (Figure 10.2). The scores in population I range from a high of 70 to a low of 50. The scores in population II range from 30 to 20. We use the range as a measure of how spread out (variable) each population is:

For population I, the scores cover a range of 20 points.

For population II, the scores cover a range of 10 points.

If we randomly select one score from population I and one score from population II and compute the difference between these two scores ($X_1 - X_2$), what range of values is possible for these differences? To answer this

question, we need to find the biggest possible difference and the smallest possible difference. As seen in Figure 10.2, the biggest difference occurs when $X_1 = 70$ and $X_2 = 20$. This is a difference of $X_1 - X_2 = 50$ points. The smallest difference occurs when $X_1 = 50$ and $X_2 = 30$. This is a difference of $X_1 - X_2 = 20$ points. Notice that the differences go from a high of 50 to a low of 20. This is a range of 30 points:

range for population I (X_1 scores) = 20 points
range for population II (X_2 scores) = 10 points
range for the differences ($X_1 - X_2$) = 30 points

The variability for the difference scores is found by *adding* together the variability for each of the two populations.

In the independent-measures *t* statistics, we compute the variability (standard error) for a sample mean difference. To compute this value, we add together the variability for each of the two sample means.

FIGURE 10.2

Two population distributions. The scores in population I vary from 50 to 70 (a 20-point spread), and the scores in population II range from 20 to 30 (a 10-point spread). If you select one score from each of these two populations, the closest two values are $X_1 = 50$ and $X_2 = 30$. The two values that are farthest apart are $X_1 = 70$ and $X_2 = 20$.

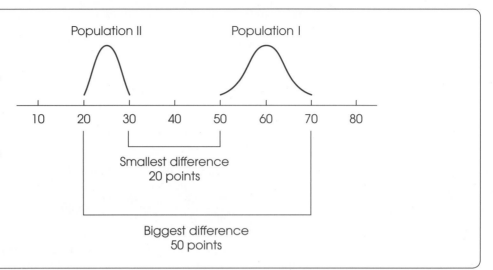

An alternative to computing pooled variance is presented in Box 10.2, p. 302.

variances equally. However, when the sample sizes are different, the two sample variances are not equally good and should not be treated equally. In Chapter 7, we introduced the law of large numbers, which states that statistics obtained from large samples tend to be better (more accurate) estimates of population parameters than statistics obtained from small samples. This same fact holds for sample variances: The variance obtained from a large sample is a more accurate estimate of σ^2 than the variance obtained from a small sample.

One method for correcting the bias in the standard error is to combine the two sample variances into a single value called the *pooled variance*. The pooled variance is obtained by averaging, or "pooling," the two sample variances using a procedure that allows the bigger sample to carry more weight in determining the final value.

You should recall that when there is only one sample, the sample variance is computed as

$$s^2 = \frac{SS}{df}$$

For the independent-measures t statistic, there are two SS values and two df values (one from each sample). The values from the two samples are combined to compute what is called the *pooled variance*. The pooled variance is identified by the symbol and is computed as

$$\text{pooled variance} = s_p^2 = \frac{SS_1 + SS_2}{df_1 + df_2} \tag{10.2}$$

With one sample, the variance is computed as SS divided by df. With two samples, the pooled variance is computed by combining the two SS values and then dividing by the combination of the two df values.

As we mentioned earlier, the pooled variance is actually an average of the two sample variances, but the average is computed so that the larger sample carries more weight in determining the final value. The following examples demonstrate this point.

Equal sample sizes We begin with two samples that are exactly the same size. The first sample has $n = 6$ scores with $SS = 50$, and the second sample has $n = 6$ scores with $SS = 30$. Individually, the two sample variances are

$$\text{Variance for sample 1: } s^2 = \frac{SS}{df} = \frac{50}{5} = 10$$

$$\text{Variance for sample 2: } s^2 = \frac{SS}{df} = \frac{30}{5} = 6$$

The pooled variance for these two samples is

$$s_p^2 = \frac{SS_1 + SS_2}{df_1 + df_2} = \frac{50 + 30}{5 + 5} = \frac{80}{10} = 8.00$$

Note that the pooled variance is exactly halfway between the two sample variances. Because the two samples are exactly the same size, the pooled variance is simply the average of the two sample variances.

Unequal sample sizes Now consider what happens when the samples are not the same size. This time the first sample has $n = 3$ scores with $SS = 20$, and the second sample has $n = 9$ scores with $SS = 48$. Individually, the two sample variances are

$$\text{Variance for sample 1: } s^2 = \frac{SS}{df} = \frac{20}{2} = 10$$

$$\text{Variance for sample 2: } s^2 = \frac{SS}{df} = \frac{48}{8} = 6$$

The pooled variance for these two samples is

$$s_p^2 = \frac{SS_1 + SS_2}{df_1 + df_2} = \frac{20 + 48}{2 + 8} = \frac{68}{10} = 6.80$$

This time the pooled variance is not located halfway between the two sample variances. Instead, the pooled value is closer to the variance for the larger sample ($n = 9$ and $s^2 = 6$) than to the variance for the smaller sample ($n = 3$ and $s^2 = 10$). The larger sample carries more weight when the pooled variance is computed.

When computing the pooled variance, the weight for each of the individual sample variances is determined by its degrees of freedom. Because the larger sample has a larger df value, it carries more weight when averaging the two variances. This produces an alternative formula for computing pooled variance.

$$\text{pooled variance} = s_p^2 = \frac{df_1 s_1^2 + df_2 s_2^2}{df_1 + df_2} \tag{10.3}$$

For example, if the first sample has $df_1 = 3$ and the second sample has $df_2 = 7$, then the formula instructs you to take 3 of the first sample variance and 7 of the second sample variance for a total of 10 variances. You then divide by 10 to obtain the average. The alternative formula is especially useful if the sample data are summarized as means and variances. Finally, you should note that because the pooled variance is an average of the two sample variances, the value obtained for the pooled variance is always located between the two sample variances.

ESTIMATED STANDARD ERROR

Using the pooled variance in place of the individual sample variances, we can now obtain an unbiased measure of the standard error for a sample mean difference. The resulting formula for the independent-measures estimated standard error is

$$\text{estimated standard error of } M_1 - M_2 = s_{(M_1-M_2)} = \sqrt{\frac{s_p^2}{n_1} + \frac{s_p^2}{n_2}} \tag{10.4}$$

Conceptually, this standard error measures how accurately the difference between two sample means represents the difference between the two population means. In a hypothesis test, H_0 specifies that $\mu_1 - \mu_2 = 0$, and the standard error also measures how much difference is expected, on average, between the two sample means. In either case, the formula combines the error for the first sample mean with the error for the second sample mean. Also note that the pooled variance from the two samples is used to compute the standard error for the sample mean difference.

THE FINAL FORMULA AND DEGREES OF FREEDOM

The complete formula for the independent-measures t statistic is as follows:

$$t = \frac{(M_1 - M_2) - (\mu_1 - \mu_2)}{s_{(M_1-M_2)}}$$

$$= \frac{\text{sample mean difference} - \text{population mean difference}}{\text{estimated standard error}} \tag{10.5}$$

In the formula, the estimated standard error in the denominator is calculated using Equation 10.4, and requires calculation of the pooled variance using either Equation 10.2 or 10.3.

The degrees of freedom for the independent-measures t statistic are determined by the df values for the two separate samples:

$$df \text{ for the } t \text{ statistic} = df \text{ for the first sample} + df \text{ for the second sample}$$
$$= df_1 + df_2$$
$$= (n_1 - 1) + (n_2 - 1) \tag{10.6}$$

Equivalently, the df value for the independent-measures t statistic can be expressed as

$$df = n_1 + n_2 - 2 \tag{10.7}$$

Note that the df formula subtracts 2 points from the total number of scores; 1 point for the first sample and 1 for the second.

The independent-measures t statistic is used for hypothesis testing. Specifically, we use the difference between two sample means $(M_1 - M_2)$ as the basis for testing hypotheses about the difference between two population means $(\mu_1 - \mu_2)$. In this context, the overall structure of the t statistic can be reduced to the following:

$$t = \frac{\text{data} - \text{hypothesis}}{\text{error}}$$

This same structure is used for both the single-sample t from Chapter 9 and the new independent-measures t that was introduced in the preceding pages. Table 10.1 identifies each component of these two t statistics and should help reinforce the point that we made earlier in the chapter; that is, the independent-measures t statistic simply doubles each aspect of the single-sample t statistic.

TABLE 10.1

The basic elements of a *t* statistic for the single-sample *t* and the independent-measures *t*.

	Sample Data	Hypothesized Population Parameter	Estimated Standard Error	Sample Variance
Single-sample *t* statistic	M	μ	$\sqrt{\dfrac{s^2}{n}}$	$s^2 = \dfrac{SS}{df}$
Independent-measures *t* statistic	$(M_1 - M_2)$	$(\mu_1 - \mu_2)$	$\sqrt{\dfrac{s_p^2}{n_1} + \dfrac{s_p^2}{n_2}}$	$s_p^2 = \dfrac{SS_1 + SS_2}{df_1 + df_2}$

LEARNING CHECK

1. What is the defining characteristic of an independent-measures research study?

2. Explain what is measured by the estimated standard error in the denominator of the independent-measures *t* statistic.

3. One sample from an independent-measures study has $n = 4$ with $SS = 100$. The other sample has $n = 8$ and $SS = 140$.

   a. Compute the pooled variance. (*Note*: Equation 10.2 works well with these data.)

   b. Compute the estimated standard error for the mean difference.

4. One sample from an independent-measures study has $n = 9$ with a variance of $s^2 = 35$. The other sample has $n = 3$ and $s^2 = 40$.

   a. Compute the pooled variance. (*Note:* Equation 10.3 works well with these data.)

   b. Compute the estimated standard error for the mean difference.

5. An independent-measures *t* statistic is used to evaluate the mean difference between two treatments with $n = 8$ in one treatment and $n = 12$ in the other. What is the *df* value for the *t* statistic?

ANSWERS

1. An independent-measures study uses a separate group of participants to represent each of the populations or treatment conditions being compared.

2. The estimated standard error measures how much difference is expected, on average, between a sample mean difference and the population mean difference. In a hypothesis test, $\mu_1 - \mu_2$ is set to zero and the standard error measures how much difference is expected between the two sample means.

3. **a.** The pooled variance is $\frac{240}{10} = 24$.

   b. The estimated standard error is 3.

4. **a.** The pooled variance is 36.

   b. The estimated standard error is 4.

5. $df = df_1 + df_2 = 7 + 11 = 18$.

10.3 **HYPOTHESIS TESTS AND EFFECT SIZE WITH THE INDEPENDENT-MEASURES *t* STATISTIC**

The independent-measures *t* statistic uses the data from two separate samples to help decide whether there is a significant mean difference between two populations or between two treatment conditions. A complete example of a hypothesis test with two independent samples follows.

EXAMPLE 10.1   Research results suggest a relationship between the TV viewing habits of 5-year-old children and their future performance in high school. For example, Anderson, Huston, Wright, and Collins (1998) report that high school students who had regularly watched Sesame Street as children had better grades in high school than their peers who had not watched Sesame Street. Suppose that a researcher intends to examine this phenomenon using a sample of 20 high school students.

The researcher first surveys the students' parents to obtain information on the family's TV-viewing habits during the time that the students were 5 years old. Based on the survey results, the researcher selects a sample of $n = 10$ students with a history of watching Sesame Street and a sample of $n = 10$ students who did not watch the program. The average high school grade is recorded for each student and the data are as follows:

Average High School Grade			
Watched Sesame Street		Did Not Watch Sesame Street	
86	99	90	79
87	97	89	83
91	94	82	86
97	89	83	81
98	92	85	92
$n = 10$		$n = 10$	
$M = 93$		$M = 85$	
$SS = 200$		$SS = 160$	

Note that this is an independent-measures study using two separate samples representing two distinct populations of high school students. The researcher would like to know whether there is a significant difference between the two types of high school student.

STEP 1   State the hypotheses and select the alpha level.

$$H_0: \mu_1 - \mu_2 = 0 \qquad \text{(No difference.)}$$

$$H_1: \mu_1 - \mu_2 \neq 0 \qquad \text{(There is a difference.)}$$

We set $\alpha = .01$.

Directional hypotheses could be used and would specify whether the students who watched Sesame Street should have higher or lower grades.

STEP 2   This is an independent-measures design. The t statistic for these data has degrees of freedom determined by

$$df = df_1 + df_2$$

$$= (n_1 - 1) + (n_2 - 1)$$

$$= 9 + 9$$

$$= 18$$

The t distribution for $df = 18$ is presented in Figure 10.3. For $\alpha = .01$, the critical region consists of the extreme 1% of the distribution and has boundaries of $t = +2.878$ and $t = -2.878$.

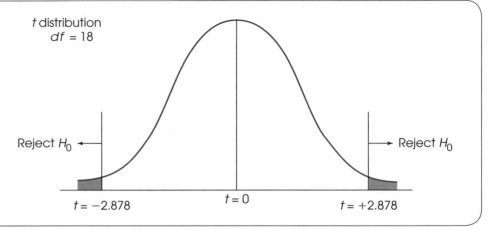

FIGURE 10.3

The critical region for the independent-measures hypothesis test in Example 10.1 with *df* = 18 and α = .01.

t distribution
df = 18

Reject H_0 ←

Reject H_0 →

$t = -2.878$

$t = 0$

$t = +2.878$

STEP 3 Obtain the data and compute the test statistic. The data are given, so all that remains is to compute the *t* statistic. As with the single-sample *t* test in Chapter 9, we recommend that the calculations be divided into three parts.

First, find the pooled variance for the two samples:

Caution: The pooled variance combines the two samples to obtain a single estimate of variance. In the formula, the two samples are combined in a single fraction.

$$s_p^2 = \frac{SS_1 + SS_2}{df_1 + df_2}$$

$$= \frac{200 + 160}{9 + 9}$$

$$= \frac{360}{18}$$

$$= 20$$

Second, use the pooled variance to compute the estimated standard error:

Caution: The standard error adds the errors from two separate samples. In the formula, these two errors are added as two separate fractions. In this case, the two errors are equal because the sample sizes are the same.

$$s_{(M_1 - M_2)} = \sqrt{\frac{s_p^2}{n_1} + \frac{s_p^2}{n_2}} = \sqrt{\frac{20}{10} + \frac{20}{10}}$$

$$= \sqrt{2 + 2}$$

$$= \sqrt{4}$$

$$= 2$$

Third, compute the *t* statistic:

$$t = \frac{(M_1 - M_2) - (\mu_1 - \mu_2)}{s_{(M_1 - M_2)}} = \frac{(93 - 85) - 0}{2}$$

$$= \frac{8}{2}$$

$$= 4$$

STEP 4   Make a decision. The obtained value ($t = 4.00$) is in the critical region. In this example, the obtained sample mean difference is four times greater than would be expected if there were no difference between the two populations. In other words, this result is very unlikely if H_0 is true. Therefore, we reject H_0 and conclude that there is a significant difference between the high school grades for students who watched Sesame Street and those who did not. Specifically, the students who watched Sesame Street had significantly higher grades than those who did not watch the program.

Note that the Sesame Street study in Example 10.1 is an example of nonexperimental research (see Chapter 1, p. 16). Specifically, the researcher did not manipulate the TV programs watched by the children and did not control a variety of variables that could influence high school grades. As a result, we cannot conclude that watching Sesame Street *causes* higher high school grades. In particular, many other, uncontrolled factors, such as the parents' level of education or family economic status, might explain the difference between the two groups. Thus, we do not know exactly why there is a relationship between watching Sesame Street and high school grades, but we do know that a relationship exists.

MEASURING EFFECT SIZE FOR THE INDEPENDENT-MEASURES *t* TEST

As noted in Chapters 8 and 9, a hypothesis test is usually accompanied by a report of effect size to provide an indication of the absolute magnitude of the treatment effect. One technique for measuring effect size is Cohen's *d*, which produces a standardized measure of mean difference. In its general form, Cohen's *d* is defined as

$$d = \frac{\text{mean difference}}{\text{standard deviation}} = \frac{\mu_1 - \mu_2}{\sigma}$$

In the context of an independent-measures research study, the difference between the two sample means ($M_1 - M_2$) is used as the best estimate of the mean difference between the two populations, and the pooled standard deviation (the square root of the pooled variance) is used to estimate the population standard deviation. Thus, the formula for estimating Cohen's *d* becomes

$$\text{estimated } d = \frac{\text{estimated mean difference}}{\text{estimated standard deviation}} = \frac{M_1 - M_2}{\sqrt{s_p^2}} \tag{10.8}$$

For the data from Example 10.1, the two sample means are 93 and 85, and the pooled variance is 20. The estimated *d* for these data is

$$d = \frac{M_1 - M_2}{\sqrt{s_p^2}} = \frac{93 - 85}{\sqrt{20}} = \frac{8}{4.7} = 1.79$$

Using the criteria established to evaluate Cohen's *d* (see Table 8.2 on p. 232), this value indicates a very large treatment effect.

The independent-measures *t* test also allows for measuring effect size by computing the percentage of variance accounted for, r^2. As we saw in Chapter 9, r^2 measures how much of the variability in the scores can be explained by the treatment effects. For example, some of the variability in the high school grades from the Sesame Street study can be explained by knowing whether a particular student watched the program; students who watched Sesame Street tend to have higher grades and students who did not watch the show tend to have lower grades. By measuring exactly how much of the variability can be explained, we can obtain a measure of how big the treatment effect actually is. The calculation of r^2 for the independent-measures t test is exactly the same as it was for the single-sample t test in Chapter 9.

$$r^2 = \frac{t^2}{t^2 + df} \qquad (10.9)$$

For the data in Example 10.1, we obtained $t = 4.00$ with $df = 18$. These values produce an r^2 of

$$r^2 = \frac{4^2}{4^2 + 18} = \frac{16}{16 + 18} = \frac{16}{34} = 0.47$$

According to the standards used to evaluate r^2 (see Table 9.3 on p. 264), this value also indicates a very large treatment effect.

Although the value of r^2 is usually obtained by using Equation 10.9, it is possible to determine the percentage of variability directly by computing SS values for the set of scores. The following example demonstrates this process using the data from the Sesame Street study in Example 10.1.

EXAMPLE 10.2　Figure 10.4(a) shows the two samples from Example 10.1 combined into a single frequency distribution of $n = 20$ scores. The overall mean for the distribution is $M = 89$ and the scores have $SS = 680$. However, it is clear that the scores for the students who watched Sesame Street tend to be clustered at the high end of the distribution. The mean for these 10 students is $M = 93$, which is 4 points higher than the overall mean for the entire group. Also, the scores for the students who did not watch the program are clustered at the low end of the distribution. For these 10 students the mean is $M = 85$, which is 4 points below the overall mean. The difference between the two types of student ($M = 85$ versus $M = 93$) is the treatment effect produced by the relationship between TV viewing and high school grades.

Now consider the distribution shown in Figure 10.4(b). To create this distribution, we started with the original scores and then eliminated the treatment effect. Specifically, we subtracted 4 points from each score in the Sesame Street group and we added 4 points to each score for students who did not watch Sesame Street. As a result, both groups now have the same mean, $M = 89$, and the treatment effect is eliminated. One consequence of removing the treatment effect is that the resulting scores are much less variable that the original scores. Recall that the original scores in Figure 10.4(a) have $SS = 680$. When the treatment effect is removed, in Figure 10.4(b), the variability is reduced to $SS = 360$. The difference between these two values is 320 points. Thus, the treatment effect accounts for 320 point of the total variability in the original scores. When expressed as a proportion of the total variability, we obtain

$$\frac{\text{variability explained by the treatment}}{\text{total variability}} = \frac{320}{680} = 0.47 = 47\%$$

You should recognize that this is exactly the same value we obtained for r^2 using Equation 10.9.

CONFIDENCE INTERVALS FOR ESTIMATING $\mu_1 - \mu_2$　As noted in Chapter 9, it is possible to compute a confidence interval as an alternative method for measuring and describing the size of the treatment effect. For the single-sample t, we used a single sample mean, M, to estimate a single population mean. For the

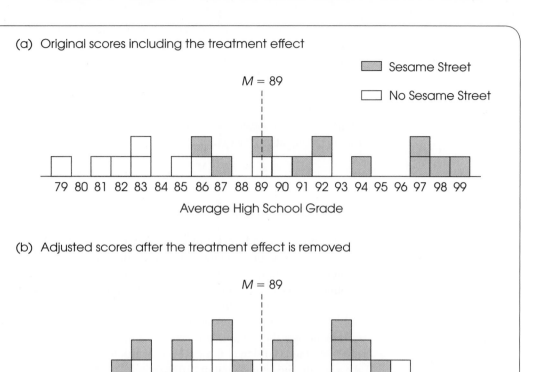

FIGURE 10.4

The two groups of scores from Example 10.1 combined into a single distribution. The original scores, including the treatment effect, are shown in part (a). Part (b) shows the adjusted scores, after the treatment effect has been removed.

independent-measures *t*, we use a sample mean difference, $M_1 - M_2$, to estimate the population mean difference, $\mu_1 - \mu_2$. In this case, the confidence interval literally estimates the size of the population mean difference between the two populations or treatment conditions.

As with the single-sample *t*, the first step is to solve the *t* equation for the unknown parameter. For the independent-measures *t* statistic, we obtain

$$\mu_1 - \mu_2 = M_1 - M_2 \pm ts_{(M_1 - M_2)} \tag{10.10}$$

In the equation, the values for $M_1 - M_2$ and for $s_{(M_1 - M_2)}$ are obtained from the sample data. Although the value for the *t* statistic is unknown, we can use the degrees of freedom for the *t* statistic and the *t* distribution table to estimate the *t* value. Using the estimated *t* and the known values from the sample, we can then compute the estimated value for $\mu_1 - \mu_2$. The following example demonstrates the process of constructing a confidence interval for a population mean difference.

EXAMPLE 10.3   Earlier we presented a research study comparing high school grades for students who had watched Sesame Street as children with the grades for students who had not watched the program (p. 289). The results of the hypothesis test indicated a significant mean difference between the two populations of students. Now, we construct a 95% confidence interval to estimate the size of the population mean difference.

The data from the study produced a mean grade of $M = 93$ for the Sesame Street group and a mean of $M = 85$ for the no–Sesame Street group, and the estimated standard error for the mean difference was $s_{(M_1 - M_2)} = 2$. With $n = 10$ scores in each sample, the independent-measures t statistic has $df = 18$. To have 95% confidence, we simply estimate that the t statistic for the sample mean difference is located somewhere in the middle 95% of all the possible t values. According to the t distribution table, with $df = 18$, 95% of the t values are located between $t = +2.101$ and $t = -2.101$. Using these values in the estimation equation, we obtain

$$\mu_1 - \mu_2 = M_1 - M_2 \pm t s_{(M_1 - M_2)}$$
$$= 93 - 85 \pm 2.101(2)$$
$$= 8 \pm 4.202$$

This produces an interval of values ranging from $8 - 4.202 = 3.798$ to $8 + 4.202 = 12.202$. Thus, our conclusion is that students who watched Sesame Street have higher grades that those who did not, and the mean difference between the two populations is somewhere between 3.798 points and 12.202 points. Furthermore, we are 95% confident that the true mean difference is in this interval because the only value estimated during the calculations was the t statistic, and we are 95% confident that the t value is located in the middle 95% of the distribution. Finally, note that the confidence interval is constructed around the sample mean difference. As a result, the sample mean difference, $M_1 - M_2 = 93 - 83 = 8$ points, is located exactly in the center of the interval.

As with the confidence interval for the single-sample t (p. 264), the confidence interval for an independent-measures t is influenced by a variety of factors other than the actual size of the treatment effect. In particular, the width of the interval depends on the percentage of confidence used, so that a larger percentage produces a wider interval. Also, the width of the interval depends on the sample size, so that a larger sample produces a narrower interval. Because the interval width is related to sample size, the confidence interval is not a pure measure of effect size like Cohen's d or r^2.

CONFIDENCE INTERVALS AND HYPOTHESIS TESTS

In addition to describing the size of a treatment effect, estimation can be used to get an indication of the *significance* of the effect. Example 10.3 presented an independent-measures research study examining the effect on high school grades of having watched Sesame Street as a child. Based on the results of the study, the 95% confidence interval estimated that the population mean difference for the two groups of students was between 3.798 and 12.202 points. The confidence interval estimate is shown in Figure 10.5. In addition to the confidence interval for $\mu_1 - \mu_2$, we have marked the spot where the mean difference is equal to zero. You should recognize that a mean difference of zero is exactly what would be predicted by the null hypothesis if we were doing a hypothesis test. You also should realize that a zero difference ($\mu_1 - \mu_2 = 0$) is *outside* of the 95% confidence interval. In other words, $\mu_1 - \mu_2 = 0$ is not an acceptable value if we want 95% confidence in our estimate. To conclude that a value of zero is *not acceptable* with 95% confidence is equivalent to concluding that a value of zero is *rejected* with 95% confidence. This conclusion is equivalent to rejecting H_0 with $\alpha = .05$. On the other hand, if a mean difference of zero were included within the 95% confidence interval, then we would have to conclude that $\mu_1 - \mu_2 = 0$ is an acceptable value, which is the same as failing to reject H_0.

The hypothesis test for these data was conducted in Example 10.1 (p. 289) and the decision was to reject H_0.

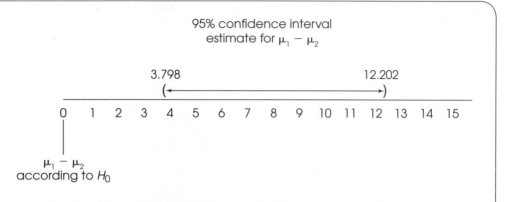

FIGURE 10.5

The 95% confidence interval for the population mean difference $(\mu_1 - \mu_2)$ from Example 10.3. Note that $\mu_1 - \mu_2 = 0$ is excluded from the confidence interval, indicating that a zero difference is not an acceptable value (H_0 would be rejected in a hypothesis test with $\alpha = .05$).

IN THE LITERATURE:

REPORTING THE RESULTS OF AN INDEPENDENT-MEASURES *t* TEST

A research report typically presents the descriptive statistics followed by the results of the hypothesis test and measures of effect size (inferential statistics). In Chapter 4 (p. 109), we demonstrated how the mean and the standard deviation are reported in APA format. In Chapter 9 (p. 267), we illustrated the APA style for reporting the results of a *t* test. Now we use the APA format to report the results of Example 10.1, an independent-measures *t* test. A concise statement might read as follows:

> The students who watched Sesame Street as children had higher high school grades ($M = 93$, $SD = 4.71$) than the students who did not watch the program ($M = 85$, $SD = 4.22$). The mean difference was significant, $t(18) = 4.00$, $p < .01$, $d = 1.79$.

You should note that standard deviation is not a step in the computations for the independent-measures *t* test, yet it is useful when providing descriptive statistics for each treatment group. It is easily computed when doing the *t* test because you need *SS* and *df* for both groups to determine the pooled variance. Note that the format for reporting *t* is exactly the same as that described in Chapter 9 (p. 267) and that the measure of effect size is reported immediately after the results of the hypothesis test.

Also, as we noted in Chapter 9, if an exact probability is available from a computer analysis, it should be reported. For the data in Example 10.1, the computer analysis reports a probability value of $p = .001$ for $t = 4.00$ with $df = 18$. In the research report, this value would be included as follows:

> The difference was significant, $t(18) = 4.00$, $p = .001$, $d = 1.79$.

Finally, if a confidence interval is reported to describe effect size, it appears immediately after the results from the hypothesis test. For the Sesame Street examples (Example 10.1 and Example 10.3), the report would be as follows:

> The difference was significant, $t(18) = 4.00$, $p = .001$, 95% CI [3.798, 12.202].

LEARNING CHECK

1. An educational psychologist would like to determine whether access to computers has an effect on grades for high school students. One group of $n = 16$ students has home room each day in a computer classroom in which each student has a computer. A comparison group of $n = 16$ students has home room in a traditional classroom. At the end of the school year, the average grade is recorded for each student. The data are as follows:

Computer	Traditional
$M = 86$	$M = 82.5$
$SS = 1005$	$SS = 1155$

   a. Is there a significant difference between the two groups? Use a two-tailed test with $\alpha = .05$.

   b. Compute Cohen's d to measure the size of the difference.

   c. Write a sentence that demonstrates how the outcome of the hypothesis test and the measure of effect size would appear in a research report.

   d. Compute the 90% confidence interval for the population mean difference between a computer classroom and a regular classroom.

2. A research report states that there is a significant difference between treatments for an independent-measures design with $t(28) = 2.27$.

   a. How many individuals participated in the research study? (*Hint:* Start with the *df* value.)

   b. Should the report state that $p > .05$ or $p < .05$?

ANSWERS

1. a. The pooled variance is 72, the standard error is 3, and $t = 1.17$. With a critical value of $t = 2.042$, fail to reject the null hypothesis.

   b. Cohen's $d = \dfrac{3.5}{\sqrt{72}} = 0.412$

   c. The results show no significant difference in grades for students with computers compared to students without computers, $t(30) = 1.17, p > .05, d = 0.412$.

   d. With $df = 30$ and 90% confidence, the t values for the confidence interval are ± 1.697. The interval is $\mu_1 - \mu_2 = 3.5 \pm 1.697(3)$. Thus, the population mean difference is estimated to be between -1.591 and 8.591. The fact that zero is an acceptable value (inside the interval) is consistent with the decision that there is no significant difference between the two population means.

2. a. The $df = 28$, so the total number of participants is 30.

   b. A significant result is indicated by $p < .05$.

DIRECTIONAL HYPOTHESES AND ONE-TAILED TESTS

When planning an independent-measures study, a researcher usually has some expectation or specific prediction for the outcome. For the Sesame Street study in Example 10.1, the researcher clearly expects the students who watched Sesame Street to have higher grades than the students who did not watch it. This kind of directional prediction can be incorporated into the statement of the hypotheses, resulting in a directional, or one-tailed, test. Recall from Chapter 8 that one-tailed tests can lead to rejecting H_0 when the mean difference is relatively small compared to the magnitude required by a two-tailed test. As a result, one-tailed tests should be used when clearly justified by theory or previous findings. The following example demonstrates the procedure for stating hypotheses and locating the critical region for a one-tailed test using the independent-measures *t* statistic.

EXAMPLE 10.4   We use the same research situation that was described in Example 10.1. The researcher is using an independent-measures design to examine the relationship between watching educational TV as a child and academic performance as a high school student. The prediction is that high school students who watched Sesame Street regularly as 5-year-old children have higher grades.

STEP 1   State the hypotheses and select the alpha level. As always, the null hypothesis says that there is no effect, and the alternative hypothesis says that there is an effect. For this example, the predicted effect is that the students who watched Sesame Street have higher grades. Thus, the two hypotheses are as follows.

$$H_0: \mu_{\text{Sesame Street}} \leq \mu_{\text{No Sesame Street}} \quad \text{(Grades are not higher with Sesame Street.)}$$

$$H_1: \mu_{\text{Sesame Street}} > \mu_{\text{No Sesame Street}} \quad \text{(Grades are higher with Sesame Street.)}$$

Note that it is usually easier to state the hypotheses in words before you try to write them in symbols. Also, it usually is easier to begin with the alternative hypothesis (H_1), which states that the treatment works as predicted. Also note that the equal sign goes in the null hypothesis, indicating *no difference* between the two treatment conditions. The idea of zero difference is the essence of the null hypothesis, and the numerical value of zero is used for ($\mu_1 - \mu_2$) during the calculation of the *t* statistic. For this test we use $\alpha = .01$.

STEP 2   Locate the critical region. For a directional test, the critical region is located entirely in one tail of the distribution. Rather than trying to determine which tail, positive or negative, is the correct location, we suggest that you identify the criteria for the critical region in a two-step process as follows. First, look at the data and determine whether the sample mean difference is in the direction that was predicted. If the answer is no, then the data obviously do not support the predicted treatment effect, and you can stop the analysis. On the other hand, if the difference is in the predicted direction, then the second step is to determine whether the difference is large enough to be significant. To test for significance, simply find the one-tailed critical value in the *t* distribution table. If the calculated *t* statistic is more extreme (either positive or negative) than the critical value, then the difference is significant.

For this example, the students who watched Sesame Street had higher grades, as predicted. With $df = 18$, the one-tailed critical value for $\alpha = .01$ is $t = 2.552$.

STEP 3   Collect the data and calculate the test statistic. The details of the calculations were shown in Example 10.1. The data produce a *t* statistic of $t = 4.00$.

STEP 4   Make a decision. The *t* statistic of $t = 4.00$ is well beyond the critical boundary of $t = 2.552$. Therefore, we reject the null hypothesis and conclude that grades for students who watched Sesame Street are significantly higher than grades for students who did not watch the program. In a research report, the one-tailed test would be clearly noted:

Grades were significantly higher for students who watched Sesame Street, $t(18) = 4.00$, $p < .01$, one tailed.

THE ROLE OF SAMPLE VARIANCE AND SAMPLE SIZE IN THE INDEPENDENT-MEASURES *t* TEST

In Chapter 9 (p. 259), we identified several factors that can influence the outcome of a hypothesis test. For the independent-measures *t*, the most obvious factor is the size of the difference between the two sample means. A larger mean difference increases the likelihood of rejecting the null hypothesis and increases measures of effect size. Two other factors that play important roles are the variability of the scores and the size of the samples. Both influence the magnitude of the estimated standard error in the denominator of the *t* statistic. Specifically, the standard error is directly related to sample variance (larger variance leads to larger error) and is inversely related to sample size (larger size leads to smaller error). As a result, larger variance produces a smaller value for the *t* statistic (closer to zero) and reduces the likelihood of finding a significant result. By contrast, a larger sample produces a larger value for the *t* statistic (farther from zero) and increases the likelihood of rejecting H_0.

Although variance and sample size both influence the hypothesis test, only variance has a large influence on measures of effect size such as Cohen's *d* and r^2; larger variance produces smaller measures of effect size. Sample size, on the other hand, has no effect on the value of Cohen's *d* and only a small influence on r^2.

The following example provides a visual demonstration of how large sample variance can obscure a mean difference between samples and lower the likelihood of rejecting H_0 for an independent-measures study.

EXAMPLE 10.5

We use the data in Figure 10.6 to demonstrate the influence of sample variance. The figure shows the results from a research study comparing two treatments. Notice that the study uses two separate samples, each with $n = 9$, and there is a 5-point mean difference between the two samples: $M = 8$ for treatment 1 and $M = 13$ for treatment 2. The frequency distribution in Figure 10.6 also shows a clear difference between the two distributions; the scores for treatment 2 are clearly higher than the scores for treatment 1.

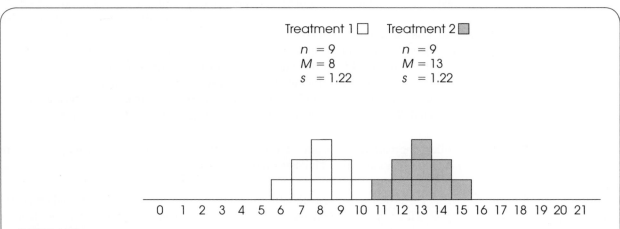

FIGURE 10.6

Two sample distributions representing two different treatments. These data show a significant difference between treatments, $t(16) = 8.62$, $p < .01$, and both measures of effect size indicate a very large treatment effect, $d = 4.10$ and $r^2 = 0.82$.

For the hypothesis test, the data produce a pooled variance of 1.50 and an estimated standard error of 0.58. The *t* statistic is

$$t = \frac{\text{mean difference}}{\text{estimated standard error}} = \frac{5}{0.58} = 8.62$$

With $df = 16$, this value is far into the critical region (for $\alpha = .05$ or $\alpha = .01$), so we reject the null hypothesis and conclude that there is a significant difference between the two treatments. These data also produce Cohen's $d = 4.10$ and $r^2 = 0.82$, both indicating a very large treatment effect.

Now consider the effect of increasing sample variance. Figure 10.7 shows the results from a second research study comparing two treatments. Notice that there are still $n = 9$ scores in each sample, and the two sample means are still $M = 8$ and $M = 13$. However, the sample variances have been greatly increased: Each sample now has $s^2 = 44.25$ as compared with $s^2 = 1.5$ for the data in Figure 10.7. Notice that the increased variance means that the scores are now spread out over a wider range, with the result that the two samples are mixed together without any clear distinction between them.

The absence of a clear difference between the two samples is supported by the hypothesis test. The pooled variance is 44.25, the estimated standard error is 3.14, and the independent-measures *t* statistic is

$$t = \frac{\text{mean difference}}{\text{estimated standard error}} = \frac{5}{3.14} = 1.59$$

With $df = 16$ and $\alpha = .05$, this value is not in the critical region. Therefore, we fail to reject the null hypothesis and conclude that there is no significant difference between the two treatments. Although there is still a 5-point difference between sample means (as in Figure 10.7), the 5-point difference is not significant with the increased variance. The measures of effect size are also substantially smaller. With the increased variance, Cohen's d is now 0.75 and $r^2 = 0.136$.

In general, large sample variance can obscure any mean differences that exist in the data, which reduces the likelihood of obtaining a significant difference in a hypothesis test and lowers measures of effect size.

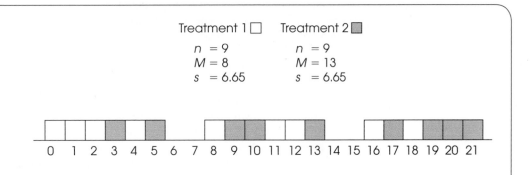

FIGURE 10.7

Two sample distributions representing two different treatments. These data show exactly the same mean difference as the scores in Figure 10.6; however, the variance has been greatly increased. With the increased variance, there is no longer a significant difference between treatments, $t(16) = 1.59$, $p > .05$, and both measures of effect size are substantially reduced, $d = 0.75$ and $r^2 = 0.14$.

10.4 ASSUMPTIONS UNDERLYING THE INDEPENDENT-MEASURES *t* FORMULA

There are three assumptions that should be satisfied before you use the independent-measures *t* formula for hypothesis testing:

1. The observations within each sample must be independent (see p. 220).

2. The two populations from which the samples are selected must be normal.

3. To justify using the pooled variance, the two populations from which the samples are selected must have equal variances.

The first two assumptions should be familiar from the single-sample *t* hypothesis test presented in Chapter 9. As before, the normality assumption is the less important of the two, especially with large samples. When there is reason to suspect that the populations are far from normal, you should compensate by ensuring that the samples are relatively large.

Remember: Adding a constant to (or subtracting a constant from) each score does not change the standard deviation.

The third assumption is referred to as *homogeneity of variance* and states that the two populations being compared must have the same variance. You may recall a similar assumption for the *z*-score hypothesis test in Chapter 8. For that test, we assumed that the effect of the treatment was to add a constant amount to (or subtract a constant amount from) each individual score. As a result, the population standard deviation after treatment was the same as it had been before treatment. We now are making essentially the same assumption, but phrasing it in terms of variances.

Recall that the pooled variance in the *t*-statistic formula is obtained by averaging together the two sample variances. It makes sense to average these two values only if they both are estimating the same population variance—that is, if the homogeneity of variance assumption is satisfied. If the two sample variances are estimating different population variances, then the average is meaningless. (*Note*: If two people are asked to estimate the same thing—for example, what you weigh—it is reasonable to average the two estimates. However, it is not meaningful to average estimates of two different things. If one person estimates your weight and another estimates the number of grapes in a pound, it is meaningless to average the two numbers.)

Homogeneity of variance is most important when there is a large discrepancy between the sample sizes. With equal (or nearly equal) sample sizes, this assumption is less critical, but still important. Violating the homogeneity of variance assumption can prevent any meaningful interpretation of the data from an independent-measures experiment. Specifically, when you compute the *t* statistic in a hypothesis test, all of the numbers in the formula come from the data except for the population mean difference, which you get from H_0. Thus, you are sure of all of the numbers in the formula except one. If you obtain an extreme result for the *t* statistic (a value in the critical region), then you conclude that the hypothesized value was wrong. But consider what happens when the homogeneity assumption is violated. In this case, you have two questionable values in the formula (the hypothesized population value and the meaningless average of the two variances). Now if you obtain an extreme *t* statistic, you do not know which of these two values is responsible. Specifically, you cannot reject the hypothesis because it may have been the pooled variance that produced the extreme *t* statistic. Without satisfying the homogeneity of variance requirement, you cannot accurately interpret a *t* statistic, and the hypothesis test becomes meaningless.

HARTLEY'S *F*-MAX TEST

How do you know whether the homogeneity of variance assumption is satisfied? One simple test involves just looking at the two sample variances. Logically, if the two population variances are equal, then the two sample variances should be very similar. When the two sample variances are reasonably close, you can be reasonably confident that the homogeneity assumption has been satisfied and proceed with the test. However, if one sample variance is more than three or four times larger than the other, then there is reason for concern. A more objective procedure involves a statistical test to evaluate the homogeneity assumption. Although there are many different statistical methods for determining whether the homogeneity of variance assumption has been satisfied, Hartley's *F*-max test is one of the simplest to compute and to understand. An additional advantage is that this test can also be used to check homogeneity of variance with more than two independent samples. Later, in Chapter 12, we examine statistical methods for comparing several different samples, and Hartley's test is useful again. The following example demonstrates the *F*-max test for two independent samples.

EXAMPLE 10.6   The *F*-max test is based on the principle that a sample variance provides an unbiased estimate of the population variance. The null hypothesis for this test states that the population variances are equal, therefore, the sample variances should be very similar. The procedure for using the *F*-max test is as follows:

1. Compute the sample variance, $s^2 = \dfrac{SS}{df}$, for each of the separate samples.

2. Select the largest and the smallest of these sample variances and compute

$$F\text{-max} = \frac{s^2\,(\text{largest})}{s^2\,(\text{smallest})}$$

   A relatively large value for *F*-max indicates a large difference between the sample variances. In this case, the data suggest that the population variances are different and that the homogeneity assumption has been violated. On the other hand, a small value of *F*-max (near 1.00) indicates that the sample variances are similar and that the homogeneity assumption is reasonable.

3. The *F*-max value computed for the sample data is compared with the critical value found in Table B.3 (Appendix B). If the sample value is larger than the table value, then you conclude that the variances are different and that the homogeneity assumption is not valid.

   To locate the critical value in the table, you need to know:

   a. *k* = number of separate samples. (For the independent-measures *t* test, *k* = 2.)

   b. $df = n - 1$ for each sample variance. The Hartley test assumes that all samples are the same size.

   c. The alpha level. The table provides critical values for $\alpha = .05$ and $\alpha = .01$. Generally a test for homogeneity would use the larger alpha level.

   Suppose, for example, that two independent samples each have *n* = 10 with sample variances of 12.34 and 9.15. For these data,

$$F\text{-max} = \frac{s^2\,(\text{largest})}{s^2\,(\text{smallest})} = \frac{12.34}{9.15} = 1.35$$

   With $\alpha = .05$, *k* = 2, and $df = n - 1 = 9$, the critical value from the table is 4.03. Because the obtained *F*-max is smaller than this critical value, you conclude that the data do not provide evidence that the homogeneity of variance assumption has been violated.

The goal for most hypothesis tests is to reject the null hypothesis to demonstrate a significant difference or a significant treatment effect. However, when testing for homogeneity of variance, the preferred outcome is to fail to reject H_0. Failing to reject H_0 with the *F*-max test means that there is no significant difference between the two population variances and the homogeneity assumption is satisfied. In this case, you may proceed with the independent-measures *t* test using pooled variance.

If the *F*-max test rejects the hypothesis of equal variances, or if you simply suspect that the homogeneity of variance assumption is not justified, you should not compute an independent-measures *t* statistic using pooled variance. However, there is an alternative procedure that does not pool the two sample variances and does not require the homogeneity assumption. The alternative is presented in Box 10.2.

BOX 10.2	**AN ALTERNATIVE TO POOLED VARIANCE**

Computing the independent-measures *t* statistic using pooled variance requires that the data satisfy the homogeneity of variance assumption. Specifically, the two distributions from which the samples are obtained must have equal variances. To avoid this assumption, many statisticians recommend an alternative formula for computing the independent-measures *t* statistic that does not require pooled variance or the homogeneity assumption. The alternative procedure consists of two steps.

1. The standard error is computed using the two separate sample variances as in Equation 10.1.
2. The value of degrees of freedom for the *t* statistic is adjusted using the following equation:

$$df = \frac{(V_1 + V_2)^2}{\dfrac{V_1^2}{n_1 - 1} + \dfrac{V_2^2}{n_2 - 1}} \quad \text{where } V_1 = \frac{s_1^2}{n_1} \text{ and } V_2 = \frac{s_2^2}{n_2}$$

Decimal values for *df* should be rounded down to the next lower integer.

The adjustment to degrees of freedom lowers the value of *df*, which pushes the boundaries for the critical region farther out. Thus, the adjustment makes the test more demanding and therefore corrects for the same bias problem that the pooled variance attempts to avoid.

Note: Many computer programs that perform statistical analysis (such as SPSS) report two versions of the independent-measures *t* statistic; one using pooled variance (with equal variances assumed) and one using the adjustment shown here (without the assumption of equal variances).

LEARNING CHECK	

1. A researcher is using an independent-measures design to evaluate the difference between two treatment conditions with $n = 8$ in each treatment. The first treatment produces $M = 63$ with a variance of $s^2 = 18$, and the second treatment has $M = 58$ with $s^2 = 14$.

   a. Use a one-tailed test with $\alpha = .05$ to determine whether the scores in the first treatment are significantly greater than the scores in the second. (*Note:* Because the two samples are the same size, the pooled variance is simply the average of the two sample variances.)

   b. Predict how the value for the *t* statistic would be affected if the two sample variances were increased to $s^2 = 68$ and $s^2 = 60$. Compute the new *t* to confirm your answer.

   c. Predict how the value for the *t* statistic for the original samples would be affected if each sample had $n = 32$ scores (instead of $n = 8$). Compute the new *t* to confirm your answer.

2. The homogeneity of variance assumption requires that the two sample variances be equal. (True or false?)

3. When you are using an F-max test to evaluate the homogeneity of variance assumption, you usually do not want to find a significant difference between the variances. (True or false?)

ANSWERS 1. **a.** The pooled variance is 16, the estimated standard error is 2, and $t(14) = 2.50$. With a one-tailed critical value of 1.761, reject the null hypothesis. Scores in the first treatment are significantly higher than scores in the second.

b. Increasing the variance should lower the value of t. The new pooled variance is 64, the estimated standard error is 4, and $t(14) = 1.25$.

c. Increasing the sample sizes should increase the value of t. The pooled variance is still 16, but the new standard error is 1, and $t(62) = 5.00$.

2. False. The assumption is that the two *population* variances are equal.

3. True. If there is a significant difference between the two variances, you cannot do the t test with pooled variance.

SUMMARY

1. The independent-measures t statistic uses the data from two separate samples to draw inferences about the mean difference between two populations or between two different treatment conditions.

2. The formula for the independent-measures t statistic has the same structure as the original z-score or the single-sample t:

$$t = \frac{\text{sample statistic} - \text{population parameter}}{\text{estimated standard error}}$$

For the independent-measures t, the sample statistic is the sample mean difference $(M_1 - M_2)$. The population parameter is the population mean difference $(\mu_1 - \mu_2)$. The estimated standard error for the sample mean difference is computed by combining the errors for the two sample means. The resulting formula is

$$t = \frac{(M_1 - M_2) - (\mu_1 - \mu_2)}{s_{(M_1 - M_2)}}$$

where the estimated standard error is

$$s_{(M_1 - M_2)} = \sqrt{\frac{s_p^2}{n_1} + \frac{s_p^2}{n_2}}$$

The pooled variance in the formula, s_p^2, is the weighted mean of the two sample variances:

$$s_p^2 = \frac{SS_1 + SS_2}{df_1 + df_2}$$

This t statistic has degrees of freedom determined by the sum of the df values for the two samples:

$$df = df_1 + df_2$$
$$= (n_1 - 1) + (n_2 - 1)$$

3. For hypothesis testing, the null hypothesis states that there is no difference between the two population means:

$$H_0: \mu_1 = \mu_2 \text{ or } \mu_1 - \mu_2 = 0$$

4. When a hypothesis test with an independent-measures t statistic indicates a significant difference, you should also compute a measure of the effect size. One measure of effect size is Cohen's d, which is a standardized measure of the mean difference. For the independent-measures t statistic, Cohen's d is estimated as follows:

$$\text{estimated } d = \frac{M_1 - M_2}{\sqrt{s_p^2}}$$

A second common measure of effect size is the percentage of variance accounted for by the treatment effect. This measure is identified by r^2 and is computed as

$$r^2 = \frac{t^2}{t^2 + df}$$

5. An alternative method for describing the size of the treatment effect is to construct a confidence interval for the population mean difference, $\mu_1 - \mu_2$. The confidence interval uses the independent-measures *t* equation, solved for the unknown mean difference:

$$\mu_1 - \mu_2 = M_1 - M_2 \pm ts_{(M_1 - M_2)}$$

First, select a level of confidence and then look up the corresponding *t* values. For example, for 95% confidence, use the range of *t* values that determine the middle 95% of the distribution. The *t* values are then used in the equation along with the values for the sample mean difference and the standard error, which are computed from the sample data.

6. Appropriate use and interpretation of the *t* statistic using pooled variance require that the data satisfy the homogeneity of variance assumption. This assumption stipulates that the two populations have equal variances. An informal test of the assumption can be made by verifying that the two sample variances are approximately equal. Hartley's *F*-max test provides a statistical technique for determining whether the data satisfy the homogeneity assumption. An alternative technique that avoids pooling variances and eliminates the need for the homogeneity assumption is presented in Box 10.2.

KEY TERMS

independent-measures research design (281)

between-subjects research design (281)

repeated-measures research design (281)

within-subjects research design (281)

independent-measures *t* statistic (282)

estimated standard error of $M_1 - M_2$ (283)

pooled variance (285)

homogeneity of variance (300)

RESOURCES

 Go to CengageBrain.com to access Psychology CourseMate, where you will find an interactive eBook, glossaries, flashcards, quizzes, statistics workshops, and more.

 aplia

If your professor has assigned Aplia:

1. Sign in to your account.
2. Complete the corresponding exercises as required by your professor.
3. When finished, click "Grade It Now" to see which areas you have mastered, which areas need more work, and detailed explanations of every answer.

SPSS

General instructions for using SPSS are presented in Appendix D. Following are detailed instructions for using SPSS to perform **The Independent-Measures *t* Test** presented in this chapter.

Data Entry

1. The scores are entered in what is called *stacked format*, which means that all of the scores from *both samples* are entered in one column of the data editor (probably

VAR00001). Enter the scores for sample #2 directly beneath the scores from sample #1 with no gaps or extra spaces.

2. Values are then entered into a second column (VAR00002) to identify the sample or treatment condition corresponding to each of the scores. For example, enter a 1 beside each score from sample #1 and enter a 2 beside each score from sample #2.

Data Analysis

1. Click **Analyze** on the tool bar, select **Compare Means,** and click on **Independent-Samples *t* Test.**
2. Highlight the column label for the set of scores (VAR0001) in the left box and click the arrow to move it into the **Test Variable(s)** box.
3. Highlight the label from the column containing the sample numbers (VAR0002) in the left box and click the arrow to move it into the **Group Variable** box.
4. Click on **Define Groups.**
5. Assuming that you used the numbers 1 and 2 to identify the two sets of scores, enter the values 1 and 2 into the appropriate group boxes.
6. Click **Continue.**
7. In addition to performing the hypothesis test, the program computes a confidence interval for the population mean difference. The confidence level is automatically set at 95%, but you can select **Options** to change the percentage.
8. Click **OK.**

SPSS Output

We used the SPSS program to analyze the data from the Sesame Street study in Example 10.1 and the program output is shown in Figure 10.8. The output includes a table of sample statistics with the mean, standard deviation, and standard error of the mean for each group. A second table, which is split into two sections in Figure 10.8, begins with the results of Levene's test for homogeneity of variance. This test should *not* be significant (you do not want the two variances to be different), so you want the reported Sig. value to be greater than .05. Next, the results of the independent-measures *t* test are presented using two different assumptions. The top row shows the outcome assuming equal variances, using the pooled variance to compute *t*. The second row does not assume equal variances and computes the *t* statistic using the alternative method presented in Box 10.2. Each row reports the calculated *t* value, the degrees of freedom, the level of significance (the *p* value for the test), the size of the mean difference, and the standard error for the mean difference (the denominator of the *t* statistic). Finally, the output includes a 95% confidence interval for the mean difference.

FOCUS ON PROBLEM SOLVING

1. As you learn more about different statistical methods, one basic problem is deciding which method is appropriate for a particular set of data. Fortunately, it is easy to identify situations in which the independent-measures *t* statistic is used. First, the data always consist of two separate samples (two *n*s, two *M*s,

Group Statistics

	VAR00002	N	Mean	Std. Deviation	Std. Error Mean
VAR00001	1.00	10	93.0000	4.71405	1.49071
	2.00	10	85.0000	4.21637	1.33333

Independent Samples Test

		Levene's Test for Equality of Variances		t-test for Equality of Means	
		F	Sig.	t	df
VAR00001	Equal variances assumed	.384	.543	4.000	18
	Equal variances not assumed			4.000	17.780

Independent Samples Test

		t-test for Equality of Means				
					95% Confidence Interval of the Difference	
		Sig. (2-tailed)	Mean Difference	Std. Error Difference	Lower	Upper
VAR00001	Equal variances assumed	.001	8.00000	2.00000	3.79816	12.20184
	Equal variances not assumed	.001	8.00000	2.00000	3.79443	12.20557

FIGURE 10.8

The SPSS output for the independent-measures hypothesis test in Example 10.1.

two *SS*s, and so on). Second, this *t* statistic is always used to answer questions about a mean difference: On the average, is one group different (better, faster, smarter) than the other group? If you examine the data and identify the type of question that a researcher is asking, you should be able to decide whether an independent-measures *t* is appropriate.

2. When computing an independent-measures *t* statistic from sample data, we suggest that you routinely divide the formula into separate stages rather than trying to do all of the calculations at once. First, find the pooled variance. Second, compute the standard error. Third, compute the *t* statistic.

3. One of the most common errors for students involves confusing the formulas for pooled variance and standard error. When computing pooled variance, you are "pooling" the two samples together into a single variance. This variance is computed as a *single fraction,* with two *SS* values in the numerator and two *df* values in the denominator. When computing the standard error, you are adding the error from the first sample and the error from the second sample. These two separate errors are added as *two separate fractions* under the square root symbol.

DEMONSTRATION 10.1

THE INDEPENDENT-MEASURES t TEST

In a study of jury behavior, two samples of participants were provided details about a trial in which the defendant was obviously guilty. Although group 2 received the same details as group 1, the second group was also told that some evidence had been withheld from the jury by the judge. Later, the participants were asked to recommend a jail sentence. The length of term suggested by each participant is presented here. Is there a significant difference between the two groups in their responses?

Group 1	Group 2
4	3
4	7
3	8
2	5
5	4
1	7
1	6
4	8

For Group 1: $M = 3$ and $SS = 16$

For Group 2: $M = 6$ and $SS = 24$

There are two separate samples in this study. Therefore, the analysis uses the independent-measures t test.

STEP 1 State the hypothesis, and select an alpha level.

$$H_0: \mu_1 - \mu_2 = 0 \qquad \text{(For the population, knowing that evidence has been withheld has no effect on the suggested sentence.)}$$

$$H_1: \mu_1 - \mu_2 \neq 0 \qquad \text{(For the population, knowing that evidence has been withheld has an effect on the jury's response.)}$$

We set the level of significance to $\alpha = .05$, two tails.

STEP 2 Identify the critical region.   For the independent-measures t statistic, degrees of freedom are determined by

$$df = df_1 + df_2$$
$$= 7 + 7$$
$$= 14$$

The t distribution table is consulted, for a two-tailed test with $\alpha = .05$ and $df = 14$. The critical t values are $+2.145$ and -2.145.

STEP 3 Compute the test statistic.   As usual, we recommend that the calculation of the t statistic be separated into three stages.

Pooled variance: For these data, the pooled variance equals

$$s_p^2 = \frac{SS_1 + SS_2}{df_1 + df_2} = \frac{16 + 24}{7 + 7} = \frac{40}{14} = 2.86$$

Estimated standard error: Now we can calculate the estimated standard error for mean differences.

$$s_{(M_1 - M_2)} = \sqrt{\frac{s_p^2}{n_1} + \frac{s_p^2}{n_2}} = \sqrt{\frac{2.86}{8} + \frac{2.86}{8}} = \sqrt{0.358 + 0.358} = \sqrt{0.716} = 0.85$$

The t statistic: Finally, the *t* statistic can be computed.

$$t = \frac{(M_1 - M_2) - (\mu_1 - \mu_2)}{s_{(M_1 - M_2)}} = \frac{(3-6) - 0}{0.85} = \frac{-3}{0.85} = -3.53$$

STEP 4   Make a decision about H_0, and state a conclusion.   The obtained *t* value of -3.53 falls in the critical region of the left tail (critical $t = \pm 2.145$). Therefore, the null hypothesis is rejected. The participants who were informed about the withheld evidence gave significantly longer sentences, $t(14) = -3.53$, $p < .05$, two tails.

DEMONSTRATION 10.2

EFFECT SIZE FOR THE INDEPENDENT-MEASURES *t*

We compute Cohen's *d* and r^2 for the jury decision data in Demonstration 10.1. For these data, the two sample means are $M_1 = 3$ and $M_2 = 6$, and the pooled variance is 2.86. Therefore, our estimate of Cohen's *d* is

$$\text{estimated } d = \frac{M_1 - M_2}{\sqrt{s_p^2}} = \frac{3-6}{\sqrt{2.86}} = \frac{3}{1.69} = 1.78$$

With a *t* value of $t = 3.53$ and $df = 14$, the percentage of variance accounted for is

$$r^2 = \frac{t^2}{t^2 + df} = \frac{(3.53)^2}{(3.53)^2 + 14} = \frac{12.46}{26.46} = 0.47 \text{ (or 47\%)}$$

PROBLEMS

1. Describe the basic characteristics of an independent-measures, or a between-subjects, research study.

2. Describe what is measured by the estimated standard error in the bottom of the independent-measures *t* statistic.

3. If other factors are held constant, explain how each of the following influences the value of the independent-measures *t* statistic and the likelihood of rejecting the null hypothesis:
   a. An increase in the mean difference between the samples.
   b. An increase in the number of scores in each sample.
   c. An increase in the variance for each sample.

4. Describe the homogeneity of variance assumption and explain why it is important for the independent-measures *t* test.

5. One sample has $SS = 36$ and a second sample has $SS = 18$.
   a. If $n = 4$ for both samples, find each of the sample variances and compute the pooled variance. Because the samples are the same size, you should find that the pooled variance is exactly halfway between the two sample variances.
   b. Now assume that $n = 4$ for the first sample and $n = 7$ for the second. Again, calculate the two sample variances and the pooled variance. You should find that the pooled variance is closer to the variance for the larger sample.

6. One sample has $SS = 70$ and a second sample has $SS = 42$.
   a. If $n = 8$ for both samples, find each of the sample variances, and calculate the pooled variance. Because the samples are the same size, you should find that the pooled variance is exactly halfway between the two sample variances.
   b. Now assume that $n = 8$ for the first sample and $n = 4$ for the second. Again, calculate the two sample variances and the pooled variance. You should find that the pooled variance is closer to the variance for the larger sample.

7. As noted on page 283, when the two population means are equal, the estimated standard error for the independent-measures t test provides a measure of how much difference to expect between two sample means. For each of the following situations, assume that $\mu_1 = \mu_2$ and calculate how much difference should be expected between the two sample means.
   a. One sample has $n = 6$ scores with $SS = 75$, and the second sample has $n = 10$ scores with $SS = 135$.
   b. One sample has $n = 6$ scores with $SS = 310$, and the second sample has $n = 10$ scores with $SS = 530$.
   c. In part b, the samples have larger variability (bigger SS values) than in part a, but the sample sizes are unchanged. How does larger variability affect the magnitude of the standard error for the sample mean difference?

8. Two samples are selected from the same population. For each of the following, calculate how much difference is expected, on average, between the two sample means.
   a. One sample has $n = 4$, the second has $n = 6$, and the pooled variance is 60.
   b. One sample has $n = 12$, the second has $n = 15$, and the pooled variance is 60.
   c. In part b, the sample sizes are larger, but the pooled variance is unchanged. How does larger sample size affect the magnitude of the standard error for the sample mean difference?

9. Two separate samples, each with $n = 15$ individuals, receive different treatments. After treatment, the first sample has $SS = 1740$ and the second has $SS = 1620$.
   a. Find the pooled variance for the two samples.
   b. Compute the estimated standard error for the sample mean difference.
   c. If the sample mean difference is 8 points, is this enough to reject the null hypothesis and conclude that there is a significant difference for a two-tailed test at the .05 level?

10. Two separate samples receive different treatments. After treatment, the first sample has $n = 9$ with $SS = 462$, and the second has $n = 7$ with $SS = 420$.
    a. Compute the pooled variance for the two samples.
    b. Calculate the estimated standard error for the sample mean difference.
    c. If the sample mean difference is 10 points, is this enough to reject the null hypothesis using a two-tailed test with $\alpha = .05$?

11. For each of the following, assume that the two samples are obtained from populations with the same mean, and calculate how much difference should be expected, on average, between the two sample means.
    a. Each sample has $n = 4$ scores with $s^2 = 68$ for the first sample and $s^2 = 76$ for the second. (*Note:* Because the two samples are the same size, the pooled variance is equal to the average of the two sample variances.)
    b. Each sample has $n = 16$ scores with $s^2 = 68$ for the first sample and $s^2 = 76$ for the second.
    c. In part b, the two samples are bigger than in part a, but the variances are unchanged. How does sample size affect the size of the standard error for the sample mean difference?

12. For each of the following, calculate the pooled variance and the estimated standard error for the sample mean difference.
    a. The first sample has $n = 4$ scores and a variance of $s^2 = 55$, and the second sample has $n = 6$ scores and a variance of $s^2 = 63$.
    b. Now the sample variances are increased so that the first sample has $n = 4$ scores and a variance of $s^2 = 220$, and the second sample has $n = 6$ scores and a variance of $s^2 = 252$.
    c. Comparing your answers for parts a and b, how does increased variance influence the size of the estimated standard error?

13. A researcher conducts an independent-measures study comparing two treatments and reports the t statistic as $t(25) = 2.071$.
    a. How many individuals participated in the entire study?
    b. Using a two-tailed test with $\alpha = .05$, is there a significant difference between the two treatments?
    c. Compute r^2 to measure the percentage of variance accounted for by the treatment effect.

14. In a recent study, Piff, Kraus, Côté, Cheng, and Keitner (2010) found that people from lower social economic classes tend to display greater prosocial behavior than their higher class counterparts. In one part of the study, participants played a game with an anonymous partner. Part of the game involved sharing points with the partner. The lower economic class participants were significantly more generous with their points compared with the upper class individuals. Results similar to those found in the study, show that $n = 12$ lower class participants shared an average of $M = 5.2$ points with

$SS = 11.91$, compared to an average of $M = 4.3$ with $SS = 9.21$ for the $n = 12$ upper class participants.

a. Are the data sufficient to conclude that there is a significant mean difference between the two economic populations? Use a two-tailed test with $\alpha = .05$.

b. Construct an 80% confidence interval to estimate the size of the population mean difference.

15. Hallam, Price, and Katsarou (2002) investigated the influence of background noise on classroom performance for children aged 10 to 12. In one part of the study, calming music led to better performance on an arithmetic task compared to a no-music condition. Suppose that a researcher selects one class of $n = 18$ students who listen to calming music each day while working on arithmetic problems. A second class of $n = 18$ serves as a control group with no music. Accuracy scores are measured for each child and the average for students in the music condition is $M = 86.4$ with $SS = 1550$ compared to an average of $M = 78.8$ with $SS = 1204$ for students in the no-music condition.

a. Is there a significant difference between the two music conditions? Use a two-tailed test with $\alpha = .05$.

b. Compute the 90% confidence interval for the population mean difference.

c. Write a sentence demonstrating how the results from the hypothesis test and the confidence interval would appear in a research report.

16. It appears that there is some truth to the old adage "That which doesn't kill us makes us stronger." Seery, Holman, and Silver (2010) found that individuals with some history of adversity report better mental health and higher well-being compared to people with little or no history of adversity. In an attempt to examine this phenomenon, a researcher surveys a group of college students to determine the negative life events that they experienced in the past 5 years and their current feeling of well-being. For $n = 18$ participants with 2 or fewer negative experiences, the average well-being score is $M = 42$ with $SS = 398$, and for $n = 16$ participants with 5 to 10 negative experiences the average score is $M = 48.6$ with $SS = 370$.

a. Is there a significant difference between the two populations represented by these two samples? Use a two-tailed test with $\alpha = .01$.

b. Compute Cohen's d to measure the size of the effect.

c. Write a sentence demonstrating how the outcome of the hypothesis test and the measure of effect size would appear in a research report.

17. Does posting calorie content for menu items affect people's choices in fast food restaurants? According to results obtained by Elbel, Gyamfi, and Kersh (2011), the answer is no. The researchers monitored the calorie content of food purchases for children and adolescents in four large fast food chains before and after mandatory labeling began in New York City. Although most of the adolescents reported noticing the calorie labels, apparently the labels had no effect on their choices. Data similar to the results obtained show an average of $M = 786$ calories per meal with $s = 85$ for $n = 100$ children and adolescents before the labeling, compared to an average of $M = 772$ calories with $s = 91$ for a similar sample of $n = 100$ after the mandatory posting.

a. Use a two-tailed test with $\alpha = .05$ to determine whether the mean number of calories after the posting is significantly different than before calorie content was posted.

b. Calculate r^2 to measure effect size for the mean difference.

18. In 1974, Loftus and Palmer conducted a classic study demonstrating how the language used to ask a question can influence eyewitness memory. In the study, college students watched a film of an automobile accident and then were asked questions about what they saw. One group was asked, "About how fast were the cars going when they smashed into each other?" Another group was asked the same question except the verb was changed to "hit" instead of "smashed into." The "smashed into" group reported significantly higher estimates of speed than the "hit" group. Suppose a researcher repeats this study with a sample of today's college students and obtains the following results.

Estimated Speed	
Smashed into	*Hit*
$n = 15$	$n = 15$
$M = 40.8$	$M = 34.0$
$SS = 510$	$SS = 414$

a. Do the results indicate a significantly higher estimated speed for the "smashed into" group? Use a one-tailed test with $\alpha = .01$.

b. Compute the estimated value for Cohen's d to measure the size of the effect.

c. Write a sentence demonstrating how the results of the hypothesis test and the measure of effect size would appear in a research report.

19. Numerous studies have found that males report higher self-esteem than females, especially for adolescents (Kling, Hyde, Showers, & Buswell, 1999). Typical results show a mean self-esteem score of $M = 39.0$ with $SS = 60.2$ for a sample of $n = 10$ male adolescents and a mean of $M = 35.4$ with $SS = 69.4$ for a sample of $n = 10$ female adolescents.

a. Do the results indicate that self-esteem is significantly higher for males? Use a one-tailed test with $\alpha = .01$.

b. Use the data to make a 95% confidence interval estimate of the mean difference in self-esteem between male and female adolescents.

c. Write a sentence demonstrating how the results from the hypothesis test and the confidence interval would appear in a research report.

20. Recent research has shown that creative people are more likely to cheat than their less creative counterparts (Gino & Ariely, 2010). Participants in the study first completed creativity assessment questionnaires and then returned to the lab several days later for a series of tasks. One task was a multiple-choice general knowledge test for which the participants circled their answers on the test sheet. Afterward, they were asked to transfer their answers to a bubble sheets for computer scoring. However, the experimenter admitted that the wrong bubble sheet had been copied so that the correct answers were still faintly visible. Thus, the participants had an opportunity to cheat and inflate their test scores. Higher scores were valuable because participants were paid based on the number of correct answers. However, the researchers had secretly coded the original tests and the bubble sheets so that they could measure the degree of cheating for each participant. Assuming that the participants were divided into two groups based on their creativity scores, the following data are similar to the cheating scores obtained in the study.

High Creativity Participants	Low Creativity Participants
$N = 27$	$N = 27$
$M = 7.41$	$M = 4.78$
$SS = 749.5$	$SS = 830$

a. Use a one-tailed test with $\alpha = .05$ to determine whether these data are sufficient to conclude that high creativity people are more likely to cheat than people with lower levels of creativity.

b. Compute Cohen's d to measure the size of the effect.

c. Write a sentence demonstrating how the results from the hypothesis test and the measure of effect size would appear in a research report.

21. When people learn a new task, their performance usually improves when they are tested the next day, but only if they get at least 6 hours of sleep (Stickgold, Whidbee, Schirmer, Patel, & Hobson, 2000). The following data demonstrate this phenomenon. The participants learned a visual discrimination task on one day, and then were tested on the task the following day. Half of the participants were allowed to have at least 6 hours of sleep and the other half were kept awake all night. Is there a significant difference between the two conditions? Use a two-tailed test with $\alpha = .05$.

Performance Scores	
6 Hours Sleep	*No Sleep*
$n = 14$	$n = 14$
$M = 72$	$M = 65$
$SS = 932$	$SS = 706$

22. Recent research has demonstrated that music-based physical training for elderly people can improve balance and walking efficiency and reduce the risk of falls (Trombetti et al., 2011). As part of the training, participants walked in time to music and responded to changes in the music's rhythm during a 1-hour per week exercise program. After 6 months, participants in the training group increased their walking speed and their stride length compared to individuals in the control group. The following data are similar to the results obtained in the study.

Exercise Group Stride Length				*Control Group Stride Length*			
24	25	22	24	26	23	20	23
26	17	21	22	20	16	21	17
22	19	24	23	18	23	16	20
23	28	25	23	25	19	17	16

Do the results indicate a significant difference in the stride length for the two groups? Use a two-tailed test with $\alpha = .05$.

23. Downs and Abwender (2002) evaluated soccer players and swimmers to determine whether the routine blows to the head experienced by soccer players produced long-term neurological deficits. In the study, neurological tests were administered to mature soccer players and swimmers and the results indicated significant differences. In a similar study, a researcher obtained the following data.

Swimmers	*Soccer players*
10	7
8	4
7	9
9	3
13	7
7	
6	
12	

a. Are the neurological test scores significantly lower for the soccer players than for the swimmers in the control group? Use a one-tailed test with $\alpha = .05$.

b. Compute the value of r^2 (percentage of variance accounted for) for these data.

24. Research has shown that people are more likely to show dishonest and self-interested behaviors in darkness than in a well-lit environment (Zhong, Bohns, & Gino, 2010). In one experiment, participants were given a set of 20 puzzles and were paid $0.50 for each one solved in a 5-minute period. However, the participants reported their own performance and there was no obvious method for checking their honesty. Thus, the task provided a clear opportunity to cheat and receive undeserved money. One group of participants was tested in a room with dimmed lighting and a second group was tested in a well-lit room. The reported number of solved puzzles was recorded for each individual. The following data represent results similar to those obtained in the study.

Well-Lit Room	Dimly-Lit Room
7	9
8	11
10	13
6	10
8	11
5	9
7	15
12	14
5	10

a. Is there a significant difference in reported performance between the two conditions? Use a two-tailed test with $\alpha = .01$.

b. Compute Cohen's d to estimate the size of the treatment effect.

CHAPTER

11

The *t* Test for Two Related Samples

Tools You Will Need
The following items are considered essential background material for this chapter. If you doubt your knowledge of any of these items, you should review the appropriate chapter or section before proceeding.

- Introduction to the *t* statistic (Chapter 9)
  - Estimated standard error
  - Degrees of freedom
  - *t* Distribution
  - Hypothesis tests with the *t* statistic

- Independent-measures design (Chapter 10)

aplia

Aplia for *Essentials of Statistics for the Behavioral Sciences*
After reading, go to "Resources" at the end of this chapter for an introduction on how to use Aplia's homework and learning resources.

11.1 INTRODUCTION TO REPEATED-MEASURES DESIGNS

In the previous chapter, we introduced the independent-measures research design as one strategy for comparing two treatment conditions or two populations. The independent-measures design is characterized by the fact that two separate samples are used to obtain the two sets of scores that are to be compared. In this chapter, we examine an alternative strategy known as a *repeated-measures design,* or a *within-subjects design.* With a repeated-measures design, two separate scores are obtained for each individual in the sample. For example, a group of patients could be measured before therapy and then measured again after therapy. Or, response time could be measured in a driving simulation task for a group of individuals who are first tested when they are sober and then tested again after two alcoholic drinks. In each case, the same variable is being measured twice for the same set of individuals; that is, we are literally repeating measurements on the same sample.

DEFINITION

> A **repeated-measures design,** or a **within-subject design,** is one in which the dependent variable is measured two or more times for each individual in a single sample. The same group of subjects is used in all of the treatment conditions.

The main advantage of a repeated-measures study is that it uses exactly the same individuals in all treatment conditions. Thus, there is no risk that the participants in one treatment are substantially different from the participants in another. With an independent-measures design, on the other hand, there is always a risk that the results are biased because the individuals in one sample are systematically different (smarter, faster, more extroverted, and so on) than the individuals in the other sample. At the end of this chapter, we present a more detailed comparison of repeated-measures studies and independent-measures studies, considering the advantages and disadvantages of both types of research.

THE MATCHED-SUBJECTS DESIGN

Occasionally, researchers try to approximate the advantages of a repeated-measures design by using a technique known as *matched subjects.* A matched-subjects design involves two separate samples, but each individual in one sample is matched one-to-one with an individual in the other sample. Typically, the individuals are matched on one or more variables that are considered to be especially important for the study. For example, a researcher studying verbal learning might want to be certain that the two samples are matched in terms of IQ and gender. In this case, a male participant with an IQ of 120 in one sample would be matched with another male with an IQ of 120 in the other sample. Although the participants in one sample are not *identical* to the participants in the other sample, the matched-subjects design at least ensures that the two samples are equivalent (or matched) with respect to some specific variables.

DEFINITION

> In a **matched-subjects design,** each individual in one sample is matched with an individual in the other sample. The matching is done so that the two individuals are equivalent (or nearly equivalent) with respect to a specific variable that the researcher would like to control.

Of course, it is possible to match participants on more than one variable. For example, a researcher could match pairs of subjects on age, gender, race, and IQ. In this case, for example, a 22-year-old white female with an IQ of 115 who was in one sample would be matched with another 22-year-old white female with an IQ of 115 in the second sample. The more variables that are used, however, the more difficult it is to find matching pairs. The goal of the matching process is to simulate a repeated-measures design as closely as possible. In a repeated-measures design, the matching is perfect because the same individual is used in both conditions. In a matched-subjects design, however, the best you can get is a degree of match that is limited to the variable(s) that are used for the matching process.

In a repeated-measures design or a matched-subjects design comparing two treatment conditions, the data consist of two sets of scores, which are grouped into sets of two, corresponding to the two scores obtained for each individual or each matched pair of subjects (Table 11.1). Because the scores in one set are directly related, one-to-one, with the scores in the second set, the two research designs are statistically equivalent and share the common name *related-samples* designs (or correlated-samples designs). In this chapter, we focus our discussion on repeated-measures designs because they are overwhelmingly the more common example of related-samples designs. However, you should realize that the statistical techniques used for repeated-measures studies also can be applied directly to data from matched-subjects studies. We should also note that a matched-subjects study occasionally is called a *matched samples design*, but the subjects in the samples must be matched one-to-one before you can use the statistical techniques in this chapter.

Now we examine the statistical techniques that allow a researcher to use the sample data from a repeated-measures study to draw inferences about the general population.

TABLE 11.1

An example of the data from a repeated-measures or a matched-subjects study using $n = 5$ participants (or matched pairs).

Participant or Matched Pair	First Score	Second Score	
#1	12	15	←The 2 scores for
#2	10	14	one participant or
#3	15	17	one matched pair
#4	17	17	
#5	12	18	

11.2 THE *t* STATISTIC FOR A REPEATED-MEASURES RESEARCH DESIGN

The *t* statistic for a repeated-measures design is structurally similar to the other *t* statistics we have examined. As we shall see, it is essentially the same as the single-sample *t* statistic covered in Chapter 9. The major distinction of the related-samples *t* is that it is based on *difference scores* rather than raw scores (*X* values). In this section, we examine difference scores and develop the *t* statistic for related samples.

DIFFERENCE SCORES: THE DATA FOR A REPEATED-MEASURES STUDY

Many over-the-counter cold medications include the warning "may cause drowsiness." Table 11.2 shows an example of data from a study that examines this phenomenon. Note that there is one sample of $n = 4$ participants, and that each individual is measured twice. The first score for each person (X_1) is a measurement of reaction time before the medication was administered. The second score (X_2) measures reaction time 1 hour after taking the medication. Because we are interested in how the medication affects reaction time, we have computed the difference between the first score and the second score for each individual. The *difference scores,* or *D* values, are shown in the last column of the table. Notice that the difference scores measure the amount of change in reaction time for each person. Typically, the difference scores are obtained by subtracting the first score (before treatment) from the second score (after treatment) for each person:

$$\text{difference score} = D = X_2 - X_1 \tag{11.1}$$

TABLE 11.2

Reaction-time measurements taken before and after taking an over-the-counter cold medication.

Person	Before Medication (X_1)	After Medication (X_2)	Difference D
A	215	210	−5
B	221	242	21
C	196	219	23
D	203	228	25

Note that M_D is the mean for the sample of D scores.

$$\Sigma D = 64$$

$$M_D = \frac{\Sigma D}{n} = \frac{64}{4} = 16$$

Note that the sign of each D score tells you the direction of the change. Person A, for example, shows a decrease in reaction time after taking the medication (a negative change), but person B shows an increase (a positive change).

The sample of difference scores (D values) serves as the sample data for the hypothesis test and all calculations are done using the D scores. To compute the t statistic, for example, we use the number of D scores (n) as well as the sample mean (M_D) and the value of SS for the sample of D scores.

THE HYPOTHESES FOR A RELATED-SAMPLES STUDY

The researcher's goal is to use the sample of difference scores to answer questions about the general population. In particular, the researcher would like to know whether there is any difference between the two treatment conditions for the general population. Note that we are interested in a population of *difference scores*. That is, we would like to know what would happen if every individual in the population were measured in two treatment conditions (X_1 and X_2) and a difference score (D) were computed for everyone. Specifically, we are interested in the mean for the population of difference scores. We identify this population mean difference with the symbol μ_D (using the subscript letter D to indicate that we are dealing with D values rather than X scores).

As always, the null hypothesis states that, for the general population, there is no effect, no change, or no difference. For a repeated-measures study, the null hypothesis states that the mean difference for the general population is zero. In symbols,

$$H_0: \mu_D = 0$$

Again, this hypothesis refers to the mean for the entire population of difference scores. Figure 11.1(a) shows an example of a population of difference scores with a mean of $\mu_D = 0$. Although the population mean is zero, the individual scores in the population are not all equal to zero. Thus, even when the null hypothesis is true, we still expect some individuals to have positive difference scores and some to have negative difference scores. However, the positives and negatives are unsystematic and in the long run balance out to $\mu_D = 0$. Also note that a sample selected from this population probably will not have a mean exactly equal to zero. As always, there will be some error between a sample mean and the population mean, so even if $\mu_D = 0$ (H_0 is true), we do not expect M_D to be exactly equal to zero.

The alternative hypothesis states that there is a treatment effect that causes the scores in one treatment condition to be systematically higher (or lower) than the scores in the other condition. In symbols,

$$H_1: \mu_D \neq 0$$

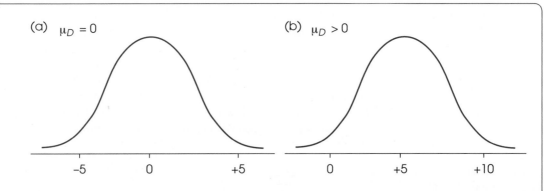

FIGURE 11.1

(a) A population of difference scores for which the mean is $\mu_D = 0$. Note that the typical difference score (*D* value) is not equal to zero. (b) A population of difference scores for which the mean is greater than zero. Note that most of the difference scores are also greater than zero.

According to H_1, the difference scores for the individuals in the population tend to be systematically positive (or negative), indicating a consistent, predictable difference between the two treatments.

Figure 11.1(b) shows an example of a population of difference scores with a positive mean difference, $\mu_D > 0$. This time, most of the individuals in the population have difference scores that are greater than zero. A sample selected from this population will contain primarily positive difference scores and will probably have a mean difference that is greater than zero, $M_D > 0$. See Box 11.1 for further discussion of H_0 and H_1.

BOX 11.1

ANALOGIES FOR H_0 AND H_1 IN THE REPEATED-MEASURES TEST

An Analogy for H_0: Intelligence is a fairly stable characteristic; that is, you do not get noticeably smarter or dumber from one day to the next. However, if we gave you an IQ test every day for a week, we probably would get seven different numbers. The day-to-day changes in your IQ score are caused by random factors such as your health, your mood, and your luck at guessing answers you do not know. Some days your IQ score is slightly higher, and some days it is slightly lower. On average, the day-to-day changes in IQ should balance out to zero. This is the situation that is predicted by the null hypothesis for a repeated-measures test. According to H_0, any changes that occur either for an individual or for a sample are just due to chance, and in the long run, they will average out to zero.

An Analogy for H_1: On the other hand, suppose that we evaluate your performance on a new video game by measuring your score every day for a week. Again, we probably will find small differences in your scores from one day to the next, just as we did with the IQ scores. However, the day-to-day changes in your game score will not be random. Instead, there should be a general trend toward higher scores as you gain more experience with the new game. Thus, most of the day-to-day changes should show an increase. This is the situation that is predicted by the alternative hypothesis for the repeated-measures test. According to H_1, the changes that occur are systematic and predictable and will not average out to zero.

THE *t* STATISTIC FOR RELATED SAMPLES

Figure 11.2 shows the general situation that exists for a repeated-measures hypothesis test. You may recognize that we are facing essentially the same situation that we encountered in Chapter 9. In particular, we have a population for which the mean and the standard deviation are unknown, and we have a sample that will be used to test a hypothesis about the unknown population. In Chapter 9, we introduced the single-sample *t* statistic, which allowed us to use a sample mean as a basis for testing hypotheses about an unknown population mean. This *t*-statistic formula is used again here to develop the repeated-measures *t* test. To refresh your memory, the single-sample *t* statistic (Chapter 9) is defined by the formula

As noted earlier, the repeated-measures *t* formula is also used for matched-subjects designs.

$$t = \frac{M - \mu}{s_M}$$

In this formula, the sample mean, *M*, is calculated from the data, and the value for the population mean, μ, is obtained from the null hypothesis. The estimated standard error, s_M, is also calculated from the data and provides a measure of how much difference it is reasonable to expect between a sample mean and the population mean if there is no treatment effect.

For the repeated-measures design, the sample data are difference scores and are identified by the letter *D*, rather than *X*. Therefore, we modify the *t* formula by adding *D*s to emphasize that we are dealing with difference scores instead of *X* values. Specifically, we are using the mean for a sample of difference scores, M_D, to test a hypothesis about the mean for the population of difference

---

FIGURE 11.2

A sample of $n = 4$ people is selected from the population. Each individual is measured twice, once in treatment I and once in treatment II, and a difference score, *D*, is computed for each individual. This sample of difference scores is intended to represent the population. Note that we are using a sample of difference scores to represent a population of difference scores. Also note that the mean for the population of difference scores is unknown. The null hypothesis states that, for the general population, there is no consistent or systematic difference between the two treatments, so the population mean difference is $\mu_D = 0$.

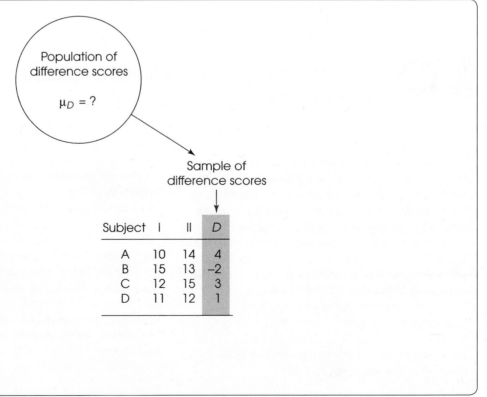

scores μ_D. With this simple change, the t formula for the repeated-measures design becomes

$$t = \frac{M_D - \mu_D}{s_{M_D}}$$

(11.2)

In this formula, the *estimated standard error for* M_D, s_{M_D}, is computed in exactly the same way as it is computed for the single-sample t statistic. The first step is to compute the variance (or the standard deviation) for the sample of D scores.

$$s^2 = \frac{SS}{n-1} = \frac{SS}{df} \qquad \text{or} \qquad s = \sqrt{\frac{SS}{df}}$$

The estimated standard error is then computed using the sample variance (or sample standard deviation) and the sample size, n.

$$s_{M_D} = \sqrt{\frac{s^2}{n}} \qquad \text{or} \qquad s_{M_D} = \frac{s}{\sqrt{n}}$$

(11.3)

Notice that all of the calculations are done using the difference scores (the D scores) and that there is only one D score for each subject. With a sample of n subjects, there are exactly n D scores, and the t statistic has $df = n - 1$. Remember that n refers to the number of D scores, not the number of X scores in the original data.

You should also note that the *repeated-measures* t *statistic* is conceptually similar to the t statistics that we have previously examined:

$$t = \frac{\text{sample statistic} - \text{population parameter}}{\text{estimated standard error}}$$

In this case, the sample data are represented by the sample mean of the difference scores (M_D), the population parameter is the value predicted by H_0 ($\mu_D = 0$), and the estimated standard error is computed from the sample data using Equation 11.3.

LEARNING CHECK

1. For the following data from a repeated-measures study, find the difference scores and compute the sample mean difference, the variance for the difference scores, and the standard error for the sample mean difference.

Participant	Treatment 1	Treatment 2
A	5	8
B	6	13
C	7	10
D	9	12

2. If the sample in the previous problem were being used to test for a significant difference between the two treatments, state the null hypothesis in words and in symbols.

ANSWERS

1. The difference scores are 3, 7, 3, and 3. The mean difference is $M_D = 4$ with $SS = 12$, $s^2 = 4$ and the standard error for the sample mean difference is 1 point.

2. The null hypothesis states that, for the general population, the average difference between the two treatments is zero. In symbols, $\mu_D = 0$.

11.3 HYPOTHESIS TESTS AND EFFECT SIZE FOR THE REPEATED-MEASURES DESIGN

In a repeated-measures study, each individual is measured in two different treatment conditions and we are interested in whether there is a systematic difference between the scores in the first treatment condition and the scores in the second treatment condition. A difference score (D value) is computed for each person and the hypothesis test uses the difference scores from the sample to evaluate the overall mean difference, μ_D, for the entire population. The hypothesis test with the repeated-measures t statistic follows the same four-step process that we have used for other tests. The complete hypothesis-testing procedure is demonstrated in Example 11.1.

EXAMPLE 11.1

Swearing is a common, almost reflexive, response to pain. Whether you knock your shin into the edge of a coffee table or smash your thumb with a hammer, most of us respond with a streak of obscenities. One question, however, is whether swearing focuses attention on the pain and, thereby, increases its intensity, or serves as a distraction that reduces pain. To address this issue, Stephens, Atkins, and Kingston (2009) conducted an experiment comparing swearing with other responses to pain. In the study, participants were asked to place one hand in icy cold water for as long as they could bear the pain. Half of the participants were told to repeat their favorite swear word over and over for as long as their hands were in the water. The other half repeated a neutral word. The researchers recorded how long each participant was able to tolerate the ice water. After a brief rest, the two groups switched words and repeated the ice water plunge. Thus, all the participants experienced both conditions (swearing and neutral) with half swearing on their first plunge and half on their second. The results clearly showed that swearing significantly increased pain tolerance and decreased the perceived level of pain. The data in Table 11.3 are representative of the results obtained in the study and represented the reports of pain level of $n = 9$ participants.

STEP 1 State the hypotheses, and select the alpha level.

$H_0: \mu_D = 0$ (There is no difference between the two conditions.)

$H_1: \mu_D \neq 0$ (There is a difference.)

For this test, we use $\alpha = .05$.

TABLE 11.3

Ratings of pain level on a scale from 1 to 10 for participants who were swearing or repeating a neutral word.

Participant	Neutral Word	Swearing	D	D²
A	9	7	−2	4
B	8	7	−1	1
C	7	3	−4	16
D	7	8	+1	1
E	8	6	−2	4
F	9	4	−5	25
G	7	6	−1	1
H	7	7	0	0
I	8	4	−4	16

$$\sum D = -18 \qquad \sum D^2 = 68$$

$$M_D = \frac{-18}{9} = -2 \quad SS = \sum D^2 - \frac{(\sum D)^2}{N} = 68 - \frac{(-18)^2}{9} = 68 - 36 = 32$$

STEP 2 Locate the critical region. For this example, $n = 9$, so the t statistic has $df = n - 1 = 8$. For $\alpha = .01$, the critical value listed in the t distribution table is ± 2.306. The critical region is shown in Figure 11.3.

STEP 3 Calculate the t statistic. Table 11.3 shows the sample data and the calculations of $M_D = -2$ and $SS = 32$. Note that all calculations are done with the difference scores. As we have done with the other t statistics, we present the calculation of the t statistic as a three-step process.

First, compute the sample variance

$$s^2 = \frac{SS}{n-1} = \frac{32}{8} = 4$$

Next, use the sample variance to compute the estimated standard error.

$$s_{M_D} = \sqrt{\frac{s^2}{n}} = \sqrt{\frac{4}{9}} = 0.667$$

Finally, use the sample mean (M_D) and the hypothesized population mean (μ_D) along with the estimated standard error to compute the value for the t statistic.

$$t = \frac{M_D - \mu_D}{s_{M_D}} = \frac{-2 - 0}{0.667} = -3.00$$

STEP 4 Make a decision. The t value we obtained falls in the critical region (see Figure 11.3). The researcher rejects the null hypothesis and concludes that cursing, as opposed to repeating a neutral work, has a significant effect on pain perception.

MEASURING EFFECT SIZE FOR THE REPEATED-MEASURES t

As we noted with other hypothesis tests, whenever a treatment effect is found to be statistically significant, it is recommended that you also report a measure of the absolute magnitude of the effect. The most commonly used measures of effect size are Cohen's d and r^2, the percentage of variance accounted for. The size of the treatment effect also can be described with a confidence interval estimating the population mean difference, μ_D. Using the data from Example 11.1, we demonstrate how these values are calculated to measure and describe effect size.

FIGURE 11.3

The critical region for the t distribution with $df = 8$ and $\alpha = .05$.

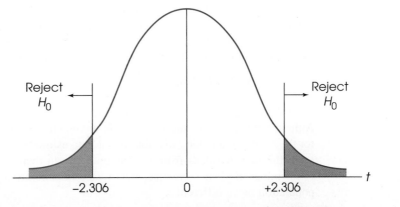

Cohen's *d* In Chapters 8 and 9, we introduced Cohen's *d* as a standardized measure of the mean difference between treatments. The standardization simply divides the population mean difference by the standard deviation. For a repeated-measures study, Cohen's *d* is defined as

$$d = \frac{\text{population mean difference}}{\text{standard deviation}} = \frac{\mu_D}{\mu_D}$$

Because we are measuring the size of the effect and not the direction, it is customary to ignore the minus sign and report Cohen's *d* as a positive value.

Because the population mean and standard deviation are unknown, we use the sample values instead. The sample mean, M_D, is the best estimate of the actual mean difference, and the sample standard deviation (square root of sample variance) provides the best estimate of the actual standard deviation. Thus, we are able to estimate the value of *d* as follows:

$$\text{estimated } d = \frac{\text{sample mean difference}}{\text{sample mean deviation}} = \frac{M_D}{s} \tag{11.4}$$

For the repeated-measures study in Example 11.1, $M_D = -2$ and the sample variance is $s^2 = 4.00$, so the data produce

$$\text{estimated } d = \frac{M_D}{s} = \frac{-2}{\sqrt{4.00}} = \frac{-2}{2} = -1.00$$

Any value greater than 0.8 is considered to be a large effect, and these data are clearly in that category (see Table 8.2 on p. 232).

The percentage of variance accounted for, r^2 Percentage of variance is computed using the obtained *t* value and the *df* value from the hypothesis test, exactly as was done for the single-sample *t* (see p. 263) and for the independent-measures *t* (see p. 292). For the data in Example 11.1, we obtain

$$r^2 = \frac{t^2}{t^2 + df} = \frac{(3.00)^2}{(3.00)^2 + 8} = \frac{9}{17} = 0.529 \text{ or } 52.9\%$$

For these data, 52.9% of the variance in the scores is explained by the effect of cursing. More specifically, swearing caused the estimated pain ratings to be consistently negative. Thus, the deviations from zero are largely explained by the treatment.

Confidence intervals for estimating μ_D As noted in the previous two chapters, it is possible to compute a confidence interval as an alternative method for measuring and describing the size of the treatment effect. For the repeated-measures *t*, we use a sample mean difference, M_D, to estimate the population mean difference, μ_D. In this case, the confidence interval literally estimates the size of the treatment effect by estimating the population mean difference between the two treatment conditions.

As with the other *t* statistics, the first step is to solve the *t* equation for the unknown parameter. For the repeated-measures *t* statistic, we obtain

$$\mu_D = M_D \pm t s_{M_D} \tag{11.5}$$

In the equation, the values for M_D and for s_{M_D} are obtained from the sample data. Although the value for the *t* statistic is unknown, we can use the degrees of freedom for the *t* statistic and the *t* distribution table to estimate the *t* value. Using the estimated *t* and the known values from the sample, we can then compute the value of μ_D. The following example demonstrates the process of constructing a confidence interval for a population mean difference.

EXAMPLE 11.2   In Example 11.1, we presented a research study demonstrating how swearing influenced the perception of pain. In the study, a sample of $n = 9$ participants rated their level of pain significantly lower when they were repeating a swear word than when they repeated a neutral word. The mean difference between treatments was $M_D = -2$ points and the estimated standard error for the mean difference was $s_{M_D} = 0.667$. Now, we construct a 95% confidence interval to estimate the size of the population mean difference.

With a sample of $n = 9$ participants, the repeated-measures t statistic has $df = 8$. To have 95% confidence, we simply estimate that the t statistic for the sample mean difference is located somewhere in the middle 95% of all the possible t values. According to the t distribution table, with $df = 8$, 95% of the t values are located between $t = +2.306$ and $t = -2.306$. Using these values in the estimation equation, together with the values for the sample mean and the standard error, we obtain

$$\mu_D = M_D \pm t s_{M_D}$$

$$= -2 \pm 2.306(0.667)$$

$$= -2 \pm 1.538$$

This produces an interval of values ranging from $-2 - 1.538 = -3.538$ to $-2 + 1.538 = -0.462$. Our conclusion is that for the general population, swearing instead of repeating a neutral word decreases the perceived pain between 0.462 and 3.538 points. We are 95% confident that the true mean difference is in this interval because the only value estimated during the calculations was the t statistic, and we are 95% confident that the t value is located in the middle 95% of the distribution. Finally, note that the confidence interval is constructed around the sample mean difference. As a result, the sample mean difference, $M_D = -2$ points, is located exactly in the center of the interval.

As with the other confidence intervals presented in Chapters 9 and 10, the confidence interval for a repeated-measures t is influenced by a variety of factors other than the actual size of the treatment effect. In particular, the width of the interval depends on the percentage of confidence used, so that a larger percentage produces a wider interval. Also, the width of the interval depends on the sample size, so that a larger sample produces a narrower interval. Because the interval width is related to sample size, the confidence interval is not a pure measure of effect size like Cohen's d or r^2.

Finally, we should note that the 95% confidence interval computed in Example 11.2 does not include the value $\mu_D = 0$. In other words, we are 95% confident that the population mean difference is not $\mu_D = 0$. This is equivalent to concluding that a null hypothesis specifying that $\mu_D = 0$ would be rejected with a test using $\alpha = .05$. If $\mu_D = 0$ were included in the 95% confidence interval, it would indicate that a hypothesis test would fail to reject H_0 with $\alpha = .05$.

LEARNING CHECK

1. A researcher is investigating the effect of a treatment by measuring performance for a sample of $n = 9$ participants before and after they receive the treatment. For this sample, performance scores increased after treatment by an average of $M = 1.9$ points with $SS = 200$.

   a. Are the data sufficient to conclude that treatment has a significant effect on performance? Use a two-tailed test with $\alpha = .05$.

   b. Compute the effect size for the treatment using both Cohen's d and r^2.

   c. Compute the 90% confidence for the population mean difference.

ANSWERS **1. a.** The null hypothesis states that the treatment has no effect, $\mu_D = 0$. The sample variance is 25, the standard error is 1.67 and $t(8) = 1.14$. With $df = 24$, the critical value is $t = 2.064$. Reject the null hypothesis and conclude that the treatment has a significant effect.

b. Cohen's $d = \frac{1.9}{5} = 0.38$ and $r^2 = \frac{10.05}{34.10} = 0.295$.

c. For 90% confidence, use $t = \pm 1.711$. The interval is $\mu_D = 1.9 \pm 1.711(0.6)$ and extends from 0.87 to 2.93.

IN THE LITERATURE
REPORTING THE RESULTS OF A REPEATED-MEASURES *t* TEST

As we have seen in Chapters 9 and 10, the APA format for reporting the results of *t* tests consists of a concise statement that incorporates the *t* value, degrees of freedom, and alpha level. One typically includes values for means and standard deviations, either in a statement or a table (Chapter 4). For Example 11.1, we observed a mean difference of $M_D = -2.00$ with $s = 2.00$. Also, we obtained a *t* statistic of $t = -3.00$ with $df = 8$, and our decision was to reject the null hypothesis at the .05 level of significance. Finally, we measured effect size by computing the percentage of variance explained and obtained $r^2 = 0.529$. A published report of this study might summarize the results as follows:

> Changing from a neutral word to a swear word reduced the perceived level of pain by an average of $M = 2.00$ points with $SD = 2.00$. The treatment effect was statistically significant, $t(8) = -3.00$, $p < .05$, $r^2 = 0.529$.

When the hypothesis test is conducted with a computer program, the printout typically includes an exact probability for the level of significance. The *p*-value from the printout is then stated as the level of significance in the research report. For example, the data from Example 11.1 produced a significance level of $p = .017$, and the results would be reported as "statistically significant, $t(8) = -3.00$, $p = .017$, $r^2 = 0.529$." Occasionally, a probability is so small that the computer rounds it off to 3 decimal points and produces a value of zero. In this situation you do not know the exact probability value and should report $p < .001$.

If the confidence interval from Example 11.2 is reported as a description of effect size together with the results from the hypothesis test, it would appear as follows:

> Changing from a neutral word to a swear word reduced the perceived level of pain, $t(8) = -3.00$, $p < .05$, 95% CI [–0.462, –3.538].

DESCRIPTIVE STATISTICS AND THE HYPOTHESIS TEST

Often, a close look at the sample data from a research study makes it easier to see the size of the treatment effect and to understand the outcome of the hypothesis test. In Example 11.1, we obtained a sample of $n = 9$ participants who produce a mean difference of $M_D = -2.00$ with a standard deviation of $s = 2.00$ points. The sample mean and standard deviation describe a set of scores centered at $M_D = -2.00$ with most of the scores located within 2.00 points of the mean. Figure 11.4 shows the actual set of difference scores that were obtained in Example 11.1. In addition to showing the scores in the sample, we have highlighted the position of $\mu_D = 0$; that is, the value specified in the null hypothesis. Notice that the scores in the sample are displaced away from zero. Specifically, the data are not consistent with a population mean of $\mu_D = 0$, which is why we rejected the null hypothesis. In addition, note that the sample mean is located 1 standard deviation below zero. This distance corresponds to the effect size measured by Cohen's $d = -1.00$. For these data, the picture of the sample distribution (see Figure 11.4) should help you to understand the measure of effect size and the outcome of the hypothesis test.

FIGURE 11.4

The sample of difference scores from Example 11.1. The mean is $M_D = -2$ and the standard deviation is $s = 2$. The difference scores are consistently negative, indicating a decrease in perceived pain, suggest that $\mu_D = 0$ (no effect) is not a reasonable hypothesis.

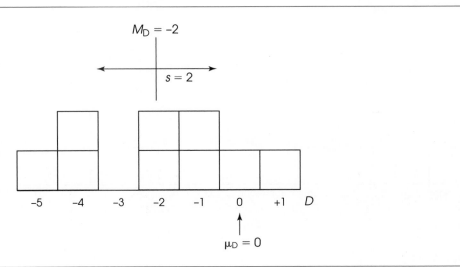

SAMPLE VARIANCE AND SAMPLE SIZE IN THE REPEATED-MEASURES *t* TEST

In Chapters 9 and 10 (p. 259 and 298), we identified several factors that can influence the outcome of a hypothesis test with the *t* statistic. The same factors apply to the repeated-measures *t*. The most obvious factor is the size of the sample mean difference. A larger mean difference increases the likelihood of rejecting the null hypothesis and increases measures of effect size. The two other factors are the variability of the scores and the size of the sample, which both influence the magnitude of the estimated standard error in the denominator of the *t* statistic. Specifically, the standard error is inversely related to sample size (larger size leads to smaller error) and is directly related to sample variance (larger variance leads to larger error). As a result, a larger sample produces a larger value for the *t* statistic (farther from zero) and increases the likelihood of rejecting H_0. Larger variance, on the other hand, produces a smaller value for the *t* statistic (closer to zero) and reduces the likelihood of finding a significant result.

Although variance and sample size both influence the hypothesis test, only variance has a large influence on measures of effect size such as Cohen's *d* and r^2; larger variance produces smaller measures of effect size. Sample size, on the other hand, has no effect on the value of Cohen's *d* and only a small influence on r^2.

VARIABILITY AS A MEASURE OF CONSISTENCY FOR THE TREATMENT EFFECT

In a repeated-measures study, the variability of the difference scores becomes a relatively concrete and easy-to-understand concept. In particular, the sample variability describes the *consistency* of the treatment effect. For example, if a treatment consistently adds a few points to each individual's score, then the set of difference scores are clustered together with relatively small variability. This is the situation that we observed in Example 11.1 (see Figure 11.4) in which nearly all of the participants had lower ratings of pain in the swearing condition. In this situation, with small variability, it is easy to see the treatment effect and it is likely to be significant.

Now consider what happens when the variability is large. Suppose that the swearing study in Example 11.1 produced a sample of $n = 9$ difference scores consisting of -11, -10, -7, -2, 0, 0, $+3$, $+4$, and $+5$. These difference scores also have a mean of $M_D = -2.00$, but now the variability is substantially increased so that $SS = 288$ and the standard deviation is $s = 6.00$. Figure 11.5 shows the new set of difference scores. Again, we have highlighted the position of $\mu_D = 0$, which is the value specified in the null hypothesis. Notice that the high variability means that there is no consistent

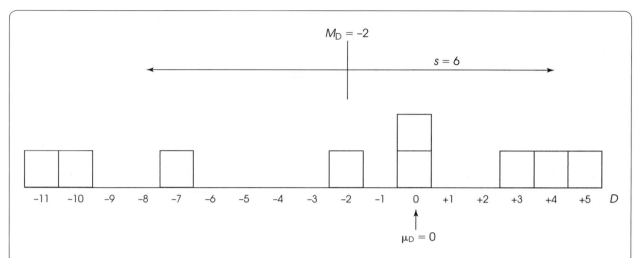

FIGURE 11.5

A sample of difference scores with a mean of $M_D = -2$ and a standard deviation of $s = 6$. The data do not show a consistent increase or decrease in scores. Because there is no consistent treatment effect, $\mu_D = 0$ is a reasonable hypothesis.

treatment effect. Some participants rate the pain higher while swearing (the positive differences) and some rate it lower (the negative differences). In the hypothesis test, the high variability increases the size of the estimated standard error and results in a hypothesis test that produces $t = 1.50$, which is not in the critical region. With these data, we would fail to reject the null hypothesis and conclude that swearing has no effect on the perceived level of pain.

With small variability (see Figure 11.4), the 2-point treatment effect is easy to see and is statistically significant. With large variability (see Figure 11.5), the 2-point effect is not easy to see and is not significant. As we have noted several times in the past, large variability can obscure patterns in the data and reduces the likelihood of finding a significant treatment effect.

DIRECTIONAL HYPOTHESIS AND ONE-TAILED TESTS

In many repeated-measures and matched-subjects studies, the researcher has a specific prediction concerning the direction of the treatment effect. For example, in the study described in Example 11.1, the researcher expects the level of perceived pain to be rated lower when the participant is cursing. This kind of directional prediction can be incorporated into the statement of the hypotheses, resulting in a directional, or one-tailed, hypothesis test. The following example demonstrates how the hypotheses and critical region are determined for a directional test.

EXAMPLE 11.3

We reexamine the experiment presented in Example 11.1. The researcher is using a repeated-measures design to investigate the effect of swearing on perceived pain. The researcher predicts that the pain ratings for the ice water will decrease when the participants are swearing compared to repeating a neutral word.

STEP 1

State the hypotheses and select the alpha level. For this example, the researcher predicts that pain ratings will decrease when the participants are swearing. The null hypothesis, on the other hand, says that the pain ratings will not decrease but rather will be unchanged or even increased with the swearing. In symbols,

$$H_0: \mu_D \geq 0 \text{ (There is no decrease with swearing.)}$$

The alternative hypothesis says that the treatment does work. For this example, H_1 says that swearing will decrease the pain ratings.

$$H_1: \mu_D < 0 \text{ (The ratings are decreased.)}$$

We use $\alpha = .01$.

STEP 2 Locate the critical region. As we demonstrated with the independent-measures t statistic (p. 297), the critical region for a one-tailed test can be located using a two-stage process. Rather than trying to determine which tail of the distribution contains the critical region, you first look at the sample mean difference to verify that it is in the predicted direction. If not, then the treatment clearly did not work as expected and you can stop the test. If the change is in the correct direction, then the question is whether it is large enough to be significant. For this example, change is in the predicted direction (the researcher predicted lower ratings and the sample mean shows a decrease). With $n = 9$, we obtain $df = 8$ and a critical value of $t = 2.896$ for a one-tailed test with $\alpha = .01$. Thus, any t statistic beyond 2.896 (positive or negative) is sufficient to reject the null hypothesis.

STEP 3 Compute the t statistic. We calculated the t statistic in Example 11.1 and obtained $t = -3.00$.

STEP 4 Make a decision. The obtained t statistic is beyond the critical boundary. Therefore, we reject the null hypothesis and conclude that swearing significantly reduced the pain ratings. In a research report, the use of a one-tailed test would be clearly noted as follows:

> Swearing, compared to repeating a neutral word, significantly decreased the pain ratings, $t(8) = -3.00$, $p < .01$, one tailed.

LEARNING CHECK

1. A researcher is investigating the effectiveness of acupuncture treatment for chronic back pain. A sample of $n = 4$ participants is obtained from a pain clinic. Each individual ranks the current level of pain and then begins a 6-week program of acupuncture treatment. At the end of the program, the pain level is rated again and the researcher records the amount of difference between the two ratings. For this sample, pain level decreased by an average of $M = 4.5$ points with $SS = 27$.

   a. Are the data sufficient to conclude that acupuncture has a significant effect on back pain? Use a two-tailed test with $\alpha = .05$.

   b. Can you conclude that acupuncture significantly reduces back pain? Use a one-tailed test with $\alpha = .05$.

2. Compute the effect size using both Cohen's d and r^2 acupuncture study in the previous question.

3. A computer printout for a repeated-measures t test reports a p value of $p = .021$.

   a. Can the researcher claim a significant effect with $\alpha = .01$?

   b. Is the effect significant with $\alpha = .05$?

ANSWERS **1. a.** For these data, the sample variance is 9, the standard error is 1.50, and $t = 3.00$. With $df = 3$, the critical values are $t = \pm3.182$. Fail to reject the null hypothesis.

b. For a one-tailed test, the critical value is $t = 2.353$. Reject the null hypothesis and conclude that acupuncture treatment significantly reduces pain.

2. $d = 4.5/3 = 1.50$ and $r^2 = 9/12 = 0.75$.

3. a. The exact *p* value, $p = .021$, is not less than $\alpha = .01$. Therefore, the effect is not significant for $\alpha = .01$ $(p > .01)$.

b. The *p* value is less than .05, so the effect is significant with $\alpha = .05$.

USES AND ASSUMPTIONS FOR REPEATED-MEASURES *t* TESTS

REPEATED-MEASURES VERSUS INDEPENDENT-MEASURES DESIGNS

In many research situations, it is possible to use either a repeated-measures design or an independent-measures design to compare two treatment conditions. The independent-measures design would use two separate samples (one in each treatment condition) and the repeated-measures design would use only one sample with the same individuals participating in both treatments. The decision about which design to use is often made by considering the advantages and disadvantages of the two designs. In general, the repeated-measures design has most of the advantages.

Number of subjects   A repeated-measures design typically requires fewer subjects than an independent-measures design. The repeated-measures design uses the subjects more efficiently because each individual is measured in both of the treatment conditions. This can be especially important when there are relatively few subjects available (for example, when you are studying a rare species or individuals in a rare profession).

Study changes over time   The repeated-measures design is especially well suited for studying learning, development, or other changes that take place over time. Remember that this design involves measuring individuals at one time and then returning to measure the same individuals at a later time. In this way, a researcher can observe behaviors that change or develop over time.

Individual differences   The primary advantage of a repeated-measures design is that it reduces or eliminates problems caused by individual differences. *Individual differences* are characteristics such as age, IQ, gender, and personality that vary from one individual to another. These individual differences can influence the scores obtained in a research study, and they can affect the outcome of a hypothesis test. Consider the data in Table 11.4. The first set of data represents the results from a typical independent-measures study, and the second set represents a repeated-measures study. Note that we have identified each participant by name to help demonstrate the effects of individual differences.

For the independent-measures data, note that every score represents a different person. For the repeated-measures study, on the other hand, the same participants are measured in both of the treatment conditions. This difference between the two designs has some important consequences.

1. We have constructed the data so that both research studies have exactly the same scores and they both show the same 5-point mean difference between treatments. In each case, the researcher would like to conclude that the 5-point difference

TABLE 11.4

Hypothetical data showing the results from an independent-measures study and a repeated-measures study. The two sets of data use exactly the same numerical scores and they both show the same 5-point mean difference between treatments.

Independent-Measures Study (2 Separate Samples)		Repeated-Measures Study (Same Sample in Both Treatments)		
Treatment 1	*Treatment 2*	*Treatment 1*	*Treatment 2*	*D*
(John) $X = 18$	(Sue) $X = 15$	(John) $X = 18$	(John) $X = 15$	-3
(Mary) $X = 27$	(Tom) $X = 20$	(Mary) $X = 27$	(Mary) $X = 20$	-7
(Bill) $X = 33$	(Dave) $X = 28$	(Bill) $X = 33$	(Bill) $X = 28$	-5
$M = 26$	$M = 21$			$M_D = -5$
$SS = 114$	$SS = 86$			$SS = 8$

was caused by the treatments. However, with the independent-measures design, there is always the possibility that the participants in treatment 1 have different characteristics than those in treatment 2. For example, the three participants in treatment 1 may be more intelligent than those in treatment 2 and their higher intelligence caused them to have higher scores. Note that this problem disappears with the repeated-measures design. Specifically, with repeated measures there is no possibility that the participants in one treatment are different from those in another treatment because the same participants are used in all of the treatments.

2. Although the two sets of data contain exactly the same scores and have exactly the same 5-point mean difference, you should realize that they are very different in terms of the variance used to compute standard error. For the independent-measures study, you calculate the *SS* or variance for the scores in each of the two separate samples. Note that in each sample there are big differences between participants. In treatment 1, for example, Bill has a score of 33 and John's score is only 18. These individual differences produce a relatively large sample variance and a large standard error. For the independent-measures study, the standard error is 5.77, which produces a *t* statistic of $t = 0.87$. For these data, the hypothesis test concludes that there is no significant difference between treatments.

In the repeated-measures study, the *SS* and variance are computed for the difference scores. If you examine the repeated-measures data in Table 11.4, you will see that the big differences between John and Bill that exist in treatment 1 and in treatment 2 are eliminated when you get to the difference scores. Because the individual differences are eliminated, the variance and standard error are dramatically reduced. For the repeated-measures study, the standard error is 1.15 and the *t* statistic is $t = -4.35$. With the repeated-measures *t*, the data show a significant difference between treatments. Thus, one big advantage of a repeated-measures study is that it reduces variance by removing individual differences, which increases the chances of finding a significant result.

TIME-RELATED FACTORS AND ORDER EFFECTS

The primary disadvantage of a repeated-measures design is that the structure of the design allows for factors other than the treatment effect to cause a participant's score to change from one treatment to the next. Specifically, in a repeated-measures design, each individual is measured in two different treatment conditions, usually *at two different times*. In this situation, outside factors that change over time may be responsible for changes in the participants' scores. For example, a participant's health or mood may change over time and cause a difference in the participant's scores. Outside factors such as the weather can also change and may have an influence on participants' scores. Because a repeated-measures study typically takes place over time, it is possible that time-related factors (other than the two treatments) are responsible for causing changes in the participants' scores.

Also, it is possible that participation in the first treatment influences the individual's score in the second treatment. If the researcher is measuring individual performance, for example, the participants may gain experience during the first treatment condition, and this extra practice may help their performance in the second condition. In this situation, the researcher would find a mean difference between the two conditions; however, the difference would not be caused by the treatments, instead it would be caused by practice effects. Changes in scores that are caused by participation in an earlier treatment are called *order effects* and can distort the mean differences found in repeated-measures research studies.

Counterbalancing   One way to deal with time-related factors and order effects is to counterbalance the order of presentation of treatments. That is, the participants are randomly divided into two groups, with one group receiving treatment 1 followed by treatment 2, and the other group receiving treatment 2 followed by treatment 1. The goal of counterbalancing is to distribute any outside effects evenly over the two treatments. For example, if practice effects are a problem, then half of the participants gain experience in treatment 1, which then helps their performance in treatment 2. However, the other half gain experience in treatment 2, which helps their performance in treatment 1. Thus, prior experience helps the two treatments equally.

Finally, if there is reason to expect strong time-related effects or strong order effects, your best strategy is not to use a repeated-measures design. Instead, use independent-measures (or a matched-subjects design) so that each individual participates in only one treatment and is measured only one time.

ASSUMPTIONS OF THE RELATED-SAMPLES *t* TEST

The related-samples *t* statistic requires two basic assumptions:

1. The observations within each treatment condition must be independent (see p. 220). Notice that the assumption of independence refers to the scores *within* each treatment. Inside each treatment, the scores are obtained from different individuals and should be independent of one another.

2. The population distribution of difference scores (*D* values) must be normal. As before, the normality assumption is not a cause for concern unless the sample size is relatively small. In the case of severe departures from normality, the validity of the *t* test may be compromised with small samples. However, with relatively large samples ($n > 30$), this assumption can be ignored.

LEARNING CHECK

1. What are the basic assumptions underlying a hypothesis test with the repeated-measures *t*?

2. A repeated-measures study and an independent-measures study are used to compare two treatments and both use a total of 20 participants. What are the *df* values for the two *t* tests?

3. Compared to an independent-measures study, a repeated-measures study tends to have less variance and a greater likelihood of detecting a treatment effect. (True or false?)

ANSWERS

1. The observations within a treatment are independent. The population distribution of *D* scores is assumed to be normal.

2. The repeated-measures *t* has $df = 19$ and the independent-measures *t* has $df = 18$.

3. True

SUMMARY

1. In a related-samples research study, the individuals in one treatment condition are directly related, one-to-one, with the individuals in the other treatment condition(s). The most common related-samples study is a repeated-measures design, in which the same sample of individuals is tested in all of the treatment conditions. This design literally repeats measurements on the same subjects. An alternative is a matched-subjects design, in which the individuals in one sample are matched one-to-one with individuals in another sample. The matching is based on a variable relevant to the study.

2. The repeated-measures t test begins by computing a difference between the first and second measurements for each subject (or the difference for each matched pair). The difference scores, or D scores, are obtained by

$$D = X_2 - X_1$$

The sample mean, M_D, and sample variance, s^2, are used to summarize and describe the set of difference scores.

3. The formula for the repeated-measures t statistic is

$$t = \frac{M_D - \mu_D}{s_{M_D}}$$

In the formula, the null hypothesis specifies $\mu_D = 0$, and the estimated standard error is computed by

$$s_{M_D} = \sqrt{\frac{s^2}{n}}$$

4. A repeated-measures design may be preferred to an independent-measures study when one wants to observe changes in behavior in the same subjects, as in learning or developmental studies. An important advantage of the repeated-measures design is that it removes or reduces individual differences, which lowers sample variability and tends to increase the chances for obtaining a significant result.

5. For a repeated-measures design, effect size can be measured using either r^2 (the percentage of variance accounted for) or Cohen's d (the standardized mean difference). The value of r^2 is computed the same way for both independent- and repeated-measures designs.

$$r^2 = \frac{t^2}{t^2 + df}$$

Cohen's d is defined as the sample mean difference divided by standard deviation for both repeated- and independent-measures designs. For repeated-measures studies, Cohen's d is estimated as

$$\text{estimated } d = \frac{M_D}{s}$$

6. An alternative method for describing the size of the treatment effect is to construct a confidence interval for the population mean difference, μ_D. The confidence interval uses the repeated-measures t equation, solved for the unknown mean difference:

$$\mu_D = M_D \pm t s_{M_D}$$

First, select a level of confidence and then look up the corresponding t values. For example, for 95% confidence, use the range of t values that determine the middle 95% of the distribution. The t values are then used in the equation along with the values for the sample mean difference and the standard error, which are computed from the sample data.

KEY TERMS

repeated-measures design (314)

within-subjects design (314)

matched-subjects design (314)

related-samples design (315)

difference scores (315)

estimated standard error for M_D (319)

repeated-measures t statistic (319)

individual differences (328)

order effects (330)

RESOURCES

Go to CengageBrain.com to access Psychology CourseMate, where you will find an interactive eBook, glossaries, flashcards, quizzes, statistics workshops, and more.

If your professor has assigned Aplia:

1. Sign in to your account.
2. Complete the corresponding exercises as required by your professor.
3. When finished, click "Grade It Now" to see which areas you have mastered, which areas need more work, and detailed explanations of every answer.

SPSS

General instructions for using SPSS are presented in Appendix D. Following are detailed instructions for using SPSS to perform **The Repeated-Measures *t* Test** presented in this chapter.

Data Entry

Enter the data into two columns (VAR0001 and VAR0002) in the data editor with the first score for each participant in the first column and the second score in the second column. The two scores for each participant must be in the same row.

Data Analysis

1. Click **Analyze** on the tool bar, select **Compare Means**, and click on **Paired-Samples T Test.**

2. One at a time, highlight the column labels for the two data columns and click the arrow to move them into the **Paired Variables** box.

3. In addition to performing the hypothesis test, the program computes a confidence interval for the population mean difference. The confidence level is automatically set at 95%, but you can select **Options** and change the percentage.

4. Click **OK.**

SPSS Output

We used the SPSS program to analyze the data from the swearing experiment in Example 11.1 and the program output is shown in Figure 11.6. The output includes a table of sample statistics with the mean and standard deviation for each treatment. A second table shows the correlation between the two sets of scores (correlations are presented in Chapter 14). The final table, which is split into two sections in Figure 11.6, shows the results of the hypothesis test, including the mean and standard deviation for the difference scores, the standard error for the mean, a 95% confidence interval for the mean difference, and the values for *t*, *df*, and the level of significance (the *p* value for the test).

FOCUS ON PROBLEM SOLVING

1. Once data have been collected, we must then select the appropriate statistical analysis. How can you tell whether the data call for a repeated-measures

Paired Samples Statistics

		Mean	N	Std. Deviation	Std. Error Mean
Pair 1	VAR00001	7.7778	9	.83333	.27778
	VAR00002	5.7778	9	1.71594	.57198

Paired Samples Correlations

		N	Correlation	Sig.
Pair 1	VAR00001 & VAR00002	9	−.126	.746

Paired Samples Test

		Paired Differences		
		Mean	Std. Deviation	Std. Error Mean
Pair 1	VAR00001 - VAR00002	2.00000	2.00000	.66667

Paired Samples Test

		Paired Differences				
		95% Confidence Interval of the Difference				
		Lower	Upper	t	df	Sig. (2-tailed)
Pair 1	VAR00001 - VAR00002	.46266	3.53734	3.000	8	.017

FIGURE 11.6

The SPSS output for the repeated-measures hypothesis test in Example 11.1.

t test? Look at the experiment carefully. Is there only one sample of subjects? Are the same subjects tested a second time? If your answers are yes to both of these questions, then a repeated-measures t test should be done. There is only one situation in which the repeated-measures t can be used for data from two samples, and that is for *matched-subjects* studies (p. 314).

2. The repeated-measures t test is based on difference scores. In finding difference scores, be sure that you are consistent with your method. That is, you may use either $X_2 - X_1$ or $X_1 - X_2$ to find D scores, but you must use the same method for all subjects.

DEMONSTRATION 11.1

A REPEATED-MEASURES t TEST

A major oil company would like to improve its tarnished image following a large oil spill. Its marketing department develops a short television commercial and tests it on a sample of $n = 7$ participants. People's attitudes about the company are measured with a short questionnaire, both before and after viewing the commercial. The data are as follows:

Person	X_1 (Before)	X_2 (After)	D (Difference)	
A	15	15	0	
B	11	13	+2	$\Sigma D = 21$
C	10	18	+8	
D	11	12	+1	$M_D = \frac{21}{7} = 3.00$
E	14	16	+2	
F	10	10	0	$SS = 74$
G	11	19	+8	

Was there a significant change? Note that participants are being tested twice—once before and once after viewing the commercial. Therefore, we have a repeated-measures design.

STEP 1 State the hypotheses, and select an alpha level.   The null hypothesis states that the commercial has no effect on people's attitude, or, in symbols,

$H_0: \mu_D = 0$ (The mean difference is zero.)

The alternative hypothesis states that the commercial does alter attitudes about the company, or

$H_1: \mu_D \neq 0$ (There is a mean change in attitudes.)

For this demonstration, we use an alpha level of .05 for a two-tailed test.

STEP 2 Locate the critical region.   Degrees of freedom for the repeated-measures *t* test are obtained by the formula

$df = n - 1$

For these data, degrees of freedom equal

$df = 7 - 1 = 6$

The *t* distribution table is consulted for a two-tailed test with $\alpha = .05$ for $df = 6$. The critical *t* values for the critical region are $t = \pm 2.447$.

STEP 3 Compute the test statistic.   Once again, we suggest that the calculation of the *t* statistic be divided into a three-part process.

Variance for the D scores: The variance for the sample of D scores is

$$s^2 = \frac{SS}{n-1} = \frac{74}{6} = 12.33$$

Estimated standard error for M_D: The estimated standard error for the sample mean difference is computed as follows:

$$s_{M_D} = \sqrt{\frac{s^2}{n}} = \sqrt{\frac{12.33}{7}} = \sqrt{1.76} = 1.33$$

The repeated-measures t statistic: Now we have the information required to calculate the t statistic.

$$t = \frac{M_D - \mu_D}{s_{M_D}} = \frac{3 - 0}{1.33} = 2.26$$

STEP 4 Make a decision about H_0, and state the conclusion.   The obtained t value is not extreme enough to fall in the critical region. Therefore, we fail to reject the null hypothesis. We conclude that there is not enough evidence to conclude that the commercial changes people's attitudes, $t(6) = 2.26$, $p > .05$, two-tailed. (Note that we state that p is *greater than* .05 because we failed to reject H_0.)

DEMONSTRATION 11.2

EFFECT SIZE FOR THE REPEATED-MEASURES *t*

We estimate Cohen's d and calculate r^2 for the data in Demonstration 11.1. The data produced a sample mean difference of $M_D = 3.00$ with a sample variance of $s^2 = 12.33$. Based on these values, Cohen's d is

$$\text{estimated } d = \frac{\text{mean difference}}{\text{standard deviation}} = \frac{M_D}{s} = \frac{3.00}{\sqrt{12.33}} = \frac{3.00}{3.51} = 0.86$$

The hypothesis test produced $t = 2.26$ with $df = 6$. Based on these values,

$$r^2 = \frac{t^2}{t^2 + df} = \frac{(2.26)^2}{(2.26)^2 + 6} = \frac{5.11}{11.11} = 0.46 \quad (\text{or } 46\%)$$

PROBLEMS

1. What is the defining characteristic of a repeated-measures or within-subjects research design?

2. Participants enter a research study with unique characteristics that produce different scores from one person to another. For an independent-measures study, these individual differences can cause problems. Identify the problems and briefly explain how they are eliminated or reduced with a repeated-measures study.

3. Explain the difference between a matched-subjects design and a repeated-measures design.

4. A researcher conducts an experiment comparing two treatment conditions with 20 scores in each treatment condition.
   a. If an independent-measures design is used, how many subjects are needed for the experiment?
   b. If a repeated-measures design is used, how many subjects are needed for the experiment?
   c. If a matched-subjects design is used, how many subjects are needed for the experiment?

5. A sample of $n = 9$ individuals participates in a repeated-measures study that produces a sample mean difference of $M_D = 4.25$ with $SS = 128$ for the difference scores.
   a. Calculate the standard deviation for the sample of difference scores. Briefly explain what is measured by the standard deviation.
   b. Calculate the estimated standard error for the sample mean difference. Briefly explain what is measured by the estimated standard error.

6. a. A repeated-measures study with a sample of $n = 16$ participants produces a mean difference of $M_D = 3$ with a standard deviation of $s = 4$. Use a two-tailed hypothesis test with $\alpha = .05$ to determine whether this sample provides evidence of a significant treatment effect.
   b. Now assume that the sample standard deviation is $s = 12$ and repeat the hypothesis test.
   c. Explain how the size of the sample standard deviation influences the likelihood of finding a significant mean difference.

7. a. A repeated-measures study with a sample of $n = 9$ participants produces a mean difference of $M_D = 3$ with a standard deviation of $s = 6$. Use a two-tailed hypothesis test with $\alpha = .05$ to determine whether it is likely that this sample came from a population with $\mu_D = 0$.

   b. Now assume that the sample mean difference is $M_D = 12$, and once again visualize the sample distribution. Use a two-tailed hypothesis test with $\alpha = .05$ to determine whether it is likely that this sample came from a population with $\mu_D = 0$.

   c. Explain how the size of the sample mean difference influences the likelihood of finding a significant mean difference.

8. A sample of difference scores from a repeated-measures experiment has a mean of $M_D = 4$ with a standard deviation of $s = 6$.

   a. If $n = 4$, is this sample sufficient to reject the null hypothesis using a two-tailed test with $\alpha = .05$?

   b. Would you reject H_0 if $n = 16$? Again, assume a two-tailed test with $\alpha = .05$.

   c. Explain how the size of the sample influences the likelihood of finding a significant mean difference.

9. When you get a surprisingly low price on a product do you assume that you got a really good deal or that you bought a low-quality product? Research indicates that you are more likely to associate low price and low quality if someone else makes the purchase rather than yourself (Yan & Sengupta, 2011). In a similar study, $n = 16$ participants were asked to rate the quality of low-priced items under two scenarios: purchased by a friend or purchased yourself. The results produced a mean difference of $M_D = 2.6$ and $SS = 135$, with self-purchases rated higher.

   a. Is the judged quality of objects significantly different for self-purchases than for purchases made by others? Use a two-tailed test with $\alpha = .05$.

   b. Compute Cohen's *d* to measure the size of the treatment effect.

10. Research has shown that losing even one night's sleep can have a significant effect on performance of complex tasks, such as problem solving (Linde & Bergstroem, 1992). To demonstrate this phenomenon, a sample of $n = 25$ college students was given a problem-solving task at noon on one day and again at noon on the following day. The students were not permitted any sleep between the two tests. For each student, the difference between the first and second score was recorded. For this sample, the students averaged $M_D = 4.7$ points better on the first test with a variance of $s^2 = 64$ for the difference scores.

   a. Do the data indicate a significant change in problem-solving ability? Use a two-tailed test with $\alpha = .05$.

   b. Compute an estimated Cohen's *d* to measure the size of the effect.

11. Strack, Martin, and Stepper (1988) reported that people rate cartoons as funnier when holding a pen in their teeth (which forced them to smile) than when holding a pen in their lips (which forced them to frown). A researcher attempted to replicate this result using a sample of $n = 25$ adults between the ages of 40 and 45. For each person, the researcher recorded the difference between the rating obtained while smiling and the rating obtained while frowning. On average the cartoons were rated as funnier when the participants were smiling, with an average difference of $M_D = 1.6$ with $SS = 150$.

   a. Do the data indicate that the cartoons are rated significantly funnier when the participants are smiling? Use a one-tailed test with $\alpha = .01$.

   b. Compute r^2 to measure the size of the treatment effect.

   c. Write a sentence describing the outcome of the hypothesis test and the measure of effect size as it would appear in a research report.

12. Masculine-themed words (such as competitive, independent, analyze, strong) are commonly used in job recruitment materials, especially for job advertisements in male-dominated areas (Gaucher, Friesen, & Kay, 2011). The same study found that these words also make the jobs less appealing to women. In a similar study, female participants were asked to read a series of job advertisements and then rate how interesting or appealing the job appeared to be. Half of the advertisements were constructed to include several masculine-themed words and the others were worded neutrally. The average rating for each type of advertisement was obtained for each participant. For $n = 25$ participants, the mean difference between the two types of advertisements is $M_D = 1.32$ points (neutral ads rated higher) with $SS = 150$ for the difference scores.

   a. Is this result sufficient to conclude that there is a significant difference in the ratings for two types of advertisements? Use a two-tailed test with $\alpha = .05$.

   b. Compute r^2 to measure the size of the treatment effect.

   c. Write a sentence describing the outcome of the hypothesis test and the measure of effect size as it would appear in a research report.

13. Research results indicate that physically attractive people are also perceived as being more intelligent (Eagly, Ashmore, Makhijani, & Longo, 1991). As a demonstration of this phenomenon, a researcher obtained a set of 10 photographs, 5 showing men who were judged to be attractive and 5 showing men who were judged to be unattractive. The photographs were shown to a sample of $n = 25$ college students and the students were asked to rate the intelligence of the person in the photo on a scale from 1 to 10.

For each student, the researcher determined the average rating for the 5 attractive photos and the average for the 5 unattractive photos, and then computed the difference between the two scores. For the entire sample, the average difference was $M_D = 2.7$ (attractive photos rated higher) with $s = 2.00$. Are the data sufficient to conclude that there was a significant difference in perceived intelligence for the two sets of photos? Use a two-tailed test at the .05 level of significance.

14. Researchers have noted a decline in cognitive functioning as people age (Bartus, 1990). However, the results from other research suggest that the antioxidants in foods such as blueberries may reduce and even reverse these age-related declines (Joseph et al., 1999). To examine this phenomenon, suppose that a researcher obtains a sample of $n = 16$ adults who are between the ages of 65 and 75. The researcher uses a standardized test to measure cognitive performance for each individual. The participants then begin a 2-month program in which they receive daily doses of a blueberry supplement. At the end of the 2-month period, the researcher again measures cognitive performance for each participant. The results show an average increase in performance of $M_D = 7.4$ with $SS = 1215$.
  a. Does this result support the conclusion that the antioxidant supplement has a significant effect on cognitive performance? Use a two-tailed test with $\alpha = .05$.
  b. Construct a 95% confidence interval to estimate the average cognitive performance improvement for the population of older adults.

15. The following data are from a repeated-measures study examining the effect of a treatment by measuring a group of $n = 6$ participants before and after they receive the treatment.
  a. Calculate the difference scores and M_D.
  b. Compute SS, sample variance, and estimated standard error.
  c. Is there a significant treatment effect? Use $\alpha = .05$, two tails.

Participant	Before Treatment	After Treatment
A	7	8
B	2	9
C	4	6
D	5	7
E	5	6
F	3	8

16. A researcher for a cereal company wanted to demonstrate the health benefits of eating oatmeal. A sample of 9 volunteers was obtained and each participant

ate a fixed diet without any oatmeal for 30 days. At the end of the 30-day period, cholesterol was measured for each individual. Then the participants began a second 30-day period in which they repeated exactly the same diet except that they added 2 cups of oatmeal each day. After the second 30-day period, cholesterol levels were measured again and the researcher recorded the difference between the two scores for each participant. For this sample, cholesterol scores averaged $M_D = 16$ points lower with the oatmeal diet with $SS = 538$ for the difference scores.
  a. Are the data sufficient to indicate a significant change in cholesterol level? Use a two-tailed test with $\alpha = .01$.
  b. Compute r^2, the percentage of variance accounted for by the treatment, to measure the size of the treatment effect.
  c. Write a sentence describing the outcome of the hypothesis test and the measure of effect size as it would appear in a research report.

17. Research indicates that the color red increases men's attraction to women (Elliot & Niesta, 2008). In the original study, men were shown women's photographs presented on either a white or a red background. Photographs presented on red were rated significantly more attractive than the same photographs mounted on white. In a similar study, a researcher prepares a set of 30 women's photographs, with 15 mounted on a white background and 15 mounted on red. One picture is identified as the test photograph and appears twice in the set, once on white and once on red. Each male participant looks through the entire set of photographs and rates the attractiveness of each woman on a 10-point scale. The following table summarizes the ratings of the test photograph for a sample of $n = 9$ men. Are the ratings for the test photograph significantly different when it is presented on a red background compared to a white background? Use a two-tailed test with $\alpha = .01$.

Participant	White Background	Red Background
A	4	7
B	6	7
C	5	8
D	5	9
E	6	9
F	4	7
G	3	9
H	8	9
I	6	9

18. One of the primary advantages of a repeated-measures design, compared to independent-measures, is that it reduces the overall variability by removing variance caused by individual differences. The following data are from a research study comparing two treatment conditions.

a. Assume that the data are from an independent-measures study using two separate samples, each with $n = 6$ participants. Compute the pooled variance and the estimated standard error for the mean difference.

b. Now assume that the data are from a repeated-measures study using the same sample of $n = 6$ participants in both treatment conditions. Compute the variance for the sample of difference scores and the estimated standard error for the mean difference. (You should find that the repeated-measures design substantially reduces the variance and the standard error.)

Treatment 1	Treatment 2	Difference
10	13	3
12	12	0
8	10	2
6	10	4
5	6	1
7	9	2
$M = 8$	$M = 10$	$M_D = 2$
$SS = 34$	$SS = 30$	$SS = 10$

19. Problem 18 shows that removing individual differences can substantially reduce variance and lower the standard error. However, this benefit only occurs if the individual differences are consistent across treatment conditions. In problem 18, for example, the first two participants (top two rows) consistently had the highest scores in both treatment conditions. Similarly, the last two participants consistently had the lowest scores in both treatments. To construct the following data, we started with the scores in problem 18 and scrambled the scores in treatment 1 to eliminate the consistency of the individual differences.

a. Assume that the data are from an independent-measures study using two separate samples, each with $n = 6$ participants. Compute the pooled variance and the estimated standard error for the mean difference.

b. Now assume that the data are from a repeated-measures study using the same sample of $n = 6$ participants in both treatment conditions. Compute the variance for the sample of difference scores and the estimated standard error for the mean difference. (This time you should find that removing the individual differences does not reduce the variance or the standard error.)

Treatment 1	Treatment 2	Difference
6	13	7
7	12	5
8	10	2
10	10	0
5	6	1
12	9	−3
$M = 8$	$M = 10$	$M_D = 2$
$SS = 34$	$SS = 30$	$SS = 64$

20. A researcher uses a matched-subjects design to investigate whether single people with pets are happier than singles without pets. A mood inventory survey is given to a group of 20- to 29-year-old non–pet owners and a similar age group of pet owners. The pet owners are matched one to one with the non–pet owners for income, number of close friendships, and general health. The data follow:

Matched Pair	Non–Pet Owner	Pet Owner
A	12	14
B	8	7
C	10	13
D	9	9
E	7	13
F	10	12

a. Is there a significant difference in the mood scores for non–pet owners versus pet owners? Test with $\alpha = .05$ for two tails.

b. Construct the 95% confidence interval to estimate the size of the mean difference in mood between the population of pet owners and the population of non–pet owners. (You should find that a mean difference of $\mu_D = 0$ is an acceptable value, which is consistent with the conclusion from the hypothesis test.)

21. Some evidence suggests that you are likely to improve your test score if you rethink and change answers on a multiple-choice exam (Johnston, 1975). To examine this phenomenon, a teacher gave the same final exam to two sections of a course. Students in one section were told to turn in their exams immediately after finishing, without changing any answers. In the other section, students were encouraged to reconsider each question and to change answers when they felt it was appropriate. Before the final, the teacher matched 9 students in the first section with 9 students in the second section based on their midterm grades. For example, a student in the no-change section with an 89 on the midterm was matched with a student in the change section who also had an 89 on the midterm. The final

exam grades for the 9 matched pairs of students are presented in the table below.

a. Do the data indicate a significant difference between the two conditions? Use a two-tailed test with $\alpha = .05$.

b. Construct a 95% confidence interval to estimate the size of the population mean difference.

c. Write a sentence demonstrating how the results of the hypothesis test and the confidence interval would appear in a research report.

Matched Pair	No-Change Section	Change Section
#1	71	86
#2	68	80
#3	91	88
#4	65	74
#5	73	82
#6	81	89
#7	85	85
#8	86	88
#9	65	76

22. The teacher from Problem 21 also tried a different approach to determining whether changing answers helps or hurts exam grades. In another class, students were told to review their final exams and change any answers they wanted to before turning them in. However, the students had to indicate both the original answer and the changed answer for each question. The teacher graded each exam twice, once using the set of original answers and once with the changes. In the class of $n = 22$ students, the exam scores improved by an average of $M_D = 2.5$ points with the changed answers. The standard deviation for the difference scores was $s = 3.1$. Are the data sufficient to conclude that rethinking and changing answers can significantly improve scores? Use a one-tailed test at the .01 level of significance.

23. At the Olympic level of competition, even the smallest factors can make the difference between winning and losing. For example, Pelton (1983) has shown that Olympic marksmen shoot much better if they fire between heartbeats, rather than squeezing the trigger during a heartbeat. The small vibration caused by a heartbeat seems to be sufficient to affect the marksman's aim. The following hypothetical data demonstrate this phenomenon. A sample of $n = 8$ Olympic marksmen fires a series of rounds while a researcher records heartbeats. For each marksman, a score is recorded for shots fired during heartbeats and for shots fired between heartbeats. Do these data indicate a significant difference? Test with $\alpha = .05$.

Participant	During Heartbeats	Between Heartbeats
A	93	98
B	90	94
C	95	96
D	92	91
E	95	97
F	91	97
G	92	95
H	93	97

24. Example 11.1 in this chapter presented a repeated-measures research study demonstrating that swearing can help reduce ratings of pain (Stephens, Atkins, & Kingston, 2009). In the study, each participant was asked to plunge a hand into icy water and keep it there as long as the pain would allow. In one condition, the participants repeated their favorite curse words while their hands were in the water. In the other condition, the participants repeated a neutral word. In addition to lowering the participants' perception of pain, swearing also increased the amount of time that they were able to tolerate the pain. Data similar to the results obtained in the study are shown in the following table.

a. Do these data indicate a significant difference in pain tolerance between the two conditions? Use a two-tailed test with $\alpha = .05$.

b. Compute r^2, the percentage of variance accounted for, to measure the size of the treatment effect.

c. Write a sentence demonstrating how the results of the hypothesis test and the measure of effect size would appear in a research report.

	Amount of Time (in Seconds)	
Participant	Swear words	Neutral words
1	94	59
2	70	61
3	52	47
4	83	60
5	46	35
6	117	92
7	69	53
8	39	30
9	51	56
10	73	61

After completing this part, you should be able to perform hypothesis tests and compute confidence intervals using t statistics. These include:

1. The single-sample t introduced in Chapter 9.
2. The independent-measures t introduced in Chapter 10.
3. The repeated-measures t introduced in Chapter 11.

In this part, we considered a set of three t statistics that are used to draw inferences about the means and mean differences for unknown populations. Because the populations are completely unknown, we rely on sample data to provide all of the necessary information. In particular, each inferential procedure begins by computing sample means and sample variances (or the corresponding SS values or standard deviations). Therefore, a good understanding of the definitions and formulas from Chapters 3 and 4 is a critical foundation for this section.

With three different t statistics available, the first problem is often deciding which one is appropriate for a specific research situation. Perhaps the best approach is to begin with a close look at the sample data.

1. For the single-sample t (Chapter 9), there is only one group of participants and only one score for each individual. With a single sample mean and a single sample variance, the t statistic can be used to test a hypothesis about a single unknown population mean or construct a confidence interval to estimate the population mean.
2. For the independent-measures t, there are two separate groups of participants who produce two groups of scores. The mean and variance are computed for each group, producing two sample means and two sample variances. After pooling the two variances, the t statistic uses the difference between the two sample means to test a hypothesis about the corresponding difference between the two unknown population means or estimate the population mean difference with a confidence interval. The null hypothesis always states that there is no difference between the two population means; $\mu_1 - \mu_2 = 0$.
3. For the repeated-measures t, there is only one group of participants but each individual is measured twice, at two different times and/or under two different treatment conditions. The two scores are then used to find a difference score for each person, and the mean and variance are computed for the sample of difference scores. The t statistic uses the sample mean difference to test a hypothesis about the corresponding population mean difference or estimate the population mean difference with a confidence interval. The null hypothesis always states that the mean for the population of difference scores is zero; $\mu_D = 0$.

REVIEW EXERCISES

1. Belsky, Weinraub, Owen, and Kelly (2001) reported on the effects of preschool childcare on the development of young children. One result suggests that children who spend more time away from their mothers are more likely to show behavioral problems in kindergarten. Using a standardized scale, the average rating of behavioral problems for kindergarten children is $\mu = 35$. A sample of $n = 16$ kindergarten children who had spent at least 20 hours per week in child care during the previous year produced a mean score of $M = 42.7$ with a standard deviation of $s = 6$.
   a. Are the data sufficient to conclude that children with a history of childcare show significantly more behavioral problems than the average kindergarten child? Use a one-tailed test with $\alpha = .01$.
   b. Compute the 90% confidence interval for the mean rating of behavioral problems for the population of kindergarten children who have a history of daycare.
   c. Write a sentence showing how the outcome of the hypothesis test and the confidence interval would appear in a research report.

2. Do you view a chocolate bar as delicious or as fattening? Your attitude may depend on your gender. In a study of American college students, Rozin, Bauer, and Catanese (2003) examined the importance of food as a source of pleasure versus concerns about food associated with weight gain and health. The following results are similar to those obtained in the study. The scores are a measure of concern about the negative aspects of eating.

Males	Females
$n = 9$	$n = 15$
$M = 33$	$M = 42$
$SS = 740$	$SS = 1240$

   a. Based on these results, is there a significant difference between the attitudes for males and for females? Use a two-tailed test with $\alpha = .05$.
   b. Compute r^2, the percentage of variance accounted for by the gender difference, to measure effect size for this study.
   c. Write a sentence demonstrating how the result of the hypothesis test and the measure of effect size would appear in a research report.

3. The stimulant Ritalin has been shown to increase attention span and improve academic performance in children with ADHD (Evans et al., 2001). To demonstrate the effectiveness of the drug, a researcher selects a sample of $n = 20$ children diagnosed with the disorder and measures each child's attention span before and after taking the drug. The data show an average increase of attention span of $M_D = 4.8$ minutes with a variance of $s^2 = 125$ for the sample of difference scores.

a. Is this result sufficient to conclude that Ritalin significantly improves attention span? Use a one-tailed test with $\alpha = .05$.

b. Compute the 80% confidence interval for the mean change in attention span for the population.

PART

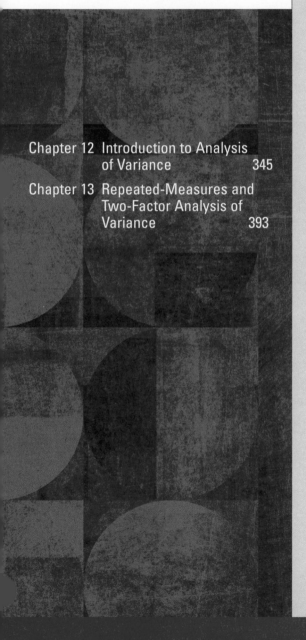

IV

Analysis of Variance: Tests for Differences Among Two or More Population Means

I n Part III, we presented a set of *t* statistics that use sample means and mean differences to draw inferences about the corresponding population means and mean differences. However, the *t* statistics are limited to situations that compare no more than two population means. Often, a research question involves the differences among more than two means and, in these situations, *t* tests are not appropriate. In this part, we introduce a new hypothesis testing technique known as analysis of variance (ANOVA). ANOVA permits researchers to evaluate the mean differences among *two or more* populations using sample data. We present three different applications of ANOVA that apply to three distinct research situations:

1. Independent-measures designs: Using two or more separate samples to draw an inference about the mean differences between two or more unknown populations.

2. Repeated-measures designs: Using one sample, with each individual tested in two or more different treatment conditions, to draw an inference about the population mean differences among the conditions.

3. Two-factor designs: Allowing two independent variables to change simultaneously within one study to create combinations of treatment conditions involving both variables. The ANOVA then evaluates the mean differences attributed to each variable acting independently and to combinations of the two variables interacting together.

In the next two chapters, we continue to examine statistical methods that use sample means as the foundation for drawing inferences about population means. The primary application of these inferential

343

methods is to help researchers interpret the outcome of their research studies. In a typical study, the goal is to demonstrate a difference between two or more treatment conditions. For example, a researcher hopes to demonstrate that a group of children who are exposed to violent TV programs behave more aggressively than children who are shown nonviolent TV programs. In this situation, the data consist of one sample mean representing the scores in one treatment condition and another sample mean representing the scores from a different treatment. The researcher hopes to find a difference between the sample means and would like to generalize the mean difference to the entire population.

The problem is that sample means can be different even when there are no differences whatsoever among the population means. As you saw in Chapter 1 (see Figure 1.2), two samples can have different means even when they are selected from the same population. Thus, even though a researcher may obtain a sample mean difference in a research study, it does not necessarily indicate that there is a mean difference in the population. As with the t tests presented in Part III, a hypothesis test is needed to determine whether the mean differences found in sample data are statistically significant. With more than two sample means, the appropriate hypothesis test is ANOVA.

CHAPTER

12

Introduction to Analysis of Variance

Tools You Will Need

The following items are considered essential background material for this chapter. If you doubt your knowledge of any of these items, you should review the appropriate chapter or section before proceeding.

- Variability (Chapter 4)
  - Sum of squares
  - Sample variance
  - Degrees of freedom
- Introduction to hypothesis testing (Chapter 8)
  - The logic of hypothesis testing
- Independent-measures *t* statistic (Chapter 10)

aplia

Aplia for *Essentials of Statistics for the Behavioral Sciences*
After reading, go to "Resources" at the end of this chapter for an introduction on how to use Aplia's homework and learning resources.

12.1 INTRODUCTION

Analysis of variance (ANOVA) is a hypothesis-testing procedure that is used to evaluate mean differences between two or more treatments (or populations). As with all inferential procedures, ANOVA uses sample data as the basis for drawing general conclusions about populations. It may appear that ANOVA and *t* tests are simply two different ways of doing exactly the same job: testing for mean differences. In some respects, this is true—both tests use sample data to test hypotheses about population means. However, ANOVA has a tremendous advantage over *t* tests. Specifically, *t* tests are limited to situations in which there are only two treatments to compare. The major advantage of ANOVA is that it can be used to compare *two or more treatments*. Thus, ANOVA provides researchers with much greater flexibility in designing experiments and interpreting results.

Figure 12.1 shows a typical research situation for which ANOVA would be used. Note that the study involves three samples representing three populations. The goal of the analysis is to determine whether the mean differences observed among the samples provide enough evidence to conclude that there are mean differences among the three populations. Specifically, we must decide between two interpretations:

1. There really are no differences between the populations (or treatments). The observed differences between the sample means are caused by random, unsystematic factors (sampling error) that differentiate one sample from another.

2. The populations (or treatments) really do have different means, and these population mean differences are responsible for causing systematic differences between the sample means.

You should recognize that these two interpretations correspond to the two hypotheses (null and alternative) that are part of the general hypothesis-testing procedure.

TERMINOLOGY IN ANOVA

Before we continue, it is necessary to introduce some of the terminology that is used to describe the research situation shown in Figure 12.1. Recall (from Chapter 1) that when a researcher manipulates a variable to create the treatment conditions in an experiment, the variable is called an *independent variable*. For example, Figure 12.1 could represent a study

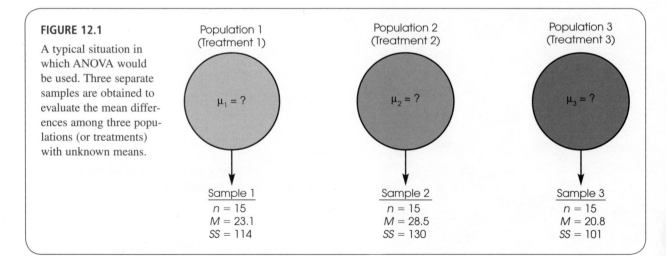

FIGURE 12.1

A typical situation in which ANOVA would be used. Three separate samples are obtained to evaluate the mean differences among three populations (or treatments) with unknown means.

Population 1 (Treatment 1) $\mu_1 = ?$

Population 2 (Treatment 2) $\mu_2 = ?$

Population 3 (Treatment 3) $\mu_3 = ?$

Sample 1
$n = 15$
$M = 23.1$
$SS = 114$

Sample 2
$n = 15$
$M = 28.5$
$SS = 130$

Sample 3
$n = 15$
$M = 20.8$
$SS = 101$

examining driving performance under three different telephone conditions: driving with no phone, talking on a hands-free phone, and talking on a hand-held phone. Note that the three conditions are created by the researcher. On the other hand, when a researcher uses a nonmanipulated variable to designate groups, the variable is called a *quasi-independent variable*. For example, the three groups in Figure 12.1 could represent 6-year-old, 8-year-old, and 10-year-old children. In the context of ANOVA, an independent variable or a quasi-independent variable is called a *factor*. Thus, Figure 12.1 could represent an experimental study in which the telephone condition is the factor being evaluated or it could represent a nonexperimental study in which age is the factor being examined.

D E F I N I T I O N

> In ANOVA, the variable (independent or quasi-independent) that designates the groups being compared is called a **factor.**

The individual groups or treatment conditions that are used to make up a factor are called the *levels* of the factor. For example, a study that examined performance under three different telephone conditions would have three levels of the factor.

D E F I N I T I O N

> The individual conditions or values that make up a factor are called the **levels** of the factor.

Like the *t* tests presented in Chapters 10 and 11, ANOVA can be used with either an independent-measures or a repeated-measures design. Recall that an independent-measures design means that there is a separate group of participants for each of the treatments (or populations) being compared. In a repeated-measures design, on the other hand, the same group is tested in all of the different treatment conditions. In addition, ANOVA can be used to evaluate the mean differences from a research study that involves more than one factor. For example, a researcher may want to compare two different therapy techniques, examining their immediate effectiveness as well as the persistence of their effectiveness over time. In this situation, the research study could involve two different groups of participants, one for each therapy, and measure each group at several different points in time. The structure of this design is shown in Figure 12.2. Notice that the study uses two factors, one independent-measures factor and one repeated-measures factor:

1. Factor 1: Therapy technique. A separate group is used for each technique (independent measures).

2. Factor 2: Time. Each group is tested at three different times (repeated measures).

In this case, the ANOVA would evaluate mean differences between the two therapies as well as mean differences between the scores obtained at different times. A study that combines two factors, like the one in Figure 12.2, is called a *two-factor design* or a *factorial design*.

The ability to combine different factors and to mix different designs within one study provides researchers with the flexibility to develop studies that address scientific questions that could not be answered by a single design using a single factor.

Although ANOVA can be used in a wide variety of research situations, this chapter introduces ANOVA in its simplest form. Specifically, we consider only *single-factor* designs. That is, we examine studies that have only one independent variable (or only one quasi-independent variable). Second, we consider only *independent-measures* designs; that is, studies that use a separate group of participants for each treatment condition. The basic logic and procedures that are presented in this chapter form the foundation for more complex applications of ANOVA. For example, in Chapter 13, we extend the

FIGURE 12.2

A research design with two factors. The research study uses two factors: One factor uses two levels of therapy technique (I versus II), and the second factor uses three levels of time (before, after, and 6 months after). Also notice that the therapy factor uses two separate groups (independent measures) and the time factor uses the same group for all three levels (repeated measures).

analysis to single-factor, repeated-measures designs and we introduce two-factor designs. But for now, in this chapter, we limit our discussion of ANOVA to *single-factor, independent-measures* research studies.

STATISTICAL HYPOTHESES FOR ANOVA

The following example introduces the statistical hypotheses for ANOVA. Suppose that a researcher examined driving performance under three different telephone conditions: no phone, a hands-free phone, and a hand-held phone. Three samples of participants are selected, one sample for each treatment condition. The purpose of the study is to determine whether using a telephone affects driving performance. In statistical terms, we want to decide between two hypotheses: the null hypothesis (H_0), which states that the telephone condition has no effect, and the alternative hypothesis (H_1), which states that the telephone condition does affect driving. In symbols, the null hypothesis states

$$H_0: \mu_1 = \mu_2 = \mu_3$$

In words, the null hypothesis states that the telephone condition has no effect on driving performance. That is, the population means for the three telephone conditions are all the same. In general, H_0 states that there is no treatment effect.

The alternative hypothesis states that the population means are not all the same:

H_1: There is at least one mean difference among the populations.

In general, H_1 states that there is a real treatment effect. As always, the hypotheses are stated in terms of population parameters, even though we use sample data to test them.

Notice that we are not stating a specific alternative hypothesis. This is because many different alternatives are possible, and it would be tedious to list them all. One alternative, for example, is that the first two populations are identical, but that the third is different. Another alternative states that the last two means are the same, but that the first is different. Other alternatives might be

$$H_1: \mu_1 \neq \mu_2 \neq \mu_3 \text{ (All three means are different.)}$$

$$H_1: \mu_1 = \mu_3, \text{ but } \mu_2 \text{ is different.}$$

We should point out that a researcher typically entertains only one (or at most a few) of these alternative hypotheses. Usually a theory or the outcomes of previous studies dictate a specific prediction concerning the treatment effect. For the sake of simplicity, we state a general alternative hypothesis rather than try to list all of the possible specific alternatives.

THE TEST STATISTIC FOR ANOVA

The test statistic for ANOVA is very similar to the independent-measures t statistic used in Chapter 10. For the t statistic, we first computed the standard error, which measures how much difference is expected between two sample means if there is no treatment effect (that is, if H_0 is true). Then we computed the t statistic with the following structure:

$$t = \frac{\text{obtained difference between two sample means}}{\text{standard error (the difference expected with no treatment effect)}}$$

For ANOVA, however, we want to compare differences among two *or more* sample means. With more than two samples, the concept of "difference between sample means" becomes difficult to define or measure. For example, if there are only two samples and they have means of $M = 20$ and $M = 30$, then there is a 10-point difference between the sample means. Suppose, however, that we add a third sample with a mean of $M = 35$. Now how much difference is there between the sample means? It should be clear that we have a problem. The solution to this problem is to use variance to define and measure the size of the differences among the sample means. Consider the following two sets of sample means:

Set 1	Set 2
$M_1 = 20$	$M_1 = 28$
$M_2 = 30$	$M_2 = 30$
$M_3 = 35$	$M_3 = 31$

If you compute the variance for the three numbers in each set, then the variance for set 1 is $s^2 = 58.33$ and the variance for set 2 is $s^2 = 2.33$. Notice that the two variances provide an accurate representation of the size of the differences. In set 1, there are relatively large differences between sample means and the variance is relatively large. In set 2, the mean differences are small and the variance is small.

Thus, we can use variance to measure sample mean differences when there are two or more samples. The test statistic for ANOVA uses this fact to compute an F-*ratio* with the following structure:

$$F = \frac{\text{variance (differences) between sample means}}{\text{variance (differences) expected with no treatment effect}}$$

Note that the F-ratio has the same basic structure as the t statistic but is based on *variance* instead of sample mean *difference*. The variance in the numerator of the F-ratio provides a single number that measures the differences among all of the sample means. The variance in the denominator of the *F*-ratio, like the standard error in the denominator of the *t* statistic, measures the mean differences that would be expected if there were no treatment effect. Thus, the *t* statistic and the *F*-ratio provide the same basic information. In each case, a large value for the test statistic provides evidence that the sample mean differences (numerator) are larger than would be expected if there were no treatment effects (denominator).

TYPE I ERRORS AND MULTIPLE-HYPOTHESIS TESTS

If we already have *t* tests for comparing mean differences, you might wonder why ANOVA is necessary. Why create a whole new hypothesis-testing procedure that simply duplicates what the *t* tests can already do? The answer to this question is based in a concern about Type I errors.

Remember that each time you do a hypothesis test, you select an alpha level that determines the risk of a Type I error. With $\alpha = .05$, for example, there is a 5%, or a 1-in-20, risk of a Type I error. Often a single experiment requires several hypothesis tests to evaluate all of the mean differences. However, each test has a risk of a Type I error, and the more tests you do, the more risk there is.

For this reason, researchers often make a distinction between the *testwise alpha level* and the *experimentwise alpha level*. The testwise alpha level is simply the alpha level that you select for each individual hypothesis test. The experimentwise alpha level is the total probability of a Type I error accumulated from all of the separate tests in the experiment. As the number of separate tests increases, so does the experimentwise alpha level.

DEFINITIONS

> The **testwise alpha level** is the risk of a Type I error, or alpha level, for an individual hypothesis test.
>
> When an experiment involves several different hypothesis tests, the **experimentwise alpha level** is the total probability of a Type I error that is accumulated from all of the individual tests in the experiment. Typically, the experimentwise alpha level is substantially greater than the value of alpha used for any one of the individual tests.

For example, an experiment involving three treatments would require three separate *t* tests to compare all of the mean differences:

Test 1 compares treatment I with treatment II.

Test 2 compares treatment I with treatment III.

Test 3 compares treatment II with treatment III.

If all tests use $\alpha = .05$, then there is a 5% risk of a Type I error for the first test, a 5% risk for the second test, and another 5% risk for the third test. The three separate tests accumulate to produce a relatively large experimentwise alpha level. The advantage of ANOVA is that it performs all three comparisons simultaneously in one hypothesis test. Thus, no matter how many different means are being compared, ANOVA uses one test with one alpha level to evaluate the mean differences, and thereby avoids the problem of an inflated experimentwise alpha level.

12.2 THE LOGIC OF ANOVA

The formulas and calculations required in ANOVA are somewhat complicated, but the logic that underlies the whole procedure is fairly straightforward. Therefore, this section gives a general picture of ANOVA before we start looking at the details. We introduce the logic of ANOVA with the help of the hypothetical data in Table 12.1.

TABLE 12.1

Hypothetical data from an experiment examining driving performance under three telephone conditions.*

Treatment 1: No Phone (Sample 1)	Treatment 2: Hand-Held Phone (Sample 2)	Treatment 3: Hands-Free Phone (Sample 3)
4	0	1
3	1	2
6	3	2
3	1	0
4	0	0
$M = 4$	$M = 1$	$M = 1$

*Note that there are three separate samples, with $n = 5$ in each sample. The dependent variable is a measure of performance in a driving simulator.

These data represent the results of an independent-measures experiment comparing performance in a driving simulator under three telephone conditions.

One obvious characteristic of the data in Table 12.1 is that the scores are not all the same. In everyday language, the scores are different; in statistical terms, the scores are variable. Our goal is to measure the amount of variability (the size of the differences) and to explain why the scores are different.

The first step is to determine the total variability for the entire set of data. To compute the total variability, we combine all of the scores from all of the separate samples to obtain one general measure of variability for the complete experiment. Once we have measured the total variability, we can begin to break it apart into separate components. The word *analysis* means dividing into smaller parts. Because we are going to analyze variability, the process is called *analysis of variance*. This analysis process divides the total variability into two basic components.

1. **Between-Treatments Variance.** Looking at the data in Table 12.1, we clearly see that much of the variability in the scores results from general differences between treatment conditions. For example, the scores in the no-phone condition tend to be much higher ($M = 4$) than the scores in the hand-held condition ($M = 1$). We calculate the variance between treatments to provide a measure of the overall differences between treatment conditions. Notice that the variance between treatments is really measuring the differences between sample means.

2. **Within-Treatment Variance.** In addition to the general differences between treatment conditions, there is variability within each sample. Looking again at Table 12.1, we see that the scores in the no-phone condition are not all the same; they are variable. The within-treatments variance provides a measure of the variability inside each treatment condition.

Analyzing the total variability into these two components is the heart of ANOVA. We now examine each of the components in more detail.

BETWEEN-TREATMENTS VARIANCE

Remember that calculating variance is simply a method for measuring how big the differences are for a set of numbers. When you see the term *variance,* you can automatically translate it into the term *differences*. Thus, the *between-treatments variance* simply measures how much difference exists between the treatment conditions. There are two possible explanations for these between-treatment differences:

1. The differences between treatments are not caused by any treatment effect but are simply the naturally occurring, random, and unsystematic differences that

exist between one sample and another. That is, the differences are the result of sampling error.

2. The differences between treatments have been caused by the *treatment effects.* For example, if using a telephone really does interfere with driving performance, then scores in the telephone conditions should be systematically lower than scores in the no-phone condition.

Thus, when we compute the between-treatments variance, we are measuring differences that could be caused by a systematic treatment effect or could simply be random and unsystematic mean differences caused by sampling error. To demonstrate that there really is a treatment effect, we must establish that the differences between treatments are bigger than would be expected by sampling error alone. To accomplish this goal, we determine how big the differences are when there is no systematic treatment effect; that is, we measure how much difference (or variance) can be explained by random and unsystematic factors. To measure these differences, we compute the variance within treatments.

WITHIN-TREATMENTS VARIANCE

Inside each treatment condition, we have a set of individuals who all receive exactly the same treatment; that is, the researcher does not do anything that would cause these individuals to have different scores. In Table 12.1, for example, the data show that five individuals were tested while talking on a hand-held phone (sample 2). Although these five individuals all received exactly the same treatment, their scores are different. Why are the scores different? The answer is that there is no specific cause for the differences. Instead, the differences that exist within a treatment represent random and unsystematic differences that occur when there are no treatment effects causing the scores to be different. Thus, the *within-treatments variance* provides a measure of how big the differences are when H_0 is true.

Figure 12.3 shows the overall ANOVA and identifies the sources of variability that are measured by each of the two basic components.

THE *F*-RATIO: THE TEST STATISTIC FOR ANOVA

Once we have analyzed the total variability into two basic components (between treatments and within treatments), we simply compare them. The comparison is made by

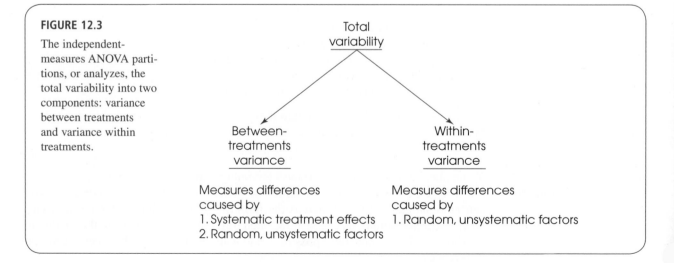

FIGURE 12.3

The independent-measures ANOVA partitions, or analyzes, the total variability into two components: variance between treatments and variance within treatments.

computing an F-*ratio*. For the independent-measures ANOVA, the *F*-ratio has the following structure:

$$F = \frac{\text{variance between treatments}}{\text{variance within treatments}} = \frac{\text{differences including any treatment effects}}{\text{differences with no treatment effects}} \qquad (12.1)$$

When we express each component of variability in terms of its sources (see Figure 12.3), the structure of the *F*-ratio is

$$F = \frac{\text{systematic treatment effects} + \text{random, unsystematic differences}}{\text{random, unsystematic differences}} \qquad (12.2)$$

The value obtained for the *F*-ratio helps to determine whether any treatment effects exist. Consider the following two possibilities:

1. When there are no systematic treatment effects, the differences between treatments (numerator) are entirely caused by random, unsystematic factors. In this case, the numerator and the denominator of the *F*-ratio are both measuring random differences and should be roughly the same size. With the numerator and denominator roughly equal, the *F*-ratio should have a value around 1.00. In terms of the formula, when the treatment effect is zero, we obtain

$$F = \frac{0 + \text{random, unsystematic differences}}{\text{random, unsystematic differences}}$$

   Thus, an *F*-ratio near 1.00 indicates that the differences between treatments (numerator) are random and unsystematic, just like the differences in the denominator. With an *F*-ratio near 1.00, we conclude that there is no evidence to suggest that the treatment has any effect.

2. When the treatment does have an effect, causing systematic differences between samples, then the combination of systematic and random differences in the numerator should be larger than the random differences alone in the denominator. In this case, the numerator of the *F*-ratio should be noticeably larger than the denominator, and we should obtain an *F*-ratio that is substantially larger than 1.00. Thus, a large *F*-ratio is evidence for the existence of systematic treatment effects; that is, there are consistent differences between treatments.

Because the denominator of the *F*-ratio measures only random and unsystematic variability, it is called the *error term*. The numerator of the *F*-ratio always includes the same unsystematic variability as in the error term, but it also includes any systematic differences caused by the treatment effect. The goal of ANOVA is to find out whether a treatment effect exists.

DEFINITION

> For ANOVA, the denominator of the *F*-ratio is called the **error term.** The error term provides a measure of the variance caused by random, unsystematic differences. When the treatment effect is zero (H_0 is true), the error term measures the same sources of variance as the numerator of the *F*-ratio, so the value of the *F*-ratio is expected to be nearly equal to 1.00.

LEARNING CHECK

LEARNING CHECK

1. Explain the difference between the testwise alpha level and the experimentwise alpha level.

2. The term "analysis" means separating or breaking a whole into parts. What is the basic analysis that takes place in analysis of variance?

3. If there is no systematic treatment effect, then what value is expected, on average, for the F-ratio in an ANOVA?

4. What is the implication when an ANOVA produces a very large value for the F-ratio?

ANSWERS

1. When a single research study involves several hypothesis tests, the testwise alpha level is the value selected for each individual test and the experimentwise alpha level is the total risk of a Type I error that is accumulated for all of the separate tests.

2. In ANOVA, the total variability for a set of scores is separated into two components: between-treatments variability and within-treatments variability.

3. When H_0 is true, the expected value for the F-ratio is 1.00 because the top and bottom of the ratio are both measuring the same variance.

4. A large F-ratio indicates the existence of a treatment effect because the differences between treatments (numerator) are much bigger than the differences that would be expected if there were no effect (denominator).

12.3 ANOVA NOTATION AND FORMULAS

Because ANOVA typically is used to examine data from more than two treatment conditions (and more than two samples), we need a notational system to keep track of all of the individual scores and totals. To help introduce this notational system, we use the hypothetical data from Table 12.1 again. The data are reproduced in Table 12.2 along with some of the notation and statistics that are described in the following list.

1. The letter k is used to identify the number of treatment conditions—that is, the number of levels of the factor. For an independent-measures study, k also specifies the number of separate samples. For the data in Table 12.2, there are three treatments, so $k = 3$.

2. The number of scores in each treatment is identified by a lowercase letter n. For the example in Table 12.2, $n = 5$ for all the treatments. If the samples are of different sizes, you can identify a specific sample by using a subscript. For example, n_2 is the number of scores in treatment 2.

3. The total number of scores in the entire study is specified by a capital letter N. When all of the samples are the same size (n is constant), $N = kn$. For the data in Table 12.2, there are $n = 5$ scores in each of the $k = 3$ treatments, so we have a total of $N = 3(5) = 15$ scores in the entire study.

4. The sum of the scores (ΣX) for each treatment condition is identified by the capital letter T (for treatment total). The total for a specific treatment can be identified by adding a numerical subscript to the T. For example, the total for the second treatment in Table 12.2 is $T_2 = 5$.

5. The sum of all of the scores in the research study (the grand total) is identified by G. You can compute G by adding up all N scores or by adding up the treatment totals: $G = \Sigma T$.

TABLE 12.2

The same data that appeared in Table 12.1 with summary values and notation appropriate for an ANOVA.

	Telephone Conditions		
Treatment 1 No Phone (Sample 1)	Treatment 2 Hand-Held Phone (Sample 2)	Treatment 3 Hands-Free Phone (Sample 3)	
4	0	1	$\Sigma X^2 = 106$
3	1	2	$G = 30$
6	3	2	$N = 15$
3	1	0	$k = 3$
4	0	0	
$T_1 = 20$	$T_2 = 5$	$T_3 = 5$	
$SS_1 = 6$	$SS_2 = 6$	$SS_3 = 4$	
$n_1 = 5$	$n_2 = 5$	$n_3 = 5$	
$M_1 = 4$	$M_2 = 1$	$M_3 = 1$	

6. Although there is no new notation involved, we also have computed SS and M for each sample, and we have calculated ΣX^2 for the entire set of $N = 15$ scores. These values are given in Table 12.2 and are important in the formulas and calculations for ANOVA.

Finally, we should note that there is no universally accepted notation for ANOVA. Although we are using Gs and Ts, for example, you may find that other sources use other symbols.

ANOVA FORMULAS

Because ANOVA requires extensive calculations and many formulas, one common problem for students is simply keeping track of the different formulas and numbers. Therefore, we examine the general structure of the procedure and look at the organization of the calculations before we introduce the individual formulas.

Because ANOVA formulas require ΣX for each treatment and ΣX for the entire set of scores, we have introduced new notation (T and G) to help identify which ΣX is being used. Remember: T stands for *treatment total,* and G stands for *grand total.*

1. The final calculation for ANOVA is the F-ratio, which is composed of two variances:

$$F = \frac{\text{variance between treatments}}{\text{variance within treatments}}$$

2. Each of the two variances in the F-ratio is calculated using the basic formula for sample variance.

$$\text{sample variance} = s^2 = \frac{SS}{df}$$

Therefore, we need to compute an SS and a df for the variance between treatments (numerator of F), and we need another SS and df for the variance within treatments (denominator of F). To obtain these SS and df values, we must go through two separate analyses: First, compute SS for the total study, and analyze it in two components (between and within). Then compute df for the total study, and analyze it in two components (between and within).

Thus, the entire process of ANOVA requires nine calculations: three values for SS, three values for df, two variances (between and within), and a final F-ratio. However, these nine calculations are all logically related and are all directed toward finding the final F-ratio. Figure 12.4 shows the logical structure of ANOVA calculations.

FIGURE 12.4

The structure and sequence of calculations for the ANOVA.

The final goal for the ANOVA is an F-ratio	$F = \dfrac{\text{Variance between treatments}}{\text{Variance within treatments}}$	
Each variance in the F-ratio is computed as SS/df	Variance between treatments $= \dfrac{SS\,\text{between}}{df\,\text{between}}$	Variance within treatments $= \dfrac{SS\,\text{within}}{df\,\text{within}}$
To obtain each of the SS and df values, the total variability is analyzed into the two components	SS total ⟋⟍ SS between SS within	df total ⟋⟍ df between df within

---

ANALYSIS OF THE SUM OF SQUARES (SS)

The ANOVA requires that we first compute a total sum of squares and then partition this value into two components: between treatments and within treatments. This analysis is outlined in Figure 12.5. We examine each of the three components separately.

1. **Total Sum of Squares, SS_{total}.** As the name implies, SS_{total} is the sum of squares for the entire set of N scores. As described in Chapter 4 (pp. 96–98), this SS value can be computed using either a definitional or a computational formula. However, ANOVA typically involves a large number of scores and the mean is often not a whole number. Therefore, it is usually much easier to calculate SS_{total} using the computational formula:

$$SS = \Sigma X^2 - \frac{(\Sigma X)^2}{N}$$

FIGURE 12.5

Partitioning the sum of squares (SS) for the independent-measures ANOVA.

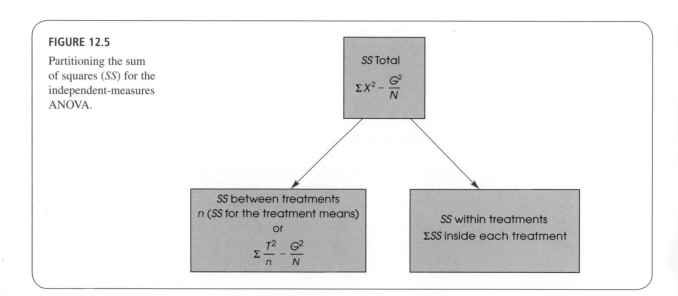

SS Total
$$\Sigma X^2 - \frac{G^2}{N}$$

SS between treatments
n (SS for the treatment means)
or
$$\Sigma \frac{T^2}{n} - \frac{G^2}{N}$$

SS within treatments
ΣSS inside each treatment

To make this formula consistent with the ANOVA notation, we substitute the letter G in place of ΣX and obtain

$$SS_{total} = \Sigma X^2 - \frac{G^2}{N} \tag{12.3}$$

Applying this formula to the set of data in Table 12.2, we obtain

$$SS_{total} = 106 - \frac{30^2}{15}$$

$$= 106 - 60$$

$$= 46$$

2. **Within-Treatments Sum of Squares, $SS_{within\ treatments}$.** Now we are looking at the variability inside each of the treatment conditions. We already have computed the SS within each of the three treatment conditions (Table 12.2): $SS_1 = 6$, $SS_2 = 6$, and $SS_3 = 4$. To find the overall within-treatment sum of squares, we simply add these values together:

$$SS_{within\ treatments} = \Sigma SS_{inside\ each\ treatment} \tag{12.4}$$

For the data in Table 12.2, this formula gives

$$SS_{within\ treatments} = 6 + 6 + 4$$

$$= 16$$

3. **Between-Treatments Sum of Squares, $SS_{within\ treatments}$.** Before we introduce any equations for $SS_{between\ treatments}$, consider what we have found so far. The total variability for the data in Table 12.2 is $SS_{total} = 46$. We intend to partition this total into two parts (see Figure 12.5). One part, $SS_{within\ treatments}$, has been found to be equal to 16. This means that $SS_{between\ treatments}$ must be equal to 30 so that the two parts (16 and 30) add up to the total (46). Thus, the value for $SS_{between\ treatments}$ can be found simply by subtraction:

$$SS_{between} = SS_{total} - SS_{within} \tag{12.5}$$

Computing $SS_{between}$ Instead of finding $SS_{between}$ by subtraction, you can compute $SS_{between}$ independently, and then check your calculations by ensuring that the two components, between and within, add up to the total. We present two different formulas for calculating $SS_{between}$ directly from the data.

To simplify the notation we use the subscripts *between* and *within* in place of *between treatments* and *within treatments*.

Recall that the variability between treatments is measuring the differences between treatment means. Conceptually, the most direct way of measuring the amount of variability among the treatment means is to compute the sum of squares for the set of sample means, SS_{means}. For the data in Table 12.2, the sample means are 4, 1, and 1. These three values produce $SS_{means} = 6$. However, each of the three means represents a group of $n = 5$ scores. Therefore, the final value for $SS_{between}$ is obtained by multiplying SS_{means} by n.

$$SS_{between} = n(SS_{means}) \tag{12.6}$$

For the data in Table 12.2, we obtain

$$SS_{between} = n(SS_{means}) = 5(6) = 30$$

Unfortunately, Equation 12.6 can only be used when all of the samples are exactly the same size (equal ns), and the equation can be very awkward, especially when the treatment means are not whole numbers. Therefore, we also present a computational formula for $SS_{between}$ that uses the treatment totals (T) instead of the treatment means.

$$SS_{between} = \Sigma \frac{T^2}{n} - \frac{G^2}{N} \tag{12.7}$$

For the data in Table 12.2, this formula produces:

$$SS_{between} = \frac{20^2}{5} + \frac{5^2}{5} + \frac{5^2}{5} - \frac{30^2}{15}$$

$$= 80 + 5 + 5 - 60$$

$$= 90 - 60$$

$$= 30$$

Note that all three techniques (Equations 12.5, 12.6, and 12.7) produce the same result, $SS_{between} = 30$.

We have presented three different equations for computing $SS_{between}$. Rather than memorizing all three, however, we suggest that you pick one formula and use it consistently. There are two reasonable alternatives to use. The simplest is Equation 12.5, which finds $SS_{between}$ simply by subtraction: First you compute SS_{total} and SS_{within}, then subtract:

$$SS_{between} = SS_{total} - SS_{within}$$

The second alternative is to use Equation 12.7, which computes $SS_{between}$ using the treatment totals (the T values). The advantage of this alternative is that it provides a way to check your arithmetic: Calculate SS_{total}, $SS_{between}$, and SS_{within} separately, and then check to be sure that the two components add up to equal SS_{total}.

Using Equation 12.6, which computes SS for the set of sample means, is usually not a good choice. Unless the sample means are all whole numbers, this equation can produce very tedious calculations. In most situations, one of the other two equations is a better alternative.

THE ANALYSIS OF DEGREES OF FREEDOM (df)

The analysis of degrees of freedom (df) follows the same pattern as the analysis of SS. First, we find df for the total set of N scores, and then we partition this value into two components: degrees of freedom between treatments and degrees of freedom within treatments. In computing degrees of freedom, there are two important considerations to keep in mind:

1. Each df value is associated with a specific SS value.

2. Normally, the value of df is obtained by counting the number of items that were used to calculate SS and then subtracting 1. For example, if you compute SS for a set of n scores, then $df = n - 1$.

With this in mind, we examine the degrees of freedom for each part of the analysis.

1. **Total Degrees of Freedom, df_{total}.** To find the df associated with SS_{total}, you must first recall that this SS value measures variability for the entire set of N scores. Therefore, the df value is

$$df_{total} = N - 1 \tag{12.8}$$

For the data in Table 12.2, the total number of scores is $N = 15$, so the total degrees of freedom are

$$df_{total} = 15 - 1$$

$$= 14$$

2. **Within-Treatments Degrees of Freedom, df_{within}.** To find the df associated with SS_{within}, we must look at how this SS value is computed. Remember, we first find SS inside of each of the treatments and then add these values together. Each of the treatment SS values measures variability for the n scores in the treatment, so each SS has $df = n - 1$. When all of these individual treatment values are added together, we obtain

$$df_{within} = \Sigma(n - 1) = \Sigma df_{\text{in each treatment}} \tag{12.9}$$

For the experiment we have been considering, each treatment has $n = 5$ scores. This means there are $n - 1 = 4$ degrees of freedom inside each treatment. Because there are three different treatment conditions, this gives a total of 12 for the within-treatments degrees of freedom.

Notice that this formula for df simply adds up the number of scores in each treatment (the n values) and subtracts 1 for each treatment. If these two stages are done separately, you obtain

$$df_{within} = N - k \tag{12.10}$$

(Adding up all the n values gives N. If you subtract 1 for each treatment, then altogether you have subtracted k because there are k treatments.) For the data in Table 12.2, $N = 15$ and $k = 3$, so

$$df_{within} = 15 - 3$$

$$= 12$$

3. **Between-Treatments Degrees of Freedom, $df_{between}$.** The df associated with $SS_{between}$ can be found by considering how the SS value is obtained. This SS formula measure the variability for the set of treatments (totals or means). To find $df_{between}$, simply count the number of treatments and subtract 1. Because the number of treatments is specified by the letter k, the formula for df is

$$df_{between} = k - 1 \tag{12.11}$$

For the data in Table 12.2, there are three different treatment conditions and

$$df_{between} = 3 - 1$$

$$= 2$$

Notice that the two parts we obtained from this analysis of degrees of freedom add up to equal the total degrees of freedom:

$$df_{total} = df_{within} + df_{between}$$

$$14 = 12 + 2$$

The complete analysis of degrees of freedom is shown in Figure 12.6.

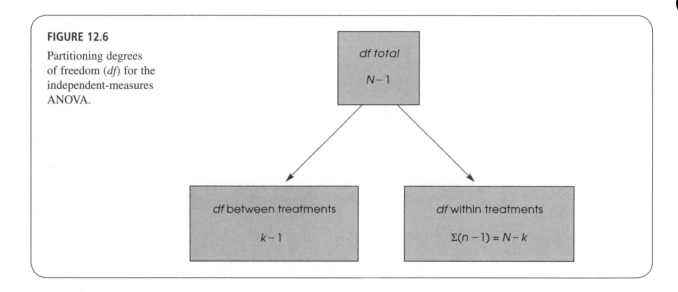

FIGURE 12.6

Partitioning degrees of freedom (*df*) for the independent-measures ANOVA.

As you are computing the *SS* and *df* values for ANOVA, keep in mind that the labels that are used for each value can help you understand the formulas. Specifically,

1. The term **total** refers to the entire set of scores. We compute *SS* for the whole set of *N* scores, and the *df* value is simply $N - 1$.

2. The term **within treatments** refers to differences that exist inside of the individual treatment conditions. Thus, we compute *SS* and *df* inside each of the separate treatments.

3. The term **between treatments** refers to differences from one treatment to another. With three treatments, for example, we are comparing three different means (or totals) and have $df = 3 - 1 = 2$.

CALCULATION OF VARIANCES (*MS*) AND THE *F*-RATIO

The next step in the ANOVA procedure is to compute the variance between treatments and the variance within treatments, which are used to calculate the *F*-ratio (see Figure 12.4).

In ANOVA, it is customary to use the term *mean square,* or simply *MS*, in place of the term *variance*. Recall (from Chapter 4) that variance is defined as the mean of the squared deviations. In the same way that we use *SS* to stand for the sum of the squared deviations, we now use *MS* to stand for the mean of the squared deviations. For the final *F*-ratio, we need an *MS* (variance) between treatments for the numerator and an *MS* (variance) within treatments for the denominator. In each case

$$MS(\text{variance}) = s^2 = \frac{SS}{df} \tag{12.12}$$

For the data we have been considering,

$$MS_{\text{between}} = s^2_{\text{between}} = \frac{SS_{\text{between}}}{df_{\text{between}}} = \frac{30}{2} = 15$$

and

$$MS_{\text{within}} = s^2_{\text{within}} = \frac{SS_{\text{within}}}{df_{\text{within}}} = \frac{16}{12} = 1.33$$

We now have a measure of the variance (or differences) between the treatments and a measure of the variance within the treatments. The F-ratio simply compares these two variances:

$$F = \frac{s_{between}^2}{s_{within}^2} = \frac{MS_{between}}{MS_{within}} \qquad (12.13)$$

For the experiment we have been examining, the data give an F-ratio of

$$F = \frac{15}{1.33} = 11.28$$

For this example, the obtained value of $F = 11.28$ indicates that the numerator of the F-ratio is substantially bigger than the denominator. If you recall the conceptual structure of the F-ratio as presented in Equations 12.1 and 12.2, the F value we obtained indicates that the differences between treatments are more than 11 times bigger than what would be expected if there were no treatment effect. Stated in terms of the experimental variables: using a telephone while driving does appear to have an effect on driving performance. However, to properly evaluate the F-ratio, we must select an α level and consult the F-distribution table that is discussed in the next section.

ANOVA summary tables   It is useful to organize the results of the analysis in one table called an *ANOVA summary table*. The table shows the source of variability (between treatments, within treatments, and total variability), SS, df, MS, and F. For the previous computations, the ANOVA summary table is constructed as follows:

Source	SS	df	MS	
Between treatments	30	2	15	$F = 11.28$
Within treatments	16	12	1.33	
Total	46	14		

Although these tables are no longer used in published reports, they are a common part of computer printouts, and they do provide a concise method for presenting the results of an analysis. (Note that you can conveniently check your work: Adding the first two entries in the SS column, $30 + 16$, produces SS_{total}. The same applies to the df column.) When using ANOVA, you might start with a blank ANOVA summary table and then fill in the values as they are calculated. With this method, you are less likely to "get lost" in the analysis, wondering what to do next.

LEARNING CHECK

1. Calculate SS_{total}, $SS_{between}$, and SS_{within} for the following set of data:

Treatment 1	Treatment 2	Treatment 3	
$n = 5$	$n = 5$	$n = 5$	$N = 15$
$T = 10$	$T = 15$	$T = 35$	$G = 60$
$SS = 21$	$SS = 16$	$SS = 23$	$\Sigma X^2 = 370$

2. A researcher reports an F-ratio with $df_{between} = 3$ and $df_{within} = 28$ for an independent-measures ANOVA. How many treatment conditions were compared in the experiment? If all the treatments have the same number of participants, then how many are in each treatment?

3. A researcher conducts an experiment comparing three treatment conditions with a separate sample of $n = 8$ in each treatment. An ANOVA is used to evaluate the data, and the results of the ANOVA are presented in the following table. Complete all missing values in the table. *Hint:* Begin with the values in the *df* column.

Source	SS	df	MS	
Between treatments	__	__	__	$F =$ ___
Within treatments	__	__	2	
Total	62	__		

ANSWERS

1. $SS_{total} = 130$; $SS_{between} = 70$; $SS_{within} = 60$

2. There were 4 treatment conditions ($df_{between} = k - 1 = 3$). A total of $N = 32$ individuals participated ($df_{within} = 30 = N - k$) with $n = 8$ in each treatment.

3.

Source	SS	df	MS	
Between treatments	20	2	10	$F = 5.00$
Within treatments	42	21	2	
Total	62	23		

12.4 THE DISTRIBUTION OF *F*-RATIOS

In ANOVA, the *F*-ratio is constructed so that the numerator and denominator of the ratio are measuring exactly the same variance when the null hypothesis is true (see Equation 12.2). In this situation, we expect the value of *F* to be around 1.00. If we obtain an *F*-ratio that is much greater than 1.00, then it is evidence that a treatment effect exists and the null hypothesis is false. The problem now is to define precisely which values are "around 1.00" and which are "much greater than 1.00." To answer this question, we need to look at all of the possible *F* values when H_0 is true—that is, the *distribution of* F-*ratios*.

Before we examine this distribution in detail, you should note two obvious characteristics:

1. Because *F*-ratios are computed from two variances (the numerator and denominator of the ratio), *F* values always are positive numbers. Remember that variance is always positive.

2. When H_0 is true, the numerator and denominator of the *F*-ratio are measuring the same variance. In this case, the two sample variances should be about the same size, so the ratio should be near 1. In other words, the distribution of *F*-ratios should pile up around 1.00.

With these two factors in mind, we can sketch the distribution of *F*-ratios. The distribution is cut off at zero (all positive values), piles up around 1.00, and then tapers off to the right (Figure 12.7). The exact shape of the *F* distribution depends on the degrees of freedom for the two variances in the *F*-ratio. You should recall that the precision of a sample variance depends on the number of scores or the degrees of freedom. In general, the variance for a large sample (large *df*) provides a more accurate estimate of the population variance. Because the precision of the *MS* values

FIGURE 12.7

The distribution of *F*-ratios with *df* = 2, 12. Of all the values in the distribution, only 5% are larger than *F* = 3.88, and only 1% are larger than *F* = 6.93.

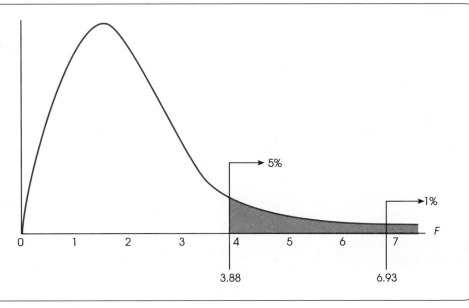

depends on *df*, the shape of the *F* distribution also depends on the *df* values for the numerator and denominator of the *F*-ratio. With very large *df* values, nearly all of the *F*-ratios are clustered very near to 1.00. With the smaller *df* values, the *F* distribution is more spread out.

THE *F* DISTRIBUTION TABLE

For ANOVA, we expect *F* near 1.00 if H_0 is true, and we expect a large value for *F* if H_0 is not true. In the *F* distribution, we need to separate those values that are reasonably near 1.00 from the values that are significantly greater than 1.00. These critical values are presented in an *F* distribution table in Appendix B. A portion of the *F* distribution table is shown in Table 12.3. To use the table, you must know the *df* values for the *F*-ratio (numerator and denominator), and you must know the alpha level for the hypothesis test. It is customary for an *F* table to have the *df* values for the numerator of the *F*-ratio printed across the top of the table. The *df* values for the denominator of *F* are printed in a column on the left-hand side. For the experiment we have been considering, the numerator of the *F*-ratio (between treatments) has *df* = 2, and the denominator of the *F*-ratio (within treatments) has *df* = 12. This *F*-ratio is said to have "degrees of freedom equal to 2 and 12." The degrees of freedom would be written as *df* = 2, 12. To use the table, you would first find *df* = 2 across the top of the table and *df* = 12 in the first column. When you line up these two values, they point to a pair of numbers in the middle of the table. These numbers give the critical cutoffs for α = .05 and α = .01. With *df* = 2, 12, for example, the numbers in the table are 3.88 and 6.93. Thus, only 5% of the distribution (α = .05) corresponds to values greater than 3.88 and only 1% of the distribution (α = .01) corresponds to values greater than 6.93 (see Figure 12.7).

In the experiment comparing driving performance under different telephone conditions, we obtained an *F*-ratio of 11.28. According to the critical cutoffs in Figure 12.7, this value is extremely unlikely (it is in the most extreme 1%). Therefore, we would reject H_0 with an α level of either .05 or .01 and conclude that the different telephone conditions significantly affect driving performance.

TABLE 12.3

A portion of the F distribution table. Entries in roman type are critical values for the .05 level of significance, and entries in bold type are for the .01 level of significance. The critical values for $df = 2, 12$ have been highlighted (see text).

Degrees of Freedom: Denominator	Degrees of Freedom: Numerator					
	1	2	3	4	5	6
10	4.96	4.10	3.71	3.48	3.33	3.22
	10.04	**7.56**	**6.55**	**5.99**	**5.64**	**5.39**
11	4.84	3.98	3.59	3.36	3.20	3.09
	9.65	**7.20**	**6.22**	**5.67**	**5.32**	**5.07**
12	4.75	3.88	3.49	3.26	3.11	3.00
	9.33	**6.93**	**5.95**	**5.41**	**5.06**	**4.82**
13	4.67	3.80	3.41	3.18	3.02	2.92
	9.07	**6.70**	**5.74**	**5.20**	**4.86**	**4.62**
14	4.60	3.74	3.34	3.11	2.96	2.85
	8.86	**6.51**	**5.56**	**5.03**	**4.69**	**4.46**

LEARNING CHECK

1. A researcher obtains $F = 4.10$ with $df = 2, 14$. Is this value sufficient to reject H_0 with $\alpha = .05$? Is it big enough to reject H_0 if $\alpha = .01$?

2. For an ANOVA evaluating the mean differences among three treatment conditions with $n = 10$ in each treatment, what is the critical value for the F-ratio with $\alpha = .05$?

ANSWERS

1. For $\alpha = .05$, the critical value is 3.74 and you should reject H_0. For $\alpha = .01$, the critical value is 6.51 and you should fail to reject H_0.

2. The F-ratio has $df = 2, 27$ and the critical value is 3.35.

12.5 EXAMPLES OF HYPOTHESIS TESTING AND EFFECT SIZE WITH ANOVA

Although we have now seen all the individual components of ANOVA, the following example demonstrates the complete ANOVA process using the standard four-step procedure for hypothesis testing.

EXAMPLE 12.1

What is the best strategy for studying before a quiz or exam? A partial answer to this question comes from a research study comparing three different strategies (Weinstein, McDermott, & Roediger, 2010). In the study, students read a passage knowing that they would be tested on the material. In one condition, participants simply reread the passage. In a second condition, the students answered prepared comprehension questions about the material, and in a third condition, the students generated and answered their own questions. The results showed that answering comprehension questions significantly improved exam performance but it did not matter whether the students had to generate their own questions.

The data in Table 12.4 are similar to those obtained in the study but use four separate groups of students and add a fourth condition in which the passage is read only once. We use an ANOVA to determine whether there are any significant differences among the four study strategies.

Before we begin the hypothesis test, note that we have already computed several summary statistics for the data in Table 12.4. Specifically, the treatment totals (T) and SS values are shown for each sample, and the grand total (G) as well as N and ΣX^2 are shown for the entire set of data. Having these summary values simplifies the computations in the hypothesis test, and we suggest that you always compute these summary statistics before you begin an ANOVA.

TABLE 12.4

Quiz scores for students using four different study strategies.

Read Once	Read and Reread	Answer Prepared Questions	Create and Answer Questions	
3	5	8	8	
3	3	5	9	$N = 24$
4	5	8	7	$G = 168$
6	7	9	10	$\Sigma X^2 = 1298$
6	8	8	10	
8	8	10	10	
$T = 30$	$T = 36$	$T = 48$	$T = 54$	
$M = 5$	$M = 6$	$M = 8$	$M = 9$	
$SS = 20$	$SS = 20$	$SS = 14$	$SS = 8$	

STEP 1: State the hypotheses and select an alpha level.

$$H_0: \mu_1 = \mu_2 = \mu_3 = \mu_4 \text{ (There is no treatment effect.)}$$

H_1: At least one of the treatment means is different.

We use $\alpha = .01$.

STEP 2: Locate the critical region.

We first must determine degrees of freedom for $MS_{\text{between treatments}}$ and $MS_{\text{within treatments}}$ (the numerator and denominator of the F-ratio), so we begin by analyzing the degrees of freedom. For these data, the total degrees of freedom are

Often it is easier to postpone finding the critical region until after step 3, where you compute the df values as part of the calculations for the F-ratio.

$$df_{\text{total}} = N - 1$$
$$= 24 - 1$$
$$= 23$$

Analyzing this total into two components, we obtain

$$df_{\text{between}} = k - 1 = 4 - 1 = 3$$

$$df_{\text{within}} = \Sigma df_{\text{inside each treatment}} = 5 + 5 + 5 + 5 = 20$$

The F-ratio for these data has $df = 3, 20$. The distribution of all the possible F-ratios with $df = 3, 20$ is presented in Figure 12.8. Note that F-ratios larger than 4.94 are extremely rare ($p < .01$) if H_0 is true and, therefore, form the critical region for the test.

STEP 3: Compute the F-ratio.

The series of calculations for computing F is presented in Figure 12.4 and can be summarized as follows:

a. Analyze the SS to obtain SS_{between} and SS_{within}.

b. Use the SS values and the df values (from step 2) to calculate the two variances, MS_{between} and MS_{within}.

c. Finally, use the two MS values (variances) to compute the F-ratio.

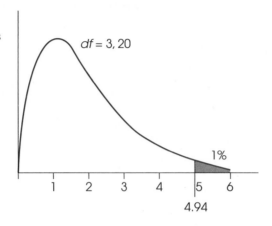

FIGURE 12.8

The distribution of *F*-ratios with *df* = 3, 20. The critical value for α = .01 is 4.94.

Analysis of SS. First, we compute the total *SS* and then the two components, as indicated in Figure 12.5.

SS_{total} is simply the *SS* for the total set of *N* = 24 scores.

$$SS_{\text{total}} = \Sigma X^2 - \frac{G^2}{N}$$

$$= 1298 - \frac{168^2}{24}$$

$$= 1298 - 1176$$

$$= 122$$

SS_{within} combines the *SS* values from inside each of the treatment conditions.

$$SS_{\text{within}} = \Sigma SS_{\text{inside each treatment}} = 20 + 20 + 14 + 8 = 62$$

SS_{between} measures the differences among the four treatment means (or treatment totals). Because we have already calculated SS_{total} and SS_{within}, the simplest way to obtain SS_{between} is by subtraction (see Equation 12.5).

$$SS_{\text{between}} = SS_{\text{total}} - SS_{\text{within}}$$

$$= 122 - 62$$

$$= 60$$

Calculation of mean squares. Because we already found $df_{\text{between}} = 3$ and $df_{\text{within}} = 16$ (Step 2), we now can compute the variance or *MS* value for each of the two components.

$$MS_{\text{between}} = \frac{SS_{\text{between}}}{df_{\text{between}}} = \frac{60}{3} = 20 \qquad MS_{\text{within}} = \frac{SS_{\text{within}}}{df_{\text{within}}} = \frac{62}{20} = 3.1$$

Calculation of F. We compute the *F*-ratio:

$$F = \frac{MS_{\text{between}}}{MS_{\text{within}}} = \frac{20}{3.1} = 6.45$$

STEP 4: Make a decision.

The F value we obtained, $F = 6.45$, is in the critical region (see Figure 12.8). It is very unlikely ($p < .01$) that we would obtain a value this large if H_0 is true. Therefore, we reject H_0 and conclude that there is a significant treatment effect.

Example 12.1 demonstrated the complete, step-by-step application of the ANOVA procedure. There are two additional points that can be made using this example.

First, you should look carefully at the statistical decision. We have rejected H_0 and concluded that not all the treatments are the same. But we have not determined which ones are different. Is generating your own questions different from using prepared questions? Is rereading different from reading only once? Unfortunately, these questions remain unanswered. We do know that at least one difference exists (we rejected H_0), but additional analysis is necessary to find out exactly where this difference is. We address this problem in Section 12.6.

Second, as noted earlier, all of the components of the analysis (the SS, df, MS, and F) can be presented together in one summary table. The summary table for the analysis in Example 12.1 is as follows:

Source	SS	df	MS	
Between treatments	60	3	20.00	$F = 6.45$
Within treatments	62	20	3.10	
Total	122	23		

Although these tables are very useful for organizing the components of an ANOVA, they are not commonly used in published reports. The current method for reporting the results from an ANOVA is presented on page 368.

MEASURING EFFECT SIZE FOR ANOVA

As we noted previously, a *significant* mean difference simply indicates that the difference observed in the sample data is very unlikely to have occurred just by chance. Thus, the term significant does not necessarily mean *large,* it simply means larger than expected by chance. To provide an indication of how large the effect actually is, researchers should report a measure of effect size in addition to the measure of significance.

For ANOVA, the simplest and most direct way to measure effect size is to compute the percentage of variance accounted for by the treatment conditions. Like the r^2 value used to measure effect size for the t tests in Chapters 9, 10, and 11, this percentage measures how much of the variability in the scores is accounted for by the differences between treatments. For ANOVA, the calculation and the concept of the percentage of variance is extremely straightforward. Specifically, we determine how much of the total SS is accounted for by the $SS_{\text{between treatments}}$.

$$\text{The percentage of variance accounted for} = \frac{SS_{\text{between treatments}}}{SS_{\text{total}}} \tag{12.14}$$

For the data in Example 12.1, we obtain

$$\text{The percentage of variance accounted for} = \frac{60}{122} = 0.492$$

In published reports of ANOVA results, the percentage of variance accounted for by the treatment effect is usually called η^2 (the Greek letter *eta* squared) instead of using r^2. Thus, for the study in Example 12.1, $\eta^2 = 0.492$.

IN THE LITERATURE
REPORTING THE RESULTS OF ANOVA

The APA format for reporting the results of ANOVA begins with a presentation of the treatment means and standard deviations in the narrative of the article, a table, or a graph. These descriptive statistics are not part of the calculations for the ANOVA, but you can easily determine the treatment means from n and T ($M = T/n$) and the standard deviations from the SS and $n - 1$ values for each treatment. Next, report the results of the ANOVA. For the study described in Example 12.1, the report might state the following:

The means and standard deviations are presented in Table 1. The analysis of variance indicates that there are significant differences among the four study strategies, $F(3, 20) = 6.45$, $p < .01$, $\eta^2 = 0.492$.

TABLE 1

Quiz scores for students using four different study strategies

	Read Once	Read and Reread	Answer Prepared Questions	Create and Answer Questions
M	5.00	6.00	8.00	9.00
SD	2.00	2.00	1.67	1.26

Note how the F-ratio is reported. In this example, degrees of freedom for between and within treatments are $df = 3, 20$, respectively. These values are placed in parentheses immediately following the symbol F. Next, the calculated value for F is reported, followed by the probability of committing a Type I error (the alpha level) and the measure of effect size.

When an ANOVA is done using a computer program, the F-ratio is usually accompanied by an exact value for p. The data from Example 12.1 were analyzed using the SPSS program (see Resources at the end of this chapter) and the computer output included a significance level of $p = .003$. Using the exact p value from the computer output, the research report would conclude, "The analysis of variance revealed significant differences among the four viewing distances, $F(3, 20) = 6.45$, $p = .003$, $\eta^2 = 0.492$."

A CONCEPTUAL VIEW OF ANOVA

Because ANOVA requires relatively complex calculations, students encountering this statistical technique for the first time often tend to be overwhelmed by the formulas and arithmetic and lose sight of the general purpose for the analysis. The following two examples are intended to minimize the role of the formulas and shift attention back to the conceptual goal of the ANOVA process.

EXAMPLE 12.2

The following data represent the outcome of an experiment using two separate samples to evaluate the mean difference between two treatment conditions. Take a minute to look at the data and, without doing any calculations, try to predict the outcome of an

ANOVA for these values. Specifically, predict what values should be obtained for the between-treatments variance (MS) and the F-ratio. If you do not "see" the answer after 20 or 30 seconds, try reading the hints that follow the data.

Treatment I	Treatment II	
4	2	$N = 8$
0	1	$G = 16$
1	0	$\Sigma X^2 = 56$
3	5	
$T = 8$	$T = 8$	
$SS = 10$	$SS = 14$	

If you are having trouble predicting the outcome of the ANOVA, read the following hints, and then go back and look at the data.

Hint 1:   Remember: $SS_{between}$ and $MS_{between}$ provide a measure of how much difference there is between treatment conditions.

Hint 2:   Find the mean or total (T) for each treatment, and determine how much difference there is between the two treatments.

You should realize by now that the data have been constructed so that there is zero difference between treatments. The two sample means (and totals) are identical, so $SS_{between} = 0$, $MS_{between} = 0$, and the F-ratio is zero.

Conceptually, the numerator of the F-ratio always measures how much difference exists between treatments. In Example 12.2, we constructed an extreme set of scores with zero difference. However, you should be able to look at any set of data and quickly compare the means (or totals) to determine whether there are big differences or small differences between treatments. We should also note that the size of the differences between treatments also directly influences measures of effect size. The data in example 12.2 have $SS_{between} = 0$, which means that $\eta^2 = 0$. As the difference between treatments increases, η^2 also increases.

Being able to estimate the magnitude of between-treatment differences is a good first step in understanding ANOVA and should help you to predict the outcome of an ANOVA. However, the *between-treatment* differences are only one part of the analysis. You must also understand the *within-treatment* differences that form the denominator of the F-ratio. The following example is intended to demonstrate the concepts underlying SS_{within} and MS_{within}. In addition, the example should give you a better understanding of how the between-treatment differences and the within-treatment differences act together within the ANOVA.

EXAMPLE 12.3   The purpose of this example is to present a visual image for the concepts of between-treatments variability and within-treatments variability. In this example, we compare two hypothetical outcomes for the same experiment. In each case, the experiment uses two separate samples to evaluate the mean difference between two treatments. The following data represent the two outcomes, which we call experiment A and experiment B.

| | Experiment A | | Experiment B | |
| | Treatment | | Treatment | |
I	II	I	II
8	12	4	12
8	13	11	9
7	12	2	20
9	11	17	6
8	13	0	16
9	12	8	18
7	11	14	3
$M = 8$	$M = 12$	$M = 8$	$M = 12$
$s = 0.82$	$s = 0.82$	$s = 6.35$	$s = 6.35$

The data from experiment A are displayed in a frequency distribution graph in Figure 12.9(a). Notice that there is a 4-point difference between the treatment means ($M_1 = 8$ and $M_2 = 12$). This is the *between-treatments* difference that contributes to the numerator of the F-ratio. Also notice that the scores in each treatment are clustered closely around the mean, indicating that the variance inside each treatment is relatively small. This is the *within-treatments* variance that contributes to the denominator of the F-ratio. Finally, you should realize that it is easy to see the mean difference between the

FIGURE 12.9

A visual representation of the between-treatments variability and the within-treatments variability that form the numerator and denominator, respectively, of the F-ratio. In (a), the difference between treatments is relatively large and easy to see. In (b), the same 4-point difference between treatments is relatively small and is overwhelmed by the within-treatments variability.

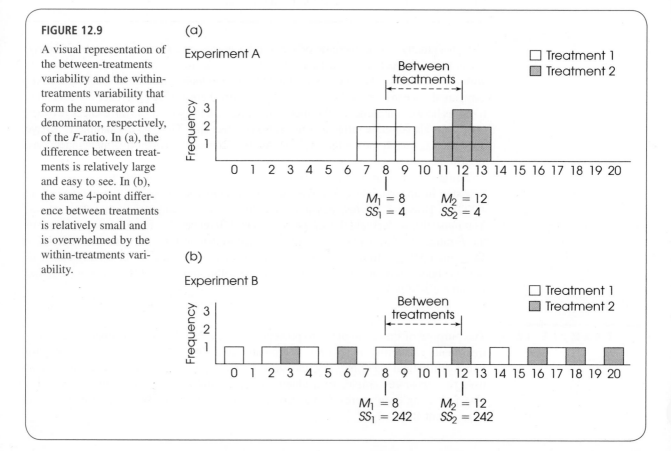

two samples. The fact that there is a clear mean difference between the two treatments is confirmed by computing the F-ratio for experiment A.

$$F = \frac{\text{between-treatments difference}}{\text{within-treatments differences}} = \frac{MS_{\text{between}}}{MS_{\text{within}}} = \frac{56}{0.667} = 83.96$$

An F-ratio of $F = 83.96$ is sufficient to reject the null hypothesis, so we conclude that there is a significant difference between the two treatments.

Now consider the data from experiment B, which are shown in Figure 12.9(b) and present a very different picture. This experiment has the same 4-point difference between treatment means that we found in experiment A ($M_1 = 8$ and $M_2 = 12$). However, for these data, the scores in each treatment are scattered across the entire scale, indicating relatively large variance inside each treatment. In this case, the large variance within treatments overwhelms the relatively small mean difference between treatments. In the figure, it is almost impossible to see the mean difference between treatments. For these data, the F-ratio confirms that there is no clear mean difference between treatments.

$$F = \frac{\text{between-treatments difference}}{\text{within-treatments differences}} = \frac{MS_{\text{between}}}{MS_{\text{within}}} = \frac{56}{40.33} = 1.39$$

For experiment B, the F-ratio is not large enough to reject the null hypothesis, so we conclude that there is no significant difference between the two treatments. Once again, the statistical conclusion is consistent with the appearance of the data in Figure 12.9(b). Looking at the figure, we see that the scores from the two samples appear to be intermixed randomly with no clear distinction between treatments.

Sample variance also influences measures of effect size. The two samples in Figure 12.9(a), with small variance, produce $\eta^2 = 56/64 = 0.875$. When the variance is increased in Figure 12.9(b), the measure of effect size is reduced to $\eta^2 = \frac{56}{540} = 0.104$.

As we have noted in previous chapters, high variability makes it difficult to see any patterns in the data. In Figure 12.9(a), the 4-point mean difference between treatments is easy to see because the sample variance is small. In Figure 12.9(b), the 4-point difference gets lost because the sample variance is large. In general, you can think of variance as measuring the amount of "noise" or "confusion" in the data. With large variance there is a lot of noise and confusion and it is difficult to see any clear patterns.

Although Examples 12.2 and 12.3 present somewhat simplified demonstrations with exaggerated data, the general point of the examples is to help you *see* what happens when you perform an ANOVA. Specifically:

1. The numerator of the F-ratio (MS_{between}) measures how much difference exists between the treatment means. Bigger mean differences produce larger F-ratios and larger measures of effect size.

2. The denominator of the F-ratio (MS_{within}) measures the variance of the scores inside each treatment; that is, the variance for each of the separate samples. In general, larger sample variance produces smaller F-ratios and smaller measures of effect size.

We should note that the number of scores in the samples also can influence the outcome of an ANOVA. As with most other hypothesis tests, if other factors are held constant, increasing the sample size tends to increase the likelihood of rejecting the null hypothesis. However, changes in sample size have little or no effect on measures of effect size such as η^2.

MS_{WITHIN} **AND POOLED VARIANCE**

You may have recognized that the two research outcomes presented in Example 12.3 are similar to those presented earlier in Example 10.5 in Chapter 10. Both examples are intended to demonstrate the role of variance in a hypothesis test. Both examples show that large values for sample variance can obscure any patterns in the data and reduce the potential for finding significant differences between means.

For the independent-measures t statistic in Chapter 10, the sample variance contributed directly to the standard error in the bottom of the t formula. Now, the sample variance contributes directly to the value of MS_{within} in the bottom of the F-ratio. In the t-statistic and in the F-ratio, the variances from the separate samples are pooled together to create one average value for sample variance. For the independent-measures t statistic, we pooled two samples together to compute

$$\text{pooled variance} = s_p^2 = \frac{SS_1 + SS_2}{df_1 + df_2}$$

Now, in ANOVA, we are combining two or more samples to calculate

$$MS_{within} = \frac{SS_{within}}{df_{within}} = \frac{\Sigma SS}{\Sigma df} = \frac{SS_1 + SS_2 + SS_3 + \ldots}{df_1 + df_2 + df_3 + \ldots}$$

Notice that the concept of pooled variance is the same whether you have exactly two samples or more than two samples. In either case, you simply add the SS values and divide by the sum of the df values. The result is an average of all of the different sample variances.

When the samples are all the same size, MS_{within} is literally the average of the sample variances. In Example, 12.1, the four samples all have $n = 6$ scores. The four SS values are 20, 20, 14, and 8, and each has $df = 5$. Therefore, the four sample variances are $\frac{20}{5} = 4.00$, $\frac{20}{5} = 4.00$, $\frac{14}{5} = 2.80$ and $\frac{8}{5} = 1.60$. The average of the four variances is $(4.0 + 4.0 + 2.8 + 1.6)/4 = 12.4/4 = 3.10$, which is exactly the value we obtained for MS_{within}. If the samples are not all the same size, MS_{within} is still the average of the sample variances, however, the average is computed so each sample variance is weighted by its sample size.

AN EXAMPLE WITH UNEQUAL SAMPLE SIZES

In the previous examples, all of the samples were exactly the same size (equal ns). However, the formulas for ANOVA can be used when the sample size varies within a research study. You also should note, however, that the general ANOVA procedure is most accurate when used to examine data with equal sample sizes. Therefore, researchers generally try to plan research studies with equal ns. However, there are circumstances in which it is impossible or impractical to have an equal number of subjects in every treatment condition. In these situations, ANOVA still provides a valid test, especially when the samples are relatively large and when the discrepancy between sample sizes is not extreme.

The following example demonstrates an ANOVA with samples of different sizes.

EXAMPLE 12.4

A researcher is interested in the amount of homework required by different academic majors. Students are recruited from Biology, English, and Psychology to participate in the study. The researcher randomly selects one course that each student is currently taking and asks the student to record the amount of out-of-class work required each week for the course. The researcher used all of the volunteer participants, which resulted in unequal sample sizes. The data are summarized in Table 12.5.

TABLE 12.5

Average hours of homework per week for one course for students in three academic majors.

Biology	English	Psychology	
$n = 4$	$n = 10$	$n = 6$	$N = 20$
$M = 9$	$M = 13$	$M = 14$	$G = 250$
$T = 36$	$T = 130$	$T = 84$	$\Sigma X^2 = 3377$
$SS = 37$	$SS = 90$	$SS = 60$	

STEP 1: State the hypotheses, and select the alpha level.

$$H_0: \mu_1 = \mu_2 = \mu_3$$

H_1: At least one population is different.

$$\alpha = .05$$

STEP 2: Locate the critical region.

To find the critical region, we first must determine the df values for the F-ratio:

$$df_{total} = N - 1 = 20 - 1 = 19$$

$$df_{between} = k - 1 = 3 - 1 = 2$$

$$df_{within} = N - k = 20 - 3 = 17$$

The F-ratio for these data has $df = 2, 17$. With $\alpha = .05$, the critical value for the F-ratio is 3.59.

STEP 3: Compute the F-ratio.

First, compute the three SS values. As usual, SS_{total} is the SS for the total set of $N = 20$ scores, and SS_{within} combines the SS values from inside each of the treatment conditions.

$$SS_{total} = \Sigma X^2 - \frac{G^2}{N} \qquad\qquad SS_{within} = \Sigma SS_{\text{inside each treatment}}$$

$$= 3377 - 3125 \qquad\qquad = 37 + 90 + 60$$

$$= 252 \qquad\qquad\qquad = 187$$

$SS_{between}$ can be found by subtraction (Equation 12.5).

$$SS_{between} = SS_{total} - SS_{within}$$

$$= 252 - 187$$

$$= 65$$

Or, $SS_{between}$ can be calculated using the computation formula (see Equation 12.7). If you use the computational formula, be careful to match each treatment total (T) with the appropriate sample size (n) as follows:

$$SS_{between} = \Sigma \frac{T^2}{n} - \frac{G^2}{N}$$

$$= \frac{36^2}{4} + \frac{130^2}{10} + \frac{84^2}{6} - \frac{250^2}{20}$$

$$= 324 + 1690 + 1176 - 3125$$

$$= 65$$

Finally, compute the *MS* values and the *F*-ratio:

$$MS_{between} = \frac{SS}{df} = \frac{65}{2} = 32.5$$

$$MS_{within} = \frac{SS}{df} = \frac{187}{17} = 11$$

$$F = \frac{MS_{between}}{MS_{within}} = \frac{32.5}{11} = 2.95$$

STEP 4: Make a decision.

Because the obtained *F*-ratio is not in the critical region, we fail to reject the null hypothesis and conclude that there are no significant differences among the three populations of students in terms of the average amount of homework each week.

LEARNING CHECK

1. A researcher used ANOVA and computed $F = 4.25$ for the following data.

	Treatments	
I	*II*	*III*
$n = 10$	$n = 10$	$n = 10$
$M = 20$	$M = 28$	$M = 35$
$SS = 1005$	$SS = 1391$	$SS = 1180$

a. If the mean for treatment III were changed to $M = 25$, what would happen to the size of the *F*-ratio (increase or decrease)?

b. If the *SS* for treatment I were changed to $SS = 1400$, what would happen to the size of the *F*-ratio (increase or decrease)?

c. If the sample means and variances were held constant but each sample size were increased to $n = 20$, then what would happen to the size of the *F*-ratio (increase or decrease)?

2. A research study comparing three treatment conditions produces $M = 5$ with $n = 4$ for the first treatment, $M = 2$ with $n = 5$ for the second treatment, and $M = 5$ with $n = 6$ for the third treatment. Calculate $SS_{between\ treatments}$ for these data.

ANSWERS

1. a. If the mean for treatment III were changed to $M = 25$, it would reduce the size of the mean differences (the three means would be closer together). This would reduce the size of $MS_{between}$ and would reduce the size of the *F*-ratio.

b. If the *SS* in treatment I were increased to $SS = 1400$, it would increase the size of the variability within treatments. This would increase MS_{within} and would reduce the size of the *F*-ratio.

c. If other factors are held constant, increasing the size of the samples increases the *F*-ratio and increases the likelihood of rejecting the null hypothesis.

2. The three sample totals are $T_1 = 20$, $T_2 = 10$, and $T_3 = 30$, which produces $G = 60$ and $N = 15$. $SS_{between} = 30$.

12.6 POST HOC TESTS

As noted earlier, the primary advantage of ANOVA (compared to *t* tests) is that it allows researchers to test for significant mean differences when there are *more than two* treatment conditions. ANOVA accomplishes this feat by comparing all of the individual mean differences simultaneously within a single test. Unfortunately, the process of combining several mean differences into a single test statistic creates some difficulty when it is time to interpret the outcome of the test. Specifically, when you obtain a significant *F*-ratio (reject H_0), it simply indicates that somewhere among the entire set of mean differences there is at least one that is statistically significant. In other words, the overall *F*-ratio only tells you that a significant difference exists; it does not tell exactly which means are significantly different and which are not.

Consider, for example, a research study that uses three samples to compare three treatment conditions. Suppose that the three sample means are $M_1 = 3$, $M_2 = 5$, and $M_3 = 10$. In this hypothetical study, there are three mean differences:

1. There is a 2-point difference between M_1 and M_2.

2. There is a 5-point difference between M_2 and M_3.

3. There is a 7-point difference between M_1 and M_3.

If an ANOVA were used to evaluate these data, a significant *F*-ratio would indicate that at least one of the sample mean differences is large enough to satisfy the criterion of statistical significance. In this example, the 7-point difference is the biggest of the three and, therefore, it must indicate a significant difference between the first treatment and the third treatment ($\mu_1 \neq \mu_3$). But what about the 5-point difference? Is it also large enough to be significant? And what about the 2-point difference between M_1 and M_2? Is it also significant? The purpose of *post hoc tests* is to answer these questions.

DEFINITION

> **Post hoc tests** (or **posttests**) are additional hypothesis tests that are done after an ANOVA to determine exactly which mean differences are significant and which are not.

As the name implies, post hoc tests are done after an ANOVA. More specifically, these tests are done after ANOVA when

1. You reject H_0 and

2. There are three or more treatments ($k \geq 3$).

Rejecting H_0 indicates that at least one difference exists among the treatments. If there are only two treatments, then there is no question about which means are different and, therefore, no need for posttests. However, with three or more treatments ($k \geq 3$), the problem is to determine exactly which means are significantly different.

POSTTESTS AND TYPE I ERRORS

In general, a post hoc test enables you to go back through the data and compare the individual treatments two at a time. In statistical terms, this is called making *pairwise comparisons*. For example, with $k = 3$, we would compare μ_1 versus μ_2, then μ_2 versus μ_3, and then μ_1 versus μ_3. In each case, we are looking for a significant mean difference.

The process of conducting pairwise comparisons involves performing a series of separate hypothesis tests, and each of these tests includes the risk of a Type I error. As you do more and more separate tests, the risk of a Type I error accumulates and is called the *experimentwise alpha level* (see p. 350).

Whenever you are conducting posttests, you must be concerned about the experimentwise alpha level. Statisticians have worked with this problem and have developed several methods for trying to control Type I errors in the context of post hoc tests. We consider two alternatives.

TUKEY'S HONESTLY SIGNIFICANT DIFFERENCE (HSD) TEST

The first post hoc test we consider is *Tukey's HSD test.* We selected Tukey's HSD test because it is a commonly used test in psychological research. Tukey's test allows you to compute a single value that determines the minimum difference between treatment means that is necessary for significance. This value, called the *honestly significant difference,* or HSD, is then used to compare any two treatment conditions. If the mean difference exceeds Tukey's HSD, then you conclude that there is a significant difference between the treatments. Otherwise, you cannot conclude that the treatments are significantly different. The formula for Tukey's HSD is

$$HSD = q\sqrt{\frac{MS_{within}}{n}} \tag{12.15}$$

The q value used in Tukey's HSD test is called a Studentized range statistic.

where the value of q is found in Table B.5 (Appendix B, p. 580), MS_{within} is the within-treatments variance from the ANOVA, and n is the number of scores in each treatment. Tukey's test requires that the sample size, n, be the same for all treatments. To locate the appropriate value of q, you must know the number of treatments in the overall experiment (k), the degrees of freedom for MS_{within} (the error term in the F-ratio), and you must select an alpha level (generally the same α used for the ANOVA).

EXAMPLE 12.5

To demonstrate the procedure for conducting post hoc tests with Tukey's HSD, we use the hypothetical data shown in Table 12.6. The data represent the results of a study comparing scores in three different treatment conditions. Note that the table displays summary statistics for each sample and the results from the overall ANOVA. With $k = 3$ treatments, $df_{within} = 24$, and $\alpha = .05$, you should find that the value of q for the test is $q = 3.53$ (see Table B.5). Therefore, Tukey's HSD is

$$HSD = q\sqrt{\frac{MS_{within}}{n}} = 3.53\sqrt{\frac{4.00}{9}} = 2.36$$

TABLE 12.6

Hypothetical results from a research study comparing three treatment conditions. Summary statistics are presented for each treatment along with the outcome from the ANOVA.

Treatment A	Treatment B	Treatment C
$n = 9$	$n = 9$	$n = 9$
$T = 27$	$T = 49$	$T = 63$
$M = 3.00$	$M = 5.44$	$M = 7.00$

Source	SS	df	MS
Between	73.19	2	36.60
Within	96.00	24	4.00
Total	169.19	26	
Overall $F(2, 24) = 9.15$			

Thus, the mean difference between any two samples must be at least 2.36 to be significant. Using this value, we can make the following conclusions:

1. Treatment A is significantly different from treatment B ($M_A - M_B = 2.44$).

2. Treatment A is also significantly different from treatment C ($M_A - M_C = 4.00$).

3. Treatment B is not significantly different from treatment C ($M_B - M_C = 1.56$).

THE SCHEFFÉ TEST

Because it uses an extremely cautious method for reducing the risk of a Type I error, the *Scheffé test* has the distinction of being one of the safest of all possible post hoc tests (smallest risk of a Type I error). The Scheffé test uses an *F*-ratio to evaluate the significance of the difference between any two treatment conditions. The numerator of the *F*-ratio is an $MS_{between}$ that is calculated using *only the two treatments you want to compare*. The denominator is the same MS_{within} that was used for the overall ANOVA. The "safety factor" for the Scheffé test comes from the following two considerations:

1. Although you are comparing only two treatments, the Scheffé test uses the value of *k* from the original experiment to compute *df* between treatments. Thus, *df* for the numerator of the *F*-ratio is $k - 1$.

2. The critical value for the Scheffé *F*-ratio is the same as was used to evaluate the *F*-ratio from the overall ANOVA. Thus, Scheffé requires that every posttest satisfy the same criterion that was used for the complete ANOVA. The following example uses the data from Table 12.6 to demonstrate the Scheffé posttest procedure.

EXAMPLE 12.6

Remember that the Scheffé procedure requires a separate $SS_{between}$, $MS_{between}$, and *F*-ratio for each comparison being made. Although Scheffé computes $SS_{between}$ using the regular computational formula (Equation 12.7), you must remember that the numbers in the formula are entirely determined by the two treatment conditions being compared. We begin by comparing treatment A (with $T = 27$ and $n = 9$) and treatment B (with $T = 49$ and $n = 9$). The first step is to compute $SS_{between}$ for these two groups. In the formula for *SS*, notice that the grand total for the two groups is $G = 27 + 49 = 76$, and the total number of scores for the two groups is $N = 9 + 9 = 18$.

$$SS_{between} = \Sigma \frac{T^2}{n} - \frac{G^2}{N}$$
$$= \frac{27^2}{9} + \frac{49^2}{9} - \frac{76^2}{18}$$
$$= 81 + 266.78 - 320.89$$
$$= 26.89$$

Although we are comparing only two groups, these two were selected from a study consisting of $k = 3$ samples. The Scheffé test uses the overall study to determine the degrees of freedom between treatments. Therefore, $df_{between} = 3 - 1 = 2$, and the $MS_{between}$ is

$$MS_{between} = \frac{SS_{between}}{df_{between}} = \frac{26.89}{2} = 13.45$$

Finally, the Scheffé procedure uses the error term from the overall ANOVA to compute the F-ratio. In this case, $MS_{within} = 4.00$ with $df_{within} = 24$. Thus, the Scheffé test produces an F-ratio of

$$F_{A \text{ versus } B} = \frac{MS_{between}}{MS_{within}} = \frac{13.45}{4.00} = 3.36$$

With $df = 2, 24$ and $\alpha = .05$, the critical value for F is 3.40 (see Table B.4). Therefore, our obtained F-ratio is not in the critical region, and we must conclude that these data show no significant difference between treatment A and treatment B.

The second comparison involves treatment B ($T = 49$) and treatment C ($T = 63$). This time the data produce $SS_{between} = 10.89$, $MS_{between} = 5.45$, and $F(2, 24) = 1.36$ (check the calculations for yourself). Once again the critical value for F is 3.40, so we must conclude that the data show no significant difference between treatment B and treatment C.

The final comparison is treatment A ($T = 27$) and treatment C ($T = 63$). This time the data produce $SS_{between} = 72$, $MS_{between} = 36$, and $F(2, 24) = 9.00$ (check the calculations for yourself). Once again the critical value for F is 3.40, and this time we conclude that the data show a significant difference.

Thus, the Scheffé posttest indicates that the only significant difference is between treatment A and treatment C.

There are two interesting points to be made from the posttest outcomes presented in the preceding two examples. First, the Scheffé test was introduced as being one of the safest of the posttest techniques because it provides the greatest protection from Type I errors. To provide this protection, the Scheffé test simply requires a larger difference between sample means before you may conclude that the difference is significant. For example, using Tukey's test in Example 12.5, we found that the difference between treatment A and treatment B was large enough to be significant. However, this same difference failed to reach significance according to the Scheffé test (Example 12.6). The discrepancy between the results is an example of the Scheffé test's extra demands: The Scheffé test simply requires more evidence and, therefore, it is less likely to lead to a Type I error.

The second point concerns the pattern of results from the three Scheffé tests in Example 12.6. You may have noticed that the posttests produce what are apparently contradictory results. Specifically, the tests show no significant difference between A and B and they show no significant difference between B and C. This combination of outcomes might lead you to suspect that there is no significant difference between A and C. However, the test did show a significant difference. The answer to this apparent contradiction lies in the criterion of statistical significance. The differences between A and B and between B and C are too small to satisfy the criterion of significance. However, when these differences are combined, the total difference between A and C is large enough to meet the criterion for significance.

LEARNING CHECK

1. With $k = 2$ treatments, are post hoc tests necessary when the null hypothesis is rejected? Explain why or why not.

2. Three treatments, each with a sample of $n = 8$ participants, have treatment totals of $T_1 = 16$, $T_2 = 32$, and $T_3 = 40$, and produce $MS_{within} = 2.5$.

   a. Use Tukey's HSD test with $\alpha = .05$ to evaluate the significance of the mean difference between treatments 1 and 2.

b. Use the Scheffé test with $\alpha = .05$ to evaluate the significance of the mean difference between treatments 1 and 2.

ANSWERS   **1.** No. Post hoc tests are used to determine which treatments are different. With only two treatment conditions, there is no uncertainty as to which two treatments are different.

2. a. For this test, $q = 3.53$ and HSD $= 1.97$. There is a 2-point mean difference between treatments 1 and 2, which is large enough to be significant.

b. For these two treatments, Scheffé produces $SS_{between} = 16$, $MS_{between} = 8$, and $F = 3.2$. With $df = 2, 21$ the critical value is 3.47. Conclude that the mean difference between treatments 1 and 2 is not significant.

12.7 THE RELATIONSHIP BETWEEN ANOVA AND *t* TESTS

When you are evaluating the mean difference from an independent-measures study comparing only two treatments (two separate samples), you can use either an independent-measures *t* test (Chapter 10) or the ANOVA presented in this chapter. In practical terms, it makes no difference which you choose. These two statistical techniques always result in the same statistical decision. In fact, the two methods use many of the same calculations and are very closely related in several other respects. The basic relationship between *t* statistics and *F*-ratios can be stated in an equation:

$$F = t^2$$

This relationship can be explained by first looking at the structure of the formulas for *F* and *t*. The *t* statistic compares *distances:* the distance between two sample means (numerator) and the distance computed for the standard error (denominator). The *F*-ratio, on the other hand, compares *variances.* You should recall that variance is a measure of squared distance. Hence, the relationship: $F = t^2$.

There are several other points to consider in comparing the *t* statistic to the *F*-ratio.

1. It should be obvious that you are testing the same hypotheses whether you choose a *t* test or an ANOVA. With only two treatments, the hypotheses for either test are

$$H_0: \mu_1 = \mu_2$$

$$H_1: \mu_1 \neq \mu_2$$

2. The degrees of freedom for the *t* statistic and the *df* for the denominator of the *F*-ratio (df_{within}) are identical. For example, if you have two samples, each with six scores, the independent-measures *t* statistic has $df = 10$, and the F-ratio has $df = 1, 10$. In each case, you are adding the *df* from the first sample $(n - 1)$ and the *df* from the second sample $(n - 1)$.

3. The distribution of *t* and the distribution of *F*-ratios match perfectly if you take into consideration the relationship $F = t^2$. Consider the *t* distribution with $df = 18$

FIGURE 12.10

The distribution of t statistics with $df = 18$ and the corresponding distribution of F-ratios with $df = 1, 18$. Notice that the critical values for $\alpha = .05$ are $t = \pm 2.101$ and $F = 2.101^2 = 4.41$.

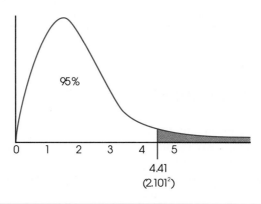

and the corresponding F distribution with $df = 1, 18$ that are presented in Figure 12.10. Notice the following relationships:

a. If each of the t values is squared, then all of the negative values become positive. As a result, the whole left-hand side of the t distribution (below zero) is flipped over to the positive side. This creates an asymmetrical, positively skewed distribution—that is, the F distribution.

b. For $\alpha = .05$, the critical region for t is determined by values greater than $+2.101$ or less than -2.101. When these boundaries are squared, you get $\pm 2.101^2 = 4.41$.

Notice that 4.41 is the critical value for $\alpha = .05$ in the F distribution. Any value that is in the critical region for t ends up in the critical region for F-ratios after it is squared.

ASSUMPTIONS FOR THE INDEPENDENT-MEASURES ANOVA

The independent-measures ANOVA requires the same three assumptions that were necessary for the independent-measures t hypothesis test:

1. The observations within each sample must be independent (see p. 220).

2. The populations from which the samples are selected must be normal.

3. The populations from which the samples are selected must have equal variances (homogeneity of variance).

Ordinarily, researchers are not overly concerned with the assumption of normality, especially when large samples are used, unless there are strong reasons to suspect that the assumption has not been satisfied. The assumption of homogeneity of variance is an important one. If a researcher suspects that it has been violated, it can be tested by Hartley's F-max test for homogeneity of variance (Chapter 10, p. 300).

LEARNING CHECK

1. A researcher uses an independent-measures t test to evaluate the mean difference obtained in a research study, and obtains a t statistic of $t = 3.00$. If the researcher used an ANOVA to evaluate the results, then what F-ratio would be obtained?

2. An ANOVA produces an F-ratio with $df = 1, 34$. Could the data have been analyzed with a t test? What would be the degrees of freedom for the t statistic?

ANSWERS

1. $F = 9$ because $F = t^2$

2. If the F-ratio has $df = 1, 34$, then the experiment compared only two treatments, and you could use a t statistic to evaluate the data. The t statistic would have $df = 34$.

SUMMARY

1. Analysis of variance (ANOVA) is a statistical technique that is used to test the significance of mean differences among two or more treatment conditions. The null hypothesis for this test states that, in the general population, there are no mean differences among the treatments. The alternative states that at least one mean is different from another.

2. The test statistic for ANOVA is a ratio of two variances called an F-ratio. The variances in the F-ratio are called mean squares, or MS values. Each MS is computed by

$$MS = \frac{SS}{df}$$

3. For the independent-measures ANOVA, the F-ratio is

$$F = \frac{MS_{between}}{MS_{within}}$$

The $MS_{between}$ measures differences between the treatments by computing the variance for the treatment means or totals. These differences are assumed to be produced by

a. Treatment effects (if they exist)

b. Random, unsystematic differences (chance)

The MS_{within} measures variance inside each of the treatment conditions. Because individuals inside a treatment condition are all treated exactly the same, any differences within treatments cannot be caused by treatment effects. Thus, the within-treatments MS is produced only by random, unsystematic differences. With these factors in mind, the F-ratio has the following structure:

$$F = \frac{\text{treatment effect} + \text{random, unsystematic differences}}{\text{random, unsystematic differences}}$$

When there is no treatment effect (H_0 is true), the numerator and the denominator of the F-ratio are measuring the same variance, and the obtained ratio should be near 1.00. If there is a significant treatment effect, then the numerator of the ratio should be larger than the denominator, and the obtained F value should be much greater than 1.00.

4. The formulas for computing each SS, df, and MS value are presented in Figure 12.11, which also shows the general structure for the ANOVA.

5. The F-ratio has two values for degrees of freedom, one associated with the MS in the numerator and one associated with the MS in the denominator. These df values are used to find the critical value for the F-ratio in the F distribution table.

6. Effect size for the independent-measures ANOVA is measured by computing eta squared, the percentage of variance accounted for by the treatment effect.

$$\eta^2 = \frac{SS_{between}}{SS_{between} + SS_{within}} = \frac{SS_{between}}{SS_{total}}$$

7. When the decision from an ANOVA is to reject the null hypothesis and when the experiment contains more than two treatment conditions, it is necessary to continue the analysis with a post hoc test, such as Tukey's HSD test or the Scheffé test. The purpose of these tests is to determine exactly which treatments are significantly different and which are not.

FIGURE 12.11

Formulas for ANOVA.

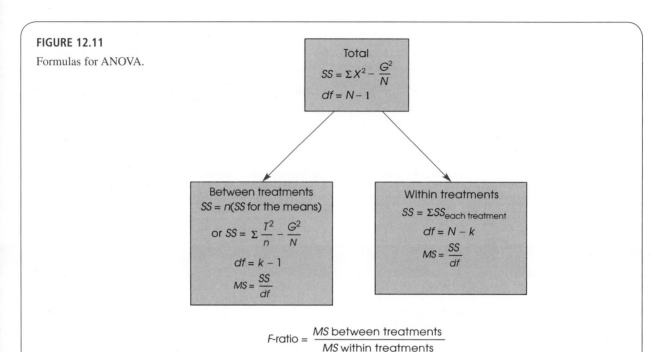

Total
$$SS = \Sigma X^2 - \frac{G^2}{N}$$
$$df = N - 1$$

Between treatments
$$SS = n(SS \text{ for the means})$$
$$\text{or } SS = \Sigma \frac{T^2}{n} - \frac{G^2}{N}$$
$$df = k - 1$$
$$MS = \frac{SS}{df}$$

Within treatments
$$SS = \Sigma SS_{\text{each treatment}}$$
$$df = N - k$$
$$MS = \frac{SS}{df}$$

$$F\text{-ratio} = \frac{MS \text{ between treatments}}{MS \text{ within treatments}}$$

KEY TERMS

analysis of variance (ANOVA) (346)

factor (347)

levels (347)

F-ratio (349)

testwise alpha level (350)

experimentwise alpha level (350)

between-treatments variance (351)

within-treatments variance (352)

treatment effect (352)

error term (353)

mean square (*MS*) (360)

ANOVA summary table (361)

distribution of *F*-ratios (362)

eta squared (η^2) (367)

post hoc tests (375)

pairwise comparisons (375)

Tukey's HSD test (376)

Scheffé test (377)

RESOURCES

Go to CengageBrain.com to access Psychology CourseMate, where you will find an interactive eBook, glossaries, flashcards, quizzes, statistics workshops, and more.

If your professor has assigned Aplia:

1. Sign in to your account.
2. Complete the corresponding exercises as required by your professor.
3. When finished, click "Grade It Now" to see which areas you have mastered, which areas need more work, and detailed explanations of every answer.

General instructions for using SPSS are presented in Appendix D. Following are detailed instructions for using SPSS to perform **The Single-Factor, Independent-Measures Analysis of Variance (ANOVA)** presented in this chapter.

Data Entry

1. The scores are entered in a *stacked format* in the data editor, which means that all of the scores from all of the different treatments are entered in a single column (VAR00001). Enter the scores for treatment #2 directly beneath the scores from treatment #1 with no gaps or extra spaces. Continue in the same column with the scores from treatment #3, and so on.

2. In the second column (VAR00002), enter a number to identify the treatment condition for each score. For example, enter a 1 beside each score from the first treatment, enter a 2 beside each score from the second treatment, and so on.

Data Analysis

1. Click **Analyze** on the tool bar, select **Compare Means,** and click on **One-Way ANOVA.**

2. Highlight the column label for the set of scores (VAR0001) in the left box and click the arrow to move it into the **Dependent List** box.

3. Highlight the label for the column containing the treatment numbers (VAR0002) in the left box and click the arrow to move it into the **Factor** box.

4. If you want descriptive statistics for each treatment, click on the **Options** box, select **Descriptives,** and click **Continue.**

5. Click **OK.**

SPSS Output

We used the SPSS program to analyze the data from the studying strategy experiment in Example 12.1, and the program output is shown in Figure 12.12. The output begins with a table showing descriptive statistics (number of scores, mean, standard deviation, standard error for the mean, a 95% confidence interval for the mean, maximum, and minimum scores) for each sample. The second part of the output presents a summary table showing the results from the ANOVA.

FOCUS ON PROBLEM SOLVING

1. It can be helpful to compute all three SS values separately, and then check to verify that the two components (between and within) add up to the total. However, you can greatly simplify the calculations if you simply find SS_{total} and SS_{within}, then obtain $SS_{between}$ by subtraction.

Descriptives

VAR00001

	N	Mean	Std. Deviation	Std. Error	95% Confidence Interval for Mean		Minimum	Maximum
					Lower Bound	Upper Bound		
1.00	6	5.0000	2.00000	.81650	2.9011	7.0989	3.00	8.00
2.00	6	6.0000	2.00000	.81650	3.9011	8.0989	3.00	8.00
3.00	6	8.0000	1.67332	.68313	6.2440	9.7560	5.00	10.00
4.00	6	9.0000	1.26491	.51640	7.6726	10.3274	7.00	10.00
Total	24	7.0000	2.30312	.47012	6.0275	7.9725	3.00	10.00

ANOVA

VAR00001

	Sum of Squares	df	Mean Square	F	Sig.
Between Groups	60.000	3	20.000	6.452	.003
Within Groups	62.000	20	3.100		
Total	122.000	23			

FIGURE 12.12

SPSS output of the ANOVA for the studying strategy experiment in Example 12.1.

2. Remember that an F-ratio has two separate values for df: a value for the numerator and one for the denominator. Properly reported, the $df_{between}$ value is stated first. You will need both df values when consulting the F distribution table for the critical F value.

3. When you encounter an F-ratio and its df values reported in the literature, you should be able to reconstruct much of the original experiment. For example, if you see "$F(2, 36) = 4.80$," you should realize that the experiment compared $k = 3$ treatment groups (because $df_{between} = k - 1 = 2$), with a total of $N = 39$ subjects participating in the experiment (because $df_{within} = N - k = 36$).

DEMONSTRATION 12.1

ANALYSIS OF VARIANCE

A human-factors psychologist studied three computer keyboard designs. Three samples of individuals were given material to type on a particular keyboard, and the number of errors committed by each participant was recorded. The data are as follows:

Keyboard A	Keyboard B	Keyboard C	
0	6	6	$N = 15$
4	8	5	$G = 60$
0	5	9	$\Sigma X^2 = 356$
1	4	4	
0	2	6	
$T = 5$	$T = 25$	$T = 30$	
$SS = 12$	$SS = 20$	$SS = 14$	

Are these data sufficient to conclude that there are significant differences in typing performance among the three keyboard designs?

STEP 1 State the hypotheses, and specify the alpha level.   The null hypothesis states that there are no differences among the keyboards in terms of number of errors committed. In symbols, we would state

$$H_0\colon \mu_1 = \mu_2 = \mu_3 \qquad \text{(Type of keyboard used has no effect.)}$$

As noted previously in this chapter, there are a number of possible statements for the alternative hypothesis. Here we state the general alternative hypothesis:

$$H_1\colon \text{ At least one of the treatment means is different.}$$

We set alpha at $\alpha = .05$.

STEP 2 Locate the critical region.   To locate the critical region, we must obtain the values for $df_{between}$ and df_{within}.

$$df_{between} = k - 1 = 3 - 1 = 2$$
$$df_{within} = N - k = 15 - 3 = 12$$

The F-ratio for this problem has $df = 2, 12$, and the critical F value for $\alpha = .05$ is $F = 3.88$.

STEP 3 Perform the analysis.   The analysis involves the following steps:

1. Perform the analysis of SS.

2. Perform the analysis of df.

3. Calculate mean squares.

4. Calculate the F-ratio.

Perform the analysis of SS. We compute SS_{total} followed by its two components.

$$SS_{total} = \Sigma X^2 - \frac{G^2}{N} = 356 - \frac{60^2}{15} = 356 - \frac{3600}{15}$$
$$= 356 - 240 = 116$$

$$SS_{within} = \Sigma SS_{inside} \text{ each treatment}$$
$$= 12 + 20 + 14$$
$$= 46$$

By subtraction, $SS_{between} = SS_{total} - SS_{within} = 116 - 46 = 70$

Analyze degrees of freedom. We compute df_{total}. Its components, $df_{between}$ and df_{within}, were previously calculated (see step 2).

$$df_{total} = N - 1 = 15 - 1 = 14$$
$$df_{between} = 2$$
$$df_{within} = 12$$

Calculate the MS values. We determine the values for $MS_{between}$ and MS_{within}.

$$MS_{between} = \frac{SS_{between}}{df_{between}} = \frac{70}{2} = 35$$
$$MS_{within} = \frac{SS_{within}}{df_{within}} = \frac{46}{12} = 3.83$$

Compute the F-ratio. Finally, we can compute F.

$$F = \frac{MS_{between}}{MS_{within}} = \frac{35}{3.83} = 9.14$$

STEP 4 Make a decision about H_0, and state a conclusion.   The obtained F of 9.14 exceeds the critical value of 3.88. Therefore, we can reject the null hypothesis. The type of keyboard used has a significant effect on the number of errors committed, $F(2, 12) = 9.14, p < .05$. The following table summarizes the results of the analysis:

Source	SS	df	MS	
Between treatments	70	2	35	$F = 9.14$
Within treatments	46	12	3.83	
Total	116	14		

DEMONSTRATION 12.2

COMPUTING EFFECT SIZE FOR ANOVA

We compute eta squared (η^2), the percentage of variance explained, for the data that were analyzed in Demonstration 12.1. The data produced a between-treatments SS of 70 and a total SS of 116. Thus,

$$\eta^2 = \frac{SS_{between}}{SS_{total}} = \frac{70}{116} = 0.60 \text{ (or 60\%)}$$

PROBLEMS

1. Explain why the F-ratio is expected to be near 1.00 when the null hypothesis is true.

2. Several factors influence the size of the F-ratio. For each of the following, indicate whether it influences the numerator or the denominator of the F-ratio, and indicate whether the size of the F-ratio would increase or decrease. In each case, assume that all other factors are held constant.
    a. An increase in the differences between the sample means.
    b. An increase in the size of the sample variances.

3. Why should you use ANOVA instead of several t tests to evaluate mean differences when an experiment consists of three or more treatment conditions?

4. Posttests are done after an ANOVA.
    a. What is the purpose of posttests?
    b. Explain why you do not need posttests if the analysis is comparing only two treatments.
    c. Explain why you do not need posttests if the decision from the ANOVA is to fail to reject the null hypothesis.

5. An independent-measures study comparing four treatment conditions with a sample of $n = 8$ in each condition produces sample means of $M_1 = 2$, $M_2 = 3$, $M_3 = 1$, and $M_4 = 6$.
    a. Compute SS for the set of 4 treatment means. (Treat the means as a set of $n = 4$ scores and compute SS.)
    b. Using the result from part a, compute $n(SS_{means})$. Note that this value is equal to $SS_{between}$ (see Equation 12.6).
    c. Now, find the 4 treatment totals and compute $SS_{between}$ with the computational formula using the T values (see Equation 12.7). You should obtain the same result as in part b.

6. The following data summarize the results from an independent-measures study comparing three treatment conditions.

	Treatment		
I	II	III	
3	5	6	$N = 12$
5	5	10	$G = 60$
3	1	10	$\Sigma X^2 = 392$
1	5	6	
$M = 3$	$M = 4$	$M = 8$	
$T = 12$	$T = 16$	$T = 32$	
$SS = 8$	$SS = 12$	$SS = 16$	

    a. Use an ANOVA with $\alpha = .05$ to determine whether there are any significant differences among the three treatment means.

    b. Calculate η^2 to measure the effect size for this study.
    c. Write a sentence demonstrating how a research report would present the results of the hypothesis test and the measure of effect size.

7. For the preceding problem you should find that there are significant differences among the three treatments. The primary reason for the significance is that the mean for treatment III is substantially larger than the means for the other two treatments. To create the following data, we started with the values from problem 6 and subtracted 3 points to each score in treatment III. Notice that subtracting a constant causes the mean to change but has no influence on the variability of the sample. In the resulting data, the mean differences are much smaller than those in problem 6.

	Treatment		
I	II	III	
3	5	3	$N = 12$
5	5	7	$G = 48$
3	1	7	$\Sigma X^2 = 236$
1	5	3	
$M = 3$	$M = 4$	$M = 5$	
$T = 12$	$T = 16$	$T = 20$	
$SS = 8$	$SS = 12$	$SS = 16$	

    a. Before you begin any calculations, predict how the change in the data should influence the outcome of the analysis. That is, how will the F-ratio and the value of η^2 for these data compare with the values obtained in problem 6?
    b. Use an ANOVA with $\alpha = .05$ to determine whether there are any significant differences among the three treatment means. (Does your answer agree with your prediction in part a?)
    c. Calculate η^2 to measure the effect size for this study. (Does your answer agree with your prediction in part a?)

8. The following data summarize the results from an independent-measures study comparing three treatment conditions.

	Treatment		
I	II	III	
4	3	8	$N = 12$
3	1	4	$G = 48$
5	3	6	$\Sigma X^2 = 238$
4	1	6	
$M = 4$	$M = 2$	$M = 6$	
$T = 16$	$T = 8$	$T = 24$	
$SS = 2$	$SS = 4$	$SS = 8$	

a. Calculate the sample variance for each of the three samples.

b. Use an ANOVA with $\alpha = .05$ to determine whether there are any significant differences among the three treatment means.

9. For the preceding problem you should find that there are significant differences among the three treatments. One reason for the significance is that the sample variances are relatively small. To create the following data, we kept the same sample means that appeared in problem 8 but increased the SS values within each sample.

Treatment			
I	*II*	*III*	
4	4	9	$N = 12$
2	0	3	$G = 48$
6	3	6	$\Sigma X^2 = 260$
4	1	6	
$M = 4$	$M = 2$	$M = 6$	
$T = 16$	$T = 8$	$T = 24$	
$SS = 8$	$SS = 10$	$SS = 18$	

a. Calculate the sample variance for each of the three samples. Describe how these sample variances compare with those from problem 8.

b. Predict how the increase in sample variance should influence the outcome of the analysis. That is, how will the F-ratio for these data compare with the value obtained in problem 8?

c. Use an ANOVA with $\alpha = .05$ to determine whether there are any significant differences among the three treatment means. (Does your answer agree with your prediction in part b?)

10. The following data summarize the results from an independent-measures study comparing three treatment conditions.

$M = 2$	$M = 3$	$M = 4$
$n = 10$	$n = 10$	$n = 10$
$T = 20$	$T = 30$	$T = 40$
$s^2 = 2.67$	$s^2 = 2.00$	$s^2 = 1.33$

a. Use an ANOVA with $\alpha = .05$ to determine whether there are any significant differences among the three treatment means. Note: Because the samples are all the same size, MS_{within} is the average of the three sample variances.

b. Calculate η^2 to measure the effect size for this study.

11. To create the following data we started with the same sample means and variances that appeared in problem 10 but increased the sample size to $n = 25$.

$M = 2$	$M = 3$	$M = 4$
$n = 25$	$n = 25$	$n = 25$
$T = 50$	$T = 75$	$T = 100$
$s^2 = 2.67$	$s^2 = 2.00$	$s^2 = 1.33$

a. Predict how the increase in sample size should affect the F-ratio for these data compared to the F-ratio in problem 10. Use an ANOVA to check your prediction. Note: Because the samples are all the same size, MS_{within} is the average of the three sample variances.

b. Predict how the increase in sample size should affect the value of η^2 for these data compared to the η^2 in problem 10. Calculate η^2 to check your prediction.

12. The following values are from an independent-measures study comparing three treatment conditions.

Treatment		
I	*II*	*III*
$n = 10$	$n = 10$	$n = 10$
$SS = 63$	$SS = 66$	$SS = 87$

a. Compute the variance for each sample.

b. Compute MS_{within}, which would be the denominator of the F-ratio for an ANOVA. Because the samples are all the same size, you should find that MS_{within} is equal to the average of the three sample variances.

13. There is some evidence that high school students justify cheating in class on the basis of poor teacher skills or low levels of teacher caring (Murdock, Miller, & Kohlhardt, 2004). Students appear to rationalize their illicit behavior based on perceptions of how their teachers view cheating. Poor teachers are thought not to know or care whether students cheat, so cheating in their classes is okay. Good teachers, on the other hand, do care and are alert to cheating, so students tend not to cheat in their classes. Following are hypothetical data similar to the actual research results. The scores represent judgments of the acceptability of cheating for the students in each sample.

Poor Teacher	Average Teacher	Good Teacher	
$n = 6$	$n = 8$	$n = 10$	$N = 24$
$M = 6$	$M = 2$	$M = 2$	$G = 72$
$SS = 30$	$SS = 33$	$SS = 42$	$\Sigma X^2 = 393$

a. Use an ANOVA with $\alpha = .05$ to determine whether there are significant differences in student judgments depending on how they see their teachers.

b. Calculate η^2 to measure the effect size for this study.

c. Write a sentence demonstrating how a research report would present the results of the hypothesis test and the measure of effect size.

14. A researcher reports an F-ratio with $df = 2, 27$ from an independent-measures research study.

a. How many treatment conditions were compared in the study?

b. What was the total number of participants in the study?

15. A research report from an independent-measures study states that there are significant differences between treatments, $F(3, 48) = 2.95, p < .05$.

a. How many treatment conditions were compared in the study?

b. What was the total number of participants in the study?

16. The following summary table presents the results from an ANOVA comparing three treatment conditions with $n = 8$ participants in each condition. Complete all missing values. (*Hint:* Start with the df column.)

Source	SS	df	MS	
Between treatments	____	____	15	$F =$ ____
Within treatments	____	____	____	
Total	93	____		

17. A pharmaceutical company has developed a drug that is expected to reduce hunger. To test the drug, two samples of rats are selected with $n = 20$ in each sample. The rats in the first sample receive the drug every day and those in the second sample are given a placebo. The dependent variable is the amount of food eaten by each rat over a 1-month period. An ANOVA is used to evaluate the difference between the two sample means and the results are reported in the following summary table. Fill in all missing values in the table. (*Hint:* Start with the df column.)

Source	SS	df	MS	
Between treatments	____	____	20	$F = 4.00$
Within treatments	____	____	____	
Total	____	____		

18. A developmental psychologist is examining the development of language skills from age 2 to age 4. Three different groups of children are obtained, one for each age, with $n = 16$ children in each group.

Each child is given a language-skills assessment test. The resulting data were analyzed with an ANOVA to test for mean differences between age groups. The results of the ANOVA are presented in the following table. Fill in all missing values.

Source	SS	df	MS	
Between treatments	20	____	____	$F =$ ____
Within treatments	____	____	____	
Total	200	____		

19. The following data were obtained from an independent-measures research study comparing three treatment conditions. Use an ANOVA with $\alpha = .05$ to determine whether there are any significant mean differences among the treatments.

	Treatment		
I	II	III	
$n = 8$	$n = 6$	$n = 4$	$N = 18$
$T = 16$	$T = 24$	$T = 32$	$G = 72$
$SS = 40$	$SS = 24$	$SS = 16$	$\Sigma X^2 = 464$

20. The following values summarize the results from an independent-measures study comparing two treatment conditions.

a. Use an independent-measures t test with $\alpha = .05$ to determine whether there is a significant mean difference between the two treatments. You should find that $F = t^2$.

b. Use an ANOVA with $\alpha = .05$ to determine whether there is a significant mean difference between the two treatments.

	Treatment	
I	II	
$n = 8$	$n = 4$	
$M = 4$	$M = 10$	$N = 12$
$T = 32$	$T = 40$	$G = 72$
$SS = 45$	$SS = 15$	$\Sigma X^2 = 588$

21. The following data are from an independent-measures study comparing two treatment conditions.

a. Use an independent-measures t test with $\alpha = .05$ to determine whether there is a significant mean difference between the two treatments.

b. Use an ANOVA with $\alpha = .05$ to determine whether there is a significant mean difference between the two treatments. You should find that $F = t^2$.

Treatment		
I	*II*	
8	2	$N = 10$
7	3	$G = 50$
6	3	$\Sigma X^2 = 306$
5	5	
9	2	
$M = 7$	$M = 3$	
$T = 35$	$T = 15$	
$SS = 10$	$SS = 6$	

22. One possible explanation for why some birds migrate and others maintain year round residency in a single location is intelligence. Specifically, birds with small brains, relative to their body size, are simply not smart enough to find food during the winter and must migrate to warmer climates where food is easily available (Sol, Lefebvre, & Rodriguez-Teijeiro, 2005). Birds with bigger brains, on the other hand, are more creative and can find food even when the weather turns harsh. Following are hypothetical data similar to the actual research results. The numbers represent relative brain size for the individual birds in each sample.

Non-Migrating	Short-Distance Migrants	Long Distance Migrants	
18	6	4	$N = 18$
13	11	9	$G = 180$
19	7	5	$\Sigma X^2 = 2150$
12	9	6	
16	8	5	
12	13	7	
$M = 15$	$M = 9$	$M = 6$	
$T = 90$	$T = 54$	$T = 36$	
$SS = 48$	$SS = 34$	$SS = 16$	

a. Use an ANOVA with $\alpha = .05$ to determine whether there are any significant mean differences among the three groups of birds.

b. Compute η^2, the percentage of variance explained by the group differences, for these data.

c. Write a sentence demonstrating how a research report would present the results of the hypothesis test and the measure of effect size.

d. Use the Tukey HSD posttest to determine which groups are significantly different.

23. There is some research indicating that college students who use Facebook while studying tend to have lower grades than non-users (Kirschner & Karpinski, 2010). A representative study surveys students to determine the amount of Facebook use during the time they are studying or doing homework. Based on the amount of time spent on Facebook, students are classified into three groups and their grade point averages are recorded. The following data show the typical pattern of results.

Facebook Use While Studying		
Non-User	*Rarely Use*	*Regularly Use*
3.70	3.51	3.02
3.45	3.42	2.84
2.98	3.81	3.42
3.94	3.15	3.10
3.82	3.64	2.74
3.68	3.20	3.22
3.90	2.95	2.58
4.00	3.55	3.07
3.75	3.92	3.31
3.88	3.45	2.80

a. Use an ANOVA with $\alpha = .05$ to determine whether there are significant mean differences among the three groups.

b. Compute η^2 to measure the size of the effect.

c. Write a sentence demonstrating how the result from the hypothesis test and the measure of effect size would appear in a research report.

24 New research suggests that watching television, especially medical shows such as Grey's Anatomy and House, can result in increased concern about personal health (Ye, 2010). Surveys administered to college students measure television viewing habits and health concerns such as fear of developing the diseases and disorders seen on television. For the following data, students are classified into three categories based on their television viewing patterns and health concerns are measured on a 10-point scale with 0 indicating "none."

Television Viewing		
Little or None	*Moderate*	*Substantial*
4	5	5
2	7	7
5	3	6
1	4	6
3	8	8
7	6	9
4	2	6
4	7	4
8	3	6
2	5	8

a. Use an ANOVA with $\alpha = .05$ to determine whether there are significant mean differences among the three groups.
b. Compute η^2 to measure the size of the effect.
c. Use Tukey's HSD test with $\alpha = .05$ to determine which groups are significantly different.

CHAPTER

13

Repeated-Measures and Two-Factor Analysis of Variance

Tools You Will Need

The following items are considered essential background material for this chapter. If you doubt your knowledge of any of these items, you should review the appropriate chapter or section before proceeding.

- Independent-measures analysis of variance (Chapter 12)
- Repeated-measures designs (Chapter 11)
- Individual differences

aplia

Aplia for *Essentials of Statistics for the Behavioral Sciences*
After reading, go to "Resources" at the end of this chapter for an introduction on how to use Aplia's homework and learning resources.

13.1 OVERVIEW

An independent variable is a manipulated variable in an experiment. A quasi-independent variable is not manipulated but defines the groups of scores in a nonexperimental design.

In the preceding chapter, we introduced ANOVA as a hypothesis-testing procedure for evaluating differences among two or more sample means. The specific advantage of ANOVA, especially in contrast to *t* tests, is that ANOVA can be used to evaluate the significance of mean differences in situations in which there are more than two sample means being compared. However, the presentation of ANOVA in Chapter 12 was limited to single-factor, independent-measures research designs. Recall that *single factor* indicates that the research study involves only one independent variable (or only one quasi-independent variable), and the term *independent-measures* indicates that the study uses a separate sample for each of the different treatment conditions being compared. In fact, ANOVA is an extremely flexible technique, with applications far beyond this single research design. In this chapter, we begin to explore some more sophisticated research situations in which ANOVA is used. Specifically, we introduce the following ANOVA topics:

1. **Repeated-Measures ANOVA.** It is possible to compare several different treatment conditions using a repeated-measures research design in which the same group of individuals participates in every treatment. We demonstrate how the ANOVA procedure can be adapted to test for mean differences from a repeated-measures study.

2. **Two-Factor ANOVA.** Often, research questions are concerned with how behavior is influenced by several different variables acting simultaneously. For example, a researcher may want to examine how weight loss is related to different combinations of diet and exercise. In this situation, two variables are manipulated (diet and exercise) while a third variable is observed (weight loss). In statistical terminology, the research study has two independent variables, or two factors. In the final section of this chapter, we show how the general ANOVA procedure from Chapter 12 can be used to test for mean differences in a two-factor research study.

13.2 REPEATED-MEASURES ANOVA

Chapter 12 introduced the general logic underlying ANOVA and presented the equations used for analyzing data from a single-factor, independent-measures research study. As we noted, the defining characteristic of an independent-measures research design is that the study uses a separate sample for each of the different treatment conditions. One concern with an independent-measures design is that the participants in one treatment condition may have characteristics that are noticeably different from participants in another condition. For example, the individuals in treatment 1 may be smarter than the individuals in treatment 2. In this case, it is impossible to explain any differences that are found between the two treatments. For example: (1) It could be that treatment 1 causes people to have higher scores, or (2) It could be that smarter people have higher scores. To avoid this problem, researchers often chose to use a *repeated-measures design*. You should recall (Chapter 11) that a repeated-measures design uses the same group of participants in all of the treatment conditions. In a repeated-measures study, it is impossible for the participants in one group to be different from those in another, because exactly the same group is in every treatment condition.

In this section we extend the ANOVA procedure to single-factor, repeated-measures designs. The analysis is used to evaluate mean differences in two general research situations:

1. An experimental study, in which the researcher manipulates an independent variable to create two or more treatment conditions, with the same group of individuals tested in all of the conditions.

2. A nonexperimental study, in which the same group of individuals is simply observed at two or more different times.

Examples of these two research situations are presented in Table 13.1. Table 13.1(a) shows data from a study in which the researcher changes the type of distraction to create three treatment conditions. One group of participants is then tested in all three conditions. In this study, the factor being examined is the type of distraction.

Table 13.1(b) shows a study in which a researcher observes depression scores for the same group of individuals at three different times. In this study, the time of measurement is the factor being examined. Another common example of this type of design is found in developmental psychology when the participants' age is the factor being studied. For example, a researcher could study the development of vocabulary skill by measuring vocabulary for a sample of 3-year-old children, then measuring the same children again at ages 4 and 5.

HYPOTHESES FOR THE REPEATED-MEASURES ANOVA

The hypotheses for the repeated-measures ANOVA are exactly the same as those for the independent-measures ANOVA presented in Chapter 12. Specifically, the null hypothesis states that, for the general population, there are no mean differences among the treatment conditions being compared. In symbols,

$$H_0: \mu_1 = \mu_2 = \mu_3 = \cdots$$

TABLE 13.1

Two sets of data representing typical examples of single-factor, repeated-measures research designs.

(a) Data from an experimental study evaluating the effects of different types of distraction on the performance of a visual detection task.

	Visual Detection Scores		
Participant	No Distraction	Visual Distraction	Auditory Distraction
A	47	22	41
B	57	31	52
C	38	18	40
D	45	32	43

(b) Data from a nonexperimental design evaluating the effectiveness of a clinical therapy for treating depression.

	Depression Scores		
Participant	Before Therapy	After Therapy	6-Month Follow-Up
A	71	53	55
B	62	45	44
C	82	56	61
D	77	50	46
E	81	54	55

The null hypothesis states that, on average, all of the treatments have exactly the same effect. According to the null hypothesis, any differences that may exist among the sample means are not caused by systematic treatment effects but rather are the result of random and unsystematic factors.

The alternative hypothesis states that there are mean differences among the treatment conditions. Rather than specifying exactly which treatments are different, we use a generic version of H_1, which simply states that differences exist:

H_1: At least one treatment mean (μ) is different from another.

Notice that the alternative says that, on average, the treatments do have different effects. Thus, the treatment conditions may be responsible for causing mean differences among the samples. As always, the goal of the ANOVA is to use the sample data to determine which of the two hypotheses is more likely to be correct.

THE *F*-RATIO FOR REPEATED-MEASURES ANOVA

The *F*-ratio for the repeated-measures ANOVA has the same structure that was used for the independent-measures ANOVA in Chapter 12. In each case, the *F*-ratio compares the actual mean differences between treatments with the amount of difference that would be expected if there were no treatment effect. The numerator of the *F*-ratio measures the actual mean differences between treatments. The denominator measures how big the differences should be if there is no treatment effect. As always, the *F*-ratio uses variance to measure the size of the differences. Thus, the *F*-ratio for both ANOVAs has the general structure

$$F = \frac{\text{variance (differences) between treatments}}{\text{variance (differences) expected if there is no treatment effect}}$$

A large value for the *F*-ratio indicates that the differences between treatments are greater than would be expected without any treatment effect. If the *F*-ratio is larger than the critical value in the *F* distribution table, then we can conclude that the differences between treatments are *significantly* larger than would be caused by chance.

Individual differences in the *F*-ratio   Although the structure of the *F*-ratio is the same for independent-measures and repeated-measures designs, there is a fundamental difference between the two designs that produces a corresponding difference in the two *F*-ratios. Specifically, individual differences are a part of one ratio but are eliminated from the other.

You should recall that the term *individual differences* refers to participant characteristics such as age, personality, and gender that vary from one person to another and may influence the measurements that you obtain for each person. Suppose, for example, that you are measuring reaction time. The first participant in your study is a 19-year-old female with an IQ of 136 who is on the college varsity volleyball team. The next participant is a 42-year-old male with an IQ of 111 who returned to college after losing his job and comes to the research study with a head cold. Would you expect to obtain the same reaction time score for these two individuals even if they receive the same treatment?

Individual differences are a part of the variance in the numerator and in the denominator of the *F*-ratio for the independent-measures ANOVA. However, individual difference are eliminated or removed from the variances in the *F*-ratio for the repeated measures ANOVA. The idea of removing individual differences was first presented in Chapter 11 when we introduced the repeated-measures design (p. 329), but we review it briefly now.

In a repeated-measures study, exactly the same individuals participate in all of the treatment conditions. Therefore, if there are any mean differences between treatments, they cannot be explained by individual differences. Thus, individual differences are automatically eliminated from the numerator of the repeated-measures F-ratio.

A repeated-measures design also allows you to remove individual differences from the variance in the denominator of the F-ratio. Because the same individuals are measured in every treatment condition, it is possible to measure the size of the individual differences. In Table 13.1(a), for example, participant A has scores that are consistently around 10 points lower than the scores for participant B. Because the individual differences are systematic and predictable, they can be measured and separated from the random, unsystematic differences in the denominator of the F-ratio.

Thus, individual differences are automatically eliminated from the numerator of the repeated-measures F-ratio. In addition, they can be measured and removed from the denominator. As a result, the structure of the final F-ratio is as follows:

$$F = \frac{\text{variance between treatments (without individual differences)}}{\text{variance with no treatment effect (individual differences removed)}}$$

The process of removing the variance caused individual differences is an important part of the procedure for a repeated-measures ANOVA.

In summary, the F-ratio for a repeated-measures ANOVA has the same basic structure as the F-ratio for independent measures (Chapter 12) except that it includes no variance caused by individual differences. The individual differences are automatically eliminated from the variance between treatments (numerator) because the repeated-measures design uses the same individuals in all treatments. In the denominator, the individual differences are subtracted during the analysis. As a result, the repeated-measures F-ratio has the following structure:

$$F = \frac{\text{between-treatments variance}}{\text{error variance}} \qquad (13.1)$$

$$= \frac{\text{treatment effects} + \text{random, unsystematic differences}}{\text{random, unsystematic differences}}$$

When there is no treatment effect, the F-ratio is balanced because the numerator and denominator are both measuring exactly the same variance. In this case, the F-ratio should have a value near 1.00. When research results produce an F-ratio near 1.00, we conclude that there is no evidence of a treatment effect and we fail to reject the null hypothesis. On the other hand, when a treatment effect does exist, it contributes only to the numerator and should produce a large value for the F-ratio. Thus, a large value for F indicates that there is a real treatment effect and, therefore, we should reject the null hypothesis.

LEARNING CHECK

1. The F-ratio for the repeated-measures ANOVA is structured so that variance caused by individual differences is eliminated.

   a. Explain why individual differences are not part of the between-treatments variance in the numerator of the F-ratio.

   b. Explain why individual differences are not part of the error variance in the denominator of the F-ratio.

ANSWERS   **1. a.** Because the individuals in one treatment are exactly the same as the individuals in every other treatment, there are no individual differences between treatments.

b. Variance caused by individual differences is measured and subtracted from the within-treatments variance to produce a measure of error variance that does not include any treatment effects or individual differences.

THE STRUCTURE OF THE REPEATED-MEASURES ANOVA

The overall structure of the repeated-measures ANOVA is shown in Figure 13.1. Note that the ANOVA can be viewed as a two-stage process. In the first stage, the total variance is partitioned into two components: *between-treatments variance* and *within-treatments variance*. This stage is identical to the analysis that we conducted for an independent-measures design in Chapter 12.

    The second stage of the analysis is intended to remove the individual differences from the denominator of the *F*-ratio. In the second stage, we begin with the variance within treatments and then measure and subtract out the *between-subject variance,* which measures the size of the individual differences. The remaining variance, often called the *residual variance,* or *error variance,* provides a measure of how much variance is reasonable to expect after the treatment effects and individual differences have been removed. The second stage of the analysis is what differentiates the repeated-measures ANOVA from the independent-measures ANOVA. Specifically, the repeated-measures design requires that the individual differences be removed.

FIGURE 13.1

The partitioning of variance for a repeated-measures experiment.

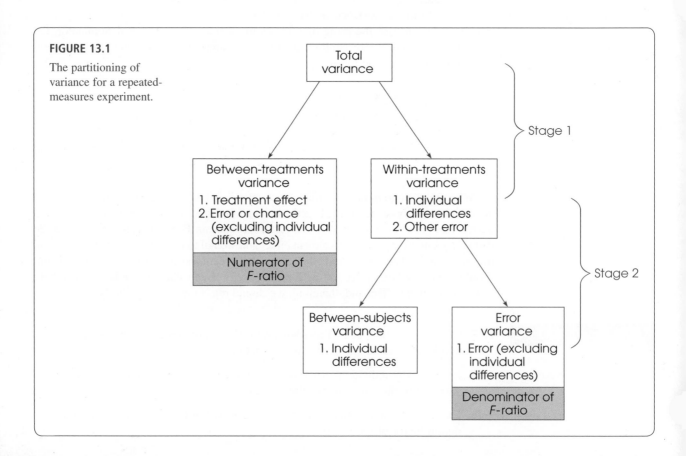

DEFINITION

In a repeated-measures ANOVA, the denominator of the F-ratio is called the **residual variance,** or the **error variance,** and measures how much variance is expected if there are no systematic treatment effects and no individual differences contributing to the variability of the scores.

NOTATION FOR THE REPEATED-MEASURES ANOVA

We use the data in Table 13.2 to introduce the notation for the repeated-measures ANOVA. The data represent the results of a study similar to one reported by Weinstein, McDermott, and Roediger (2010), comparing different strategies for studying text passages in preparation for a quiz or exam. Four strategies were evaluated—reading once, rereading, answering prepared comprehension questions, creating and answering your own comprehension questions. After studying a passage, each participant was given a 10-point quiz on the material. After a short break, the participant moved on to a new passage and a new studying strategy. This process continued until all participants had completed all four strategies. You may notice that this research study and the numerical values in the table are identical to those used to demonstrate the independent-measures ANOVA in the previous chapter (Example 12.1, page 364). In this case, however, the data represent a repeated-measures study in which the same group of $n = 6$ individuals is tested in all four treatment conditions.

You should recognize that most of the notation in Table 13.2 is identical to the notation used in an independent-measures analysis (Chapter 12) For example, there are $n = 6$ participants who are tested in $k = 4$ treatment conditions, producing a total of $N = 24$ scores that add up to a grand total of $G = 168$. Note, however, that $N = 24$ now refers to the total number of scores in the study, not the number of participants.

The repeated-measures ANOVA introduces only one new notational symbol. The letter P is used to represent the total of all of the scores for each individual in the study. You can think of the P values as "Person totals" or "Participant totals." In Table 13.2, for example, participant A had scores of 3, 5, 8, and 8 for a total of $P = 24$. The P values are used to define and measure the magnitude of the individual differences in the second stage of the analysis.

EXAMPLE 13.1

We use the data in Table 13.2 to demonstrate the repeated-measures ANOVA. Again, the goal of the test is to determine whether there are any significant differences among the four strategies being compared. Specifically, are any of the mean differences in the

TABLE 13.2

Quiz scores for students using four different strategies for studying text passages. *Note:* For comparison, the scores are identical to the values in Example 12.1.

Strategies for Studying Text Passages

Student	Read Once	Read and Reread	Answer Prepared Questions	Create and Answer Questions	Person Totals		
A	3	5	8	8	$P = 24$	$n =$	6
B	3	3	5	9	$P = 20$	$k =$	4
C	4	5	8	7	$P = 24$	$N =$	24
D	6	7	9	10	$P = 32$	$G =$	168
E	6	8	8	10	$P = 32$	$\Sigma X^2 =$	1298
F	8	8	10	10	$P = 36$		
	$T = 30$	$T = 36$	$T = 48$	$T = 54$			
	$M = 5$	$M = 6$	$M = 8$	$M = 9$			
	$SS = 20$	$SS = 20$	$SS = 14$	$SS = 8$			

data greater than would be expected if there were no systematic differences among the four strategies?

STAGE 1 OF THE REPEATED-MEASURES ANOVA

The first stage of the repeated-measures analysis is identical to the independent-measures ANOVA that was presented in Chapter 12. Specially, the SS and df for the total set of scores are analyzed into within-treatments and between-treatments components.

Because the numerical values in Table 13.2 are the same as the values used in Example 12.1 (p. 364), the computations for the first stage of the repeated-measures analysis are identical to those in Example 12.1. Rather than repeating the same arithmetic, the results of the first stage of the repeated-measures analysis can be summarized as follows:

Total:

$$SS_{total} = \Sigma X^2 - \frac{G^2}{N} = 1298 - \frac{168^2}{24} = 1298 - 1176 = 122$$
$$df_{total} = N - 1 = 23$$

Within treatments:

$$SS_{within\ treatments} = \Sigma SS_{inside\ each\ treatment} = 20 + 20 + 14 + 8 = 62$$
$$df_{within\ treatments} = \Sigma df_{inside\ each\ treatment} = 5 + 5 + 5 + 5 = 20$$

Between treatments:
For this example we find $SS_{between\ treatments}$ by subtraction.

$$SS_{between\ treatments} = SS_{total} - SS_{within\ treatments}$$
$$= 122 - 62 = 60$$
$$df_{between\ treatments} = k - 1 = 3$$

For more details on the formulas and calculations, see Example 12.1, pages 364–366.

This completes the first stage of the repeated-measures ANOVA. Note that the two components, between and within, add up to the total for the SS values and for the df values. Also note that the between-treatments SS and df values provide a measure of the mean differences between treatments and are used to compute the variance in the numerator of the final F-ratio.

STAGE 2 OF THE REPEATED-MEASURES ANOVA

The second stage of the analysis involves removing the individual differences from the denominator of the F-ratio. Because the same individuals are used in every treatment, it is possible to measure the size of the individual differences. For the data in Table 13.2, for example, participants A, B, and C tend to have the lowest scores and participants D, E, and F tend to have the highest scores. These individual differences are reflected in the P values, or person totals, in the right-hand column. We use these P values to create a computational formula for $SS_{between\ subjects}$ in much the same way that we used the treatment totals, the T values, in the computational formula for $SS_{between\ treatments}$. Specifically, the formula for the between-subjects SS is

$$SS_{between\ subjects} = \Sigma \frac{P^2}{k} - \frac{G^2}{N}$$

(13.2)

Notice that the formula for the between-subjects SS has exactly the same structure as the computational formula for the between-treatments SS (see the calculation on p. 358). In this case, we use the person totals (P values) instead of the treatment totals (T values). Each P value is squared and divided by the number of scores that were added to obtain the total. In this case, each person has k scores, one for each treatment. Box 13.1 presents another demonstration of the similarity of the formulas for SS between subjects and SS between treatments. For the data in Table 13.2,

$$SS_{\text{between subjects}} = \frac{24^2}{4} + \frac{20^2}{4} + \frac{24^2}{4} + \frac{32^2}{4} + \frac{32^2}{4} + \frac{36^2}{4} - \frac{168^2}{24}$$
$$= 144 + 100 + 144 + 256 + 256 + 324 - 1176$$
$$= 48$$

The value of $SS_{\text{between subjects}}$ provides a measure of the size of the individual differences—that is, the differences between subjects. In the second stage of the analysis, we simply subtract the individual differences to obtain the measure of error that forms the denominator of the F-ratio. Thus, the final step in the analysis of SS is

$$SS_{\text{error}} = SS_{\text{within treatments}} - SS_{\text{between subjects}} \qquad (13.3)$$

We have already computed $SS_{\text{within treatments}} = 62$ and $SS_{\text{between subjects}} = 48$, therefore

$$SS_{\text{error}} = 62 - 48 = 14$$

BOX 13.1 $SS_{\text{between subjects}}$ **AND** $SS_{\text{between treatments}}$

The data for a repeated-measures study are normally presented in a matrix, with the treatment conditions determining the columns and the participants defining the rows. The data in Table 13.2 demonstrate this normal presentation. The calculation of $SS_{\text{between treatments}}$ provides a measure of the differences between treatment conditions—that is, a measure of the mean differences between the *columns* in the data matrix. For the data in Table 13.2, the column totals are 30, 36, 48, and 54. These values are variable, and $SS_{\text{between treatments}}$ measures the amount of variability.

The following table reproduces the data from Table 13.2, but now we have turned the data matrix on its side so that the participants define the columns and the treatment conditions define the rows.

In this new format, the differences between the columns represent the *between-subjects variance*. The column totals are now P values (instead of T values) and the number of scores in each column is now

identified by k (instead of n). With these changes in notation, the formula for $SS_{\text{between subjects}}$ has exactly the same structure as the formula for $SS_{\text{between treatments}}$. If you examine the two equations, the similarity should be clear.

	Participant						
	A	B	C	D	E	F	
Read Once	3	3	4	6	6	8	$T = 30$
Read and Reread	5	3	5	7	8	8	$T = 36$
Answer Prepared Questions	8	5	8	9	8	10	$T = 48$
Create and Answer Questions	8	9	7	10	10	10	$T = 54$
	$P = 24$	$P = 20$	$P = 24$	$P = 32$	$P = 32$	$P = 36$	

The analysis of degrees of freedom follows exactly the same pattern that was used to analyze SS. Remember that we are using the P values to measure the magnitude of the individual differences. The number of P values corresponds to the number of subjects, n, so the corresponding df is

$$df_{\text{between subjects}} = n - 1 \tag{13.4}$$

For the data in Table 13.2, there are $n = 6$ subjects and

$$df_{\text{between subjects}} = 6 - 1 = 5$$

Next, we subtract the individual differences from the within-subjects component to obtain a measure of error. In terms of degrees of freedom,

$$df_{\text{error}} = df_{\text{within treatments}} - df_{\text{between subjects}} \tag{13.5}$$

For the data in Table 13.2,

$$df_{\text{error}} = 20 - 5 = 15$$

An algebraically equivalent formula for df_{error} uses only the number of treatment conditions (k) and the number of participants (n):

$$df_{\text{error}} = (k - 1)(n - 1) \tag{13.6}$$

The usefulness of equation 13.6 is discussed in Box 13.2.

Remember: The purpose for the second stage of the analysis is to measure the individual differences and then remove the individual differences from the denominator of the F-ratio. This goal is accomplished by computing SS and df between subjects (the individual differences) and then subtracting these values from the within-treatments values. The result is a measure of variability resulting from error with the individual differences removed. This error variance (SS and df) is used in the denominator of the F-ratio.

BOX 13.2	USING THE ALTERNATIVE FORMULA FOR df_{error}

The statistics presented in a research report not only describe the significance of the results but typically provide enough information to reconstruct the research design. The alternative formula for df_{error} is particularly useful for this purpose. Suppose, for example, that a research report for a repeated-measures study includes an F-ratio with $df = 2, 10$. How many treatment conditions were compared in the study and how many individuals participated?

To answer these question, begin with the first df value, which is $df_{\text{between treatments}} = 2 = k - 1$. From this value, it is clear that $k = 3$ treatments. Next, use the

second df value, which is $df_{\text{error}} = 10$. Using this value and the fact that $k - 1 = 2$, use equation 13.6 to find the number of participants.

$$df_{\text{error}} = 10 = (k - 1)(n - 1) = 2(n - 1)$$

If $2(n - 1) = 10$, then $n - 1$ must equal 5. Therefore, $n = 6$.

Therefore, we conclude that a repeated-measures study producing an F-ratio with $df = 2, 10$ must have compared 3 treatment conditions using a sample of 6 participants.

CALCULATION OF THE VARIANCES (*MS* VALUES) AND THE *F*-RATIO

The final calculation in the analysis is the *F*-ratio, which is a ratio of two variances. Each variance is called a *mean square,* or *MS*, and is obtained by dividing the appropriate *SS* by its corresponding *df* value. The *MS* in the numerator of the *F*-ratio measures the size of the differences between treatments and is calculated as

$$MS_{\text{between treatments}} = \frac{SS_{\text{between treatments}}}{df_{\text{between treatments}}} \quad\quad (13.7)$$

For the data in Table 13.2,

$$MS_{\text{between treatments}} = \frac{SS_{\text{between treatments}}}{df_{\text{between treatments}}} = \frac{60}{3} = 20$$

The denominator of the *F*-ratio measures how much difference is reasonable to expect if there are no systematic treatment effects and the individual differences have been removed. This is the error variance, or the residual variance, obtained in stage 2 of the analysis.

$$MS_{\text{error}} = \frac{SS_{\text{error}}}{df_{\text{error}}} \quad\quad (13.8)$$

For the data in Table 13.2,

$$MS_{\text{error}} = \frac{SS_{\text{error}}}{df_{\text{error}}} = \frac{14}{15} = 0.933$$

Finally, the *F*-ratio is computed as

$$F = \frac{MS_{\text{between treatments}}}{MS_{\text{error}}} \qu\quad (13.9)$$

For the data in Table 13.2,

$$F = \frac{MS_{\text{between treatments}}}{MS_{\text{error}}} = \frac{20}{0.933} = 21.43$$

Once again, notice that the repeated-measures ANOVA uses MS_{error} in the denominator of the *F*-ratio. This *MS* value is obtained in the second stage of the analysis, after the individual differences have been removed. As a result, individual differences are completely eliminated from the repeated-measures *F*-ratio, so that the general structure is

$$F = \frac{\text{treatment effects} + \text{unsystematic differences (without individual diffs)}}{\text{unsystematic differences (without individual diffs)}}$$

For the data we have been examining, the *F*-ratio is $F = 21.43$, indicating that the differences between treatments (numerator) are 22 times bigger than you would expect without any treatment effects (denominator). A ratio this large provides clear evidence that there is a real treatment effect. To verify this conclusion you must consult the *F* distribution table to determine the appropriate critical value for the test. The degrees of freedom for the F-ratio are determined by the two variances that form the numerator and the denominator. For a repeated-measures ANOVA, the df values for the F-ratio are reported as

$$df = df_{\text{between treatments}}, df_{\text{error}}$$

For the example we are considering, the F-ratio has $df = 3, 15$ ("degrees of freedom equal three and fifteen"). Using the F distribution table (p. 577) with $\alpha = .05$, the critical value is $F = 3.29$, and with $\alpha = .01$ the critical value is $F = 5.42$. Our obtained F-ratio, $F = 21.43$, is well beyond either of the critical values, so we can conclude that the differences between treatments are *significantly* greater than expected by chance using either $\alpha = .05$ or $\alpha = .01$.

The summary table for the repeated-measures ANOVA from Example 13.1 is presented in Table 13.3. Although these tables are no longer commonly used in research reports, they provide a concise format for displaying all of the elements of the analysis.

MEASURING EFFECT SIZE FOR THE REPEATED-MEASURES ANOVA

The most common method for measuring effect size with ANOVA is to compute the percentage of variance that is explained by the treatment differences. In the context of ANOVA, the percentage of variance is commonly identified as η^2 (eta squared). In Chapter 12, for the independent-measures analysis, we computed η^2 as

$$\eta^2 = \frac{SS_{\text{between treatments}}}{SS_{\text{between treatments}} + SS_{\text{within treatments}}} = \frac{SS_{\text{between treatments}}}{SS_{\text{total}}}$$

The intent is to measure how much of the total variability is explained by the differences between treatments. With a repeated-measures design, however, there is another component that can explain some of the variability in the data. Specifically, part of the variability is caused by differences between individuals. In Table 13.2, for example, person A consistently scored lower than person F. This consistent difference explains some of the variability in the data. When computing the size of the treatment effect, it is customary to remove any variability that can be explained by other factors, and then compute the percentage of the remaining variability that can be explained by the treatment effects. Thus, for a repeated-measures ANOVA, the variability from the individual differences is removed before computing η^2. As a result, η^2 is computed as

$$\eta^2 = \frac{SS_{\text{between treatments}}}{SS_{\text{total}} - SS_{\text{between subjects}}} \tag{13.10}$$

TABLE 13.3

A summary table for the repeated-measures ANOVA for the data from Example 13.1.

Source	SS	df	MS	F
Between treatments	60	3	20.00	$F(3,15) = 21.43$
Within treatments	62	20		
Between subjects	48	5		
Error	14	15	0.933	
Total	122	23		

Because Equation 13.10 computes a percentage that is not based on the total variability of the scores (one part, $SS_{\text{between subjects}}$, is removed), the result is often called a *partial* eta squared.

The general goal of Equation 13.10 is to calculate a percentage of the variability that has not already been explained by other factors. Thus, the denominator of Equation 13.10 is limited to variability from the treatment differences and variability that is exclusively from random, unsystematic factors. With this in mind, an equivalent version of the η^2 formula is

$$\eta^2 = \frac{SS_{\text{between treatments}}}{SS_{\text{between treatments}} + SS_{\text{error}}} \tag{13.11}$$

In this new version of the eta-squared formula, the denominator consists of the variability that is explained by the treatment differences plus the other *unexplained* variability. Using either formula, the data from Example 13.1 produce

$$\eta^2 = \frac{60}{74} = 0.811 \quad (\text{or } 81.1\%)$$

This result means that 81.1% of the variability in the data (except for the individual differences) is accounted for by the differences between treatments.

IN THE LITERATURE

REPORTING THE RESULTS OF A REPEATED-MEASURES ANOVA

As described in Chapter 12 (p. 368), the format for reporting ANOVA results in journal articles consists of

1. A summary of descriptive statistics (at least treatment means and standard deviations, and tables or graphs as needed)

2. A concise statement of the outcome of the ANOVA

For the study in Example 13.1, the report could state:

The means and variances of the quiz scores for the four strategies are shown in Table 1. A repeated-measures analysis of variance indicated significant mean differences in the four methods for studying text passages, $F(3, 15) = 21.43$, $p < .01$, $\eta^2 = 0.811$.

TABLE 1

Quiz scores for students using four different study strategies

	Read Once	Read and Reread	Answer Prepared Questions	Create and Answer Questions
M	5.00	6.00	8.00	9.00
SD	2.00	2.00	1.67	1.26

POST HOC TESTS WITH REPEATED-MEASURES ANOVA

Recall that ANOVA provides an overall test of significance for the mean differences between treatments. When the null hypothesis is rejected, it indicates only that there is a difference between at least two of the treatment means. If $k = 2$, it is obvious which two treatments are different. However, when k is greater than 2, the situation becomes more complex. To determine exactly where significant differences exist, the researcher must follow the ANOVA with post hoc tests. In Chapter 12, we used Tukey's HSD and the Scheffé test to make these multiple comparisons among treatment means. These two procedures attempt to control the overall alpha level by making adjustments for the number of potential comparisons.

For a repeated-measures ANOVA, Tukey's HSD and the Scheffé test can be used in the exact same manner as was done for the independent-measures ANOVA, *provided* that you substitute MS_{error} in place of $MS_{within\ treatments}$ in the formulas and use df_{error} in place of $df_{within\ treatments}$ when locating the critical value in a statistical table. For example, the study in Example 13.1 compared four treatments and produced $MS_{error} = 0.933$ with $df_{error} = 15$ and $n = 6$. Using Tukey's HSD posttest, we find $q = 4.08$ and obtain

$$\text{HSD} = q\sqrt{\frac{MS_{error}}{n}} = 4.08\sqrt{\frac{0.933}{6}} = 4.08(0.394) = 1.61$$

Thus, any mean difference greater than 1.61 points is significant with $\alpha = .05$. For this study, reading once is not significantly different from rereading, and answering prepared questions is not significantly different from creating and answering your own questions. However, answering either type of comprehension questions produces significantly better performance than simply reading. Note: This is the same pattern of results that was obtained in the original study.

ASSUMPTIONS OF THE REPEATED-MEASURES ANOVA

The basic assumptions for the repeated-measures ANOVA are identical to those required for the independent-measures ANOVA.

1. The observations within each treatment condition must be independent (see p. 220).

2. The population distribution within each treatment must be normal. (As before, the assumption of normality is important only with small samples.)

3. The variances of the population distributions for each treatment should be equivalent.

For the repeated-measures ANOVA, there is an additional assumption, called homogeneity of covariance. Basically, it refers to the requirement that the relative standing of each subject be maintained in each treatment condition. This assumption is violated if the effect of the treatment is not consistent for all of the subjects or if order effects exist for some, but not other, subjects. This issue is very complex and is beyond the scope of this book. However, methods do exist for dealing with violations of this assumption (for a discussion, see Keppel, 1973).

ADVANTAGES AND DISADVANTAGES OF THE REPEATED-MEASURES DESIGN

As we noted in Chapter 11 (p. 328), a repeated-measures design has some distinct advantages and some disadvantages compared to an independent-measures design. On the positive side, a repeated-measures design typically requires fewer subjects than an independent-measures design. The repeated-measures design uses only one group of subjects, which can be an asset if relatively few subjects are available. The primary advantage of repeated-measures designs, however, is that they remove variance caused by individual differences from the analysis. If individual differences are relatively large, they may obscure a treatment effect in an independent-measures design. In this situation, a repeated-measures design is more likely to detect the treatment effect and produce a significant result.

The primary disadvantage of a repeated-measures design is that it often creates the opportunity for factors other than the treatment effect to cause a participant's score to change from one treatment to the next. Specifically, when participants are measured in different treatment conditions at different times, outside factors that change over time, such as the weather, may cause changes in the participants' scores. It also is possible that experience gained in one treatment condition may influence performance in later treatments. For example, practicing a task in one condition may lead to improved performance in a later treatment. In this case, the participant's scores are changing from one treatment to another but the changes are not being caused by the treatments.

LEARNING CHECK

1. A repeated-measures study is used to evaluate the mean differences among four treatment conditions using a sample of $n = 10$ participants. What are the df values for the F-ratio?

2. A research report includes a repeated-measures F-ratio with $df = 3, 24$. How many treatment conditions were compared and how many individuals participated in the study? (See Box 13.2.)

3. For the following data, compute $SS_{\text{within treatments}}$, $SS_{\text{between subjects}}$ and SS_{error}.

		Treat	ment		
Subject	1	2	3	4	
A	2	2	2	2	$G = 32$
B	4	0	0	4	$\Sigma X^2 = 96$
C	2	0	2	0	
D	4	2	2	4	
	$T = 12$	$T = 4$	$T = 6$	$T = 10$	
	$SS = 4$	$SS = 4$	$SS = 3$	$SS = 11$	

ANSWERS

1. $df = 3, 27$

2. There were 4 treatment conditions ($k - 1 = 3$) and 9 participants ($n - 1 = 8$).

3. $SS_{\text{within treatments}} = 22$, $SS_{\text{between subjects}} = 8$, and $SS_{\text{error}} = 22 - 8 = 14$.

REPEATED-MEASURES ANOVA AND THE REPEATED-MEASURES t TEST

As we noted in Chapter 12 (pp. 379–380), whenever you are evaluating the difference between two sample means, you can use either a t test or ANOVA. In Chapter 12 we demonstrated that the two tests are related in many respects, including:

1. The two tests always reach the same conclusion about the null hypothesis.

2. The basic relationship between the two test statistics is $F = t^2$.

3. The df value for the t statistic is identical to the df value for the denominator of the F-ratio.

4. If you square the critical value for the two-tailed t test, you obtain the critical value for the F-ratio. Again, the basic relationship is $F = t^2$.

In Chapter 12, these relationships were demonstrated for the independent-measures tests, but they are also true for repeated-measures designs comparing two treatment conditions. The following example demonstrates the relationships.

EXAMPLE 13.2 The following table shows the data from a repeated-measures study comparing two treatment conditions. We have structured the data in a format that is compatible with the repeated-measures t test. Note that the calculations for the t test are based on the difference scores (D values) in the final column.

Participant	Treatment I	II	D
A	3	5	2
B	4	14	10
C	5	7	2
D	4	6	2

$$M_D = 4$$
$$SS_D = 48$$

The repeated-measures t test   The null hypothesis for the t test states that, for the general population, there is no mean difference between the two treatment conditions.

$$H_0: \mu_D = 0$$

With $n = 4$ participants, the test has $df = 3$ and the critical boundaries for a two-tailed test with $\alpha = .05$ are t = ±3.182.

For these data, the sample mean difference is $M_D = 4$, the variance for the difference scores is $s^2 = 16$, and the standard error is $s_{M_D} = 2$ points. These values produce a t statistic of

$$t = \frac{M_D - \mu_D}{s_{M_D}} = \frac{4 - 0}{2} = 2.00$$

The t value is not in the critical region, so we fail to reject H_0 and conclude that there is no significant difference between the two treatments.

The repeated-measures ANOVA   Now we reorganize the data into a format that is compatible with a repeated-measures ANOVA. Notice that the ANOVA uses the original scores (not the difference scores) and requires the P totals for each participant.

Participant	Treatment I	II	P	
A	3	5	8	$G = 48$
B	4	14	18	$\Sigma X^2 = 372$
C	5	7	12	$N = 8$
D	4	6	10	

Again, the null hypothesis states that, for the general population, there is no mean difference between the two treatment conditions.

$$H_0: \mu_1 = \mu_2$$

For this study, $df_{\text{between treatments}} = 1$, $df_{\text{within treatments}} = 6$, $df_{\text{between subjects}} = 3$, which produce $df_{\text{error}} = (6 - 3) = 3$. Thus, the F-ratio has $df = 1, 3$ and the critical value for $\alpha = .05$ is $F = 10.13$. Note that the denominator of the F-ratio has the same df value as the t statistic ($df = 3$) and that the critical value for F is equal to the squared critical value for t ($10.13 = 3.182^2$).

For these data,

$$SS_{total} = 84$$

$$SS_{within} = 52$$

$$SS_{between\ treatments} = (84 - 52) = 32$$

$$SS_{between\ subjects} = 28$$

$$SS_{error} = (52 - 28) = 24$$

The two variances in the F-ratio are

$$MS_{between\ treatments} = \frac{SS_{between\ treatments}}{df_{between\ treatments}} = \frac{32}{1} = 32$$

and $$MS_{error} = \frac{SS_{error}}{df_{error}} = \frac{24}{3} = 8$$

and the F-ratio is $$F = \frac{MS_{between\ treatments}}{MS_{error}} = \frac{32}{8} = 4.00$$

Notice that the F-ratio and the t statistic are related by the equation $F = t^2$ ($4 = 2^2$). The F-ratio (like the t statistic) is not in the critical region so, once again, we fail to reject H_0 and conclude that there is no significant difference between the two treatments.

LEARNING CHECK

1. A repeated-measures study is used to evaluate the mean differences between two treatment conditions using a sample of $n = 20$ participants.

   a. If a repeated-measures t is used for the hypothesis test, what are the df values for the t statistic?

   b. If a repeated-measures ANOVA is used for the hypothesis test, what are the df values for the F-ratio?

2. A research report includes a repeated-measures F-ratio of $F = 4.00$ with $df = 1, 24$.

   a. Could the researchers have used a t statistic instead of an F-ratio to evaluate the mean difference? Explain your answer.

   b. If a t statistic were used, then what value would be obtained for t?

ANSWERS

1. a. $df = 19$

   b. $df = 1, 19$

2. a. The study compared only 2 treatments ($df_{between\ treatments} = 1$), so a t statistic could be used.

   b. $t = \sqrt{4} = 2$

13.3 TWO-FACTOR ANOVA (INDEPENDENT MEASURES)

In most research situations, the goal is to examine the relationship between two variables. Typically, the research study attempts to isolate the two variables to eliminate or reduce the influence of any outside variables that may distort the relationship being studied. A typical experiment, for example, focuses on one independent variable (which is expected to influence behavior) and one dependent variable (which is a measure of the behavior). In real life, however, variables rarely exist in isolation. That is, behavior usually is influenced by a variety of different variables acting and interacting simultaneously. To examine these more complex, real-life situations, researchers often design research studies that include more than one independent variable. Thus, researchers systematically change two (or more) variables and then observe how the changes influence another (dependent) variable.

An independent variable is a manipulated variable in an experiment. A quasi-independent variable is not manipulated but defines the groups of scores in a nonexperimental study.

In Chapter 12 and earlier in this chapter, we examined ANOVA for *single-factor* research designs—that is, designs that included only one independent variable or only one quasi-independent variable. When a research study involves more than one factor, it is called a *factorial design.* In this chapter, we consider the simplest version of a factorial design. Specifically, we examine ANOVA as it applies to research studies with exactly two factors. In addition, we limit our discussion to studies that use a separate sample for each treatment condition—that is, independent-measures designs. Finally, we consider only research designs for which the sample size (n) is the same for all treatment conditions. In the terminology of ANOVA, this chapter examines *two-factor, independent-measures, equal* n *designs.* The following example demonstrates the general elements of this kind of research design.

EXAMPLE 13.3

Imagine that you are seated at your desk, ready to take the final exam in statistics. Just before the exams are handed out, a television crew appears and sets up a camera and lights aimed directly at you. They explain they are filming students during exams for a television special. You are told to ignore the camera and go ahead with your exam.

Would the presence of a TV camera affect your performance on an exam? For some of you, the answer to this question is "definitely yes," and for others, "probably not." In fact, both answers are right; whether or not the TV camera affects performance depends on your personality. Some of you would become terribly distressed and self-conscious, while others really could ignore the camera and go on as if everything were normal.

In an experiment that duplicates the situation we have described, Shrauger (1972) tested participants on a concept formation task. Half the participants worked alone (no audience), and half worked with an audience of people who claimed to be interested in observing the experiment. Shrauger also divided the participants into two groups on the basis of personality: those high in self-esteem and those low in self-esteem. Table 13.4 shows the structure of Shrauger's study. Note that the study

TABLE 13.4

The structure of a two-factor experiment presented as a matrix. The two factors are self-esteem and presence/absence of an audience, with two levels for each factor.

		Factor B: Audience Condition	
		No Audience	Audience
Factor A: Self-Esteem	Low	Scores for a group of participants who are classified as low self-esteem and are tested with no audience.	Scores for a group of participants who are classified as low self-esteem and are tested with an audience.
	High	Scores for a group of participants who are classified as high self-esteem and are tested with no audience.	Scores for a group of participants who are classified as high self-esteem and are tested with an audience.

involves two separate factors: One factor is manipulated by the researcher, changing from no-audience to audience, and the second factor is self-esteem, which varies from high to low. The two factors are used to create a *matrix* with the different levels of self-esteem defining the rows and the different audience conditions defining the columns. The resulting two-by-two matrix shows four different combinations of the variables, producing four different conditions. Thus, the research study would require four separate samples, one for each *cell*, or box, in the matrix. The dependent variable for the study is the number of errors on the concept formation task for people observed in each of the four conditions.

The two-factor ANOVA tests for mean differences in research studies that are structured like the audience-and-self-esteem example in Table 13.4. For this example, the two-factor ANOVA evaluates three separate sets of mean differences:

1. What happens to the mean number of errors when the audience is added or taken away?

2. Is there a difference in the mean number of errors for participants with high self-esteem compared to those with low self-esteem?

3. Is the mean number of errors affected by specific combinations of self-esteem and audience? (For example, an audience may have a large effect on participants with low self-esteem but only a small effect for those with high self-esteem.)

Thus, the two-factor ANOVA allows us to examine three types of mean differences within one analysis. In particular, we conduct three separate hypotheses tests for the same data, with a separate F-ratio for each test. The three F-ratios have the same basic structure:

$$F = \frac{\text{variance (differences) between treatments}}{\text{variance (differences) expected if there is no treatment effect}}$$

In each case, the numerator of the F-ratio measures the actual mean differences in the data, and the denominator measures the differences that would be expected if there is no treatment effect. As always, a large value for the F-ratio indicates that the sample mean differences are greater than would be expected by chance alone, and, therefore, provides evidence of a treatment effect. To determine whether the obtained F-ratios are *significant*, we need to compare each F-ratio with the critical values found in the F-distribution table in Appendix B.

MAIN EFFECTS AND INTERACTIONS   As noted in the previous section, a two-factor ANOVA actually involves three distinct hypothesis tests. In this section, we examine these three tests in more detail.

Traditionally, the two independent variables in a two-factor experiment are identified as factor A and factor B. For the study presented in Table 13.4, self-esteem is factor A, and the presence or absence of an audience is factor B. The goal of the study is to evaluate the mean differences that may be produced by either of these factors acting independently or by the two factors acting together.

Main effects   One purpose of the study is to determine whether differences in self-esteem (factor A) result in differences in performance. To answer this question, we compare the mean score for all of the participants with low self-esteem with the mean for those with high self-esteem. Note that this process evaluates the mean difference between the top row and the bottom row in Table 13.4.

To make this process more concrete, we present a set of hypothetical data in Table 13.5. The table shows the mean score for each of the treatment conditions (cells) as well as the overall mean for each column (each audience condition) and the overall mean for each row (each self-esteem group). These data indicate that the low self-esteem participants (the top row) had an overall mean of $M = 8$ errors. This overall mean was obtained by computing the average of the two means in the top row. In contrast, the high self-esteem participants had an overall mean of $M = 4$ errors (the mean for the bottom row). The difference between these means constitutes what is called the *main effect* for self-esteem, or the *main effect for factor* A.

Similarly, the main effect for factor B (audience condition) is defined by the mean difference between the columns of the matrix. For the data in Table 13.5, the two groups of participants tested with no audience had an overall mean score of $M = 5$ errors. Participants tested with an audience committed an overall average of $M = 7$ errors. The difference between these means constitutes the *main effect* for the audience conditions, or the *main effect for factor* B.

DEFINITION

> The mean differences among the levels of one factor are referred to as the **main effect** of that factor. When the design of the research study is represented as a matrix with one factor determining the rows and the second factor determining the columns, then the mean differences among the rows describe the main effect of one factor, and the mean differences among the columns describe the main effect for the second factor.

The mean differences between columns or rows simply *describe* the main effects for a two-factor study. As we have observed in earlier chapters, the existence of sample mean differences does not necessarily imply that the differences are *statistically significant*. In general, two samples are not expected to have exactly the same means. There will always be small differences from one sample to another, and you should not automatically assume that these differences are an indication of a systematic treatment effect. In the case of a two-factor study, any main effects that are observed in the data must be evaluated with a hypothesis test to determine whether they are statistically significant effects. Unless the hypothesis test demonstrates that the main effects are significant, you must conclude that the observed mean differences are simply the result of sampling error.

The evaluation of main effects accounts for two of the three hypothesis tests in a two-factor ANOVA. We state hypotheses concerning the main effect of factor A and the main effect of factor B and then calculate two separate F-ratios to evaluate the hypotheses.

For the example we are considering, factor A involves the comparison of two different levels of self-esteem. The null hypothesis would state that there is no difference between the two levels; that is, self-esteem has no effect on performance. In symbols,

$$H_0 : \mu_{A_1} = \mu_{A_2}$$

TABLE 13.5

Hypothetical data for an experiment examining the effect of an audience on participants with different levels of self-esteem.

	No Audience	Audience	
Low Self-Esteem	$M = 7$	$M = 9$	$M = 8$
High Self-Esteem	$M = 3$	$M = 5$	$M = 4$
	$M = 5$	$M = 7$	

The alternative hypothesis is that the two different levels of self-esteem do produce different scores:

$$H_1 : \mu_{A_1} \neq \mu_{A_2}$$

To evaluate these hypotheses, we compute an F-ratio that compares the actual mean differences between the two self-esteem levels versus the amount of difference that would be expected without any systematic treatment effects.

$$F = \frac{\text{variance for (differences between) the means for factor } A}{\text{variance (differences) expected if there is no treatment effect}}$$

$$F = \frac{\text{variance for (differences between) the row means}}{\text{variance (differences) expected if there is no treatment effect}}$$

Similarly, factor B involves the comparison of the two different audience conditions. The null hypothesis states that there is no difference in the mean number of errors between the two conditions. In symbols,

$$H_0 : \mu_{B_1} = \mu_{B_2}$$

As always, the alternative hypothesis states that the means are different:

$$H_1 : \mu_{B_1} \neq \mu_{B_2}$$

Again, the F-ratio compares the obtained mean difference between the two audience conditions versus the amount of difference that would be expected if there is no systematic treatment effect.

$$F = \frac{\text{variance for (differences between) the means for factor } B}{\text{variance (differences) expected if there is no treatment effect}}$$

$$F = \frac{\text{variance for (differences between) the column means}}{\text{variance (differences) expected if there is no treatment effect}}$$

Interactions   In addition to evaluating the main effect of each factor individually, the two-factor ANOVA allows you to evaluate other mean differences that may result from unique combinations of the two factors. For example, specific combinations of self-esteem and an audience acting together may have effects that are different from the effects of self-esteem or an audience acting alone. Any "extra" mean differences that are not explained by the main effects are called an *interaction,* or an *interaction between factors.* The real advantage of combining two factors within the same study is the ability to examine the unique effects caused by an interaction.

D E F I N I T I O N

> An **interaction** between two factors occurs whenever the mean differences between individual treatment conditions, or cells, are different from what would be predicted from the overall main effects of the factors.

To make the concept of an interaction more concrete, we reexamine the data shown in Table 13.5. For these data, there is no interaction; that is, there are no extra mean differences that are not explained by the main effects. For example, within each audience condition (each column of the matrix), the average number of errors for the low self-esteem participants is 4 points higher than the average for the high self-esteem participants. This 4-point mean difference is exactly what is predicted by the overall main effect for self-esteem.

The data in Table 13.6 show the same pattern of results that was obtained in Shrauger's research study.

Now consider a different set of data shown in Table 13.6. These new data show exactly the same main effects that existed in Table 13.5 (the column means and the row means have not been changed). But now there is an interaction between the two factors. For example, for the low self-esteem participants (top row), there is a 4-point difference in the number of errors committed with an audience and without an audience. This 4-point difference cannot be explained by the 2-point main effect for the audience factor. Also, for the high self-esteem participants (bottom row), the data show no difference between the two audience conditions. Again, the zero difference is not what would be expected based on the 2-point main effect for the audience factor. Mean differences that are not explained by the main effects are an indication of an interaction between the two factors.

To evaluate the interaction, the two-factor ANOVA first identifies mean differences that are not explained by the main effects. The extra mean differences are then evaluated by an F-ratio with the following structure:

$$F = \frac{\text{variance (mean differences) not explained by the main effects}}{\text{variance (mean differences) expected if there are no treatment effects}}$$

The null hypothesis for this F-ratio simply states that there is no interaction:

H_0: There is no interaction between factors A and B. All of the mean differences between treatment conditions are explained by the main effects of the two factors.

The alternative hypothesis states that there is an interaction between the two factors:

H_1: There is an interaction between factors. The mean differences between treatment conditions are not what would be predicted from the overall main effects of the two factors.

More about interactions In the previous section, we introduced the concept of an interaction as the unique effect produced by two factors working together. This section presents two alternative definitions of an interaction. These alternatives are intended to help you understand the concept of an interaction and to help you identify an interaction when you encounter one in a set of data. You should realize that the new definitions are equivalent to the original and simply present slightly different perspectives on the same concept.

The first new perspective on the concept of an interaction focuses on the notion of independence for the two factors. More specifically, if the two factors are independent, so that one factor does not influence the effect of the other, then there is no interaction. On the other hand, when the two factors are not independent, so that the effect of one factor *depends on* the other, then there is an interaction. The notion of dependence between factors is consistent with our earlier discussion of interactions. If one factor influences the effect of the other, then unique combinations of the factors produce unique effects.

TABLE 13.6

Hypothetical data for an experiment examining the effect of an audience on participants with different levels of self-esteem. The data show the same main effects as the values in Table 13.5, but the individual treatment means have been modified to create an interaction.

	No Audience	Audience	
Low Self-Esteem	$M = 6$	$M = 10$	$M = 8$
High Self-Esteem	$M = 4$	$M = 4$	$M = 4$
	$M = 5$	$M = 7$	

DEFINITION

> When the effect of one factor depends on the different levels of a second factor, then there is an **interaction** between the factors.

This definition of an interaction should be familiar in the context of a "drug interaction." Your doctor and pharmacist are always concerned that the effect of one medication may be altered or distorted by a second medication that is being taken at the same time. Thus, the effect of one drug (factor A) depends on a second drug (factor B), and you have an interaction between the two drugs.

Returning to Table 13.5, you will notice that the size of the audience effect (first column versus second column) *does not depend* on the self-esteem of the participants. For these data, adding an audience produces the same 2-point increase in errors for both groups of participants. Thus, the audience effect does not depend on self-esteem, and there is no interaction. Now consider the data in Table 13.6. This time, the effect of adding an audience *depends on* the self-esteem of the participants. For example, there is a 4-point increase in errors for the low self-esteem participants but adding an audience has no effect on the errors for the high self-esteem participants. Thus, the audience effect depends on the level of self-esteem, which means that there is an interaction between the two factors.

The second alternative definition of an interaction is obtained when the results of a two-factor study are presented in a graph. In this case, the concept of an interaction can be defined in terms of the pattern displayed in the graph. Figure 13.2 shows the two sets of data we have been considering. The original data from Table 13.5, where there is no interaction, are presented in Figure 13.2(a). To construct this figure, we selected one of the factors to be displayed on the horizontal axis; in this case, the different levels of the audience factor are displayed. The dependent variable, the number of errors, is shown on the vertical axis. Note that the figure actually contains two separate graphs: The top line shows the relationship between the audience factor and errors for the low self-esteem participants, and the bottom line shows the relationship for the high self-esteem participants. In general, the picture in the graph matches the structure of the data

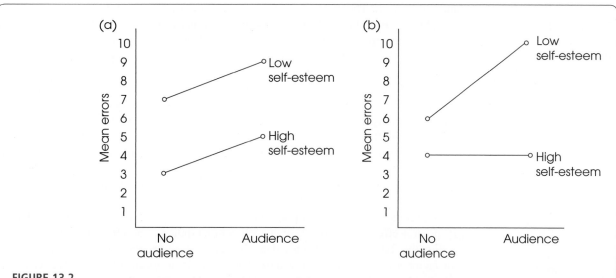

FIGURE 13.2

(a) Graph showing the treatment means from Table 13.5, for which there is no interaction.

(b) Graph for Table 13.6, for which there is an interaction.

matrix; the columns of the matrix appear as values along the *X*-axis, and the rows of the matrix appear as separate lines in the graph.

For the original set of data, Figure 13.2(a), note that the two lines are parallel; that is, the distance between lines is constant. In this case, the distance between lines reflects the 2-point difference in mean errors between low and high self-esteem participants, and this 2-point difference is the same for both audience conditions.

Now look at a graph that is obtained when there is an interaction in the data. Figure 13.2(b) shows the data from Table 13.6. This time, note that the lines in the graph are not parallel. The distance between the lines changes as you scan from left to right. For these data, the distance between the lines corresponds to the self-esteem effect—that is, the mean difference in errors for low versus high self-esteem participants. The fact that this difference depends on the audience condition is an indication of an interaction between the two factors.

DEFINITION

> When the results of a two-factor study are presented in a graph, the existence of nonparallel lines (lines that cross or diverge) indicates an **interaction** between the two factors.

For many students, the concept of an interaction is easiest to understand using the perspective of interdependency; that is, an interaction exists when the effects of one variable *depend* on another factor. However, the easiest way to identify an interaction within a set of data is to draw a graph showing the treatment means. The presence of nonparallel lines is an easy way to spot an interaction.

INDEPENDENCE OF MAIN EFFECTS AND INTERACTIONS

The two-factor ANOVA consists of three hypothesis tests, each evaluating specific mean differences: the *A* effect, the *B* effect, and the $A \times B$ interaction. As we have noted, these are three *separate* tests, but you should also realize that the three tests are *independent*. That is, the outcome for any one of the three tests is totally unrelated to the outcome for either of the other two. Thus, it is possible for data from a two-factor study to display any possible combination of significant and/or not significant main effects and interactions. The data sets in Table 13.7 show several possibilities.

The $A \times B$ interaction typically is called "*A* by *B*" interaction. If there is an interaction between an audience and self-esteem, it may be called the "audience by self-esteem" interaction.

Table 13.7(a) shows data with mean differences between levels of factor *A* (an *A* effect) but no mean differences for factor *B* and no interaction. To identify the *A* effect, notice that the overall mean for A_1 (the top row) is 10 points higher than the overall mean for A_2 (the bottom row). This 10-point difference is the main effect for factor *A*. To evaluate the *B* effect, notice that both columns have exactly the same overall mean, indicating no difference between levels of factor *B*; hence, there is no *B* effect. Finally, the absence of an interaction is indicated by the fact that the overall *A* effect (the 10-point difference) is constant within each column; that is, the *A* effect *does not depend* on the levels of factor *B*. (Alternatively, the data indicate that the overall *B* effect is constant within each row.)

Table 13.7(b) shows data with an *A* effect and a *B* effect but no interaction. For these data, the *A* effect is indicated by the 10-point mean difference between rows, and the *B* effect is indicated by the 20-point mean difference between columns. The fact that the 10-point *A* effect is constant within each column indicates no interaction.

Finally, Table 13.7(c) shows data that display an interaction but no main effect for factor *A* or for factor *B*. For these data, there is no mean difference between rows (no *A* effect) and no mean difference between columns (no *B* effect). However, within each row (or within each column), there are mean differences. The "extra" mean differences within the rows and columns cannot be explained by the overall main effects and therefore indicate an interaction.

TABLE 13.7

Three sets of data showing different combinations of main effects and interaction for a two-factor study. (The numerical value in each cell of the matrices represents the mean value obtained for the sample in that treatment condition.)

a. Data showing a main effect for factor A but no B effect and no interaction

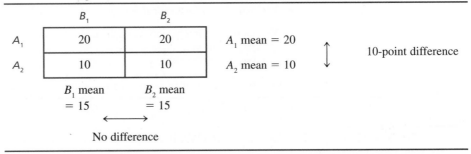

b. Data showing main effects for both factor A and factor B but no interaction

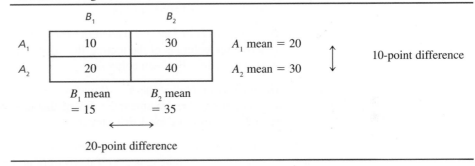

c. Data showing no main effect for either factor but an interaction

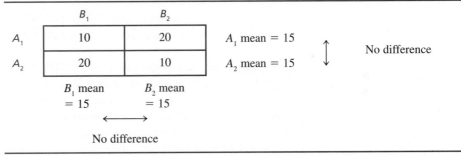

LEARNING CHECK

1. The following matrix shows the results from a two-factor experiment.

   a. What means are compared to evaluate the main effect for factor A?

   b. What means are compared to evaluate the main effect for factor B?

   c. Does there appear to be an interaction between the two factors? Explain your answer.

	B_1	B_2	
A_1	$M = 20$	$M = 30$	$M = 25$
A_2	$M = 10$	$M = 10$	$M = 10$
	$M = 15$	$M = 25$	

2. It is impossible to have an interaction unless you also have main effects for at least one of the two factors. (True or false?)

ANSWERS   **1. a.** The main effect for factor A compares $M = 25$ and $M = 10$.

b. The main effect for factor B compares $M = 15$ and $M = 25$.

c. Yes, there is an interaction. In A_1 there is a 10-point difference between the two levels of factor B, but in A_2 there is no mean difference. Thus, the B effect depends on the levels of factor A.

2. False. The existence of an interaction is completely independent of the main effects.

THE STRUCTURE OF THE TWO-FACTOR ANOVA

The two-factor ANOVA is composed of three distinct hypothesis tests:

1. The main effect of factor A (often called the A-effect). Assuming that factor A is used to define the rows of the matrix, the main effect of factor A evaluates the mean differences between rows.

2. The main effect of factor B (called the B-effect). Assuming that factor B is used to define the columns of the matrix, the main effect of factor B evaluates the mean differences between columns.

3. The interaction (called the $A \times B$ interaction). The interaction evaluates mean differences between treatment conditions that are not predicted from the overall main effects from factor A or factor B.

For each of these three tests, we are looking for mean differences between treatments that are larger than would be expected if there were no treatment effects. In each case, the significance of the treatment effect is evaluated by an F-ratio. All three F-ratios have the same basic structure:

$$F = \frac{\text{variance (mean differences) between treatments}}{\text{variance (mean differences) expected if there is no treatment effect}} \quad (13.12)$$

The general structure of the two-factor ANOVA is shown in Figure 13.3. Note that the overall analysis is divided into two stages. In the first stage, the total variability is separated into two components: between-treatments variability and within-treatments variability. This first stage is identical to the single-factor ANOVA introduced in Chapter 12 with each cell in the two-factor matrix viewed as a separate treatment condition. The within-treatments variability that is obtained in stage 1 of the analysis is used to compute the denominator for the F-ratios. As we noted in Chapter 12, within each treatment, all of the participants are treated exactly the same. Thus, any differences that exist within the treatments cannot be caused by treatment effects. As a result, the within-treatments variability provides a measure of the differences that exist when there are no systematic treatment effects influencing the scores (see Equation 13.12).

The between-treatments variability obtained in stage 1 of the analysis combines all the mean differences produced by factor A, factor B, and the interaction. The purpose of the second stage is to partition the differences into three separate components: differences attributed to factor A, differences attributed to factor B, and any remaining mean differences that define the interaction. These three components form the numerators for the three F-ratios in the analysis.

The goal of this analysis is to compute the variance values needed for the three F-ratios. We need three between-treatments variances (one for factor A, one for factor B, and one for the interaction), and we need a within-treatments variance. Each of these variances (or mean squares) is determined by a sum of squares value (SS) and a degrees of freedom value (df):

Remember that in ANOVA a variance is called a mean square, or MS.

$$\text{mean square} = MS = \frac{SS}{df}$$

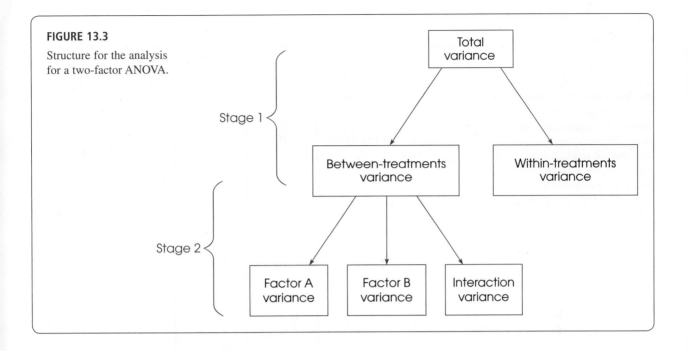

FIGURE 13.3

Structure for the analysis for a two-factor ANOVA.

EXAMPLE 13.4

To demonstrate the two-factor ANOVA, we will use a research study based on previous work by Ackerman and Goldsmith (2011). Their study compared learning performance by students who studied text either from printed pages or from a computer screen. The results from the study indicate that students do much better studying from printed pages if their study time is self-regulated. However, when the researchers fixed the time spent studying, there was no difference between the two conditions. Apparently, students are less accurate predicting their learning performance or have trouble regulating study time when working with a computer screen compared to working with paper. Table 13.8 shows data from a two-factor study replicating the Ackerman and Goldsmith experiment. The two factors are mode of presentation (paper or computer screen) and time control (self-regulated or fixed). A separate group of $n = 5$ students was tested in each of the four conditions. The dependent variable is student performance on a 10-point quiz covering the text that was studied.

The data are displayed in a matrix with the two levels of time control (factor A) making up the rows and the two levels of presentation mode (factor B) making up the columns. Note that the data matrix has a total of four *cells* or treatment conditions with a separate sample of $n = 5$ participants in each condition. Most of the notation should be familiar from the single-factor ANOVA presented in Chapter 12. Specifically, the treatment totals are identified by T values, the total number of scores in the entire study is $N = 20$, and the grand total (sum) of all 20 scores is $G = 155$. In addition to these familiar values, we have included the totals for each row and for each column in the matrix. The goal of the ANOVA is to determine whether the mean differences observed in the data are significantly greater than would be expected if there were no treatment effects.

STAGE 1 OF THE TWO-FACTOR ANALYSIS

The first stage of the two-factor analysis separates the total variability into two components: between-treatments and within-treatments. The formulas for this stage are identical to the formulas used in the single-factor ANOVA in Chapter 12 with the provision

TABLE 13.8

Data for a two-factor study comparing two levels of time control (self-regulated or fixed by the researchers) and two levels of text presentation (paper and computer screen). The dependent variable is performance on a quiz covering the text that was presented. The study involves four treatment conditions with $n = 5$ participants in each treatment.

		Factor B: Text Presentation Mode		
		Paper	Computer Screen	
	Self-regulated	11 8 9 10 7 $M = 9$ $T = 45$ $SS = 10$	4 4 8 5 4 $M = 5$ $T = 25$ $SS = 12$	$T_{row} = 70$
Factor A: Time Control				$N = 20$ $G = 155$ $\Sigma X^2 = 1303$
	Fixed	10 7 10 6 7 $M = 8$ $T = 40$ $SS = 14$	10 6 10 10 9 $M = 9$ $T = 45$ $SS = 12$	$T_{row} = 85$
		$T_{col} = 85$	$T_{col} = 70$	

that each cell in the two-factor matrix is treated as a separate treatment condition. The formulas and the calculations for the data in Table 13.8 are as follows:

Total variability

$$SS_{total} = \Sigma X^2 - \frac{G^2}{N}$$

(13.13)

For these data,

$$\begin{aligned} SS_{total} &= 1303 - \frac{155^2}{20} \\ &= 1303 - 1201.25 \\ &= 101.75 \end{aligned}$$

This SS value measures the variability for all $N = 20$ scores and has degrees of freedom given by

$$df_{total} = N - 1$$

(13.14)

For the data in Table 13.8, $df_{total} = 19$.

Within-treatments variability To compute the variance within treatments, we first compute SS and $df = n - 1$ for each of the individual treatment conditions. Then the within-treatments SS is defined as

$$SS_{within\ treatments} = \Sigma SS_{each\ treatment}$$

(13.15)

And the within-treatments df is defined as

$$df_{\text{within treatments}} = \Sigma df_{\text{each treatment}} \qquad (13.16)$$

For the four treatment conditions in Table 13.8,

$$SS_{\text{within treatments}} = 10 + 12 + 14 + 12$$

$$= 48$$

$$df_{\text{within treatments}} = 4 + 4 + 4 + 4$$

$$= 16$$

Between-treatments variability   Because the two components in stage 1 must add up to the total, the easiest way to find $SS_{\text{between treatments}}$ is by subtraction.

$$SS_{\text{between treatments}} = SS_{\text{total}} - SS_{\text{within}} \qquad (13.17)$$

For the data in Table 13.8, we obtain

$$SS_{\text{between treatments}} = 101.75 - 48 = 53.75$$

However, you can also use the computational formula to calculate $SS_{\text{between treatments}}$ directly.

$$SS_{\text{between treatments}} = \Sigma \frac{T^2}{n} - \frac{G^2}{N} \qquad (13.18)$$

For the data in Table 13.8, there are four treatments (four T values), each with $n = 5$ scores, and the between-treatments SS is

$$SS_{\text{between treatments}} = \frac{45^2}{5} + \frac{25^2}{5} + \frac{40^2}{5} + \frac{45^2}{5} + \frac{155^2}{20}$$
$$= 405 + 125 + 320 + 405 - 1201.25$$
$$= 53.75$$

The between-treatments df value is determined by the number of treatments (or the number of T values) minus one. For a two-factor study, the number of treatments is equal to the number of cells in the matrix. Thus,

$$df_{\text{between treatments}} = \text{number of cells} - 1 \qquad (13.19)$$

For these data, $df_{\text{between treatments}} = 3$.

This completes the first stage of the analysis. Note that the two components add to equal the total for both SS values and df values.

$$SS_{\text{between treatments}} + SS_{\text{within treatments}} = SS_{\text{total}}$$

$$53.75 + 48 = 101.75$$

$$df_{\text{between treatments}} + df_{\text{within treatments}} = df_{\text{total}}$$

$$3 + 16 = 19$$

STAGE 2 OF THE TWO-FACTOR ANALYSIS

The second stage of the analysis determines the numerators for the three F-ratios. Specifically, this stage determines the between-treatments variance for factor A, factor B, and the interaction.

1. **Factor A.** The main effect for factor A evaluates the mean differences between the levels of factor A. For this example, factor A defines the rows of the matrix, so we are evaluating the mean differences between rows. To compute the SS for factor A, we calculate a between-treatment SS using the row totals in exactly the same way as we computed $SS_{\text{between treatments}}$ using the treatment totals (T values) earlier. For factor A, the row totals are 70 and 85, and each total was obtained by adding 10 scores.

Therefore,

$$SS_A = \Sigma \frac{T^2_{ROW}}{n_{ROW}} - \frac{G^2}{N} \tag{13.20}$$

For our data,

$$SS_A = \frac{70^2}{10} + \frac{85^2}{10} - \frac{155^2}{20}$$
$$= 490 + 722.5 - 1201.25$$
$$= 11.25$$

Factor A involves two treatments (or two rows), easy and difficult, so the df value is

$$df_A = \text{number of rows} - 1 \tag{13.21}$$
$$= 2 - 1$$
$$= 1$$

2. **Factor B.** The calculations for factor B follow exactly the same pattern that was used for factor A, except for substituting columns in place of rows. The main effect for factor B evaluates the mean differences between the levels of factor B, which define the columns of the matrix.

$$SS_B = \Sigma \frac{T^2_{COL}}{n_{COL}} - \frac{G^2}{N} \tag{13.22}$$

For our data, the column totals are 85 and 70, and each total was obtained by adding 10 scores. Thus,

$$SS_B = \frac{85^2}{10} + \frac{70^2}{10} + \frac{155^2}{10}$$
$$= 725.5 + 490 - 1201.25$$
$$= 11.25$$

$$df_B = \text{number of columns} - 1 \tag{13.23}$$
$$= 2 - 1$$
$$= 1$$

3. The $A \times B$ Interaction. The $A \times B$ interaction is defined as the "extra" mean differences not accounted for by the main effects of the two factors. We use this definition to find the SS and df values for the interaction by simple subtraction. Specifically, the between-treatments variability is partitioned into three parts: the A effect, the B effect, and the interaction (see Figure 13.3). We have already computed the SS and df values for A and B, so we can find the interaction values by subtracting to find out how much is left. Thus,

$$SS_{A \times B} = SS_{\text{between treatments}} - SS_A - SS_B \qquad (13.24)$$

For our data,

$$SS_{A \times B} = 53.75 - 11.25 - 11.25$$
$$= 31.25$$

Similarly,

$$df_{A \times B} = df_{\text{between treatments}} - df_A - df_B \qquad (13.25)$$

$$= 3 - 1 - 1$$
$$= 1$$

An easy to remember alternative formula for $df_{A \times B}$ is

$$df_{A \times B} = df_A \times df_B \qquad (13.26)$$

$$= 1 \times 1 = 1$$

MEAN SQUARES AND *F*-RATIOS FOR THE TWO-FACTOR ANOVA

The two-factor ANOVA consists of three separate hypothesis tests with three separate F-ratios. The denominator for each F-ratio is intended to measure the variance (differences) that would be expected if there are no treatment effects. As we saw in Chapter 12, the within-treatments variance is the appropriate denominator for an independent-measures design (see page 352). The within-treatments variance is called a *mean square,* or MS, and is computed as follows:

$$MS_{\text{within treatments}} = \frac{SS_{\text{within treatments}}}{df_{\text{within treatments}}}$$

For the data in Table 13.8,

$$MS_{\text{within treatments}} = \frac{48}{16} = 3$$

This value forms the denominator for all three F-ratios.

The numerators of the three F-ratios all measured variance or differences between treatments: differences between levels of factor A, differences between levels of factor B, and extra differences that are attributed to the $A \times B$ interaction. These three variances are computed as follows:

$$MS_A = \frac{SS_A}{df_A} \qquad MS_B = \frac{SS_B}{df_B} \qquad MS_{A \times B} = \frac{SS_{A \times B}}{df_{A \times B}}$$

For the data in Table 13.9, the three MS values are

$$MS_A = \frac{11.25}{1} = 11.25 \qquad MS_B = \frac{11.25}{1} = 11.25 \qquad MS_{A \times B} = \frac{31.25}{1} = 31.25$$

Finally, the three F-ratios are

$$F_A = \frac{MS_A}{MS_{\text{within treatments}}} = \frac{11.25}{3} = 3.75$$

$$F_B = \frac{MS_B}{MS_{\text{within treatments}}} = \frac{11.25}{3} = 3.75$$

$$F_{A \times B} = \frac{MS_{A \times B}}{MS_{\text{within treatments}}} = \frac{31.25}{3} = 10.41$$

To determine the significance of each F-ratio, we must consult the F distribution table using the df values for each of the individual F-ratios. For this example, all three F-ratios have $df = 1$ for the numerator and $df = 16$ for the denominator. Checking the table with $df = 1$, 16, we find a critical value of 4.49 for $\alpha = .05$ and a critical value of 8.53 for $\alpha = .01$. For both main effects, we obtained $F = 3.75$, so neither of the main effects is significant. For the interaction, we obtained $F = 10.41$, which exceeds both of the critical values, so we conclude that there is a significant interaction between the two factors. That is, the difference between the two modes of presentation depends on how studying time is controlled.

Table 13.9 is a summary table for the complete two-factor ANOVA from Example 13.4. Although these tables are no longer commonly used in research reports, they provide a concise format for displaying all of the elements of the analysis.

TABLE 13.9

A summary table for the two-factor ANOVA for the data from Example 13.4.

Source	SS	df	MS	F
Between treatments	53.75	3		
Factor A (time control)	11.25	1	11.25	$F(1, 16) = 3.75$
Factor B (presentation)	11.25	1	11.25	$F(1, 16) = 3.75$
$A \times B$	31.25	1	31.25	$F(1, 16) = 10.42$
Within treatments	48	16	3	
Total	101.75	19		

LEARNING CHECK

1. Explain why the within-treatment variability is the appropriate denominator for the two-factor independent-measures F-ratios.

2. The following data summarize the results from a two-factor independent-measures experiment:

		Factor B		
		B_1	B_2	B_3
Factor A	A_1	$n = 5$ $T = 0$ $SS = 30$	$n = 5$ $T = 10$ $SS = 40$	$n = 5$ $T = 20$ $SS = 50$
	A_2	$n = 5$ $T = 10$ $SS = 60$	$n = 5$ $T = 10$ $SS = 50$	$n = 5$ $T = 10$ $SS = 40$

a. Calculate SS for factor A.

b. Calculate SS for factor B.

c. Given that the between-treatments (or between-cells) SS is equal to 40, what is the SS for the interaction?

3. The following table summarizes the results from a two-factor ANOVA with 2 levels of factor A, 3 levels of factor B, and n = 6 in each treatment condition. Fill in all of the blank cells.

Source	SS	df	MS	
Between Treat.	75	—		
Factor A	—	—	—	$F = \_\_$
Factor B	—	—	15	$F = \_\_$
$A \times B$	—	—	—	$F = 6.00$
Within Treat.	—	—	—	
Total	165	—		

ANSWERS

1. Within each treatment condition, all individuals are treated in exactly the same way. Therefore, the within-treatment variability measures the differences that exist between one score and another when there is no treatment effect causing the scores to be different. This is exactly the variance that is needed for the denominator of the F-ratios.

2. a. The totals for factor A are 30 and 30, and each total is obtained by adding 15 scores. $SS_A = 0$.

b. The totals for factor B are 10, 20, and 30, and each total is obtained by adding 10 scores. $SS_B = 20$.

c. The interaction is determined by differences that remain after the main effects have been accounted for. For these data,

$$SS_{A \times B} = SS_{\text{between treatments}} - SS_A - SS_B$$

$$= 40 - 0 - 20$$

$$= 20$$

3.

Source	SS	df	MS	
Between Treat.	75	5		
Factor A	9	1	9	$F = 3.00$
Factor B	30	2	15	$F = 5.00$
$A \times B$	36	2	18	$F = 6.00$
Within Treat.	90	30	3	
Total	165	35		

MEASURING EFFECT SIZE FOR THE TWO-FACTOR ANOVA

The general technique for measuring effect size with an ANOVA is to compute a value for η^2, the percentage of variance that is explained by the treatment effects. For a two-factor ANOVA, we compute three separate values for η^2: one measuring how much of the variance is explained by the main effect for factor A, one for factor B, and a third for the interaction. As we did with the repeated-measures ANOVA (page 404), we remove any variability that can be explained by other sources before we calculate the percentage for each of the three specific treatment effects. Thus, for example, before we compute the η^2 for factor A, we remove the variability that is explained by factor B and the variability explained by the interaction. The resulting equation is,

$$\text{for factor } A, \ \eta^2 = \frac{SS_A}{SS_{\text{total}} - SS_B - SS_{A \times B}} \tag{13.27}$$

Note that the denominator of Equation 13.27 consists of the variability that is explained by factor A and the other *unexplained* variability. Thus, an equivalent version of the equation is,

$$\text{for factor } A, \ \eta^2 = \frac{SS_A}{SS_A + SS_{\text{within treatments}}} \tag{13.28}$$

Similarly, the η^2 formulas for factor B and for the interaction are as follows:

$$\text{for factor } B, \ \eta^2 = \frac{SS_B}{SS_{\text{total}} - SS_A - SS_{A \times B}} = \frac{SS_B}{SS_B + SS_{\text{within treatments}}} \tag{13.29}$$

$$\text{for } A \times B, \ \eta^2 = \frac{SS_{A \times B}}{SS_{\text{total}} - SS_A - SS_B} = \frac{SS_{A \times B}}{SS_{A \times B} + SS_{\text{within treatments}}} \tag{13.30}$$

Because each of the η^2 equations computes a percentage that is not based on the total variability of the scores, the results are often called *partial* eta squares. For the data in Example 13.4, the equations produce the following values:

$$\eta^2 \text{ for factor } A \text{ (time control)} = \frac{11.25}{11.25 + 48} = 0.190$$

$$\eta^2 \text{ for factor } B \text{ (presentation mode)} = \frac{11.25}{11.25 + 48} = 0.190$$

$$\eta^2 \text{ for factor } A \times B \text{ interation} = \frac{31.25}{31.25 + 48} = 0.394$$

IN THE LITERATURE

REPORTING THE RESULTS OF A TWO-FACTOR ANOVA

The APA format for reporting the results of a two-factor ANOVA follows the same basic guidelines as the single-factor report. First, the means and standard deviations are reported. Because a two-factor design typically involves several treatment conditions, these descriptive statistics often are presented in a table or a graph. Next, the results of all three hypothesis tests (*F*-ratios) are reported. The results for the study in Example 13.4 could be reported as follows:

> The means and standard deviations for all treatment conditions are shown in Table 1. The two-factor analysis of variance showed no significant main effect for time control, $F(1, 16) = 3.75, p > .05, \eta^2 = 0.190$, or for presentation mode, $F(1, 16) = 3.75, p > .05, \eta^2 = 0.190$. However, the interaction between factors was significant, $F(1, 16) = 10.41, p < .01, \eta^2 = 0.394$.

INTERPRETING THE RESULTS FROM A TWO-FACTOR ANOVA

Because the two-factor ANOVA involves three separate tests, you must consider the overall pattern of results rather than focusing on the individual main effects or the interaction. In particular, whenever there is a significant interaction, you should be cautious about accepting the main effects at face value (whether they are significant or not). Remember, an interaction means that the effect of one factor *depends on* the level of the second factor. Because the effect changes from one level to the next, there is no consistent "main effect."

Figure 13.4 shows the sample means obtained from the paper versus computer screen study. Recall that the analysis showed that both main effects were not significant but the interaction was significant. Although both main effects were too small to be significant, it would be incorrect to conclude that neither factor influenced behavior. For this example, the difference between studying text presented on paper versus on a computer screen depends on how studying time is controlled. Specifically, there is little or no difference between paper and a computer screen when the time spent studying is fixed by the researchers. However, studying text from paper produces much higher quiz scores when participants regulate their own study time. Thus, the difference between studying from paper and studying from a computer screen *depends on* how the time spent studying is controlled. This interdependence between factors is the source of the significant interaction.

ASSUMPTIONS FOR THE TWO-FACTOR ANOVA

The validity of the ANOVA presented in this chapter depends on the same three assumptions that we have encountered with other hypothesis tests for independent-measures designs (the *t* test in Chapter 10 and the single-factor ANOVA in Chapter 12):

1. The observations within each sample must be independent (see page 220).

2. The populations from which the samples are selected must be normal.

3. The populations from which the samples are selected must have equal variances (homogeneity of variance).

As before, the assumption of normality generally is not a cause for concern, especially when the sample size is relatively large. The homogeneity of variance

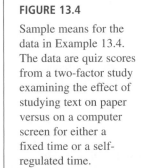

FIGURE 13.4

Sample means for the data in Example 13.4. The data are quiz scores from a two-factor study examining the effect of studying text on paper versus on a computer screen for either a fixed time or a self-regulated time.

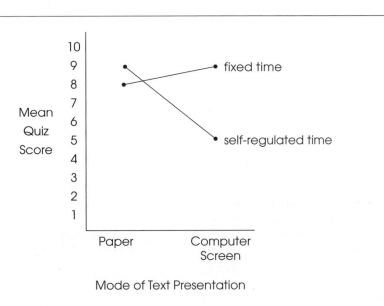

assumption is more important, and if it appears that your data fail to satisfy this requirement, you should conduct a test for homogeneity before you attempt the ANOVA. Hartley's F-max test (see page 301) allows you to use the sample variances from your data to determine whether there is evidence for any differences among the population variances. Remember, for the two-factor ANOVA, there is a separate sample for each cell in the data matrix. The test for homogeneity applies to all these samples and the populations they represent.

SUMMARY

1. The repeated-measures ANOVA is used to evaluate the mean differences obtained in a research study comparing two or more treatment conditions using the same sample of individuals in each condition. The test statistic is an F-ratio, in which the numerator measures the variance (differences) between treatments and the denominator measures the variance (differences) that is expected without any treatment effects or individual differences.

$$F = \frac{MS_{\text{between treatments}}}{MS_{\text{error}}}$$

2. The first stage of the repeated-measures ANOVA is identical to the independent-measures ANOVA and separates the total variability into two components: between-treatments and within-treatments. Because a repeated-measures design uses the same subjects in every treatment condition, the differences between treatments cannot be caused by individual differences. Thus, individual differences are automatically eliminated from the between-treatments variance in the numerator of the F-ratio.

3. In the second stage of the repeated-measures analysis, individual differences are computed and removed from the denominator of the F-ratio. To remove the individual differences, you first compute the variability between subjects (SS and df) and then subtract these values from the corresponding within-treatments values. The residual provides a measure of error excluding individual differences, which is the appropriate denominator for the repeated-measures F-ratio.

4. Effect size for the repeated-measures ANOVA is measured by computing eta squared, the percentage of variance accounted for by the treatment effect. For the repeated-measures ANOVA

$$\eta^2 = \frac{SS_{\text{between treatments}}}{SS_{\text{total}} - SS_{\text{between subjects}}}$$

$$= \frac{SS_{\text{between treatments}}}{SS_{\text{between treatments}} + SS_{\text{error}}}$$

Because part of the variability (the SS caused by individual differences) is removed before computing η^2, this measure of effect size is often called a partial eta squared.

5. A research study with two independent variables is called a two-factor design. Such a design can be diagramed as a matrix with the levels of one factor defining the rows and the levels of the other factor defining the columns. Each cell in the matrix corresponds to a specific combination of the two factors.

6. Traditionally, the two factors are identified as factor A and factor B. The purpose of the ANOVA is to determine whether there are any significant mean differences among the treatment conditions or cells in the experimental matrix. These treatment effects are classified as follows:
   a. The A-effect: Overall mean differences among the levels of factor A.
   b. The B-effect: Overall mean differences among the levels of factor B.
   c. The $A \times B$ interaction: Extra mean differences that are not accounted for by the main effects.

7. The two-factor ANOVA produces three F-ratios: one for factor A, one for factor B, and one for the $A \times B$ interaction. Each F-ratio has the same basic structure:

$$F = \frac{MS_{\text{treatment effect}} \text{ (either } A \text{ or } B \text{ or } A \times B)}{MS_{\text{within treatments}}}$$

The formulas for the SS, df, and MS values for the two-factor ANOVA are presented in Figure 13.5.

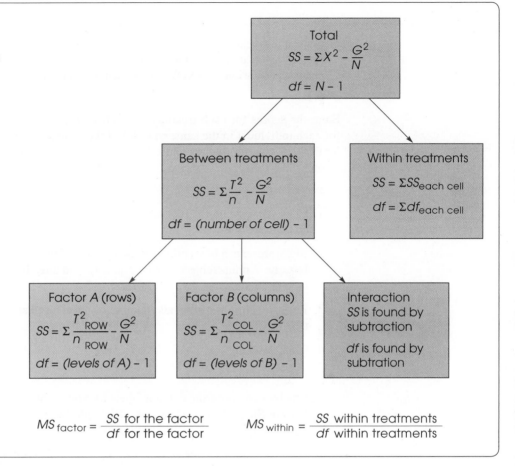

FIGURE 13.5

The ANOVA for an independent-measures two-factor design.

$$MS_{factor} = \frac{SS \text{ for the factor}}{df \text{ for the factor}} \qquad MS_{within} = \frac{SS \text{ within treatments}}{df \text{ within treatments}}$$

KEY TERMS

individual differences (396)

between-treatments variance (398)

error variance (398)

between-subjects variance (398)

two-factor design (410)

matrix (411)

cell (411)

main effect (411)

interaction (413)

RESOURCES

Go to CengageBrain.com to access Psychology CourseMate, where you will find an interactive eBook, glossaries, flashcards, quizzes, statistics workshops, and more.

aplia

If your professor has assigned Aplia:

1. Sign in to your account.
2. Complete the corresponding exercises as required by your professor.
3. When finished, click "Grade It Now" to see which areas you have mastered, which areas need more work, and detailed explanations of every answer.

General instructions for using SPSS are presented in Appendix D. Following are detailed instructions for using SPSS to perform the Single-Factor, **Repeated-Measures Analysis of Variance (ANOVA)** presented in this chapter.

Data Entry

Enter the scores for each treatment condition in a separate column, with the scores for each individual in the same row. All of the scores for the first treatment go in the VAR00001 column, the second treatment scores go in the VAR00002 column, and so on.

Data Analysis

1. Click **Analyze** on the tool bar, select **General Linear Model,** and click on **Repeated-Measures.**

2. SPSS presents a box entitled **Repeated-Measures Define Factors.** Within the box, the Within-Subjects Factor Name should already contain **Factor 1.** If not, type in Factor 1.

3. Enter the **Number of levels** (number of different treatment conditions) in the next box.

4. Click **Add.**

5. Click **Define.**

6. One by one, move the column labels for your treatment conditions into the **Within Subjects Variables** box. (Highlight the column label on the left and click the arrow to move it into the box.)

7. If you want descriptive statistics for each treatment, click on the **Options** box, select **Descriptives,** and click **Continue.**

8. Click **OK.**

SPSS Output

We used the SPSS program to analyze the data from the study comparing different strategies for studying that was presented in Example 13.1. Portions of the program output are shown in Figure 13.6. Note that large portions of the SPSS output are not relevant for our purposes and are not included in Figure 13.6. The first item of interest is the table of **Descriptive Statistics,** which presents the mean, standard deviation, and number of scores for each treatment. Next, we skip to the table showing **Tests of Within-Subjects Effects.** The top line of the factor1 box (Sphericity Assumed) shows the between-treatments sum of squares, degrees of freedom, and mean square that form the numerator of the F-ratio. The same line reports the value of the F-ratio and the level of significance (the p value or alpha level). Similarly, the top line of the Error (factor1) box shows the sum of squares, the degrees of freedom, and the mean square for the error term (the denominator of the F-ratio). The final box in the output (not shown in Figure 13.6) is labeled **Tests of Between-Subjects Effects** and the bottom line (Error) reports the between-subjects sum of squares and degrees of freedom (ignore the mean square and F-ratio, which are not part of the repeated-measures ANOVA).

Following are detailed instructions for using SPSS to perform the **Two-Factor, Independent-Measures Analysis of Variance (ANOVA)** presented in this chapter.

Descriptive Statistics

	Mean	Std. Deviation	N
VAR00001	5.0000	2.00000	6
VAR00002	6.0000	2.00000	6
VAR00003	8.0000	1.67332	6
VAR00004	9.0000	1.26491	6

Tests of Within-Subjects Effects

Measure:MEASURE_1

Source		Type III Sum of Squares	df	Mean Square	F	Sig.
factor 1	Sphericity Assumed	60.000	3	20.000	21.429	.000
	Greenhouse-Geisser	60.000	2.178	27.551	21.429	.000
	Huynh-Feldt	60.000	3.000	20.000	21.429	.000
	Lower-bound	60.000	1.000	60.000	21.429	.006
Error (factor 1)	Sphericity Assumed	14.000	15	.933		
	Greenhouse-Geisser	14.000	10.889	1.286		
	Huynh-Feldt	14.000	15.000	.933		
	Lower-bound	14.000	5.000	2.800		

FIGURE 13.6

Portions of the SPSS output for the repeated-measures ANOVA for the study evaluating different strategies for studying in Example 13.1.

Data Entry

1. The scores are entered into the SPSS data editor in a *stacked format,* which means that all of the scores from all of the different treatment conditions are entered in a single column (VAR00001).

2. In a second column (VAR00002) enter a code number to identify the level of factor *A* for each score. If factor *A* defines the rows of the data matrix, enter a 1 beside each score from the first row, enter a 2 beside each score from the second row, and so on.

3. In a third column (VAR00003) enter a code number to identify the level of factor *B* for each score. If factor *B* defines the columns of the data matrix, enter a 1 beside each score from the first column, enter a 2 beside each score from the second column, and so on.

Thus, each row of the SPSS data editor will have one score and two code numbers, with the score in the first column, the code for factor A in the second column, and the code for factor B in the third column.

Data Analysis

1. Click **Analyze** on the tool bar, select **General Linear Model,** and click on **Univariant.**

2. Highlight the column label for the set of scores (VAR0001) in the left box and click the arrow to move it into the **Dependent Variable** box.

3. One by one, highlight the column labels for the two factor codes and click the arrow to move them into the **Fixed Factors** box.

4. If you want descriptive statistics for each treatment, click on the **Options** box, select **Descriptives,** and click **Continue.**

5. Click **OK.**

SPSS Output

We used the SPSS program to analyze the data from the study in Example 13.4, and part of the program output is shown in Figure 13.7. The output begins with a table listing the factors (not shown in Figure 13.7), followed by a table showing descriptive statistics, including the mean and standard deviation for each cell or treatment condition. The results of the ANOVA are shown in the table labeled **Tests of Between-Subjects Effects**. The top row (*Corrected Model*) presents the between-treatments *SS* and *df* values. The second row (*Intercept*) is not relevant for our purposes. The next three rows present the two main effects and the interaction (the *SS, df,* and *MS* values, as well as the *F*-ratio and the level of significance), with each factor identified by its column number from the SPSS data editor. The next row (*Error*) describes the error term (denominator of the *F*-ratio), and the final row (*Corrected Total*) describes the total variability for the entire set of scores. (Ignore the row labeled *Total*.)

FOCUS ON PROBLEM SOLVING

1. Before you begin a repeated-measures ANOVA, complete all of the preliminary calculations needed for the ANOVA formulas. This requires that you find the total for each treatment (Ts), the total for each person (Ps), the grand total (G), the SS for each treatment condition, and ΣX^2 for the entire set of N scores. As a partial check on these calculations, be sure that the T values add up to G and that the P values have a sum of G.

2. To help remember the structure of repeated-measures ANOVA, keep in mind that a repeated-measures experiment eliminates the contribution of individual differences. There are no individual differences contributing to the numerator of the F-ratio ($MS_{\text{between treatments}}$) because the same individuals are used for all treatments. Therefore, you must also eliminate individual differences in the denominator. This is accomplished in the second stage of the analysis by subtracting the between-subjects variance from the within subjects variance to produce an error term for the F-ratio.

FIGURE 13.7

Portions of the SPSS output for the two-factor ANOVA for the study in Example 13.4.

Descriptive Statistics

Dependent Variable: VAR00001

VAR00002	VAR00003	Mean	Std. Deviation	N
1.00	1.00	9.0000	1.58114	5
	2.00	5.0000	1.73205	5
	Total	7.0000	2.62467	10
2.00	1.00	8.0000	1.87083	5
	2.00	9.0000	1.73205	5
	Total	8.5000	1.77951	10
Total	1.00	8.5000	1.71594	10
	2.00	7.0000	2.66667	10
	Total	7.7500	2.31414	20

Tests of Between-Subjects Effects

Dependent Variable: VAR00001

Source	Type III Sum of Squares	df	Mean Square	F	Sig.
Corrected Model	53.750[a]	3	17.917	5.972	.006
Intercept	1201.250	1	1201.250	400.417	.000
VAR00002	11.250	1	11.250	3.750	.071
VAR00003	11.250	1	11.250	3.750	.071
VAR00002 * VAR00003	31.250	1	31.250	10.417	.005
Error	48.000	16	3.000		
Total	1303.000	20			
Corrected Total	101.750	19			

3. Before you begin a two-factor ANOVA, take time to organize and summarize the data. It is best if you summarize the data in a matrix with rows corresponding to the levels of one factor and columns corresponding to the levels of the other factor. In each cell of the matrix, show the number of scores (n), the total and mean for the cell, and the SS within the cell. Also compute the row totals and column totals that are needed to calculate main effects.

4. For a two-factor ANOVA, there are three separate F-ratios. Although the three F-ratios use the same error term in the denominator (MS_{within}), they have different numerators, which may have different df values.

DEMONSTRATION 13.1

REPEATED-MEASURES ANOVA

The following data were obtained from a research study examining the effect of sleep deprivation on motor-skills performance. A sample of five participants was tested on a motor-skills task after 24 hours of sleep deprivation, tested again after 36 hours, and tested once more after 48 hours. The dependent variable is the number of errors made on the motor-skills task. Do these data indicate that the number of hours of sleep deprivation has a significant effect on motor skills performance?

Participant	24 Hours	36 Hours	48 Hours	P totals	
A	0	0	6	6	$N = 15$
B	1	3	5	9	$G = 45$
C	0	1	5	6	$\Sigma X^2 = 245$
D	4	5	9	18	
E	0	1	5	6	
	$T = 5$	$T = 10$	$T = 30$		
	$SS = 12$	$SS = 16$	$SS = 12$		

STEP 1 State the hypotheses, and specify alpha.　The null hypothesis states that, for the general population, there are no differences among the three deprivation conditions. Any differences that exist among the samples are simply the result of chance or error. In symbols,

$$H_0: \mu_1 = \mu_2 = \mu_3$$

The alternative hypothesis states that there are differences among the conditions.

H_1: At least one of the treatment means is different.

We use $\alpha = .05$.

STEP 2 Locate the critical region.　Rather than compute the df values and look for a critical value for F at this time, we proceed directly to the ANOVA.

STAGE 1 The first stage of the analysis is identical to the independent-measures ANOVA presented in Chapter 12.

$$SS_{total} = \Sigma X^2 - \frac{G^2}{N} = 245 - \frac{45^2}{15} = 110$$

$$SS_{within} = \Sigma SS_{inside\ each\ treatment} = 12 + 16 + 12 = 40$$

$$SS_{between} = \Sigma \frac{T^2}{n} - \frac{G^2}{N} = \frac{5^2}{5} + \frac{10^2}{5} + \frac{30^2}{5} - \frac{45^2}{15} = 70$$

and the corresponding degrees of freedom are

$$df_{total} = N - 1 = 14$$

$$df_{within} = \Sigma df = 4 + 4 + 4 = 12$$

$$df_{between} = k - 1 = 2$$

STAGE 2 The second stage of the repeated-measures analysis measures and removes the individual differences from the denominator of the F-ratio.

$$SS_{\text{between subjects}} = \Sigma \frac{P^2}{k} - \frac{G^2}{N}$$

$$= \frac{6^2}{3} + \frac{9^2}{3} + \frac{6^2}{3} + \frac{18^2}{3} + \frac{6^2}{3} - \frac{45^2}{15}$$

$$= 36$$

$$SS_{\text{error}} = SS_{\text{within}} - SS_{\text{between subjects}}$$

$$= 40 - 36$$

$$= 4$$

and the corresponding df values are

$$df_{\text{between subjects}} = n - 1 = 4$$

$$df_{\text{error}} = df_{\text{within}} - df_{\text{between subjects}}$$

$$= 12 - 4$$

$$= 8$$

The mean square values that form the F-ratio are as follows:

$$MS_{\text{between}} = \frac{SS_{\text{between}}}{df_{\text{between}}} = \frac{70}{2} = 35$$

$$MS_{\text{error}} = \frac{SS_{\text{error}}}{df_{\text{error}}} = \frac{4}{8} = 0.50$$

Finally, the F-ratio is

$$F = \frac{MS_{\text{between}}}{MS_{\text{error}}} = \frac{35}{0.50} = 70.00$$

STEP 3 Make a decision and state a conclusion.   With $df = 2, 8$ and $\alpha = .05$, the critical value is $F = 4.46$. Our obtained F-ratio ($F = 70.00$) is well into the critical region, so our decision is to reject the null hypothesis and conclude that there are significant differences among the three levels of sleep deprivation.

DEMONSTRATION 13.2

TWO-FACTOR ANOVA

The following data are from a two-factor study comparing performance in three treatment conditions for males and females. There is a separate sample of $n = 10$ participants in each of the six groups. We use a two-factor ANOVA to evaluate the significance of the mean differences.

Factor B (Treatment Condition)

		B_1	B_2	B_3
Factor A	Male	$T = 10$ $M = 1$ $SS = 195$	$T = 50$ $M = 5$ $SS = 235$	$T = 30$ $M = 3$ $SS = 220$
	Female	$T = 30$ $M = 3$ $SS = 237$	$T = 30$ $M = 3$ $SS = 240$	$T = 90$ $M = 9$ $SS = 225$
		$N = 60$	$G = 240$	$\Sigma X^2 = 2312$

STEP 1   State the hypotheses, and select alpha.

For a two-factor study, there are three separate hypotheses, the two main effects and the interaction.

For factor A, the null hypothesis states that there is no difference in performance for males versus females. In symbols,

$$H_0: \mu_{males} = \mu_{females}$$

For factor B, the null hypothesis states that there is no difference in performance among the three treatment conditions. In symbols,

$$H_0: \mu_{B_1} = \mu_{B_2} = \mu_{B_3}$$

For the $A \times B$ interaction, the null hypothesis states that the effect of either factor does not depend on the levels of the other factor.

We will use $\alpha = .05$ for all tests.

STEP 2   Locate the critical region.

Rather than compute the df values and look up critical values for F at this time, we proceed directly to the ANOVA.

STAGE 1   The first stage of the analysis is identical to the independent-measures ANOVA presented in Chapter 12, where each cell in the data matrix is considered a separate treatment condition.

$$SS_{total} = \Sigma X^2 - \frac{G^2}{N}$$

$$= 2312 - \frac{240^2}{60} = 1352$$

$$SS_{within\ treatments} = \Sigma SS_{each\ treatment}$$

$$= 195 + 275 + 220 + 237 + 240 + 225 = 972$$

$$SS_{between\ treatments} = \Sigma \frac{T^2}{n} - \frac{G^2}{N}$$

$$= \frac{10^2}{10} + \frac{50^2}{10} + \frac{30^2}{10} + \frac{30^2}{10} + \frac{30^2}{10} + \frac{90^2}{10} + \frac{240^2}{60}$$

$$= 380$$

The corresponding degrees of freedom are

$$df_{total} = N - 1 = 59$$

$$df_{within\ treatments} = \Sigma df_{each\ treatment} = 9 + 9 + 9 + 9 + 9 + 9 = 54$$

$$df_{between\ treatments} = number\ of\ cells - 1 = 5$$

STAGE 2 The second stage of the analysis partitions the between-treatments variability into three components: the main effect for factor A, the main effect for factor B, and the $A \times B$ interaction.

a. **Factor A.** The main effect for factor A evaluates the mean differences between the levels of factor A. For this example, factor A defines the rows of the matrix, so we are evaluating the mean differences between rows. To compute the SS for factor A, we calculate a between-treatment SS using the row totals exactly the same as we computed $SS_{between\ treatments}$ using the treatment totals (T values) earlier. For factor A, the row totals are 90 and 150, and each total was obtained by adding 30 scores.

For factor A (male, female)

$$SS_A = \Sigma \frac{T_{ROW}^2}{n_{ROW}^2} - \frac{G^2}{N}$$

$$= \frac{90^2}{30} + \frac{150^2}{30} - \frac{240^2}{60}$$

$$= 60$$

For factor B (treatments)

$$SS_B = \Sigma \frac{T_{COL}^2}{n_{COL}^2} - \frac{G^2}{N}$$

$$= \frac{40^2}{20} + \frac{80^2}{20} - \frac{120^2}{20} - \frac{240^2}{60}$$

$$= 160$$

For the $A \times B$ interaction

$$SS_{A \times B} = SS_{between\ treatments} - SS_A - SS_B$$

$$= 380 - 60 - 160$$

$$= 160$$

The corresponding degrees of freedom are

$$df_A = number\ of\ rows - 1 = 1$$

$$df_B = number\ of\ columns - 1 = 2$$

$$df_{A \times B} = df_{between\ treatments} - df_A - df_B = 5 - 1 - 2 = 2$$

The *MS* value needed for the *F*-ratios are

$$MS_A = \frac{60}{1} = 60$$

$$MS_B = \frac{160}{2} = 80$$

$$MS_{A \times B} = \frac{160}{2} = 80$$

$$MS_{\text{within treatments}} = \frac{972}{54} = 18$$

Finally, the three *F*-ratios are

$$F_A = \frac{MS_A}{MS_{\text{within treatments}}} = \frac{60}{18} = 3.33$$

$$F_B = \frac{MS_B}{MS_{\text{within treatments}}} = \frac{80}{18} = 4.44$$

$$F_{A \times B} = \frac{MS_{A \times B}}{MS_{\text{within treatments}}} = \frac{80}{18} = 4.44$$

STEP 3 Make a decision and state a conclusion.

The *F*-ratio for factor *A* has *df* = 1, 54. With α = .05, the critical *F* value is 4.03 (using *df* = 1, 50 from the table). For these data, factor *A* has no significant effect. Statistically, there is no difference in performance between males and females.

Factor *B* and the interaction both have *df* = 2, 54. With α = .05, the critical *F* value is 3.18 (using *df* = 1, 50 from the table). For these data, there are significant differences among the levels of factor *B* and there is a significant interaction. The interaction indicates that the differences among treatments are not the same for males as they are for females.

PROBLEMS

1. How does the denominator of the *F*-ratio (the error term) differ for a repeated-measures ANOVA compared to an independent-measures ANOVA?

2. The repeated-measures ANOVA can be viewed as a two-stage process. What is the purpose of the second stage?

3. A researcher conducts an experiment comparing three treatment conditions with *n* = 10 scores in each condition.
   a. If the researcher uses an independent-measures design, how many individuals are needed for the study and what are the *df* values for the *F*-ratio?
   b. If the researcher uses a repeated-measures design, how many individuals are needed for the study and what are the *df* values for the *F*-ratio?

4. A researcher conducts a repeated-measures experiment using a sample of *n* = 8 subjects to evaluate the differences among four treatment conditions. If

the results are examined with an ANOVA, what are the *df* values for the *F*-ratio?

5. A researcher uses a repeated-measures ANOVA to evaluate the results from a research study and reports an *F*-ratio with *df* = 2, 30.
   a. How many treatment conditions were compared in the study?
   b. How many individuals participated in the study?

6. A published report of a repeated-measures research study includes the following description of the statistical analysis. "The results show significant differences among the treatment conditions, $F(3, 21) = 6.10$, $p < .01$."
   a. How many treatment conditions were compared in the study?
   b. How many individuals participated in the study?

7. The following data were obtained from a repeated-measures study comparing two treatment conditions.
   a. Use a repeated-measures *t* test with α = .05 to determine whether there are significant mean differences between the two treatments. Note that

you will need to find the difference score (D) for each person.

b. Use a repeated-measures ANOVA with $\alpha = .05$ to determine whether there are significant mean differences between the two treatments. Within rounding error, you should find that $F = t^2$.

Person	Treatments I	II	Person Totals
A	3	5	$P = 8$
B	5	9	$P = 14$ $N = 16$
C	1	5	$P = 6$ $G = 80$
D	1	7	$P = 8$ $\Sigma X^2 = 500$
E	5	9	$P = 14$
F	3	7	$P = 10$
G	2	6	$P = 8$
H	4	8	$P = 12$

$$M = 3 \quad M = 7$$
$$T = 24 \quad T = 56$$
$$SS = 18 \quad SS = 18$$

8. A recent study examined how applicants with a facial blemish such as a scar or birthmark fared in job interviews (Madera & Hebl, 2011). The results indicate that interviewers recalled less information and gave lower ratings to applicants with a blemish. In a similar study, participants conducted computer-simulated interviews with a series of applicants including one with a facial scar and one with a facial birthmark. The following data represent the ratings given to each applicant.
a. Use a repeated-measures ANOVA with $\alpha = .05$ to determine whether there are significant mean differences among the three conditions.
b. Compute η^2, the percentage of variance accounted for by the mean differences, to measure the size of the treatment effects.
c. Write a sentence demonstrating how a research report would present the results of the hypothesis test and the measure of effect size.

Participant	Scar	Birthmark	No Blemish	Person Total
A	1	1	4	$P = 6$
B	3	4	8	$P = 15$ $N = 15$
C	0	2	7	$P = 9$ $G = 45$
D	0	0	6	$P = 6$ $\Sigma X^2 = 231$
E	1	3	5	$P = 9$

$$M = 1 \quad M = 2 \quad M = 6$$
$$T = 5 \quad T = 10 \quad T = 30$$
$$SS = 6 \quad SS = 10 \quad SS = 10$$

9. One of the primary advantages of a repeated-measures design, compared to an independent-measures design, is that it reduces the overall variability by removing variance caused by individual differences. The following data are from a research study comparing three treatment conditions.
a. Assume that the data are from an independent-measures study using three separate samples, each with $n = 6$ participants. Ignore the column of P totals and use an independent-measures ANOVA with $\alpha = .05$ to test the significance of the mean differences.
b. Now assume that the data are from a repeated-measures study using the same sample of $n = 6$ participants in all three treatment conditions. Use a repeated-measures ANOVA with $\alpha = .05$ to test the significance of the mean differences.
c. Explain why the two analyses lead to different conclusions.

Treatment 1	Treatment 2	Treatment 3	P
6	9	12	27
8	8	8	24 $N = 18$
5	7	9	21 $G = 108$
0	4	8	12 $\Sigma X^2 = 800$
2	3	4	9
3	5	7	15

$$M = 4 \quad M = 6 \quad M = 8$$
$$T = 24 \quad T = 36 \quad T = 48$$
$$SS = 42 \quad SS = 28 \quad SS = 34$$

10. The following data are from an experiment comparing three different treatment conditions:

A	B	C	
0	1	2	$N = 15$
2	5	5	$\Sigma X^2 = 354$
1	2	6	
5	4	9	
2	8	8	
$T = 10$	$T = 20$	$T = 30$	
$SS = 14$	$SS = 30$	$SS = 30$	

a. If the experiment uses an *independent-measures design*, can the researcher conclude that the treatments are significantly different? Test at the .05 level of significance.
b. If the experiment is done with a *repeated-measures design*, should the researcher conclude that the treatments are significantly different? Set alpha at .05 again.
c. Explain why the analyses in parts a and b lead to different conclusions.

11. A researcher is evaluating customer satisfaction with the service and coverage of two phone carriers. Each individual in a sample of $n = 25$ uses one carrier for two weeks and then switches to the other. Each participant then rates the two carriers. The following table presents the results from the repeated-measures ANOVA comparing the average ratings. Fill in the missing values in the table. (*Hint:* Start with the *df* values.)

Source	SS	df	MS	
Between treatments	___	___	2	F = ___
Within treatments	___	___		
Between subjects	___	___		
Error	12	___	___	
Total	23	___		

12. The following summary table presents the results from a repeated-measures ANOVA comparing three treatment conditions with a sample of $n = 11$ subjects. Fill in the missing values in the table. (*Hint:* Start with the *df* values.)

Source	SS	df	MS	
Between treatments	___	___	___	F = 5.00
Within treatments	80	___		
Between subjects	___	___		
Error	60	___	___	
Total	___	___		

13. A recent study indicates that simply giving college students a pedometer can result in increased walking (Jackson & Howton, 2008). Students were given pedometers for a 12-week period, and asked to record the average number of steps per day during weeks 1, 6, and 12. The following data are similar to the results obtained in the study.

	Number of steps (×1000)				
	Week				
Participant	1	6	12	P	
A	6	8	10	24	
B	4	5	6	15	
C	5	5	5	15	G = 72
D	1	2	3	6	$\Sigma X^2 = 400$
E	0	1	2	3	
F	2	3	4	9	

T = 18	T = 24	T = 30
SS = 28	SS = 32	SS = 40

a. Use a repeated-measures ANOVA with $\alpha = .05$ to determine whether the mean number of steps changes significantly from one week to another.

b. Compute η^2 to measure the size of the treatment effect.

c. Write a sentence demonstrating how a research report would present the results of the hypothesis test and the measure of effect size.

14. The following data represent the typical results from a delayed discounting study. The participants are asked how much they would take today instead of waiting for a specific delay period to receive $1000. Each participant responds to all 5 of the delay periods. Use a repeated-measures ANOVA with $\alpha = .01$ to determine whether there are significant differences among the 5 delay periods for the following data:

Participant	1 month	6 months	1 year	2 years	5 years
A	950	850	800	700	550
B	800	800	750	700	600
C	850	750	650	600	500
D	750	700	700	650	550
E	950	900	850	800	650
F	900	900	850	750	650

15. The endorphins released by the brain act as natural painkillers. For example, Gintzler (1980) monitored endorphin activity and pain thresholds in pregnant rats during the days before they gave birth. The data showed an increase in pain threshold as the pregnancy progressed. The change was gradual until 1 or 2 days before birth, at which point there was an abrupt increase in pain threshold. Apparently a natural painkilling mechanism was preparing the animals for the stress of giving birth. The following data represent pain-threshold scores similar to the results obtained by Gintzler. Do these data indicate a significant change in pain threshold? Use a repeated-measures ANOVA with $\alpha = .01$.

	Days Before Giving Birth			
Subject	7	5	3	1
A	39	40	49	52
B	38	39	44	55
C	44	46	50	60
D	40	42	46	56
E	34	33	41	52

16. The structure of a two-factor study can be presented as a matrix with the levels of one factor determining the rows and the levels of the second factor determining the columns. With this structure in mind, describe the mean differences that are evaluated by each of the three hypothesis tests that make up a two-factor ANOVA.

17. Briefly explain what happens during the second stage of the two-factor ANOVA.

18. The following matrix presents the results from an independent-measures, two-factor study with a sample of $n = 10$ participants in each treatment condition. Note that one treatment mean is missing.

	Factor B	
	B_1	B_2
A_1	$M = 20$	$M = 30$
A_2	$M = 40$	

Factor A

a. What value for the missing mean would result in no main effect for factor A?
b. What value for the missing mean would result in no main effect for factor B?
c. What value for the missing mean would result in no interaction?

19. The following matrix presents the results of a two-factor study with $n = 10$ scores in each of the six treatment conditions. Note that one of the treatment means is missing.

	Factor B		
	B_1	B_2	B_3
A_1	$M = 10$	$M = 20$	$M = 40$
A_2	$M = 20$	$M = 30$	

Factor A

a. What value for the missing mean would result in no main effect for factor A?
b. What value for the missing mean would result in no interaction?

20. A researcher conducts an independent-measures, two-factor study using a separate sample of $n = 15$ participants in each treatment condition. The results are evaluated using an ANOVA and the researcher reports an F-ratio with $df = 1, 84$ for factor A, and an F-ratio with $df = 2, 84$ for factor B.
a. How many levels of factor A were used in the study?
b. How many levels of factor B were used in the study?
c. What are the df values for the F-ratio evaluating the interaction?

21. A researcher conducts an independent-measures, two-factor study with two levels of factor A and three levels of factor B, using a sample of $n = 12$ participants in each treatment condition.
a. What are the df values for the F-ratio evaluating the main effect of factor A?
b. What are the df values for the F-ratio evaluating the main effect of factor B?
c. What are the df values for the F-ratio evaluating the interaction?

22. Some people like to pour beer gently down the side of the glass to preserve bubbles. Others, splash it down the center to release the bubbles into a foamy head and free the aromas. Champagne, however is best when the bubbles remain concentrated in the wine. According to an article in the *Journal of Agricultural and Food Chemistry,* a group of French scientists recently verified the difference between the two pouring methods by measuring the amount of bubbles in each glass of champagne poured two different ways and at three different temperatures (*Journal of Agricultural and Food Chemistry,* 2010). The following data present the pattern of results obtained in the study.

	Champagne Temperature (°F)		
	40°	46°	52°
Gentle Pour	$n = 10$ $M = 7$ $SS = 64$	$n = 10$ $M = 3$ $SS = 57$	$n = 10$ $M = 2$ $SS = 47$
Splashing Pour	$n = 10$ $M = 5$ $SS = 56$	$n = 10$ $M = 1$ $SS = 54$	$n = 10$ $M = 0$ $SS = 46$

a. Use a two-factor ANOVA with $\alpha = .05$ to evaluate the mean differences.
b. Briefly explain how temperature and pouring influence the bubbles in champagne according to this pattern of results.

23. Example 13.1 in this chapter described a two-factor study examining performance under two audience conditions (factor B) for high and low self-esteem participants (factor A). The following summary table presents possible results from the analysis of that study. Assuming that the study used a separate sample of $n = 15$ participants in each treatment condition (each cell), fill in the missing values in the table. (*Hint:* Start with the df values.)

Source	SS	df	MS	
Between treatments	67	___		
Audience	___	___	___	$F = $ ___
Self-esteem	29	___	___	$F = $
Interaction	___	___	___	$F = 5.50$
Within treatments	___	___	4	
Total	___	___		

24. The following table summarizes the results from a two-factor study with 2 levels of factor A and 3 levels of factor B using a separate sample of $n = 11$ participants in each treatment condition. Fill in the missing values. (*Hint:* Start with the df values.)

Source	SS	df	MS	
Between treatments	___	___		
Factor A	___	___	___	$F = 7$
Factor B	___	___	___	$F = 8$
$A \times B$ Interaction	___	___	___	$F = 3$
Within treatments	240	___	___	
Total	___	___		

25. The following data are from a two-factor study examining the effects of two treatment conditions on males and females.
   a. Use an ANOVA with $\alpha = .05$ for all tests to evaluate the significance of the main effects and the interaction.
   b. Compute η^2 to measure the size of the effect for each main effect and the interaction.

Factor B: Treatment

	B_1	B_2	B_3	
Male	3	1	10	
	1	4	10	
	1	8	14	
	6	6	7	$T_{ROW1} = 90$
	4	6	9	
	$M = 3$	$M = 5$	$M = 10$	
	$T = 15$	$T = 25$	$T = 50$	
	$SS = 18$	$SS = 28$	$SS = 26$	$N = 30$
Factor A: Gender	0	2	1	$G = 120$
	2	7	1	$\Sigma X^2 = 860$
	0	2	1	
	0	2	6	$T_{ROW2} = 30$
Female	3	2	1	
	$M = 1$	$M = 3$	$M = 2$	
	$T = 5$	$T = 15$	$T = 10$	
	$SS = 8$	$SS = 20$	$SS = 20$	

$T_{COL1} = 20 \quad T_{COL2} = 40 \quad T_{COL3} = 60$

26. Research indicates that paying students to improve their grades simply does not work (Fryer, 2011). However, paying students for specific tasks such as reading books, attending class, or doing homework does have a significant effect. Apparently, students on their own do not understand how to get good grades. If they are told exactly what to do, however, the incentives work. The following data represent a two-factor study attempting to replicate this result.

	Paid for Homework	Not Paid for Homework
Paid for Grades	14	2
	7	7
	10	5
	9	7
	11	3
	9	6
Not Paid for Grades	13	7
	7	2
	9	4
	7	2
	11	6
	7	3

   a. Use a two-factor ANOVA with $\alpha = .05$ to evaluate the significance of the main effects and the interaction.
   b. Calculate the η^2 values to measure the effect size for the two main effects and the interaction.
   c. Describe the pattern of results. (How does paying for grades influence performance? How does paying for homework influence performance? Does the effect of paying for homework depend on whether you also pay for grades?)

27. In Chapter 12 (page 390), we described a study reporting that college students who are on Facebook (or have it running in the background) while studying had lower grades than students who did not use the social network (Kirschner & Karpinski, 2010). A researcher would like to know if the same result extends to students in lower grade levels. The researcher planned a two-factor study comparing Facebook users with non-users for middle school students, high school students, and college students. For consistency across groups, grades were converted into six categories, numbered 0 to 5 from low to high. The results are presented in the following matrix.
   a. Use a two-factor ANOVA with $\alpha = .05$ to evaluate the mean differences.
   b. Describe the pattern of results.

	Middle School	High School	College
Non-user	3	5	5
	5	5	4
	5	2	2
	3	4	5
User	5	1	1
	3	2	0
	2	3	0
	2	2	3

28. In Chapter 11, we described a research study in which the color red appeared to increase men's attraction to women (Elliot & Niesta, 2008). The same researchers have published other results showing that red also increases women's attraction to men but does not appear to affect judgments of same-sex individuals (Elliot et al., 2010). Combining these results into one study produces a two-factor design in which men judge photographs of both women and men, which are shown on both red and white backgrounds.

The dependent variable is a rating of attractiveness for the person shown in the photograph. The study uses a separate group of participants for each condition. The following table presents data similar to the results from previous research.

		Person Shown in Photograph	
		Female	Male
Background Color for Photograph	White	$n = 10$ $M = 4.5$ $SS = 6$	$n = 10$ $M = 4.4$ $SS = 7$
	Red	$n = 10$ $M = 7.5$ $SS = 9$	$n = 10$ $M = 4.6$ $SS = 8$

a. Use a two-factor ANOVA with $\alpha = .05$ to evaluate the main effects and the interaction.
b. Describe the effect of background color on judgments of males and females.

After completing this part, you should be able to perform an ANOVA to evaluate the significance of mean differences in three research situations. These include:

1. The single-factor independent-measures design introduced in Chapter 12.
2. The single-factor repeated-measures design introduced in Chapter 13.
3. The two-factor independent-measures design introduced in Chapter 13.

In this part, we introduce three applications of ANOVA that use an F-ratio statistic to evaluate the mean differences among two or more populations. In each case, the F-ratio has the following structure:

$$F = \frac{\text{variance between treatments}}{\text{variance from random unsystematic sources}}$$

The numerator of the F-ratio measures the mean differences that exist from one treatment condition to another, including any systematic differences caused by the treatments. The denominator measures the differences that exist when there are no systematic factors that cause one score to be different from another. The F-ratio is structured so that the numerator and denominator are measuring exactly the same variance when the null hypothesis is true and there are no systematic treatment effects. In this case, the F-ratio should have a value near 1.00. Thus, an F-ratio near 1.00 is evidence that the null hypothesis is true. Similarly, an F-ratio that is much larger than 1.00 provides evidence that a systematic treatment effect does exist and the null hypothesis should be rejected.

For independent-measures designs, either single-factor or two-factor, the denominator of the F-ratio is obtained by computing the variance within treatments. Inside each treatment condition, all participants are treated exactly the same so there are no systematic treatment effects that cause the scores to vary.

For a repeated-measures design, the same individuals are used in every treatment condition, so any differences between treatments cannot be caused by individual differences. Thus, the numerator of the F-ratio does not include any individual differences. Therefore, individual differences must also be eliminated from the denominator to balance the F-ratio. As a result, the repeated-measures ANOVA is a two-stage process. The first stage separates the between-treatments variance (numerator) and the within-treatments variance. The second stage removes the systematic individual differences from the within-treatments variance to produce the appropriate denominator for the F-ratio.

For a two-factor design, the mean differences between treatments can be caused by either of the two factors or by specific combinations of factors. The goal of the ANOVA is to separate these possible treatment effects so that each can be evaluated independent of the others. To accomplish this, the two-factor ANOVA is a two-stage process. The first stage separates the between-treatments variance and the within-treatments variance (denominator). The second stage analyzes the between-treatments variance into three components: the main effect from the first factor, the main effect from the second factor, and the interaction.

Note that the repeated-measures ANOVA and the two-factor ANOVA are both two-stage processes. Both begin by separating the between-treatments variance and the within-treatments variance. However, the second stages of these two ANOVAs serve different purposes and focus on different components. The repeated-measures ANOVA focuses on the within-treatments variance and is intended to remove the individual differences. The two-factor ANOVA focuses on the between-treatments variance and is intended to separate the main effects and the interaction.

REVIEW EXERCISES

1. A researcher examining the jet lag that people experience when flying long distances obtained the following data measuring the number of days required to adjust after a long flight. Do the data indicate significant differences in jet lag depending on the direction of travel? Test with $\alpha = .05$.

Westbound	Eastbound	Same Time Zone
2	6	1
1	4	0
3	6	1
3	8	1
2	5	0
4	7	0
$M = 2.5$	$M = 6$	$M = 0.5$
$SS = 5.5$	$SS = 10$	$SS = 1.5$

2. The following data were obtained from a repeated-measures study comparing three treatment conditions.

		Treatments		
Person	I	II	III	Person Totals
A	0	4	2	$P = 6$
B	1	5	6	$P = 12$
C	3	3	3	$P = 9$
D	0	1	5	$P = 6$
E	0	2	4	$P = 6$
F	2	3	4	$P = 9$

$N = 18$
$G = 48$
$\Sigma X^2 = 184$

$M = 1$ $M = 3$ $M = 4$
$T = 6$ $T = 18$ $T = 24$
$SS = 8$ $SS = 10$ $SS = 10$

a. Do the data indicate significant differences among the three treatments? Test at the .05 level of significance.

b. Calculate η^2 to measure the size of the effect.

c. Write a sentence demonstrating how the outcome of the hypothesis test and the measure of effect size would appear in a research report.

3. Briefly describe what is meant by an interaction between factors in a two-factor research study.

4. Most sports injuries are immediate and obvious, like a broken leg. However, some can be more subtle, like the neurological damage that may occur when soccer players repeatedly head a soccer ball. To examine long-term effects of repeated heading, Downs and Abwender (2002) examined two different age groups of soccer players and swimmers. The dependent variable was performance on a conceptual thinking task. Following are hypothetical data, similar to the research results.

a. Use a two-factor ANOVA with $\alpha = .05$ to evaluate the main effects and interaction.

b. Calculate the effects size (η^2) for the main effects and the interaction.

c. Briefly describe the outcome of the study.

		Factor B: Age	
		College	Older
Factor A: Sport	Soccer	$n = 20$ $M = 9$ $T = 180$ $SS = 380$	$n = 20$ $M = 4$ $T = 80$ $SS = 390$
	Swimming	$n = 20$ $M = 9$ $T = 180$ $SS = 350$	$n = 20$ $M = 8$ $T = 160$ $SS = 400$

$\Sigma X^2 = 6360$

Correlations and Nonparametric Tests

Back in Chapter 1, we stated that the primary goal of science is to establish relationships between variables. Until this point, the statistics we have presented all attempt to accomplish this goal by comparing *groups of scores* using *means and variances* as the basic statistical measures. Typically, one variable is used to define the groups, and a second variable is measured to obtain a set of scores within each group. Means and variances are then computed for the scores, and the sample means are used to test hypotheses about population means. If the hypothesis test indicates a significant mean difference, then we conclude that there is a relationship between the variables.

However, many research situations do not involve comparing groups, and many do not produce data that allow you to calculate means and variances. For example, a researcher can investigate the relationship between two variables (for example, IQ and creativity) by measuring both variables within a single group of individuals. Also, the measurement procedure may not produce numerical scores. For example, participants can indicate their color preferences by simply picking a favorite color or by ranking several choices. Without numerical scores, it is impossible to calculate means and variances. Instead, the data consist of proportions or frequencies. For example, a research study may investigate what proportion of people select red as their favorite color and whether this proportion is different for introverted people compared with extroverted people.

Notice that these new research situations are still asking questions about the relationships between variables, and they are still using sample data to make inferences about populations. However, they are no longer comparing groups and they are no longer based on means and variances. In this part, we introduce the statistical methods that have been developed for these other kinds of research.

CHAPTER

14

Correlation

Tools You Will Need

The following items are considered essential background material for this chapter. If you doubt your knowledge of any of these items, you should review the appropriate chapter or section before proceeding.

- Sum of squares (SS) (Chapter 4)
  - Computational formula
  - Definitional formula

- z-scores (Chapter 5)
- Hypothesis testing (Chapter 8)
- Analysis of Variance (Chapter 12)
  - *MS* values and *F*-ratios

aplia

Aplia for *Essentials of Statistics for the Behavioral Sciences*
After reading, go to "Resources" at the end of this chapter for an introduction on how to use Aplia's homework and learning resources.

14.1   INTRODUCTION

Correlation is a statistical technique that is used to measure and describe the relationship between two variables. Usually the two variables are simply observed as they exist naturally in the environment—there is no attempt to control or manipulate the variables. For example, a researcher could check high school records (with permission) to obtain a measure of each student's academic performance, and then survey each family to obtain a measure of income. The resulting data could be used to determine whether there is a relationship between high school grades and family income. Notice that the researcher is not manipulating any student's grade or any family's income, but is simply observing what occurs naturally. You also should notice that a correlation requires two scores for each individual (one score from each of the two variables). These scores normally are identified as *X* and *Y*. The pairs of scores can be listed in a table, or they can be presented graphically in a scatter plot (Figure 14.1). In the scatter plot, the values for the *X* variable are listed on the horizontal axis and the *Y* values are listed on the vertical axis. Each individual is then represented by a single point in the graph so that the horizontal position corresponds to the individual's *X* value and the vertical position corresponds to the *Y* value. The value of a scatter plot is that it allows you to see any patterns or trends that exist in the data. The scores in Figure 14.1, for example, show a clear relationship between family income and student grades; as income increases, grades also increase.

THE CHARACTERISTICS OF A RELATIONSHIP

A correlation is a numerical value that describes and measures three characteristics of the relationship between *X* and *Y*. These three characteristics are as follows:

1. **The Direction of the Relationship.** The sign of the correlation, positive or negative, describes the direction of the relationship.

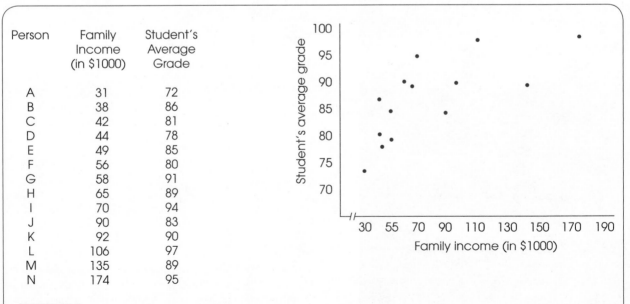

Person	Family Income (in $1000)	Student's Average Grade
A	31	72
B	38	86
C	42	81
D	44	78
E	49	85
F	56	80
G	58	91
H	65	89
I	70	94
J	90	83
K	92	90
L	106	97
M	135	89
N	174	95

FIGURE 14.1

Correlational data showing the relationship between family income (*X*) and student grades (*Y*) for a sample of *n* = 14 high school students. The scores are listed in order from lowest to highest family income and are shown in a scatter plot.

DEFINITIONS

> In a **positive correlation,** the two variables tend to change in the same direction: As the value of the *X* variable increases from one individual to another, the *Y* variable also tends to increase; when the *X* variable decreases, the *Y* variable also decreases.
>
> In a **negative correlation,** the two variables tend to go in opposite directions. As the *X* variable increases, the *Y* variable decreases. That is, it is an inverse relationship.

The following examples illustrate positive and negative relationships.

EXAMPLE 14.1   Suppose you run the drink concession at the football stadium. After several seasons, you begin to notice a relationship between the temperature at game time and the beverages you sell. Specifically, you have noted that when the temperature is low, you sell relatively little beer. However, as the temperature goes up, beer sales also go up (Figure 14.2). This is an example of a positive correlation. You also have noted a relationship between temperature and coffee sales: On cold days, you sell a lot of coffee, but coffee sales go down as the temperature goes up. This is an example of a negative relationship.

2. **The Form of the Relationship.** In the preceding coffee and beer examples, the relationships tend to have a linear form; that is, the points in the scatter plot tend to cluster around a straight line. We have drawn a line through the middle of the data points in each figure to help show the relationship. The most common use of correlation is to measure straight-line relationships. However, other forms of

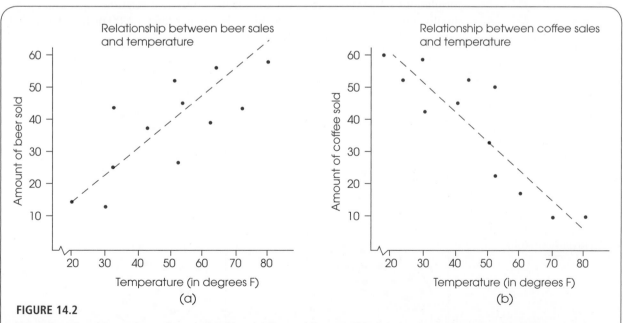

FIGURE 14.2

Examples of positive and negative relationships. (a) Beer sales are positively related to temperature. (b) Coffee sales are negatively related to temperature.

relationships do exist and there are special correlations used to measure them. (We examine alternatives in Section 14.5.)

3. **The Strength or Consistency of the Relationship.** Finally, the correlation measures the consistency of the relationship. For a linear relationship, for example, the data points could fit perfectly on a straight line. Every time X increases by one point, the value of Y also changes by a consistent and predictable amount. Figure 14.3(a) shows an example of a perfect linear relationship. However, relationships are usually not perfect. Although there may be a tendency for the value of Y to increase whenever X increases, the amount that Y changes is not always the same, and occasionally, Y decreases when X increases. In this situation, the data points do not fall perfectly on a straight line. The consistency of the relationship is measured by the numerical value of the correlation. A *perfect correlation* always is identified by a correlation of 1.00 and indicates a perfectly consistent relationship. For a correlation of 1.00 (or –1.00), each change in X is accompanied by a perfectly predictable change in Y. At the other extreme, a correlation of 0 indicates no consistency at all. For a correlation of 0, the data points are scattered randomly with no clear trend [see Figure 14.3(b)]. Intermediate values between 0 and 1 indicate the degree of consistency.

Examples of different values for linear correlations are shown in Figure 14.3. In each example we have sketched a line around the data points. This line, called an *envelope* because it encloses the data, often helps you to see the overall trend in the data. As a rule of thumb, when the envelope is shaped roughly like a football, the correlation is around 0.7. Envelopes that are fatter than a football indicate correlations closer to 0, and narrower shapes indicate correlations closer to 1.00.

You should also note that the sign (+ or −) and the strength of a correlation are independent. For example, a correlation of 1.00 indicates a perfectly consistent relationship whether it is positive (+1.00) or negative (−1.00). Similarly, correlations of +0.80 and −0.80 are equally consistent relationships. Finally, you should notice that a correlation can never be greater than +1.00 or less than −1.00.

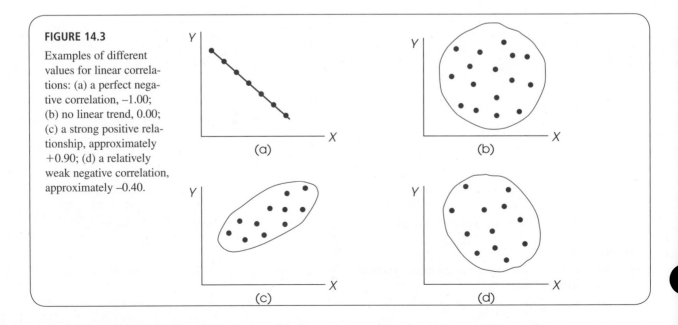

FIGURE 14.3

Examples of different values for linear correlations: (a) a perfect negative correlation, –1.00; (b) no linear trend, 0.00; (c) a strong positive relationship, approximately +0.90; (d) a relatively weak negative correlation, approximately –0.40.

LEARNING CHECK

1. For each of the following, indicate whether you would expect a positive or a negative correlation.

   a. Model year and price for a used Honda

   b. IQ and grade point average for high school students

   c. Daily high temperature and daily energy consumption for 30 winter days in New York City

2. The data points would be clustered more closely around a straight line for a correlation of −0.80 than for a correlation of +0.05. (True or false?)

3. If the data points are clustered close to a line that slopes up from left to right, then a good estimate of the correlation would be +0.90. (True or false?)

4. If a scatter plot shows a set of data points that form a circular pattern, the correlation should be near zero. (True or false?)

ANSWERS

1. **a.** Positive: Higher model years tend to have higher prices.

   b. Positive: More intelligent students tend to get higher grades.

   c. Negative: Higher temperature tends to decrease the need for heating.

2. True. The numerical value indicates the strength of the relationship. The sign only indicates direction.

3. True.

4. True.

14.2 THE PEARSON CORRELATION

By far the most common correlation is the *Pearson correlation* (or the Pearson product–moment correlation) which measures the degree of straight-line relationship.

DEFINITION

> The **Pearson correlation** measures the degree and the direction of the linear relationship between two variables.

The Pearson correlation is identified by the letter r. Conceptually, this correlation is computed by

$$r = \frac{\text{degree to which } X \text{ and } Y \text{ vary together}}{\text{degree to which } X \text{ and } Y \text{ vary separately}}$$

$$= \frac{\text{covariability of } X \text{ and } Y}{\text{variability of } X \text{ and } Y \text{ separately}}$$

When there is a perfect linear relationship, every change in the X variable is accompanied by a corresponding change in the Y variable. In Figure 14.3(a), for example, every time the value of X increases, there is a perfectly predictable decrease in the value of Y. The result is a perfect linear relationship, with X and Y always varying together. In this case, the covariability (X and Y together) is identical to the variability of X and Y separately, and the formula produces a correlation with a magnitude of 1.00 or −1.00. At the other extreme, when there is no linear relationship, a change in the X variable does not correspond to any predictable change in the Y variable. In this case, there is no covariability, and the resulting correlation is zero.

THE SUM OF PRODUCTS OF DEVIATIONS

To calculate the Pearson correlation, it is necessary to introduce one new concept: the *sum of products* of deviations, or SP. This new value is similar to SS (the sum of squared deviations), which is used to measure variability for a single variable. Now, we use SP to measure the amount of covariability between two variables. The value for SP can be calculated with either a definitional formula or a computational formula.

The *definitional formula* for the sum of products is

$$SP = \Sigma(X - M_x)(Y - M_y) \tag{14.1}$$

where M_x is the mean for the X scores and M_y is the mean for the Ys.

The definitional formula instructs you to perform the following sequence of operations:

1. Find the X deviation and the Y deviation for each individual.

2. Find the product of the deviations for each individual.

3. Add the products.

Notice that this process "defines" the value being calculated: the sum of the products of the deviations.

The *computational formula* for the sum of products of deviations is

$$SP = \Sigma XY - \frac{\Sigma X \Sigma Y}{n} \tag{14.2}$$

Caution: The n in this formula refers to the number of pairs of scores.

Because the computational formula uses the original scores (X and Y values), it usually results in easier calculations than those required with the definitional formula, especially if M_x or M_y is not a whole number. However, both formulas always produce the same value for SP.

You may have noted that the formulas for SP are similar to the formulas you have learned for SS (sum of squares). The relationship between the two sets of formulas is described in Box 14.1. The following example demonstrates the calculation of SP with both formulas.

EXAMPLE 14.2

The same set of $n = 4$ pairs of scores is used to calculate SP, first using the definitional formula and then using the computational formula.

For the definitional formula, you need deviation scores for each of the X values and each of the Y values. Note that the mean for the Xs is $M_x = 3$ and the mean for the Ys is $M_y = 5$. The deviations and the products of deviations are shown in the following table:

Scores		Deviations		Products
X	Y	$X - M_x$	$Y - M_y$	$(X - M_x)(Y - M_y)$
1	3	-2	-2	$+4$
2	6	-1	$+1$	-1
4	4	$+1$	-1	-1
5	7	$+2$	$+2$	$+4$
				$+6 = SP$

Caution: The signs (+ and −) are critical in determining the sum of products, *SP*.

For these scores, the sum of the products of the deviations is $SP = +6$.

For the computational formula, you need the X value, the Y value, and the XY product for each individual. Then you find the sum of the Xs, the sum of the Ys, and the sum of the XY products. These values are as follows:

X	Y	XY	
1	3	3	
2	6	12	
4	4	16	
5	7	35	
12	20	66	Totals

Substituting the totals in the formula gives

$$SP = \Sigma XY - \frac{\Sigma X \Sigma Y}{n}$$

$$= 66 - \frac{12(20)}{4}$$

$$= 66 - 60$$

$$= 6$$

Both formulas produce the same result, $SP = 6$.

BOX 14.1 COMPARING THE *SP* AND *SS* FORMULAS

It will help you to learn the formulas for *SP* if you note the similarity between the two *SP* formulas and the corresponding formulas for *SS* that were presented in Chapter 4. The definitional formula for *SS* is

$$SS = \Sigma(X - M)^2$$

In this formula, you must square each deviation, which is equivalent to multiplying it by itself. With this in mind, the formula can be rewritten as

$$SS = \Sigma(X - M)(X - M)$$

The similarity between the *SS* formula and the *SP* formula should be obvious—the *SS* formula uses squares and the *SP* formula uses products. This same relationship exists for the computational formulas. For *SS*, the computational formula is

$$SS = \Sigma X^2 - \frac{(\Sigma X)^2}{n}$$

As before, each squared value can be rewritten so that the formula becomes

$$SP = \Sigma XX - \frac{\Sigma X \Sigma X}{n}$$

Again, note the similarity in structure between the *SS* formula and the *SP* formula. If you remember that *SS* uses squares and *SP* uses products, the two new formulas for the sum of products should be easy to learn.

CALCULATION OF THE PEARSON CORRELATION

As noted earlier, the Pearson correlation consists of a ratio comparing the covariability of X and Y (the numerator) with the variability of X and Y separately (the denominator). In the formula for the Pearson r, we use SP to measure the covariability of X and Y. The variability of X is measured by computing SS for the X scores and the variability of Y is measured by SS for the Y scores. With these definitions, the formula for the Pearson correlation becomes

$$r = \frac{SP}{\sqrt{SS_X SS_Y}} \tag{14.3}$$

Note that you *multiply* SS for X by SS for Y in the denominator of the Pearson formula.

The following example demonstrates the use of this formula with a simple set of scores.

EXAMPLE 14.3

The Pearson correlation is computed for the following set of $n = 5$ pairs of scores.

X	Y
0	2
10	6
4	2
8	4
8	6

Before starting any calculations, it is useful to put the data in a scatter plot and make a preliminary estimate of the correlation. These data have been graphed in Figure 14.4. Looking at the scatter plot, it appears that there is a very good (but not perfect) positive correlation. You should expect an approximate value of $r = +0.8$ or $+0.9$. To find the Pearson correlation, we need SP, SS for X, and SS for Y. The calculations for each of these values, using the definitional formulas, are presented in Table 14.1. (Note that the mean for the X values is $M_X = 6$ and the mean for the Y scores is $M_Y = 4$.)

Using the values from Table 14.1, the Pearson correlation is

$$r = \frac{SP}{\sqrt{(SS_X)(SS_Y)}} = \frac{28}{\sqrt{(64)(16)}} = \frac{28}{32} = +0.875$$

FIGURE 14.4

Scatter plot of the data from Example 14.3.

TABLE 14.1

Calculation of SS_X, SS_Y, and SP for a sample of $n = 5$ pairs of scores.

Scores		Deviations		Squared Deviations		Products
X	Y	$X - M_X$	$Y - M_Y$	$(X - M_X)^2$	$(Y - M_Y)^2$	$(X - M_X)(Y - M_Y)$
0	2	−6	−2	36	4	+12
10	6	+4	+2	16	4	+8
4	2	−2	−2	4	4	+4
8	4	+2	0	4	0	0
8	6	+2	+2	4	4	+4
				$SS_X = 64$	$SS_Y = 16$	$SP = +28$

Correlation and the pattern of data points   Note that the value we obtained for the correlation in Example 14.3 is perfectly consistent with the pattern formed by the data points in Figure 14.4. The positive sign for the correlation indicates that the points are clustered around a line that slopes up to the right. Second, the high value for the correlation (near 1.00) indicates that the points are very tightly clustered close to the line. Thus, the value of the correlation describes the relationship that exists in the data.

Because the Pearson correlation describes the pattern formed by the data points, any factor that does not change the pattern also does not change the correlation. For example, if 5 points were added to each of the X values in Figure 14.4, then each data point would move to the right. However, because all of the data points shift to the right, the overall pattern is not changed, it is simply moved to a new location. Similarly, if 5 points were subtracted from each X value, the pattern would shift to the left. In either case, the overall pattern stays the same and the correlation is not changed. In the same way, adding a constant to (or subtracting a constant from) each Y value simply shifts the pattern up (or down) but does not change the pattern and, therefore, does not change the correlation. Multiplying each X and/or Y value by a constant also does not change the pattern formed by the data points. For example, if each of the X values in Figure 14.4 were multiplied by 2, then the same scatter plot could be used to display either the original scores or the new scores. The current figure shows the original scores, but if the values on the X-axis (0, 1, 2, 3, and so on) are doubled (0, 2, 4, 6, and so on), then the same figure would show the pattern formed by the new scores. In summary, adding a constant to (or subtracting a constant from) each X and/or Y value does not change the pattern of data points and does not change the correlation. Also, multiplying (or dividing) each X and/or Y value by a constant does not change the pattern and does not change the value of the correlation.

THE PEARSON CORRELATION AND Z-SCORES

The Pearson correlation measures the relationship between an individual's location in the X distribution and his or her location in the Y distribution. For example, a positive correlation means that individuals who have a high X score also tend to have a high Y score. Similarly, a negative correlation indicates that individuals with high X scores tend to have low Y scores.

Recall from Chapter 5 that z-scores identify the exact location of each individual score within a distribution. With this in mind, each X value can be transformed into a z-score, z_X, using the mean and standard deviation for the set of Xs. Similarly, each Y score can be transformed into z_Y. If the X and Y values are viewed as a sample, then the transformation is completed using the sample formula for z (Equation 5.3). If the X and Y values form a complete population, then the z-scores are computed using Equation 5.1. After the transformation, the formula for the Pearson correlation can be expressed entirely in terms of z-scores.

For a sample, $r = \dfrac{\Sigma z_X z_Y}{(n-1)}$ (14.4)

$$\text{For a population,} \rho = \frac{\Sigma z_X z_y}{N} \tag{14.5}$$

Note that the population value is identified with a Greek letter, in this case the letter rho (ρ), which is the Greek equivalent of the letter r.

1. Can SP ever have a value less than zero?

2. Calculate the sum of products of deviations (SP) for the following set of scores. Use the definitional formula and then the computational formula. Verify that you get the same answer with both formulas.

X	Y
0	1
4	3
5	3
2	2
4	1

3. For the following data:

   a. Sketch a scatter plot and make an estimate of the Pearson correlation.

   b. Compute the Pearson correlation.

X	Y
2	6
1	5
3	3
0	7
4	4

ANSWERS 1. Yes. SP can be positive, negative, or zero depending on the relationship between X and Y.

2. $SP = 5$

3. b. $r = -\frac{8}{10} = -0.80$

14.3   USING AND INTERPRETING THE PEARSON CORRELATION

WHERE AND WHY CORRELATIONS ARE USED

Although correlations have a number of different applications, a few specific examples are presented next to give an indication of the value of this statistical measure.

1. **Prediction.** If two variables are known to be related in a systematic way, then it is possible to use one of the variables to make predictions about the other. For example, when you applied for admission to college, you were required to submit a great deal of personal information, including your scores on the Scholastic Achievement Test (SAT). College officials want this information because it helps to predict your chances of success in college. It has been demonstrated over several years that SAT scores and college grade point averages are correlated. Students

who do well on the SAT tend to do well in college; students who have difficulty with the SAT tend to have difficulty in college. Based on this relationship, college admissions officers can predict the potential success of each applicant. You should note that this prediction is not perfectly accurate. Not everyone who does poorly on the SAT has trouble in college. That is why you also submit letters of recommendation, high school grades, and other information with your application.

2. **Validity.** Suppose that a psychologist develops a new test for measuring intelligence. How could you show that this test truly measures what it claims; that is, how could you demonstrate the validity of the test? One common technique for demonstrating validity is to use a correlation. If the test actually measures intelligence, then the scores on the test should be related to other measures of intelligence—for example, standardized IQ tests, performance on learning tasks, problem-solving ability, and so on. The psychologist could measure the correlation between the new test and each of these other measures of intelligence to demonstrate that the new test is valid.

3. **Reliability.** In addition to evaluating the validity of a measurement procedure, correlations are used to determine reliability. A measurement procedure is considered reliable to the extent that it produces stable, consistent measurements. That is, a reliable measurement procedure produces the same (or nearly the same) scores when the same individuals are measured twice under the same conditions. For example, if your IQ were measured as 113 last week, you would expect to obtain nearly the same score if your IQ were measured again this week. One way to evaluate reliability is to use correlations to determine the relationship between two sets of measurements. When reliability is high, the correlation between two measurements should be strong and positive.

4. **Theory Verification.** Many psychological theories make specific predictions about the relationship between two variables. For example, a theory may predict a relationship between brain size and learning ability; a developmental theory may predict a relationship between the parents' IQs and the child's IQ; a social psychologist may have a theory predicting a relationship between personality type and behavior in a social situation. In each case, the prediction of the theory could be tested by determining the correlation between the two variables.

INTERPRETING CORRELATIONS

When you encounter correlations, there are four additional considerations that you should bear in mind:

1. Correlation simply describes a relationship between two variables. It does not explain why the two variables are related. Specifically, a correlation should not and cannot be interpreted as proof of a cause-and-effect relationship between the two variables.

2. The value of a correlation can be affected greatly by the range of scores represented in the data.

3. One or two extreme data points, often called *outliers,* can have a dramatic effect on the value of a correlation.

4. When judging how "good" a relationship is, it is tempting to focus on the numerical value of the correlation. For example, a correlation of +0.5 is halfway between 0 and 1.00 and, therefore, appears to represent a moderate degree of relationship. However, a correlation should not be interpreted as a proportion. Although a correlation of 1.00 does mean that there is a 100% perfectly predictable relationship

between X and Y, a correlation of 0.5 does not mean that you can make predictions with 50% accuracy. To describe how accurately one variable predicts the other, you must square the correlation. Thus, a correlation of $r = 0.5$ means that one variable *partially* predicts the other, but the predictable portion is only $r^2 = 0.5^2 = 0.25$ (or 25%) of the total variability.

We now discuss each of these four points in detail.

CORRELATION AND CAUSATION

One of the most common errors in interpreting correlations is to assume that a correlation necessarily implies a cause-and-effect relationship between the two variables. (Even Pearson blundered by asserting causation from correlational data [Blum, 1978].) We constantly are bombarded with reports of relationships: Cigarette smoking is related to heart disease; alcohol consumption is related to birth defects; carrot consumption is related to good eyesight. Do these relationships mean that cigarettes cause heart disease or carrots cause good eyesight? The answer is *no*. Although there may be a causal relationship, the simple existence of a correlation does not prove it. Earlier, for example, we discussed a study showing a relationship between high school grades and family income. However, this result does not mean that having a higher family income *causes* students to get better grades. For example, if mom gets an unexpected bonus at work, it is unlikely that her child's grades will also show a sudden increase. To establish a cause-and-effect relationship, it is necessary to conduct a true experiment (see p. 13) in which one variable is manipulated by a researcher and other variables are rigorously controlled. The fact that a correlation does not establish causation is demonstrated in the following example.

EXAMPLE 14.4

Suppose we select a variety of different cities and towns throughout the United States and measure the number of churches (X variable) and the number of serious crimes (Y variable) for each. A scatter plot showing hypothetical data for this study is presented in Figure 14.5. Notice that this scatter plot shows a strong, positive correlation between churches and crime. You also should note that these are realistic data. It is reasonable that small towns would have less crime and fewer churches and that large cities would have large values for both variables. Does this relationship mean that churches cause crime? Does it mean that crime causes churches? It should be clear that both answers are no. Although a strong correlation exists between number of churches and crime, the real cause of the relationship is the size of the population.

CORRELATION AND RESTRICTED RANGE

Whenever a correlation is computed from scores that do not represent the full range of possible values, you should be cautious in interpreting the correlation. Suppose, for example, that you are interested in the relationship between IQ and creativity. If you select a sample of your fellow college students, your data probably will represent only a limited range of IQ scores (most likely from 110 to 130). The correlation within this *restricted range* could be completely different from the correlation that would be obtained from a full range of IQ scores. For example, Figure 14.6 shows a strong positive relationship between X and Y when the entire range of scores is considered. However, this relationship is obscured when the data are limited to a restricted range.

To be safe, you should not generalize any correlation beyond the range of data represented in the sample. For a correlation to provide an accurate description for the general population, there should be a wide range of X and Y values in the data.

FIGURE 14.5

Hypothetical data showing the logical relationship between the number of churches and the number of serious crimes for a sample of U.S. cities.

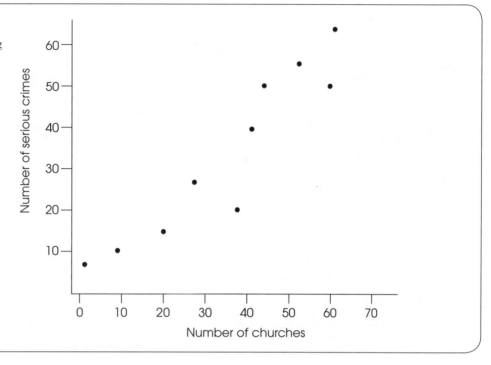

FIGURE 14.6

In this example, the full range of X and Y values shows a strong, positive correlation, but the restricted range of scores produces a correlation near zero.

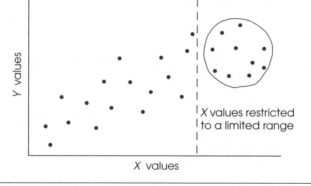

OUTLIERS An outlier is an individual with X and/or Y value that is substantially different (larger or smaller) from the values obtained for the other individuals in the data set. The data point of a single outlier can have a dramatic influence on the value obtained for the correlation. This effect is illustrated in Figure 14.7. Figure 14.7(a) shows a set of $n = 5$ data points for which the correlation between the X and Y variables is nearly zero (actually $r = -0.08$). In Figure 14.7(b), one extreme data point (14, 12) has been added to the original data set. When this outlier is included in the analysis, a strong, positive correlation emerges (now $r = +0.85$). Note that the single outlier drastically alters the value for the correlation and, thereby, can affect one's interpretation of the relationship between variables X and Y. Without the outlier, one would conclude there is no relationship between the two variables. With the extreme data point, $r = +0.85$, which implies a strong relationship with Y increasing consistently as X increases. The problem of outliers is a good reason for looking at a scatter plot, instead of simply basing your interpretation on the numerical value of the correlation. If you only

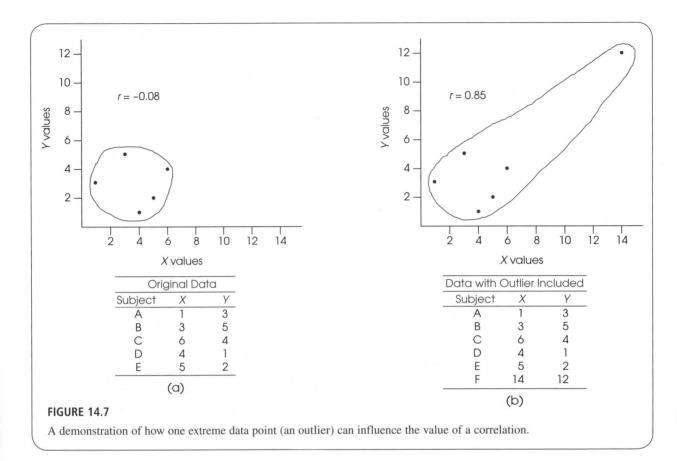

FIGURE 14.7

A demonstration of how one extreme data point (an outlier) can influence the value of a correlation.

"go by the numbers," you might overlook the fact that one extreme data point inflated the size of the correlation.

CORRELATION AND THE STRENGTH OF THE RELATIONSHIP

A correlation measures the degree of relationship between two variables on a scale from 0 to 1.00. Although this number provides a measure of the degree of relationship, many researchers prefer to square the correlation and use the resulting value to measure the strength of the relationship.

One of the common uses of correlation is for prediction. If two variables are correlated, you can use the value of one variable to predict the other. For example, college admissions officers do not just guess which applicants are likely to do well; they use other variables (SAT scores, high school grades, and so on) to predict which students are most likely to be successful. These predictions are based on correlations. By using correlations, the admissions officers expect to make more accurate predictions than would be obtained by chance. In general, the squared correlation (r^2) measures the gain in accuracy that is obtained from using the correlation for prediction. The squared correlation measures the proportion of variability in the data that is explained by the relationship between X and Y. It is sometimes called the *coefficient of determination*.

DEFINITION

> The value r^2 is called the **coefficient of determination** because it measures the proportion of variability in one variable that can be determined from the relationship with the other variable. A correlation of $r = 0.80$ (or –0.80), for example, means that $r^2 = 0.64$ (or 64%) of the variability in the Y scores can be predicted from the relationship with X.

In earlier chapters (see pp. 262, 291, and 322), we introduced r^2 as a method for measuring effect size for research studies where mean differences were used to compare treatments. Specifically, we measured how much of the variance in the scores was accounted for by the differences between treatments. In experimental terminology, r^2 measures how much of the variance in the dependent variable is accounted for by the independent variable. Now we are doing the same thing, except that there is no independent or dependent variable. Instead, we simply have two variables, X and Y, and we use r^2 to measure how much of the variance in one variable can be determined from its relationship with the other variable. The following example demonstrates this concept.

EXAMPLE 14.5   Figure 14.8 shows three sets of data representing different degrees of linear relationship. The first set of data [Figure 14.8(a)] shows the relationship between IQ and shoe size. In this case, the correlation is $r = 0$ (and $r^2 = 0$), and you have no ability to predict a person's IQ based on his or her shoe size. Knowing a person's shoe size provides no information (0%) about the person's IQ. In this case, shoe size provides no help explaining why different people have different IQs.

Now consider the data in Figure 14.8(b). These data show a moderate, positive correlation, $r = +0.60$, between IQ scores and college grade point averages (GPA). Students with high IQs tend to have higher grades than students with low IQs. From this relationship, it is possible to predict a student's GPA based on his or her IQ. However, you should realize that the prediction is not perfect. Although students with high IQs *tend* to have high GPAs, this is not always true. Thus, knowing a student's IQ provides some information about the student's grades, or knowing a student's grades provides some information about the student's IQ. In this case, IQ scores help explain the fact that different students have different GPAs. Specifically, you can say that *part* of the differences in GPA are accounted for by IQ. With a correlation of $r = +0.60$, we obtain $r^2 = 0.36$, which means that 36% of the variance in GPA can be explained by IQ.

Finally, consider the data in Figure 14.8(c). This time we show a perfect linear relationship ($r = +1.00$) between monthly salary and yearly salary for a group of college employees. With $r = 1.00$ and $r^2 = 1.00$, there is 100% predictability. If you know a person's monthly salary, you can predict perfectly the person's annual salary. If two people have different annual salaries, the difference can be completely explained (100%) by the difference in their monthly salaries.

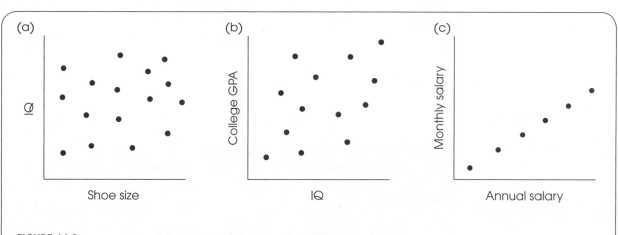

FIGURE 14.8

Three sets of data showing three different degrees of linear relationship.

Just as r^2 was used to evaluate effect size for mean differences in Chapters 9, 10, and 11, r^2 can now be used to evaluate the size or strength of the correlation. The same standards that were introduced in Table 9.3 (p. 264) apply to both uses of the r^2 measure. Specifically, an r^2 value of 0.01 indicates a small effect or a small correlation, an r^2 value of 0.09 indicates a medium correlation, and an r^2 of 0.25 or larger indicates a large correlation.

More information about the coefficient of determination (r^2) is presented in Section 14.5. For now, you should realize that whenever two variables are consistently related, it is possible to use one variable to predict values for the second variable.

<table>
<tr><td>**LEARNING CHECK**</td><td>

1. A researcher finds a correlation of $r = -0.71$ between the time spent playing video games each week and grade point average for a group of high school boys. This means that playing video games causes students to get lower grades. (True or false?)

2. A researcher finds a correlation of $r = 0.60$ between salary and the number of years of education for a group of 40-year-old men. How much of the variance in salary is explained by the years of education?

</td></tr>
<tr><td>**ANSWERS**</td><td>

1. False. You cannot conclude that there is a cause-and-effect relationship based on a correlation.

2. $r^2 = 0.36$, or 36%

</td></tr>
</table>

14.4 HYPOTHESIS TESTS WITH THE PEARSON CORRELATION

The Pearson correlation is generally computed for sample data. As with most sample statistics, however, a sample correlation is often used to answer questions about the corresponding population correlation. For example, a psychologist would like to know whether there is a relationship between IQ and creativity. This is a general question concerning a population. To answer the question, a sample would be selected, and the sample data would be used to compute the correlation value. You should recognize this process as an example of inferential statistics: using samples to draw inferences about populations. In the past, we have been concerned primarily with using sample means as the basis for answering questions about population means. In this section, we examine the procedures for using a sample correlation as the basis for testing hypotheses about the corresponding population correlation.

THE HYPOTHESES

The basic question for this hypothesis test is whether a correlation exists in the population. The null hypothesis is "No. There is no correlation in the population," or "The population correlation is zero." The alternative hypothesis is "Yes. There is a real, nonzero correlation in the population." Because the population correlation is traditionally represented by ρ (the Greek letter rho), these hypotheses would be stated in symbols as

$$H_0: \rho = 0 \quad \text{(There is no population correlation.)}$$

$$H_1: \rho \neq 0 \quad \text{(There is a real correlation.)}$$

When there is a specific prediction about the direction of the correlation, it is possible to do a directional, or one-tailed, test. For example, if a researcher is predicting a positive relationship, the hypotheses would be

H_0: $\rho \leq 0$ (The population correlation is not positive.)

H_1: $\rho > 0$ (The population correlation is positive.)

The correlation from the sample data is used to evaluate the hypotheses. For the regular, nondirectional test, a sample correlation near zero provides support for H_0 and a sample value far from zero tends to refute H_0. For a directional test, a positive value for the sample correlation would tend to refute a null hypothesis stating that the population correlation is not positive.

Although sample correlations are used to test hypotheses about population correlations, you should keep in mind that samples are not expected to be identical to the populations from which they come; there is some discrepancy (sampling error) between a sample statistic and the corresponding population parameter. Specifically, you should always expect some error between a sample correlation and the population correlation it represents. One implication of this fact is that, even when there is no correlation in the population ($\rho = 0$), you are still likely to obtain a nonzero value for the sample correlation. This is particularly true for small samples. Figure 14.9 illustrates how a small sample from a population with a near-zero correlation could result in a correlation that deviates from zero. The colored dots in the figure represent the entire population and the three circled dots represent a random sample. Note that the three sample points show a relatively good, positive correlation even through there is no linear trend ($\rho = 0$) for the population.

FIGURE 14.9

Scatter plot of a population of X and Y values with near-zero correlation. However, a small sample of $n = 3$ data points from this population shows a relatively strong, positive correlation. Data points in the sample are circled.

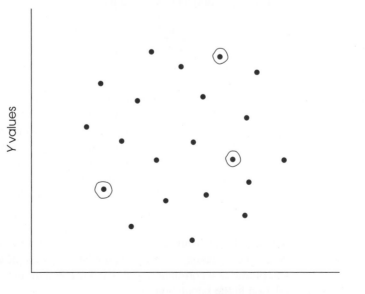

When you obtain a nonzero correlation for a sample, the purpose of the hypothesis test is to decide between the following two interpretations:

1. There is no correlation in the population ($\rho = 0$), and the sample value is the result of sampling error. Remember, a sample is not expected to be identical to the population. There always is some error between a sample statistic and the corresponding population parameter. This is the situation specified by H_0.

2. The nonzero sample correlation accurately represents a real, nonzero correlation in the population. This is the alternative stated in H_1.

The correlation from the sample helps to determine which of these two interpretations is more likely. A sample correlation near zero supports the conclusion that the population correlation is also zero. A sample correlation that is substantially different from zero supports the conclusion that there is a real, nonzero correlation in the population.

THE HYPOTHESIS TEST

The hypothesis test evaluating the significance of a correlation can be conducted using either a t statistic or an F-ratio. The F-ratio is discussed later (pp. 493–496), and we focus on the t statistic here. The t statistic for a correlation has the same general structure as t statistics introduced in Chapters 9, 10, and 11.

$$t = \frac{\text{sample statistic} - \text{population parameter}}{\text{standard error}}$$

In this case, the sample statistic is the sample correlation (r) and the corresponding parameter is the population correlation (ρ). The null hypothesis specifies that the population correlation is $\rho = 0$. The final part of the equation is the standard error, which is determined by

$$\text{standard error for } r = s_r = \sqrt{\frac{1 - r^2}{n - 2}} \tag{14.6}$$

Thus, the complete t statistic is

$$t = \frac{r - \rho}{\sqrt{\frac{(1 - r^2)}{(n - 2)}}} \tag{14.7}$$

The t statistic has degrees of freedom defined by $df = n - 2$. An intuitive explanation for this value is that a sample with only $n = 2$ data points has no degrees of freedom. Specifically, if there are only two points, they will fit perfectly on a straight line, and the sample produces a perfect correlation of $r = +1.00$ or $r = -1.00$. Because the first two points always produce a perfect correlation, the sample correlation is free to vary only when the data set contains more than two points. Thus, $df = n - 2$.

The following examples demonstrate the hypothesis test.

EXAMPLE 14.6

A researcher is using a regular, two-tailed test with $\alpha = .05$ to determine whether a nonzero correlation exists in the population. A sample of $n = 30$ individuals is obtained and produces a correlation of $r = 0.35$. The null hypothesis states that there is no correlation in the population.

$$H_0: \rho = 0$$

For this example, $df = 28$ and the critical values are $t = \pm 2.048$. With $r^2 = 0.35^2 = 0.1225$, the data produce

$$t = \frac{0.35 - 0}{\sqrt{(1 - 0.1225)/28}} = \frac{0.35}{0.177} = 1.97$$

The t value is not in the critical region so we fail to reject the null hypothesis. The sample correlation is not large enough to reject the null hypothesis.

EXAMPLE 14.7 With a sample of $n = 30$ and a correlation of $r = 0.35$, this time we use a directional, one-tailed test to determine whether there is a positive correlation in the population.

$$H_0: \rho \leq 0 \text{ (There is not a positive correlation.)}$$

$$H_1: \rho > 0 \text{ (There is a positive correlation.)}$$

The sample correlation is positive, as predicted, so we simply need to determine whether it is large enough to be significant. For a one-tailed test with $df = 28$ and $\alpha = .05$, the critical value is $t = 1.701$. In the previous example, we found that this sample produces $t = 1.97$, which is beyond the critical boundary. For the one-tailed test, we reject the null hypothesis and conclude that there is a significant positive correlation in the population.

As with most hypothesis tests, if other factors are held constant, the likelihood of finding a significant correlation increases as the sample size increases. For example, a sample correlation of $r = 0.50$ produces a nonsignificant $t(8) = 1.63$ for a sample of $n = 10$, but the same correlation produces a significant $t(18) = 2.45$ if the sample size is increased to $n = 20$.

IN THE LITERATURE
REPORTING CORRELATIONS

Correlations are typically reported using APA format. The statement should include the sample size, the calculated value for the correlation, whether it is a statistically significant relationship, the probability level, and the type of test used (one- or two-tailed). For example, a correlation might be reported as follows:

> A correlation for the data revealed a significant relationship between amount of education and annual income, $r = +0.65$, $n = 30$, $p < .01$, two tails.

Sometimes a study might look at several variables, and correlations between all possible variable pairings are computed. Suppose, for example, that a study measured people's annual income, amount of education, age, and intelligence. With four variables, there are six possible pairings leading to six different correlations. The results from multiple correlations are most easily reported in a table called a *correlation matrix*, using footnotes to indicate which correlations are significant. For example, the report might state:

The analysis examined the relationships among income, amount of education, age, and intelligence for $n = 30$ participants. The correlations between pairs of variables are reported in Table 1. Significant correlations are noted in the table.

TABLE 1

Correlation matrix for income, amount of education, age, and intelligence

	Education	Age	IQ
Income	+.65*	+.41**	+.27
Education		+.11	+.38**
Age			−.02

$n = 30$
*$p < .01$, two tails
**$p < .05$, two tails

LEARNING CHECK

1. A researcher obtains a correlation of $r = -0.39$ for a sample of $n = 25$ individuals. Does this sample provide sufficient evidence to conclude that there is a significant, nonzero correlation in the population? Assume a two-tailed test with $\alpha = .05$.

2. As sample size gets smaller, what happens to the magnitude of the correlation necessary for significance? Explain why this occurs.

ANSWERS

1. No. The sample correlation produces $t = -2.03$. With $df = 23$ and $\alpha = .05$, the critical value is 2.069. The sample value is not in the critical region.

2. As the sample size gets smaller, the magnitude of the correlation needed for significance gets larger. With a small sample, it is easy to get a relatively large correlation just by chance. Therefore, a small sample requires a very large correlation before you can be confident there is a real (nonzero) relationship in the population.

PARTIAL CORRELATIONS

Occasionally a researcher may suspect that the relationship between two variables is being distorted by the influence of a third variable. Earlier in the chapter, for example, we found a strong positive relationship between the number of churches and the number of serious crimes for a sample of different towns and cities (see Example 14.4, p 460). However, it is unlikely that there is a direct relationship between churches and crime. Instead, both variables are influenced by population: Large cities have a lot of churches and high crime rates compared to smaller towns, which have fewer churches and less crime. If population were controlled, there probably would be no real correlation between churches and crime.

Fortunately, there is a statistical technique, known as *partial correlation,* that allows a researcher to measure the relationship between two variables while controlling or holding constant the influence of a third variable. Thus, a researcher could use a partial correlation to examine the relationship between churches and crime without the risk that the relationship is distorted by the size of the population.

DEFINITION

> A **partial correlation** measures the relationship between two variables while controlling the influence of a third variable by holding it constant.

In a situation with three variables, X, Y, and Z, it is possible to compute three individual Pearson correlations:

1. r_{XY}, measuring the correlation between X and Y

2. r_{XZ}, measuring the correlation between X and Z

3. r_{YZ}, measuring the correlation between Y and Z

These three individual correlations can then be used to compute a partial correlation. For example, the partial correlation between X and Y, holding Z constant, is determined by the formula

$$r_{XY-Z} = \frac{r_{XY} - (r_{XZ}r_{YZ})}{\sqrt{(1 - r_{XZ}^2)(1 - r_{YZ}^2)}}$$

(14.8)

The following example demonstrates the calculation and interpretation of a partial correlation.

EXAMPLE 14.8   We begin with the hypothetical data shown in Table 14.2. These scores have been constructed to simulate the church/crime/population situation for a sample of $n = 15$ cities. The X variable represents the number of churches, Y represents the number of crimes, and Z represents the population for each city. Note that there are three categories for the size of the population (three values for Z) corresponding to small, medium, and large cities. For these scores, the individual Pearson correlations are all large and positive:

a. The correlation between churches and crime is $r_{XY} = 0.923$.

b. The correlation between churches and population is $r_{XZ} = 0.961$.

c. The correlation between crime and population is $r_{YZ} = 0.961$.

TABLE 14.2

Hypothetical data showing the relationship between the number of churches, the number of crimes, and the population of a set of $n = 15$ cities.

Number of Churches (X)	Number of Crimes (Y)	Population (Z)
1	4	1
2	3	1
3	1	1
4	2	1
5	5	1
7	8	2
8	11	2
9	9	2
10	7	2
11	10	2
13	15	3
14	14	3
15	16	3
16	17	3
17	13	3

The data points for the 15 cities are shown in the scatter plot in Figure 14.10. Notice that the population variable, Z, separates the scores into three distinct groups: When $Z = 1$, the population is low and churches and crime (X and Y) are also low; when $Z = 2$, the population is moderate and churches and crime (X and Y) are also moderate; and when $Z = 3$, the population is large and churches and crime are both high. Thus, as the population increases from one city to another, the number of churches and crimes also increase, and the result is a strong positive correlation between churches and crime.

Within each of the three population categories, however, there is no linear relationship between churches and crime. Specifically, within each group, the population variable is constant and the five data points for X and Y form a circular pattern, indicating no consistent linear relationship. The partial correlation allows us to hold population

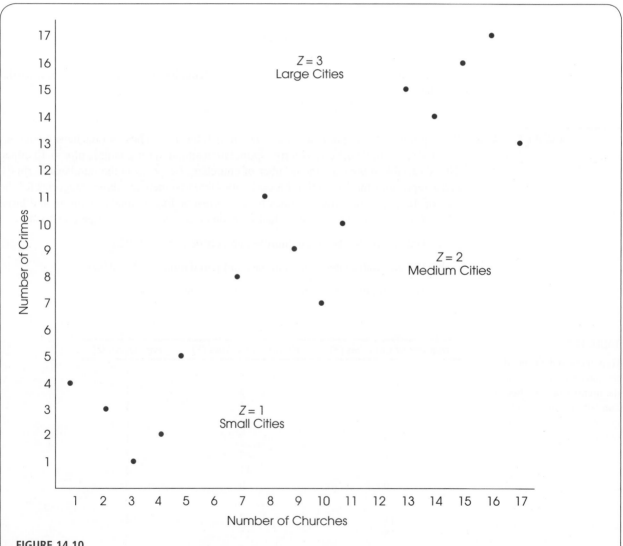

FIGURE 14.10

Hypothetical data showing the relationship between the number of churches and the number of crimes for three groups of cities. Those with small populations ($Z = 1$), those with medium populations ($Z = 2$), and those with large populations ($Z = 3$).

constant across the entire sample and measure the underlying relationship between churches and crime without any influence from population. For these data, the partial correlation is

$$r_{XY-Z} = \frac{0.923 - 0.961(0.961)}{\sqrt{(1 - 0.961^2)(1 - 0.961^2)}}$$

$$= \frac{0}{0.076}$$

$$= 0$$

Thus, when the population differences are eliminated, there is no correlation remaining between churches and crime ($r = 0$).

In Example 14.8, the population differences, which correspond to the different values of the Z variable, were eliminated mathematically in the calculation of the partial correlation. However, it is possible to visualize how these differences are eliminated in the actual data. Looking at Figure 14.10, focus on the five points in the bottom left corner. These are the five cities with small populations, few churches, and little crime. The five points in the upper right corner represent the five cities with large populations, many churches, and a lot of crime. The partial correlation controls population size by mathematically equalizing the populations for all 15 cities. Population is increased for the five small cities. However, increasing the population also increases churches and crime. Similarly, population is decreased for the five large cities, which also decreases churches and crime. In Figure 14.10, imagine the five points in the bottom left moving up and to the right so that they overlap with the points in the center. At the same time, the five points in the upper right move down and to the left so that they also overlap the points in the center. When population is equalized, all 15 data points are clustered in the center of the figure with no clear positive or negative trend. In other words, the remaining correlation between churches and crime is $r = 0$.

In Example 14.8 we used a partial correlation to demonstrate that an apparent relationship between churches and crime was actually caused by the influence of a third variable, population. It also is possible to use partial correlations to demonstrate that a relationship is not caused by the influence of a third variable. As an example, consider research examining the relationship between exposure to sexual content on television and sexual behavior among adolescents (Collins et al., 2004). The study consisted of a survey of 1,792 adolescents, 12 to 17 years old, who reported their television viewing habits and their sexual behaviors. The results showed a clear relationship between television viewing and behaviors. Specifically, the more sexual content the adolescents watched on television, the more likely they were to engage in sexual behaviors. One concern for the researchers was that the observed relationship may be influenced by the age of the participants. For example, the older adolescents (age 17) probably watch more programs with sexual content and engage in more sexual behaviors than the younger adolescents (age 12) do. Although the viewing of sexual content on television and the participants' sexual behaviors increase together, the observed relationship may simply be the result of age differences. To address this problem, the researcher used a partial correlation technique to control or hold constant the age variable. The results clearly showed that a relationship still exists between television sexual content and sexual behavior even after the influence of the participants' ages was accounted for.

1. Sales figures show a positive relationship between temperature and ice cream consumption; as temperature increases, ice cream consumption also increases. Other research shows a positive relationship between temperature and crime rate (Cohn & Rotton, 2000). When the temperature increases, both ice cream consumption and crime rates tend to increase. As a result, there is a positive correlation between ice cream consumption and crime rate. However, what do you think is the true relationship between ice cream consumption and crime rate? Specifically, what value would you predict for the partial correlation between the two variables if temperature were held constant?

ANSWER 1. There should be no systematic relationship between ice cream consumption and crime rate. The partial correlation should be near zero.

 ## ALTERNATIVES TO THE PEARSON CORRELATION

The Pearson correlation measures the degree of linear relationship between two variables when the data (*X* and *Y* values) consist of numerical scores from an interval or ratio scale of measurement. However, other correlations have been developed for nonlinear relationships and for other types of data. In this section, we examine three additional correlations: the Spearman correlation, the point-biserial correlation, and the phi-coefficient. As you will see, all three can be viewed as special applications of the Pearson correlation.

THE SPEARMAN CORRELATION

When the Pearson correlation formula is used with data from an ordinal scale (ranks), the result is called the *Spearman correlation*. The Spearman correlation is used in two situations.

First, the Spearman correlation is used to measure the relationship between *X* and *Y* when both variables are measured on ordinal scales. Recall from Chapter 1 that an ordinal scale typically involves ranking individuals rather than obtaining numerical scores. Rank-order data are fairly common because they are often easier to obtain than interval or ratio scale data. For example, a teacher may feel confident about rank-ordering students' leadership abilities but would find it difficult to measure leadership on some other scale.

In addition to measuring relationships for ordinal data, the Spearman correlation can be used as a valuable alternative to the Pearson correlation, even when the original raw scores are on an interval or a ratio scale. As we have noted, the Pearson correlation measures the degree of *linear relationship* between two variables—that is, how well the data points fit on a straight line. However, a researcher often expects the data to show a consistently one-directional relationship but not necessarily a linear relationship. For example, Figure 14.11 shows the typical relationship between practice and performance. For nearly any skill, increasing amounts of practice tend to be associated with improvements in performance (the more you practice, the better you get). However, it is not a straight-line relationship. When you are first learning a new skill, practice produces large improvements in performance. After you have been performing a skill for several years, however, additional practice produces only minor changes in performance. Although there is a consistent relationship between the amount of practice and the quality of performance, it clearly is not linear. If the Pearson correlation were computed for these data, it would not produce a correlation of 1.00 because the data do not fit perfectly on a straight line. In a situation like this, the Spearman correlation can be used to measure the consistency of the relationship, independent of its form.

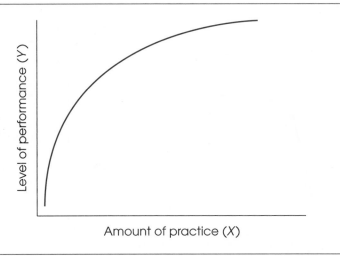

FIGURE 14.11

Hypothetical data showing the relationship between practice and performance. Although this relationship is not linear, there is a consistent positive relationship. An increase in performance tends to accompany an increase in practice.

The reason that the Spearman correlation measures consistency, rather than form, comes from a simple observation: When two variables are consistently related, their ranks are linearly related. For example, a perfectly consistent positive relationship means that every time the X variable increases, the Y variable also increases. Thus, the smallest value of X is paired with the smallest value of Y, the second-smallest value of X is paired with the second smallest value of Y, and so on. Every time the rank for X goes up by 1 point, the rank for Y also goes up by 1 point. As a result, the ranks fit perfectly on a straight line. This phenomenon is demonstrated in the following example.

EXAMPLE 14.9

Table 14.3 presents X and Y scores for a sample of $n = 4$ people. Note that the data show a perfectly consistent relationship. Each increase in X is accompanied by an increase in Y. However, the relationship is not linear, as can be seen in the graph of the data in Figure 14.12(a).

Next, we convert the scores to ranks. The lowest X is assigned a rank of 1, the next lowest a rank of 2, and so on. The Y scores are then ranked in the same way. The ranks are listed in Table 14.3 and shown in Figure 14.12(b). Note that the perfect consistency for the scores produces a perfect linear relationship for the ranks.

The preceding example demonstrates that a consistent relationship among scores produces a linear relationship when the scores are converted to ranks. Thus, if you want to measure the consistency of a relationship for a set of scores, you can simply convert the scores to ranks and then use the Pearson correlation formula to measure the linear relationship for the ranked data. The degree of linear relationship for the ranks provides a measure of the degree of consistency for the original scores.

TABLE 14.3

Scores and ranks for Example 14.9.

Person	X	Y	X-Rank	Y-Rank
A	4	9	3	3
B	2	2	1	1
C	10	10	4	4
D	3	8	2	2

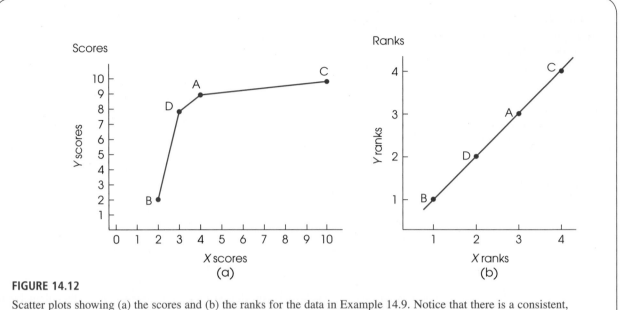

FIGURE 14.12

Scatter plots showing (a) the scores and (b) the ranks for the data in Example 14.9. Notice that there is a consistent, positive relationship between the X and Y scores, although it is not a linear relationship. Also notice that the scatter plot of the ranks shows a perfect linear relationship.

To summarize, the Spearman correlation measures the relationship between two variables when both are measured on ordinal scales (ranks). There are two general situations in which the Spearman correlation is used:

1. Spearman is used when the original data are ordinal. In this case, you rank the ordinal scores and apply the Pearson correlation formula to the set of ranks.

2. Spearman is used when the original scores are numerical values from an interval or ratio scale and the goal is to measure the consistency of the relationship between X and Y, independent of the specific form of the relationship. In this case, the original scores are first converted to ranks, and then the Pearson correlation formula is used with the ranks. Because the Pearson formula measures the degree to which the ranks fit on a straight line, it also measures the degree of consistency in the relationship for the original scores. Incidentally, when there is a consistently one-directional relationship between two variables, the relationship is said to be *monotonic*. Thus, the Spearman correlation measures the degree of monotonic relationship between two variables.

The word *monotonic* describes a sequence that is consistently increasing (or decreasing). Like the word *monotonous*, it means constant and unchanging.

In either case, the Spearman correlation is identified by the symbol r_s to differentiate it from the Pearson correlation. The complete process of computing the Spearman correlation, including ranking scores, is demonstrated in Example 14.10.

EXAMPLE 14.10   The following data show a nearly perfect monotonic relationship between X and Y. When X increases, Y tends to decrease, and there is only one reversal in this general trend. To compute the Spearman correlation, we first rank the X and Y values, and we then compute the Pearson correlation for the ranks.

We have listed the X values in order so that the trend is easier to recognize.

Original Data		Ranks		
X	Y	X	Y	XY
3	12	1	5	5
4	10	2	3	6
10	11	3	4	12
11	9	4	2	8
12	2	5	1	5
				$36 = \Sigma XY$

To compute the correlation, we need SS for X, SS for Y, and SP. Remember that all of these values are computed with the ranks, not the original scores. The X ranks are simply the integers 1, 2, 3, 4, and 5. These values have $\Sigma X = 15$ and $\Sigma X^2 = 55$. The SS for the X ranks is

$$SS_X = \Sigma X^2 - \frac{(\Sigma X)^2}{n} = 55 - \frac{(15)^2}{5} = 10$$

Note that the ranks for Y are identical to the ranks for X; that is, they are the integers 1, 2, 3, 4, and 5. Therefore, the SS for Y is identical to the SS for X:

$$SS_Y = 10$$

To compute the SP value, we need ΣX, ΣY, and ΣXY for the ranks. The XY values are listed in the table with the ranks, and we already have found that both the Xs and the Ys have a sum of 15. Using these values, we obtain

$$SP = \Sigma XY - \frac{(\Sigma X)(\Sigma Y)}{n} = 36 - \frac{(15)(15)}{5} = -9$$

Finally, the Spearman correlation simply uses the Pearson formula for the ranks.

$$r_s = \frac{SP}{\sqrt{(SS_X)(SS_Y)}} = \frac{-9}{\sqrt{10(10)}} = -0.9$$

The Spearman correlation indicates that the data show a consistent (nearly perfect) negative trend.

RANKING TIED SCORES   When you are converting scores into ranks for the Spearman correlation, you may encounter two (or more) identical scores. Whenever two scores have exactly the same value, their ranks should also be the same. This is accomplished by the following procedure:

1. List the scores in order from smallest to largest. Include tied values in the list.

2. Assign a rank (first, second, etc.) to each position in the ordered list.

3. When two (or more) scores are tied, compute the mean of their ranked positions, and assign this mean value as the final rank for each score.

The process of finding ranks for tied scores is demonstrated here. These scores have been listed in order from smallest to largest.

Scores	Rank Position	Final Rank	
3	1	1.5	Mean of 1 and 2
3	2	1.5	
5	3	3	
6	4	5	Mean of 4, 5, and 6
6	5	5	
6	6	5	
12	7	7	

Note that this example has seven scores and uses all seven ranks. For $X = 12$, the largest score, the appropriate rank is 7. It cannot be given a rank of 6 because that rank has been used for the tied scores.

If the original scores are ordinal values, then they are ranked using exactly the same process for ranking tied scores. For example, suppose a researcher has the following letter grades for a sample of $n = 7$ students: A, A, B, C, C, D, and F. The grades would receive the following ranks: 1.5, 1.5, 3, 4.5, 4.5, 6, and 7.

SPECIAL FORMULA FOR THE SPEARMAN CORRELATION

After the original X values and Y values have been ranked, the calculations necessary for SS and SP can be greatly simplified. First, you should note that the X ranks and the Y ranks are really just a set of integers: 1, 2, 3, 4, ... , n. To compute the mean for these integers, you can locate the midpoint of the series by $M = (n + 1)/2$. Similarly, the SS for this series of integers can be computed by

$$SS = \frac{n(n^2 - 1)}{12} \quad \text{(Try it out.)}$$

Also, because the X ranks and the Y ranks are the same values, the SS for X is identical to the SS for Y.

Because calculations with ranks can be simplified and because the Spearman correlation uses ranked data, these simplifications can be incorporated into the final calculations for the Spearman correlation. Instead of using the Pearson formula after ranking the data, you can put the ranks directly into a simplified formula:

$$r_s = 1 - \frac{6 \Sigma D^2}{n(n^2 - 1)} \tag{14.9}$$

Caution: In this formula, you compute the value of the fraction and then subtract from 1. The 1 is not part of the fraction.

where D is the difference between the X rank and the Y rank for each individual. This formula produces the same result that would be obtained from the Pearson formula. However, note that this special formula can be used only after the scores have been converted to ranks and only when there are no ties among the ranks. If there are relatively few tied ranks, the formula still may be used, but it loses accuracy as the number of ties increases. The application of this formula is demonstrated in the following example.

EXAMPLE 14.11

To demonstrate the special formula for the Spearman correlation, we use the same data that were presented in Example 14.10. The ranks for these data are shown again here:

Ranks		Difference	
X	Y	D	D^2
1	5	4	16
2	3	1	1
3	4	1	1
4	2	−2	4
5	1	−4	16
			$38 = \Sigma D^2$

Using the special formula for the Spearman correlation, we obtain

$$r_s = 1 - \frac{6 \Sigma D^2}{n(n^2 - 1)} = 1 - \frac{6(38)}{5(25 - 1)} = 1 - \frac{228}{120} = 1 - 1.90 = -0.90$$

This is exactly the same answer that we obtained in Example 14.10, using the Pearson formula on the ranks.

LEARNING CHECK

1. Describe what is measured by a Spearman correlation, and explain how this correlation is different from the Pearson correlation.

2. If the following scores are converted into ranks, what rank will be assigned to the individuals who have scores of $X = 7$?

   Scores: 1, 1, 1, 3, 6, 7, 7, 8, 10

3. Rank the following scores and compute the Spearman correlation:

X	Y
2	7
12	3
9	16
14	5

ANSWERS

1. The Spearman correlation measures the consistency of the direction of the relationship between two variables. The Spearman correlation does not depend on the form of the relationship, whereas the Pearson correlation measures how well the data fit a linear form.

2. Both scores get a rank of 6.5 (the average of 6 and 7).

3. $r_s = -0.60$

THE POINT-BISERIAL CORRELATION AND MEASURING EFFECT SIZE WITH R^2

In Chapters 9, 10, and 11, we introduced r^2 as a measure of effect size that often accompanies a hypothesis test using the t statistic. The r^2 used to measure effect size and the r used to measure a correlation are directly related, and we now have an opportunity to demonstrate the relationship. Specifically, we compare the independent-measures t test (Chapter 10) and a special version of the Pearson correlation known as the *point-biserial correlation*.

The point-biserial correlation is used to measure the relationship between two variables in situations in which one variable consists of regular, numerical scores, but the second variable has only two values. A variable with only two values is called a *dichotomous variable* or a *binomial variable*. Some examples of dichotomous variables are

1. Male versus female

2. College graduate versus not a college graduate

3. First-born child versus later-born child

4. Success versus failure on a particular task

5. Older than 30 years versus younger than 30 years

It is customary to use the numerical values 0 and 1, but any two different numbers would work equally well and would not affect the value of the correlation.

To compute the point-biserial correlation, the dichotomous variable is first converted to numerical values by assigning a value of zero (0) to one category and a value of one (1) to the other category. Then, the regular Pearson correlation formula is used with the converted data.

To demonstrate the point-biserial correlation and its association with the r^2 measure of effect size, we use the data from Example 10.1 (p. 289). The original example compared high school grades for two groups of students: one group who regularly watched Sesame Street as 5-year-old children and one who did not watch the program. The data from the independent-measures study are presented on the left side of Table 14.4. Notice that the data consist of two separate samples and the independent-measures t was used to determine whether there was a significant mean difference between the two populations represented by the samples.

TABLE 14.4

The same data are organized in two different formats. On the left-hand side, the data appear as two separate samples appropriate for an independent-measures t hypothesis test. On the right-hand side, the same data are shown as a single sample, with two scores for each individual: the original high school grade and a dichotomous score (Y) that identifies the group in which the participant is located (Sesame Street = 1 and No-Sesame Street = 0). The data on the right are appropriate for a point-biserial correlation.

Data for the independent-measures t test. Two separate samples, each with n 5 10 scores.

Average High School Grade			
Watched Sesame Street		Did Not Watch Sesame Street	
86	99	90	79
87	97	89	83
91	94	82	86
97	89	83	81
98	92	85	92
$n = 10$		$n = 10$	
$M = 93$		$M = 85$	
$SS = 200$		$SS = 160$	

Data for the point-biserial correlation. Two scores, X and Y, for each of the $n = 20$ participants.

Participant	Grade X	Group Y
A	86	1
B	87	1
C	91	1
D	97	1
E	98	1
F	99	1
G	97	1
H	94	1
I	89	1
J	92	1
K	90	0
L	89	0
M	82	0
N	83	0
O	85	0
P	79	0
Q	83	0
R	86	0
S	81	0
T	92	0

On the right-hand side of Table 14.4 we have reorganized the data into a form that is suitable for a point-biserial correlation. Specifically, we used each student's high school grade as the X value and we have created a new variable, Y, to represent the group, or condition, for each student. In this case, we have used $Y = 1$ for students who watched Sesame Street and $Y = 0$ for students who did not watch the program.

When the data in Table 14.4 were originally presented in Chapter 10, we conducted an independent-measures t hypothesis test and obtained $t = 4.00$ with $df = 18$. We measured the size of the treatment effect by calculating r^2, the percentage of variance accounted for, and obtained $r^2 = 0.47$.

Calculating the point-biserial correlation for these data also produces a value for r. Specifically, the X scores produce $SS = 680$; the Y values produce $SS = 5.00$, and the sum of the products of the X and Y deviations produces $SP = 40$. The point-biserial correlation is

$$r = \frac{SP}{\sqrt{(SS_X)(SS_Y)}} = \frac{40}{\sqrt{(680)(5)}} = \frac{40}{58.31} = 0.686$$

Notice that squaring the value of the point-biserial correlation produces $r^2 = (0.686)^2 = 0.47$, which is exactly the value of r^2 we obtained measuring effect size.

In some respects, the point-biserial correlation and the independent-measures hypothesis test are evaluating the same thing. Specifically, both are examining the relationship between the TV-viewing habits of 5-year-old children and their future academic performance in high school.

1. The correlation is measuring the *strength* of the relationship between the two variables. A large correlation (near 1.00 or −1.00) would indicate that there is a consistent, predictable relationship between high school grades and watching Sesame Street as a 5-year-old child. In particular, the value of r^2 measures how much of the variability in grades can be predicted by knowing whether the participants watched Sesame Street.

2. The t test evaluates the *significance* of the relationship. The hypothesis test determines whether the mean difference in grades between the two groups is greater than can be reasonably explained by chance alone.

As we noted in Chapter 10 (p. 291–295), the outcome of the hypothesis test and the value of r^2 are often reported together. The t value measures statistical significance and r^2 measures the effect size. Also, as we noted in Chapter 10, the values for t and r^2 are directly related. In fact, either can be calculated from the other by the equations

$$r^2 = \frac{t^2}{t^2 + df} \quad \text{and} \quad t^2 = \frac{r^2}{\left(1 - r^2\right) / df}$$

where df is the degrees of freedom for the t statistic.

However, you should note that r^2 is determined entirely by the size of the correlation, whereas t is influenced by the size of the correlation and the size of the sample. For example, a correlation of $r = 0.30$ produces $r^2 = 0.09$ (9%) no matter how large the sample may be. On the other hand, a point-biserial correlation of $r = 0.30$ for a total sample of 10 people ($n = 5$ in each group) produces a nonsignificant value of $t = 0.889$. If the sample is increased to 50 people ($n = 25$ in each group), the same correlation produces a significant t value of $t = 2.18$. Although t and r are related, they are measuring different things.

THE PHI-COEFFICIENT   When both variables (X and Y) measured for each individual are dichotomous, the correlation between the two variables is called the *phi-coefficient*. To compute phi (ϕ), you follow a two-step procedure:

1. Convert each of the dichotomous variables to numerical values by assigning a 0 to one category and a 1 to the other category for each of the variables.

2. Use the regular Pearson formula with the converted scores.

This process is demonstrated in the following example.

EXAMPLE 14.12   A researcher is interested in examining the relationship between birth-order position and personality for individuals who have at least one sibling. A random sample of $n = 8$ participants is obtained, and each individual is classified in terms of birth-order position as first-born versus later-born. Then, each individual's personality is classified as either introvert or extrovert.

The original measurements are then converted to numerical values by the following assignments:

Birth Order	Personality
First-born child = 0	Introvert = 0
Later-born child = 1	Extrovert = 1

The original data and the converted scores are as follows:

Original Data		Converted Scores	
Birth Order (X)	Personality (Y)	Birth Order (X)	Personality (Y)
1st	Introvert	0	0
3rd	Extrovert	1	1
1st	Extrovert	0	1
2nd	Extrovert	1	1
4th	Extrovert	1	1
2nd	Introvert	1	0
1st	Introvert	0	0
3rd	Extrovert	1	1

The Pearson correlation formula is then used with the converted data to compute the phi-coefficient.

Because the assignment of numerical values is arbitrary (either category could be designated 0 or 1), the sign of the resulting correlation is meaningless. As with most correlations, the *strength* of the relationship is best described by the value of r^2, the coefficient of determination, which measures how much of the variability in one variable is predicted or determined by the association with the second variable.

We also should note that although the phi-coefficient can be used to assess the relationship between two dichotomous variables, the more common statistical procedure is a chi-square statistic, which is examined in Chapter 15.

LEARNING CHECK

1. The following data represent job-related stress scores for a sample of $n = 8$ individuals. These people also are classified by salary level.

   a. Convert the data into a form suitable for the point-biserial correlation.

   b. Compute the point-biserial correlation for these data.

Salary More than $40,000	Salary Less than $40,000
8	4
6	2
5	1
3	3

2. A researcher would like to know whether there is a relationship between gender and manual dexterity for 3-year-old children. A sample of $n = 10$ boys and $n = 10$ girls is obtained and each child is given a manual-dexterity test. Five of the girls failed the test and only two of the boys failed. Describe how these data could be coded into a form suitable for computing a phi-coefficient to measure the strength of the relationship.

ANSWERS

1. **a.** Salary level is a dichotomous variable and can be coded as $Y = 1$ for individuals with salary more than $40,000 and $Y = 0$ for salary less than $40,000. The stress scores produce $SS_X = 36$, the salary codes produce $SS_Y = 2$, and $SP = 6$.

   b. The point-biserial correlation is 0.71.

2. Gender could be coded with male = 0 and female = 1. Manual dexterity could be coded with failure = 0 and success = 1. Eight boys would have scores of 0 and 1 and two would have scores of 0 and 0. Five girls would have scores of 1 and 1 and five would have scores of 1 and 0.

14.6 INTRODUCTION TO LINEAR EQUATIONS AND REGRESSION

Earlier in the chapter, we introduced the Pearson correlation as a technique for describing and measuring the linear relationship between two variables. Figure 14.13 presents hypothetical data showing the relationship between SAT scores and college grade point average (GPA). Note that the figure shows a good, but not perfect, positive relationship. Also note that we have drawn a line through the middle of the data points. This line serves several purposes:

1. The line makes the relationship between SAT scores and GPA easier to see.

2. The line identifies the center, or *central tendency,* of the relationship, just as the mean describes central tendency for a set of scores. Thus, the line provides a simplified description of the relationship. For example, if the data points were removed, the straight line would still give a general picture of the relationship between SAT scores and GPA.

3. Finally, the line can be used for prediction. The line establishes a precise, one-to-one relationship between each X value (SAT score) and a corresponding Y value (GPA). For example, an SAT score of 620 corresponds to a GPA of 3.25 (see Figure 14.13). Thus, the college admissions officers could use the straight-line relationship to predict that a student entering college with an SAT score of 620 should achieve a college GPA of approximately 3.25.

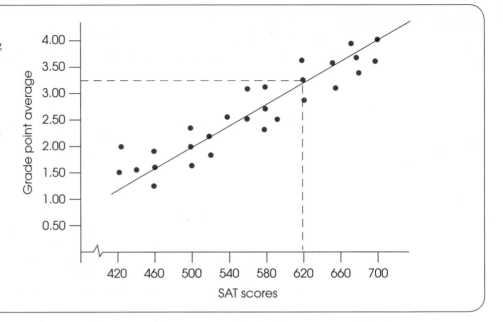

FIGURE 14.13

Hypothetical data showing the relationship between SAT scores and GPA with a regression line drawn through the data points. The regression line defines a precise, one-to-one relationship between each X value (SAT score) and its corresponding Y value (GPA).

Our goal in this section is to develop a procedure that identifies and defines the straight line that provides the best fit for any specific set of data. This straight line does not have to be drawn on a graph; it can be presented in a simple equation. Thus, our goal is to find the equation for the line that best describes the relationship for a set of X and Y data.

LINEAR EQUATIONS

In general, a *linear relationship* between two variables X and Y can be expressed by the equation

$$Y = bX + a \qquad (14.10)$$

where a and b are fixed constants.

For example, a local video store charges an annual membership fee of $5, which allows you to rent videos and games for $2 each. With this information, the total cost for 1 year can be computed using a *linear equation* that describes the relationship between the total cost (Y) and the number of videos and games rented (X).

$$Y = 2X + 5$$

Note that a positive slope means that Y increases when X is increased, and a negative slope indicates that Y decreases when X is increased.

In the general linear equation, the value of b is called the *slope*. The slope determines how much the Y variable changes when X is increased by 1 point. For the video store example, the slope is $b = 2$ and indicates that your total cost increases by $2 for each video you rent. The value of a in the general equation is called the Y-*intercept* because it determines the value of Y when $X = 0$. (On a graph, the a value identifies the point where the line intercepts the Y-axis.) For the video-store example, $a = 5$; there is a $5 membership charge even if you never rent a video.

Figure 14.14 shows the general relationship between the annual cost and number of videos for the video store example. Notice that the relationship results in a straight line. To obtain this graph, we picked any two values of X and then used the equation to compute the corresponding values for Y. For example,

When X = 3:	When X = 8:
$Y = bX + a$	$Y = bX + a$
$= \$2(3) + \$5$	$= \$2(8) + \$5$
$= \$6 + \$5$	$= \$16 + \$5$
$= \$11$	$= \$21$

When drawing a graph of a linear equation, it is wise to compute and plot at least three points to be certain that you have not made a mistake.

Next, these two points are plotted on the graph: one point at $X = 3$ and $Y = 11$, the other point at $X = 8$ and $Y = 21$. Because two points completely determine a straight line, we simply drew the line so that it passed through these two points.

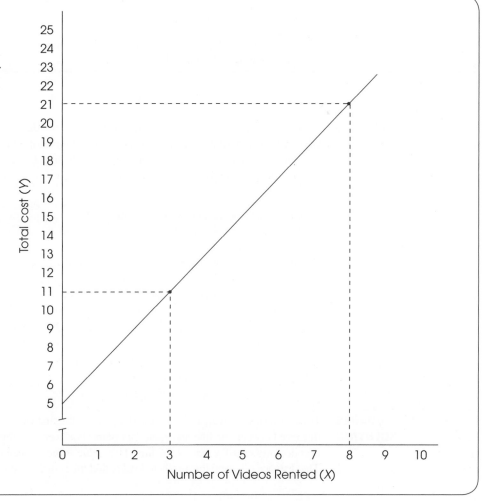

FIGURE 14.14

The relationship between total cost and number of videos rented each month. The video store charges a $5 monthly membership fee and $2 for each video or game rented. The relationship is described by a linear equation, $Y = 2X + 5$, where Y is the total cost and X is the number of videos.

LEARNING CHECK

1. A local gym charges a $25 monthly membership fee plus $2 per hour for aerobics classes. What is the linear equation that describes the relationship between the total monthly cost (Y) and the number of class hours each month (X)?

2. For the linear equation, $Y = -3X + 7$, what happens to the value of Y each time X is increased by 1 point?

3. Use the linear equation $Y = 2X - 7$ to determine the value of Y for each of the following values of X: 1, 3, 5, 10.

4. If the slope constant (b) in a linear equation is positive, then a graph of the equation is a line tilted from lower left to upper right. (True or false?)

ANSWERS

1. $Y = 2X + 25$

2. The slope is -3, so Y decreases by 3 points each time X increases by 1 point.

3.

X	Y
1	-5
3	-1
5	3
10	13

4. True. A positive slope indicates that Y increases (goes up in the graph) when X increases (goes to the right in the graph).

REGRESSION

Because a straight line can be extremely useful for describing a relationship between two variables, a statistical technique has been developed that provides a standardized method for determining the best-fitting straight line for any set of data. The statistical procedure is *regression*, and the resulting straight line is called the *regression line.*

DEFINITION

> The statistical technique for finding the best-fitting straight line for a set of data is called **regression,** and the resulting straight line is called the **regression line.**

The goal for regression is to find the best-fitting straight line for a set of data. To accomplish this goal, however, it is first necessary to define precisely what is meant by "best fit." For any particular set of data, it is possible to draw lots of different straight lines that all appear to pass through the center of the data points. Each of these lines can be defined by a linear equation of the form $Y = bX + a$ where b and a are constants that determine the slope and Y-intercept of the line, respectively. Each individual line has its own unique values for b and a. The problem is to find the specific line that provides the best fit to the actual data points.

THE LEAST-SQUARES SOLUTION

To determine how well a line fits the data points, the first step is to define mathematically the distance between the line and each data point. For every X value in the data, the linear equation determines a Y value on the line. This value is the predicted Y and is called $\hat{Y}$ ("Y hat"). The distance between this predicted value and the actual Y value in the data is determined by

$$\text{distance} = Y - \hat{Y}$$

Note that we simply are measuring the vertical distance between the actual data point (Y) and the predicted point on the line. This distance measures the error between the line and the actual data (Figure 14.15).

Because some of these distances are positive and some are negative, the next step is to square each distance to obtain a uniformly positive measure of error. Finally, to determine the total error between the line and the data, we add the squared errors for all of the data points. The result is a measure of overall squared error between the line and the data:

$$\text{total squared error} = \Sigma(Y - \hat{Y})^2$$

Now we can define the *best-fitting* line as the one that has the smallest total squared error. For obvious reasons, the resulting line is commonly called the *least-squared-error solution*. In symbols, we are looking for a linear equation of the form

$$\hat{Y} = bX + a$$

For each value of X in the data, this equation determines the point on the line ($\hat{Y}$) *that gives the best prediction of Y*. The problem is to find the specific values for a and b that make this the best-fitting line.

The calculations that are needed to find this equation require calculus and some sophisticated algebra, so we do not present the details of the solution. The results, however, are relatively straightforward, and the solutions for b and a are as follows:

$$b = \frac{SP}{SS_X} \tag{14.11}$$

where SP is the sum of products and SS_x is the sum of squares for the X scores.

A commonly used alternative formula for the slope is based on the standard deviations for X and Y. The alternative formula is

$$b = r\frac{s_y}{s_x} \tag{14.12}$$

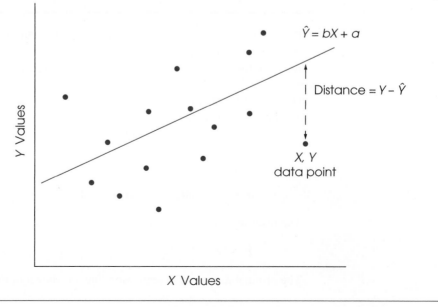

FIGURE 14.15

The distance between the actual data point (Y) and the predicted point on the line ($\hat{Y}$) is defined as $Y - \hat{Y}$. The goal of regression is to find the equation for the line that minimizes these distances.

where s_Y is the standard deviation for the Y scores, s_X is the standard deviation for the X scores, and r is the Pearson correlation for X and Y. The value of the constant a in the equation is determined by

$$a = M_Y - bM_X \qquad (14.13)$$

Note that these formulas determine the linear equation that provides the best prediction of Y values. This equation is called the *regression equation for* Y.

DEFINITION

> The **regression equation for** Y is the linear equation.
>
> $$\hat{Y} = bX + a \qquad (14.14)$$
>
> where the constant b is determined by Equation 14.11, or 14.12 and the constant a is determined by Equation 14.13. This equation results in the least squared error between the data points and the line.

EXAMPLE 14.13   The scores in the following table are used to demonstrate the calculation and use of the regression equation for predicting Y.

X	Y	$X - M_X$	$Y - M_Y$	$(X - M_X)^2$	$(Y - M_Y)^2$	$(X - M_X)(Y - M_Y)$
5	10	1	3	1	9	3
1	4	−3	−3	9	9	9
4	5	0	−2	0	4	0
7	11	3	4	9	16	12
6	15	2	8	4	64	16
4	6	0	−1	0	1	0
3	5	−1	−2	1	4	2
2	0	−2	−7	4	49	14
				$SS_X = 28$	$SS_Y = 156$	$SP = 56$

For these data, $\Sigma X = 32$, so $M_X = 4$. Also, $\Sigma Y = 56$, so $M_Y = 7$. These values have been used to compute the deviation scores for each X and Y value. The final three columns show the squared deviations for X and for Y, and the products of the deviation scores.

Our goal is to find the values for b and a in the regression equation. Using Equations 14.11 and 14.13, the solutions for b and a are

$$b = \frac{SP}{SS_X} = \frac{56}{28} = 2$$

$$a = M_Y - bM_X = 7 - 2(4) = -1$$

The resulting equation is

$$\hat{Y} = 2X - 1$$

The original data and the regression line are shown in Figure 14.16.

FIGURE 14.16

The X and Y data points and the regression line for the $n = 8$ pairs of scores in Example 14.13.

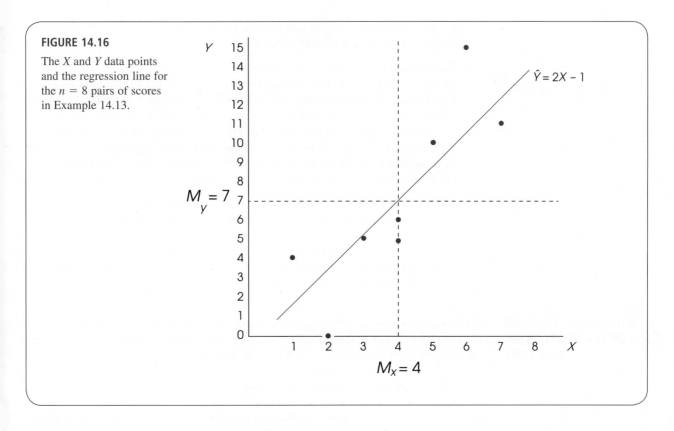

The regression line shown in Figure 14.16 demonstrates some simple and very predictable facts about regression. First, the calculation of the Y-intercept (Equation 14.13) ensures that the regression line passes through the point defined by the mean for X and the mean for Y. That is, the point identified by the coordinates M_x, M_Y will always be on the line. We have included the two means in Figure 14.16 to show that the point they define is on the regression line. Second, the sign of the correlation ($+$ or $-$) is the same as the sign of the slope of the regression line. Specifically, if the correlation is positive, then the slope is also positive and the regression line slopes up to the right. On the other hand, if the correlation is negative, then the slope is negative and the line slopes down to the right. A correlation of zero means that the slope is also zero and the regression equation produces a horizontal line that passes through the data at a level equal to the mean for the Y values. Note that the regression line in Figure 14.16 has a positive slope. One consequence of this fact is that all of the points on the line that are above the mean for X are also above the mean for Y. Similarly, all of the points below the mean for X are also below the mean for Y. Thus, every individual with a positive deviation for X is predicted to have a positive deviation for Y, and everyone with a negative deviation for X is predicted to have a negative deviation for Y.

USING THE REGRESSION EQUATION FOR PREDICTION

As we noted at the beginning of this section, one common use of regression equations is for prediction. For any given value of X, we can use the equation to compute a predicted value for Y. For the equation from Example 14.13, an individual with a score of $X = 3$ would be predicted to have a Y score of

$$\hat{Y} = 2X - 1 = 6 - 1 = 5$$

Although regression equations can be used for prediction, a few cautions should be considered whenever you are interpreting the predicted values:

1. The predicted value is not perfect (unless $r = +1.00$ or -1.00). If you examine Figure 14.16, it should be clear that the data points do not fit perfectly on the line. In general, there is some error between the predicted Y values (on the line) and the actual data. Although the amount of error varies from point to point, on average the errors are directly related to the magnitude of the correlation. With a correlation near 1.00 (or -1.00), the data points generally are clustered close to the line and the error is small. As the correlation gets nearer to zero, the points move away from the line and the magnitude of the error increases.

2. The regression equation should not be used to make predictions for X values that fall outside of the range of values covered by the original data. For Example 14.13, the X values ranged from $X = 1$ to $X = 7$, and the regression equation was calculated as the best-fitting line within this range. Because you have no information about the X-Y relationship outside this range, the equation should not be used to predict Y for any X value lower than 1 or greater than 7.

STANDARDIZED FORM OF THE REGRESSION EQUATIONS

So far, we have presented the regression equation in terms of the original values, or raw scores, for X and Y. Occasionally, however, researchers standardize the scores by transforming the X and Y values into z-scores before finding the regression equation. The resulting equation is often called the standardized form of the regression equation and is greatly simplified compared to the raw-score version. The simplification comes from the fact that z-scores have standardized characteristics. Specifically, the mean for a set of z-scores is always zero and the standard deviation is always 1. As a result, the standardized form of the regression equation becomes

$$\hat{z}_Y = (\text{beta}) \, z_X \tag{14.15}$$

First notice that we are now using the z-score for each X (z_X) to predict the z-score for the corresponding Y (z_Y). Also, note that the slope constant that was identified as b in the raw-score formula is now identified as beta. Because both sets of z-scores have a mean of zero, the constant a disappears from the regression equation. Finally, when one variable, X, is being used to predict a second variable, Y, the value of beta is equal to the Pearson correlation for X and Y. Thus, the standardized form of the regression equation can also be written as

$$\hat{z}_Y = r z_X \tag{14.16}$$

Because the process of transforming all of the original scores into z-scores can be tedious, researchers usually compute the raw-score version of the regression equation (Equation 14.14) instead of the standardized form. However, most computer programs report the value of beta as part of the output from linear regression, and you should understand what this value represents.

LEARNING CHECK

1. Sketch a scatter plot for the following data—that is, a graph showing the X, Y data points:

X	Y
4	13
2	5
5	12
1	6

    a. Find the regression equation for predicting Y from X. Draw this line on your graph. Does it look like the best-fitting line?

    b. Use the regression equation to find the predicted Y value corresponding to each X in the data.

ANSWERS   **1. a.** $SS_X = 10$, $SP = 20$, $b = 2$, $a = 3$. The equation is $\hat{Y} = 2X + 3$.

    b. The predicted Y values are 11, 7, 13, and 5.

THE STANDARD ERROR OF ESTIMATE

It is possible to determine a regression equation for any set of data by simply using the formulas already presented. The linear equation you obtain is then used to generate predicted Y values for any known value of X. However, it should be clear that the accuracy of this prediction depends on how well the points on the line correspond to the actual data points—that is, the amount of error between the predicted values, $\hat{Y}$, and the actual scores, Y values. Figure 14.17 shows two different sets of data that have exactly the same regression equation. In one case, there is a perfect correlation ($r = +1$) between X and Y, so the linear equation fits the data perfectly. For the second set of data, the predicted Y values on the line only approximate the real data points.

A regression equation, by itself, allows you to make predictions, but it does not provide any information about the accuracy of the predictions. To measure the precision of the regression, it is customary to compute a *standard error of estimate.*

DEFINITION

The **standard error of estimate** gives a measure of the standard distance between the predicted Y values on the regression line and the actual Y values in the data.

Conceptually, the standard error of estimate is very much like a standard deviation: Both provide a measure of standard distance. Also, the calculation of the standard error of estimate is very similar to the calculation of standard deviation.

To calculate the standard error of estimate, we first find the sum of squared deviations (SS). Each deviation measures the distance between the actual Y value (from the data) and the predicted Y value (from the regression line). This sum of squares is commonly called SS_{residual} because it is based on the remaining distance between the actual Y scores and the predicted values on the line.

$$SS_{\text{residual}} = \Sigma(Y - \hat{Y})^2 \tag{14.17}$$

The obtained SS value is then divided by its degrees of freedom to obtain a measure of variance. This procedure should be very familiar:

$$\text{Variance} = \frac{SS}{df}$$

The degrees of freedom for the standard error of estimate are $df\ 5\ n - 2$. The reason for having $n - 2$ degrees of freedom, rather than the customary $n - 1$, is that we now are measuring deviations from a line rather than deviations from a mean. To find the equation for the regression line, you must know the means for both the X and the Y scores. Specifying these two means places two restrictions on the variability of the data, with the result that the scores have only $n - 2$ degrees of freedom. (*Note*: the $df\ 5\ n - 2$ for SS_{residual} is the same $df\ 5\ n - 2$ that we encountered when testing the significance of the Pearson correlation on page 466.)

Recall that variance measures the average squared distance.

The final step in the calculation of the standard error of estimate is to take the square root of the variance to obtain a measure of standard distance. The final equation is

$$\text{standard error of estimate} = \sqrt{\frac{SS_{\text{residual}}}{df}} = \sqrt{\frac{\Sigma(Y - \hat{Y})^2}{n-2}}$$

(14.18)

The following example demonstrates the calculation of this standard error.

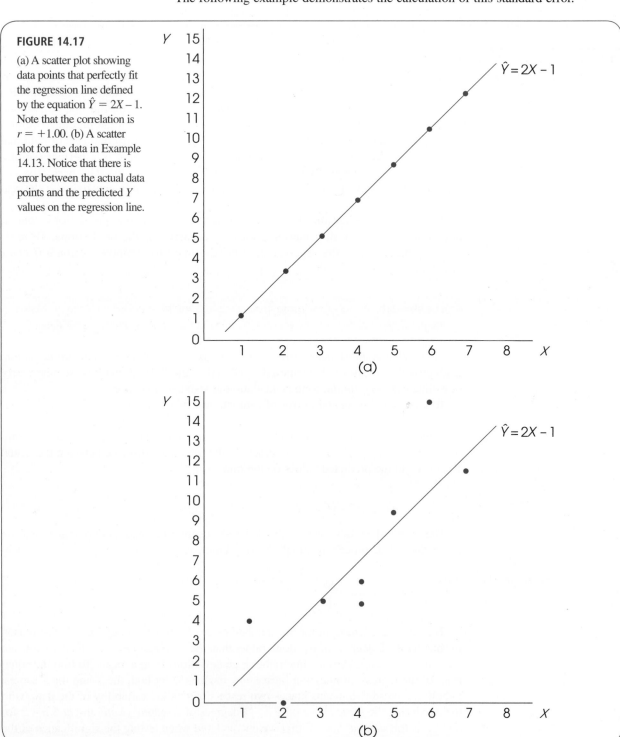

FIGURE 14.17

(a) A scatter plot showing data points that perfectly fit the regression line defined by the equation $\hat{Y} = 2X - 1$. Note that the correlation is $r = +1.00$. (b) A scatter plot for the data in Example 14.13. Notice that there is error between the actual data points and the predicted Y values on the regression line.

EXAMPLE 14.14

The same data that were used in Example 14.13 are used here to demonstrate the calculation of the standard error of estimate. These data have the regression equation

$$\hat{Y} = 2X - 1$$

Using this regression equation, we have computed the predicted Y value, the residual, and the squared residual for each individual, using the data from Example 14.13.

Data		Predicted Y value	Residual	Squared Residual
X	Y	$\hat{Y} = 2X - 1$	$Y - \hat{Y}$	$(Y - \hat{Y})^2$
5	10	9	1	1
1	4	1	3	9
4	5	7	−2	4
7	11	13	−2	4
6	15	11	4	16
4	6	7	−1	1
3	5	5	0	0
2	0	3	−3	9
			0	$SS_{residual} = 44$

First note that the sum of the residuals is equal to zero. In other words, the sum of the distances above the line is equal to the sum of the distances below the line. This is true for any set of data and provides a way to check the accuracy of your calculations. The squared residuals are listed in the final column. For these data, the sum of the squared residuals is $SS_{residual} = 244$. With $n = 8$, the data have $df = n - 2 = 6$, so the standard error of estimate is

$$\text{standard error of estimate} = \sqrt{\frac{SS_{residual}}{df}} = \sqrt{\frac{44}{6}} = 2.708$$

Remember: The standard error of estimate provides a measure of how accurately the regression equation predicts the Y values. In this case, the standard distance between the actual data points and the regression line is measured by standard error of estimate = 2.708.

RELATIONSHIP BETWEEN THE STANDARD ERROR AND THE CORRELATION

It should be clear from Example 14.14 that the standard error of estimate is directly related to the magnitude of the correlation between X and Y. If the correlation is near 1.00 (or −1.00), then the data points are clustered close to the line, and the standard error of estimate is small. As the correlation gets nearer to zero, the data points become more widely scattered, the line provides less accurate predictions, and the standard error of estimate grows larger.

Earlier (p. 462), we observed that squaring the correlation provides a measure of the accuracy of prediction. The squared correlation, r^2, is called the coefficient of determination because it determines what proportion of the variability in Y is predicted by the relationship with X. Because r^2 measures the predicted portion of the variability in the Y scores, we can use the expression $(1 - r^2)$ to measure the unpredicted portion. Thus,

$$\text{predicted variability} = SS_{\text{regression}} = r^2 SS_Y \tag{14.19}$$

$$\text{unpredicted variability} = SS_{\text{residual}} = (1 - r^2)SS_Y \tag{14.20}$$

For example, if $r = 0.80$, then the *predicted variability* is $r^2 = 0.64$ (or 64%) of the total variability for the Y scores and the remaining 36% $(1 - r^2)$ is the *unpredicted variability*. Note that when $r = 1.00$, the prediction is perfect and there are no residuals. As the correlation approaches zero, the data points move farther off the line and the residuals grow larger. Using Equation 14.20 to compute SS_{residual}, the standard error of estimate can be computed as

$$\text{standard error of estimate} = \sqrt{\frac{SS_{\text{residual}}}{df}} = \sqrt{\frac{(1 - r^2)SS_Y}{n - 2}} \tag{14.21}$$

Because it is usually much easier to compute the Pearson correlation than to compute the individual $(Y - \hat{Y})^2$ values, Equation 14.20 is usually the easiest way to compute SS_{residual}, and Equation 14.21 is usually the easiest way to compute the standard error of estimate for a regression equation. The following example demonstrates this new formula.

EXAMPLE 14.15   We use the same data used in Examples 14.13 and 14.14, which produced $SS_X = 28$, $SS_Y = 156$, and $SP = 56$. For these data, the Pearson correlation is

$$r = \frac{56}{\sqrt{28(156)}} = \frac{56}{66.09} = 0.847$$

With $SS_Y = 156$ and a correlation of $r = 0.847$, the predicted variability from the regression equation is

$$SS_{\text{regression}} = r^2 SS_Y = (0.847^2)(156) = 0.718(156) = 112.01$$

Similarly, the unpredicted variability is

$$SS_{\text{residual}} = (1 - r^2)SS_Y = (1 - 0.847^2)(156) = 0.282(156) = 43.99$$

Notice that the new formula for SS_{residual} produces the same value, within rounding error, that we obtained by adding the squared residuals in Example 14.14. Also note that this new formula is generally much easier to use because it requires only the correlation value (r) and the SS for Y. The primary point of this example, however, is that SS_{residual} and the standard error of estimate are closely related to the value of the correlation. With a large correlation (near $+1.00$ or -1.00), the data points are close to the regression line, and the standard error of estimate is small. As a correlation gets smaller (near zero), the data points move away from the regression line, and the standard error of estimate gets larger.

Because it is possible to have the same regression equation for several different sets of data, it is also important to consider r^2 and the standard error of estimate. The regression equation simply describes the best-fitting line and is used for making predictions. However, r^2 and the standard error of estimate indicate how accurate these predictions are.

<table>
<tr><td>LEARNING CHECK</td><td>

1. Describe what is measured by the standard error of estimate for a regression equation.

2. As the numerical value of a correlation increases, what happens to the standard error of estimate?

3. A sample of $n = 6$ pairs of X and Y scores produces a correlation of $r = 0.80$ and $SS_Y = 100$. What is the standard error of estimate for the regression equation?
</td></tr>
<tr><td>ANSWERS</td><td>

1. The standard error of estimate measures the average, or standard, distance between the predicted Y values on the regression line and the actual Y values in the data.

2. A larger correlation means that the data points are clustered closer to the line, which means the standard error of estimate is smaller.

3. The standard error of estimate $= \sqrt{\dfrac{36}{4}} = 3$.
</td></tr>
</table>

ANALYSIS OF REGRESSION: TESTING THE SIGNIFICANCE OF THE REGRESSION EQUATION

As we noted earlier in the chapter, a sample correlation is expected to be representative of its population correlation. For example, if the population correlation is zero, then the sample correlation is expected to be near zero. Note that we do not expect the sample correlation to be exactly equal to zero. This is the general concept of *sampling error* that was introduced in Chapter 1 (p. 8). The principle of sampling error is that there is typically some discrepancy or error between the value obtained for a sample statistic and the corresponding population parameter. Thus, when there is no relationship whatsoever in the population, a correlation of $\rho = 0$, you are still likely to obtain a nonzero value for the sample correlation. In this situation, however, the sample correlation is caused by chance and a hypothesis test usually demonstrates that the correlation is not significant.

Whenever you obtain a nonzero value for a sample correlation, you also obtain real, numerical values for the regression equation. However, if there is no real relationship in the population, both the sample correlation and the regression equation are meaningless—they are simply the result of sampling error and should not be viewed as an indication of any relationship between X and Y. In the same way that we tested the significance of a Pearson correlation, we can test the significance of the regression equation. In fact, when a single variable, X, is being used to predict a single variable, Y, the two tests are equivalent. In each case, the purpose for the test is to determine whether the sample correlation represents a real relationship or is simply the result of sampling error. For both tests, the null hypothesis states that there is no relationship between the two variables in the population. For a correlation,

H_0: the population correlation is $\rho = 0$

For the regression equation,

H_0: the slope of the regression equation (b or beta) is zero

The process of testing the significance of a regression equation is called *analysis of regression* and is very similar to the analysis of variance (ANOVA) presented in Chapter 12. As with ANOVA, the regression analysis uses an F-ratio to determine whether the variance predicted by the regression equation is significantly greater than would be expected if there were no relationship between X and Y. The F-ratio is a ratio of two variances, or mean square (MS) values, and each variance is obtained by dividing an SS value by its corresponding degrees of freedom. The numerator of the F-ratio is $MS_{\text{regression}}$, which is the variance in the Y scores that is predicted by the regression equation. This variance measures the systematic changes in Y that occur when the value of X

increases or decreases. The denominator is MS_{residual}, which is the unpredicted variance in the Y scores. This variance measures the changes in Y that are independent of changes in X. The two MS value are defined as

$$MS_{\text{regression}} = \frac{SS_{\text{regression}}}{df_{\text{regression}}} \text{ with } df = 1 \text{ and } MS_{\text{residuals}} = \frac{SS_{\text{residual}}}{df_{\text{residual}}} \text{ with } df = n - 2$$

The F-ratio is

$$F = \frac{MS_{\text{regression}}}{MS_{\text{residual}}} \text{ with } df = 1, \ n - 2 \qquad (14.22)$$

The complete analysis of SS and degrees of freedom is diagrammed in Figure 14.18. The analysis of regression procedure is demonstrated in the following example, using the same data that we used in Examples 14.13, 14.14, and 14.15.

EXAMPLE 14.16 The data consist of $n = 8$ pairs of scores with a correlation of $r = 0.847$ and $SS_Y = 156$. The null hypothesis states either that there is no relationship between X and Y in the population, or that the regression equation does not account for a significant portion of the variance for the Y scores. The F-ratio for the analysis of regression has $df = 1, n - 2$. For these data, $df = 1, 6$. With $\alpha = .05$, the critical value is 5.99.

As noted in the previous section, the SS for the Y scores can be separated into two components: the predicted portion corresponding to r^2 and the unpredicted, or residual, portion corresponding to $(1 - r^2)$. With $r = 0.847$, we obtain $r^2 = 0.718$ and

$$\text{predicted variability} = SS_{\text{regression}} = 0.718(156) = 112.01$$

$$\text{unpredicted variability} = SS_{\text{residual}} = (1 - 0.718)(156) = 0.282(156) = 43.99$$

Using these SS values and the corresponding df values, we calculate a variance, or MS, for each component. For these data the MS values are

$$MS_{\text{regression}} = \frac{SS_{\text{regression}}}{df_{\text{regression}}} = \frac{112.01}{1} = 112.01$$

$$MS_{\text{residual}} = \frac{SS_{\text{residual}}}{df_{\text{residual}}} = \frac{43.99}{6} = 7.33$$

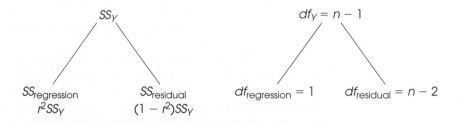

FIGURE 14.18

The partitioning of SS and df for analysis of regression. The variability in the original Y scores (both SS_Y and df_Y) is partitioned into two components: (1) the variability that is explained by the regression equation, and (2) the residual variability.

Finally, the F-ratio for evaluating the significance of the regression equation is

$$F = \frac{MS_{\text{regression}}}{MS_{\text{residual}}} = \frac{112.01}{7.33} = 15.28$$

The F-ratio is in the critical region, so we reject the null hypothesis and conclude that the regression equation does account for a significant portion of the variance for the Y scores. The complete analysis of regression is summarized in Table 14.5 which is a common format for computer printouts of regression analysis.

SIGNIFICANCE OF REGRESSION AND SIGNIFICANCE OF THE CORRELATION

In a situation with a single X variable and a single Y variable, testing the significance of the regression equation is equivalent to testing the significance of the Pearson correlation. Therefore, whenever the correlation between two variables is significant, you can conclude that the regression equation is also significant. Similarly, if a correlation is not significant, then the regression equation is also not significant. Earlier in the chapter (p. 466), we introduced a hypothesis test using the following t statistic to evaluate the significance of a correlation.

$$t = \frac{r - \rho}{\sqrt{\dfrac{(1 - r^2)}{(n - 2)}}}$$

We now demonstrate that this t statistic is equivalent to the F-ratio used for analysis of regression. Specifically, the two test statistics are related by the basic equality $F = t^2$ that was introduced in Chapters 12 and 13 (pp. 397 and 407). Recall that a t statistic with $df = n - 1$ can be squared to produce an equivalent F-ratio with $df = 1, n - 1$.

We begin the demonstration of equivalence by removing the population correlation, ρ, from the t equation. This value is always zero, as specified by the null hypothesis, and its removal does not affect the equation. Next, we square the t statistic to produce the corresponding F-ratio.

$$t^2 = F = \frac{r^2}{\dfrac{(1 - r^2)}{(n - 2)}}$$

Finally, multiply the numerator and the denominator by SS_Y to produce

$$t^2 = F = \frac{r^2(SS_Y)}{\dfrac{(1 - r^2)(SS_Y)}{(n - 2)}}$$

You should recognize the numerator of the new F-ratio as $SS_{\text{regression}}$ (see Equation 14.19). Dividing by $df = 1$, which does not change the value, produces $MS_{\text{regression}}$. Similarly, the

TABLE 14.5

A summary table showing the results of the analysis of regression in Example 14.16.

Source	SS	df	MS	F
Regression	112.01	1	112.01	15.28
Residual	43.99	6	7.33	
Total	156.00	7		

denominator of the F-ratio is SS_{residual} (see Equation 14.20) divided by $df = n - 2$, which is MS_{residual}. Thus, the squared t value is identical to the F-ratio used in analysis of regression (Equation 14.22) to evaluate the significance of the regression equation.

LEARNING CHECK

1. A set of $n = 18$ pairs of scores produces a Pearson correlation of $r = 0.60$ with $SS_Y = 100$. Find $SS_{\text{regression}}$ and SS_{residual} and compute the F-ratio to evaluate the significance of the regression equation of predicting Y.

ANSWER

1. $SS_{\text{regression}} = 36$ with $df = 1$. $SS_{\text{residual}} = 64$ with $df = 16$. $F = 9.00$. With $df = 1, 16$, the F-ratio is significant with either $\alpha = .05$ or $\alpha = .01$.

SUMMARY

1. A correlation measures the relationship between two variables, X and Y. The relationship is described by three characteristics:
   a. *Direction.* The sign of the correlation ($+$ or $-$) specifies the direction.
   b. *Form.* The Pearson correlation measures the degree of straight line relationship, but other correlations measure the consistency or strength of the relationship, independent of any specific form.
   c. *Strength or consistency.* The numerical value of the correlation measures the strength or consistency of the relationship from 0 (not consistent) to 1.00 (perfect).

2. The most commonly used correlation is the Pearson correlation, which measures the degree of linear relationship. The Pearson correlation is identified by the letter r and is computed by

$$r = \frac{SP}{\sqrt{SS_X SS_Y}}$$

In this formula, SP is the sum of products of deviations.

definitional formula: $SP = \Sigma(X - M_X)(Y - M_Y)$

computational formula: $SP = \Sigma XY - \frac{\Sigma X \Sigma Y}{n}$

3. A correlation between two variables should not be interpreted as implying a causal relationship. Simply because X and Y are related does not mean that X causes Y or that Y causes X.

4. To evaluate the strength of a relationship, you square the value of the correlation. The resulting value, r^2, is called the *coefficient of determination* because it measures the portion of the variability in one variable that can be predicted using the relationship with the second variable.

5. A sample correlation, r, can be used to evaluate the significance of the corresponding population correlation, ρ, using a t statistic with $df = n - 2$.

$$t = \frac{r - \rho}{\sqrt{\dfrac{(1 - r^2)}{(n - 2)}}}$$

6. A partial correlation measures the linear relationship between two variables by eliminating the influence of a third variable by holding it constant.

7. The Spearman correlation (r_s) measures the consistency of direction in the relationship between X and Y—that is, the degree to which the relationship is one-directional, or monotonic. The Spearman correlation is computed by a two-stage process:
   a. Rank the X scores and the Y scores separately.
   b. Compute the Pearson correlation using the ranks.

8. The point-biserial correlation is used to measure the strength of the relationship when one of the two variables is dichotomous. The dichotomous variable is coded using values of 0 and 1, and the regular Pearson formula is applied. Squaring the point-biserial correlation produces the same r^2 value that is obtained to measure effect size for the independent-measures t test. When both variables, X and Y, are dichotomous, the phi-coefficient can be used to measure the strength of the relationship. Both variables are coded 0 and 1, and the Pearson formula is used to compute the correlation.

9. When there is a general linear relationship between two variables, X and Y, it is possible to construct a linear equation that allows you to predict the Y value corresponding to any known value of X.

predicted Y value $= \hat{Y} = bX + a$

The technique for determining this equation is called regression. By using a *least-squares* method to minimize the error between the predicted Y values and the actual Y values, the best-fitting line is achieved when the linear equation has

$$b = \frac{SP}{SS_X} = r\frac{s_Y}{s_X} \text{ and } a = M_Y - bM_X$$

10. The linear equation generated by regression (called the regression equation) can be used to compute a predicted Y value for any value of X. However, the prediction is not perfect, so for each Y value, there is a predicted portion and an unpredicted, or residual, portion. Overall, the predicted portion of the Y score variability is measured by r^2, and the residual portion is measured by $1 - r^2$.

$$\text{predicted variability} = SS_{\text{regression}} = r^2 SS_Y$$

$$\text{unpredicted variability} = SS_{\text{residual}} = (1 - r^2)SS_Y$$

11. The residual variability can be used to compute the standard error of estimate, which provides a measure of the standard distance (or error) between the predicted Y values on the line and the actual data points. The standard error of estimate is computed by

$$\text{standard error of estimate} = \sqrt{\frac{SS_{\text{residual}}}{n-2}} = \sqrt{MS_{\text{residual}}}$$

It is also possible to compute an F-ratio to evaluate the significance of the regression equation. The process is called analysis of regression and determines whether the equation predicts a significant portion of the variance for the Y scores. First a variance, or MS, value is computed for the predicted variability and the residual variability,

$$MS_{\text{regression}} = \frac{SS_{\text{regression}}}{df_{\text{regression}}} \quad MS_{\text{residual}} = \frac{SS_{\text{residual}}}{df_{\text{residual}}}$$

where $df_{\text{regression}} = 1$ and $df_{\text{residual}} = n - 2$.

$$F = \frac{MS_{\text{regression}}}{MS_{\text{residual}}} \text{ with } df = 1, \ n - 2$$

The F-ratio for analysis of regression is equivalent to the t statistic evaluating the significance of the correlation.

KEY TERMS

correlation (450)

positive correlation (451)

negative correlation (451)

perfect correlation (452)

Pearson correlation (453)

sum of products (*SP*) (454)

restricted range (460)

coefficient of determination (462)

correlation matrix (467)

partial correlation (463)

Spearman correlation (472)

linear relationship (477)

point-biserial correlation (478)

dichotomous variable (478)

phi-coefficient (480)

linear equation (482)

slope (482)

Y-intercept (482)

regression (484)

regression line (484)

least-squared-error solution (485)

regression equation for Y (486)

standard error of estimate (489)

predicted variability ($SS_{\text{regression}}$) (492)

unpredicted variability (SS_{residual}) (492)

analysis of regression (493)

RESOURCES

Go to CengageBrain.com to access Psychology CourseMate, where you will find an interactive eBook, glossaries, flashcards, quizzes, statistics workshops, and more.

If your professor has assigned Aplia:

1. Sign in to your account.
2. Complete the corresponding exercises as required by your professor.
3. When finished, click "Grade It Now" to see which areas you have mastered, which areas need more work, and detailed explanations of every answer.

SPSS

General instructions for using SPSS are presented in Appendix D. Following are detailed instructions for using SPSS to perform **The Pearson, Spearman, point-biserial, and partial correlations.** *Note:* We focus on the Pearson correlation and then describe how slight modifications to this procedure can be made to compute the Spearman, point-biserial, and partial correlations. Separate instructions for the **phi-coefficient** are presented at the end of this section.

Data Entry

The data are entered into two columns in the data editor, one for the X values (VAR00001) and one for the Y values (VAR00002), with the two scores for each individual in the same row.

Data Analysis

1. Click **Analyze** on the tool bar, select **Correlate,** and click on **Bivariate.**

2. One by one, move the labels for the two data columns into the **Variables** box. (Highlight each label and click the arrow to move it into the box.)

3. The **Pearson** box should be checked but, at this point, you can switch to the Spearman correlation by clicking the appropriate box.

4. Click **OK.**

SPSS Output

We used SPSS to compute the correlation for the data in Example 14.13, and the output is shown in Figure 14.19. The program produces a correlation matrix showing all of the possible correlations, including the correlation of X with X and the correlation of Y with Y (both are perfect correlations). You want the correlation of X and Y, which is contained in the upper right corner (or the lower left). The output includes the significance level (p value or alpha level) for the correlation.

To compute a partial correlation, click **Analyze** on the tool bar, select **Correlate,** and click on **Partial.** Move the column labels for the two variables to be correlated into the **Variables** box and move the column label for the variable to be held constant into the **Controlling for** box and click **OK.**

To compute the **Spearman** correlation, enter either the X and Y ranks or the X and Y scores into the first two columns. Then follow the same Data Analysis instructions that were presented for the Pearson correlation. At step 3 in the instructions, click on the **Spearman** box before the final OK. (*Note:* If you enter X and Y scores into the data editor, SPSS converts the scores to ranks before computing the Spearman correlation.)

FIGURE 14.19

The SPSS output showing the correlation for the data in Example 14.13.

Correlations

		VAR00001	VAR00002
VAR00001	Pearson Correlation	1	.847
	Sig. (2-tailed)		.008
	N	8	8
VAR00002	Pearson Correlation	.847**	1
	Sig. (2-tailed)	.008	
	N	8	8

**. Correlation is significant at the 0.01 level (2-tailed).

To compute the **point-biserial** correlation, enter the scores (X values) in the first column and enter the numerical values (usually 0 and 1) for the dichotomous variable in the second column. Then, follow the same Data Analysis instructions that were presented for the Pearson correlation.

The **phi-coefficient** can also be computed by entering the complete string of 0s and 1s into two columns of the SPSS data editor, then following the same Data Analysis instructions that were presented for the Pearson correlation. However, this can be tedious, especially with a large set of scores. The following is an alternative procedure for computing the phi-coefficient with large data sets.

Data Entry

1. Enter the values 0, 0, 1, 1 (in order) into the first column of the SPSS data editor.

2. Enter the values 0, 1, 0, 1 (in order) into the second column.

3. Count the number of individuals in the sample who are classified with $X = 0$ and $Y = 0$. Enter this frequency in the top box in the third column of the data editor. Then, count how many have $X = 0$ and $Y = 1$ and enter the frequency in the second box of the third column. Continue with the number who have $X = 1$ and $Y = 0$, and finally the number who have $X = 1$ and $Y = 1$. You should end up with 4 values in column three.

4. Click **Data** on the Tool Bar at the top of the SPSS Data Editor page and select **Weight Cases** at the bottom of the list.

5. Click the circle labeled **Weight cases by,** and then highlight the label for the column containing your frequencies (VAR00003) on the left and move it into the **Frequency Variable** box by clicking on the arrow.

6. Click **OK**.

7. Click **Analyze** on the tool bar, select **Correlate,** and click on **Bivariate.**

8. One by one, move the labels for the two data columns containing the 0s and 1s (probably VAR00001 and VAR00002) into the **Variables** box. (Highlight each label and click the arrow to move it into the box.)

9. Verify that the **Pearson** box is checked.

10. Click **OK.**

SPSS Output

The program produces the same correlation matrix that was described for the Pearson correlation. Again, you want the correlation between *X* and *Y*, which is in the upper right corner (or lower left). Remember, with the phi-coefficient, the sign of the correlation is meaningless.

Following are detailed instructions for using SPSS to perform the **Linear Regression** presented in this chapter.

Data Entry

Enter the *X* values in one column and the *Y* values in a second column of the SPSS data editor.

Data Analysis

1. Click **Analyze** on the tool bar, select **Regression,** and click on **Linear.**

2. In the left-hand box, highlight the column label for the *Y* values, then click the arrow to move the column label into the **Dependent Variable** box.

3. Highlight the column label for the *X* values and click the arrow to move it into the **Independent Variable(s)** box.

4. Click **OK.**

SPSS Output

We used SPSS to perform regression for the data in Examples 14.13, 14.14, and 14.15 and the output is shown in Figure 14.20. The Model Summary table presents the values for *R*, R^2, and the standard error of estimate. (*Note: R* is simply the Pearson correlation between *X* and *Y*.) The ANOVA table presents the analysis of regression evaluating the significance of the regression equation, including the *F*-ratio and the level of significance (the *p* value or alpha level for the test). The **Coefficients** table summarizes both the unstandardized and the standardized coefficients for the regression equation. The table shows the values for the constant (*a*) and the coefficient (*b*). The standardized coefficient is the beta values. Again, beta is simply the Pearson correlation between *X* and *Y*. Finally, the table uses a *t* statistic to evaluate the significance of the predictor variable. This is identical to the significance of the regression equation and you should find that *t* is equal to the square root of the *F*-ratio from the analysis of regression.

FOCUS ON PROBLEM SOLVING

1. A correlation always has a value from +1.00 to –1.00. If you obtain a correlation outside this range, then you have made a computational error.

Model Summary

Model	R	R Square	Adjusted R Square	Std. Error of the Estimate
1	.847[a]	.718	.671	2.70801

ANOVA[b]

Model		Sum of Squares	df	Mean Square	F	Sig.
1	Regression	112.000	1	112.000	15.273	.008[a]
	Residual	44.000	6	7.333		
	Total	156.000	7			

Coefficients[a]

Model		Unstandardized Coefficients		Standardized Coefficients		
		B	Std. Error	Beta	t	Sig.
1	(Constant)	-1.000	2.260		-.442	.674
	VAR00001	2.000	.512	.847	3.908	.008

FIGURE 14.20

Portions of the SPSS output from the analysis of regression for the data in Examples 14.13, 14.14, and 14.15.

2. When interpreting a correlation, the sign and the numerical value must be considered separately. Remember that the sign indicates the direction of the relationship between X and Y. The numerical value reflects the strength of the relationship. Therefore, a correlation of -0.90 is as strong as a correlation of $+0.90$.

3. Before you begin to calculate a correlation, sketch a scatter plot of the data and make an estimate of the correlation. (Is it positive or negative? Is it near 1 or near 0?) After computing the correlation, compare your final answer with your original estimate.

4. The F-ratio for analysis of regression is usually calculated using the actual $SS_{regression}$ and $SS_{residual}$. However, you can simply use r^2 in place of $SS_{regression}$ and you can use $1 - r^2$ in place of $SS_{residual}$. Note: You must still use the correct df values for the numerator and the denominator.

DEMONSTRATION 14.1

CORRELATION AND REGRESSION

Calculate the Pearson correlation for the following data:

Person	X	Y	
A	0	4	$M_X = 4$ with $SS_X = 40$
B	2	1	$M_Y = 6$ with $SS_Y = 54$
C	8	10	$SP = 40$
D	6	9	
E	4	6	

STEP 1 Sketch a scatter plot. We have constructed a scatter plot for the data (Figure 14.21) and placed an envelope around the data points to make a preliminary estimate of the correlation. Note that the envelope is narrow and elongated. This indicates that the correlation is large—perhaps 0.80 to 0.90. Also, the correlation is positive because increases in X are generally accompanied by increases in Y. We also have sketched a straight line through the middle of the data points, roughly approximating the slope and Y-intercept of the regression line.

STEP 2 Compute the Pearson correlation. For these data, the Pearson correlation is

$$r = \frac{SP}{\sqrt{SS_X SS_Y}} = \frac{40}{\sqrt{40(54)}} = \frac{40}{\sqrt{2160}} = \frac{40}{46.48} = 0.861$$

In step 1, our preliminary estimate for the correlation was between $+0.80$ and $+0.90$. The calculated correlation is consistent with this estimate.

STEP 3 Compute the values for the regression equation. The general form of the regression equation is

$$\hat{Y} = bX + a \quad \text{where } b = \frac{SP}{SS_X} \text{ and } a = M_Y - bM_X$$

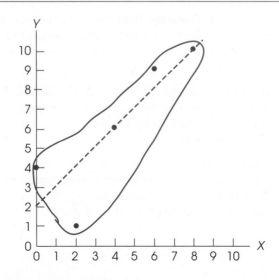

FIGURE 14.21

The scatter plot for the data of Demonstration 14.1. An envelope is drawn around the points to estimate the magnitude of the correlation. A line is drawn through the middle of the envelope.

For these data, $b = \dfrac{40}{40} = 1.00$ and $a = 6 - 1(4) = +2.00$

Thus, the regression equation is $\hat{Y} = (1)X + 2.00$ or simply, $\hat{Y} = X + 2$.

STEP 4 Evaluate the significance of the correlation and the regression equation.   The null hypothesis states that, for the population, there is no linear relationship between X and Y, and that the values obtained for the sample correlation and the regression equation are simply the result of sampling error. In terms of the correlation, H_0 says that the population correlation is zero ($\rho = 0$). In terms of the regression equation, H_0 says that the equation does not predict a significant portion of the variance, or that the beta value is zero. The test can be conducted using either the t statistic for a correlation or the F-ratio for analysis of regression. Using the F-ratio, we obtain

$$SS_{regression} = r^2(SS_Y) = (0.861)^2(54) = 40.03 \text{ with } df = 1$$

$$SS_{residual} = (1 - r^2)(SS_Y) = (1 - 0.861^2)(54) = 13.97 \text{ with } df = n = 2 = 3$$

$$F = \frac{MS_{regression}}{MS_{residual}} = \frac{40.03/1}{13.97/3} = 8.60$$

With $df = 1, 3$ and $\alpha = .05$, the critical value is 10.13. Fail to reject the null hypothesis. The correlation and the regression equation are both not significant.

PROBLEMS

1. a. What information is provided by the sign ($+$ or $-$) of the Pearson correlation?
b. What information is provided by the numerical value of the Pearson correlation?

2. Calculate SP (the sum of products of deviations) for the following scores. *Note:* Both means are whole numbers, so the definitional formula works well.

X	Y
0	2
1	4
4	5
3	3
7	6

3. Calculate SP (the sum of products of deviations) for the following scores. *Note:* Both means are decimal values, so the computational formula works well.

X	Y
0	2
0	1
1	0
2	1
1	2
0	3

4. For the following scores,

X	Y
1	3
3	5
2	1
2	3

a. Sketch a scatter plot and estimate the Pearson correlation.
b. Compute the Pearson correlation.

5. For the following scores,

X	Y
1	7
4	2
1	3
1	6
2	0
0	6
2	3
1	5

a. Sketch a scatter plot and estimate the Pearson correlation.
b. Compute the Pearson correlation.

6. For the following scores,

X	Y
1	6
4	1
1	4
1	3
3	1

a. Sketch a scatter plot and estimate the value of the Pearson correlation.

b. Compute the Pearson correlation.

7. With a small sample, a single point can have a large effect on the magnitude of the correlation. To create the following data, we started with the scores from problem 8 and changed the first X value from X = 1 to X = 6.

X	Y
6	6
4	1
1	4
1	3
3	1

a. Sketch a scatter plot and estimate the value of the Pearson correlation.

b. Compute the Pearson correlation.

8. For the following set of scores,

X	Y
6	4
3	1
5	0
6	7
4	2
6	4

a. Compute the Pearson correlation.

b. Add 2 points to each X value and compute the correlation for the modified scores. How does adding a constant to every score affect the value of the correlation?

c. Multiply each of the original X values by 2 and compute the correlation for the modified scores. How does multiplying each score by a constant affect the value of the correlation?

9. Judge and Cable (2010) report the results of a study demonstrating a negative relationship between weight and income for a group of women professionals. Following are data similar to those obtained in the study. To simplify the weight variable, the women are classified into five categories that measure actual weight relative to height, from 1 = thinnest to 5 = heaviest. Income figures are annual income (in thousands), rounded to the nearest $1,000.

a. Calculate the Pearson correlation for these data.

b. Is the correlation statistically significant? Use a two-tailed test with $\alpha = .05$.

Weight (X)	Income (Y)
1	125
2	78
4	49
3	63
5	35
2	84
5	38
3	51
1	93
4	44

10. The researchers cited in the previous problem also examined the weight/salary relationship for men and found a positive relationship, suggesting that we have very different standards for men than for women (Judge & Cable, 2010). The following are data similar to those obtained for working men. Again, weight relative to height is coded in five categories from 1 = thinnest to 5 = heaviest. Income is recorded as thousands earned annually.

a. Calculate the Pearson correlation for these data.

b. Is the correlation statistically significant? Use a two-tailed test with $\alpha = .05$.

Weight (X)	Income (Y)
4	156
3	88
5	49
2	73
1	45
3	92
1	53
5	148

11. Identifying individuals with a high risk of Alzheimer's disease usually involves a long series of cognitive tests. However, researchers have developed a 7-Minute Screen, which is a quick and easy way to accomplish the same goal. The question is whether the 7-Minute Screen is as effective as the complete series of tests. To address this question, Ijuin et al. (2008) administered both tests to a group of patients and compared the results. The following data represent results similar to those obtained in the study.

Patient	7-Minute Screen	Cognitive Series
A	3	11
B	8	19
C	10	22
D	8	20
E	4	14
F	7	13
G	4	9
H	5	20
I	14	25

a. Compute the Pearson correlation to measure the degree of relationship between the two test scores.

b. Is the correlation statistically significant? Use a two-tailed test with $\alpha = .01$.

c. What percentage of variance for the cognitive scores is predicted from the 7-Minute Screen scores? (Compute the value of r^2.)

12. As we have noted in previous chapters, even a very small effect can be significant if the sample is large enough. Suppose, for example, that a researcher obtains a correlation of $r = 0.60$ for a sample of $n = 10$ participants.

a. Is this sample sufficient to conclude that a significant correlation exists in the population? Use a two-tailed test with $\alpha = .05$.

b. If the sample had $n = 25$ participants, is the correlation significant? Again, use a two-tailed test with $\alpha = .05$.

13. A researcher measures three variables, X, Y, and Z, for each individual in a sample of $n = 25$. The Pearson correlations for this sample are $r_{XY} = 0.8$, $r_{XZ} = 0.6$, and $r_{YZ} = 0.7$.

a. Find the partial correlation between X and Y, holding Z constant.

b. Find the partial correlation between X and Z, holding Y constant. (*Hint:* Simply switch the labels for the variables Y and Z to correspond with the labels in the equation.)

14. Problem 9 presented data showing a negative relationship between weight and income for a sample of working women. However, weight was coded in five categories, which could be viewed as an ordinal scale rather than an interval or ratio scale. If so, a Spearman correlation is more appropriate than a Pearson correlation. Convert the weights and the incomes into ranks and compute the Spearman correlation for the scores in problem 9.

15. Problem 23 in Chapter 10 presented data showing that mature soccer players, who have a history of hitting soccer balls with their heads, had significantly lower cognitive scores than mature swimmers, who do not suffer repeated blows to the head. The independent-measures t test produced $t = 2.11$ with $df = 11$ and a value of $r^2 = 0.288$ (28.8%).

a. Convert the data from this problem into a form suitable for the point-biserial correlation (use 1 for the swimmers and 0 for the soccer players), and then compute the correlation.

b. Square the value of the point-biserial correlation to verify that you obtain the same r^2 value that was computed in Chapter 10.

16. Studies have shown that people with high intelligence are generally more likely to volunteer as participants in research, but not for research that involves unusual experiences such as hypnosis. To examine this phenomenon, a researcher administers a questionnaire to a sample of college students. The survey asks for the student's grade point average (as a measure of intelligence) and whether the student would like to take part in a future study in which participants would be hypnotized. The results showed that 7 of the 10 lower-intelligence people were willing to participant but only 2 of the 10 higher-intelligence people were willing.

a. Convert the data to a form suitable for computing the phi-coefficient. (Code the two intelligence categories as 0 and 1 for the X variable, and code the willingness to participate as 0 and 1 for the Y variable.)

b. Compute the phi-coefficient for the data.

17. Sketch a graph showing the line for the equation $Y = -2X + 4$. On the same graph, show the line for $Y = X - 4$.

18. The regression equation is intended to be the "best fitting" straight line for a set of data. What is the criterion for "best fitting"?

19. A set of $n = 20$ pairs of scores (X and Y values) has $SS_X = 16$, $SS_Y = 100$, and $SP = 32$. If the mean for the X values is $M_X = 6$ and the mean for the Y values is $M_Y = 20$,

a. Calculate the Pearson correlation for the scores.

b. Find the regression equation for predicting Y from the X values.

20. A set of $n = 25$ pairs of scores (X and Y values) produces a regression equation of $\hat{Y} = 3X - 2$. Find the predicted Y value for each of the following X scores: 0, 1, 3, -2.

21. For the following set of data,

a. Find the linear regression equation for predicting Y from X.

b. Calculate the standard error of estimate for the regression equation.

X	Y
7	6
9	6
6	3
12	5
9	6
5	4

22. Does the regression equation from problem 21 account for a significant portion of the variance in the Y scores? Use $\alpha = .05$ to evaluate the F-ratio.

23. For the following scores,

X	Y
3	6
6	1
3	4
3	3
5	1

a. Find the regression equation for predicting Y from X.
b. Calculate the predicted Y value for each X.

24. Although you might suspect that dissatisfied people would be the most likely individuals to participate in political activities in an attempt to change things, research tends to show just the opposite. Flavin and Keane (2011) found a positive relationship between life satisfaction and political participation, which included activities such as attending rallies, contributing to candidates, and displaying a yard sign. Following are data similar to those obtained in the study.

Life Satisfaction	Political Participation
5	4
8	7
3	2
6	9
3	5
1	3
4	6
2	4

a. Find the regression equation for predicting political participation from life satisfaction.
b. Using $\alpha = .05$, test the significance of the regression equation.

25. Problem 9 examined the relationship between weight and income for a sample of $n = 10$ women. Weights were classified in five categories and had a mean of $M = 3$ with $SS = 20$. Income, measured in thousands, had a mean score of $M = 66$ with $SS = 7430$, and $SP = -359$.
   a. Find the regression equation for predicting income from weight. (Identify the income scores as X values and the weight scores as Y values.)
   b. What percentage of the variance in the income is accounted for by the regression equation? (Compute the correlation, r, then find r^2.)
   c. Does the regression equation account for a significant portion of the variance in income? Use $\alpha = .05$ to evaluate the F-ratio.

26. There appears to be some evidence suggesting that earlier retirement may lead to memory decline (Rohwedder & Willis, 2010). The researchers gave a memory test to men and women aged 60 to 64 years in several countries that have different retirement ages. For each country, the researchers recorded the average memory score and the percentage of individuals in the 60 to 64 age range who were retired. Note that a higher percentage retired indicates a younger retirement age for that country. The following data are similar to the results from the study. Use the data to find the regression equation for predicting memory scores from the percentage of people aged 60 to 64 who are retired.

Country	% Retired (X)	Memory Score (Y)
Sweden	39	9.3
U.S.A.	48	10.9
England	59	10.7
Germany	70	9.1
Spain	74	6.4
Netherlands	78	9.1
Italy	81	7.2
France	87	7.9
Belgium	88	8.5
Austria	91	9.0

27. The regression equation is computed for a set of $n = 18$ pairs of X and Y values with a correlation of $r = +80$ and $SS_Y = 100$.
   a. Find the standard error of estimate for the regression equation.
   b. How big would the standard error be if the sample size were $n = 38$?

28. a. One set of 20 pairs of scores, X and Y values, produces a correlation of $r = 0.70$. If $SS_Y = 150$, find the standard error of estimate for the regression line.

   b. A second set of 20 pairs of X and Y values produces a correlation of $r = 0.30$. If $SS_Y = 150$, find the standard error of estimate for the regression line.

29. a. A researcher computes the regression equation for a sample of $n = 25$ pairs of scores, X and Y values. If an analysis of regression is used to test the significance of the equation, what are the df values for the F-ratio?

   b. A researcher evaluating the significance of a regression equation obtains an F-ratio with $df = 1, 18$. How many pairs of scores, X and Y values, are in the sample?

CHAPTER

15

The Chi-Square Statistic: Tests for Goodness of Fit and Independence

Tools You Will Need

The following items are considered essential background material for this chapter. If you doubt your knowledge of any of these items, you should review the appropriate chapter or section before proceeding.

• Proportions (math review, Appendix A)
• Frequency distributions (Chapter 2)

aplia

Aplia for *Essentials of Statistics for the Behavioral Sciences*
After reading, go to "Resources" at the end of this chapter for an introduction on how to use Aplia's homework and learning resources.

15.1 PARAMETRIC AND NONPARAMETRIC STATISTICAL TESTS

All of the statistical tests that we have examined thus far are designed to test hypotheses about specific population parameters. For example, we used t tests to assess hypotheses about a population mean (μ) or mean difference ($\mu_1 - \mu_2$). In addition, these tests typically make assumptions about other population parameters. Recall that, for analysis of variance (ANOVA), the population distributions are assumed to be normal and homogeneity of variance is required. Because these tests all concern parameters and require assumptions about parameters, they are called *parametric tests*.

Another general characteristic of parametric tests is that they require a numerical score for each individual in the sample. The scores then are added, squared, averaged, and otherwise manipulated using basic arithmetic. In terms of measurement scales, parametric tests require data from an interval or a ratio scale (see Chapter 1).

Often, researchers are confronted with experimental situations that do not conform to the requirements of parametric tests. In these situations, it may not be appropriate to use a parametric test. Remember that, when the assumptions of a test are violated, the test may lead to an erroneous interpretation of the data. Fortunately, there are several hypothesis-testing techniques that provide alternatives to parametric tests. These alternatives are called *nonparametric tests*.

In this chapter, we introduce two commonly used examples of nonparametric tests. Both tests are based on a statistic known as chi-square and both tests use sample data to evaluate hypotheses about the proportions or relationships that exist within populations. Note that the two chi-square tests, like most nonparametric tests, do not state hypotheses in terms of a specific parameter and they make few (if any) assumptions about the population distribution. For the latter reason, nonparametric tests sometimes are called *distribution-free tests*.

One of the most obvious differences between parametric and nonparametric tests is the type of data they use. All of the parametric tests that we have examined so far require numerical scores. For nonparametric tests, on the other hand, the participants are usually just classified into categories such as Democrat and Republican, or High, Medium, and Low IQ. Note that these classifications involve measurement on nominal or ordinal scales, and they do not produce numerical values that can be used to calculate means and variances. Instead, the data for many nonparametric tests are simply frequencies—for example, the number of Democrats and the number of Republicans in a sample of $n = 100$ registered voters.

Occasionally, you have a choice between using a parametric and a nonparametric test. Changing to a nonparametric test usually involves transforming the data from numerical scores to nonnumerical categories. For example, you could start with numerical scores measuring self-esteem and create three categories consisting of high, medium, and low self-esteem. In most situations, the parametric test is preferred because it is more likely to detect a real difference or a real relationship. However, there are situations for which transforming scores into categories might be a better choice.

1. Occasionally, it is simpler to obtain category measurements. For example, it is easier to classify students as high, medium, or low in leadership ability than to obtain a numerical score measuring each student's ability.

2. The original scores may violate some of the basic assumptions that underlie certain statistical procedures. For example, the t tests and ANOVA assume that the data come from normal distributions. Also, the independent-measures tests assume that the different populations all have the same variance (the homogeneity-of-variance assumption). If a researcher suspects that the data do not satisfy these

assumptions, it may be safer to transform the scores into categories and use a nonparametric test to evaluate the data.

3. The original scores may have unusually high variance. Variance is a major component of the standard error in the denominator of t statistics and the error term in the denominator of F-ratios. Thus, large variance can greatly reduce the likelihood that these parametric tests will find significant differences. Converting the scores to categories essentially eliminates the variance. For example, all individuals fit into three categories (high, medium, and low) no matter how variable the original scores are.

4. Occasionally, an experiment produces an undetermined, or infinite, score. For example, a rat may show no sign of solving a particular maze after hundreds of trials. This animal has an infinite, or undetermined, score. Although there is no absolute number that can be assigned, you can say that this rat is in the highest category, and then classify the other scores according to their numerical values.

15.2   THE CHI-SQUARE TEST FOR GOODNESS OF FIT

Parameters such as the mean and the standard deviation are the most common way to describe a population, but there are situations in which a researcher has questions about the proportions or relative frequencies for a distribution. For example,

How does the number of women lawyers compare with the number of men in the profession?

Of the two leading brands of cola, which is preferred by most Americans?

In the past 10 years, has there been a significant change in the proportion of college students who declare a business major?

The name of the test comes from the Greek letter χ (chi, pronounced "kye"), which is used to identify the test statistic.

Note that each of the preceding examples asks a question about proportions in the population. In particular, we are not measuring a numerical score for each individual. Instead, the individuals are simply classified into categories and we want to know what proportion of the population is in each category. The *chi-square test for goodness of fit* is specifically designed to answer this type of question. In general terms, this chi-square test uses the proportions obtained for sample data to test hypotheses about the corresponding proportions in the population.

DEFINITION

The **chi-square test for goodness of fit** uses sample data to test hypotheses about the shape or proportions of a population distribution. The test determines how well the obtained sample proportions fit the population proportions specified by the null hypothesis.

Recall from Chapter 2 that a frequency distribution is defined as a tabulation of the number of individuals located in each category of the scale of measurement. In a frequency distribution graph, the categories that make up the scale of measurement are listed on the X-axis. In a frequency distribution table, the categories are listed in the first column. With chi-square tests, however, it is customary to present the scale of measurement as a series of boxes, with each box corresponding to a separate category on the scale. The frequency corresponding to each category is simply presented as a number written inside the box. Figure 15.1 shows how the grade distribution for a class of $n = 40$ students can be presented as a graph, a table, or a series of boxes. The scale of measurement for this example consists of five grade categories (A, B, C, D, and F).

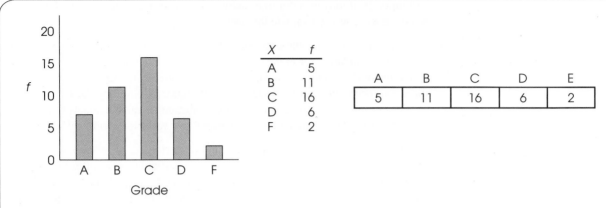

FIGURE 15.1

A distribution of grades for a sample of $n = 40$ students. The same frequency distribution is shown as a bar graph, as a table, and with the frequencies written in a series of boxes.

THE NULL HYPOTHESIS FOR THE GOODNESS-OF-FIT TEST

For the chi-square test of goodness of fit, the null hypothesis specifies the proportion (or percentage) of the population in each category. For example, a hypothesis might state that 50% of all lawyers are men and 50% are women. The simplest way of presenting this hypothesis is to put the hypothesized proportions in the series of boxes representing the scale of measurement:

	Men	Women
H_0:	50%	50%

Although it is conceivable that a researcher could choose any proportions for the null hypothesis, there usually is some well-defined rationale for stating a null hypothesis. Generally H_0 falls into one of the following categories:

1. **No Preference, Equal Proportions.** The null hypothesis often states that there is no preference among the different categories. In this case, H_0 states that the population is divided equally among the categories. For example, a hypothesis stating that there is no preference among the three leading brands of soft drinks would specify a population distribution as follows:

	Brand X	Brand Y	Brand Z
H_0:	$\frac{1}{3}$	$\frac{1}{3}$	$\frac{1}{3}$

(Preferences in the population are equally divided among the three soft drinks.)

The no-preference hypothesis is used in situations in which a researcher wants to determine whether there are any preferences among the categories, or whether the proportions differ from one category to another.

Because the null hypothesis for the goodness-of-fit test specifies an exact distribution for the population, the alternative hypothesis (H_1) simply states that the population distribution has a different shape from that specified in H_0. If the null hypothesis states that the population is equally divided among three categories, then the alternative hypothesis says that the population is not divided equally.

2. **No Difference from a Known Population.** The null hypothesis can state that the proportions for one population are not different from the proportions that are known to exist for another population. For example, suppose it is known that 28% of the licensed drivers in the state are younger than 30 years old and 72% are 30 or older. A researcher might wonder whether this same proportion holds for the distribution of speeding tickets. The null hypothesis would state that tickets are handed out equally across the population of drivers, so there is no difference between the age distribution for drivers and the age distribution for speeding tickets. Specifically, the null hypothesis would be

	Tickets Given to Drivers Younger than 30	Tickets Given to Drivers 30 or Older
H_0:	28%	72%

(Proportions for the population of tickets are not different from proportions for drivers.)

The no-difference hypothesis is used when a specific population distribution is already known. For example, you may have a known distribution from an earlier time, and the question is whether there has been any change in the proportions. Or, you may have a known distribution for one population (drivers) and the question is whether a second population (speeding tickets) has the same proportions.

Again, the alternative hypothesis (H_1) simply states that the population proportions are not equal to the values specified by the null hypothesis. For this example, H_1 would state that the number of speeding tickets is disproportionately high for one age group and disproportionately low for the other.

THE DATA FOR THE GOODNESS-OF-FIT TEST

The data for a chi-square test are remarkably simple. There is no need to calculate a sample mean or SS; you just select a sample of n individuals and count how many are in each category. The resulting values are called *observed frequencies*. The symbol for observed frequency is f_o. For example, the following data represent observed frequencies for a sample of 40 college students. The students were classified into three categories based on the number of times they reported exercising each week.

No Exercise	1 Time a Week	More Than Once a Week
15	19	6

$n = 40$

Notice that each individual in the sample is classified into one and only one of the categories. Thus, the frequencies in this example represent three completely separate groups of students: 15 who do not exercise regularly, 19 who average once a week, and 6 who exercise more than once a week. Also note that the observed frequencies add up to the total sample size: $\Sigma f_o = n$. Finally, you should realize that we are not assigning individuals to categories. Instead, we are simply measuring individuals to determine the category in which they belong.

D E F I N I T I O N

> The **observed frequency** is the number of individuals from the sample who are classi-fied in a particular category. Each individual is counted in one and only one category.

EXPECTED
FREQUENCIES

The general goal of the chi-square test for goodness of fit is to compare the data (the observed frequencies) with the null hypothesis. The problem is to determine how well the data fit the distribution specified in H_0—hence the name *goodness of fit*.

The first step in the chi-square test is to construct a hypothetical sample that represents how the sample distribution would look if it were in perfect agreement with the proportions stated in the null hypothesis. Suppose, for example, the null hypothesis states that the population is distributed in three categories with the following proportions:

	Category A	Category B	Category C
H_0:	25%	50%	25%

(The population is distributed across the three categories with 25% in category A, 50% in category B, and 25% in category C.)

If this hypothesis is correct, how would you expect a random sample of $n = 40$ individuals to be distributed among the three categories? It should be clear that your best strategy is to predict that 25% of the sample would be in category A, 50% would be in category B, and 25% would be in category C. To find the exact frequency expected for each category, multiply the sample size (n) by the proportion (or percentage) from the null hypothesis. For this example, you would expect

$$25\% \text{ of } 40 = 0.25(40) = 10 \text{ individuals in category A}$$

$$50\% \text{ of } 40 = 0.50(40) = 20 \text{ individuals in category B}$$

$$25\% \text{ of } 40 = 0.25(40) = 10 \text{ individuals in category C}$$

The frequency values predicted from the null hypothesis are called *expected fre-quencies*. The symbol for expected frequency is f_e, and the expected frequency for each category is computed by

$$\text{expected frequency} = f_e = pn \qquad (15.1)$$

where p is the proportion stated in the null hypothesis and n is the sample size.

D E F I N I T I O N

> The **expected frequency** for each category is the frequency value that is pre-dicted from the proportions in the null hypothesis and the sample size (n). The expected frequencies define an ideal, *hypothetical* sample distribution that would be obtained if the sample proportions were in perfect agreement with the propor-tions specified in the null hypothesis.

Note that the no-preference null hypothesis always produces equal f_e values for all categories because the proportions (p) are the same for all categories. On the other hand, the no-difference null hypothesis typically does not produce equal values for the expected frequencies because the hypothesized proportions typically vary from one category to another. You also should note that the expected frequen-cies are calculated, hypothetical values and the numbers that you obtain may be decimals or fractions. The observed frequencies, on the other hand, always repre-sent real individuals and always are whole numbers.

THE CHI-SQUARE STATISTIC

The general purpose of any hypothesis test is to determine whether the sample data support or refute a hypothesis about the population. In the chi-square test for goodness of fit, the sample is expressed as a set of observed frequencies (f_o values), and the null hypothesis is represented by a set of expected frequencies (f_e values). The *chi-square statistic* simply measures how well the data (f_o) fit the hypothesis (f_e). The symbol for the chi-square statistic is χ^2. The formula for the chi-square statistic is

$$\text{chi-square} = \chi^2 = \Sigma \frac{(f_o - f_e)^2}{f_e} \tag{15.2}$$

As the formula indicates, the value of chi-square is computed by the following steps:

1. Find the difference between f_o (the data) and f_e (the hypothesis) for each category.

2. Square the difference. This ensures that all values are positive.

3. Next, divide the squared difference by f_e.

4. Finally, add the values from all of the categories.

The first two steps determine the numerator of the chi-square statistic and should be easy to understand. Specifically, the numerator measures how much difference there is between the data (the f_o values) and the hypothesis (represented by the f_e values). The final step is also reasonable: we add the values to obtain the total discrepancy between the data and the hypothesis. Thus, a large value for chi-square indicates that the data do not fit the hypothesis, and leads us to reject the null hypothesis.

However, the third step, which determines the denominator of the chi-square statistic, is not so obvious. Why must we divide by f_e before we add the category values? The answer to this question is that the obtained discrepancy between f_o and f_e is viewed as *relatively* large or *relatively* small depending on the size of the expected frequency. This point is demonstrated in the following analogy.

Suppose that you were going to throw a party and you *expected* 1,000 people to show up. However, at the party you counted the number of guests and *observed* that 1,040 actually showed up. Forty more guests than expected are no major problem when all along you were planning for 1,000. There probably will be enough beer and potato chips for everyone. On the other hand, suppose you had a party and you expected 10 people to attend but instead 50 actually showed up. Forty more guests in this case spell big trouble. How "significant" the discrepancy is depends in part on what you were originally expecting. With very large expected frequencies, allowances are made for more error between f_o and f_e. This is accomplished in the chi-square formula by dividing the squared discrepancy for each category, $(f_o - f_e)^2$, by its expected frequency.

THE CHI-SQUARE DISTRIBUTION AND DEGREES OF FREEDOM

It should be clear from the chi-square formula that the numerical value of chi-square is a measure of the discrepancy between the observed frequencies (data) and the expected frequencies (H_0). As usual, the sample data are not expected to provide a perfectly accurate representation of the population. In this case, the proportions, or observed frequencies, in the sample are not expected to be exactly equal to the proportions in the population. Thus, if there are small discrepancies between the f_o and f_e values, we obtain a small value for chi-square and we conclude that there is a good fit between the data and the hypothesis (fail to reject H_0). However, when there are large discrepancies between f_o and f_e, we obtain a large value for chi-square and conclude that the data do not fit the hypothesis (reject H_0). To decide whether a particular chi-square value is "large" or "small," we must refer to a *chi-square distribution*. This distribution is the set of chi-square values for all of the possible random samples when H_0 is true. Much like other distributions that we have examined (*t* distribution, *F* distribution), the chi-square distribution is a theoretical distribution with well-defined characteristics. Some of these characteristics are easy to infer from the chi-square formula.

1. The formula for chi-square involves adding squared values, so you can never obtain a negative value. Thus, all chi-square values are zero or larger.

2. When H_0 is true, you expect the data (f_o values) to be close to the hypothesis (f_e values). Thus, we expect chi-square values to be small when H_0 is true.

These two factors suggest that the typical chi-square distribution is positively skewed (Figure 15.2). Note that small values, near zero, are expected when H_0 is true and large values (in the right-hand tail) are very unlikely. Thus, unusually large values of chi-square form the critical region for the hypothesis test.

Although the typical chi-square distribution is positively skewed, there is one other factor that plays a role in the exact shape of the chi-square distribution—the number of categories. Recall that the chi-square formula requires that you add values from every category. The more categories you have, the more likely it is that you will obtain a large sum for the chi-square value. On average, chi-square is larger when you are adding values from 10 categories than when you are adding values from only 3 categories. As a result, there is a whole family of chi-square distributions, with the exact shape of each distribution determined by the number of categories used in the study. Technically, each specific chi-square distribution is identified by degrees of freedom (*df*), which are determined by the number of categories. For the goodness-of-fit test, the degrees of freedom are

$$df = C - 1 \tag{15.3}$$

Caution: The *df* for a chi-square test is *not* related to sample size (*n*), as it is in most other tests.

where C is the number of categories. A brief discussion of this *df* formula is presented in Box 15.1. Figure 15.3 shows the general relationship between *df* and the shape of the chi-square distribution. Note that the chi-square values tend to get larger (shift to the right) as the number of categories and the degrees of freedom increase.

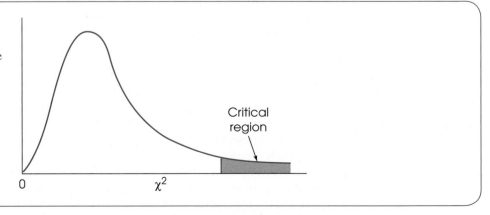

FIGURE 15.2

Chi-square distributions are positively skewed. The critical region is placed in the extreme tail, which reflects large chi-square values.

BOX 15.1 A CLOSER LOOK AT DEGREES OF FREEDOM

Degrees of freedom for the chi-square test literally measure the number of free choices that exist when you are determining the null hypothesis or the expected frequencies. For example, when you are classifying individuals into three categories, you have exactly two free choices in stating the null hypothesis. You may select any two proportions for the first two categories, but then the third proportion is determined. If you hypothesize 25% in the first category and 50% in the second category, then the third category must be 25% to account for 100% of the population.

Category A	Category B	Category C
25%	50%	?

In general, you are free to select proportions for all but one of the categories, but then the final proportion is determined by the fact that the entire set must total 100%. Thus, you have $C - 1$ free choices, where C is the number of categories: degrees of freedom, df, equal $C - 1$.

LOCATING THE CRITICAL REGION FOR A CHI-SQUARE TEST

Recall that a large value for the chi-square statistic indicates a big discrepancy between the data and the hypothesis, and suggests that we reject H_0. To determine whether a particular chi-square value is significantly large, you must consult the table entitled The Chi-Square Distribution (Appendix B). A portion of the chi-square table is shown in Table 15.1. The first column lists df values for the chi-square test, and the other column heads are proportions (alpha levels) in the extreme right-hand tail of the distribution. The numbers in the body of the table are the critical values of chi-square. The table shows, for example, that when the null hypothesis is true and $df = 3$, only 5% ($\alpha = .05$) of the chi-square values are greater than 7.81, and only 1% ($\alpha = .01$) are greater than 11.34. Thus, with $df = 3$, any chi-square value greater than 7.81 has a probability of $p < .05$, and any value greater than 11.34 has a probability of $p < .01$.

FIGURE 15.3

The shape of the chi-square distribution for different values of df. As the number of categories increases, the peak (mode) of the distribution has a larger chi-square value.

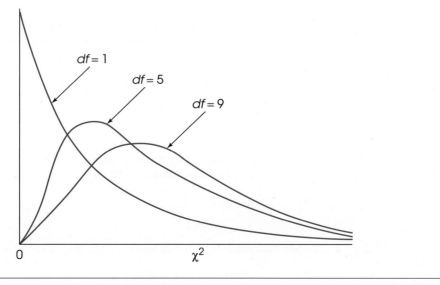

TABLE 15.1

A portion of the table of critical values for the chi-square distribution.

df	Proportion in Critical Region				
	0.10	0.05	0.025	0.01	0.005
1	2.71	3.84	5.02	6.63	7.88
2	4.61	5.99	7.38	9.21	10.60
3	6.25	7.81	9.35	11.34	12.84
4	7.78	9.49	11.14	13.28	14.86
5	9.24	11.07	12.83	15.09	16.75
6	10.64	12.59	14.45	16.81	18.55
7	12.02	14.07	16.01	18.48	20.28
8	13.36	15.51	17.53	20.09	21.96
9	14.68	16.92	19.02	21.67	23.59

EXAMPLE OF THE CHI-SQUARE TEST FOR GOODNESS OF FIT

The following example demonstrates the complete process of hypothesis testing with the goodness-of-fit test.

EXAMPLE 15.1   A psychologist examining art appreciation selected an abstract painting that had no obvious top or bottom. Hangers were placed on the painting so that it could be hung with any one of the four sides at the top. The painting was shown to a sample of $n = 50$ participants, and each was asked to hang the painting in the orientation that looked correct. The following data indicate how many people chose each of the four sides to be placed at the top:

Top up (correct)	Bottom up	Left side up	Right side up
18	17	7	8

The question for the hypothesis test is whether there are any preferences among the four possible orientations. Are any of the orientations selected more (or less) often than would be expected simply by chance?

STEP 1   State the hypotheses and select an alpha level. The hypotheses can be stated as follows:

H_0:   In the general population, there is no preference for any specific orientation. Thus, the four possible orientations are selected equally often, and the population distribution has the following proportions:

Top up (correct)	Bottom up	Left side up	Right side up
25%	25%	25%	25%

H_1:   In the general population, one or more of the orientations is preferred over the others.

We use $\alpha = .05$.

STEP 2   Locate the critical region. For this example, the value for degrees of freedom is

$$df = C - 1 = 4 - 1 = 3$$

For $df = 3$ and $\alpha = .05$, the table of critical values for chi-square indicates that the critical χ^2 has a value of 7.81. The critical region is sketched in Figure 15.4.

STEP 3   Calculate the chi-square statistic. The calculation of chi-square is actually a two-stage process. First, you must compute the expected frequencies from H_0 and then calculate the value of the chi-square statistic. For this example, the null hypothesis specifies that one-quarter of the population ($p = 25\%$) will be in each of the four categories. According to this hypothesis, we should expect one-quarter of the sample to be in each category. With a sample of $n = 50$ individuals, the expected frequency for each category is

Expected frequencies are computed and may be decimal values. Observed frequencies are always whole numbers.

$$f_e = pn = \frac{1}{4}(50) = 12.5$$

The observed frequencies and the expected frequencies are presented in Table 15.2.

Using these values, the chi-square statistic may now be calculated.

$$
\begin{aligned}
\chi^2 &= \Sigma\frac{(f_o - f_e)^2}{f_e} \\
&= \frac{(18-12.5)^2}{12.5} + \frac{(17-12.5)^2}{12.5} + \frac{(7-12.5)^2}{12.5} + \frac{(8-12.5)^2}{12.5} \\
&= \frac{30.25}{12.5} + \frac{20.25}{12.5} + \frac{30.25}{12.5} + \frac{20.25}{12.5} \\
&= 2.42 + 1.62 + 2.42 + 1.62 \\
&= 8.08
\end{aligned}
$$

STEP 4   State a decision and a conclusion. The obtained chi-square value is in the critical region. Therefore, H_0 is rejected, and the researcher may conclude that the four orientations are not equally likely to be preferred. Instead, there are significant differences among the four orientations, with some selected more often and others less often than would be expected by chance.

FIGURE 15.4

For Example 15.1, the critical region begins at a chi-square value of 7.81.

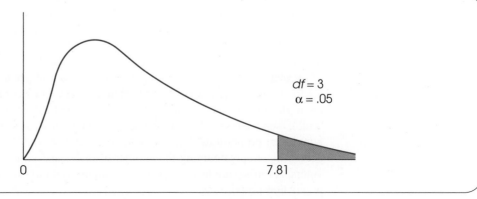

TABLE 15.2

The observed frequencies and the expected frequencies for the chi-square test in Example 15.1.

	Top up (Correct)	Bottom up	Left Side up	Right Side up
Observed Frequencies	18	17	7	8
Expected Frequencies	12.5	12.5	12.5	12.5

IN THE LITERATURE
REPORTING THE RESULTS FOR CHI-SQUARE

APA style specifies the format for reporting the chi-square statistic in scientific journals. For the results of Example 15.1, the report might state:

> The participants showed significant preferences among the four orientations for hanging the painting, $\chi^2(3, n = 50) = 8.08, p < .05$.

Note that the form of the report is similar to that of other statistical tests we have examined. Degrees of freedom are indicated in parentheses following the chi-square symbol. Also contained in the parentheses is the sample size (n). This additional information is important because the degrees of freedom value is based on the number of categories (C), not sample size. Next, the calculated value of chi-square is presented, followed by the probability that a Type I error has been committed. Because we obtained an extreme, very unlikely value for the chi-square statistic, the probability is reported as *less than* the alpha level. Additionally, the report may provide the observed frequencies (f_o) for each category. This information may be presented in a simple sentence or in a table.

GOODNESS OF FIT AND THE SINGLE-SAMPLE *t* TEST

We began this chapter with a general discussion of the difference between parametric tests and nonparametric tests. In this context, the chi-square test for goodness of fit is an example of a nonparametric test; that is, it makes no assumptions about the parameters of the population distribution, and it does not require data from an interval or ratio scale. In contrast, the single-sample *t* test introduced in Chapter 9 is an example of a parametric test: It assumes a normal population, it tests hypotheses about the population mean (a parameter), and it requires numerical scores that can be added, squared, divided, and so on.

Although the chi-square test and the single-sample *t* are clearly distinct, they are also very similar. In particular, both tests are intended to use the data from a single sample to test hypotheses about a single population.

The primary factor that determines whether you should use the chi-square test or the *t* test is the type of measurement that is obtained for each participant. If the sample data consist of numerical scores (from an interval or ratio scale), then it is appropriate to compute a sample mean and use a *t* test to evaluate a hypothesis about the population mean. For example, a researcher could measure the IQ for each individual in a sample of registered voters. A *t* test could then be used to evaluate a hypothesis about the mean IQ for the entire population of registered voters. On the other hand, if the individuals in the sample are classified into nonnumerical categories (on a nominal or ordinal scale), then the researcher would use a chi-square test to evaluate a hypothesis about the population proportions. For example, a researcher could classify people according to gender by simply counting the number of males and females in a sample of registered voters. A chi-square test would then be appropriate to evaluate a hypothesis about the population proportions.

LEARNING CHECK

1. For a chi-square test, the observed frequencies are always whole numbers. (True or false?)

2. For a chi-square test, the expected frequencies are always whole numbers. (True or false?)

3. A researcher has developed three different designs for a computer keyboard. A sample of $n = 60$ participants is obtained, and each individual tests all three keyboards and identifies his or her favorite. The frequency distribution of preferences is as follows:

Design A	Design B	Design C
23	12	25

$n = 60$

    a. What is the *df* value for the chi-square statistic?

    b. Assuming that the null hypothesis states that there are no preferences among the three designs, find the expected frequencies for the chi-square test.

ANSWERS

1. True. Observed frequencies are obtained by counting people in the sample.

2. False. Expected frequencies are computed and may be fractions or decimal values.

3. **a.** $df = 2$

    b. According to the null hypothesis, one-third of the population would prefer each design. The expected frequencies should show one-third of the sample preferring each design. The expected frequencies are all 20.

THE CHI-SQUARE TEST FOR INDEPENDENCE

The chi-square statistic may also be used to test whether there is a relationship between two variables. In this situation, each individual in the sample is measured or classified on two separate variables. For example, Table 15.3 shows the data from a classic experiment demonstrating how eyewitness memory can be influenced by the questions that witnesses are asked (Loftus and Palmer, 1974). In the study, a sample of 150 students watched a film of an automobile accident. After watching the film, the students were separated into three groups and questioned about the accident. One group was asked, "About how fast were the cars going when they smashed into each other?" Another group received the same question except that the verb was changed to "hit" instead of "smashed into." A third group served as a control and was not asked any question about the speed of the two cars. A week later, the participants returned and were asked if they remembered seeing any broken glass in the accident. (There was no broken glass in the film.) Notice that the researchers are manipulating the form of the initial question and then measuring a yes/no response to a follow-up question 1 week later. Table 15.3 shows the structure of this design as a matrix with the independent variable (different groups) determining the rows of the matrix and the two categories for the dependent variable (yes/no) determining the columns. The number in each cell of the matrix is the frequency count showing how many participants are classified in that category. For example, of the 50 students who heard the word *smashed,* there were 16 (32%) who claimed to remember seeing broken glass even though there was none in the film. By comparison, only 7 of the 50 students (14%) who heard the word *hit* said they re-called seeing broken glass. Note that the data consist of frequencies, not scores, from a

TABLE 15.3

A frequency distribution table showing the number of participants who answered either yes or no when asked whether they recalled seeing any broken glass 1 week after witnessing a video of an automobile accident. Immediately after the video, one group was asked how fast the cars were going when they "smashed into" each other. A second group was asked how fast the cars were going when they "hit" each other. A third group served as a control and was not asked about the speed of the cars.

		Response to the Question: Did You See Any Broken Glass?	
		Yes	No
Verb Used to Ask About the Speed of the Cars	Smashed into	16	34
	Hit	7	43
	Control (Not Asked)	6	44

sample. The researchers would like to use the frequencies from the sample to test a hypothesis about the corresponding frequency distribution in the population. Specifically, the researchers would like to know whether the sample data provide enough evidence to conclude that there is a significant relationship between eyewitnesses' memories and the questions they were asked during the initial interview.

You should recognize that the eyewitness study shown in Table 15.3 is an example of experimental research (Chapter 1, page 13). The researchers manipulated an independent variable and controlled other variables by randomly assigning the participants to groups or treatment conditions. However, similar data are often obtained from non-experimental studies. For example, Table 15.4 presents hypothetical data for a sample of $n = 200$ students who have been classified by personality and color preference. The number in each box, or cell, of the matrix indicates the frequency, or number of individuals in that particular group. In Table 15.4, for example, there are 10 students who were classified as introverted and who selected red as their preferred color. To obtain these data, the researcher first selects a random sample of $n = 200$ students. Each student is then given a personality test and is asked to select a preferred color from among the four choices. Note that the classification is based on the measurements for each student; the researcher does not assign students to categories. Once again, the goal is to use the frequencies from the sample to test a hypothesis about the population frequency distribution. Specifically, are these data sufficient to conclude that there is a significant relationship between personality and color preference in the population of students?

The procedure for using sample frequencies to evaluate hypotheses concerning relationships between variables involves another test using the chi-square statistic. In this situation, however, the test is called the *chi-square test for independence*.

DEFINITION

> The **chi-square test for independence** uses the frequency data from a sample to evaluate the relationship between two variables in the population. Each individual in the sample is classified on both of the two variables, creating a two-dimensional frequency-distribution matrix. The frequency distribution for the sample is then used to test hypotheses about the corresponding frequency distribution for the population.

TABLE 15.4

Color preferences according to personality types.

	Red	Yellow	Green	Blue	
Introvert	10	3	15	22	50
Extrovert	90	17	25	18	150
	100	20	40	40	$n = 200$

THE NULL HYPOTHESIS FOR THE CHI-SQUARE TEST FOR INDEPENDENCE

The null hypothesis for the chi-square test for independence states that the two variables being measured are independent; that is, for each individual, the value obtained for one variable is not related to (or influenced by) the value for the second variable. This general hypothesis can be expressed in two different conceptual forms, each viewing the data and the test from slightly different perspectives. The data in Table 15.4 describing color preference and personality are used to present both versions of the null hypothesis.

H_0 **version 1**   For this version of H_0, the data are viewed as a single sample with each individual measured on two variables. The goal of the chi-square test is to evaluate the relationship between the two variables. For the example we are considering, the goal is to determine whether there is a consistent, predictable relationship between personality and color preference. That is, if I know your personality, will it help me to predict your color preference? The null hypothesis states that there is no relationship. The alternative hypothesis, H_1, states that there is a relationship between the two variables.

> H_0: For the general population of students, there is no relationship between color preference and personality.

This version of H_0 demonstrates the similarity between the chi-square test for independence and a correlation. In each case, the data consist of two measurements (X and Y) for each individual, and the goal is to evaluate the relationship between the two variables. The correlation, however, requires numerical scores for X and Y. The chi-square test, on the other hand, simply uses frequencies for individuals classified into categories.

H_0 **version 2**   For this version of H_0, the data are viewed as two (or more) separate samples representing two (or more) populations or treatment conditions. The goal of the chi-square test is to determine whether there are significant differences between the populations. For the example we are considering, the data in Table 15.4 would be viewed as a sample of $n = 50$ introverts (top row) and a separate sample of $n = 150$ extroverts (bottom row). The chi-square test determines whether the distribution of color preferences for introverts is significantly different from the distribution of color preferences for extroverts. From this perspective, the null hypothesis is stated as follows:

> H_0: In the population of students, the distribution of color preferences for introverts has the same shape as the distribution for extroverts. The two distributions have the same proportions.

Notice that the null hypothesis does not say that the two distributions are identical; it simply says that they have the same proportions. For example, if 10% of the introverts prefer yellow, then 10% of the extroverts should also prefer yellow.

The second version of H_0 demonstrates the similarity between the chi-square test and an independent-measures t test (or ANOVA). In each case, the data consist of two (or more) separate samples that are being used to test for differences between two (or more) populations. The t test (or ANOVA) requires numerical scores to compute means and mean differences. However, the chi-square test simply uses frequencies for individuals classified into categories. The null hypothesis for the chi-square test states that the populations have the same proportions (same shape). The alternative hypothesis, H_1, simply states that the populations have different proportions. For the example we are considering, H_1 states that the shape of the distribution of color preferences for introverts is different from the shape of the distribution of color preferences for extroverts.

Equivalence of H_0 version 1 and H_0 version 2   Although we have presented two different statements of the null hypothesis, these two versions are equivalent. The first version of H_0 states that color preference is not related to personality. If this hypothesis is correct, then the distribution of color preferences should not depend on personality. In other words, the distribution of color preferences should have the same proportions for introverts and for extroverts, which is the second version of H_0.

For example, if we found that 60% of the introverts preferred red, then H_0 would predict that we also should find that 60% of the extroverts prefer red. In this case, knowing that an individual prefers red does not help you predict his or her personality. Note that finding the *same proportions* indicates *no relationship*.

On the other hand, if the proportions were different, it would suggest that there is a relationship. For example, if red is preferred by 60% of the extroverts but only 10% of the introverts, then there is a clear, predictable relationship between personality and color preference. (If I know your personality, then I can predict your color preference.) Thus, finding *different proportions* means that there is *a relationship* between the two variables.

DEFINITION

> Two variables are **independent** when there is no consistent, predictable relationship between them. In this case, the frequency distribution for one variable is not dependent on the categories of the second variable. As a result, when two variables are independent, the frequency distribution for one variable has the same shape (same proportions) for all categories of the second variable.

Thus, stating that there is no relationship between two variables (version 1 of H_0) is equivalent to stating that the distributions have equal proportions (version 2 of H_0).

OBSERVED AND EXPECTED FREQUENCIES

The chi-square test for independence uses the same basic logic that was used for the goodness-of-fit test. First, a sample is selected and each individual is classified or categorized. Because the test for independence considers two variables, every individual is classified on both variables, and the resulting frequency distribution is presented as a two-dimensional matrix (see Table 15.4). As before, the frequencies in the sample distribution are called *observed frequencies* and are identified by the symbol f_o.

The next step is to find the expected frequencies, or f_e values, for this chi-square test. As before, the *expected frequencies* define an ideal hypothetical distribution that is in perfect agreement with the null hypothesis. Once the expected frequencies are obtained, we compute a chi-square statistic to determine how well the data (observed frequencies) fit the null hypothesis (expected frequencies).

The easiest way to find the expected frequencies is to begin with the null hypothesis stated in terms of equal proportions. For the example we are considering, the null hypothesis states

H_0:   The frequency distribution of color preference has the same shape (same proportions) for both categories of personality.

To find the expected frequencies, we first determine the overall distribution of color preferences and then apply this distribution to both categories of personality. Table 15.5 shows an empty matrix corresponding to the data from Table 15.4. Notice that the empty matrix includes all of the row totals and column totals from the original sample data. The row totals and column totals are essential for computing the expected frequencies.

TABLE 15.5

An empty frequency distribution matrix showing only the row totals and column totals. (These numbers describe the basic characteristics of the sample from Table 15.4.)

The column totals for the matrix describe the overall distribution of color preferences. For these data, 100 people selected red as their preferred color. Because the total sample consists of 200 people, the proportion selecting red is 100 out of 200, or 50%. The complete set of color preference proportions is as follows:

$$100 \text{ out of } 200 = 50\% \text{ prefer red}$$

$$20 \text{ out of } 200 = 10\% \text{ prefer yellow}$$

$$40 \text{ out of } 200 = 20\% \text{ prefer green}$$

$$40 \text{ out of } 200 = 20\% \text{ prefer blue}$$

The row totals in the matrix define the two samples of personality types. For example, the matrix in Table 15.5 shows a total of 50 introverts (the top row) and a sample of 150 extroverts (the bottom row). According to the null hypothesis, both personality groups should have the same proportions for color preferences. To find the expected frequencies, we simply apply the overall distribution of color preferences to each sample. Beginning with the sample of 50 introverts in the top row, we obtain expected frequencies of

50% prefer red:	$f_e = 50\%$ of $50 = 0.50(50) = 25$
10% prefer yellow:	$f_e = 10\%$ of $50 = 0.10(50) = 5$
20% prefer green:	$f_e = 20\%$ of $50 = 0.20(50) = 10$
20% prefer blue:	$f_e = 20\%$ of $50 = 0.20(50) = 10$

Using exactly the same proportions for the sample of $n = 150$ extroverts in the bottom row, we obtain expected frequencies of

50% prefer red:	$f_e = 50\%$ of $150 = 0.50(50) = 75$
10% prefer yellow:	$f_e = 10\%$ of $150 = 0.10(50) = 15$
20% prefer green:	$f_e = 20\%$ of $150 = 0.20(50) = 30$
20% prefer blue:	$f_e = 20\%$ of $150 = 0.20(50) = 30$

The complete set of expected frequencies is shown in Table 15.6. Notice that the row totals and the column totals for the expected frequencies are the same as those for the original data (the observed frequencies) in Table 15.4.

A simple formula for determining expected frequencies Although expected frequencies are derived directly from the null hypothesis and the sample characteristics, it is not necessary to go through extensive calculations to find f_e values. In fact, there is a simple formula that determines f_e for any cell in the frequency distribution matrix:

$$f_e = \frac{f_c f_r}{n} \tag{15.4}$$

TABLE 15.6

Expected frequencies corresponding to the data in Table 15.4. (This is the distribution predicted by the null hypothesis.)

	Red	Yellow	Green	Blue	
Introvert	25	5	10	10	50
Extrovert	75	15	30	30	150
	100	20	40	40	

where f_c is the frequency total for the column (column total), f_r is the frequency total for the row (row total), and n is the number of individuals in the entire sample. To demonstrate this formula, we compute the expected frequency for introverts selecting yellow in Table 15.6. First, note that this cell is located in the top row and second column in the table. The column total is $f_c = 20$, the row total is $f_r = 50$, and the sample size is $n = 200$. Using these values in formula 15.4, we obtain

$$f_e = \frac{f_c f_r}{n} = \frac{20(50)}{200} = 5$$

This is identical to the expected frequency we obtained using percentages from the overall distribution.

THE CHI-SQUARE STATISTIC AND DEGREES OF FREEDOM

The chi-square test for independence uses exactly the same chi-square formula as the test for goodness of fit:

$$\chi^2 = \Sigma \frac{(f_o - f_e)^2}{f_e}$$

As before, the formula measures the discrepancy between the data (f_o values) and the hypothesis (f_e values). A large discrepancy produces a large value for chi-square and indicates that H_0 should be rejected. To determine whether a particular chi-square statistic is significantly large, you must first determine degrees of freedom (df) for the statistic and then consult the chi-square distribution in Appendix B. For the chi-square test of independence, degrees of freedom are based on the number of cells for which you can freely choose expected frequencies. Recall that the f_e values are partially determined by the sample size (n) and by the row totals and column totals from the original data. These various totals restrict your freedom in selecting expected frequencies. This point is illustrated in Table 15.7. Notice that we have filled in only three of the f_e values in the table. However, these three values determine all of the other expected frequencies. For example, the bottom number in the first column must be 75 to produce a column total of 100. Similarly, the final value in the first row must be 10 to produce a row total of 50. In general, the entire bottom

TABLE 15.7

Degrees of freedom and expected frequencies. (Once three values have been selected, all of the remaining expected frequencies are determined by the row totals and the column totals. This example has only three free choices, so $df = 3$.)

	Red	Yellow	Green	Blue	
	25	5	10	?	50
	?	?	?	?	150
	100	20	40	40	

row and the entire last column are restricted by the row totals and the column totals. As a result, we may freely choose all but one f_e in each row and all but one f_e in each column. If R is the number of rows and C is the number of columns, and you remove the last column and the bottom row from the matrix, you are left with a smaller matrix that has $C - 1$ columns and $R - 1$ rows. This smaller matrix determines the df value. Specifically, the total number of f_e values that you can freely choose is $(R - 1)(C - 1)$, and the degrees of freedom for the chi-square test of independence are given by the formula

$$df = (R - 1)(C - 1) \tag{15.5}$$

Also note that once you calculate the expected frequencies to fill the smaller matrix, the rest of the f_e values can be found by subtraction.

AN EXAMPLE OF THE CHI-SQUARE TEST FOR INDEPENDENCE

The following example demonstrates the complete hypothesis-testing procedure for the chi-square test for independence.

EXAMPLE 15.2

Many parents allow their underage children to drink alcohol in limited situations when an adult is present to supervise. The idea is that teens will learn responsible drinking habits if they first experience alcohol in a controlled environment. Other parents take a strict no-drinking approach with the idea that they are sending a clear message about what is right and what is wrong. Recent research, however, suggests that the more permissive approach may actually result in more negative consequences (McMorris, et al., 2011). In the study, teens who were allowed to drink with their parents were significantly more likely to experience alcohol-related problems than teens who were not allowed to drink. In an attempt to replicate this study, researchers surveyed a sample of 150 students each year from age 14 to 17. The students were asked about their alcohol use and about alcohol-related problems such as binge drinking, fights, and blackouts. The results are shown in Table 15.8. Do the data show a significant relationship between the parents' rules about alcohol and subsequent alcohol-related problems?

STEP 1

State the hypotheses, and select a level of significance. According to the null hypothesis, the two variables are independent. This general hypothesis can be stated in two different ways:

Version 1

H_0: In the general population, there is no relationship between parents' rules for alcohol use and the development of alcohol-related problems.

This version of H_0 emphasizes the similarity between the chi-square test and a correlation.

TABLE 15.8

A frequency distribution showing experience with alcohol-related problems according to parents' rules concerning underage drinking.

	Experience with Alcohol-Related Problems		
	No	Yes	
Not Allowed to Drink	71	9	80
Allowed to Drink	89	31	120
	160	40	$n = 200$

Version 2

> H_0: In the general population, the distribution of alcohol-related problems has the same proportions for teenagers whose parents permit drinking and for those whose parents do not.

The second version of H_0 emphasizes the similarity between the chi-square test and the independent-measures t test.

The alternative hypothesis states that there is a relationship between the two variables (version 1), or that the two distributions are different (version 2). Remember that the two versions for the hypotheses are equivalent. The choice between them is largely determined by how the researcher wants to describe the outcome. For example, a researcher may want to emphasize the *relationship* between variables or the *difference* between groups.

For this test, we use $\alpha = .05$.

STEP 2 Determine the degrees of freedom and locate the critical region. For the chi-square test for independence,

$$df = (R - 1)(C - 1) = (2 - 1)(2 - 1) = 1$$

With $df = 2$ and $\alpha = .05$, the critical value for chi-square is 3.84 (see Table B.6 in Appendix B, p. 581).

STEP 3 Determine the expected frequencies, and compute the chi-square statistic. The following table shows an empty matrix with the same row totals and column totals as the original data. The expected frequencies must maintain the same row totals and column totals, and create an ideal frequency distribution that perfectly represents the null hypothesis. Specifically, the proportions for the group of 80 teens for whom alcohol was not allowed must be the same as the proportions for the group of 120 who were permitted to drink.

	Experience with Alcohol-Related Problems		
	No	Yes	
Not Allowed to Drink			80
Allowed to Drink			120
	160	40	$n = 200$

The column totals describe the overall distribution of alcohol-related problems. These totals indicate that 160 out of 200 participants reported that they did not experience any alcohol-related problems. This proportion corresponds to $\frac{160}{200}$, or 80% of the total sample. Similarly, $\frac{40}{200}$, or 20% reported that they did experience alcohol-related problems. The null hypothesis (version 2) states that these proportions are the same for both groups of participants. Therefore, we simply apply the proportions to each group to obtain the expected frequencies. For the group of 80 teens who were not allowed to drink (top row), we obtain

$$80\% \text{ of } 80 = 64 \text{ expected to experience problems}$$

$$20\% \text{ of } 80 = 16 \text{ expected not to experience problems}$$

For the group of 120 teens who were allowed to drink (bottom row), we expect

80% of 120 = 96 expected to experience problems

20% of 120 = 24 expected not to experience problems

These expected frequencies are summarized in Table 15.9.

The chi-square statistic is now used to measure the discrepancy between the data (the observed frequencies in Table 15.8) and the null hypothesis that was used to generate the expected frequencies in Table 15.9.

$$\chi^2 = \frac{(17-64)^2}{64} = \frac{(9-16)^2}{16} = \frac{(89-96)^2}{96} = \frac{(31-24)^2}{24}$$
$$= 0.766 + 3.063 + 0.510 + 2.042$$
$$= 6.381$$

STEP 4   Make a decision regarding the null hypothesis and the outcome of the study. The obtained chi-square value exceeds the critical value (3.84). Therefore, the decision is to reject the null hypothesis. In the literature, this would be reported as a significant result with $\chi^2(1, n = 200) = 6.381$, $p < .05$. According to version 1 of H_0, this means that we have decided that there is a significant relationship between parents' rules about alcohol and subsequent problems. Expressed in terms of version 2 of H_0, the data show a significant difference in alcohol-related problems between teens whose parents allowed drinking and those whose parents did not. To describe the details of the significant result, you must compare the original data (Table 15.8) with the expected frequencies in Table 15.9. Looking at the two tables, it should be clear that teens whose parents allowed drinking experienced more alcohol-related problems than would be expected if the two variables were independent.

TABLE 15.9

The expected frequencies (f_e values) if experience with alcohol-related problems is completely independent of parents' rules concerning underage drinking.

	Experience with Alcohol-Related Problems		
	No	Yes	
Allowed to Drink	64	16	80
Not Allowed to Drink	96	24	120
	160	40	$n = 200$

THE RELATIONSHIP BETWEEN CHI-SQUARE AND OTHER STATISTICAL PROCEDURES

We have noted that the hypotheses for the chi-square test for independence can be stated in terms of the relationship between variables (version 1) or the difference between groups (version 2). The first version emphasizes the relationship between the chi-square test and the Pearson correlation, and the second version emphasizes the relationship between chi-square and the independent-measures t or ANOVA.

Chi-square and the Pearson correlation   The chi-square test for independence and the Pearson correlation are both intended to evaluate the relationship between two variables. The type of data obtained in a research study determines which of the two statistical procedures is appropriate. Suppose, for example, that a researcher is interested in the relationship between self-esteem and academic performance for 10-year-old children. If the researcher obtained numerical scores for both variables, then the resulting data would be similar to the values shown in Table 15.10(a) and the researcher could use a Pearson correlation to evaluate the relationship. On the other hand, if both variables are classified into non-numerical categories as in Table 15.10(b), then the data consist of frequencies and the relationship could be evaluated with a chi-square test for independence.

Chi-square and the independent-measures t and ANOVA   Once again, consider a researcher investigating the relationship between self-esteem and academic performance for 10-year-old children. This time, suppose that the researcher measured academic performance by simply classifying individuals into two categories, high and low, and then obtained a numerical score for each individual's self-esteem. The resulting data would be similar to the scores in Table 15.11(a), and an independent-measures t test would be used to evaluate the mean difference between the two groups of scores. Alternatively, the researcher could measure self-esteem by classifying individuals into three categories: high, medium, and low. If a numerical score is then obtained for each individual's academic performance, the resulting data would look like the scores in Table 15.11(b), and an ANOVA would be used to evaluate the mean differences among the three groups. Finally, if both variables are classified into non-numerical categories, then the data would look like the scores shown earlier in Table 15.10(b) and a chi-square test for independence would be used to evaluate the difference between the two academic-performance groups or the differences among the three self-esteem groups.

The point of these examples is that the chi-square test for independence, the Pearson correlation, and tests for mean differences can all be used to evaluate the relationship between two variables. One main distinction among the different statistical procedures is the form of the data. However, another distinction is the fundamental purpose of these different statistics. The chi-square test and the tests for mean differences (t and ANOVA) evaluate the *significance* of the relationship; that is, they determine whether the relationship observed in the sample provides enough evidence to conclude that there is a corresponding relationship in the population. You can also evaluate the significance of a Pearson correlation; however, the main purpose of a correlation is to measure the *strength* of the relationship. In particular, squaring the correlation, r^2, provides a measure of effect size, describing the proportion of variance in one variable that is accounted for by its relationship with the other variable.

TABLE 15.10

Two possible data structures for research studies examining the relationship between self-esteem and academic performance. In part (a), there are numerical scores for both variables and the data are suitable for a correlation. In part (b), both variables are classified into categories and the data are frequencies suitable for a chi-square test.

(a)

Participant	Self-Esteem X	Academic Performance Y
A	13	73
B	19	88
C	10	71
D	22	96
E	20	90
F	15	82

(b)

Academic Performance		Level of Self-Esteem			
		High	Medium	Low	
	High	17	32	11	60
	Low	13	43	34	90
		30	75	45	$n = 150$

TABLE 15.11

Data appropriate for an independent-measures *t* test or an ANOVA. In part (a), self-esteem scores are obtained for two groups of students differing in level of academic performance. In part (b), academic performance scores are obtained for three groups of students differing in level of self-esteem.

(a) Self-esteem scores for two groups of students.

Academic Performance	
High	Low
17	13
21	15
16	14
24	20
18	17
15	14
19	12
20	19
18	16

(b) Academic performance scores for three groups of students.

Self-Esteem		
High	Medium	Low
94	83	80
90	76	72
85	70	81
84	81	71
89	78	77
96	88	70
91	83	78
85	80	72
88	82	75

LEARNING CHECK

1. A researcher would like to know which factors are most important to people who are buying a new car. A sample of $n = 200$ customers between the ages of 20 and 29 are asked to identify the most important factor in the decision process: Performance, Reliability, or Style. The researcher would like to know whether there is a difference between the factors identified by women compared to those identified by men. The data are as follows:

Observed Frequencies of Most Important Factor According to Gender

	Performance	Reliability	Style	Totals
Male	21	33	26	80
Female	19	67	34	120
Totals	40	100	60	

   a. State the null hypotheses.

   b. Determine the value for *df* for the chi-square test.

   c. Compute the expected frequencies.

ANSWERS

1. a. H_0: In the population, the distribution of preferred factors for men has the same proportions as the distribution for women.

   b. $df = 2$

   c. f_e values are as follows:

Expected frequencies

	Performance	Reliability	Style
Male	16	40	24
Female	24	60	36

15.4 **MEASURING EFFECT SIZE FOR THE CHI-SQUARE TEST FOR INDEPENDENCE**

A hypothesis test, like the chi-square test for independence, evaluates the statistical significance of the results from a research study. Specifically, the intent of the test is to determine whether it is likely that the patterns or relationships observed in the sample data could have occurred without any corresponding patterns or relationships in the population. Tests of significance are influenced not only by the size or strength of the treatment effects but also by the size of the samples. As a result, even a small effect can be statistically significant if it is observed in a very large sample. Because a significant effect does not necessarily mean a large effect, it is generally recommended that the outcome of a hypothesis test be accompanied by a measure of the effect size. This general recommendation also applies to the chi-square test for independence.

THE PHI-COEFFICIENT AND CRAMÉR'S V

In Chapter 14 (p. 480), we introduced the *phi-coefficient* as a measure of correlation for data consisting of two dichotomous variables (both variables have exactly two values). This same situation exists when the data for a chi-square test for independence form a 2×2 matrix (again, each variable has exactly two values). In this case, it is possible to compute the correlation phi (ϕ) in addition to the chi-square hypothesis test for the same set of data. Because phi is a correlation, it measures the strength of the relationship, rather than the significance, and thus provides a measure of effect size. The value for the phi-coefficient can be computed directly from chi-square by the following formula:

Caution: The value of χ^2 is already a squared value. Do not square it again.

$$\phi = \sqrt{\frac{\chi^2}{n}}$$ (15.6)

The value of the phi-coefficient is determined entirely by the *proportions* in the 2×2 data matrix and is completely independent of the absolute size of the frequencies. The chi-square value, however, is influenced by the proportions and by the size of the frequencies. This distinction is demonstrated in the following example.

EXAMPLE 15.3

The following data show a frequency distribution evaluating the relationship between gender and preference between two candidates for student president.

	Candidate	
	A	B
Male	5	10
Female	10	5

Note that the data show that males prefer candidate B by a 2-to-1 margin and females prefer candidate A by 2 to 1. Also note that the sample includes a total of 15 males and 15 females. We will not perform all the arithmetic here, but these data produce chi-square equal to 3.33 (which is not significant) and a phi-coefficient of 0.333.

Next we keep exactly the same proportions in the data, but double all of the frequencies. The resulting data are as follows:

	Candidate	
	A	B
Male	10	20
Female	20	10

Once again, males prefer candidate B by 2 to 1 and females prefer candidate A by 2 to 1. However, the sample now contains 30 males and 30 females. For these new data, the value of chi-square is 6.66, twice as big as it was before (and now significant with $\alpha = .05$), but the value of the phi-coefficient is still 0.333.

Because the proportions are the same for the two samples, the value of the phi-coefficient is unchanged. However, the larger sample provides more convincing evidence than the smaller sample, so the larger sample is more likely to produce a significant result.

The interpretation of ϕ follows the same standards used to evaluate a correlation (Table 9.3, p. 264 shows the standards for squared correlations): a correlation of 0.10 is a small effect, 0.30 is a medium effect, and 0.50 is a large effect. Occasionally, the value of ϕ is squared (ϕ^2) and is reported as a percentage of variance accounted for, exactly the same as r^2.

When the chi-square test involves a matrix larger than 2×2, a modification of the phi-coefficient, known as *Cramér's V*, can be used to measure effect size.

$$V = \sqrt{\frac{\chi^2}{n(df^*)}}$$

(15.7)

Note that the formula for Cramér's V (15.7) is identical to the formula for the phi-coefficient (15.6) except for the addition of df^* in the denominator. The df^* value is *not* the same as the degrees of freedom for the chi-square test, but it is related. Recall that the chi-square test for independence has $df = (R - 1)(C - 1)$, where R is the number of rows in the table and C is the number of columns. For Cramér's V, the value of df^* is the smaller of either $(R - 1)$ or $(C - 1)$.

Cohen (1988) has also suggested standards for interpreting Cramér's V that are shown in Table 15.12. Note that when $df^* = 1$, as in a 2×2 matrix, the criteria for interpreting V are exactly the same as the criteria for interpreting a regular correlation or a phi-coefficient.

In a research report, the measure of effect size appears immediately after the results of the hypothesis test. For the study in Example 15.2, for example, we obtained $\chi^2 = 6.381$ for a sample of $n = 200$ participants. Because the data form a 2×2 matrix, the phi-coefficient is the appropriate measure of effect size and the data produce

$$\phi = \sqrt{\frac{\chi^2}{n}} = \sqrt{\frac{6.381}{200}} = 0.179$$

For these data, the results from the hypothesis test and the measure of effect size would be reported as follows:

The results showed a significant relationship between parents' rules about alcohol and subsequent alcohol-related problems, $\chi^2(1, n = 200) = 6.381$, $p < .05$, $\phi = 0.179$. Specifically, teenagers whose parents allowed supervised drinking were more likely to experience problems.

TABLE 15.12

Standards for interpreting Cramér's V as proposed by Cohen (1988).

	Small Effect	Medium Effect	Large Effect
For $df^* = 1$	0.10	0.30	0.50
For $df^* = 2$	0.07	0.21	0.35
For $df^* = 3$	0.06	0.17	0.29

15.5 ASSUMPTIONS AND RESTRICTIONS FOR CHI-SQUARE TESTS

To use a chi-square test for goodness of fit or a test of independence, several conditions must be satisfied. For any statistical test, violation of assumptions and restrictions casts doubt on the results. For example, the probability of committing a Type I error may be distorted when assumptions of statistical tests are not satisfied. Some important assumptions and restrictions for using chi-square tests are the following:

1. **Independence of Observations.** This is *not* to be confused with the concept of independence between *variables,* as seen in the chi-square test for independence (Section 15.3). One consequence of independent observations is that each observed frequency is generated by a different individual. A chi-square test would be inappropriate if a person could produce responses that can be classified in more than one category or contribute more than one frequency count to a single category. (See p. 220 for more information on independence.)

2. **Size of Expected Frequencies.** A chi-square test should not be performed when the expected frequency of any cell is less than 5. The chi-square statistic can be distorted when f_e is very small. Consider the chi-square computations for a single cell. Suppose that the cell has values of $f_e = 1$ and $f_o = 5$. Note that there is a 4-point difference between the observed and expected frequencies. However, the total contribution of this cell to the total chi-square value is

$$\text{cell} = \frac{\left(f_o - f_e\right)^2}{f_e} = \frac{(5-1)^2}{1} = \frac{4^2}{1} = 16$$

Now consider another instance, in which $f_e = 10$ and $f_o = 14$. The difference between the observed and the expected frequencies is still 4, but the contribution of this cell to the total chi-square value differs from that of the first case:

$$\text{cell} = \frac{\left(f_o - f_e\right)^2}{f_e} = \frac{(14-10)^2}{10} = \frac{4^2}{10} = 1.6$$

It should be clear that a small f_e value can have a great influence on the chi-square value. This problem becomes serious when f_e values are less than 5. When f_e is very small, what would otherwise be a minor discrepancy between f_o and f_e results in large chi-square values. The test is too sensitive when f_e values are extremely small. One way to avoid small expected frequencies is to use large samples.

1. A researcher completes a chi-square test for independence and obtains $\chi^2 = 6.2$ for a sample of $n = 40$ participants.

   a. If the frequency data formed a 2×2 matrix, what is the phi-coefficient for the test?

   b. If the frequency data formed a 3×3 matrix, what is Cramér's V for the test?

2. Explain why a very small value for an expected frequency can distort the results of a chi-square test.

ANSWERS

1. **a.** $\phi = 0.394$

   b. $V = 0.278$

2. With a very small value for an expected frequency, even a minor discrepancy between the observed frequency and the expected frequency can produce a large number that is added into the chi-square statistic. This inflates the value of chi-square and can distort the outcome of the test.

SUMMARY

1. Chi-square tests are nonparametric techniques that test hypotheses about the form of the entire frequency distribution. Two types of chi-square tests are the test for goodness of fit and the test for independence. The data for these tests consist of the frequency of, or number of individuals who are located in, each category.

2. The test for goodness of fit compares the frequency distribution for a sample to the population distribution that is predicted by H_0. The test determines how well the observed frequencies (sample data) fit the expected frequencies (data predicted by H_0).

3. The expected frequencies for the goodness-of-fit test are determined by

$$\text{expected frequency} = f_e = pn$$

where p is the hypothesized proportion (according to H_0) of observations falling into a category and n is the size of the sample.

4. The chi-square statistic is computed by

$$\text{chi-square} = \chi^2 = \Sigma \frac{(f_o - f_e)^2}{f_e}$$

where f_o is the observed frequency for a particular category and f_e is the expected frequency for that category. Large values for χ^2 indicate that there is a large discrepancy between the observed (f_o) and the expected (f_e) frequencies and may warrant rejection of the null hypothesis.

5. Degrees of freedom for the test for goodness of fit are

$$df = C - 1$$

where C is the number of categories.

6. The chi-square distribution is positively skewed and begins at the value of zero. Its exact shape is determined by degrees of freedom.

7. The test for independence evaluates the relationship between two variables using the same chi-square formula as the test for goodness of fit. The null hypothesis states that the two variables in question are independent of each other. That is, the frequency distribution for one variable does not depend on the categories of the second variable.

8. For the test for independence, the expected frequencies for H_0 can be directly calculated from the marginal frequency totals,

$$f_e = \frac{f_c f_r}{n}$$

where f_c is the total column frequency and f_r is the total row frequency for the cell in question.

9. Degrees of freedom for the test for independence are computed by

$$df = (R - 1)(C - 1)$$

where R is the number of row categories and C is the number of column categories.

10. The chi-square statistic is distorted when f_e values are very small. Chi-square tests, therefore, should not be performed when the expected frequency of any cell is less than 5.

11. The effect size for a chi-square test for independence is measured by computing a phi-coefficient for data that form a 2×2 matrix or computing Cramér's V for a matrix that is larger than 2×2.

$$\text{phi} = \sqrt{\frac{\chi^2}{n}} \quad \text{Cramér's } V = \sqrt{\frac{\chi^2}{n(df^*)}}$$

where df^* is the smaller of $(R - 1)$ and $(C - 1)$. Both phi and Cramér's V are evaluated using the criteria in Table 15.12.

KEY TERMS

parametric test (p. 510)

nonparametric test (p. 510)

distribution-free tests (p. 510)

chi-square test for goodness-of-fit (p. 511)

observed frequencies (p. 513)

expected frequencies (p. 514)

chi-square statistic (p. 515)

chi-square distribution (p. 516)

chi-square test for independence (p. 522)

phi-coefficient (p. 532)

Cramér's V (p. 533)

RESOURCES

 Go to CengageBrain.com to access Psychology CourseMate, where you will find an interactive eBook, glossaries, flashcards, quizzes, statistics workshops, and more.

 aplia

If your professor has assigned Aplia:

1. Sign in to your account.
2. Complete the corresponding exercises as required by your professor.
3. When finished, click "Grade It Now" to see which areas you have mastered, which areas need more work, and detailed explanations of every answer.

SPSS

General instructions for using SPSS are presented in Appendix D. Following are detailed instructions for using SPSS to perform **The Chi-Square Tests for Goodness of Fit and for Independence** that are presented in this chapter.

The Chi-Square Test for Goodness of Fit

Data Entry

1. Enter the set of observed frequencies in the first column of the SPSS data editor. If there are four categories, for example, enter the four observed frequencies.

2. In the second column, enter the numbers 1, 2, 3, and so on, so that there is a number beside each of the observed frequencies in the first column.

Data Analysis

1. Click **Data** on the tool bar at the top of the page and select **weight cases** at the bottom of the list.

2. Click the **Weight cases by** circle, then highlight the label for the column containing the observed frequencies (VAR00001) on the left and move it into the **Frequency Variable** box by clicking on the arrow.

3. Click **OK.**

4. Click **Analyze** on the tool bar, select **Nonparametric Tests,** and click on **One-Sample.**

5. Click the **Settings** tab on the top of the next page, choose **Customize,** and select Chi-Square.

6. Click on **Options** and set the expected probabilities to all equal or customized values. Enter the expected probabilities if they are different values.

7. Click **OK.**

8. Click **Run.**

SPSS Output

The program produces a table reporting either a significant or a not significant result and gives the p value or α level for the test. It does not report a value for the chi-square statistic.

The Chi-Square Test for Independence

Data Entry

1. Enter the complete set of observed frequencies in one column of the SPSS data editor (VAR00001).

2. In a second column, enter a number (1, 2, 3, etc.) that identifies the row corresponding to each observed frequency. For example, enter a 1 beside each observed frequency that came from the first row.

3. In a third column, enter a number (1, 2, 3, etc.) that identifies the column corresponding to each observed frequency. Each value from the first column gets a 1, and so on.

Data Analysis

1. Click **Data** on the tool bar at the top of the page and select **weight cases** at the bottom of the list.

2. Click the **Weight cases by** circle, then highlight the label for the column containing the observed frequencies (VAR00001) on the left and move it into the **Frequency Variable** box by clicking on the arrow.

3. Click **OK.**

4. Click **Analyze** on the tool bar at the top of the page, select **Descriptive Statistics,** and click on **Crosstabs.**

5. Highlight the label for the column containing the rows (VAR00002) and move it into the **Rows** box by clicking on the arrow.

6. Highlight the label for the column containing the columns (VAR00003) and move it into the **Columns** box by clicking on the arrow.

7. Click on **Statistics,** select **Chi-Square,** and click **Continue.**

8. Click **OK.**

SPSS Output

We used SPSS to conduct the chi-square test for independence for the data in Example 15.2, examining the relationship between parents' rules concerning teenage drinking and subsequent alcohol-related problems, and the output is shown in Figure 15.5. The first table in the output simply lists the variables and is not shown in the figure. The **Crosstabulation** table simply shows the matrix of observed frequencies. The final table, labeled **Chi-Square Tests,** reports the results. Focus on the top row, the **Pearson**

VAR00002 * VAR00003 Crosstabulation

Count

		VAR00003		Total
		1.00	2.00	
VAR00002	1.00	71	9	80
	2.00	89	31	120
Total		160	40	200

Chi-Square Tests

	Value	df	Asymp. Sig. (2-sided)	Exact Sig. (2-sided)	Exact Sig. (1-sided)
Pearson Chi-Square	6.380[a]	1	.012		
Continuity Correction[b]	5.501	1	.019		
Likelihood Ratio	6.774	1	.009		
Fisher's Exact Test				.012	.008
Linear-by-Linear Association	6.348	1	.012		
N of Valid Cases	200				

a. 0 cells (.0%) have expected count less than 5. The minimum expected count is 16.00.
b. Computed only for a 2x2 table

FIGURE 15.5

The SPSS output for the chi-square test for independence in Example 15.2.

Chi-Square, which reports the calculated chi-square value, the degrees of freedom, and the level of significance (the *p* value, or the alpha level, for the test).

FOCUS ON PROBLEM SOLVING

1. The expected frequencies that you calculate must satisfy the constraints of the sample. For the goodness-of-fit test, $\Sigma f_e = \Sigma f_o = n$. For the test for independence, the row totals and column totals for the expected frequencies should be identical to the corresponding totals for the observed frequencies.

2. It is entirely possible to have fractional (decimal) values for expected frequencies. Observed frequencies, however, are always whole numbers.

3. Whenever $df = 1$, the difference between observed and expected frequencies $(f_o = f_e)$ is identical (the same value) for all cells. This makes the calculation of chi-square easier.

4. Although you are advised to compute expected frequencies for all categories (or cells), you should realize that it is not essential to calculate all f_e values separately. Remember that df for chi-square identifies the number of f_e values that are free to vary. Once you have calculated that number of f_e values, the remaining f_e values are determined. You can get these remaining values by subtracting the calculated f_e values from their corresponding row or column totals.

5. Remember that, unlike previous statistical tests, the degrees of freedom (*df*) for a chi-square test are *not* determined by the sample size (*n*). Be careful!

DEMONSTRATION 15.1

TEST FOR INDEPENDENCE

A manufacturer of watches would like to examine preferences for digital versus analog watches. A sample of $n = 200$ people is selected, and these individuals are classified by age and preference. The manufacturer would like to know whether there is a relationship between age and watch preference. The observed frequencies (f_o) are as follows:

	Digital	Analog	Undecided	Totals
Younger than 30	90	40	10	140
30 or Older	10	40	10	60
Column Totals	100	80	20	$n = 200$

STEP 1 State the hypotheses, and select an alpha level.   The null hypothesis states that there is no relationship between the two variables.

H_0: Preference is independent of age. That is, the frequency distribution of preferences has the same form for people younger than 30 as for people 30 or older.

The alternative hypothesis states that there is a relationship between the two variables.

H_1: Preference is related to age. That is, the type of watch preferred depends on a person's age.

We set alpha to $\alpha = .05$.

STEP 2 Locate the critical region. Degrees of freedom for the chi-square test for independence are determined by

$$df = (C - 1)(R - 1)$$

For these data,

$$df = (3 - 1)(2 - 1) = 2(1) = 2$$

For $df = 2$ with $\alpha = .05$, the critical chi-square value is 5.99. Thus, our obtained chi-square must exceed 5.99 to be in the critical region and to reject H_0.

STEP 3 Compute the test statistic. Two calculations are required: finding the expected frequencies and calculating the chi-square statistic.

Expected frequencies, f_e. For the test for independence, the expected frequencies can be found using the column totals (f_c), the row totals (f_r), and the following formula:

$$f_e = \frac{f_c f_r}{n}$$

For people younger than 30, we obtain the following expected frequencies:

$$f_e = \frac{100(140)}{200} = \frac{14,000}{200} = 70 \text{ for digital}$$

$$f_e = \frac{80(140)}{200} = \frac{11,200}{200} = 56 \text{ for analog}$$

$$f_e = \frac{20(140)}{200} = \frac{2800}{200} = 14 \text{ for undecided}$$

For individuals 30 or older, the expected frequencies are as follows:

$$f_e = \frac{100(60)}{200} = \frac{6000}{200} = 30 \text{ for digital}$$

$$f_e = \frac{80(60)}{200} = \frac{4800}{200} = 24 \text{ for analog}$$

$$f_e = \frac{20(60)}{200} = \frac{1200}{200} = 6 \text{ for undecided}$$

The following table summarizes the expected frequencies:

	Digital	Analog	Undecided
Younger than 30	70	56	14
30 or Older	30	24	6

The chi-square statistic. The chi-square statistic is computed from the formula

$$\chi^2 = \Sigma \frac{(f_o - f_e)^2}{f_e}$$

The following table summarizes the calculations:

Cell	f_o	f_e	$(f_o - f_e)$	$(f_o - f_e)^2$	$(f_o - f_e)^2/f_e$
Younger than 30—digital	90	70	20	400	5.71
Younger than 30—analog	40	56	−16	256	4.57
Younger than 30—undecided	10	14	−4	16	1.14
30 or older—digital	10	30	−20	400	13.33
30 or older—analog	40	24	16	256	10.67
30 or older—undecided	10	6	4	16	2.67

Finally, add the values in the last column to get the chi-square statistic.

$$\chi^2 = 5.71 + 4.57 + 1.14 + 13.33 + 10.67 + 2.67$$

$$= 38.09$$

STEP 4 Make a decision about H_0, and state the conclusion. The chi-square value is in the critical region. Therefore, we reject the null hypothesis. There is a relationship between watch preference and age, $\chi^2(2, n = 200) = 38.09, p < .05$.

DEMONSTRATION 15.2

EFFECT SIZE WITH CRAMÉR'S *V*

Because the data matrix is larger than 2 × 2, we compute Cramér's *V* to measure effect size.

$$\text{Cramér's } V = \sqrt{\frac{\chi^2}{n(df^*)}} = \sqrt{\frac{38.09}{200(1)}} = \sqrt{0.19} = 0.436$$

PROBLEMS

1. Parametric tests (such as *t* or ANOVA) differ from nonparametric tests (such as chi-square) primarily in terms of the assumptions they require and the data they use. Explain these differences.

2. Güven, Elaimis, Binokay, and Tan (2003) studied the distribution of paw preferences in rats using a computerized food-reaching test. For a sample of $n = 144$ rats, they found 104 right-handed animals. Is this significantly different from what would be expected if right- and left-handed rats are equally common in the population? Test with $\alpha = .01$.

3. In Chapter 9 (p. 257), we described a study showing that newborn infants spend more time looking at attractive faces when they are shown together with less attractive faces (Slater, et al., 1998). In the study, a pair of faces is shown on a screen and the researchers record the amount of time the baby spends looking at each face. In a sample of $n = 40$ infants, suppose that 26 spent the majority of their time looking at the more attractive face and only 14 spent the majority of time looking at the unattractive face. Is this result significantly different from what would be expected if there were no preference between the two faces? Test with $\alpha = .05$.

4. Data from the department of motor vehicles indicate that 80% of all licensed drivers are older than age 25.

a. In a sample of $n = 60$ people who recently received speeding tickets, 38 were older than 25 years and the other 22 were age 25 or younger. Is the age distribution for this sample significantly different from the distribution for the population of licensed drivers? Use $\alpha = .05$.

b. In a sample of $n = 60$ people who recently received parking tickets, 43 were older than 25 years and the other 17 were age 25 or younger. Is the age distribution for this sample significantly different from the distribution for the population of licensed drivers? Use $\alpha = .05$.

5. Research has demonstrated that people tend to be attracted to others who are similar to themselves. One study demonstrated that individuals are disproportionately more likely to marry those with surnames that begin with the same letter as their own (Jones, Pelham, Carvallo, & Mirenberg, 2004). The researchers began by looking at marriage records and recording the surname for each groom and the maiden name of each bride. From these records it is possible to calculate the probability of randomly matching a bride and a groom whose last names begin with the same letter. Suppose that this probability is only 6.5%. Next, a sample of $n = 200$ married couples is selected and the number who shared the same last initial at the time they were married is counted. The resulting observed frequencies are as follows:

Same Initial	Different Initials	
19	181	200

Do these data indicate that the number of couples with the same last initial is significantly different than would be expected if couples were matched randomly? Test with $\alpha = .05$.

6. Suppose that the researcher from the previous problem repeated the study of married couples' initials using twice as many participants and obtaining observed frequencies that exactly double the original values. The resulting data are as follows:

Same Initial	Different Initials	
38	362	400

a. Use a chi-square test to determine whether the number of couples with the same last initial is significantly different than would be expected if couples were matched randomly. Test with $\alpha = .05$.

b. You should find that the data lead to rejecting the null hypothesis. However, in problem 5 the decision was fail to reject. How do you explain the fact that the two samples have the same proportions but lead to different conclusions?

7. A normal distribution is a common assumption underlying many statistical tests. Although the assumption is usually not important, it is possible to test whether it is plausible. Specifically, the unit normal table lists proportions for individual sections of a normal distribution, and a chi-square test for goodness of fit can be used to evaluate whether a specific distribution fits the proportions. For example, if a normal distribution is divided into sections using z-score values, then proportions in each section should be as follows:

$z < -1.5$	$-1.5 < z$ < -0.5	$-0.5 < z$ < 0.5	$0.5 < z$ < 1.5	$z > 1.5$
6.68%	24.17%	38.30%	24.17%	6.68%

Use these proportions to test whether the following sample of $n = 90$ scores is significantly different from a normal distribution. Test with $\alpha = .05$.

$z < -1.5$	$-1.5 < z$ < -0.5	$-0.5 < z <$ 0.5	$0.5 < z$ < 1.5	$z > 1.5$
8	19	31	23	9

8. Automobile insurance is much more expensive for teenage drivers than for older drivers. To justify this cost difference, insurance companies claim that the younger drivers are much more likely to be involved in costly accidents. To test this claim, a researcher obtains information about registered drivers from the department of motor vehicles (DMV) and selects a sample of $n = 300$ accident reports from the police department. The DMV reports the percentage of registered drivers in each age category as follows: 16% are younger than age 20; 28% are 20 to 29 years old; and 56% are age 30 or older. The number of accident reports for each age group is as follows:

Under age 20	Age 20–29	Age 30 or older
68	92	140

a. Do the data indicate that the distribution of accidents for the three age groups is significantly different from the distribution of drivers? Test with $\alpha = .05$.

b. Write a sentence demonstrating how the outcome of the hypothesis test would appear in a research report.

9. The color red is often associated with anger and male dominance. Based on this observation, Hill and Barton (2005) monitored the outcome of four combat sports (boxing, tae kwan do, Greco-Roman wrestling, and freestyle wrestling) during the 2004 Olympic games and found that participants wearing red outfits won significantly more often than those wearing blue.

   a. In 50 wrestling matches involving red versus blue, suppose that the red outfit won 31 times and lost 19 times. Is this result sufficient to conclude that red wins significantly more than would be expected by chance? Test at the .05 level of significance.

   b. In 100 matches, suppose red won 62 times and lost 38. Is this sufficient to conclude that red wins significantly more than would be expected by chance? Again, use $\alpha = .05$.

   c. Note that the winning percentage for red uniforms in part a is identical to the percentage in part b (31 out of 50 is 62%, and 62 out of 100 is also 62%). Although the two samples have an identical winning percentage, one is significant and the other is not. Explain why the two samples lead to different conclusions.

10. Research suggests that romantic background music increases the likelihood that a woman will give her phone number to a man she has just met (Guéguen & Jacob, 2010). In the study, women spent time in a waiting room with background music playing. In one condition, the music was a popular love song and for the other condition the music was a neutral song. The participant was then moved to another room in which she was instructed to discuss two food products with a young man. The men were part of the study and were selected because they had been rated as average in attractiveness. The experimenter returned to end the study and asked the pair to wait alone for a few minutes. During this time, the man used a scripted line to ask the woman for her phone number. The following table presents data similar to those obtained in the study, showing the number of women who did or did not give their numbers for each music condition.

	Phone Number	No Number	
Romantic Music	21	19	40
Neutral Music	9	31	40
	30	50	

   Is there a significant difference between the two types of music? Test with $\alpha = .05$.

11. Mulvihill, Obuseh, and Caldwell (2008) conducted a survey evaluating healthcare providers' perception of a new state children's insurance program. One question asked the providers whether they viewed the reimbursement from the new insurance as higher, lower, or the same as private insurance. Another question assessed the providers' overall satisfaction with the new insurance. The following table presents observed frequencies similar to the study results.

	Satisfied	Not Satisfied	
Less Reimbursement	46	54	100
Same or More Reimbursement	42	18	60
	88	72	

   Do the results indicate that the providers' satisfaction of the new program is related to their perception of the reimbursement rates? Test with $\alpha = .05$.

12. Research has demonstrated strong gender differences in teenagers' approaches to dealing with mental health issues (Chandra & Minkovitz, 2006). In a typical study, eighth-grade students are asked to report their willingness to use mental health services in the event they were experiencing emotional or other mental health problems. Typical data for a sample of $n = 150$ students are shown in the following table.

   a. Do the data show a significant relationship between gender and willingness to seek mental health assistance? Test with $\alpha = .05$.

   b. Compute Cramér's V to measure the size of the effect.

	Willingness to Use Mental Health Services			
	Probably No	Maybe	Probably Yes	
Males	17	32	11	60
Females	13	43	34	90
	30	75	45	$n = 150$

13. Research indicates that playing a prosocial video game tends to increase prosocial behaviors (Greitemeyer & Osswald, 2010). In a similar experiment, participants were assigned to play a prosocial, a violent (antisocial), or a neutral video game. Near the end of each session, the experimenter accidentally spilled a box of pencils on the floor and then

recorded whether the participant stopped to help pick them up. The data are as follows:

	Prosocial	Violent	Neutral	
Helped	12	7	8	27
Did not Help	3	8	7	18
	15	15	15	

Do the data indicate a significant relationship between the type of game played and helping behavior? Test with $\alpha = .05$.

14. The data from problem 13 show no significant relationship between the type of game and helping behavior. To construct the following data, we simply doubled the sample size from problem 13 so that all of the individual frequencies are twice as big. Notice that the sample *proportions* have not changed.

	Prosocial	Violent	Neutral	
Helped	24	14	16	54
Did not Help	6	16	14	36
	30	30	30	

  a. Test for a significant relationship using $\alpha = .05$. How does the decision compare with the decision in problem 13? You should find that a larger sample increases the likelihood of a significant result.
  b. Compute the phi-coefficient for these data and compare it with the result from problem 13. You should find that the sample size has no effect on the strength of the relationship.

15. Earlier in this chapter, we discussed a study investigating the relationship between memory for eyewitnesses and the questions they are asked (Loftus & Palmer, 1974). In the study, participants watched a film of an automobile accident and then were questioned about the accident. One group was asked how fast the cars were going when they "smashed into" each other. A second group was asked about the speed when the cars "hit" each other, and a third group was not asked any question about the speed of the cars. A week later, the participants returned to answer additional questions about the accident, including whether they recalled seeing any broken glass. Although there was no broken glass

in the film, several students claimed to remember seeing it. The following table shows the frequency distribution of responses for each group.

		Response to the Question: Did You See Any Broken Glass?	
		Yes	No
Verb Used to Ask About the Speed of the Cars	Smashed into	16	34
	Hit	7	43
	Control (Not Asked)	6	44

  a. Does the proportion of participants who claim to remember broken glass differ significantly from group to group? Test with $\alpha = .05$.
  b. Compute Cramérs V to measure the size of the treatment effect.
  c. Describe how the phrasing of the question influenced the participants' memories.
  d. Write a sentence demonstrating how the outcome of the hypothesis test and the measure of effect size would be reported in a journal article.

16. Research suggests that liberals and conservatives respond differently to gaze cuing, which is the tendency to shift attention in the direction suggested by another person's eye movements (Dodd, Hibbing, & Smith, 2011). In the study, participants watched a drawing of a face on a computer screen. The eyes on the face would then look either left or right and, shortly afterward, a dot would appear on either the left or right side of the screen. Participants had to respond as quickly as possible indicating the side on which the dot appeared. Liberals tended to shift their attention to the side indicated by the eyes and were significantly faster when the dot appeared on that side but significantly slower when the dot was on the opposite side. Conservatives, on the other hand were not influenced by the eye direction and were equally fast no matter where the dot appeared. One possible explanation is that liberals are more empathetic and more likely to be influenced by others. The following data are simply measures of whether participants shifted their gaze in the direction of another person's eye movements.

  a. Do these results indicate a significant difference between the two political groups? Test with $\alpha = .05$.
  b. The relationship between responding to gaze cues and political tendency can also be evaluated with a phi-coefficient. Compute the phi-coefficient for these data.

Shifted Gaze

	No	Yes	Totals
Liberal	7	23	30
Conservative	15	9	24
Totals	22	32	

17. Research results suggest that IQ scores for boys are more variable than IQ scores for girls (Arden & Plomin, 2006). A typical study looking at 10-year-old children classifies participants by gender and by low, average, or high IQ. Following are hypothetical data representing the research results. Do the data indicate a significant difference between the frequency distributions for males and females? Test at the .05 level of significance and describe the difference.

IQ

	Low	Average	High	
Boys	18	42	20	80
Girls	12	54	14	80

$n = 160$

18. Gender differences in dream content are well documented (see Winget & Kramer, 1979). Suppose a researcher studies aggression content in the dreams of men and women. Each participant reports his or her most recent dream. Then each dream is judged by a panel of experts to have low, medium, or high aggression content. The observed frequencies are shown in the following matrix:

Aggression Content

		Low	Medium	High
Gender	Female	18	4	2
	Male	4	17	15

Is there a relationship between gender and the aggression content of dreams? Test with $\alpha = .01$.

19. In a study similar to one conducted by Fallon and Rozin (1985), a psychologist prepared a set of silhouettes showing different female body shapes ranging from somewhat thin to somewhat heavy and asked a group of women to indicate which body figure they thought men would consider the most attractive. Then a group of men were shown the same set of profiles and asked which image they considered the most attractive. The following hypothetical data show the number of individuals who selected each of the four body image profiles.

a. Do the data indicate a significant difference between the actual preferences for the men and the preferences predicted by the women? Test at the .05 level of significance.

b. Compute the phi-coefficient to measure the strength of the relationship.

Body Image Profiles

	Somewhat Thin	Slightly Thin	Slightly Heavy	Somewhat Heavy	
Women	29	25	18	8	80
Men	11	15	22	12	60
	40	40	40	20	

20. A recent study indicates that people tend to select video game avatars with characteristics similar to those of their creators (Bélisle & Onur, 2010). Participants who had created avatars for a virtual community game completed a questionnaire about their personalities. An independent group of viewers examined the avatars and recorded their impressions of the avatars. One personality characteristic considered was introverted/extroverted. Following is the frequency distribution of personalities for participants and the avatars they created.

Participant Personality

	Introverted	Extroverted	
Introverted Avatar	22	23	45
Extroverted Avatar	16	39	55
	38	62	

a. Is there a significant relationship between the personalities of the participants and the personalities of their avatars? Test with $\alpha = .05$.

b. Compute the phi-coefficient to measure the size of the effect.

21. Research indicates that people who volunteer to participate in research studies tend to have higher intelligence than nonvolunteers. To test this phenomenon, a researcher obtains a sample of 200 high school students. The students are given a description of a psychological research study and asked whether they would volunteer to participate. The researcher also obtains an IQ score for each student and classifies the students into high, medium, and low IQ groups. Do the following data indicate a significant relationship between IQ and volunteering? Test at the .05 level of significance.

	IQ			
	High	Medium	Low	
Volunteer	43	73	34	150
Not Volunteer	7	27	16	50
	50	100	50	

22. Although the phenomenon is not well understood, it appears that people born during the winter months are slightly more likely to develop schizophrenia than people born at other times (Bradbury & Miller, 1985). The following hypothetical data represent a sample of 50 individuals diagnosed with schizophrenia and a sample of 100 people with no psychotic diagnosis. Each individual is also classified according to the season in which he or she was born. Do the data indicate a significant relationship between schizophrenia and the season of birth? Test at the .05 level of significance.

	Season of Birth				
	Summer	Fall	Winter	Spring	
No Disorder	26	24	22	28	100
Schizophrenia	9	11	18	12	50
	35	35	40	40	

After completing this part, you should be able to calculate and interpret correlations, find linear regression equations, and conduct the chi-square tests for goodness of fit and for independence.

The most commonly used correlation is the Pearson correlation, which measures the direction and degree of linear relationship between two variables (X and Y) that have been measured on interval or ratio scales (numerical scores). The regression equation determines the best fitting line to describe the relationship between X and Y, and to compute predicted Y values for each value of X. A partial correlation can be used to reveal the underlying relationship between X and Y when the influence of a third variable is eliminated.

The Pearson formula is also used in a variety of other situations to compute special correlations. The Spearman correlation uses the Pearson formula when X and Y are both measured on ordinal scales (ranks). The Spearman correlation measures the direction and the degree to which the relationship is consistently one directional. When one of the variables consists of numerical scores and the other has only two values, the two values of the dichotomous variable can be coded as 0 and 1, and the Pearson formula can be used to find the point-biserial correlation. The point-biserial correlation measures the strength of the relationship between X and Y, and can be squared to produce the same r^2 value that is used to measure effect size for the independent-measures t test. When both variables are dichotomous, they can both be coded as 0 and 1, and the Pearson formula can be used to find the phi-coefficient. As a correlation, the phi-coefficient measures the strength of the relationship and is often used as a measure of effect size to accompany a chi-square test for independence for a 2 × 2 data matrix.

The chi-square test for goodness of fit uses the frequency distribution from a sample to evaluate a hypothesis about the corresponding population distribution. The null hypothesis for the goodness-of-fit test typically falls into one of two categories:

1. Equal proportions: The null hypothesis states that the population is equally distributed across the set of categories.
2. No difference: The null hypothesis states that the distribution for one population is not different from the known distribution for another population.

The chi-square test for independence uses frequency data from a sample to evaluate a hypothesis about the relationship between two variables in the population. The null hypothesis for this test can be phrased two different ways:

1. No relationship: The null hypothesis states that there is no relationship between the two variables in the population.

2. No difference: One variable is viewed as defining a set of different populations. The null hypothesis states that the frequency distribution for the second variable has the same shape (same proportions) for all of the different populations.

REVIEW EXERCISES

1. For the following scores,

X	Y
7	6
9	6
6	3
12	5
9	6
5	4

   a. Sketch a scatter plot showing the six data points.
   b. Just looking at the scatter plot, estimate the value of the Pearson correlation.
   c. Compute the Pearson correlation.

2. For the following data:

X	Y
1	2
4	7
3	5
2	1
5	14
3	7

   a. Find the regression equation for predicting Y from X.
   b. Does the regression equation account for a significant portion of the variance in the Y scores? Use $\alpha = .05$ to evaluate the F-ratio.

3. A developmental psychologist would like to determine whether infants display any color preferences. A stimulus consisting of four color patches (red, green, blue, and yellow) is projected onto the ceiling above a crib. Infants are placed in the crib, one at a time, and the psychologist records how much time each infant spends looking at each of the four colors. The color that receives the most attention during a 100-second test period is identified as the preferred color for that infant. The preferred colors for a sample of 60 infants are shown in the following table:

Red	Green	Blue	Yellow
20	12	18	10

a. Do the data indicate any significant preferences among the four colors? Test at the .05 level of significance.

b. Write a sentence demonstrating how the outcome of the hypothesis test would appear in a research report.

4. A communications company has developed three new designs for a cell phone. To evaluate consumer response, a sample of 60 college students and 60 older adults is selected and each person is given all three phones to use for 1 week. At the end of the week, the participants must identify which of the three designs they prefer. The distribution of preference is as follows:

	Design 1	Design 2	Design 3	
Student	27	20	13	60
Older Adult	21	34	5	60
	48	54	18	

a. Do the data indicate that the distribution of preferences for older adults is significantly different from the distribution for college students? Test with $\alpha = .05$.

b. Compute the phi-coefficient to measure the strength of the relationship.

APPENDIX A   **Basic Mathematics Review**

PREVIEW

This appendix reviews some of the basic math skills that are necessary for the statistical calculations presented in this book. Many students already will know some or all of this material. Others will need to do extensive work and review. To help you assess your own skills, we include a skills assessment exam here. You should allow approximately 30 minutes to complete the test. When you finish, grade your test using the answer key on page 569.

Notice that the test is divided into five sections. If you miss more than three questions in any section of the test, you probably need help in that area. Turn to the section of this appendix that corresponds to your problem area. In each section, you will find a general review, examples, and additional practice problems. After reviewing the appropriate section and doing the practice problems, turn to the end of the appendix. You will find another version of the skills assessment exam. If you still miss more than three questions in any section of the exam, continue studying. Get assistance from an instructor or a tutor if necessary. At the end of this appendix is a list of recommended books for individuals who need a more extensive review than can be provided here. We stress that mastering this material now will make the rest of the course much easier.

SKILLS ASSESSMENT PREVIEW EXAM

SECTION 1

(corresponding to Section A.1 of this appendix)

1. $3 + 2 \times 7 = ?$
2. $(3 + 2) \times 7 = ?$
3. $3 + 2^2 - 1 = ?$
4. $(3 + 2)^2 - 1 = ?$
5. $12/4 + 2 = ?$
6. $12/(4 + 2) = ?$
7. $12/(4 + 2)^2 = ?$
8. $2 \times (8 - 2^2) = ?$
9. $2 \times (8 - 2)^2 = ?$
10. $3 \times 2 + 8 - 1 \times 6 = ?$
11. $3 \times (2 + 8) - 1 \times 6 = ?$
12. $3 \times 2 + (8 - 1) \times 6 = ?$

SECTION 2

(corresponding to Section A.2 of this appendix)

1. The fraction $\frac{3}{4}$ corresponds to a percentage of _____.
2. Express 30% as a fraction.
3. Convert $\frac{12}{40}$ to a decimal.
4. $\frac{2}{13} + \frac{8}{13} = ?$
5. $1.375 + 0.25 = ?$
6. $\frac{2}{5} \times \frac{1}{4} = ?$
7. $\frac{1}{8} + \frac{2}{3} = ?$
8. $3.5 \times 0.4 = ?$
9. $\frac{1}{5} \div \frac{3}{4} = ?$
10. $3.75/0.5 = ?$
11. In a group of 80 students, 20% are psychology majors. How many psychology majors are in this group?
12. A company reports that two-fifths of its employees are women. If there are 90 employees, how many are women?

SECTION 3

(corresponding to Section A.3 of this appendix)

1. $3 + (-2) + (-1) + 4 = ?$
2. $6 - (-2) = ?$
3. $-2 - (-4) = ?$
4. $6 + (-1) - 3 - (-2) - (-5) = ?$
5. $4 \times (-3) = ?$
6. $-2 \times (-6) = ?$
7. $-3 \times 5 = ?$
8. $-2 \times (-4) \times (-3) = ?$
9. $12 \div (-3) = ?$
10. $-18 \div (-6) = ?$
11. $-16 \div 8 = ?$
12. $-100 \div (-4) = ?$

SECTION 4

(corresponding to Section A.4 of this appendix)

For each equation, find the value of X.

1. $X + 6 = 13$
2. $X - 14 = 15$
3. $5 = X - 4$
4. $3X = 12$
5. $72 = 3X$
6. $X/5 = 3$
7. $10 = X/8$
8. $3X + 5 = -4$
9. $24 = 2X + 2$
10. $(X + 3)/2 = 14$
11. $(X - 5)/3 = 2$
12. $17 = 4X - 11$

SECTION 5

(corresponding to Section A.5 of this appendix)

1. $4^3 = ?$
2. $\sqrt{25 - 9} = ?$
3. If $X = 2$ and $Y = 3$, then $XY^3 = ?$
4. If $X = 2$ and $Y = 3$, then $(X + Y)^2 = ?$
5. If $a = 3$ and $b = 2$, then $a^2 + b^2 = ?$
6. $(-3)^3 = ?$
7. $(-4)^4 = ?$
8. $\sqrt{4} \times 4 = ?$
9. $36/\sqrt{9} = ?$
10. $(9 + 2)2 = ?$
11. $5^2 + 2^3 = ?$
12. If $a = 3$ and $b = -1$, then $a^2b^3 = ?$

The answers to the skills assessment exam are at the end of the appendix (pages 569−570).

A.1   SYMBOLS AND NOTATION

Table A.1 presents the basic mathematical symbols that you should know, along with examples of their use. Statistical symbols and notation are introduced and explained throughout this book as they are needed. Notation for exponents and square roots is covered separately at the end of this appendix.

Parentheses are a useful notation because they specify and control the order of computations. Everything inside the parentheses is calculated first. For example,

$$(5 + 3) \times 2 = 8 \times 2 = 16$$

Changing the placement of the parentheses also changes the order of calculations. For example,

$$5 + (3 \times 2) = 5 + 6 = 11$$

ORDER OF OPERATIONS   Often a formula or a mathematical expression will involve several different arithmetic operations, such as adding, multiplying, squaring, and so on. When you encounter these situations, you must perform the different operations in the correct sequence. Following is a list of mathematical operations, showing the order in which they are to be performed.

1. Any calculation contained within parentheses is done first.

2. Squaring (or raising to other exponents) is done second.

3. Multiplying and/or dividing is done third. A series of multiplication and/or division operations should be done in order from left to right.

4. Adding and/or subtracting is done fourth.

The following examples demonstrate how this sequence of operations is applied in different situations.

To evaluate the expression

$$(3 + 1)^2 - 4 \times 7/2$$

first, perform the calculation within parentheses:

$$(4)^2 - 4 \times 7/2$$

Next, square the value as indicated:

$$16 - 4 \times 7/2$$

TABLE A.1

Symbol	Meaning	Example
$+$	Addition	$5 + 7 = 12$
$-$	Subtraction	$8 - 3 = 5$
$\times$, ( )	Multiplication	$3 \times 9 = 27,\ 3(9) = 27$
$\div$, /	Division	$15 \div 3 = 5,\ 15/3 = 5,\ \frac{15}{3} = 5$
$>$	Greater than	$20 > 10$
$<$	Less than	$7 < 11$
$\neq$	Not equal to	$5 \neq 6$

Then perform the multiplication and division:

$$16 - 14$$

Finally, do the subtraction:

$$16 - 14 = 2$$

A sequence of operations involving multiplication and division should be performed in order from left to right. For example, to compute $12/2 \times 3$, you divide 12 by 2 and then multiply the result by 3:

$$12/2 \times 3 = 6 \times 3 = 18$$

Notice that violating the left-to-right sequence can change the result. For this example, if you multiply before dividing, you will obtain

$$12/2 \times 3 = 12/6 = 2 \qquad \text{(This is wrong.)}$$

A sequence of operations involving only addition and subtraction can be performed in any order. For example, to compute $3 + 8 - 5$, you can add 3 and 8 and then subtract 5:

$$(3 + 8) - 5 = 11 - 5 = 6$$

or you can subtract 5 from 8 and then add the result to 3:

$$3 + (8 - 5) = 3 + 3 = 6$$

A mathematical expression or formula is simply a concise way to write a set of instructions. When you evaluate an expression by performing the calculation, you simply follow the instructions. For example, assume you are given these instructions:

1. First, add 3 and 8.
2. Next, square the result.
3. Next, multiply the resulting value by 6.
4. Finally, subtract 50 from the value you have obtained.

You can write these instructions as a mathematical expression.

1. The first step involves addition. Because addition is normally done last, use parentheses to give this operation priority in the sequence of calculations:

$$(3 + 8)$$

2. The instruction to square a value is noted by using the exponent 2 beside the value to be squared:

$$(3 + 8)^2$$

3. Because squaring has priority over multiplication, you can simply introduce the multiplication into the expression:

$$6 \times (3 + 8)^2$$

4. Addition and subtraction are done last, so simply write in the requested subtraction:

$$6 \times (3 + 8)^2 - 50$$

To calculate the value of the expression, you work through the sequence of operations in the proper order:

$$6 \times (3 + 8)^2 - 50 = 6 \times (11)^2 - 50$$

$$= 6 \times (121) - 50$$

$$= 726 - 50$$

$$= 676$$

As a final note, you should realize that the operation of squaring (or raising to any exponent) applies only to the value that immediately precedes the exponent. For example,

$$2 \times 3^2 = 2 \times 9 = 18 \qquad \text{(Only the 3 is squared.)}$$

If the instructions require multiplying values and then squaring the product, you must use parentheses to give the multiplication priority over squaring. For example, to multiply 2 times 3 and then square the product, you would write

$$(2 \times 3)^2 = (6)^2 = 36$$

LEARNING CHECK

1. Evaluate each of the following expressions:

    a. $4 \times 8/2^2$

    b. $4 \times (8/2)^2$

    c. $100 - 3 \times 12/(6 - 4)^2$

    d. $(4 + 6) \times (3 - 1)^2$

    e. $(8 - 2)/(9 - 8)^2$

    f. $6 + (4 - 1)^2 - 3 \times 4^2$

    g. $4 \times (8 - 3) + 8 - 3$

ANSWERS   **1. a.** 8   **b.** 64   **c.** 91   **d.** 40   **e.** 6   **f.** -33 **g.** 25

A.2 PROPORTIONS: FRACTIONS, DECIMALS, AND PERCENTAGES

A proportion is a part of a whole and can be expressed as a fraction, a decimal, or a percentage. For example, in a class of 40 students, only 3 failed the final exam.

The proportion of the class that failed can be expressed as a fraction

$$\text{fraction} = \frac{3}{40}$$

or as a decimal value

$$\text{decimal} = 0.075$$

or as a percentage

percentage $= 7.5\%$

In a fraction, such as $\frac{3}{4}$, the bottom value (the denominator) indicates the number of equal pieces into which the whole is split. Here the "pie" is split into 4 equal pieces:

If the denominator has a larger value—say, 8—then each piece of the whole pie is smaller:

A larger denominator indicates a smaller fraction of the whole.

The value on top of the fraction (the numerator) indicates how many pieces of the whole are being considered. Thus, the fraction $\frac{3}{4}$ indicates that the whole is split evenly into 4 pieces and that 3 of them are being used:

A fraction is simply a concise way of stating a proportion: "Three out of four" is equivalent to $\frac{3}{4}$. To convert the fraction to a decimal, you divide the numerator by the denominator:

$$\frac{3}{4} = 3 \div 4 = 0.75$$

To convert the decimal to a percentage, simply multiply by 100, and place a percent sign (%) after the answer:

$$0.75 \times 100 = 75\%$$

The U.S. money system is a convenient way of illustrating the relationship between fractions and decimals. "One quarter," for example, is one-fourth $\left(\frac{1}{4}\right)$ of a dollar, and its decimal equivalent is 0.25. Other familiar equivalencies are as follows:

	Dime	Quarter	50 Cents	75 Cents
Fraction	$\frac{1}{10}$	$\frac{1}{4}$	$\frac{1}{2}$	$\frac{3}{4}$
Decimal	0.10	0.25	0.50	0.75
Percentage	10%	25%	50%	75%

FRACTIONS

1. **Finding Equivalent Fractions.** The same proportional value can be expressed by many equivalent fractions. For example,

$$\frac{1}{2} = \frac{2}{4} = \frac{10}{20} = \frac{50}{100}$$

To create equivalent fractions, you can multiply the numerator and denominator by the same value. As long as both the numerator and the denominator of the fraction are multiplied by the same value, the new fraction will be equivalent to the original. For example,

$$\frac{3}{10} = \frac{9}{30}$$

because both the numerator and the denominator of the original fraction have been multiplied by 3. Dividing the numerator and denominator of a fraction by the same value will also result in an equivalent fraction. By using division, you can reduce a fraction to a simpler form. For example,

$$\frac{40}{100} = \frac{2}{5}$$

because both the numerator and the denominator of the original fraction have been divided by 20.

You can use these rules to find specific equivalent fractions. For example, find the fraction that has a denominator of 100 and is equivalent to $\frac{3}{4}$. That is,

$$\frac{3}{4} = \frac{?}{100}$$

Notice that the denominator of the original fraction must be multiplied by 25 to produce the denominator of the desired fraction. For the two fractions to be equal, both the numerator and the denominator must be multiplied by the same number. Therefore, we also multiply the top of the original fraction by 25 and obtain

$$\frac{3 \times 25}{4 \times 25} = \frac{75}{100}$$

2. **Multiplying Fractions.** To multiply two fractions, you first multiply the numerators and then multiply the denominators. For example,

$$\frac{3}{4} \times \frac{5}{7} = \frac{3 \times 5}{4 \times 7} = \frac{15}{28}$$

3. **Dividing Fractions.** To divide one fraction by another, you invert the second fraction and then multiply. For example,

$$\frac{1}{2} \div \frac{1}{4} = \frac{1}{2} \times \frac{4}{1} = \frac{1 \times 4}{2 \times 1} = \frac{4}{2} = \frac{2}{1} = 2$$

4. **Adding and Subtracting Fractions.** Fractions must have the same denominator before you can add or subtract them. If the two fractions already have a common denominator, you simply add (or subtract as the case may be) *only* the values in the numerators. For example,

$$\frac{2}{5} + \frac{1}{5} = \frac{3}{5}$$

Suppose you divided a pie into five equal pieces (fifths). If you first ate two-fifths of the pie and then another one-fifth, the total amount eaten would be three-fifths of the pie:

If the two fractions do not have the same denominator, you must first find equivalent fractions with a common denominator before you can add or subtract. The product of the two denominators will always work as a common denominator for equivalent fractions (although it may not be the lowest common denominator). For example,

$$\frac{2}{3} + \frac{1}{10} = ?$$

Because these two fractions have different denominators, it is necessary to convert each into an equivalent fraction and find a common denominator. We will use $3 \times 10 = 30$ as the common denominator. Thus, the equivalent fraction of each is

$$\frac{2}{3} = \frac{20}{30} \quad \text{and} \quad \frac{1}{10} = \frac{3}{30}$$

Now the two fractions can be added:

$$\frac{20}{30} + \frac{3}{30} = \frac{23}{30}$$

5. **Comparing the Size of Fractions.** When comparing the size of two fractions with the same denominator, the larger fraction will have the larger numerator. For example,

$$\frac{5}{8} > \frac{3}{8}$$

The denominators are the same, so the whole is partitioned into pieces of the same size. Five of these pieces are more than three of them:

When two fractions have different denominators, you must first convert them to fractions with a common denominator to determine which is larger. Consider the following fractions:

$$\frac{3}{8} \quad \text{and} \quad \frac{7}{16}$$

If the numerator and denominator of $\frac{3}{8}$ are multiplied by 2, the resulting equivalent fraction will have a denominator of 16:

$$\frac{3}{8} = \frac{3 \times 2}{8 \times 2} = \frac{6}{16}$$

Now a comparison can be made between the two fractions:

$$\frac{6}{16} < \frac{7}{16}$$

Therefore,

$$\frac{3}{8} < \frac{7}{16}$$

DECIMALS

1. **Converting Decimals to Fractions.** Like a fraction, a decimal represents part of the whole. The first decimal place to the right of the decimal point indicates how many tenths are used. For example,

$$0.1 = \frac{1}{10} \qquad 0.7 = \frac{7}{10}$$

The next decimal place represents $\frac{1}{100}$, the next $\frac{1}{1000}$, the next $\frac{1}{10,000}$, and so on. To change a decimal to a fraction, just use the number without the decimal point for the numerator. Use the denominator that the last (on the right) decimal place represents. For example,

$$0.32 = \frac{32}{100} \qquad 0.5333 = \frac{5333}{10,000} \qquad 0.05 = \frac{5}{100} \qquad 0.001 = \frac{1}{1000}$$

2. **Adding and Subtracting Decimals.** To add and subtract decimals, the only rule is that you must keep the decimal points in a straight vertical line. For example,

$$
\begin{array}{r}
0.27 \\
+\ 1.326 \\
\hline
1.526
\end{array}
\qquad
\begin{array}{r}
3.595 \\
-\ 0.67 \\
\hline
2.925
\end{array}
$$

3. **Multiplying Decimals.** To multiply two decimal values, you first multiply the two numbers, ignoring the decimal points. Then you position the decimal point in the answer so that the number of digits to the right of the decimal point is equal to the total number of decimal places in the two numbers being multiplied. For example,

1.73 (two decimal places)	0.25 (two decimal places)
$\times$ 0.251 (three decimal places)	$\times$ 0.005 (three decimal places)
173	125
865	00
346	00
0.43423 (five decimal places)	0.00125 (five decimal places)

4. **Dividing Decimals.** The simplest procedure for dividing decimals is based on the fact that dividing two numbers is identical to expressing them as a fraction:

$$0.25 \div 1.6 \text{ is identical to } \frac{0.25}{1.6}$$

You now can multiply both the numerator and the denominator of the fraction by 10, 100, 1000, or whatever number is necessary to remove the decimal places. Remember that multiplying both the numerator and the denominator of a fraction by the *same* value will create an equivalent fraction. Therefore,

$$\frac{0.25}{1.6} = \frac{0.25 \times 100}{1.6 \times 100} = \frac{25}{100} = \frac{5}{32}$$

The result is a division problem without any decimal places in the two numbers.

PERCENTAGES

1. **Converting a Percentage to a Fraction or a Decimal.** To convert a percentage to a fraction, remove the percent sign, place the number in the numerator, and use 100 for the denominator. For example,

$$52\% = \frac{52}{100} \qquad 5\% = \frac{5}{100}$$

To convert a percentage to a decimal, remove the percent sign and divide by 100, or simply move the decimal point two places to the left. For example,

$$83\% = \underline{83}. \qquad = 0.83$$

$$14.5\% = \underline{14}.5 = 0.145$$

$$5\% = \underline{5}. = 0.05$$

2. **Performing Arithmetic Operations with Percentages.** There are situations in which it is best to express percent values as decimals in order to perform certain arithmetic operations. For example, what is 45% of 60? This question may be stated as

$$45\% \times 60 = ?$$

The 45% should be converted to decimal form to find the solution to this question. Therefore,

$$0.45 \times 60 = 27$$

LEARNING CHECK

1. Convert $\frac{3}{25}$ to a decimal.

2. Convert $\frac{3}{8}$ to a percentage.

3. Next to each set of fractions, write "True" if they are equivalent and "False" if they are not:

   a. $\frac{3}{8} = \frac{9}{24}$ _____   **b.** $\frac{7}{9} = \frac{17}{19}$ _____

   c. $\frac{2}{7} = \frac{4}{14}$ _____

4. Compute the following:

   a. $\frac{1}{6} \times \frac{7}{10}$ **b.** $\frac{7}{8} - \frac{1}{2}$ **c.** $\frac{9}{10} \div \frac{2}{3}$ **d.** $\frac{7}{22} + \frac{2}{3}$

5. Identify the larger fraction of each pair:

   a. $\frac{7}{10}, \frac{21}{100}$ **b.** $\frac{3}{4}, \frac{7}{12}$ **c.** $\frac{22}{3}, \frac{19}{3}$

6. Convert the following decimals into fractions:

   a. 0.012   **b.** 0.77   **c.** 0.005

7. $2.59 \times 0.015 = ?$

8. $1.8 \div 0.02 = ?$

9. What is 28% of 45?

ANSWERS   **1.** 0.12   **2.** 37.5%   **3. a.** True   **b.** False   **c.** True

4. a. $\frac{7}{60}$ **b.** $\frac{3}{8}$ **c.** $\frac{27}{20}$ **d.** $\frac{65}{66}$ **5. a.** $\frac{7}{10}$ **b.** $\frac{3}{4}$ **c.** $\frac{22}{3}$

6. a. $\frac{12}{1000} = \frac{3}{250}$ **b.** $\frac{77}{100}$ **c.** $\frac{5}{1000} = \frac{1}{200}$ **7.** 0.03885   **8.** 90   **9.** 12.6

A.3   NEGATIVE NUMBERS

Negative numbers are used to represent values less than zero. Negative numbers may occur when you are measuring the difference between two scores. For example, a researcher may want to evaluate the effectiveness of a propaganda film by measuring people's attitudes with a test both before and after viewing the film:

	Before	After	Amount of Change
Person A	23	27	+4
Person B	18	15	−3
Person C	21	16	−5

Notice that the negative sign provides information about the direction of the difference: A plus sign indicates an increase in value, and a minus sign indicates a decrease.

Because negative numbers are frequently encountered, you should be comfortable working with these values. This section reviews basic arithmetic operations using negative numbers. You should also note that any number without a sign (+ or −) is assumed to be positive.

1. **Adding Negative Numbers.** When adding numbers that include negative values, simply interpret the negative sign as subtraction. For example,

$$3 + (-2) + 5 = 3 - 2 + 5 = 6$$

When adding a long string of numbers, it often is easier to add all of the positive values to obtain the positive sum and then to add all of the negative values to obtain the negative sum. Finally, you subtract the negative sum from the positive sum. For example,

$$-1 + 3 + (-4) + 3 + (-6) + (-2)$$

positive sum = 6   negative sum = 13

Answer: $6 - 13 = -7$

2. **Subtracting Negative Numbers.** To subtract a negative number, change it to a positive number, and add. For example,

$$4 - (-3) = 4 + 3 = 7$$

This rule is easier to understand if you think of positive numbers as financial gains and negative numbers as financial losses. In this context, taking away a debt is equivalent to a financial gain. In mathematical terms, taking away a negative number is equivalent to adding a positive number. For example, suppose you are meeting a friend for lunch. You have $7, but you owe your friend $3. Thus, you really have only $4 to spend for lunch. But your friend forgives (takes away) the $3 debt. The result is that you now have $7 to spend. Expressed as an equation,

$$\$4 \text{ minus a } \$3 \text{ debt} = \$7$$

$$4 - (-3) = 4 + 3 = 7$$

3. **Multiplying and Dividing Negative Numbers.** When the two numbers being multiplied (or divided) have the same sign, the result is a positive number. When the two numbers have different signs, the result is negative. For example,

$$3 \times (-2) = -6$$

$$-4 \times (-2) = +8$$

The first example is easy to explain by thinking of multiplication as repeated addition. In this case,

$$3 \times (-2) = (-2) + (-2) + (-2) = -6$$

You add three negative 2s, which results in a total of negative 6. In the second example, we are multiplying by a negative number. This amounts to repeated subtraction. That is,

$$-4 \times (-2) = -(-2) - (-2) - (-2) - (-2)$$

$$= 2 + 2 + 2 + 2 = 8$$

By using the same rule for both multiplication and division, we ensure that these two operations are compatible. For example,

$$-6 \div 3 = -2$$

which is compatible with

$$3 \times (-2) = -6$$

Also,

$$8 \div (-4) = -2$$

which is compatible with

$$-4 \times (-2) = +8$$

1. Complete the following calculations:

a. $3 + (-8) + 5 + 7 + (-1) + (-3)$

b. $5 - (-9) + 2 - (-3) - (-1)$

c. $3 - 7 - (-21) + (-5) - (-9)$

d. $4 - (-6) - 3 + 11 - 14$

e. $9 + 8 - 2 - 1 - (-6)$

f. $9 \times (-3)$

g. $-7 \times (-4)$

h. $-6 \times (-2) \times (-3)$

i. $-12 \div (-3)$

j. $18 \div (-6)$

ANSWERS   **1. a.** 3   **b.** 20   **c.** 21   **d.** 4   **e.** 20

f. -27 **g.** 28   **h.** -36 **i.** 4   **j.** -3

A.4   BASIC ALGEBRA: SOLVING EQUATIONS

An equation is a mathematical statement that indicates two quantities are identical. For example,

$$12 = 8 + 4$$

Often an equation will contain an unknown (or variable) quantity that is identified with a letter or symbol, rather than a number. For example,

$$12 = 8 + X$$

In this event, your task is to find the value of X that makes the equation "true," or balanced. For this example, an X value of 4 will make a true equation. Finding the value of X is usually called *solving the equation*.

To solve an equation, there are two points to keep in mind:

1. Your goal is to have the unknown value (X) isolated on one side of the equation. This means that you need to remove all of the other numbers and symbols that appear on the same side of the equation as the X.

2. The equation remains balanced, provided that you treat both sides exactly the same. For example, you could add 10 points to *both* sides, and the solution (the X value) for the equation would be unchanged.

FINDING THE SOLUTION FOR AN EQUATION

We will consider four basic types of equations and the operations needed to solve them.

1. When X Has a Value Added to It. An example of this type of equation is

$$X + 3 = 7$$

Your goal is to isolate X on one side of the equation. Thus, you must remove the $+3$ on the left-hand side. The solution is obtained by subtracting 3 from *both* sides of the equation:

$$X + 3 - 3 = 7 - 3$$
$$X = 4$$

The solution is $X = 4$. You should always check your solution by returning to the original equation and replacing X with the value you obtained for the solution. For this example,

$$X + 3 = 7$$
$$4 + 3 = 7$$
$$7 = 7$$

2. **When X Has a Value Subtracted From It.** An example of this type of equation is

$$X - 8 = 12$$

In this example, you must remove the -8 from the left-hand side. Thus, the solution is obtained by adding 8 to *both* sides of the equation:

$$X - 8 + 8 = 12 + 8$$
$$X = 20$$

Check the solution:

$$X - 8 = 12$$
$$20 - 8 = 12$$
$$12 = 12$$

3. **When X Is Multiplied by a Value.** An example of this type of equation is

$$4X = 24$$

In this instance, it is necessary to remove the 4 that is multiplied by X. This may be accomplished by dividing both sides of the equation by 4:

$$\frac{4X}{4} = \frac{24}{4}$$
$$X = 6$$

Check the solution:

$$4X = 24$$
$$4(6) = 24$$
$$24 = 24$$

4. **When X Is Divided by a Value.** An example of this type of equation is

$$\frac{X}{3} = 9$$

Now the X is divided by 3, so the solution is obtained by multiplying by 3. Multiplying both sides yields

$$3\left(\frac{X}{3}\right) = 9(3)$$

$$X = 27$$

For the check,

$$\frac{X}{3} = 9$$

$$\frac{27}{3} = 9$$

$$9 = 9$$

SOLUTIONS FOR MORE COMPLEX EQUATIONS

More complex equations can be solved by using a combination of the preceding simple operations. Remember that at each stage you are trying to isolate X on one side of the equation. For example,

$$3X + 7 = 22$$

$$3X + 7 - 7 = 22 - 7 \qquad \text{(Remove } +7 \text{ by subtracting 7 from both sides.)}$$

$$3X = 15$$

$$\frac{3X}{3} = \frac{15}{3} \qquad \text{(Remove 3 by dividing both sides by 3.)}$$

$$X = 5$$

To check this solution, return to the original equation, and substitute 5 in place of X:

$$3X + 7 = 22$$

$$3(5) + 7 = 22$$

$$15 + 7 = 22$$

$$22 = 22$$

Following is another type of complex equation frequently encountered in statistics:

$$\frac{X + 3}{4} = 2$$

First, remove the 4 by multiplying both sides by 4:

$$4\left(\frac{X + 3}{4}\right) = 2(4)$$

$$X + 3 = 8$$

Now remove the $+3$ by subtracting 3 from both sides:

$$X + 3 - 3 = 8 - 3$$

$$X = 5$$

To check this solution, return to the original equation, and substitute 5 in place of *X:*

$$\frac{X+3}{4} = 2$$

$$\frac{5+3}{4} = 2$$

$$\frac{8}{4} = 2$$

$$2 = 2$$

1. Solve for *X*, and check the solutions:

   a. $3X = 18$ **b.** $X + 7 = 9$ **c.** $X - 4 = 18$ **d.** $5X - 8 = 12$

   e. $\dfrac{X}{9} = 5$ **f.** $\dfrac{X+1}{6} = 4$ **g.** $X + 2 = -5$ **h.** $\dfrac{X}{5} = -5$

   i. $\dfrac{2X}{3} = 12$ **j.** $\dfrac{X}{3} + 1 = 3$

ANSWERS   1. **a.** $X = 6$ **b.** $X = 2$ **c.** $X = 22$ **d.** $X = 4$ **e.** $X = 45$

   f. $X = 23$ **g.** $X = -7$ **h.** $X = -25$ **i.** $X = 18$ **j.** $X = 6$

A.5   EXPONENTS AND SQUARE ROOTS

EXPONENTIAL NOTATION

A simplified notation is used whenever a number is being multiplied by itself. The notation consists of placing a value, called an *exponent,* on the right-hand side of and raised above another number, called a *base*. For example,

$$7^3 \leftarrow \text{exponent}$$
$$\uparrow$$
$$\text{base}$$

The exponent indicates how many times the base is used as a factor in multiplication. Following are some examples:

$7^3 = 7(7)(7)$ (Read "7 cubed" or "7 raised to the third power")
$5^2 = 5(5)$ (Read "5 squared")
$2^5 = 2(2)(2)(2)(2)$ (Read "2 raised to the fifth power")

There are a few basic rules about exponents that you will need to know for this course. They are outlined here.

1. **Numbers Raised to One or Zero.** Any number raised to the first power equals itself. For example,

   $$6^1 = 6$$

Any number (except zero) raised to the zero power equals 1. For example,

$$9^0 = 1$$

2. **Exponents for Multiple Terms**. The exponent applies only to the base that is just in front of it. For example,

$$XY^2 = XYY$$

$$a^2b^3 = aabbb$$

3. **Negative Bases Raised to an Exponent.** If a negative number is raised to a power, then the result will be positive for exponents that are even and negative for exponents that are odd. For example,

$$(-4)^3 = -4(-4)(-4)$$
$$= 16(-4)$$
$$= -64$$

and

$$(-3)^4 = -3(-3)(-3)(-3)$$
$$= 9(-3)(-3)$$
$$= 9(9)$$
$$= 81$$

Note: The parentheses are used to ensure that the exponent applies to the entire negative number, including the sign. Without the parentheses there is some ambiguity as to how the exponent should be applied. For example, the expression -3^2 could have two interpretations:

$$-3^2 = (-3)(-3) = 9 \quad \text{or} \quad -3^2 = -(3)(3) = -9$$

4. **Exponents and Parentheses.** If an exponent is present outside of parentheses, then the computations within the parentheses are done first, and the exponential computation is done last:

$$(3 + 5)^2 = 8^2 = 64$$

Notice that the meaning of the expression is changed when each term in the parentheses is raised to the exponent individually:

$$3^2 + 5^2 = 9 + 25 = 34$$

Therefore,

$$X^2 + Y^2 \neq (X + Y)^2$$

5. **Fractions Raised to a Power.** If the numerator and denominator of a fraction are each raised to the same exponent, then the entire fraction can be raised to that exponent. That is,

$$\frac{a^2}{b^2} = \left(\frac{a}{b}\right)^2$$

For example,

$$\frac{3^2}{4^2} = \left(\frac{3}{4}\right)^2$$

$$\frac{9}{16} = \frac{3}{4}\left(\frac{3}{4}\right)$$

$$\frac{9}{16} = \frac{9}{16}$$

SQUARE ROOTS   The square root of a value equals a number that, when multiplied by itself, yields the original value. For example, the square root of 16 equals 4, because 4 times 4 equals 16. The symbol for the square root is called a *radical*, $\sqrt{}$. The square root is taken for the number under the radical. For example,

$$\sqrt{16} = 4$$

Finding the square root is the inverse of raising a number to the second power (squaring). Thus,

$$\sqrt{a^2} = a$$

For example,

$$\sqrt{3^2} = \sqrt{9} = 3$$

Also,

$$\left(\sqrt{b}\right)^2 = b$$

For example,

$$\left(\sqrt{64}\right)^2 = 8^2 = 64$$

Computations under the same radical are performed *before* the square root is taken. For example,

$$\sqrt{9 + 16} = \sqrt{25} = 5$$

Note that with addition (or subtraction), separate radicals yield a different result:

$$\sqrt{9} + \sqrt{16} = 3 + 4 = 7$$

Therefore,

$$\sqrt{X} + \sqrt{Y} \neq \sqrt{X + Y}$$
$$\sqrt{X} - \sqrt{Y} \neq \sqrt{X - Y}$$

If the numerator and denominator of a fraction each have a radical, then the entire fraction can be placed under a single radical:

$$\frac{\sqrt{16}}{\sqrt{4}} = \sqrt{\frac{16}{4}}$$

$$\frac{4}{2} = \sqrt{4}$$

$$2 = 2$$

Therefore,

$$\frac{\sqrt{X}}{\sqrt{Y}} = \sqrt{\frac{X}{Y}}$$

Also, if the square root of one number is multiplied by the square root of another number, then the same result would be obtained by taking the square root of the product of both numbers. For example,

$$\sqrt{9} \times \sqrt{16} = \sqrt{9 \times 16}$$

$$3 \times 4 = \sqrt{144}$$

$$12 = 12$$

Therefore,

$$\sqrt{a} \times \sqrt{b} = \sqrt{ab}$$

LEARNING CHECK

1. Perform the following computations:
   a. $(-6)^3$
   b. $(3 + 7)^2$
   c. a^3b^2 when $a = 2$ and $b = -5$
   d. a^4b^3 when $a = 2$ and $b = 3$
   e. $(XY)^2$ when $X = 3$ and $Y = 5$
   f. $X^2 + Y^2$ when $X = 3$ and $Y = 5$
   g. $(X + Y)^2$ when $X = 3$ and $Y = 5$
   h. $\sqrt{5 + 4}$
   i. $\left(\sqrt{9}\right)^2$
   j. $\dfrac{\sqrt{16}}{\sqrt{4}}$

ANSWERS   1. a. -216 b. 100   c. 200   d. 432   e. 225

f. 34   g. 64   h. 3   i. 9   j. 2

PROBLEMS FOR APPENDIX A   Basic Mathematics Review

1. $50/(10 - 8) = ?$
2. $(2 + 3)^2 = ?$
3. $20/10 \times 3 = ?$
4. $12 - 4 \times 2 + 6/3 = ?$
5. $24/(12 - 4) + 2 \times (6 + 3) = ?$
6. Convert $\frac{7}{20}$ to a decimal.
7. Express $\frac{9}{25}$ as a percentage.
8. Convert 0.91 to a fraction.
9. Express 0.0031 as a fraction.
10. Next to each set of fractions, write "True" if they are equivalent and "False" if they are not:

   a. $\dfrac{4}{1000} = \dfrac{2}{100}$ _____

   b. $\dfrac{5}{6} = \dfrac{52}{62}$ _____

   c. $\dfrac{1}{8} = \dfrac{7}{56}$ _____

11. Perform the following calculations:

   a. $\dfrac{4}{5} \times \dfrac{2}{3} = ?$ b. $\dfrac{7}{9} \div \dfrac{2}{3} = ?$

   c. $\dfrac{3}{8} + \dfrac{1}{5} = ?$ d. $\dfrac{5}{18} - \dfrac{1}{6} = ?$

12. $2.51 \times 0.017 = ?$
13. $3.88 \times 0.0002 = ?$
14. $3.17 + 17.0132 = ?$
15. $5.55 + 10.7 + 0.711 + 3.33 + 0.031 = ?$

16. $2.04 \div 0.2 = ?$
17. $0.36 \div 0.4 = ?$
18. $5 + 3 - 6 - 4 + 3 = ?$
19. $9 - (-1) - 17 + 3 - (-4) + 5 = ?$
20. $5 + 3 - (-8) - (-1) + (-3) - 4 + 10 = ?$
21. $8 \times (-3) = ?$
22. $-22 \div (-2) = ?$
23. $-2(-4) \_ (-3) = ?$
24. $84 \div (-4) = ?$

Solve the equations in problems $25-32$ for X.

25. $X - 7 = -2$
26. $9 = X + 3$
27. $\dfrac{X}{4} = 11$
28. $-3 = \dfrac{X}{3}$
29. $\dfrac{X + 3}{5} = 2$
30. $\dfrac{X + 1}{3} = -8$
31. $6X - 1 = 11$
32. $2X + 3 = -11$
33. $(-5)^2 = ?$
34. $(-5)^3 = ?$
35. If $a = 4$ and $b = 3$, then $a^2 + b^4 = ?$
36. If $a = -1$ and $b = 4$, then $(a + b)^2 = ?$
37. If $a = -1$ and $b = 5$, then $ab^2 = ?$
38. $\dfrac{8}{\sqrt{4}} = ?$
39. $\sqrt{\dfrac{20}{5}} = ?$

SKILLS ASSESSMENT FINAL EXAM

SECTION 1

1. $4 + 8/4 = ?$
2. $(4 + 8)/4 = ?$
3. $4 \times 3^2 = ?$
4. $(4 \times 3)^2 = ?$
5. $10/5 \times 2 = ?$
6. $10/(5 \times 2) = ?$
7. $40 - 10 \times 4/2 = ?$
8. $(5 - 1)^2/2 = ?$
9. $3 \times 6 - 3^2 = ?$
10. $2 \times (6 - 3)^2 = ?$
11. $4 \times 3 - 1 + 8 \times 2 = ?$
12. $4 \times (3 - 1 + 8) \times 2 = ?$

SECTION 2

1. Express $\frac{14}{80}$ as a decimal.
2. Convert $\frac{6}{25}$ to a percentage.

3. Convert 18% to a fraction.
4. $\frac{3}{5} \times \frac{2}{3} = ?$
5. $\frac{5}{24} + \frac{5}{6} = ?$
6. $\frac{7}{12} \div \frac{5}{6} = ?$
7. $\frac{5}{9} - \frac{1}{3} = ?$
8. $6.11 \times 0.22 = ?$
9. $0.18 \div 0.9 = ?$
10. $8.742 + 0.76 = ?$
11. In a statistics class of 72 students, three-eighths of the students received a B on the first test. How many Bs were earned?
12. What is 15% of 64?

SECTION 3

1. $3 - 1 - 3 + 5 - 2 + 6 = ?$
2. $-8 - (-6) = ?$
3. $2 - (-7) - 3 + (-11) - 20 = ?$
4. $-8 - 3 - (-1) - 2 - 1 = ?$
5. $8(-2) = ?$
6. $-7(-7) = ?$
7. $-3(-2)(-5) = ?$
8. $-3(5)(-3) = ?$
9. $-24 \div (-4) = ?$
10. $36 \div (-6) = ?$
11. $-56/7 = ?$
12. $-7/(-1) = ?$

SECTION 4

Solve for X.

1. $X + 5 = 12$
2. $X - 11 = 3$
3. $10 = X + 4$
4. $4X = 20$
5. $\dfrac{X}{2} = 15$
6. $18 = 9X$
7. $\dfrac{X}{5} = 35$
8. $2X + 8 = 4$

9. $\dfrac{X + 1}{3} = 6$
10. $4X + 3 = -13$
11. $\dfrac{X + 3}{3} = -7$
12. $23 = 2X - 5$

SECTION 5

1. $5^3 = ?$
2. $(-4)^3 = ?$
3. $(-2)^5 = ?$
4. $(-2)^6 = ?$
5. If $a = 4$ and $b = 2$, then $ab^2 = ?$
6. If $a = 4$ and $b = 2$, then $(a + b)^3 = ?$
7. If $a = 4$ and $b = 2$, then $a^2 + b^2 = ?$
8. $(11 + 4)^2 = ?$
9. $\sqrt{7^2} = ?$
10. If $a = 36$ and $b = 64$, then $\sqrt{a + b} = ?$
11. $\dfrac{25}{\sqrt{25}} = ? = ?$
12. If $a = -1$ and $b = 2$, then $a^3b^4 = ?$

ANSWER KEY Skills Assessment Exams

PREVIEW EXAM

SECTION 1

1. 17
2. 35
3. 6
4. 24
5. 5
6. 2
7. $\dfrac{1}{3}$
8. 8
9. 72
10. 8
11. 24
12. 48

SECTION 2

1. 75%
2. $\dfrac{30}{100}$, or $\dfrac{3}{10}$
3. 0.3
4. $\dfrac{10}{13}$
5. 1.625
6. $\dfrac{2}{20}$, or $\dfrac{1}{10}$
7. $\dfrac{19}{24}$
8. 1.4
9. $\dfrac{4}{15}$
10. 7.5
11. 16
12. 36

SECTION 3

1. 4
2. 8
3. 2
4. 9
5. -12
6. 12
7. -15
8. -24
9. -4
10. 3
11. -2
12. 25

FINAL EXAM

SECTION 1

1. 6
2. 3
3. 36
4. 144
5. 4
6. 1
7. 20
8. 8
9. 9
10. 18
11. 27
12. 80

SECTION 2

1. 0.175
2. 24%
3. $\dfrac{18}{100}$, or $\dfrac{9}{50}$
4. $\dfrac{6}{15}$, or $\dfrac{2}{5}$
5. $\dfrac{25}{24}$
6. $\dfrac{42}{60}$, or $\dfrac{7}{10}$
7. $\dfrac{2}{9}$
8. 1.3442
9. 0.2
10. 9.502
11. 27
12. 9.6

SECTION 3

1. 8
2. -2
3. -25
4. -13
5. -16
6. 49
7. -30
8. 45
9. 6
10. -6
11. -8
12. 7

PREVIEW EXAM

SECTION 4

1. $X = 7$	**2.** $X = 29$	**3.** $X = 9$
4. $X = 4$	**5.** $X = 24$	**6.** $X = 15$
7. $X = 80$	**8.** $X = -3$	**9.** $X = 11$
10. $X = 25$	**11.** $X = 11$	**12.** $X = 7$

SECTION 5

1. 64	**2.** 4	**3.** 54
4. 25	**5.** 13	**6.** -27
7. 256	**8.** 8	**9.** 12
10. 121	**11.** 33	**12.** -9

FINAL EXAM

SECTION 4

1. $X = 7$	**2.** $X = 14$	**3.** $X = 6$
4. $X = 5$	**5.** $X = 30$	**6.** $X = 2$
7. $X = 175$	**8.** $X = -2$	**9.** $X = 17$
10. $X = -4$	**11.** $X = -24$	**12.** $X = 14$

SECTION 5

1. 125	**2.** -64	**3.** -32
4. 64	**5.** 16	**6.** 216
7. 20	**8.** 225	**9.** 7
10. 10	**11.** 5	**12.** -16

SOLUTIONS TO SELECTED PROBLEMS FOR APPENDIX A   Basic Mathematics Review

1. 25	**3.** 6	**17.** 0.9	**19.** 5
5. 21	**6.** 0.35	**21.** -24	**22.** 11
7. 36%	**9.** $\dfrac{31}{10{,}000}$	**25.** $X = 5$	**28.** $X = -9$
10. b. False		**30.** $X = -25$	**31.** $X = 2$
11. a. $\dfrac{8}{15}$ **b.** $\dfrac{21}{18}$ **c.** $\dfrac{23}{40}$		**34.** -125	**36.** 9
12. 0.04267	**14.** 20.1832	**37.** -25	**39.** 2

SUGGESTED REVIEW BOOKS

There are many basic mathematics books available if you need a more extensive review than this appendix can provide. Several are probably available in your library. The following books are but a few of the many that you may find helpful:

Gustafson, R. D., Karr, R., & Massey, M. (2011). *Beginning Algebra* (9th ed.). Belmont, CA: Brooks/Cole.

Lial, M. L., Salzman, S.A., & Hestwood, D.L. (2010). *Basic College Mathematics* (8th ed). Reading MA: Addison-Wesley.

McKeague, C. P. (2010). *Basic College Mathematics: A Text/Workbook.* (7th ed.). Belmont, CA: Brooks/Cole.

Statistical Tables

TABLE B.1   THE UNIT NORMAL TABLE*

*Column A lists z-score values. A vertical line drawn through a normal distribution at a z-score location divides the distribution into two sections.
Column B identifies the proportion in the larger section, called the *body*.
Column C identifies the proportion in the smaller section, called the *tail*.
Column D identifies the proportion between the mean and the z-score.
Note: Because the normal distribution is symmetrical, the proportions for negative z-scores are the same as those for positive z-scores.

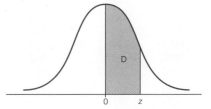

(A) z	(B) Proportion in Body	(C) Proportion in Tail	(D) Proportion Between Mean and z	(A) z	(B) Proportion in Body	(C) Proportion in Tail	(D) Proportion Between Mean and z
0.00	.5000	.5000	.0000	0.25	.5987	.4013	.0987
0.01	.5040	.4960	.0040	0.26	.6026	.3974	.1026
0.02	.5080	.4920	.0080	0.27	.6064	.3936	.1064
0.03	.5120	.4880	.0120	0.28	.6103	.3897	.1103
0.04	.5160	.4840	.0160	0.29	.6141	.3859	.1141
0.05	.5199	.4801	.0199	0.30	.6179	.3821	.1179
0.06	.5239	.4761	.0239	0.31	.6217	.3783	.1217
0.07	.5279	.4721	.0279	0.32	.6255	.3745	.1255
0.08	.5319	.4681	.0319	0.33	.6293	.3707	.1293
0.09	.5359	.4641	.0359	0.34	.6331	.3669	.1331
0.10	.5398	.4602	.0398	0.35	.6368	.3632	.1368
0.11	.5438	.4562	.0438	0.36	.6406	.3594	.1406
0.12	.5478	.4522	.0478	0.37	.6443	.3557	.1443
0.13	.5517	.4483	.0517	0.38	.6480	.3520	.1480
0.14	.5557	.4443	.0557	0.39	.6517	.3483	.1517
0.15	.5596	.4404	.0596	0.40	.6554	.3446	.1554
0.16	.5636	.4364	.0636	0.41	.6591	.3409	.1591
0.17	.5675	.4325	.0675	0.42	.6628	.3372	.1628
0.18	.5714	.4286	.0714	0.43	.6664	.3336	.1664
0.19	.5753	.4247	.0753	0.44	.6700	.3300	.1700
0.20	.5793	.4207	.0793	0.45	.6736	.3264	.1736
0.21	.5832	.4168	.0832	0.46	.6772	.3228	.1772
0.22	.5871	.4129	.0871	0.47	.6808	.3192	.1808
0.23	.5910	.4090	.0910	0.48	.6844	.3156	.1844
0.24	.5948	.4052	.0948	0.49	.6879	.3121	.1879

(A) z	(B) Proportion in Body	(C) Proportion in Tail	(D) Proportion Between Mean and z	(A) z	(B) Proportion in Body	(C) Proportion in Tail	(D) Proportion Between Mean and z
0.50	.6915	.3085	.1915	1.00	.8413	.1587	.3413
0.51	.6950	.3050	.1950	1.01	.8438	.1562	.3438
0.52	.6985	.3015	.1985	1.02	.8461	.1539	.3461
0.53	.7019	.2981	.2019	1.03	.8485	.1515	.3485
0.54	.7054	.2946	.2054	1.04	.8508	.1492	.3508
0.55	.7088	.2912	.2088	1.05	.8531	.1469	.3531
0.56	.7123	.2877	.2123	1.06	.8554	.1446	.3554
0.57	.7157	.2843	.2157	1.07	.8577	.1423	.3577
0.58	.7190	.2810	.2190	1.08	.8599	.1401	.3599
0.59	.7224	.2776	.2224	1.09	.8621	.1379	.3621
0.60	.7257	.2743	.2257	1.10	.8643	.1357	.3643
0.61	.7291	.2709	.2291	1.11	.8665	.1335	.3665
0.62	.7324	.2676	.2324	1.12	.8686	.1314	.3686
0.63	.7357	.2643	.2357	1.13	.8708	.1292	.3708
0.64	.7389	.2611	.2389	1.14	.8729	.1271	.3729
0.65	.7422	.2578	.2422	1.15	.8749	.1251	.3749
0.66	.7454	.2546	.2454	1.16	.8770	.1230	.3770
0.67	.7486	.2514	.2486	1.17	.8790	.1210	.3790
0.68	.7517	.2483	.2517	1.18	.8810	.1190	.3810
0.69	.7549	.2451	.2549	1.19	.8830	.1170	.3830
0.70	.7580	.2420	.2580	1.20	.8849	.1151	.3849
0.71	.7611	.2389	.2611	1.21	.8869	.1131	.3869
0.72	.7642	.2358	.2642	1.22	.8888	.1112	.3888
0.73	.7673	.2327	.2673	1.23	.8907	.1093	.3907
0.74	.7704	.2296	.2704	1.24	.8925	.1075	.3925
0.75	.7734	.2266	.2734	1.25	.8944	.1056	.3944
0.76	.7764	.2236	.2764	1.26	.8962	.1038	.3962
0.77	.7794	.2206	.2794	1.27	.8980	.1020	.3980
0.78	.7823	.2177	.2823	1.28	.8997	.1003	.3997
0.79	.7852	.2148	.2852	1.29	.9015	.0985	.4015
0.80	.7881	.2119	.2881	1.30	.9032	.0968	.4032
0.81	.7910	.2090	.2910	1.31	.9049	.0951	.4049
0.82	.7939	.2061	.2939	1.32	.9066	.0934	.4066
0.83	.7967	.2033	.2967	1.33	.9082	.0918	.4082
0.84	.7995	.2005	.2995	1.34	.9099	.0901	.4099
0.85	.8023	.1977	.3023	1.35	.9115	.0885	.4115
0.86	.8051	.1949	.3051	1.36	.9131	.0869	.4131
0.87	.8078	.1922	.3078	1.37	.9147	.0853	.4147
0.88	.8106	.1894	.3106	1.38	.9162	.0838	.4162
0.89	.8133	.1867	.3133	1.39	.9177	.0823	.4177
0.90	.8159	.1841	.3159	1.40	.9192	.0808	.4192
0.91	.8186	.1814	.3186	1.41	.9207	.0793	.4207
0.92	.8212	.1788	.3212	1.42	.9222	.0778	.4222
0.93	.8238	.1762	.3238	1.43	.9236	.0764	.4236
0.94	.8264	.1736	.3264	1.44	.9251	.0749	.4251
0.95	.8289	.1711	.3289	1.45	.9265	.0735	.4265
0.96	.8315	.1685	.3315	1.46	.9279	.0721	.4279
0.97	.8340	.1660	.3340	1.47	.9292	.0708	.4292
0.98	.8365	.1635	.3365	1.48	.9306	.0694	.4306
0.99	.8389	.1611	.3389	1.49	.9319	.0681	.4319

(A) z	(B) Proportion in Body	(C) Proportion in Tail	(D) Proportion Between Mean and z	(A) z	(B) Proportion in Body	(C) Proportion in Tail	(D) Proportion Between Mean and z
1.50	.9332	.0668	.4332	2.00	.9772	.0228	.4772
1.51	.9345	.0655	.4345	2.01	.9778	.0222	.4778
1.52	.9357	.0643	.4357	2.02	.9783	.0217	.4783
1.53	.9370	.0630	.4370	2.03	.9788	.0212	.4788
1.54	.9382	.0618	.4382	2.04	.9793	.0207	.4793
1.55	.9394	.0606	.4394	2.05	.9798	.0202	.4798
1.56	.9406	.0594	.4406	2.06	.9803	.0197	.4803
1.57	.9418	.0582	.4418	2.07	.9808	.0192	.4808
1.58	.9429	.0571	.4429	2.08	.9812	.0188	.4812
1.59	.9441	.0559	.4441	2.09	.9817	.0183	.4817
1.60	.9452	.0548	.4452	2.10	.9821	.0179	.4821
1.61	.9463	.0537	.4463	2.11	.9826	.0174	.4826
1.62	.9474	.0526	.4474	2.12	.9830	.0170	.4830
1.63	.9484	.0516	.4484	2.13	.9834	.0166	.4834
1.64	.9495	.0505	.4495	2.14	.9838	.0162	.4838
1.65	.9505	.0495	.4505	2.15	.9842	.0158	.4842
1.66	.9515	.0485	.4515	2.16	.9846	.0154	.4846
1.67	.9525	.0475	.4525	2.17	.9850	.0150	.4850
1.68	.9535	.0465	.4535	2.18	.9854	.0146	.4854
1.69	.9545	.0455	.4545	2.19	.9857	.0143	.4857
1.70	.9554	.0446	.4554	2.20	.9861	.0139	.4861
1.71	.9564	.0436	.4564	2.21	.9864	.0136	.4864
1.72	.9573	.0427	.4573	2.22	.9868	.0132	.4868
1.73	.9582	.0418	.4582	2.23	.9871	.0129	.4871
1.74	.9591	.0409	.4591	2.24	.9875	.0125	.4875
1.75	.9599	.0401	.4599	2.25	.9878	.0122	.4878
1.76	.9608	.0392	.4608	2.26	.9881	.0119	.4881
1.77	.9616	.0384	.4616	2.27	.9884	.0116	.4884
1.78	.9625	.0375	.4625	2.28	.9887	.0113	.4887
1.79	.9633	.0367	.4633	2.29	.9890	.0110	.4890
1.80	.9641	.0359	.4641	2.30	.9893	.0107	.4893
1.81	.9649	.0351	.4649	2.31	.9896	.0104	.4896
1.82	.9656	.0344	.4656	2.32	.9898	.0102	.4898
1.83	.9664	.0336	.4664	2.33	.9901	.0099	.4901
1.84	.9671	.0329	.4671	2.34	.9904	.0096	.4904
1.85	.9678	.0322	.4678	2.35	.9906	.0094	.4906
1.86	.9686	.0314	.4686	2.36	.9909	.0091	.4909
1.87	.9693	.0307	.4693	2.37	.9911	.0089	.4911
1.88	.9699	.0301	.4699	2.38	.9913	.0087	.4913
1.89	.9706	.0294	.4706	2.39	.9916	.0084	.4916
1.90	.9713	.0287	.4713	2.40	.9918	.0082	.4918
1.91	.9719	.0281	.4719	2.41	.9920	.0080	.4920
1.92	.9726	.0274	.4726	2.42	.9922	.0078	.4922
1.93	.9732	.0268	.4732	2.43	.9925	.0075	.4925
1.94	.9738	.0262	.4738	2.44	.9927	.0073	.4927
1.95	.9744	.0256	.4744	2.45	.9929	.0071	.4929
1.96	.9750	.0250	.4750	2.46	.9931	.0069	.4931
1.97	.9756	.0244	.4756	2.47	.9932	.0068	.4932
1.98	.9761	.0239	.4761	2.48	.9934	.0066	.4934
1.99	.9767	.0233	.4767	2.49	.9936	.0064	.4936

(A) z	(B) Proportion in Body	(C) Proportion in Tail	(D) Proportion Between Mean and z	(A) z	(B) Proportion in Body	(C) Proportion in Tail	(D) Proportion Between Mean and z
2.50	.9938	.0062	.4938	2.95	.9984	.0016	.4984
2.51	.9940	.0060	.4940	2.96	.9985	.0015	.4985
2.52	.9941	.0059	.4941	2.97	.9985	.0015	.4985
2.53	.9943	.0057	.4943	2.98	.9986	.0014	.4986
2.54	.9945	.0055	.4945	2.99	.9986	.0014	.4986
2.55	.9946	.0054	.4946	3.00	.9987	.0013	.4987
2.56	.9948	.0052	.4948	3.01	.9987	.0013	.4987
2.57	.9949	.0051	.4949	3.02	.9987	.0013	.4987
2.58	.9951	.0049	.4951	3.03	.9988	.0012	.4988
2.59	.9952	.0048	.4952	3.04	.9988	.0012	.4988
2.60	.9953	.0047	.4953	3.05	.9989	.0011	.4989
2.61	.9955	.0045	.4955	3.06	.9989	.0011	.4989
2.62	.9956	.0044	.4956	3.07	.9989	.0011	.4989
2.63	.9957	.0043	.4957	3.08	.9990	.0010	.4990
2.64	.9959	.0041	.4959	3.09	.9990	.0010	.4990
2.65	.9960	.0040	.4960	3.10	.9990	.0010	.4990
2.66	.9961	.0039	.4961	3.11	.9991	.0009	.4991
2.67	.9962	.0038	.4962	3.12	.9991	.0009	.4991
2.68	.9963	.0037	.4963	3.13	.9991	.0009	.4991
2.69	.9964	.0036	.4964	3.14	.9992	.0008	.4992
2.70	.9965	.0035	.4965	3.15	.9992	.0008	.4992
2.71	.9966	.0034	.4966	3.16	.9992	.0008	.4992
2.72	.9967	.0033	.4967	3.17	.9992	.0008	.4992
2.73	.9968	.0032	.4968	3.18	.9993	.0007	.4993
2.74	.9969	.0031	.4969	3.19	.9993	.0007	.4993
2.75	.9970	.0030	.4970	3.20	.9993	.0007	.4993
2.76	.9971	.0029	.4971	3.21	.9993	.0007	.4993
2.77	.9972	.0028	.4972	3.22	.9994	.0006	.4994
2.78	.9973	.0027	.4973	3.23	.9994	.0006	.4994
2.79	.9974	.0026	.4974	3.24	.9994	.0006	.4994
2.80	.9974	.0026	.4974	3.30	.9995	.0005	.4995
2.81	.9975	.0025	.4975	3.40	.9997	.0003	.4997
2.82	.9976	.0024	.4976	3.50	.9998	.0002	.4998
2.83	.9977	.0023	.4977	3.60	.9998	.0002	.4998
2.84	.9977	.0023	.4977	3.70	.9999	.0001	.4999
2.85	.9978	.0022	.4978	3.80	.99993	.00007	.49993
2.86	.9979	.0021	.4979	3.90	.99995	.00005	.49995
2.87	.9979	.0021	.4979	4.00	.99997	.00003	.49997
2.88	.9980	.0020	.4980				
2.89	.9981	.0019	.4981				
2.90	.9981	.0019	.4981				
2.91	.9982	.0018	.4982				
2.92	.9982	.0018	.4982				
2.93	.9983	.0017	.4983				
2.94	.9984	.0016	.4984				

TABLE B.2   THE *t* DISTRIBUTION

Table entries are values of *t* corresponding to proportions in one tail or in two tails combined.

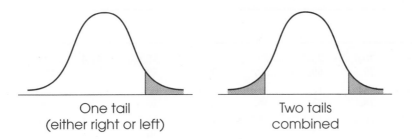

One tail
(either right or left)

Two tails
combined

df	Proportion in One Tail					
	0.25	0.10	0.05	0.025	0.01	0.005
	Proportion in Two Tails Combined					
	0.50	0.20	0.10	0.05	0.02	0.01
1	1.000	3.078	6.314	12.706	31.821	63.657
2	0.816	1.886	2.920	4.303	6.965	9.925
3	0.765	1.638	2.353	3.182	4.541	5.841
4	0.741	1.533	2.132	2.776	3.747	4.604
5	0.727	1.476	2.015	2.571	3.365	4.032
6	0.718	1.440	1.943	2.447	3.143	3.707
7	0.711	1.415	1.895	2.365	2.998	3.499
8	0.706	1.397	1.860	2.306	2.896	3.355
9	0.703	1.383	1.833	2.262	2.821	3.250
10	0.700	1.372	1.812	2.228	2.764	3.169
11	0.697	1.363	1.796	2.201	2.718	3.106
12	0.695	1.356	1.782	2.179	2.681	3.055
13	0.694	1.350	1.771	2.160	2.650	3.012
14	0.692	1.345	1.761	2.145	2.624	2.977
15	0.691	1.341	1.753	2.131	2.602	2.947
16	0.690	1.337	1.746	2.120	2.583	2.921
17	0.689	1.333	1.740	2.110	2.567	2.898
18	0.688	1.330	1.734	2.101	2.552	2.878
19	0.688	1.328	1.729	2.093	2.539	2.861
20	0.687	1.325	1.725	2.086	2.528	2.845
21	0.686	1.323	1.721	2.080	2.518	2.831
22	0.686	1.321	1.717	2.074	2.508	2.819
23	0.685	1.319	1.714	2.069	2.500	2.807
24	0.685	1.318	1.711	2.064	2.492	2.797
25	0.684	1.316	1.708	2.060	2.485	2.787
26	0.684	1.315	1.706	2.056	2.479	2.779
27	0.684	1.314	1.703	2.052	2.473	2.771
28	0.683	1.313	1.701	2.048	2.467	2.763
29	0.683	1.311	1.699	2.045	2.462	2.756
30	0.683	1.310	1.697	2.042	2.457	2.750
40	0.681	1.303	1.684	2.021	2.423	2.704
60	0.679	1.296	1.671	2.000	2.390	2.660
120	0.677	1.289	1.658	1.980	2.358	2.617
∞	0.674	1.282	1.645	1.960	2.326	2.576

Table III of Fisher, R. A., & Yates, F. (1974). *Statistical Tables for Biological, Agricultural and Medical Research* (6th ed.). London: Longman Group Ltd., 1974 (previously published by Oliver and Boyd Ltd., Edinburgh). Copyright ©1963 R. A. Fisher and F. Yates. Adapted and reprinted with permission of Pearson Education Limited.

TABLE B.3   CRITICAL VALUES FOR THE *F*-MAX STATISTIC*

*The critical values for $\alpha = .05$ are in lightface type, and for $\alpha = .01$, they are in boldface type.

$n - 1$	2	3	4	5	k = Number of Samples 6	7	8	9	10	11	12
4	9.60 **23.2**	15.5 **37.**	20.6 **49.**	25.2 **59.**	29.5 **69.**	33.6 **79.**	37.5 **89.**	41.4 **97.**	44.6 **106.**	48.0 **113.**	51.4 **120.**
5	7.15 **14.9**	10.8 **22.**	13.7 **28.**	16.3 **33.**	18.7 **38.**	20.8 **42.**	22.9 **46.**	24.7 **50.**	26.5 **54.**	28.2 **57.**	29.9 **60.**
6	5.82 **11.1**	8.38 **15.5**	10.4 **19.1**	12.1 **22.**	13.7 **25.**	15.0 **27.**	16.3 **30.**	17.5 **32.**	18.6 **34.**	19.7 **36.**	20.7 **37.**
7	4.99 **8.89**	6.94 **12.1**	8.44 **14.5**	9.70 **16.5**	10.8 **18.4**	11.8 **20.**	12.7 **22.**	13.5 **23.**	14.3 **24.**	15.1 **26.**	15.8 **27.**
8	4.43 **7.50**	6.00 **9.9**	7.18 **11.7**	8.12 **13.2**	9.03 **14.5**	9.78 **15.8**	10.5 **16.9**	11.1 **17.9**	11.7 **18.9**	12.2 **19.8**	12.7 **21.**
9	4.03 **6.54**	5.34 **8.5**	6.31 **9.9**	7.11 **11.1**	7.80 **12.1**	8.41 **13.1**	8.95 **13.9**	9.45 **14.7**	9.91 **15.3**	10.3 **16.0**	10.7 **16.6**
10	3.72 **5.85**	4.85 **7.4**	5.67 **8.6**	6.34 **9.6**	6.92 **10.4**	7.42 **11.1**	7.87 **11.8**	8.28 **12.4**	8.66 **12.9**	9.01 **13.4**	9.34 **13.9**
12	3.28 **4.91**	4.16 **6.1**	4.79 **6.9**	5.30 **7.6**	5.72 **8.2**	6.09 **8.7**	6.42 **9.1**	6.72 **9.5**	7.00 **9.9**	7.25 **10.2**	7.48 **10.6**
15	2.86 **4.07**	3.54 **4.9**	4.01 **5.5**	4.37 **6.0**	4.68 **6.4**	4.95 **6.7**	5.19 **7.1**	5.40 **7.3**	5.59 **7.5**	5.77 **7.8**	5.93 **8.0**
20	2.46 **3.32**	2.95 **3.8**	3.29 **4.3**	3.54 **4.6**	3.76 **4.9**	3.94 **5.1**	4.10 **5.3**	4.24 **5.5**	4.37 **5.6**	4.49 **5.8**	4.59 **5.9**
30	2.07 **2.63**	2.40 **3.0**	2.61 **3.3**	2.78 **3.5**	2.91 **3.6**	3.02 **3.7**	3.12 **3.8**	3.21 **3.9**	3.29 **4.0**	3.36 **4.1**	3.39 **4.2**
60	1.67 **1.96**	1.85 **2.2**	1.96 **2.3**	2.04 **2.4**	2.11 **2.4**	2.17 **2.5**	2.22 **2.5**	2.26 **2.6**	2.30 **2.6**	2.33 **2.7**	2.36 **2.7**

Table 31 of Pearson, E., and Hartley, H.O. (1958). *Biometrika Tables for Statisticians* (2nd ed.). New York: Cambridge University Press. Adapted and reprinted with permission of the Biometrika trustees.

TABLE B.4   THE *F* DISTRIBUTION*

*Table entries in lightface type are critical values for the .05 level of significance. Boldface type values are for the .01 level of significance.

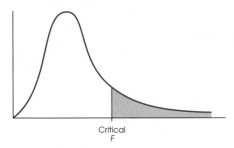

Critical
F

Degrees of Freedom: Denominator	Degrees of Freedom: Numerator														
	1	2	3	4	5	6	7	8	9	10	11	12	14	16	20
1	161	200	216	225	230	234	237	239	241	242	243	244	245	246	248
	4052	**4999**	**5403**	**5625**	**5764**	**5859**	**5928**	**5981**	**6022**	**6056**	**6082**	**6106**	**6142**	**6169**	**6208**
2	18.51	19.00	19.16	19.25	19.30	19.33	19.36	19.37	19.38	19.39	19.40	19.41	19.42	19.43	19.44
	98.49	**99.00**	**99.17**	**99.25**	**99.30**	**99.33**	**99.34**	**99.36**	**99.38**	**99.40**	**99.41**	**99.42**	**99.43**	**99.44**	**99.45**
3	10.13	9.55	9.28	9.12	9.01	8.94	8.88	8.84	8.81	8.78	8.76	8.74	8.71	8.69	8.66
	34.12	**30.92**	**29.46**	**28.71**	**28.24**	**27.91**	**27.67**	**27.49**	**27.34**	**27.23**	**27.13**	**27.05**	**26.92**	**26.83**	**26.69**
4	7.71	6.94	6.59	6.39	6.26	6.16	6.09	6.04	6.00	5.96	5.93	5.91	5.87	5.84	5.80
	21.20	**18.00**	**16.69**	**15.98**	**15.52**	**15.21**	**14.98**	**14.80**	**14.66**	**14.54**	**14.45**	**14.37**	**14.24**	**14.15**	**14.02**
5	6.61	5.79	5.41	5.19	5.05	4.95	4.88	4.82	4.78	4.74	4.70	4.68	4.64	4.60	4.56
	16.26	**13.27**	**12.06**	**11.39**	**10.97**	**10.67**	**10.45**	**10.27**	**10.15**	**10.05**	**9.96**	**9.89**	**9.77**	**9.68**	**9.55**
6	5.99	5.14	4.76	4.53	4.39	4.28	4.21	4.15	4.10	4.06	4.03	4.00	3.96	3.92	3.87
	13.74	**10.92**	**9.78**	**9.15**	**8.75**	**8.47**	**8.26**	**8.10**	**7.98**	**7.87**	**7.79**	**7.72**	**7.60**	**7.52**	**7.39**
7	5.59	4.74	4.35	4.12	3.97	3.87	3.79	3.73	3.68	3.63	3.60	3.57	3.52	3.49	3.44
	12.25	**9.55**	**8.45**	**7.85**	**7.46**	**7.19**	**7.00**	**6.84**	**6.71**	**6.62**	**6.54**	**6.47**	**6.35**	**6.27**	**6.15**
8	5.32	4.46	4.07	3.84	3.69	3.58	3.50	3.44	3.39	3.34	3.31	3.28	3.23	3.20	3.15
	11.26	**8.65**	**7.59**	**7.01**	**6.63**	**6.37**	**6.19**	**6.03**	**5.91**	**5.82**	**5.74**	**5.67**	**5.56**	**5.48**	**5.36**
9	5.12	4.26	3.86	3.63	3.48	3.37	3.29	3.23	3.18	3.13	3.10	3.07	3.02	2.98	2.93
	10.56	**8.02**	**6.99**	**6.42**	**6.06**	**5.80**	**5.62**	**5.47**	**5.35**	**5.26**	**5.18**	**5.11**	**5.00**	**4.92**	**4.80**
10	4.96	4.10	3.71	3.48	3.33	3.22	3.14	3.07	3.02	2.97	2.94	2.91	2.86	2.82	2.77
	10.04	**7.56**	**6.55**	**5.99**	**5.64**	**5.39**	**5.21**	**5.06**	**4.95**	**4.85**	**4.78**	**4.71**	**4.60**	**4.52**	**4.41**
11	4.84	3.98	3.59	3.36	3.20	3.09	3.01	2.95	2.90	2.86	2.82	2.79	2.74	2.70	2.65
	9.65	**7.20**	**6.22**	**5.67**	**5.32**	**5.07**	**4.88**	**4.74**	**4.63**	**4.54**	**4.46**	**4.40**	**4.29**	**4.21**	**4.10**
12	4.75	3.88	3.49	3.26	3.11	3.00	2.92	2.85	2.80	2.76	2.72	2.69	2.64	2.60	2.54
	9.33	**6.93**	**5.95**	**5.41**	**5.06**	**4.82**	**4.65**	**4.50**	**4.39**	**4.30**	**4.22**	**4.16**	**4.05**	**3.98**	**3.86**
13	4.67	3.80	3.41	3.18	3.02	2.92	2.84	2.77	2.72	2.67	2.63	2.60	2.55	2.51	2.46
	9.07	**6.70**	**5.74**	**5.20**	**4.86**	**4.62**	**4.44**	**4.30**	**4.19**	**4.10**	**4.02**	**3.96**	**3.85**	**3.78**	**3.67**
14	4.60	3.74	3.34	3.11	2.96	2.85	2.77	2.70	2.65	2.60	2.56	2.53	2.48	2.44	2.39
	8.86	**6.51**	**5.56**	**5.03**	**4.69**	**4.46**	**4.28**	**4.14**	**4.03**	**3.94**	**3.86**	**3.80**	**3.70**	**3.62**	**3.51**
15	4.54	3.68	3.29	3.06	2.90	2.79	2.70	2.64	2.59	2.55	2.51	2.48	2.43	2.39	2.33
	8.68	**6.36**	**5.42**	**4.89**	**4.56**	**4.32**	**4.14**	**4.00**	**3.89**	**3.80**	**3.73**	**3.67**	**3.56**	**3.48**	**3.36**
16	4.49	3.63	3.24	3.01	2.85	2.74	2.66	2.59	2.54	2.49	2.45	2.42	2.37	2.33	2.28
	8.53	**6.23**	**5.29**	**4.77**	**4.44**	**4.20**	**4.03**	**3.89**	**3.78**	**3.69**	**3.61**	**3.55**	**3.45**	**3.37**	**3.25**

TABLE B.4   (continued)

Degrees of Freedom: Denominator	Degrees of Freedom: Numerator														
	1	2	3	4	5	6	7	8	9	10	11	12	14	16	20
17	4.45	3.59	3.20	2.96	2.81	2.70	2.62	2.55	2.50	2.45	2.41	2.38	2.33	2.29	2.23
	8.40	**6.11**	**5.18**	**4.67**	**4.34**	**4.10**	**3.93**	**3.79**	**3.68**	**3.59**	**3.52**	**3.45**	**3.35**	**3.27**	**3.16**
18	4.41	3.55	3.16	2.93	2.77	2.66	2.58	2.51	2.46	2.41	2.37	2.34	2.29	2.25	2.19
	8.28	**6.01**	**5.09**	**4.58**	**4.25**	**4.01**	**3.85**	**3.71**	**3.60**	**3.51**	**3.44**	**3.37**	**3.27**	**3.19**	**3.07**
19	4.38	3.52	3.13	2.90	2.74	2.63	2.55	2.48	2.43	2.38	2.34	2.31	2.26	2.21	2.15
	8.18	**5.93**	**5.01**	**4.50**	**4.17**	**3.94**	**3.77**	**3.63**	**3.52**	**3.43**	**3.36**	**3.30**	**3.19**	**3.12**	**3.00**
20	4.35	3.49	3.10	2.87	2.71	2.60	2.52	2.45	2.40	2.35	2.31	2.28	2.23	2.18	2.12
	8.10	**5.85**	**4.94**	**4.43**	**4.10**	**3.87**	**3.71**	**3.56**	**3.45**	**3.37**	**3.30**	**3.23**	**3.13**	**3.05**	**2.94**
21	4.32	3.47	3.07	2.84	2.68	2.57	2.49	2.42	2.37	2.32	2.28	2.25	2.20	2.15	2.09
	8.02	**5.78**	**4.87**	**4.37**	**4.04**	**3.81**	**3.65**	**3.51**	**3.40**	**3.31**	**3.24**	**3.17**	**3.07**	**2.99**	**2.88**
22	4.30	3.44	3.05	2.82	2.66	2.55	2.47	2.40	2.35	2.30	2.26	2.23	2.18	2.13	2.07
	7.94	**5.72**	**4.82**	**4.31**	**3.99**	**3.76**	**3.59**	**3.45**	**3.35**	**3.26**	**3.18**	**3.12**	**3.02**	**2.94**	**2.83**
23	4.28	3.42	3.03	2.80	2.64	2.53	2.45	2.38	2.32	2.28	2.24	2.20	2.14	2.10	2.04
	7.88	**5.66**	**4.76**	**4.26**	**3.94**	**3.71**	**3.54**	**3.41**	**3.30**	**3.21**	**3.14**	**3.07**	**2.97**	**2.89**	**2.78**
24	4.26	3.40	3.01	2.78	2.62	2.51	2.43	2.36	2.30	2.26	2.22	2.18	2.13	2.09	2.02
	7.82	**5.61**	**4.72**	**4.22**	**3.90**	**3.67**	**3.50**	**3.36**	**3.25**	**3.17**	**3.09**	**3.03**	**2.93**	**2.85**	**2.74**
25	4.24	3.38	2.99	2.76	2.60	2.49	2.41	2.34	2.28	2.24	2.20	2.16	2.11	2.06	2.00
	7.77	**5.57**	**4.68**	**4.18**	**3.86**	**3.63**	**3.46**	**3.32**	**3.21**	**3.13**	**3.05**	**2.99**	**2.89**	**2.81**	**2.70**
26	4.22	3.37	2.98	2.74	2.59	2.47	2.39	2.32	2.27	2.22	2.18	2.15	2.10	2.05	1.99
	7.72	**5.53**	**4.64**	**4.14**	**3.82**	**3.59**	**3.42**	**3.29**	**3.17**	**3.09**	**3.02**	**2.96**	**2.86**	**2.77**	**2.66**
27	4.21	3.35	2.96	2.73	2.57	2.46	2.37	2.30	2.25	2.20	2.16	2.13	2.08	2.03	1.97
	7.68	**5.49**	**4.60**	**4.11**	**3.79**	**3.56**	**3.39**	**3.26**	**3.14**	**3.06**	**2.98**	**2.93**	**2.83**	**2.74**	**2.63**
28	4.20	3.34	2.95	2.71	2.56	2.44	2.36	2.29	2.24	2.19	2.15	2.12	2.06	2.02	1.96
	7.64	**5.45**	**4.57**	**4.07**	**3.76**	**3.53**	**3.36**	**3.23**	**3.11**	**3.03**	**2.95**	**2.90**	**2.80**	**2.71**	**2.60**
29	4.18	3.33	2.93	2.70	2.54	2.43	2.35	2.28	2.22	2.18	2.14	2.10	2.05	2.00	1.94
	7.60	**5.42**	**4.54**	**4.04**	**3.73**	**3.50**	**3.33**	**3.20**	**3.08**	**3.00**	**2.92**	**2.87**	**2.77**	**2.68**	**2.57**
30	4.17	3.32	2.92	2.69	2.53	2.42	2.34	2.27	2.21	2.16	2.12	2.09	2.04	1.99	1.93
	7.56	**5.39**	**4.51**	**4.02**	**3.70**	**3.47**	**3.30**	**3.17**	**3.06**	**2.98**	**2.90**	**2.84**	**2.74**	**2.66**	**2.55**
32	4.15	3.30	2.90	2.67	2.51	2.40	2.32	2.25	2.19	2.14	2.10	2.07	2.02	1.97	1.91
	7.50	**5.34**	**4.46**	**3.97**	**3.66**	**3.42**	**3.25**	**3.12**	**3.01**	**2.94**	**2.86**	**2.80**	**2.70**	**2.62**	**2.51**
34	4.13	3.28	2.88	2.65	2.49	2.38	2.30	2.23	2.17	2.12	2.08	2.05	2.00	1.95	1.89
	7.44	**5.29**	**4.42**	**3.93**	**3.61**	**3.38**	**3.21**	**3.08**	**2.97**	**2.89**	**2.82**	**2.76**	**2.66**	**2.58**	**2.47**
36	4.11	3.26	2.86	2.63	2.48	2.36	2.28	2.21	2.15	2.10	2.06	2.03	1.98	1.93	1.87
	7.39	**5.25**	**4.38**	**3.89**	**3.58**	**3.35**	**3.18**	**3.04**	**2.94**	**2.86**	**2.78**	**2.72**	**2.62**	**2.54**	**2.43**
38	4.10	3.25	2.85	2.62	2.46	2.35	2.26	2.19	2.14	2.09	2.05	2.02	1.96	1.92	1.85
	7.35	**5.21**	**4.34**	**3.86**	**3.54**	**3.32**	**3.15**	**3.02**	**2.91**	**2.82**	**2.75**	**2.69**	**2.59**	**2.51**	**2.40**
40	4.08	3.23	2.84	2.61	2.45	2.34	2.25	2.18	2.12	2.07	2.04	2.00	1.95	1.90	1.84
	7.31	**5.18**	**4.31**	**3.83**	**3.51**	**3.29**	**3.12**	**2.99**	**2.88**	**2.80**	**2.73**	**2.66**	**2.56**	**2.49**	**2.37**

TABLE B.4   (continued)

Degrees of Freedom: Denominator	Degrees of Freedom: Numerator														
	1	2	3	4	5	6	7	8	9	10	11	12	14	16	20
42	4.07	3.22	2.83	2.59	2.44	2.32	2.24	2.17	2.11	2.06	2.02	1.99	1.94	1.89	1.82
	7.27	**5.15**	**4.29**	**3.80**	**3.49**	**3.26**	**3.10**	**2.96**	**2.86**	**2.77**	**2.70**	**2.64**	**2.54**	**2.46**	**2.35**
44	4.06	3.21	2.82	2.58	2.43	2.31	2.23	2.16	2.10	2.05	2.01	1.98	1.92	1.88	1.81
	7.24	**5.12**	**4.26**	**3.78**	**3.46**	**3.24**	**3.07**	**2.94**	**2.84**	**2.75**	**2.68**	**2.62**	**2.52**	**2.44**	**2.32**
46	4.05	3.20	2.81	2.57	2.42	2.30	2.22	2.14	2.09	2.04	2.00	1.97	1.91	1.87	1.80
	7.21	**5.10**	**4.24**	**3.76**	**3.44**	**3.22**	**3.05**	**2.92**	**2.82**	**2.73**	**2.66**	**2.60**	**2.50**	**2.42**	**2.30**
48	4.04	3.19	2.80	2.56	2.41	2.30	2.21	2.14	2.08	2.03	1.99	1.96	1.90	1.86	1.79
	7.19	**5.08**	**4.22**	**3.74**	**3.42**	**3.20**	**3.04**	**2.90**	**2.80**	**2.71**	**2.64**	**2.58**	**2.48**	**2.40**	**2.28**
50	4.03	3.18	2.79	2.56	2.40	2.29	2.20	2.13	2.07	2.02	1.98	1.95	1.90	1.85	1.78
	7.17	**5.06**	**4.20**	**3.72**	**3.41**	**3.18**	**3.02**	**2.88**	**2.78**	**2.70**	**2.62**	**2.56**	**2.46**	**2.39**	**2.26**
55	4.02	3.17	2.78	2.54	2.38	2.27	2.18	2.11	2.05	2.00	1.97	1.93	1.88	1.83	1.76
	7.12	**5.01**	**4.16**	**3.68**	**3.37**	**3.15**	**2.98**	**2.85**	**2.75**	**2.66**	**2.59**	**2.53**	**2.43**	**2.35**	**2.23**
60	4.00	3.15	2.76	2.52	2.37	2.25	2.17	2.10	2.04	1.99	1.95	1.92	1.86	1.81	1.75
	7.08	**4.98**	**4.13**	**3.65**	**3.34**	**3.12**	**2.95**	**2.82**	**2.72**	**2.63**	**2.56**	**2.50**	**2.40**	**2.32**	**2.20**
65	3.99	3.14	2.75	2.51	2.36	2.24	2.15	2.08	2.02	1.98	1.94	1.90	1.85	1.80	1.73
	7.04	**4.95**	**4.10**	**3.62**	**3.31**	**3.09**	**2.93**	**2.79**	**2.70**	**2.61**	**2.54**	**2.47**	**2.37**	**2.30**	**2.18**
70	3.98	3.13	2.74	2.50	2.35	2.23	2.14	2.07	2.01	1.97	1.93	1.89	1.84	1.79	1.72
	7.01	**4.92**	**4.08**	**3.60**	**3.29**	**3.07**	**2.91**	**2.77**	**2.67**	**2.59**	**2.51**	**2.45**	**2.35**	**2.28**	**2.15**
80	3.96	3.11	2.72	2.48	2.33	2.21	2.12	2.05	1.99	1.95	1.91	1.88	1.82	1.77	1.70
	6.96	**4.88**	**4.04**	**3.56**	**3.25**	**3.04**	**2.87**	**2.74**	**2.64**	**2.55**	**2.48**	**2.41**	**2.32**	**2.24**	**2.11**
100	3.94	3.09	2.70	2.46	2.30	2.19	2.10	2.03	1.97	1.92	1.88	1.85	1.79	1.75	1.68
	6.90	**4.82**	**3.98**	**3.51**	**3.20**	**2.99**	**2.82**	**2.69**	**2.59**	**2.51**	**2.43**	**2.36**	**2.26**	**2.19**	**2.06**
125	3.92	3.07	2.68	2.44	2.29	2.17	2.08	2.01	1.95	1.90	1.86	1.83	1.77	1.72	1.65
	6.84	**4.78**	**3.94**	**3.47**	**3.17**	**2.95**	**2.79**	**2.65**	**2.56**	**2.47**	**2.40**	**2.33**	**2.23**	**2.15**	**2.03**
150	3.91	3.06	2.67	2.43	2.27	2.16	2.07	2.00	1.94	1.89	1.85	1.82	1.76	1.71	1.64
	6.81	**4.75**	**3.91**	**3.44**	**3.14**	**2.92**	**2.76**	**2.62**	**2.53**	**2.44**	**2.37**	**2.30**	**2.20**	**2.12**	**2.00**
200	3.89	3.04	2.65	2.41	2.26	2.14	2.05	1.98	1.92	1.87	1.83	1.80	1.74	1.69	1.62
	6.76	**4.71**	**3.88**	**3.41**	**3.11**	**2.90**	**2.73**	**2.60**	**2.50**	**2.41**	**2.34**	**2.28**	**2.17**	**2.09**	**1.97**
400	3.86	3.02	2.62	2.39	2.23	2.12	2.03	1.96	1.90	1.85	1.81	1.78	1.72	1.67	1.60
	6.70	**4.66**	**3.83**	**3.36**	**3.06**	**2.85**	**2.69**	**2.55**	**2.46**	**2.37**	**2.29**	**2.23**	**2.12**	**2.04**	**1.92**
1000	3.85	3.00	2.61	2.38	2.22	2.10	2.02	1.95	1.89	1.84	1.80	1.76	1.70	1.65	1.58
	6.66	**4.62**	**3.80**	**3.34**	**3.04**	**2.82**	**2.66**	**2.53**	**2.43**	**2.34**	**2.26**	**2.20**	**2.09**	**2.01**	**1.89**
∞	3.84	2.99	2.60	2.37	2.21	2.09	2.01	1.94	1.88	1.83	1.79	1.75	1.69	1.64	1.57
	6.64	**4.60**	**3.78**	**3.32**	**3.02**	**2.80**	**2.64**	**2.51**	**2.41**	**2.32**	**2.24**	**2.18**	**2.07**	**1.99**	**1.87**

TABLE B.5   THE STUDENTIZED RANGE STATISTIC (q)*

*The critical values for q corresponding to $\alpha = .05$ (lightface type) and $\alpha = .01$ (boldface type).

df for Error Term	k = Number of Treatments										
	2	3	4	5	6	7	8	9	10	11	12
5	3.64	4.60	5.22	5.67	6.03	6.33	6.58	6.80	6.99	7.17	7.32
	5.70	**6.98**	**7.80**	**8.42**	**8.91**	**9.32**	**9.67**	**9.97**	**10.24**	**10.48**	**10.70**
6	3.46	4.34	4.90	5.30	5.63	5.90	6.12	6.32	6.49	6.65	6.79
	5.24	**6.33**	**7.03**	**7.56**	**7.97**	**8.32**	**8.61**	**8.87**	**9.10**	**9.30**	**9.48**
7	3.34	4.16	4.68	5.06	5.36	5.61	5.82	6.00	6.16	6.30	6.43
	4.95	**5.92**	**6.54**	**7.01**	**7.37**	**7.68**	**7.94**	**8.17**	**8.37**	**8.55**	**8.71**
8	3.26	4.04	4.53	4.89	5.17	5.40	5.60	5.77	5.92	6.05	6.18
	4.75	**5.64**	**6.20**	**6.62**	**6.96**	**7.24**	**7.47**	**7.68**	**7.86**	**8.03**	**8.18**
9	3.20	3.95	4.41	4.76	5.02	5.24	5.43	5.59	5.74	5.87	5.98
	4.60	**5.43**	**5.96**	**6.35**	**6.66**	**6.91**	**7.13**	**7.33**	**7.49**	**7.65**	**7.78**
10	3.15	3.88	4.33	4.65	4.91	5.12	5.30	5.46	5.60	5.72	5.83
	4.48	**5.27**	**5.77**	**6.14**	**6.43**	**6.67**	**6.87**	**7.05**	**7.21**	**7.36**	**7.49**
11	3.11	3.82	4.26	4.57	4.82	5.03	5.20	5.35	5.49	5.61	5.71
	4.39	**5.15**	**5.62**	**5.97**	**6.25**	**6.48**	**6.67**	**6.84**	**6.99**	**7.13**	**7.25**
12	3.08	3.77	4.20	4.51	4.75	4.95	5.12	5.27	5.39	5.51	5.61
	4.32	**5.05**	**5.50**	**5.84**	**6.10**	**6.32**	**6.51**	**6.67**	**6.81**	**6.94**	**7.06**
13	3.06	3.73	4.15	4.45	4.69	4.88	5.05	5.19	5.32	5.43	5.53
	4.26	**4.96**	**5.40**	**5.73**	**5.98**	**6.19**	**6.37**	**6.53**	**6.67**	**6.79**	**6.90**
14	3.03	3.70	4.11	4.41	4.64	4.83	4.99	5.13	5.25	5.36	5.46
	4.21	**4.89**	**5.32**	**5.63**	**5.88**	**6.08**	**6.26**	**6.41**	**6.54**	**6.66**	**6.77**
15	3.01	3.67	4.08	4.37	4.59	4.78	4.94	5.08	5.20	5.31	5.40
	4.17	**4.84**	**5.25**	**5.56**	**5.80**	**5.99**	**6.16**	**6.31**	**6.44**	**6.55**	**6.66**
16	3.00	3.65	4.05	4.33	4.56	4.74	4.90	5.03	5.15	5.26	5.35
	4.13	**4.79**	**5.19**	**5.49**	**5.72**	**5.92**	**6.08**	**6.22**	**6.35**	**6.46**	**6.56**
17	2.98	3.63	4.02	4.30	4.52	4.70	4.86	4.99	5.11	5.21	5.31
	4.10	**4.74**	**5.14**	**5.43**	**5.66**	**5.85**	**6.01**	**6.15**	**6.27**	**6.38**	**6.48**
18	2.97	3.61	4.00	4.28	4.49	4.67	4.82	4.96	5.07	5.17	5.27
	4.07	**4.70**	**5.09**	**5.38**	**5.60**	**5.79**	**5.94**	**6.08**	**6.20**	**6.31**	**6.41**
19	2.96	3.59	3.98	4.25	4.47	4.65	4.79	4.92	5.04	5.14	5.23
	4.05	**4.67**	**5.05**	**5.33**	**5.55**	**5.73**	**5.89**	**6.02**	**6.14**	**6.25**	**6.34**
20	2.95	3.58	3.96	4.23	4.45	4.62	4.77	4.90	5.01	5.11	5.20
	4.02	**4.64**	**5.02**	**5.29**	**5.51**	**5.69**	**5.84**	**5.97**	**6.09**	**6.19**	**6.28**
24	2.92	3.53	3.90	4.17	4.37	4.54	4.68	4.81	4.92	5.01	5.10
	3.96	**4.55**	**4.91**	**5.17**	**5.37**	**5.54**	**5.69**	**5.81**	**5.92**	**6.02**	**6.11**
30	2.89	3.49	3.85	4.10	4.30	4.46	4.60	4.72	4.82	4.92	5.00
	3.89	**4.45**	**4.80**	**5.05**	**5.24**	**5.40**	**5.54**	**5.65**	**5.76**	**5.85**	**5.93**
40	2.86	3.44	3.79	4.04	4.23	4.39	4.52	4.63	4.73	4.82	4.90
	3.82	**4.37**	**4.70**	**4.93**	**5.11**	**5.26**	**5.39**	**5.50**	**5.60**	**5.69**	**5.76**
60	2.83	3.40	3.74	3.98	4.16	4.31	4.44	4.55	4.65	4.73	4.81
	3.76	**4.28**	**4.59**	**4.82**	**4.99**	**5.13**	**5.25**	**5.36**	**5.45**	**5.53**	**5.60**
120	2.80	3.36	3.68	3.92	4.10	4.24	4.36	4.47	4.56	4.64	4.71
	3.70	**4.20**	**4.50**	**4.71**	**4.87**	**5.01**	**5.12**	**5.21**	**5.30**	**5.37**	**5.44**
∞	2.77	3.31	3.63	3.86	4.03	4.17	4.28	4.39	4.47	4.55	4.62
	3.64	**4.12**	**4.40**	**4.60**	**4.76**	**4.88**	**4.99**	**5.08**	**5.16**	**5.23**	**5.29**

Table 29 of Pearson, E., and Hartley, H. O. (1966). *Biometrika Tables for Statisticians* (3rd ed.). New York: Cambridge University Press. Adapted and reprinted with permission of the Biometrika trustees.

TABLE B.6   CRITICAL VALUES FOR THE PEARSON CORRELATION*

*To be significant, the sample correlation, r, must be greater than or equal to the critical value in the table.

	Level of Significance for One-Tailed Test			
	.05	.025	.01	.005
	Level of Significance for Two-Tailed Test			
$df = n - 2$	.10	.05	.02	.01
1	.988	.997	.9995	.9999
2	.900	.950	.980	.990
3	.805	.878	.934	.959
4	.729	.811	.882	.917
5	.669	.754	.833	.874
6	.622	.707	.789	.834
7	.582	.666	.750	.798
8	.549	.632	.716	.765
9	.521	.602	.685	.735
10	.497	.576	.658	.708
11	.476	.553	.634	.684
12	.458	.532	.612	.661
13	.441	.514	.592	.641
14	.426	.497	.574	.623
15	.412	.482	.558	.606
16	.400	.468	.542	.590
17	.389	.456	.528	.575
18	.378	.444	.516	.561
19	.369	.433	.503	.549
20	.360	.423	.492	.537
21	.352	.413	.482	.526
22	.344	.404	.472	.515
23	.337	.396	.462	.505
24	.330	.388	.453	.496
25	.323	.381	.445	.487
26	.317	.374	.437	.479
27	.311	.367	.430	.471
28	.306	.361	.423	.463
29	.301	.355	.416	.456
30	.296	.349	.409	.449
35	.275	.325	.381	.418
40	.257	.304	.358	.393
45	.243	.288	.338	.372
50	.231	.273	.322	.354
60	.211	.250	.295	.325
70	.195	.232	.274	.302
80	.183	.217	.256	.283
90	.173	.205	.242	.267
100	.164	.195	.230	.254

TABLE B.7   THE CHI-SQUARE DISTRIBUTION*

*The table entries are critical values of x^2.

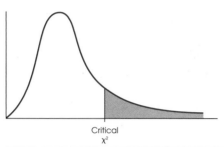

Critical
x^2

df	Proportion in Critical Region				
	0.10	0.05	0.025	0.01	0.005
1	2.71	3.84	5.02	6.63	7.88
2	4.61	5.99	7.38	9.21	10.60
3	6.25	7.81	9.35	11.34	12.84
4	7.78	9.49	11.14	13.28	14.86
5	9.24	11.07	12.83	15.09	16.75
6	10.64	12.59	14.45	16.81	18.55
7	12.02	14.07	16.01	18.48	20.28
8	13.36	15.51	17.53	20.09	21.96
9	14.68	16.92	19.02	21.67	23.59
10	15.99	18.31	20.48	23.21	25.19
11	17.28	19.68	21.92	24.72	26.76
12	18.55	21.03	23.34	26.22	28.30
13	19.81	22.36	24.74	27.69	29.82
14	21.06	23.68	26.12	29.14	31.32
15	22.31	25.00	27.49	30.58	32.80
16	23.54	26.30	28.85	32.00	34.27
17	24.77	27.59	30.19	33.41	35.72
18	25.99	28.87	31.53	34.81	37.16
19	27.20	30.14	32.85	36.19	38.58
20	28.41	31.41	34.17	37.57	40.00
21	29.62	32.67	35.48	38.93	41.40
22	30.81	33.92	36.78	40.29	42.80
23	32.01	35.17	38.08	41.64	44.18
24	33.20	36.42	39.36	42.98	45.56
25	34.38	37.65	40.65	44.31	46.93
26	35.56	38.89	41.92	45.64	48.29
27	36.74	40.11	43.19	46.96	49.64
28	37.92	41.34	44.46	48.28	50.99
29	39.09	42.56	45.72	49.59	52.34
30	40.26	43.77	46.98	50.89	53.67
40	51.81	55.76	59.34	63.69	66.77
50	63.17	67.50	71.42	76.15	79.49
60	74.40	79.08	83.30	88.38	91.95
70	85.53	90.53	95.02	100.42	104.22
80	96.58	101.88	106.63	112.33	116.32
90	107.56	113.14	118.14	124.12	128.30
100	118.50	124.34	129.56	135.81	140.17

Appendix C Solutions for Odd-Numbered Problems in the Text

CHAPTER 1 INTRODUCTION TO STATISTICS

1. a. The population is the entire set of adolescent boys who take medication for depression.
b. The sample is the group of 30 boys who were tested in the study.

3. Descriptive statistics are used to simplify and summarize data. Inferential statistics use sample data to make general conclusions about populations.

5. A correlational study has only one group of individuals and measures two different variables for each individual. Other rese arch evaluating relationships between variables compares two (or more) different groups of scores.

7. The independent variable is the amount of control over office design. The dependent variables are productivity and well-being.

9. a. This is a nonexperimental study. The researcher is simply observing two variables. No variable is manipulated to create the two groups.
b. This is an experiment. The researcher is manipulating the amount of vitamin C and should control other variables by using equivalent groups of participants.

11. This is not an experiment because there is no manipulation. Instead, the study is comparing two preexisting groups (state university and religious college students).

13. a. Time is continuous.
b. Discrete

c. Discrete
d. The underlying variable is knowledge, which is continuous.

15. a. The independent variable is Tai Chi versus no Tai Chi (control).
b. The independent variable is measured on a nominal scale.
c. The dependent variable is the amount of arthritis pain.
d. The dependent variable is measured on an interval or ratio scale.

17. a. The independent variable is whether the motivational signs were posted, and the dependent variable is amount of use of the stairs.
b. Posting versus not posting is measured on a nominal scale.

19. a. $\Sigma X^2 = 48$
b. $(\Sigma X)^2 = 14^2 = 196$
c. $\Sigma(X - 1) = 9$
d. $\Sigma(X - 1)^2 = 25$

21. a. $\Sigma X = 4$
b. $\Sigma Y = 18$
c. $\Sigma XY = 11$

23. a. $\Sigma X^2 = 50$
b. $(\Sigma X)^2 = 12^2 = 144$
c. $\Sigma(X - 3) = 0$
d. $\Sigma(X - 3)^2 = 14$

CHAPTER 2 FREQUENCY DISTRIBUTIONS

1.

X	f
7	2
6	3
5	1
4	1
3	4
2	6
1	3

3. a. $n = 12$
b. $\Sigma X = 40$
c. $\Sigma X^2 = 148$

5. a.

X	f
50–54	2
45–49	2
40–44	2
35–39	1
30–34	3
25–29	5
20–24	3
15–19	6

b.

X	f
50–50	2
40–49	4
30–39	4
20–29	8
10–19	6

7. a. 5 points wide and around 7 intervals
b. 2 points wide and around 9 intervals
c. 10 points wide and around 8 intervals

9. A bar graph leaves a space between adjacent bars and is used with data from nominal or ordinal scales. In a histogram, adjacent bars touch at the real limits. Histograms are used to display data from interval or ratio scales.

11.

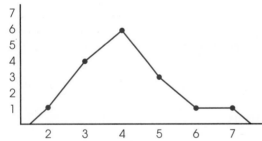

13. a. Histogram or polygon (ratio scale)
b. Bar graph (ordinal scale)
c. Bar graph (nominal scale)
d. Bar graph (nominal scale)

15.

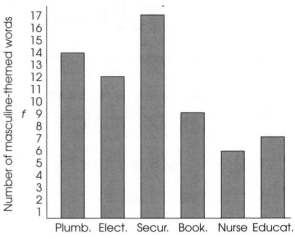

17. a.

X	f
9	1
8	1
7	4
6	5
5	7
4	2

b. The distribution is positively skewed

19. a.

X	f
10	2
9	4
8	5
7	4
6	3
5	2
4	2
3	1
2	1

b.

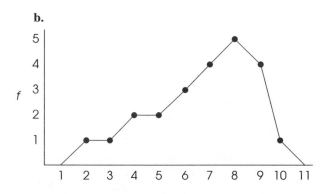

c. 1) The distribution is negatively skewed.

  2) The scores are centered around $X = 7$ or $X = 8$.

  3) The scores are clustered at the high end of the scale.

21.

X	f_{low}	f_{high}
5	1	5
4	2	6
3	4	3
2	5	1
1	3	0

The scores for children from the high number-talk parents are noticeably higher.

CHAPTER 3   MEASURES OF CENTRAL TENDENCY

1. The purpose of central tendency is to identify a single score that serves as the best representative for an entire distribution, usually a score from the center of the distribution.

3. The mean is $\frac{51}{9} = 5.67$, the median is 6, and the mode is 3.

5. The mean is $\frac{66}{3} = 5.08$, the median is 5, and the mode is 5.

7. $\mu = \frac{12}{15} = 8$

9. $N = 5$.

11. The original sample has $n = 6$ and $\Sigma X = 78$. The new sample has $n = 5$ and $\Sigma X = 75$. The new mean is $M = 15$.

13. The original sample has $n = 10$ and $\Sigma X = 90$. The new sample has $n = 9$ and the total is still $\Sigma X = 90$. The new mean is $M = 10$.

15. The original sample has $n = 7$ and $\Sigma X = 112$. The new sample has $n = 7$ and $\Sigma X = 126$. The new mean is $M = 18$.

17. The original population has $N = 8$ and $\Sigma X = 128$. The new population has $N = 7$ and $\Sigma X = 105$. The removed score must be $X = 23$.

19. The original sample has $n = 9$ and $\Sigma X = 180$. The new sample has $n = 9$ and $\Sigma X = 198$. The total (ΣX) increased by 18 points. If the score was $X = 7$, it was increased to $X = 25$.

21. a. The combined sample mean is $M = 12$.

  b. The combined sample mean is $(24 + 80)/8 = 13$.

  c. The combined sample mean is $(40 + 48)/8 = 11$.

23. With a skewed distribution, the extreme scores in the tail can displace the mean out toward the tail. The result is that the mean is often not a very representative value.

25. The participants recalled an average of $M = \frac{68}{16} = 4.25$ humorous sentences compared to $M = \frac{49}{16} = 3.06$ nonhumorous sentences. Humor does appear to improve memory performance.

27. The average rating with no alcohol was $M = \frac{53}{15} = 3.53$ and with moderate alcohol consumption it was $M = \frac{74}{15} = 4.93$. The woman is judged to be more attractive when the participants have consumed some alcohol.

CHAPTER 4   MEASURES OF VARIABILITY

1. a. *SS* is the sum of squared deviation scores.

   b. Variance is the mean squared deviation.

   c. Standard deviation is the square root of the variance. It provides a measure of the standard distance from the mean.

3. Variance and standard deviation are always greater than or equal to zero. They are measures of distance that are based on squared deviations, which are always positive.

5. Variance is defined as the mean squared deviation and, for a population, is computed as the sum of squared deviations divided by *N*. However, if this same definition is used for a sample, the sample variance will be biased and will consistently underestimate the corresponding population value. Therefore, the formula for sample variance includes an adjustment to correct for the bias. The adjustment involves dividing by $df = n - 1$ rather than *n*.

7. a. With a standard deviation of $s = 2$, you are above the mean by 3 standard deviations.

   b. With a standard deviation of $s = 10$, you are below the mean by less than half of a standard deviation.

9. a.

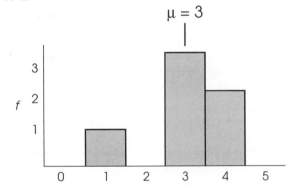

b. The mean is $\mu = \frac{18}{6} = 3$ and the standard deviation appears to be about 1.5 points.

   c. $SS = 6$, $\sigma^2 = 1$, $\sigma = 1$

11. a. The range is either 11 or 12, and the standard deviation is $\sigma = 4$.

   b. After adding 2 points to each score, the range is still either 11 or 12, and the standard deviation is still $\sigma = 4$. Adding a constant to every score does not affect measures of variability.

13. a. The new mean is $\mu = 35$ and the standard deviation is still $\sigma = 5$.

   b. The new mean is $\mu = 90$ and the new standard deviation is $\sigma = 15$.

15. a. The simplified scores had $M = 4.5$, $SS = 27$, and $s = 3$.

   b. The original scores had $M = 84.5$, $SS = 27$, and $s = 3$.

17. a. The mean is $M = 4$ and the standard deviation is $s = \sqrt{9} = 3$.

   b. The new mean is $M = 6$ and the new standard deviation is $\sqrt{49} = 7$.

   c. Changing one score changes both the mean and the standard deviation.

19. The mean is $\mu = 1.50$, $SS = 32$, $\sigma^2 = 4$, and $\sigma = 2$.

21. The mean is $M = 7$, $SS = 24$, $s^2 = 6$ and $s = \sqrt{6} = 2.45$.

23. a. For the older adults, the mean is $M = 5.47$, $SS = 65.73$, $s^2 = 4.70$, and $s = 2.17$. For the younger adults, the mean is $M = 7.27$, $SS = 18.93$, $s^2 = 1.35$, and $s = 1.16$.

   b. The younger adults had a higher average and were much less variable.

PART 1   REVIEW

1. a. The goal for descriptive statistics is to simplify, organize, and summarize data so that it is easier for researchers to see patterns.

   b. A frequency distribution provides an organized summary of the complete set of scores.

   c. A measure of central tendency summarizes an entire set of scores with a single value that is representative of the whole set.

   d. A measure of variability provides a single number that describes the differences that exist from one score to another.

2. a.

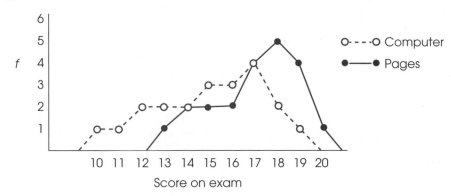

The students who studied from printed pages appear to have higher scores than those who studied from a computer screen.

b. The students who studied printed pages had an average score of $M = 17$ compared to an average of only $M = 15$ for the students who studied on the computer.

c. For the printed-pages group, $SS = 74$, the variance is $s^2 = 3.7$ and the standard deviation is $s = 1.92$. For the computer-screen group, $SS = 122$, the variance is $s^2 = 6.1$ and the standard deviation is $s = 2.47$. The scores for the computer-screen are more variable.

CHAPTER 5   *z*-SCORES: LOCATION OF SCORES AND STANDARDIZED DISTRIBUTIONS

1. The sign of the *z*-score tells whether the location is above (+) or below (−) the mean, and the magnitude tells the distance from the mean in terms of the number of standard deviations.

3. a. above the mean by 40 points
   b. above the mean by 10 points
   c. below the mean by 20 points
   d. below the mean by 5 points

5.

X	z	X	z	X	z
45	0.36	52	1.09	41	0.09
30	−0.82	25	−1.36	38	−0.18

7. a.

X	z	X	z	X	z
69	0.75	84	2.00	63	0.25
54	−0.50	48	−1.00	45	−1.25

b.

X	z	X	z	X	z
66	0.50	78	1.50	30	−2.50
57	−0.25	54	−0.50	75	1.25

9.

X	z	X	z	X	z
27	0.40	31	1.20	35	2.00
21	−0.80	22	−0.60	18	−1.40

11. a. $X = 41$
   b. $X = 42$
   c. $X = 44$
   d. $X = 48$

13. $\sigma = 6$

15. $M = 53$

17. $\sigma = 4$

19. $\mu = 50$ and $\sigma = 6$. The distance between the two scores is 9 points, which is equal to 1.5 standard deviations.

21. a. $\sigma = 8$

  b. $\sigma = 4$

23. a. $X = 52$ ($z = 0.20$)

  b. $X = 60$ ($z = 1.00$)

  c. $X = 44$ ($z = -0.60$)

  d. $X = 30$ ($z = -2.00$)

25. a. $\mu = 5$ and $\sigma = 4$

  b. & c.

Original X	z-score	Transformed X
0	-1.25	75
6	0.25	105
4	-0.25	95
3	-0.50	90
12	1.75	135

CHAPTER 6   **PROBABILITY**

1. a. $p = \frac{1}{50} = 0.02$

  b. $p = \frac{10}{50} = 0.20$

  c. $p = \frac{20}{50} = 0.40$

3. The two requirements for a random sample are: (1) each individual has an equal chance of being selected, and (2) if more than one individual is selected, the probabilities must stay constant for all selections.

5. a. body to the left, $p = 0.9938$

  b. body to the left, $p = 0.7881$

  c. body to the right, $p = 0.6915$

  d. body to the right, $p = 0.7794$

7. a. $p = 0.1974$

  b. $p = 0.4972$

  c. $p = 0.7698$

9. a. $z = -1.64$ or -1.65

  b. $z = 0.52$

  c. $z = 0.39$

  d. $z = -0.84$

11. a. tail to the right, $p = 0.4013$

  b. tail to the right, $p = 0.2266$

  c. tail to the left, $p = 0.3085$

  d. tail to the left, $p = 0.1056$

13. a. $p(z > 0.50) = 0.3085$

  b. $p(z < 0.80) = 0.7881$

  c. $p(-1.00 < z < 1.00) = 0.6826$

15. a. $z = 1.04$, $X = 604$

  b. $z = 1.28$, $X = 628$

  c. $z = 2.05$, $X = 705$

17. a. $p(z > 1.20) = 0.1151$

  b. $p(z < -1.60) = 0.0548$

19. a. $z = 0.60$, $p = 0.2743$

  b. $z = -1.40$, $p = 0.0808$

  c. $z = 0.84$, $X = \$206$ or more

21. $p(X > 36) = p(z > 2.17) = 0.0150$ or 1.50%

CHAPTER 7   **PROBABILITY AND SAMPLES: THE DISTRIBUTION OF SAMPLE MEANS**

1. The distribution of sample means will be normal (because $n > 30$), have an expected value of $\mu = 40$, and a standard error of $\sigma_M = \frac{10}{\sqrt{100}} = 1$.

3. The distribution of sample means will *not* be normal when it is based on small samples ($n < 30$) selected from a population that is not normal.

5. a. $= \frac{20}{\sqrt{4}}$ 10 points

  b. $\frac{20}{\sqrt{16}} = 5$ points

  c. $\frac{20}{\sqrt{25}} = 4$ points

7. a. $n > 9$

  b. $n > 16$

  c. $n > 36$

9. a. $\sigma_M = 6$ points and $z = 0.50$

  b. $\sigma_M = 3$ points and $z = 1.00$

  c. $\sigma_M = 2$ points and $z = 1.50$

11. a. With a standard error of 9, $M = 67$ corresponds to $z = 0.78$, which is not extreme.

  b. With a standard error of 3, $M = 67$ corresponds to $z = 2.33$, which is extreme.

13. a. $\sigma_M = 5$, $z = -0.60$, and $p = 0.7257$

  b. $\sigma_M = 3$, $z = -1.00$, and $p = 0.8413$

15. **a.** $z = -0.50$ and $p = 0.3085$
   b. $\sigma_M = 3$, $z = -1.00$ and $p = 0.1587$
   c. $\sigma_M = 1$, $z = -3.00$ and $p = 0.0013$
17. **a.** $\sigma_M = 4$, $z = \pm 1.96$ and the range is 42.16 to 57.84
   b. $\sigma_M = 4$, $z = \pm 2.58$ and the range is 39.68 to 60.32
19. **a.** $z = 0.33$ and $p = 0.3707$
   b. $z = -3.00$ and $p = 0.0013$
   c. $p\,(0 < z < 1.00) = 0.3413$

21. **a.** With a standard error of $\sigma_M = 3.3$, $M = 38.9$ corresponds to $z = -0.42$ and $p = 0.3372$. This is not an unusual sample. It is representative of the population.
   b. With a standard error of $\sigma_M = 2.2$, $M = 36.2$ corresponds to $z = -1.86$ and $p = 0.0314$. The sample mean is unusually small and not representative.

23.

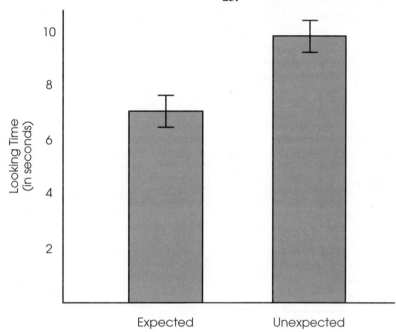

CHAPTER 8   INTRODUCTION TO HYPOTHESIS TESTING

1. **a.** A larger difference produces a larger value in the numerator, which produces a larger z-score.
   b. A larger standard deviation produces larger standard error in the denominator, which produces a smaller z-score.
   c. A larger sample produces a smaller standard error in the denominator, which produces a larger z-score.
3. **a.** The null hypothesis states that the herb has no effect on memory scores.
   b. H_0: $\mu = 50$ (even with the herbs, the mean is still 50). H_1: $\mu \neq 50$ (the mean has changed). The critical region consists of z-scores beyond ± 1.96. For these data, the standard error is 3 and $z = \frac{4}{3} = 1.33$. Fail to reject the null hypothesis. The herbal supplements do not have a significant effect on memory scores.

5. **a.** H_0: $\mu = 80$. With $\sigma = 12$, the sample mean corresponds to $z = \frac{-4}{3} = -1.33$. This is not sufficient to reject the null hypothesis. You cannot conclude that the course has a significant effect.
   b. H_0: $\mu = 80$. With $\sigma = 6$, the sample mean corresponds to $z = -\frac{-4}{1.5} = -2.67$. This is sufficient to reject the null hypothesis and conclude that the course does have a significant effect.
   c. There is a 4-point difference between the sample and the hypothesis. In part a, the standard error is 3 points and the 4-point difference is not significant. However, in part b, the standard error is only 1.5 points and the 4-point difference is now significantly more than is expected by chance. In general, a larger standard deviation produces a larger standard error, which reduces the likelihood of rejecting the null hypothesis.

7. a. With $\sigma = 5$, the standard error is 1, and $z = \frac{4}{1} = 4.00$. Reject H_0.

   b. With $\sigma = 15$, the standard error is 3, and $z = \frac{4}{3} = 1.33$. Fail to reject H_0.

   c. Larger variability reduces the likelihood of rejecting H_0.

9. a. With a 4-point treatment effect, for the z-score to be greater than 1.96, the standard error must be smaller than 2.03. The sample size must be greater than 96.12; a sample of $n = 97$ or larger is needed.

   b. With a 2-point treatment effect, for the z-score to be greater than 1.96, the standard error must be smaller than 1.02. The sample size must be greater than 384.47; a sample of $n = 385$ or larger is needed.

11. a. The null hypothesis states that there is no effect on reaction time, $\mu = 400$. The critical region consists of z-scores beyond $z = \pm1.96$. For these data, the standard error is 6.67 and $z = -8/6.67 = -1.20$. Fail to reject H_0. There is no significant change in reaction time.

   b. Cohen's $d = \frac{8}{40} = 0.20$.

   c. The caffeine did not have a significant effect on reaction time, $z = -1.20, p > .05, d = 0.20$.

13. With $n = 4$, the standard error is 0.95 and the sample mean corresponds to $z = 2.37$. This is well beyond the critical boundary of 1.96. Reject the null hypothesis and conclude that the past 4 years do not constitute a representative sample from a population with a mean of $\mu = 9.6$.

15. a. H_0: $\mu = 45$ (the supplement has no effect). The standard error is 2.25 and $z = 2.31$, which is beyond the critical boundary of 1.96. Reject the null hypothesis and conclude that the supplement has a significant effect on cognitive performance.

   b. Cohen's $d = \frac{5.2}{9} = 0.578$

   c. The blueberry supplement had a significant effect on cognitive skill scores, $z = 2.31, p < .05, d = 0.578$.

17. a. With no treatment effect the distribution of sample means is centered at $\mu = 75$ with a standard error of 1.90 points. The critical boundary of $z = 1.96$ corresponds to a sample mean of $M = 78.72$. With a 4-point treatment effect, the distribution of sample means is centered at $\mu = 79$. In this distribution a mean of $M = 78.72$ corresponds to $z = -0.15$. The power for the test is the probability of obtaining a z-score greater than -0.15, which is $p = 0.5596$.

   b. With a one-tailed test, critical boundary of $z = 1.65$ corresponds to a sample mean of $M = 78.14$. With a 4-point treatment effect, the distribution of sample means is centered at $\mu = 79$. In this distribution a mean of $M = 78.14$ corresponds to $z = -0.45$. The power for the test is the probability of obtaining a z-score greater than -0.45, which is $p = 0.6736$.

19. a. Increasing alpha increases power.

   b. Changing from one- to two-tailed decreases power.

21. a. For a sample of $n = 16$, the standard error would be 5 points, and the critical boundary for $z = 1.96$ corresponds to a sample mean of $M = 89.8$. With a 12-point effect, the distribution of sample means would be centered at $\mu = 92$. In this distribution, the critical boundary of $M = 89.8$ corresponds to $z = -0.44$. The power for the test is $p\,(z > -0.44) = 0.6700$ or 67%.

   b. For a sample of $n = 25$, the standard error would be 4 points, and the critical boundary for $z = 1.96$ corresponds to a sample mean of $M = 87.84$. With a 12-point effect, the distribution of sample means would be centered at $\mu = 92$. In this distribution, the critical boundary of $M = 87.84$ corresponds to $z = -1.04$. The power for the test is $p(z > -1.04) = 0.8508$, or 85.08%.

PART II   REVIEW

1. a. $z = 0.10$

   b. $X = 40$

   c. If the entire population of X values is transformed into z-scores, the set of z-scores will have a mean of 0 and a standard deviation of 1.00.

   d. The standard error is 10 points and $z = -0.80$.

   e. The standard error is 5 points and $z = -1.60$.

3. a. H_0: $\mu \leq 1.85$ (not more than average) For the males, the standard error is 0.2 and $z = 3.00$. With a critical value of $z = 2.33$, reject the null hypothesis.

   b. H_0: $\mu \geq 1.85$ (not fewer than average) For the females, the standard error is 0.24 and $z = -2.38$. With a critical value of $z = -2.33$, reject the null hypothesis.

CHAPTER 9   INTRODUCTION TO THE T STATISTIC

1. A z-score is used when the population standard deviation (or variance) is known. The t statistic is used when the population variance or standard deviation is unknown. The t statistic uses the sample variance or standard deviation in place of the unknown population values.

3. **a.** The sample variance is 16 and the estimated standard error is 2.
   b. The sample variance is 54 and the estimated standard error is 3.
   c. The sample variance is 12 and the estimated standard error is 1.

5. **a.** $t = \pm 2.571$
   b. $t = \pm 2.201$
   c. $t = \pm 2.069$

7. **a.** $M = 7$ and $s = \sqrt{24} = 4.90$
   b. $s_M = 2$.

9. **a.** With $n = 16$, $s_M = 0.75$ and $t = \frac{1.3}{0.75} = 1.73$. This is not greater than the critical value of 2.131, so there is no significant effect.
   b. With $n = 36$, $s_M = 0.50$ and $t = \frac{1.3}{0.50} = 2.60$. This value is greater than the critical value of 2.042 (using $df = 30$), so we reject the null hypothesis and conclude that there is a significant treatment effect.
   c. As the sample size increases, the likelihood of rejecting the null hypothesis also increases.

11. **a.** With a two-tailed test, the critical boundaries are ± 2.306 and the obtained value of $t = \frac{3.3}{1.5} = 2.20$ is not sufficient to reject the null hypothesis.
   b. For the one-tailed test the critical value is 1.860, so we reject the null hypothesis and conclude that participants significantly overestimated the number who noticed.

13. **a.** With $df = 15$, the critical values are ± 2.947. For these data, the sample variance is 16, the estimated standard error is 1, and $t = \frac{8.2}{1} = 8.20$. Reject the null hypothesis and conclude that there has been a significant change in the level of anxiety.
   b. With $df = 15$, the t values for 90% confidence are ± 1.753, and the interval extends from 21.547 to 25.053.
   c. The data indicate a significant change in the level of anxiety, $t(15) = 8.20, p < .01$, 95% CI [21.547, 25.053].

15. **a.** With $df = 63$, the critical values are ± 2.660 (using $df = 60$ in the table). For these data, the estimated standard error is 1.50, and $t = \frac{7}{1.50} = 4.67$. Reject the null hypothesis and conclude that there has been a significant change in the average IQ score.
   b. Using $df = 60$, the t values for 80% confidence are ± 1.296, and the interval extends from 105.056 to 108.944.

17. **a.** The estimated standard error is 1.9, and $t = \frac{4.5}{1.9} = 2.37$. For a two-tailed test, the critical value is 2.306. Reject the null hypothesis, scores for students with e-books are significantly different.
   b. For 90% confidence, use $t = \pm 1.860$. The interval is $77.2 \pm (1.860)1.9$ and extends from 73.666 to 80.734.
   c. The results show that exam scores were significantly different for students using e-books than for other students, $t(8) = 2.37, p < .05$, 90% CI [73.666, 80.734].

19. **a.** With $n = 9$ the estimated standard error is 4 and $t = \frac{4}{4} = 1$. $r^2 = \frac{1}{9} = 0.111$. Cohen's $d = \frac{4}{12} = 0.333$.
   b. With $n = 16$ the estimated standard error is 3 and $t = \frac{4}{3} = 1.33$. $r^2 = \frac{1.77}{16.77} = 0.106$. Cohen's $d = \frac{4}{12} = 0.333$.
   c. The sample size does not have any influence on Cohen's d and has only a minor effect on r^2.

21. **a.** H_0: $\mu \leq 4$ (not greater than neutral). The estimated standard error is 0.26 and $t = 2.04$. With a critical value of 1.753, reject H_0 and conclude that the males with a great sense of humor were rated significantly higher than neutral.
   b. H_0: $\mu \geq 4$ (not lower than neutral). The estimated standard error is 0.295 and $t = -2.37$. With a critical value of -1.753, reject H_0 and conclude that the males with a no sense of humor were rated significantly lower than neutral.

23. **a.** H_0: $\mu = 50$. With $df = 9$ the critical values are $t = \pm 3.250$. For these data, $M = 55.5$, $SS = 162.5$, $s^2 = 18.06$, the standard error is 1.34, and $t = 4.10$. Reject H_0 and conclude that mathematical achievement scores for children with a history of daycare are significantly different from scores for other children
   b. Cohen's $d = \frac{5.5}{4.25} = 1.29$.
   c. The results indicate that mathematics test scores for children with a history of daycare are significantly different from scores for children without daycare experience, $t(9) = 4.10, p < .01, d = 1.29$.

CHAPTER 10 **THE *t* TEST FOR TWO INDEPENDENT SAMPLES**

1. An independent-measures study uses a separate sample for each of the treatments or populations being compared.

3. **a.** The size of the mean difference is the numerator of the *t* statistic. The larger the mean difference, the larger the value for *t*.

   b. The size of the two samples influences the magnitude of the estimated standard error in the denominator of the *t* statistic. As sample size increases, the value of *t* also increases (moves farther from zero), and the likelihood of rejecting H_0 also increases.

   c. The variability of the scores influences the estimated standard error in the denominator. As the variability of the scores increases, the value of *t* decreases (becomes closer to zero), and the likelihood of rejecting H_0 decreases.

5. **a.** The first sample has $s^2 = 12$ and the second has $s^2 = 6$. The pooled variance is $\frac{54}{6} = 9$ (halfway between).

   b. The first sample has $s^2 = 12$ and the second has $s^2 = 3$. The pooled variance is $\frac{54}{9} = 6$ (closer to the variance for the larger sample).

7. **a.** The pooled variance is 15 and the estimated standard error is 2.

   b. The pooled variance is 60 and the estimated standard error is 4.

   c. Larger variability produces a larger standard error.

9. **a.** The pooled variance is 120.

   b. The estimated standard error is 4.00.

   c. A mean difference of 8 would produce $t = \frac{8}{4} = 2.00$. With $df = 28$ the critical values are ±2.048. Fail to reject H_0.

11. **a.** The estimated standard error for the sample mean difference is 6 points.

    b. The estimated standard error for the sample mean difference is 3 points.

    c. Larger samples produce a smaller standard error.

13. **a.** The two samples combined have a total of 27 participants.

    b. With $df = 25$ and $\alpha = .05$, the critical region consists of *t* values beyond ±2.060. The *t* statistic is in the critical region. Reject H_0 and conclude that there is a significant difference.

    c. $r^2 = \frac{4.29}{29.29} = 0.146$ or 14.6%

15. **a.** Using $df = 30$, because 34 is not listed in the table, and $\alpha = .05$, the critical region consists of *t* values beyond ±2.042. The pooled variance is 81, the estimated standard error is 3, and $t(34) = \frac{7.6}{3} = 2.53$. The *t* statistic is in the critical region. Reject H_0 and conclude that there is a significant difference.

    b. For 90% confidence, the *t* values are ±1.697 (using $df = 30$), and the interval extends from 2.509 to 12.691 points higher with the calming music.

    c. Classroom performance was significantly better with background music, $t(34) = 2.53, p < .05$, 95% CI [2.509, 12.691].

17. **a.** The pooled variance is 7753, the estimated standard error is 12.45, and $t = \frac{14}{12.45} = 1.12$. With $df = 198$ the critical value is 1.98 (using $df = 120$). Fail to reject the null hypothesis and conclude that there was no significant change in calorie consumption after the mandatory posting.

    b. $r^2 = \frac{1.25}{199.25} = 0.0063$ or 0.63%

19. **a.** The pooled variance is 7.2, the estimated standard error is 1.2, and $t(18) = 3.00$. For a one-tailed test with $df = 18$ the critical value is 2.552. Reject the null hypothesis. There is a significant difference between the two groups.

    b. For 95% confidence, the *t* values are ±2.101, and the interval extends from 1.079 to 6.121 points higher for boys.

    c. The results indicate that adolescent males have significantly higher self-esteem than girls, $t(18) = 3.00, p < .01$, one tailed, 95% CI [1.079, 6.121].

21. The pooled variance is 63, the estimated standard error is 3.00, and $t = \frac{7}{3} = 2.33$. With $df = 26$ the critical value is 2.056. Reject the null hypothesis and conclude that there is a significant difference between the two sleep conditions.

23. **a.** The null hypothesis states that the type of sport does not affect neurological performance. For a one-tailed test, the critical boundary is $t = 1.796$. For the swimmers, $M = 9$ and $SS = 44$. For the soccer players, $M = 6$ and $SS = 24$. The pooled variance is 6.18 and $t(11) = 2.11$. Reject H_0. The data show that the soccer players have significantly lower scores.

    b. For these data, $r^2 = 0.288$ (28.8%).

CHAPTER 11   **THE *t* TEST FOR TWO RELATED SAMPLES**

1. A repeated-measures design uses the same group of participants in all of the treatment conditions.

3. For a repeated-measures design the same subjects are used in both treatment conditions. In a matched-subjects design, two different sets of subjects are used. However, in a matched-subjects design, each subject in one condition is matched with respect to a specific variable with a subject in the second condition so that the two separate samples are equivalent with respect to the matching variable.

5. **a.** The standard deviation is 4 points and measures the average distance between an individual score and the sample mean.
   b. The estimated standard error is 1.33 points and measures the average distance between a sample mean and the population mean.

7. **a.** The estimated standard error is 2 points and $t(8) = 1.50$. With a critical boundary of ±2.306, fail to reject the null hypothesis.
   b. With $M_D = 12$, $t(8) = 6.00$. With a critical boundary of ±2.306, reject the null hypothesis.
   c. The larger the mean difference, the greater the likelihood of finding a significant difference.

9. **a.** The sample variance is 9, the estimated standard error is 0.75, and $t(15) = \frac{2.6}{0.75} = 3.46$. With critical boundaries of ±2.131, reject H_0.
   b. Cohen's $d = \frac{2.6}{3} = 0.867$

11. **a.** The null hypothesis says that there is no difference in judgments for smiling versus frowning. For these data, the sample variance is 6.25, the estimated standard error is 0.5, and $t = \frac{1.6}{0.5} = 3.20$. For a one-tailed test with $df = 24$, the critical value is 2.492. Reject the null hypothesis.
   b. $r^2 = \frac{10.24}{34.24} = 0.299$ (29.9%)
   c. The cartoons were rated significantly funnier when people held a pen in their teeth compared to holding a pen in their lips, $t(24) = 3.20$, $p < .01$, one tailed, $r^2 = 0.299$.

13. The null hypothesis states that there is no difference in the perceived intelligence between attractive and unat-tractive photos. For these data, the estimated standard error is 0.4 and $t = \frac{2.7}{0.4} = 6.75$. With $df = 24$, the critical value is 2.064. Reject the null hypothesis.

15. **a.** The difference scores are 1, 7, 2, 2, 1, and 5. $M_D = 3$.
   b. $SS = 30$, sample variance is 6, and the estimated standard error is 1.
   c. With $df = 5$ and $\alpha = .05$, the critical values are $t = \pm2.571$. For these data, $t = 3.00$. Reject H_0. There is a significant treatment effect.

17. The null hypothesis states that the background color has no effect on judged attractiveness. For these data, $M_D = 3$, $SS = 18$, the sample variance is 2.25, the estimated standard error is 0.50, and $t(8) = 6.00$. With $df = 8$ and $\alpha = .01$, the critical values are $t = \pm3.355$. Reject the null hypothesis, the background color does have a significant effect.

19. **a.** The pooled variance is 6.4 and the estimated standard error is 1.46.
   b. For the difference scores the variance is 12.8 and the estimated standard error is 1.46.

21. **a.** The null hypothesis says that changing answers has no effect, H_0: $\mu_D = 0$. With $df = 8$ and $\alpha = .05$, the critical values are $t = \pm2.306$. For these data, $M_D = 7$, $SS = 288$, the standard error is 2, and $t(8) = 3.50$. Reject H_0 and conclude that changing answers has a significant effect on exam performance.
   b. For 95% confidence use $t = \pm2.306$. The interval extends from 2.388 to 11.612.
   c. Changing answers resulted in significantly higher exam scores, $t(8) = 3.50$, $p < .05$, 95% CI [2.388, 11.612].

23. The null hypothesis says that there is no difference between shots fired during versus between heart beats, H_0: $\mu_D = 0$. With $\alpha = .05$, the critical region consists of t values beyond ±2.365. For these data, $M_D = 3$, $SS = 36$, $s^2 = 5.14$, the standard error is 0.80, and $t(7) = 3.75$. Reject H_0 and conclude that the timing of the shot has a significant effect on the marksmen's scores.

PART III   **REVIEW**

1. **a.** The estimated standard error is 1.50, and $t = \frac{7.7}{1.50} = 5.13$. For a one-tailed test, the critical value is 2.602. Reject the null hypothesis, children with a history of day care have significantly more behavioral problems.
   b. For 90% confidence use $t = \pm1.753$. The interval is $\mu = 7.7 \pm1.753(1.5)$ and extends from 5.07 to 10.33.
   c. The results show that kindergarten children with a history of day care have significantly more behav-

ioral problems than other kindergarten children, $t(15) = 5.13, p < .01$, 90% CI[5.07, 10.33].

3. a. The estimated standard error is 2.5 and $t(19) =$ 1.92. With a critical value of 1.729, reject the null hypothesis and conclude that attention span is significantly longer with the medication.

b. The confidence interval is $\mu_D = 4.8 \pm 1.328(2.5)$ and extends from 1.48 to 8.12.

CHAPTER 12 INTRODUCTION TO ANALYSIS OF VARIANCE

1. When there is no treatment effect, the numerator and the denominator of the F-ratio are both measuring the same sources of variability (random, unsystematic differences from sampling error). In this case, the F-ratio is balanced and should have a value near 1.00.

3. With 3 or more treatment conditions, you need three or more t tests to evaluate all the mean differences. Each test involves a risk of a Type I error. The more tests you do, the more risk there is of a Type I error. The ANOVA performs all of the tests simultaneously with a single, fixed alpha level.

5. a. The three means produce $SS = 14$.

b. $n(SS_{means}) = 112$

c. The four totals are 32, 72, 8, and 48 with $G = 96$. $SS_{between} = 112$

7. a. With smaller mean differences the F-ratio and η^2 should both be smaller than the values obtained in problem 6.

b.

Source	SS	df	MS	
Between treatments	8	2	4	$F(2, 9) = 1$
Within treatments	36	9	4	
Total	44	11		

b. With $\alpha = .05$, the critical value is $F = 4.26$. Fail to reject the null hypothesis and conclude that there are no significant differences among the three treatments. The F-ratio is much smaller as predicted.

c. For these data, $\eta^2 = \frac{8}{44} = 0.182$ which is much smaller than the value in problem 6.

9. a. The sample variances are 2.67, 3.33, and 6.00. These values are much larger than the variances in problem 8.

b. The larger variances should result in a smaller F-ratio that is less likely to reject the null hypothesis.

c.

Source	SS	df	MS	
Between treatments	32	2	16	$F(2, 9) = 4.00$
Within treatments	36	9	4	
Total	68	11		

With $\alpha = .05$, the critical value is $F = 4.26$. Fail to reject the null hypothesis and conclude that there are no significant differences among the three treatments. The F-ratio is much smaller as predicted.

11. a. Larger samples should increase the F-ratio.

Source	SS	df	MS	
Between treatments	50	2	25	$F(2, 72) = 12.50$
Within treatments	144	72	2	
Total	194	74		

The F-ratio is much larger than it was in problem 10.

b. Increasing the sample size should have little or no effect on η^2. $\eta^2 = \frac{50}{144} = 0.258$, which is about the same as the value obtained in problem 10.

13. a.

Source	SS	df	MS	
Between treatments	72	2	36	$F(2, 21) = 7.20$
Within treatments	105	21	5	
Total	177	23		

With $\alpha = .05$, the critical value is $F = 3.47$. Reject the null hypothesis and conclude that there are significant differences among the three types of teachers.

b. For these data, $\eta^2 = \frac{72}{177} = 0.407$.

c. The results indicate significant differences in the students' acceptability of cheating for the three different types of teacher, $F(2, 21) = 7.20$, $p <$ .05, $\eta^2 = 0.407$.

15. a. $k = 4$ treatment conditions.

b. The study used a total of $N = 52$ participants.

17.

Source	SS	df	MS	
Between treatments	20	1	20	$F = 4.00$
Within treatments	190	38	5	
Total	210	39		

19.

Source	SS	df	MS	
Between treatments	96	2	48	$F(2, 15) = 9.01$
Within treatments	80	15	5.33	
Total	176	17		

With $df = 2, 15$, the critical value for $\alpha = .05$ is 3.68. Reject the null hypothesis.

21. a. The pooled variance is 2, the estimated standard error is 0.894 and $t(8) = 4.47$. With $df = 8$, the critical value is 2.306. Reject the null hypothesis.

b.

Source	SS	df	MS	
Between treatments	40	1	40	$F(1, 8) = 20$
Within treatments	16	8	2	
Total	56	9		

With $df = 1, 8$, the critical value is 5.32. Reject the null hypothesis. Within rounding error, note that $F = t^2$.

23. a. The means and standard deviations are

Non-user	Rarely	Regularly
$M = 3.71$	$M = 3.46$	$M = 3.01$
$s = 0.302$	$s = 0.298$	$s = 0.268$

Source	SS	df	MS	
Between treatments	2.517	2	1.258	$F(2, 27) = 14.98$
Within treatments	2.265	27	0.084	
Total	4.781	29		

With $df = 2, 27$ the critical value is 3.35. Reject the null hypothesis.

b. $\eta^2 = \frac{2.517}{4.781} = 0.526$

c. The results show significant differences in mean grade point averages between groups, $F(2, 27) = 14.98$, $p < .05$, $\eta^2 = 0.526$.

CHAPTER 13 REPEATED-MEASURES AND TWO-FACTOR ANALYSIS OF VARIANCE

1. For an independent measures design, the variability within treatments is the appropriate error term. For repeated measures, however, you must subtract out variability caused by individual differences from the variability within treatments to obtain a measure of error.

3. a. A total of 30 participants is needed; three separate samples, each with $n = 10$. The F-ratio has $df = 2, 27$.

b. One sample of $n = 10$ is needed. The F-ratio has $df = 2, 18$.

5. a. 3 treatments

b. 16 participants

7. a. The mean difference is $MD = 4$ and the difference scores have $SS = 8$. With an estimated standard error of 0.378, $t(7) = 10.582$. With a critical value of ± 2.306, reject the null hypothesis and conclude that there is a significant difference between treatments.

b.

Source	SS	df	MS	
Between treatments	64	1	64	$F(1, 7) = 112.28$
Within treatments	36	14		
Between subjects	32	7		
Error	4	7	0.57	
Total	100	15		

With $df = 1, 7$, the critical value is 5.59. Reject H_0. There is a significant difference between the two treatments. Note that $t^2 = (10.582)^2 = 111.98$, which is within rounding error of $F = 112.28$.

9. a. For the independent-measures ANOVA, we obtain:

Source	SS	df	MS	
Between treatments	48	2	24	$F(2, 15) = 3.46$
Within treatments	104	15	6.93	
Total	152	17		

With a critical value of 3.68 for $\alpha = .05$, fail to reject the null hypothesis.

b. For the repeated-measures ANOVA,

Source	SS	df	MS	
Between treatments	48	2	24	$F(2, 10) = 12.00$
Within treatments	104	15		
Between subjects	84	5		
Error	20	10	2	
Total	152	17		

With a critical value of 4.10 for $\alpha = .05$, reject the null hypothesis.

c. The repeated-measures ANOVA reduces the error variance by removing individual differences. This increases the likelihood that the ANOVA will find significant differences.

11.

Source	SS	df	MS	
Between treatments	2	1	2	$F(1, 24) = 4.00$
Within treatments	21	48		
Between subjects	9	24		
Error	12	24	0.5	
Total	23	49		

13.

Source	SS	df	MS	
Between treatments	12	2	6	$F(2, 10) = 15.00$
Within treatments	100	15		
Between subjects	96	5		
Error	4	10	0.4	
Total	112	17		

15. The means and standard deviations for the four measurement days are as follows:

7 Days	5 Days	3 Days	1 Day
$M = 39$	$M = 40$	$M = 46$	$M = 55$
$s = 3.61$	$s = 4.73$	$s = 3.67$	$s = 3.32$

Source	SS	df	MS	
Between treatments	810	3	270	$F(3, 12) = 101.25$
Within treatments	240	16		
Between subjects	208	4		
Error	32	12	2.67	
Total	1050	19		

With $\alpha = .01$, the critical value is 5.95. There are significant differences.

17. During the second stage of the two-factor ANOVA, the mean differences between treatments are analyzed into differences from each of the two main effects and differences from the interaction.

19. a. $M = 20$
   b. $M = 50$

21. a. $df = 1, 66$
   b. $df = 2, 66$
   c. $df = 2, 66$

23.

Source	SS	df	MS	
Between treatments	67	3		
Achievement need	16	1	16	$F(1, 56) = 4.00$
Task difficulty	29	1	29	$F(1, 56) = 7.25$
Interaction	22	1	22	$F(1, 56) = 5.50$
Within treatments	224	56	4	
Total	291	59		

25. a.

Source	SS	df	MS	
Between treatments	260	5		
Gender	120	1	120	$F(1, 24) = 24$
Treatments	80	2	40	$F(2, 24) = 8$
Gender x treatment	60	2	30	$F(2, 24) = 6$
Within treatments	120	24	5	
Total	380	29		

With $df = 1, 24$, the critical value is 4.26, and with $df = 2, 24$, the critical value is 3.40. Both main effects and the interaction are significant.

b. For gender, $\eta^2 = \frac{120}{240} - 0.50$
   For treatments, $\eta^2 = \frac{10}{200} = 0.4$
   For the interaction, $\eta^2 = \frac{60}{180} = 0.33$

27. a. The means for the six groups are as follows:

	Middle School	High School	College
Non-user	4.00	4.00	4.00
User	3.00	2.00	1.00

Source	SS	df	MS	
Between treatments	32	5		
Use	24	1	24	$F(1, 18) = 14.4$
School level	4	2	2	$F(2, 18) = 1.2$
Interaction	4	2	2	$F(2, 18) = 1.2$
Within treatments	30	18	1.67	
Total	62	23		

For $df = 1$, 18 the critical value is 4.41 and for $df = 2$, 18 it is 3.55. The main effect for Facebook use is significant but the other main effect and the interaction are not.

b. Grades are significantly lower for Facebook users. A difference exists for all three grade levels but appears to increase as the students get older, although there is no significant interaction.

PART IV   REVIEW

1. The null hypothesis states that the direction of flight has no effect on jet lag. For $\alpha = .05$, the critical value is 3.68

Source	SS	df	MS	
Between treatments	93	2	46.50	$F(2, 15) = 41.15$
Within treatments	17	15	1.13	
Total	110	17		

Reject the null hypothesis.

2. a.

Source	SS	df	MS	
Between treatments	28	2	14	$F(2, 10) = 7.78$
Within treatments	28	15		
Between subjects	10	5		
Error	18	10	1.8	
Total	56	17		

With $df = 2$, 10, the critical value is 4.10. Reject H_0. There are significant differences among the three treatments.

b. $\eta^2 = \frac{28}{46} = .609$

c. The data indicate significant differences among treatments, $F(2, 10) = 7.78$, $p < .05$, $\eta^2 = 0.609$.

3. An interaction indicates that the effect of one factor depends on the levels of the other factor. Alternatively, it indicates that the main effects for one factor are not consistent across the levels of the other factor.

4. a.

Source	SS	df	MS	
Between treatments	340	3		
A	80	1	80	$F(1, 76) = 4.00$
B	180	1	180	$F(1, 76) = 9.00$
A $\times$ B	80	1	80	$F(1, 76) = 4.00$
Within treatments	1520	76	20	
Total	1860	79		

The critical value for all three F-ratios is 3.98 (using $df = 1$, 70). Both main effects and the interaction are significant.

b. For the sport factor, eta squared is $\frac{80}{1600} = 0.050$. For the age factor, eta squared is $\frac{180}{1700} = 0.106$. For the interaction, eta squared is $\frac{80}{1600} = 0.050$.

c. For the swimmers, there is little or no difference between the younger and older age groups, but the older soccer players show noticeably lower scores than the younger players.

CHAPTER 14   CORRELATION

1. a. A positive correlation indicates that X and Y change in the same direction: As X increases, Y also increases. A negative correlation indicates that X and Y tend to change in opposite directions: As X increases, Y decreases.

b. The numerical value of the Pearson correlation indicates how well the data points fit a straight line. A value of 1.00 (or -1.00) indicates a perfect linear fit and a value of zero indicates no linear trend.

3. $SP = -2$

5. a. The scatter plot shows points moderately scattered around a line sloping down to the right.

b. $SS_X = 10$, $SS_Y = 40$, and $SP = -13$. The correlation is $r = \frac{-13}{20} = -0.65$.

7. a. The scatter plot shows points clustered around a line sloping up to the right.

b. $SS_X = 18$, $SS_Y = 18$, and $SP = 5$. The correlation is $r = \frac{5}{18} = 0.278$.

9. a. For the weights, $SS = 20$ and for the incomes, $SS = 7430$. $SP = -359$. The correlation is $r = -0.931$.

b. With $n = 10$, $df = 8$ and the critical value is 2.306. $t(8) = 7.22$. The correlation is significant.

11. a. For these data, $SS_{7min} = 98$, $SS_{cognitive} = 236$, and $SP = 127$. $r = 0.835$.

b. With $df = 7$, the critical value is 2.365. $t(7) = 4.01$. The correlation is significant.

c. $r^2 = 0.697$ or 69.7%

13. a. $r_{XY-Z} = \frac{0.38}{0.57} = 0.667$

b. $r_{XZ-Y} = \frac{0.04}{0.428} = 0.093$

15. a. $r = 0.538$

b. $r^2 = 0.289$. Within rounding error this is the same as the r^2 obtained with the t test in Chapter 10.

17.

19. a. $r = 0.80$

b. $\hat{Y} = 2X + 8$

21. $SS_X = 32$, $SS_Y = 8$, $SP = 8$. The regression equation is $\hat{Y} = 0.25X + 3$

23. a. $SS_X = 8$, $SP = -10$, $\hat{Y} = -1.25X + 8$

b.

X	$\hat{Y}$
3	4.25
6	0.50
3	4.25
3	4.25
5	1.75

25. a. $SS_{weight} = 20$, $SS_{income} = 7430$, $SP = -359$. $\hat{Y} = -17.95X + 119.85$

b. $r = -0.931$ and $r^2 = 0.867$

c. $F = 52.15$ with $df = 1, 8$. The regression equation is significant with $\alpha = .05$ or $\alpha = .01$.

27. a. The standard error of estimate is $\frac{\sqrt{36}}{\sqrt{16}} = 1.50$.

b. The standard error of estimate is $\frac{\sqrt{36}}{\sqrt{36}} = 1.00$.

29. a. $df = 1, 23$

b. $n = 20$ pairs of scores

CHAPTER 15   **CHI-SQUARE STATISTIC: TESTS FOR GOODNESS OF FIT AND INDEPENDENCE**

1. Nonparametric tests make few, if any, assumptions about the populations from which the data are obtained. For example, the populations do not need to form normal distributions, nor is it required that different populations in the same study have equal variances (homogeneity of variance assumption). Parametric tests require data measured on an interval or ratio scale. For nonparametric tests, any scale of measurement is acceptable.

3. The null hypothesis states that there is no preference between the two faces. The expected frequency is $f_e = 20$ for both categories, and chi-square $= 3.60$. With $df = 1$, the critical value is 3.84. Fail to reject H_0 and conclude that there are no significant preferences.

5. The null hypothesis states that couples with the same initial do not occur more often than would be expected by chance. For a sample of 200, the expected frequencies are 13 with the same initial and 187 with different initials. With $df = 1$ the critical value is 3.84, and the data produce a chi-square of 2.96. Fail to reject the null hypothesis.

7. The null hypothesis states that the sample distribution has the same proportions as a normal distribution. The expected frequencies for the five sections are 6.01, 21.75, 34,47, 21.75, and 6.01. With df = 4, the critical value is 9.49. For this sample, chi-square = 2.92. Fail to reject the null hypothesis. The sample is not significantly different from a normal distribution.

9. **a.** The null hypothesis states that there is no advantage (no preference) for red or blue. With $df = 1$, the critical value is 3.84. The expected frequency is 25 wins for each color, and chi-square = 2.88. Fail to reject H_0 and conclude that there is no significant advantage for one color over the other.

   b. The null hypothesis states that there is no advantage (no preference) for red or blue. With $df = 1$, the critical value is 3.84. The expected frequency is 50 wins for each color, and chi-square = 5.76. Reject H_0 and conclude that there is a significant advantage for the color red.

   c. Although the proportions are identical for the two samples, the sample in part b is twice as big as the sample in part a. The larger sample provides more convincing evidence of an advantage for red than does the smaller sample.

11. The null hypothesis states that the distribution of satisfaction scores is the same for both groups. With $df = 1$, the critical value is 3.84. The expected frequencies are:

	Satisfied	Not Satisfied	
Less Reimbursement	55	45	100
Same or More Reimbursement	33	27	60
	88	72	

Chi-square = 8.73. Reject H_0.

13. **a.** The null hypothesis states that there is no relationship between helping behavior and the type of game played. For the three groups who helped, the expected frequencies are all $f_e = 9$ and for the three groups who did not help the expected frequencies are all $f_e = 6$. With $df = 2$, the critical value is 5.99. Chi-square = 3.88. Fail to reject the null hypothesis.

   b. Cramér's $V = 0.294$

15. **a.** The null hypothesis states that the proportion who falsely recall seeing broken glass should be the same for all three groups. The expected frequency of saying yes is 9.67 for all groups, and the expected frequency

for saying no is 40.33 for all groups. With $df = 2$, the critical value is 5.99. For these data, chi-square = 7.78. Reject the null hypothesis and conclude that the likelihood of recalling broken glass is depends on the question that the participants were asked.

   b. Cramérs $V = 0.228$.

   c. Participants who were asked about the speed when the cars "smashed into" each other were more than two times more likely to falsely recall seeing broken glass.

   d. The results of the chi-square test indicate that the phrasing of the question had a significant effect on the participants' recall of the accident, $\chi^2(2, N = 150) = 7.78, p < .05, V = 0.228$.

17. The null hypothesis states that IQ and gender are independent. The distribution of IQ scores for boys should be the same as the distribution for girls. With $df = 2$ and and $\alpha = .05$, the critical value is 5.99. The expected frequencies are 15 low IQ, 48 medium, and 17 high for both boys and girls. For these data, chi-square is 3.76. Fail to reject the null hypothesis. These data do not provide evidence for a significant relationship between IQ and gender.

19. The null hypothesis states that there is no difference between the distribution of preferences predicted by women and the actual distribution for men. With $df = 3$ and $\alpha = .05$, the critical value is 7.81. The expected frequencies are:

	Somewhat Thin	Slightly Thin	Slightly Heavy	Somewhat Heavy
Women	22.9	22.9	22.9	11.4
Men	17.1	17.1	17.1	8.6

Chi-square = 9.13. Reject H_0 and conclude that there is a significant difference in the preferences predicted by women and the actual preferences expressed by men.

21. **a.** The null hypothesis states that there is no relationship between IQ and volunteering. With $df = 2$ and $\alpha = .05$, the critical value is 5.99. The expected frequencies are:

	IQ		
	High	Medium	Low
Volunteer	37.5	75	37.5
Not Volunteer	12.5	25	12.5

The chi-square statistic is 4.75. Fail to reject H_0, with $\alpha = .05$ and $df = 2$.

PART V   REVIEW

1. a. The scatter plot shows points widely scattered around a line sloping up to the right.

   b. The correlation is small but positive; around 0.4 to 0.6.

   c. For these scores, $SS_X = 32$, $SS_Y = 8$, and $SP = 8$. The correlation is $r = \frac{8}{16} = 0.50$.

3. a. The null hypothesis states that there is no preference among the four colors; $p = \frac{1}{4}$ for all categories. The expected frequencies are $f_e = 15$ for all categories, and chi-square $= 4.53$. With $df = 3$, the critical value is 7.81. Fail to reject H_0 and conclude that there are no significant preferences.

   b. The results indicate that there are no significant preferences among the four colors, $\chi^2(3, N = 60) = 4.53$, $p > .05$.

APPENDIX D **General Instructions for Using SPSS**

The Statistical Package for the Social Sciences, commonly known as SPSS, is a computer program that performs statistical calculations and is widely available on college campuses. Detailed instructions for using SPSS for specific statistical calculations (such as computing sample variance or performing an independent-measures t test) are presented at the end of the appropriate chapter in the text. Look for the SPSS logo in the Resources section at the end of each chapter. In this appendix, we provide a general overview of the SPSS program.

SPSS consists of two basic components: A data editor and a set of statistical commands. The **data editor** is a huge matrix of numbered rows and columns. To begin any analysis, you must type your data into the data editor. Typically, the scores are entered into columns of the editor. Before scores are entered, each of the columns is labeled "var." After scores are entered, the first column becomes VAR00001, the second column becomes VAR00002, and so on. To enter data into the editor, the **Data View** tab must be set at the bottom left of the screen. If you want to name a column (instead of using VAR00001), click on the **Variable View** tab at the bottom of the data editor. You will get a description of each variable in the editor, including a box for the name. You may type in a new name using up to 8 lowercase characters (no spaces, no hyphens). Click the **Data View** tab to go back to the data editor.

The **statistical commands** are listed in menus that are made available by clicking on **Analyze** in the tool bar at the top of the screen. When you select a statistical command, SPSS typically asks you to identify exactly where the scores are located and exactly what other options you want to use. This is accomplished by identifying the column(s) in the data editor that contain the needed information. Typically, you are presented with a display similar to the figure at the top of the following page. On the left is a box that lists all of the columns in the data editor that contain information. In this example, we have typed values into columns 1, 2, 3, and 4. On the right is an empty box that is waiting for you to identify the correct column. For example, suppose that you wanted to do a statistical calculation using the scores in column 3. You should highlight VAR00003 by clicking on it in the left-hand box, then click the arrow to move the column label into the right-hand box. (If you make a mistake, you can highlight the variable in the right-hand box, which will reverse the arrow so that you can move the variable back to the left-hand box.)

Variable(s)

VAR00001 VAR00002 VAR00003 VAR00004	➤	

SPSS DATA FORMATS   The SPSS program uses two basic formats for entering scores into the data matrix. Each is described and demonstrated as follows:

1. The first format is used when the data consist of several scores (more than one) for each individual. This includes data from a repeated-measures study, in which each person is measured in all of the different treatment conditions, and data from a correlational study where there are two scores, X and Y, for each individual. Table D1 illustrates this kind of data and shows how the scores would appear in the SPSS data matrix. Note that the scores in the data matrix have exactly the same structure as the scores in the original data. Specifically, each row of the data matrix contains the scores for an individual participant, and each column contains the scores for one treatment condition.

TABLE D1

Data for a repeated-measures or correlational study with several scores for each individual. The left half of the table (a) shows the original data, with three scores for each person; and the right half (b) shows the scores as they would be entered into the SPSS data matrix. Note: SPSS automatically adds the two decimal points for each score. For example, you type in 10 and it appears as 10.00 in the matrix.

(a) Original data

	Treatments		
Person	I	II	III
A	10	14	19
B	9	11	15
C	12	15	22
D	7	10	18
E	13	18	20

(b) Data as entered into the SPSS data matrix

	VAR0001	VAR0002	VAR0003	var
1	10.00	14.00	19.00	
2	9.00	11.00	15.00	
3	12.00	15.00	22.00	
4	7.00	10.00	18.00	
5	13.00	18.00	20.00	

2. The second format is used for data from an independent-measures study using a separate group of participants for each treatment condition. This kind of data is entered into the data matrix in a *stacked* format. Instead of having the scores from different treatments in different columns, all of the scores from all of the treatment conditions are entered into a single column so that the scores from one treatment condition are literally stacked on top of the scores from another treatment condition. A code number is then entered into a second column beside each score to tell the computer which treatment condition corresponds to each score. For example, you could enter a value of 1 beside each score from treatment #1, enter a 2 beside each score from treatment #2, and so on. Table D2 illustrates this kind of data and shows how the scores would be entered into the SPSS data matrix.

TABLE D2

Data for an independent-measures study with a different group of participants in each treatment condition. The left half of the table shows the original data, with three separate groups, each with five participants, and the right half shows the scores as they would be entered into the SPSS data matrix. Note that the data matrix lists all 15 scores in the same column, then uses code numbers in a second column to indicate the treatment condition corresponding to each score.

(a) Original data

	Treatments	
I	*II*	*III*
10	14	19
9	11	15
12	15	22
7	10	18
13	18	20

(b) Data as entered into the SPSS data matrix

	VAR0001	VAR0002	var
1	10.00	1.00	
2	9.00	1.00	
3	12.00	1.00	
4	7.00	1.00	
5	13.00	1.00	
6	14.00	2.00	
7	11.00	2.00	
8	15.00	2.00	
9	10.00	2.00	
10	18.00	2.00	
11	19.00	3.00	
12	15.00	3.00	
13	22.00	3.00	
14	18.00	3.00	
15	20.00	3.00	

Statistics Organizer: Finding the Right Statistics for Your Data

OVERVIEW: THREE BASIC DATA STRUCTURES

After students have completed a statistics course, they occasionally are confronted with situations in which they have to apply the statistics they have learned. For example, in the context of a research methods course, or while working as a research assistant, students are presented with the results from a study and asked to do the appropriate statistical analysis. The problem is that many of these students have no idea where to begin. Although they have learned the individual statistics, they cannot match the statistical procedures to a specific set of data. The Statistics Organizer attempts to help you find the right statistics by providing an organized overview for most of the statistical procedures presented in this book.

We assume that you know (or can anticipate) what your data look like. Therefore, we begin by presenting some basic categories of data so you can find the one that matches your own data. For each data category, we then present the potential statistical procedures and identify the factors that determine which are appropriate for you based on the specific characteristics of your data. Most research data can be classified in one of three basic categories.

Category 1: A single group of participants with one score per participant.

Category 2: A single group of participants with two variables measured for each participant.

Category 3: Two (or more) groups of scores with each score a measurement of the same variable.

In this section, we present examples of each structure. Once you match your own data to one of the examples, you can proceed to the section of the chapter in which we describe the statistical procedures that apply to that example.

SCALES OF MEASUREMENT

Before we begin discussion of the three categories of data, there is one other factor that differentiates data within each category and helps to determine which statistics are appropriate. In Chapter 1, we introduced four scales of measurement and noted that different measurement scales allow different kinds of mathematical manipulation, which result in different statistics. For most statistical applications, however, ratio and interval scales are equivalent, so we group them together for the following review.

Ratio scales and **interval scales** produce numerical scores that are compatible with the full range of mathematical manipulation. Examples include measurements of height in inches, weight in pounds, the number of errors on a task, and IQ scores.

Ordinal scales consist of ranks or ordered categories. Examples include classifying cups of coffee as small, medium, and large or ranking job applicants as 1st, 2nd, and 3rd.

Nominal scales consist of named categories. Examples include gender (male/female), academic major, or occupation.

Within each category of data, we present examples representing these three measurement scales and discuss the statistics that apply to each.

CATEGORY 1:
A SINGLE GROUP
OF PARTICIPANTS
WITH ONE SCORE PER
PARTICIPANT

This type of data often exists in research studies that are conducted simply to describe individual variables as they exist naturally. For example, a recent news report stated that half of American teenagers, ages 12 through 17, send 50 or more text messages a day. To get this number, the researchers had to measure the number of text messages for each individual in a large sample of teenagers. The resulting data consist of one score per participant for a single group.

It is also possible that the data are a portion of the results from a larger study examining several variables. For example a college administrator may conduct a survey to obtain information describing the eating, sleeping, and study habits of the college's students. Although several variables are being measured, the intent is to look at them one at a time. For example, the administrator will look at the number of hours each week that each student spends studying. These data consist of one score for each individual in a single group. The administrator will then shift attention to the number of hours per day that each student spends sleeping. Again, the data consist of one score for each person in a single group. The identifying feature for this type of research (and this type of data) is that there is no attempt to examine relationships between different variables. Instead, the goal is to describe individual variables, one at a time.

Table 1 presents three examples of data in this category. Note that the three data sets differ in terms of the scale of measurement used to obtain the scores. The first set (a) shows numerical scores measured on an interval or ratio scale. The second set (b) consists of ordinal, or rank ordered categories, and the third set (c) shows nominal measurements. The statistics used for data in this category are discussed in Section I.

TABLE 1

Three examples of data with one score per participant for one group of participants.

(a) Number of Text Messages Sent in Past 24 Hours	(b) Rank in Class for High School Graduation	(c) Got a Flu Shot Last Season
X	X	X
6	23rd	No
13	18th	No
28	5th	Yes
11	38th	No
9	17th	Yes
31	42nd	No
18	32nd	No

CATEGORY 2: A SINGLE GROUP OF PARTICIPANTS WITH TWO VARIABLES MEASURED FOR EACH PARTICIPANT

These research studies are specifically intended to examine relationships between variables. Note that different variables are being measured, so each participant has two or more scores, each representing a different variable. Typically, there is no attempt to manipulate or control the variables; they are simply observed and recorded as they exist naturally.

Although several variables may be measured, researchers usually select pairs of variables to evaluate specific relationships. Therefore, we present examples showing pairs of variables and focus on statistics that evaluate relationships between two variables. Table 2 presents four examples of data in this category. Once again, the four data sets differ in terms of the scales of measurement that are used. The first set of data (a) shows numerical scores for each set of measurements. For the second set (b) we have ranked the scores from the first set and show the resulting ranks. The third data set (c) shows numerical scores for one variable and nominal scores for the second variable. In the fourth set (d), both scores are measured on a nominal scale of measurement. The appropriate statistical analyses for these data are discussed in Section II.

CATEGORY 3: TWO OR MORE GROUPS OF SCORES WITH EACH SCORE A MEASUREMENT OF THE SAME VARIABLE

A second method for examining relationships between variables is to use the categories of one variable to define different groups and then measure a second variable to obtain a set of scores within each group. The first variable, defining the groups, usually falls into one of the following general categories:

a. Participant Characteristic: For example, gender or age.

b. Time: For example, before versus after treatment.

c. Treatment Conditions: For example, with caffeine versus without caffeine.

TABLE 2

Examples of data with two scores for each participant for one group of participants.

(a) SAT Score (X) and College Freshman GPA (Y)		(b) Ranks for the Scores in Set (a)	
X	Y	X	Y
620	3.90	7	8
540	3.12	3	2
590	3.45	6	5
480	2.75	1	1
510	3.20	2	3
660	3.85	8	7
570	3.50	5	6
560	3.24	4	4

(c) Age (X) and Wrist Watch Preference (Y)		(d) Gender (X) and Academic Major (Y)	
X	Y	X	Y
27	Digital	M	Sciences
43	Analogue	M	Humanities
19	Digital	F	Arts
34	Digital	M	Professions
37	Digital	F	Professions
49	Analogue	F	Humanities
22	Digital	F	Arts
65	Analogue	M	Sciences
46	Digital	F	Humanities

If the scores in one group are consistently different from the scores in another group, then the data indicate a relationship between variables. For example, if the performance scores for a group of females are consistently higher than the scores for a group of males, then there is a relationship between performance and gender.

Another factor that differentiates data sets in this category is the distinction between independent-measures and repeated-measures designs. Independent-measures designs were introduced in Chapters 10 and 12, and repeated-measures designs were presented in Chapters 11 and 13. You should recall that an *independent-measures design,* also known as a *between-subjects design,* requires a separate group of participants for each group of scores. For example, a study comparing scores for males with scores for females would require two groups of participants. On the other hand, a *repeated-measures design,* also known as a *within-subjects design,* obtains several groups of scores from the same group of participants. A common example of a repeated-measures design is a before/after study in which one group of individuals is measured before a treatment and then measured again after the treatment.

Examples of data sets in this category are presented in Table 3. The table includes a sampling of independent-measures and repeated-measures designs as well as examples representing measurements from several different scales of measurement. The appropriate statistical analyses for data in this category are discussed in Section III.

TABLE 3

Examples of data comparing two or more groups of scores with all scores measuring the same variable.

(a) Attractiveness Ratings for a Woman in a Photograph Shown on a Red or a White Background

White	Red
5	7
4	5
4	4
3	5
4	6
3	4
4	5

(b) Performance Scores Before and After 24 Hours of Sleep Deprivation

Participant	Before	After
A	9	7
B	7	6
C	7	5
D	8	8
E	5	4
F	9	8
G	8	5

(c) Success or Failure on a Task for Participants Working Alone or in a Group

Alone	Group
Fail	Succeed
Succeed	Succeed
Succeed	Succeed
Succeed	Succeed
Fail	Fail
Fail	Succeed
Succeed	Succeed
Fail	Succeed

(d) Amount of Time Spent on Facebook (Small, Medium, Large) for Students from Each High School Class

Freshman	Sophomore	Junior	Senior
Med	Small	Med	Large
Small	Large	Large	Med
Small	Med	Large	Med
Med	Med	Large	Large
Small	Med	Med	Large
Large	Large	Med	Large
Med	Large	Small	Med
Small	Med	Large	Large

SECTION I: STATISTICAL PROCEDURES FOR DATA FROM A SINGLE GROUP OF PARTICIPANTS WITH ONE SCORE PER PARTICIPANT

One feature of this data category is that the researcher typically does not want to examine a relationship between variables but rather simply intends to describe individual variables as they exist naturally. Therefore, the most commonly used statistical procedures for these data are descriptive statistics that are used to summarize and describe the group of scores.

SCORES FROM RATIO OR INTERVAL SCALES: NUMERICAL SCORES

When the data consist of numerical values from interval or ratio scales, there are several options for descriptive and inferential statistics. We consider the most likely statistics and mention some alternatives.

Descriptive statistics   The most often used descriptive statistics for numerical scores are the mean (Chapter 3) and the standard deviation (Chapter 4). If there are a few extreme scores or the distribution is strongly skewed, the median (Chapter 3) may be better than the mean as a measure of central tendency.

Inferential statistics   If there is a basis for a null hypothesis concerning the mean of the population from which the scores were obtained, a single-sample t test (Chapter 9) can be used to evaluate the hypothesis. Some potential sources for a null hypothesis are as follows:

1. If the scores are from a measurement scale with a well-defined neutral point, then the t test can be used to determine whether the sample mean is significantly different from (higher than or lower than) the neutral point. On a 7-point rating scale, for example, a score of $X = 4$ is often identified as neutral. The null hypothesis would state that the population mean is equal to $\mu = 4$.

2. If the mean is known for a comparison population, then the t test can be used to determine whether the sample mean is significantly different from (higher than or lower than) the known value. For example, it may be known that the average score on a standardized reading achievement test for children finishing first grade is $\mu = 20$. If a researcher uses a sample of second-grade children to determine whether there is a significant difference between the two grade levels, then the null hypothesis would state that the mean for the population of second-grade children is also equal to 20. The known mean could also be from an earlier time, for example 10 years ago. The hypothesis test would then determine whether a sample from today's population indicates a significant change in the mean during the past 10 years.

The single-sample t test evaluates the statistical significance of the results. A significant result means that the data are very unlikely ($p < \alpha$) to have been produced by random, chance factors. However, the test does not measure the size or strength of the effect. Therefore, a t test should be accompanied by a measure of effect size, such as Cohen's d or the percentage of variance accounted for, r^2.

SCORES FROM ORDINAL SCALES: RANKS OR ORDERED CATEGORIES

Descriptive statistics   Occasionally, the original scores are measurements on an ordinal scale. It is also possible that the original numerical scores have been transformed into ranks or ordinal categories (for example, small, medium, and large). In either case, the median is appropriate for describing central tendency for ordinal measurements and proportions can be used to describe the distribution of individuals across categories. For example, a researcher might report that 60% of the students were in the high–self-esteem category, 30% in the moderate–self-esteem category, and only 10% in the low–self-esteem category.

Inferential statistics   If there is a basis for a null hypothesis specifying the proportions in each ordinal category for the population from which the scores were obtained, then a chi-square test for goodness of fit (Chapter 15) can be used to evaluate the hypothesis. For example, it may be reasonable to hypothesize that the categories occur equally often (equal proportions) in the population and the test would determine whether the sample proportions are significantly different.

SCORES FROM A NOMINAL SCALE

For these data, the scores simply indicate the nominal category for each individual. For example, individuals could be classified as male/female or grouped into different occupational categories.

Descriptive statistics   The only descriptive statistics available for these data are the mode (Chapter 3) for describing central tendency or using proportions (or percentages) to describe the distribution across categories.

Inferential statistics   If there is a basis for a null hypothesis specifying the proportions in each category for the population from which the scores were obtained, then a chi-square test for goodness of fit (Chapter 15) can be used to evaluate the hypothesis. For example, it may be reasonable to hypothesize that the categories occur equally often (equal proportions) in the population. If proportions are known for a comparison population or for a previous time, the null hypothesis could specify that the proportions are the same for the population from which the scores were obtained. For example, if it is known that 35% of the adults in the United States get a flu shot each season, then a researcher could select a sample of college students and count how many got a shot and how many did not [see the data in Table 1(c)]. The null hypothesis for the chi-square test would state that the distribution for college students is not different from the distribution for the general population.

Figure 1 summarizes the statistical procedures used for data in category 1.

SECTION II: STATISTICAL PROCEDURES FOR DATA FROM A SINGLE GROUP OF PARTICIPANTS WITH TWO VARIABLES MEASURED FOR EACH PARTICIPANT

The goal of the statistical analysis for data in this category is to describe and evaluate the relationships between variables, typically focusing on two variables at a time. With only two variables, the appropriate statistics are correlations and regression (Chapter 14), and the chi-square test for independence (Chapter 15). With three variables, another alternative is a partial correlation (Chapter 14), which evaluates the relationship between two variables while controlling the influence of the third.

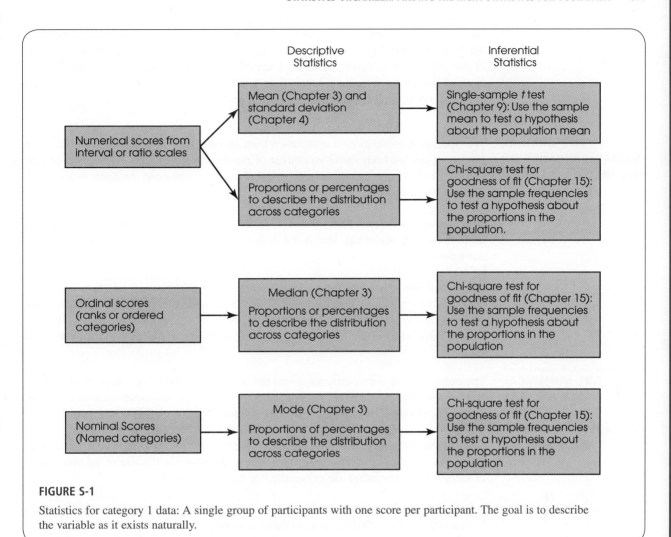

FIGURE S-1

Statistics for category 1 data: A single group of participants with one score per participant. The goal is to describe the variable as it exists naturally.

TWO NUMERICAL VARIABLES FROM INTERVAL OR RATIO SCALES

The Pearson correlation measures the degree and direction of linear relationship between the two variables (see Example 14.3 on p. 456). Linear regression determines the equation for the straight line that gives the best fit to the data points. For each X value in the data, the equation produces a predicted Y value on the line so that the squared distances between the actual Y values and the predicted Y values are minimized.

Descriptive statistics   The Pearson correlation serves as its own descriptive statistic. Specifically, the sign and magnitude of the correlation describe the linear relationship between the two variables. The squared correlation is often used to describe the strength of the relationship. The linear regression equation provides a mathematical description of the relationship between X values and Y. The slope constant describes the amount that Y changes each time the X value is increased by 1 point. The constant (Y intercept) value describes the value of Y when X is equal to zero.

Inferential statistics   The statistical significance of the Pearson correlation is evaluated with a t statistic or by comparing the sample correlation with critical values listed in Table B.6. A significant correlation means that it is very unlikely ($p < \alpha$) that the sample correlation would occur without a corresponding relationship in the population. Analysis of regression is a hypothesis-testing procedure that evaluates the significance of the regression equation. Statistical significance means that the equation predicts more of the variance in the Y scores than would be reasonable to expect if there were not a real underlying relationship between X and Y.

TWO ORDINAL VARIABLES (RANKS OR ORDERED CATEGORIES)

The Spearman correlation is used when both variables are measured on ordinal scales (ranks). If one or both variables consist of numerical scores from an interval or ratio scale, then the numerical values can be transformed to ranks and the Spearman correlation can be computed.

Descriptive statistics   The Spearman correlation describes the degree and direction of monotonic relationship; that is the degree to which the relationship is consistently one directional.

Inferential statistics   A test for significance of the Spearman correlation is not presented in this book but can be found in more advanced texts such as Gravetter and Wallnau (2013). A significant correlation means that it is very unlikely ($p < \alpha$) that the sample correlation would occur without a corresponding relationship in the population.

ONE NUMERICAL VARIABLE AND ONE DICHOTOMOUS VARIABLE (A VARIABLE WITH EXACTLY 2 VALUES)

The point-biserial correlation measures the relationship between a numerical variable and a dichotomous variable. The two categories of the dichotomous variable are coded as numerical values, typically 0 and 1, to calculate the correlation.

Descriptive statistics   Because the point-biserial correlation uses arbitrary numerical codes, the direction of relationship is meaningless. However, the size of the correlation, or the squared correlation, describes the degree of relationship.

Inferential statistics   The data for a point-biserial correlation can be regrouped into a format suitable for an independent-measures t hypothesis test, or the t value can be computed directly from the point-biserial correlation (see the example on pages 477–479). The t value from the hypothesis test determines the significance of the relationship.

TWO DICHOTOMOUS VARIABLES

The phi-coefficient is used when both variables are dichotomous. For each variable, the two categories are numerically coded, typically as 0 and 1, to calculate the correlation.

Descriptive statistics   Because the phi-coefficient uses arbitrary numerical codes, the direction of relationship is meaningless. However, the size of the correlation, or the squared correlation, describes the degree of relationship.

Inferential statistics   The data from a phi-coefficient can be regrouped into a format suitable for a 2×2 chi-square test for independence, or the chi-square value can be computed directly from the phi-coefficient (see Chapter 15, p. 532). The chi-square value determines the significance of the relationship.

TWO VARIABLES FROM ANY MEASUREMENT SCALES

The chi-square test for independence (Chapter 15) provides an alternative to correlations for evaluating the relationship between two variables. For the chi-square test, each of the two variables can be measured on any scale, provided that the number of categories is reasonably small. For numerical scores covering a wide range of value, the scores can be grouped into a smaller number of ordinal intervals. For example, IQ scores ranging from 93 to 137 could be grouped into three categories described as high, medium, and low IQ.

For the chi-square test, the two variables are used to create a matrix showing the frequency distribution for the data. The categories for one variable define the rows of the matrix and the categories of the second variable define the columns. Each cell of the matrix contains the frequency, or number of individuals whose scores correspond to the row and column of the cell. For example, the gender and academic major scores in Table 2(d) could be reorganized in a matrix as follows:

	Arts	Humanities	Sciences	Professions
Female				
Male				

The value in each cell is the number of students with the gender and major identified by the cell's row and column. The null hypothesis for the chi-square test would state that there is no relationship between gender and academic major.

Descriptive statistics   The chi-square test is an inferential procedure that does not include the calculation of descriptive statistics. However, it is customary to describe the data by listing or showing the complete matrix of observed frequencies. Occasionally researchers describe the results by pointing out cells that have exceptionally large discrepancies. For example, in Chapter 15 we described a study investigating eyewitness memory. Participants watched a video of an automobile accident and were questioned about what they saw. One group was asked to estimate the speed of the cars when they "smashed into" each other and another group was asked to estimate speed when the cars "hit" each other. A week later, they were asked additional questions, including whether they recalled seeing broken glass. Part of the description of the results focuses on cells reporting "Yes" responses. Specifically, the "smashed into" group had more than twice as many "Yes" responses than the "hit" group.

Inferential statistics   The chi-square test evaluates the significance of the relationship between the two variables. A significant result means that the distribution of frequencies in the data is very unlikely to occur ($p < \alpha$) if there is no underlying relationship between variables in the population. As with most hypothesis tests, a significant result does not provide information about the size or strength of the relationship. Therefore, either a phi-coefficient or Cramér's V is used to measure effect size.

Figure 2 summarizes the statistical procedures used for data in category 2.

SECTION III: STATISTICAL PROCEDURES FOR DATA CONSISTING OF TWO (OR MORE) GROUPS OF SCORES WITH EACH SCORE A MEASUREMENT OF THE SAME VARIABLE

Data in this category includes single-factor and two-factor designs. In a single-factor study, the values of one variable are used to define different groups and a second variable (the dependent variable) is measured to obtain a set of scores in each group. For a two-factor design, two variables are used to construct a matrix with the values of

FIGURE S-2

Statistics for category 2 data: One group of participants with two variables measured for each participant. The goal is to describe and evaluate the relationship between variables.

one variable defining the rows and the values of the second variable defining the columns. A third variable (the dependent variable) is measured to obtain a set of scores in each cell of the matrix. To simplify discussion, we focus on single-factor designs now and address two-factor designs in a separate section at the end of this section.

The goal for a single-factor research design is to demonstrate a relationship between the two variables by showing consistent differences between groups. The scores in each group can be numerical values measured on interval or ratio scales, ordinal values (ranks), or simply categories on a nominal scale. The different measurement scales permit different types of mathematics and result in different statistical analyses.

SCORES FROM INTERVAL OR RATIO SCALES: NUMERICAL SCORES

Descriptive statistics   When the scores in each group are numerical values, the standard procedure is to compute the mean (Chapter 3) and the standard deviation (Chapter 4) as descriptive statistics to summarize and describe each group. For a repeated-measures study comparing exactly two groups, it also is common to compute the difference between the two scores for each participant and then report the mean and the standard deviation for the difference scores.

Inferential statistics   Analysis of variance (ANOVA) and t tests are used to evaluate the statistical significance of the mean differences between the groups of scores. With only two groups, the two tests are equivalent and either may be used. With more than two groups, mean differences are evaluated with an ANOVA. For independent-measures designs (between-subjects designs), the independent-measures t (Chapter 10) and independent-measures ANOVA (Chapter 12) are appropriate. For repeated-measures designs, the repeated-measures t (Chapter 11) and repeated-measures ANOVA (Chapter 13) are used. For all tests, a significant result indicates that the sample mean differences in the data are very unlikely ($p < \alpha$) to occur if there are not corresponding mean differences in the population. For an ANOVA comparing more than two means, a significant F-ratio indicates that post tests such as Scheffé or Tukey (Chapter 12) are necessary to determine exactly which sample means are significantly different. Significant results from a t test should be accompanied by a measure of effect size such as Cohen's d or r^2. For ANOVA, effect size is measured by computing the percentage of variance accounted for, η^2.

SCORES FROM NOMINAL OR ORDINAL SCALES

Descriptive statistics   For nominal or ordinal data, the data are usually described by the distribution of individuals across categories. For example, the scores in one group may be clustered in one category or set of categories and the scores in another group may be clustered in different categories.

Inferential statistics   With a relatively small number of nominal categories, the data can be displayed as a frequency-distribution matrix with the groups defining the rows and the nominal categories defining the columns. The number in each cell is the frequency, or number of individuals in the group, identified by the cell's row, with scores corresponding to the cell's column. For example, the data in Table 3(c) show success or failure on a task for participants who are working alone or working in a group. These data could be regrouped as follows:

	Success	Failure
Work Alone		
Work in a Group		

Ordinal data are treated in exactly the same way. For example, a researcher could group high school students by class (Freshman, Sophomore, Junior, Senior) and measure the amount of time each student spends on Facebook by classifying students into three ordinal categories (small, medium, large). An example of the resulting data is shown in Table 3(d). However, the same data could be regrouped into a frequency-distribution matrix as follows:

Amount of Time Spent on Facebook		
	Small	Medium	Large
Freshman			
Sophomore			
Junior			
Senior			

In each case, a chi-square test for independence (Chapter 15) can be used to evaluate differences between groups. A significant result indicates that the sample distributions would be very unlikely ($p < \alpha$) to occur if the corresponding population distributions all have the same proportions (same shape).

TWO-FACTOR DESIGNS WITH SCORES FROM INTERVAL OR RATIO SCALES

Research designs with two independent (or quasi-independent) variables are known as two-factor designs. These designs can be presented as a matrix with the levels of one factor defining the rows and the levels of the second factor defining the columns. A third variable (the dependent variable) is measured to obtain a group of scores in each cell of the matrix (see Example 13.4 on page 419).

Descriptive statistics   When the scores in each group are numerical values, the standard procedure is to compute the mean (Chapter 3) and the standard deviation (Chapter 4) as descriptive statistics to summarize and describe each group.

Inferential Statistics   A two-factor ANOVA is used to evaluate the significance of the mean differences between cells. The ANOVA separates the mean differences into three categories and conducts three separate hypothesis tests:

1. The main effect for factor *A* evaluates the overall mean differences for the first factor; that is, the mean differences between rows in the data matrix.

2. The main effect for factor *B* evaluates the overall mean differences for the second factor; that is, the mean differences between columns in the data matrix.

3. The interaction between factors evaluates the mean differences between cells that are not accounted for by the main effects.

For each test, a significant result indicates that the sample mean differences in the data are very unlikely ($p < \alpha$) to occur if there are not corresponding mean differences in the population. For each of the three tests, effect size is measured by computing the percentage of variance accounted for, η^2.

Figure 3 summarizes the statistical procedures used for data in category 3.

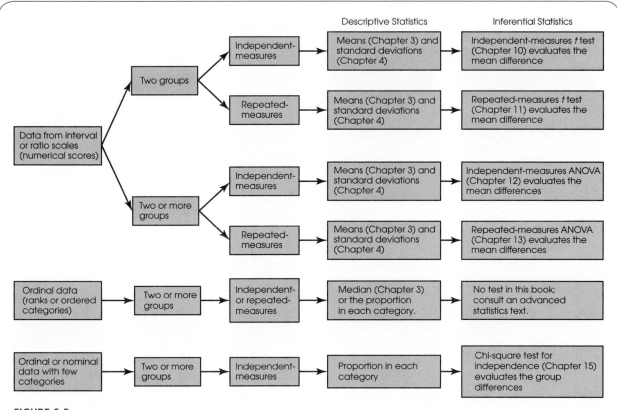

FIGURE S-3

Statistics for category 3 data: Two or more groups of scores with with one score per participant. The goal is to evaluate differences between groups of scores.

References

Note: Numbers in **bold** type indicate the textbook page(s) on which each reference is mentioned.

Ackerman, R., & Goldsmith, M. (2011). Metacognitive regulation of text learning: On screen versus on paper. *Journal of Experimental Psychology: Applied, 17,* 18–32. doi: 10.1037/a0022086

American Psychological Association (APA). (2010). *Publication manual of the American Psychological Association* (6th ed.) Washington, DC: Author. **(p. 78)**

Anderson, D. R., Huston, A. C., Wright, J. C., & Collins, P. A. (1998). Initial findings on the long term impact of Sesame Street and educational television for children: The recontact study. In R. Noll and M. Price (Eds.), *A communication cornucopia: Markle Foundation essays on information policy* (pp. 279–296). Washington, DC: Brookings Institution. **(p. 289)**

Arden, R., & Plomin, R. (2006). Sex differences in variance of intelligence across childhood. *Personality and Individual Differences, 41*, 39–48. **(pp. 117, 545)**

Athos, E. A., Levinson, B., Kistler, A., Zemansky, J., Bostrom, A., Freimer, N., & Gitschier, J. (2007). Dichotomy and perceptual distortions in absolute pitch ability. *Proceedings of the National Academy of Science of the United States of America, 104*, 14795–14800. **(p. 74)**

Bartus, R. T. (1990). Drugs to treat age-related neurodegenerative problems: The final frontier of medical science? *Journal of the American Geriatrics Society, 38*, 680–695. **(pp. 243, 337)**

Bélisle, J., & Bodur, H. O. (2010). Avatars as information: Perception of consumers based on the avatars in virtual worlds. *Psychology & Marketing, 27,* 741–765. **(p. 545)**

Belsky, J., Weinraub, M., Owen, M., & Kelly, J. (2001). Quality of childcare and problem behavior. In J. Belsky (Chair), *Early childcare and children's development prior to school entry.* Symposium conducted at the 2001 Biennial Meetings of the Society for Research in Child Development, Minneapolis, MN. **(p. 341)**

Blum, J. (1978). P*seudoscience and mental ability: The origins and fallacies of the IQ controversy.* New York: Monthly Review Press. **(p. 456)**

Bradbury, T. N., & Miller, G. A. (1985). Season of birth in schizophrenia: A review of evidence, methodology, and etiology. *Psychological Bulletin, 98,* 569–594. **(p. 546)**

Broberg, A. G., Wessels, H., Lamb, M. E., & Hwang, C. P. (1997). Effects of day care on the development of cognitive abilities in 8-year-olds: A longitudinal study. *Development Psychology, 33,* 62–69. **(p. 278)**

Brunt, A., Rhee, Y., & Zhong, L. (2008). Differences in dietary patterns among college students according to body mass index. *Journal of American College Health. 56,* 629–634. **(p. 242)**

Callahan, L. F. (2009). Physical activity programs for chronic arthritis. *Current Opinion in Rheumatology, 21,* 177–182. **(pp. 34, 202)**

Candappa, R. (2000). *The little book of wrong shui.* Kansas City: Andrews McMeel Publishing. **(p. 4)**

Chandra, A., & Minkovitz, C. S. (2006). Stigma starts early: Gender differences in teen willingness to use mental health services. *Journal of Adolescent Health, 38,* 754.el–754.e8. **(p. 543)**

Cohen, J. (1988). *Statistical power analysis for the behavioral sciences.* Hillsdale, NJ: Lawrence Erlbaum Associates. **(pp. 230, 231, 264, 533)**

Cohn, E. J., & Rotton, J. (2000). Weather, disorderly conduct, and assaults: From social contact to social avoidance. *Environment and Behavior, 32,* 651–673. **(p. 472)**

Collins, R. L., Elliott, M. N., Berry, S. H., Kanouse, D. E., Kunkel, D., Hunter, S. B., & Miu, A. (2004). Watching sex on television predicts adolescent initiation of sexual behavior. *Pediatrics, 114,* e280–e289. **(p. 471)**

Cowles, M., & Davis, C. (1982). On the origins of the .05 level of statistical significance. *American Psychologist, 37,* 553–558. **(p. 216)**

Dodd, M. D., Hibbing, J. R., and Smith K. B. (2011) The politics of attention: Gaze-cuing effects are moderated by political temperament. *Attention, Perception, and Psychophysics, 73,* 24-29. **(p. 544)**

Downs, D. S., & Abwender, D. (2002). Neuropsychological impairment in soccer athletes. *Journal of Sports Medicine and Physical Fitness, 42,* 103–107. **(pp. 311, 446)**

Eagly, A. H., Ashmore, R. D., Makhijani, M. G., & Longo, L. C. (1991). What is beautiful is good but . . . : meta-analytic review of research on the physical attractiveness stereotype. *Psychological Bulletin,110,* 109–128. **(p. 336)**

Elbel, B., Gyamfi, J., and Kersh, R. (2011). Child and adolescent fast-food choice and the influence of calorie labeling: a natural experiment. *International Journal of Obesity*, *35*, 493–500. doi: 10.1038/ijo.2011.4. **(p. 310)**

Elliot, A. J., Niesta, K., Greitemeyer, T., Lichtenfeld, S., Gramzow, R., Maier, M. A., & Liu, H. (2010). Red, rank, and romance in women viewing men. *Journal of Experimental Psychology: General, 139,* 399–417. **(p. 443)**

Elliot, A. J., & Niesta, D. (2008). Romantic red: Red enhances men's attraction to women. *Journal of Personality and Social Psychology, 95,* 1150–1164. **(pp. 337, 443)**

Evans, S. W., Pelham, W. E., Smith, B. H., Bukstein, O., Gnagy, E. M., Greiner, A. R., Atenderfer, L. B., & Baron-Myak, C. (2001). Dose-response effects of methylphenidate on ecologically valid measures of academic performance and classroom behavior in adolescents with ADHD. *Experimental and Clinical Psychopharmacology, 9,* 163–175. **(p. 342)**

Fallon, A. E., & Rozin, P. (1985). Sex differences in perceptions of desirable body shape. *Journal of Abnormal Psychology, 94,* 102–105. **(p. 545)**

Flavin, P, and Keane, M. (2012). Life satisfaction and political participation: Evidence from the United States. *Journal of Happiness Studies, 13*, 63-78. Doi: 10.1007/s10902-011-9250-1. **(p. 506)**

Flynn, J. R. (1984). The mean IQ of Americans: Massive gains 1932 to 1978. *Psychological Bulletin. 95,* 29–51. **(p. 276)**

Flynn, J. R. (1999). Searching for justice: The discovery of IQ gains over time. *American Psychologist, 54,* 5–20. **(p. 276)**

Ford, A. M., & Torok, D. (2008). Motivational signage increases physical activity on a college campus. *Journal of American College Health, 57,* 242–244. **(p. 34)**

Fowler, J. H., & Christakis, N. A. (2008). Dynamic spread of happiness in a large social network: Longitudinal analysis over 20 years in the Framingham heart study. *British Medical Journal (Clinical Research ed.), 337*, pp a2338 (electronic publication). **(p. 58)**

Fryer, R. (2011). Financial Incentives and Student Achievement: Evidence from Randomized Trials; *The Quarterly Journal of Economics, 126,* 1755–1798. **(p. 442)**

Gaucher, D., Friesen, J., and Kay, A. C. (2011). Evidence that gendered wording in job advertisements exists and sustains gender inequality. *Journal of Personality and Social Psychology, 101*, 109–128. **(pp. 57, 336)**

Gilovich, T., Medvec, V. H., & Savitsky, K. (2000). The spotlight effect in social judgment: An egocentric bias in estimates of the salience of one's own actions and appearance. *Journal of Personality and Social Psychology, 78,* 211–222. **(p. 276)**

Gino, F. and Ariely, D. (2012). The dark side of creativity: original thinkers can be more dishonest. *Journal of Personality and Social Psychology, 102,* 445-459. doi: 10.1037/a0026406. **(p. 311)**

Gintzler, A. R. (1980). Endorphin-mediated increases in pain threshold during pregnancy. *Science, 210,* 193–195. **(p. 440)**

Greitemeyer, T., and Osswald, S. (2010). Effects of prosocial video games on prosocial behavior. *Journal of Personality and Social Psychology, 98*, 211-221. doi: 10.1037/a0016997. **(pp. 18, 543)**

Guéguen, N., & Jacob, C. (2010). 'Love is in the air': Effects of songs with romantic lyrics on compliance with a courtship request. Psychology of Music, 38, 303–307. **(p. 543)**

Güven, M., Elaimis, D. D., Binokay, S., & Tan, O. (2003). Population-level right-paw preference in rats assessed by a new computerized food-reaching test. **(p. 541)**

Hallam, S., Price, J., & Katsarou, G. (2002). The effects of background music on primary school pupils, task performance. *Educational Studies, 28,* 111–122. **(p. 310)**

Hill, R. A., & Barton, R. A. (2005). Red enhances human performance in contests. *Nature, 435,* 293. **(p. 543)**

Hunter, J. E. (1997). Needed: A ban on the significance test. *Psychological Science, 8,* 3–7. **(p. 227)**

Ijuin, M., Homma, A., Mimura, M., Kitamura, S., Kawai, Y., Imai, Y., & Gondo, Y. (2008). Validation of the 7-minute screen for the detection of early-stage Alzheimer's disease. *Dementia and Geriatric Cognitive Disorders, 25,* 248–255. **(p. 504)**

Jackson, E. M., & Howton, A. (2008). Increasing walking in college students using a pedometer intervention: Differences according to body mass index. *Journal of American College Health, 57,* 159–164. **(p. 440)**

Johnston, J. J. (1975). Sticking with first responses on multiple-choice exams: For better or worse? *Teaching of Psychology, 2,* 178–179. **(p. 338)**

Jones, B. T, Jones, B. C. Thomas, A. P., & Piper, J. (2003). Alcohol consumption increases attractiveness ratings of opposite sex faces: a possible third route to risky sex. *Addiction, 98,* 1069–1075. Doi: 10.1046/j.1360-0443.2003.00426.x. **(pp. 67, 86)**

Jones, J. T, Pelham, B. W., Carvallo, M., & Mirenberg, M. C. (2004). How do I love thee, let me count the Js: Implicit egotism and interpersonal attraction. *Journal of Personality and Social Behavior, 87,* 665–683. **(p. 542)**

Joseph. J. A., Shukitt-Hale. B., Denisova. N. A., Bielinuski, D., Martin, A., McEwen. J. J., & Bickford, P. C. (1999). Reversals of age-related declines in neuronal signal transduction, cognitive, and motor behavioral deficits with blueberry, spinach, or strawberry dietary supplementation. *Journal of Neuroscience, 19,* 8114–8121. **(pp. 243, 337)**

Judge, T. A., & Cable, D. M. (2010). When it comes to pay, do the thin win? The effect of weight on pay for men and women. *Journal of Applied Psychology, 96,* 95–112. doi: 10.1037/a0020860. **(pp. 33, 504)**

Kadosh, R. C., Soskic, S., Iuculano, T., Kanai, R. and Walsh, V. (2010). Modulating neuronal activity produces specific and long-lasting changes in numerical competence. *Current Biology, 20,* 2016–2020. **(p. 206)**

Keppel, G. (1973). *Design and analysis: A researcher's handbook.* Englewood Cliffs, NJ: Prentice-Hall. **(p. 406)**

Killeen. P. R. (2005). An alternative to null-hypothesis significance tests. *Psychological Science, 16,* 345–353. **(p. 227)**

Kirschner, P. A., & Karpinski, A. C. (2010). Facebook and academic performance. *Computers in Human Behavior, 26,* 1237–1245. Doi: 10.1016/j. chb.2010.03.024 **(pp. 390, 442)**

Kling, K. C., Hyde, J. S., Showers, C. J., & Buswell, B. N. (1999). Gender differences in self-esteem: A meta-analysis. *Psychological Bulletin, 125,* 470–500. **(p. 310)**

Knight, C., Haslam, S. A., and England, A. H. (2010). The relative merits of lean, enriched, and empowered offices: An experimental examination of the impact of workspace management strategies on well-being and productivity. *Journal of Experimental Psychology: Applied, 16,* 158–172. **(p. 33)**

Kosfeld, M., Heinrichs, M., Zak, P. J., Fischblacher, U., & Fehr, R. (2005). Oxytocin increases trust in humans. *Nature, 435,* 673–676. **(p. 34)**

Kuo, M., Adlaf. E. M., Lee, H., Gliksman, L., Demers, A., & Wechsler, H. (2002). More Canadian students drink but American students drink more: Comparing college alcohol use in two countries. *Addiction, 97,* 1583–1592. **(p. 19)**

Levine, S. C., Suriyakham, L. W., Rowe, M. L., Huttenlocher, J., and Gunderson, E. A. 2010, What counts in the development of young children's number knowledge? *Developmental Psychology, 46,* 1309–1319. **(p. 58)**

Liger-Belair, G., Bourget, M., Villaume, S., Jeandet, P., Pron, H., & and Polidori, G. (2010). On the losses of dissolved CO2 during Champagne serving. *Journal of Agricultural and Food Chemistry, 58,* 8768–8775. DOI: 10.1021/jf101239w. **(p. 441)**

Liguori, A., & Robinson, J. H. (2001). Caffeine antagonism of alcohol-induced driving impairment. *Drug and Alcohol Dependence, 63,* 123–129. doi:10.1016/S0376-8716(00)00196-4. **(p. 242)**

Linde, L., & Bergstroem, M, (1992). The effect of one night without sleep on problem-solving and immediate recall. *Psychological Research, 54,* 127–136. **(p. 336)**

Loftus, E. F., & Palmer, J. C. (1974). Reconstruction of automobile destruction: An example of the interaction between language and memory. *Journal of Verbal Learning & Verbal Behavior, 13,* 585–589. **(pp. 310, 521, 544)**

Loftus, G. R. (1996). Psychology will be a much better science when we change the way we analyze data. *Current Directions in Psychological Science, 5,* 161–171. **(p. 227)**

Madera, J. M., and Hebl, M. R. ((2011). Discrimination against facially stigmatized applicants in interviews: An eye-tracking and face-to-face investigation. Journal of Applied Psychology, 97, 317–330. doi: 10.1037/a0025799. **(p. 439)**

McGee, E., & Shevliln, M. (2009). Effect of humor on interpersonal attraction and mate selection. *Journal of Psychology, 143,* 67–77. **(p. 277)**

McGee, R., Williams, S., Howden-Chapman, P., Martin, J., & Kawachi. I. (2006). Participation in clubs and groups from childhood to adolescence and its effects on attachment and self-esteem. *Journal of Adolescence, 29,* 1–17. **(p. 241)**

McMorris, B. J., Catalano, R. F., Kim, M. J. Toumbourou, J. W., and Hemphill, S. A. (2011). Influence of family factors and supervised alcohol use on adolescent alcohol use and harms: similarities between youth in different alcohol policy contexts. *Journal of Studies on Alcohol and Drugs, 72,* 418-428. **(p. 527)**

Montarello, S., & Martens, B. K. (2005). Effects of interspersed brief problems on students' endurance at completing math work. *Journal of Behavioral Education, 14,* 249–266. **(p. 243)**

Morse, C. K. (1993). Does variability increase with age? An archival study of cognitive measures. *Psychology and Aging, 8,* 156–164. **(p. 117)**

Miller, K. E. (2008). Wired: Energy drinks, jock identity, masculine norms, and risk taking. *Journal of American College Health, 56,* 481–490. **(p. 245)**

Mulvihill, B. A., Obuseh, F. A., & Caldwell, C. (2008). Healthcare providers' satisfaction with a State Children's Health Insurance Program (SCHIP). *Maternal & Child Health Journal, 12,* 260–265. **(p. 543)**

Murdock. T. B., Miller, M., & Kohlhardt, J. (2004). Effects of classroom context variables on high school students' judgments of the acceptability and likelihood of cheating. *Journal of Educational Psychology, 96,* 765–777. **(p. 388)**

Oishi, S. (2010). Residential mobility, well-being, and mortality. *Journal of Personality and Social Psychology, 98,* 980–994. **(p. 278)**

Pelton, T. (1983). The shootists. Science83, 4(4), 84–86. **(p. 339)**

Persson, J., Bringlov, E., Nilsson, L., & Nyberg. L. (2004). The memory-enhancing effects of Ginseng and Ginkgo biloba in health volunteers. *Psychopharmacology, 172,* 430–434. **(p. 241)**

Piff, P. K., Kraus, M. W., Cote, S., Cheng, B. H., and Keitner, D. (2010). Having less, giving more: the influence of social class on prosocial behavior. *Journal of Personality and Social Psychology, 99,* 771–784. **(p. 309)**

Resenhoeft, A., Villa, J., & Wiseman, D. (2008). Tattoos can harm perceptions: A study and suggestions. *Journal of American College Health, 56,* 593–596. **(p. 243)**

Rohwedder, S., & Willis, R. J. (2010). Mental retirement. *Journal of Economic Perspectives, 24,* 119–138. Doi: 10.1257/jep.24.1.119. **(p. 506)**

Rozin, P., Bauer, R., & Cantanese, D. (2003). Food and life, pleasure and worry, among American college students: Gender differences and regional similarities. *Journal of Personality and Social Psychology, 85,* 132–141. **(p. 341)**

Scaife, M. (1976). The response to eye-like shapes by birds. I. The effect of context: A predator and a strange bird. *Animal Behaviour, 24,* 195–199. **(p. 276)**

Schmidt, S. R. (1994). Effects of humor on sentence memory. *Journal of Experimental Psychology: Learning, Memory, & Cognition, 20,* 953–967. **(p. 86)**

Seery, M. D., Holman, E. A., and Silver, R. C. (2010). Whatever does not kill us: Cumulative lifetime adversity, vulnerability, and resilience. Journal of Personality and Social Psychology, 99, 1025–1041. doi: 10.1037/a0021344. **(p. 310)**

Shrauger, J. S. (1972). Self-esteem and reactions to being observed by others. *Journal of Personality and Social Psychology, 23,* 192–200. **(p. 410)**

Siegfried, T. (2010). Odds are, it's wrong. *Science News, 177,* 26–29. **(p. 228)**

Slater, A., Von der Schulenburg, C., Brown, E., Badenoch, M., Butterworth, G., Parsons, S., & Samuels, C. (1998). Newborn infants prefer attractive faces. *Infant Behavior and Development, 21,* 345–354. **(pp. 257, 541)**

Sol, D., Lefebvre, L., & Rodriguez-Teijeiro, J. D. (2005). Brain size, innovative propensity and migratory behavior in temperate Palaearctic birds. *Proceedings [Proc Biol Sci], 272,* 1433–441. **(p. 390)**

Stephens, R., Atkins, J., & Kingston, A. (2009). Swearing as a response to pain. *NeuroReport: For Rapid Communication of Neuroscience Research, 20,* 1056–1060. Doi: 10.1097/WNR.0b013e32832e64b1 **(pp. 19, 86, 320, 339)**

Stickgold, R., Whidbee, D., Schirmer B., Patel, V., & Hobson, J. A. (2000). Visual discrimination task improvement: A multi-step process occurring during sleep. *Journal of Cognitive Neuroscience, 12,* 246–254. **(p. 311)**

Strack, F., Martin, L. L., & Stepper, S. (1988). Inhibiting and facilitating conditions of the human smile: A non-obtrusive test of the facial feedback hypothesis. *Journal of Personality & Social Psychology, 54,* 768–777. **(p. 336)**

Trockel, M. T., Barnes, M. D., & Egget, D. L. (2000). Health-related variables and academic performance among first-year college students: Implications for sleep and other behaviors. *Journal of American College Health, 49,* 125–131. **(p. 12)**

Trombetti, A, Hars, M. Herrmann, F.R., Kressig, R. W., Ferrari, S., and Rizzoli, R. (2011). Effect of music-based multitask training on gait, balance, and fall risk in elderly people: a randomized controlled trial. *Archives of Internal Medicine, 171,* 525–533. **(p. 311)**

Twenge, J. M. (2000). The age of anxiety? Birth cohort change in anxiety and neuroticism, 1952-1993. *Journal of Personality and Social Psychology, 79,* 1007–1021. **(p. 276)**

U.S. Census Bureau. (2005). *Americans spend more than 100 hours commuting to work each year, Census Bureau reports.* Retrieved January 14, 2009, from www.census.gov/Press-Release/www/releases/archives/american_community_survey_acs/004489.html **(p. 166)**

von Hippel, P. T. (2005). Mean, median, and skew: Correcting a textbook rule. *Journal of Statistics Education, 13,* 2. **(p. 81)**

Wegesin, D. J., & Stern, Y. (2004). Inter- and intra-individual variability in recognition memory: Effects of aging and estrogen use. *Neuropsychology, 18,* 646–657. **(p. 117)**

Weinstein, Y., McDermott, K. B., and Roediger, H. L. III (2010). A comparison of study strategies for passages: Rereading, answering questions, and generating questions.. *Journal of Experimental Psychology: Applied, 16,* 308–316. **(pp. 33, 277, 364, 399)**

Wells, G. M. (2010). The effect of religiosity and campus alcohol culture on collegiate alcohol consumption, *Journal of American College Health. 58,* 295–304. **(p. 33)**

Wilkinson, L., and the Task Force on Statistical Inference. (1999). Statistical methods in psychology journals. *American Psychologist, 54,* 594–604. **(p. 230)**

Winget, C., & Kramer, M. (1979). *Dimensions of dreams.* Gainesville: University Press of Florida. **(p. 545)**

Xu, F., & Garcia, V. (2008). Intuitive statistics by 8-month-old infants. *Proceedings of the National Academy of Sciences of the United States of America, 105,* 5012–5015. **(p. 202)**

Yan, D. and Sengupta, J. (2011). Effects of construal level on the price-quality relationship. *Journal of Consumer Research, 38*, 376–389. doi: 10.1086/659755. **(p. 336)**

Ye, Y. Beyond materialism: The role of health-related beliefs in the relationship between television viewing and life satisfaction among college students. *Mass Communication and Society, 13,* 458–478. Doi: 10.1080/15205430903296069 **(p. 390)**

Zhong, C., Bohns, V. K., & Gino, F. (2010). Good lamps are the best police: Darkness increases dishonesty and self-interested behavior. *Psychological Science, 21,* 311–314. **(p. 312)**

Zhou, X., Vohs, K. D., & Baumeister, R. F. (2009). The symbolic power of money: Reminders of money after social distress and physical pain. *Psychological Science, 20,* 700–706. **(p. 14)**

Index

SUMMARY OF STATISTICS FORMULAS

THE MEAN

Population: $\mu = \dfrac{\Sigma X}{N}$ Sample: $M = \dfrac{\Sigma X}{n}$

SUM OF SQUARES

Definitional: $SS = \Sigma(X - \mu)^2$

Computational: $SS = \Sigma X^2 - \dfrac{(\Sigma X)^2}{N}$

VARIANCE

Population: $\sigma^2 = \dfrac{SS}{N}$ Sample: $s^2 = \dfrac{SS}{n-1}$

STANDARD DEVIATION

Population: $\sigma = \sqrt{\dfrac{SS}{N}}$ Sample: $s = \sqrt{\dfrac{SS}{n-1}}$

z-SCORE (FOR LOCATING AN X VALUE)

$z = \dfrac{X - \mu}{\sigma}$

z-SCORE (FOR LOCATING A SAMPLE MEAN)

$z = \dfrac{M - \mu}{\sigma_M}$ where $\sigma_M = \dfrac{\sigma}{\sqrt{n}} = \sqrt{\dfrac{\sigma^2}{n}}$

t STATISTIC (SINGLE SAMPLE)

$t = \dfrac{M - \mu}{s_M}$ where $s_M = \sqrt{\dfrac{s^2}{n}}$

t STATISTIC (INDEPENDENT MEASURES)

$t = \dfrac{(M_1 - M_2) - (\mu_1 - \mu_2)}{s_{(M_1 - M_2)}}$

where $s_{(M_1 - M_2)} = \sqrt{\dfrac{s_p^2}{n_1} + \dfrac{s_p^2}{n_2}}$ and $s_p^2 = \dfrac{SS_1 + SS_2}{df_1 + df_2}$

t STATISTIC (RELATED SAMPLES)

$t = \dfrac{M_D - \mu_D}{s_{M_D}}$ where $s_{M_D} = \sqrt{\dfrac{s^2}{n}}$

ESTIMATION

t Statistic (Single Sample)

$\mu = M \pm ts_M$

t Statistic (Independent Measures)

$\mu_1 - \mu_2 = M_1 - M_2 \pm ts_{(M_1 - M_2)}$

t Statistic (Related Samples)

$\mu_D = M_D \pm ts_{M_D}$

INDEPENDENT-MEASURES ANOVA

$SS_{\text{total}} = \Sigma X^2 - \dfrac{G^2}{N}$ $df_{\text{total}} = N - 1$

$SS_{\text{between}} = \Sigma \dfrac{T^2}{n} - \dfrac{G^2}{N}$ $df_{\text{between}} = k - 1$

$SS_{\text{within}} = \Sigma SS_{\text{inside each treatment}}$ $df_{\text{within}} = N - k$

$F = \dfrac{MS_{\text{between}}}{MS_{\text{within}}}$ where each $MS = \dfrac{SS}{df}$

REPEATED-MEASURES ANOVA

$SS_{\text{between}} = \Sigma \dfrac{T^2}{n} - \dfrac{G^2}{N}$ $df_{\text{between}} = k - 1$

$SS_{\text{error}} = SS_{\text{within}} - SS_{\text{subjects}}$

$df_{\text{error}} = (N - k) - (n - 1)$

where $SS_{\text{within}} = \Sigma SS_{\text{inside each treatment}}$

and $SS_{\text{subjects}} = \Sigma \dfrac{P^2}{k} - \dfrac{G^2}{N}$

$F = \dfrac{MS_{\text{between}}}{MS_{\text{error}}}$ where each $MS = \dfrac{SS}{df}$

Study Tips for Success

C. DOMINIK GÜSS, University of North Florida

Your classmate got another A, as usual, and you catch yourself thinking, "Sure she got an A. It's easy for her. She's so smart, she always gets As." But this is fallacious thinking based on the belief that some people are gifted and do not have to put much effort into learning and studying, while others are not so fortunate. Such thinking is not only defeating, it is incorrect—most of us can get As. Using the following "Indomitable Dozen" study tips can help make anyone successful in their studies. Not convinced? Let's start with a scientific study that supports this idea.

Psychologists have found that people can memorize about 5 to 9 numbers in a row (scientists refer to this magic number as 7 ± 2, which is easier to remember than 5 to 9). Thus, if people are instructed to memorize as many numbers as possible out of a list of about 30, they can repeat around 7 in correct order. One college student, let's call him S.F., volunteered for an experiment in which he listened to lists of digits (e.g., 3 5 9 3 2 6 8 5 6) and then repeated them. This example is quite easy; you might even be able to recall the whole list correctly. Initially, S.F. was also able to recall eight digits; then, however, he continued to learn and recall such lists of digits for about 200 hours over a time period of two years. How many digits do you think he was able to recall correctly by the end of the experiment? As it turns out, he was able to recall 81 random digits presented at a rate of one digit per second (Chase & Ericsson, 1982). From lesson to lesson, his digit span increased from the original average digit span of 8 to 81. S.F. would be able to recall, for example, the following list:

8 3 6 2 3 4 1 1 5 7 6 4 3 7 8 7 7 9 3 2 2 4 5 6 3 2 6 7 8 4
5 6 4 4 7 0 0 7 5 3 1 1 2 4 6 7 4 3 2 4 6 8 8 9 5 4 3 2 3 4
6 7 4 3 2 4 5 6 7 8 4 3 3 5 4 1 7 9 0 2 3

We will come back to S.F. later to answer the question of why he was able to perform so well. For now, these results show us that our human brain is able to perform extraordinary tasks. So, how can we improve our memories and become experts like S.F.? The main goal is to encode information effectively, store it in our memories, and retrieve the information at the right time. To put it another way, we need to get the information into our heads, keep it there, and access it when we need it. Let's see if you read carefully. What were the initials of the student who did the experiment? Did you remember S.F.? If you did, maybe you associated it with something like San Francisco. The city name might have helped you in remembering the name of the student.

Before you continue reading, please notice the photos included in each section of this module. These photos were not selected for their visual appeal; they were chosen to help you remember the essential points of the section. For example, when you see the picture of a row of dumbbells, you might remember the tip about the importance of repetition.

The following tips refer first to encoding, then to storing, and finally to retrieving information.

Focus

So, what was the introduction about? Can you repeat it in your own words?

This is simple, but important: We have to put effort into what we are doing, like S.F. This first tip tells us that to encode information we have to focus and pay attention when we study. Our all too human minds can only focus on a limited amount of information at any given time. For instance, we cannot watch TV, eat popcorn, and read a complicated textbook at the same time. We can perform two or more tasks only if they are well practiced, e.g., watching TV and eating popcorn. Eating popcorn does not take away "mental energy" because all the necessary movements of our arms and mouth are well practiced and automatic. However, textbook material and class notes usually contain novel information, and our mind needs all its capacity to focus on it. If we try to limit distractions, we will study more successfully and better retain the information we study.

Let's do a brief activity: Repeat the word "silk" eight times, as fast as you can. Say it out loud and very fast. Now answer the question: "What do cows drink?" You might answer "milk" if you have not heard this joke before. But, think again: the correct answer is "water." We answer milk because milk rhymes with silk, because the concepts "cow" and "milk" are closely related in our memory, and because we did not think much before answering the question. If we had visualized a cow eating grass and drinking while focusing on this question, we would have come up with the answer right away. So pay attention—and do not fall for that one again!

Attitude Counts

Enjoying an activity can motivate us to excel in it. Playing chess several hours a day might be a joy for one person, and it might be a nightmare for another. Let us say Paola is fascinated by chess and forgets the time, not to mention the rest of the world, while playing. Pedro, on the other hand, finds it boring and looks at his watch every five minutes to see how much time has passed. Consider this: We spend a lot of time doing the things we enjoy, such as shopping, watching TV, or playing games on the computer.

Imagine you are a freshman and you think to yourself: "I am excited. Now I can take my *Introduction to Psychology* textbook and learn something new about altered states of consciousness, like why I had that crazy dream last night and what it meant, or what effects drugs have on the human mind, or what hypnosis is and how it works." With such an attitude, it is much easier for you to encode and store information than if you say to yourself: "I have to study for this dumb test, so let's get it over with."

So positive thinking helps. And one way to help yourself think positively is by incorporating an attitude of appreciation for what you have. Consider the following statistics; they may help you maintain the realization of what an amazing opportunity and privilege it is to be a college student.

Enjoying an activity motivates us.

Eight hundred and fifty million people go to bed hungry each night (Food and Agriculture Organization of the United Nations, 2006). According to the article "Where and Why Are 10 Million Children Dying Every Year?" by Black, Morris, and Bryce (2003), one child dies every five seconds from hunger-related causes. In 2004, almost 1 billion people earned less than $1 per day and lived below the international poverty line (World Bank, 2007). Worldwide, only 6% of all people complete a college education—for developing countries, this figure drops to 3% (World Bank, 2000). In the U.S., one in four adults (25%) has attained at least a bachelor's degree (U.S. Census Bureau, 2003). So if you graduate from college, you will be among that 25%. Did you notice that the education statistics for the U.S. in the earlier sentence were written to pertain specifically to you? Making something personal helps us remember.

Of course, knowing all this, it is still not easy to study. Initial excitement fades and we need some motivation to keep going. Moreover, you might have a professor whose class lectures are boring. What we need, then, is to change our attitude about the subject material, as described above, and to be disciplined. After all, we study for ourselves, for our own advancement—not for our parents, and not for our teachers.

Take Notes

While sitting in class, listening to the professor's lecture, much of what is said may seem quite sensible; so sensible, in fact, that you might not think to take notes. But then, several days pass. You are at home trying to study for the next exam, and as you look through your notes, you realize that you did not write much down. At this point, you cannot remember all the specifics of the lecture and you find yourself fervently wishing you had more detailed notes. You copy a couple of friends' notes, but they are hard to understand. What did they write down? What does this mean? Why did they write that down? The point is that it is a really good idea to take notes. Professors often ask questions on their exams that refer to materials they discussed in class. By any chance, have you been taking notes on this module? If you have, then you are on your way to learning and remembering.

Of course, there is always the other extreme. Some students make the mistake of writing down everything the professor says. When they look through their notes, they cannot see a structure because they have simply copied what the professor said. If these students learned to listen more carefully to the lectures, write down key information, and organize the information with headings and subheadings, their notes would make more sense.

Another tip: reread your notes relatively soon after each class; if you wait four weeks to start reading those notes just before the exam, you might have a hard time understanding what you wrote down. Too much time will have passed, and many other things will have transpired to distract you.

Organize and Summarize

Can you repeat the first three study tips again? We will repeat them at the end of this section, but you can test yourself now.

Some textbooks are not well written and some professors' lectures are not as well structured as they could be. It can be difficult at times to figure out what an author wanted to say on some pages of a textbook or what point a professor wanted to make during the last ten minutes of a lecture. In such cases, you need to do the organizing yourself. Try to summarize the text you read or part of the lecture. Figure out the key topics and terms. What are the most important points? What is the take home message? Some students use flashcards, some write out the main points of the chapter, and still others ask the professor when something is truly confusing.

Why is this necessary? Unfortunately, it is human to forget. No student can remember every single detail from 400 pages of *Introduction to Psychology*, which is just as well, as not all of the details are relevant. If you can summarize each page in four or five sentences, then you have only about 30 pages out of that 400 to remember. Sounds more manageable, doesn't it?

So, if you have the essential information summarized, you can 1) concentrate on it; 2) enjoy what you are read-

Repetition is the key to success.

ing; 3) have better structured notes; and 4) read it over and rehearse it (our next tip), thus decreasing the likelihood that you will forget it. This is what we have discussed so far—not to mention a fine example of identifying what the important points are.

Repeat, Repeat, Repeat

"Repetition is the mother of wisdom," says a proverb. There is no other way but repetition to become an expert in any area. Tiger Woods practices specific movements for hours each day—and has done so for years. A scientist reads books and articles continuously to stay on top of his or her field. A student has to read and reread and reread book chapters and lecture notes so that the material can be stored effectively in his or her long-term memory.

Now, there is a difference between reading and "*reading.*" One can simply repeat what was read (maintenance rehearsal), or one can actively elaborate on it (elaborative rehearsal; Craik & Lockhart, 1972) by asking questions like:

- "What does this remind me of?"
- "What concrete example can I use from my life to give this meaning to me?"
- "How would I repeat this sentence in my own words?"
- "What important message can I take from the paragraph I read?"
- "How can I apply this information?"

All of these questions activate our brain and help link new information with our existing knowledge, making it more likely that we will retain it so we can remember it later. We can repeat by reading out loud, writing it down, explaining the concept to our dog, or talking to ourselves in the mirror. William Glasser (as cited in Teele, 1992) once said: "We learn 10 percent of what is read, 20 percent of what we hear, 30 percent of what we see, 50 percent of what we both see and hear, 70 percent of what is discussed with others, 80 percent of what is experienced personally, 95 percent of what we teach to someone else." When you can teach a concept to your dog, you probably have it mastered.

Use Mnemonic Devices

We talked before about S.F. and his amazing ability to recall 80 digits. How was he able to store those digits? He did not get special instructions from the experimenter or any specific help. Here is what S.F. did: He grouped the digits together in meaningful units, using a process called *chunking*. For instance, the three digits 3 5 0 could be grouped together as one chunk, as in "3 minutes 50 seconds—close to the world record mile time." This made sense to S.F.

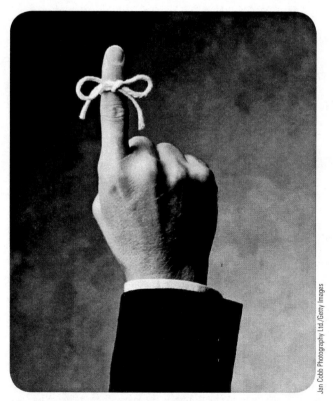

Mnemonics are strategies to improve our memory.

because he was a long-distance runner. By chunking the digits, he could convert three or four digits into one chunk (such as the world record mile time). Assuming an average digit span of 7 ± 2, this process would have allowed him to store more than 20 digits, but still not 80 digits. However, S.F. then developed a strategy to recall roughly 20 lists of three to four digits each.

A strategy many people use to remember lists is to build *acronyms*, i.e., a word that consists of the initial letters of several other words. Assume you have to learn the BIG 5 personality traits (McCrae & Costa, 1987), a very popular concept in personality psychology. The BIG 5 are: open-mindedness, conscientiousness, extraversion, agreeableness, and neuroticism. These are five long words. You might want to learn the acronym OCEAN, which consists of the first letter of each of the five words. This acronym is easy to remember and might help you during the exam to remember the BIG 5. You might have learned the acronym HOMES in high school for the names of the Great Lakes, Roy G Biv for the colors of the rainbow, and Every Good Boy Does Fine for the musical chords EGBDF.

If you are musically inclined, you could also use the melody of one of your favorite songs and change the words. One student, Andrea Cagle, a preschool teacher, taught her class the Frère Jacques song (Brother John) and changed the words to:

>Are you sleeping? Are you sleeping?
>Brother John? Brother John?
>Morning bells are ringing. Morning bells are ringing.
>Ding, Ding, Dong! Ding, Ding, Dong!
>Follow directions. Follow directions.
>Do not fight! Do not fight!
>Do not touch your classmate. Do not touch your classmate.
>Always do what's right! Always do what's right!
>Aim high and do your best. Aim high and do your best.
>Do not yell. Do not yell.
>Be kind to everybody. Be kind to everybody.
>And you will do just well. And you will do just well.

Her class liked the song and learned it very quickly—along with its important educational message. Mnemonics are techniques that help our minds to recall information better. Chunking, acronyms, music, and rhymes are all examples of mnemonics. Why do they help us? We can imagine our memory as a web of billions of interconnected neurons. These neurons store information. If you connect information with an acronym or rhyme, it becomes easier to recall all the parts stored in this web of neurons.

Jan Cobb Photography Ltd./Getty Images

Images are another mnemonic device being used throughout this module. This use of images helps you connect the images with what you read. When you see the picture of the hand and index finger, you will remember S.F. and his exceptional ability to recall digits. When you see a scuba diver, you will remember the importance of context-dependent memory, our next tip.

Context Matters

Let's repeat the tips we have discussed so far. First, we encode, store, and retrieve information and work on it like S.F., by concentrating; second, we have a good attitude; third, we take notes in class; fourth, we organize the material; fifth, we repeat; and sixth, we use mnemonics. Once you have learned your material and stored it in your memory, the time will come when you have to retrieve this information. You might sit in your chair reading the exam and think, "Yes, I know the answer. I remember. The information was on the right page next to the photo of the dog." You concentrate and try to remember, but you simply cannot remember the answer to the question. This could be due to two factors. One factor is called *context-dependent memory*. People usually retrieve more information if they are in the same environment in which they learned it. So the best place for you to study would be in the classroom in the chair where you will take the exam. The library might be the second best choice.

Mood can affect our memory and learning.

In a 1975 study, Godden and Baddeley gave scuba divers a list of 40 unrelated words. Some learned it while 20 feet under water, and some learned it while on land, but all were wearing scuba gear. Then they split each group and had them recall as many words as possible, either underwater or on land. The two groups that performed best out of the four total groups were in the same environment when they learned and when they retrieved the information (underwater/underwater, on land/on land). Recall was about 50 percent better when the divers were in the same environment during learning and recall. When the learning and retrieval environments differed, the scuba divers did not perform as well.

Of course, we cannot spend evenings or weekends in our classroom studying, but we can a) come often to class, sit in our chairs, and listen to a lot of information relevant to the exam (and take notes), and b) study in many different environments (e.g., the library, a friend's house, the living room, etc) to reduce the context effect.

Mood Matters, Too

The second factor affecting information retrieval is called *mood-dependent memory*. If you are in the same mood during learning and retrieval of information, you perform better than if your moods are different (Eich, 1995). If you

In Godden and Baddeley's study, scuba divers had to study either on land or underwater.

are, for example, relaxed at home studying your lecture notes, and then during the exam you become nervous, your two mood states are different. It will be harder to answer the exam questions because it will be harder to remember. Being nervous blocks our access to the information we have learned. So try to use some relaxation techniques such as a) breathing deeply; b) imagining a nice, beautiful, relaxing place (like the beach) before you start reading the exam questions; and c) giving yourself a pep talk: "I studied well and I know a lot, I can do this!" Our bodies cannot be in two emotional states, i.e., nervous and relaxed, at the same time. So when you feel nervous, try to tense and release several muscles, such as the muscles in your hand, arm, foot, or leg. You will soon realize that you feel more relaxed and you will be able to focus better on the exam questions.

One professor found that students did significantly better on exams when they were asked to give themselves positive messages affirming their preparation for the exam, their ability to do well on it, and their belief in themselves five minutes before sitting down to take the exam.

Create a Study Group

Shall we go through the list of tips again, and use a mnemonic? Like a song, perhaps? Sing to the tune of "Twinkle, Twinkle, Little Star."

> Focus, Focus, Attitude counts,
> Take your notes and Organize
> Rehearse and use Mnemonics
> Context, Mood, Study groups,
> Manage time, Eat and Sleep well,
> Don't forget to Know thyself!

Another tip for enhancing academic performance and practicing retrieval is to join or create a study group. This does not mean a study group that meets the night before an exam for the first time, or one whose members spend the evening talking about friendships, movies, celebrity gossip, the latest fashion, etc. It means a study group that meets regularly and actually discusses the class materials with the goal of studying and helping each other. Such a study group can be very helpful. While it does not reduce the amount of time each member must spend reading, it offers a place where you can ask each other questions, explain concepts to each other, give examples, and apply what you have learned. If you can do this in a study group, then you will be well prepared for your exams.

See if this sounds familiar to you: You studied alone, read over your text and thought to yourself, "I'm really getting this—this makes perfect sense." But later, when you are

Time pressure can cause stress.

talking with a friend trying to explain the concept you read, you are not able to express yourself clearly and your friend cannot understand what you are saying. There is a difference between reading (and comprehending what you are reading) and explaining materials to someone. While reading we fall easily into a passive state. When we explain, we have to be actively engaged. Explaining is harder, but if we explain well, it can show us that we really are the master of the material.

A study group can be a wonderful avenue for getting feedback on how much you know. It is also a time you reserve for studying together. Especially in your first year at a university, a study group is an opportunity to make friends and get to know people. It may also be easier to ask the members of the group about topics you did not understand than the instructor of an Introduction to Psychology class with 200 students.

Manage Your Time

People make plans about the future and reserve a certain amount of time for the completion of tasks. Kelly might say, "I have to write a paper; it is due on Monday, October 10, so if I start October 7, I should be fine, because I have the whole weekend to finish the paper." This is called the "planning fallacy," and we all fall for it at one time or another (Buehler, Griffin, & Ross, 1994). We all underestimate how long it takes to complete a task. Most of us have experienced extreme time pressure to complete something simply because we did not start early enough. If you are a perpetual procrastinator, you will probably argue that you are able to write a much better paper when under pressure. You might think that, but it is very likely that the professor who reads your paper thinks otherwise.

Let's get back to Kelly. Here it is, October 8, and guess what has happened: Her friend has invited her to a party. What do you suppose Kelly will do? Finish the paper? So, start on your assignments early. If you feel you are starting too early, then you are starting at the right time. Often, unforeseen things happen in life; if you start early, you are prepared for both the paper and the unforeseen events, like having your printer break down or your computer crash right when you need them the most. You never know what will come up, and if you start early, you will be ready to counteract the planning fallacy. You might even have time to go to your friend's party.

When you reserve time for studying or writing papers, try to commit yourself and write it down in your calendar or schedule. The day has only 24 hours minus about 7.5 hours for sleep. Reserve time for yourself. Being a student is not easy and you also need time to relax or go to the movie theatre once in a while. You might give yourself such a reward after a difficult exam, for example. You could use the following principle: Use the activities you like the most as rewards for doing those activities you like less (e.g., going shopping after having written a paper, reading a chapter on abnormal behavior after you have done your statistics homework, etc.).

Sleep and Eat Well

It is important to see that our minds are connected with our bodies. As the Romans said, "*Mens sana in corpore sano*" (A healthy mind is in a healthy body). Body and mind are inseparable. If we only sleep four hours, then our mind cannot focus and studying will be very difficult. If we fast and do not eat well during study periods, we will have a hard time retaining information and performing well. According to Shaw and Tiggerman (2004):

> There is also an emerging body of evidence linking dieting with a range of impairments in cognitive functioning. Specifically, female dieters have been found to exhibit poorer sustained attention, poorer immediate free recall and longer simple reaction times than their non-dieting counterparts. . . . Furthermore, performance has been found to be poorer, with the same individuals, when dieting than when not dieting.

So let's take care of our bodies, so that our minds can perform well.

Know Yourself

Written in Greek in the Temple of Apollo at Delphi were the words "Know Thyself." The writer is unknown; perhaps Socrates, Pythagoras, or Solon. It is apparent, however, that the Greeks of 2000 years ago understood how important it is to know oneself. Of course, the statement refers more to a moral and philosophical life-goal, but it also applies to studying.

The tips we have discussed so far can help you to master your materials and perform well on your exams. However, every one of us is unique. The more you know yourself and your strengths and weaknesses regarding studying, the easier it will be for you to make progress. Then you will know what to change in order to perform even better.

One person may, for example, be able to read and focus for two hours, while another person can focus well

Man is what he eats. A healthy mind is in a healthy body.

It is important to know yourself.

only for 30 minutes before needing a short break. It would be less efficient if the second person forced herself to study for two hours when she would be able to continue studying with a clear mind again after just a ten-minute break. One person may be very sensitive to visual stimuli, while another person is more sensitive to sound and likes reading the passages of the textbook out loud. So think about when and how you study best.

The following questions refer to the topics we have discussed so far. The questions can help you to reflect on your studying behavior and hopefully will give you some ideas about what you can change and improve. Remember, "Know Thyself."

Self Assessment

1. How many pairs of tips and pictures do you remember? Write them down.
2. Why do you think you remembered those specific tips and pictures?
3. Which of the tips were most helpful for you? Which tip do you think would help you most? Commit yourself to trying it out.
4. What other things do you do while studying that are not mentioned here but are helpful for you?
5. What do you see as your strengths and weaknesses from the following list of 12 points?

Twelve Questions on Study Habits and Skills

The more often you answer with a "yes" (a "3" or a "4"), the better your study habits. So, ideally, you should have around 40 points.

		No			Yes
1.	**Focus.**				
	I am able to focus well on my study materials for a long time.	1	2	3	4
2.	**Attitude counts.**				
	I like the classes I am taking.	1	2	3	4
3.	**Take notes.**				
	I take extensive (but not too extensive) notes in class.	1	2	3	4
4.	**Organize and summarize.**				
	I summarize textbook chapters on flashcards or in a separate document.	1	2	3	4
5.	**Repeat, repeat, repeat.**				
	I usually read my class notes and textbook chapters three times before an exam.	1	2	3	4
6.	**Use mnemonic devices.**				
	I often build acronyms or use other strategies to memorize material.	1	2	3	4
7.	**Context matters.**				
	I study in many different locations.	1	2	3	4
8.	**Mood matters, too.**				
	I am quite relaxed when I am taking exams.	1	2	3	4
9.	**Create a study group.**				
	I am part of a well-functioning study group.	1	2	3	4
10.	**Manage your time.**				
	I start studying for exams and doing my assignments ahead of time.	1	2	3	4
11.	**Sleep and eat well.**				
	I am eating well and sleeping well	1	2	3	4
12.	**Know yourself.**				
	I can describe my study habits quite well to a friend.	1	2	3	4

References

Black, R., Morris, S., & Bryce, J. (2003). Where and why are 10 million children dying every year? *The Lancet, 361*, 2226-2234.

Buehler, R., Griffin, D., & Ross, M. (1994). Exploring the "planning fallacy": Why people underestimate their task completion times. *Journal of Personality and Social Psychology, 67*, 366–381.

Chase, W. G., & Ericsson, K. A. (1982). Skill and working memory. In G. H. Bower (Ed.), *The psychology of learning and motivation* (Vol. 16, pp. 1–58). New York: Academic Press.

Craik, F. I. M., & Lockhart, R. S. (1972). Levels of processing. A framework for memory research. *Journal of Verbal Learning and Verbal Behaviour, 11*, 671-684.

Eich, E. (1995). Searching for mood dependent memory. *Psychological Science, 6*(2), 67-75.

Food and Agriculture Organization of the United Nations (2006). *State of food insecurity in the world, 2006*. Rome, Italy: FAO.

Godden, D. R., & Baddeley, A. D. (1975). Context-dependent memory in two natural environments: On land and underwater. *British Journal of Psychology, 66*, 325-332.

McCrae, R. R., & Costa, P. T., Jr. (1987). Validation of the five-factor model of personality across instruments and observers. *Journal of Personality and Social Psychology, 52*(1), 81-90.

Premack, D. (1959). Toward empirical behavioral laws: I. Positive reinforcement. *Psychological Review, 66*, 219-233.

Shaw, J., & Tiggerman, M. (2004). Dieting and working memory: Preoccupying cognitions and the role of the articulatory control process. *British Journal of Health Psychology, 9*(2), 175-186.

Teele, S. (1992). Discussant for Joseph Walters' application of multiple intelligences research in alternative assessment. *Proceedings of the Second National Research Symposium on Limited English Proficient Student Issues: Focus on Evaluation and Measurement. OBEMLA, 1992*. Retrieved from http://www.ncela.gwu.edu/pubs/symposia/second/vol1/application-discussants.htm

The World Bank (2000). Educational attainment of the total population aged 15 and over. Retrieved from http://devdata.worldbank.org/edstats/ThematicDataOnEducation/RegionData/Region15.xls

The World Bank (2007). *World development indicators, 2007*. Washington, DC: The World Bank.

U.S. Census Bureau (2003). Educational attainment in the United States: 2003 (P20-550). Retrieved from http://www.census.gov/prod/2004pubs/p20-550.pdf

Website showing many of the study tips we discussed:

http://www.how-to-study.com/pqr.htm

Website showing what world champions can do with their memories:

http://www.worldmemorychampionships.com

Acknowledgements

I would like to thank Ma. Teresa Tuason and Shannon McLeish for their thoughtful comments on an earlier version of this module and especially my students from whom I learn so much.

WADSWORTH
CENGAGE Learning™

Wadsworth Psychology Module: Study Tips for Success
C. Dominik Güss

© 2009 Wadsworth, Cengage Learning

Library of Congress Control Number: 2008920397

ISBN-13: 978-0-495-59486-4

ISBN-10: 0-495-59486-5

Wadsworth
10 Davis Drive
Belmont, CA 94002-3098
USA

Cengage Learning is a leading provider of customized learning solutions with office locations around the globe, including Singapore, the United Kingdom, Australia, Mexico, Brazil, and Japan. Locate your local office at **international.cengage.com/region.**

Cengage Learning products are represented in Canada by Nelson Education, Ltd.

For product information and technology assistance, contact us at
Cengage Learning Academic Resource Center, 1-800-423-0563

For permission to use material from this text or product,
submit all requests online at **www.cengage.com/permissions**
Further permissions questions can be emailed to
permissionrequest@cengage.com

For your course and learning solutions, visit **academic.cengage.com**

Purchase any of our products at your local college store or at our preferred online store **www.ichapters.com**

Printed in Canada
1 2 3 4 5 6 7 12 11 10 09 08

WADSWORTH
CENGAGE Learning™

For your course and learning solutions, visit **academic.cengage.com**
Purchase any of our products at your local college store or at our preferred online store **www.ichapters.com**

ISBN-13: 978-0-495-59486-4
ISBN-10: 0-495-59486-5

900

9 780495 594864